THE FEDERAL CENSUS

of

1860

for

MONROE COUNTY, OHIO

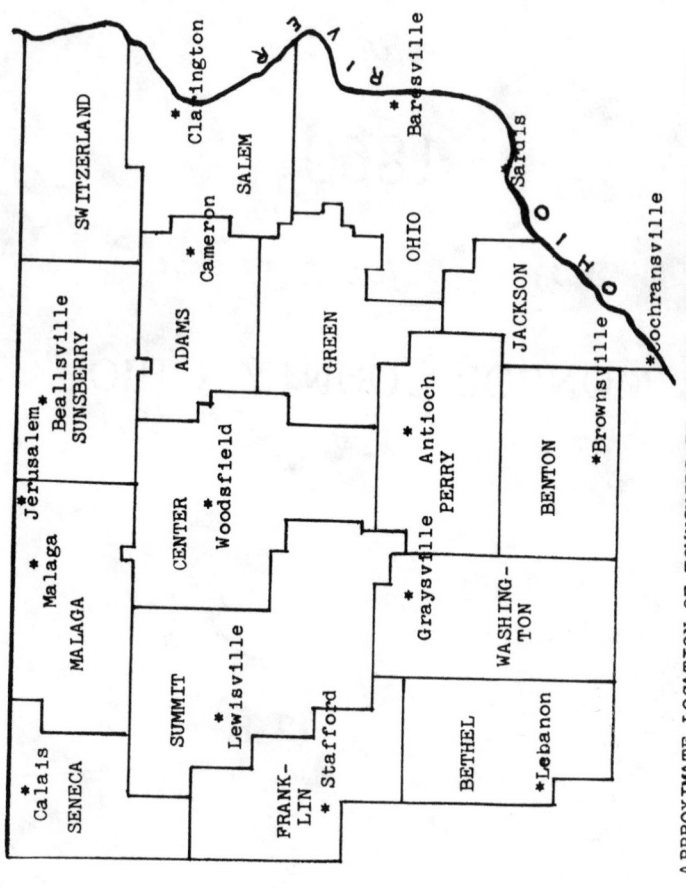

APPROXIMATE LOCATION OF TOWNSHIPS IN MONROE COUNTY, OHIO, IN 1860.
Based on "Map of Monroe County, Ohio, by Jno. B. Noll, 1869."
Published at Cincinnati by Ergott, Forbriger & Co.

THE FEDERAL CENSUS

of

1860

for

MONROE COUNTY, OHIO

Compiled and Indexed

by

Wilma S. Davis

PICTON PRESS

CAMDEN, MAINE

First Printing October 1967
Second Printing October 1996

This book is available from:

Monroe County Historical Society
PO Box 538
Woodsfield, OH 43793
Tel: (614) 472-1933

and also from

Picton Press
PO Box 250
Rockport, ME 04856-0250

Visa/MasterCard orders:
1-207-236-6565
FAX orders: 1-207-236-6713

Manufactured in the United States of America
Printed on 50# acid-free paper

PUBLISHER'S PREFACE TO THE 1996 PRINTING

Wilma S. Davis meticulously transcribed, arranged, and indexed both the 1850 and 1860 Federal censuses of Monroe County, Ohio some thirty years ago. She published the 1850 census in Washington, DC in 1965; the 1860 census there in 1967. The Monroe County Historical Society was subsequently established in Monroe County, Ohio on 28 February 1974, and has now grown to approximately 400 members. For many years the Society distributed both Ms Davis' 1860 Federal census of Monroe County and her companion work on the 1850 Federal census of Monroe County.

However all copies of both books have been sold out for some time now, and as a new generation of researchers has come along, the usefulness and ease of access to the census records offered by Ms Davis' books has been greatly missed.

The Monroe County Historical Society and Picton Press are therefore extremely pleased to be able to bring you a new printing of Wilma Davis' 1860 census, hoping that it will offer you the information you seek. Researchers who are interested in Monroe County and its environs are encouraged to join the Society and support its activities. The Society may be contacted at: Monroe County Historical Society, PO Box 538, Woodsfield, OH 43793.

Picton Press 17 July 1996

INTRODUCTION

Monroe County, Ohio, was created from Belmont, Guernsey, and Washington counties on January 29, 1813. It is located in the southeastern part of the state, with the Ohio River forming most of its eastern boundary. On March 11, 1851, Monroe County contributed several of her western townships to the formation of Ohio's newest county--Noble--and this resulted in the re-drawing of township limits as well as the western boundary of the county itself. Thus a comparison of the map contained in my transcript of the 1850 census with the one included in this volume will reveal a number of changes during the ten-year period.

As stated in my previous volume, the courthouses at Woodsfield experienced several fires, climaxing with a rather serious one in 1867. Consequently many records of value to historians and genealogists interested in the earlier years of the county have been either lost or destroyed. In order to make supplemental records available to researchers, therefore, Catherine Foreaker Fedorchak of Gary, Indiana, and Sara Dolph Foraker of Topeka, Kansas, included a transcript of the federal census of 1820 for this county in their Monroe County, Ohio, Genealogical Records, Volume III, published in 1964. The following year, I published an indexed transcript of the 1850 census for the same county. The present edition of the 1860 census is being offered, therefore, as another attempt to fill the gap created by the loss of early county records.

A comparison of the present volume with my previous one will reveal several changes in format. These changes are the result of comments and suggestions received from a number of my readers. It is hoped that these changes will facilitate the use of the transcript by both individuals and libraries. The material reproduced here was first prepared from a microfilm copy and then compared with the original volume now in the collections of The National Archives here in Washington, D. C.

In compiling the original census records, the enumerator transcribed his information on large printed sheets. Each side of the sheet was imprinted with: (1) a heading which provided space for the name of the county, the township or district, the post-office, date, page and name of the enumerator; (2) fourteen vertical columns of information; (3) forty numbered lines for the names of the individuals being counted; and lastly, (4) space for totaling information inserted in various columns. At a later date, the sheets for an entire county were collected and bound into volumes. During this process each sheet was numbered consecutively in the upper right-hand corner. Since this stamped number is usually more accurate than the pagination inserted by each enumerator, citing this sheet number in describing the location of an individual or family in the records is generally preferred. Accordingly, the beginning of each sheet is indicated on the following pages by listing the enumerator's page at the left margin, giving the date in the middle of the line, and then providing the sheet number or its verso at the right-hand margin.

1

Then, because of the lack of space across the ordinary typed page, the fourteen columns of the original census sheet have been combined in the following manner:

1. The first column is the numbered line of the original sheet. Occasionally two names were inserted in one line by the enumerator; in which case, the line number is given twice. Where the enumerators failed to use all the lines on his sheet, only the lines used are indicated.

2. Dwelling houses numbered in order of visitation/ Families numbered in order of visitation.

3. Name of every person whose usual place of abode on the first day of June, 1860, was in this family. The names have not been edited for spelling and have been transcribed just as the enumerator wrote them, or as read where the legibility was poor.

4. Age.

5. Sex.

6. Color. If white, no notation was made in this column. M was used to denote a Mulatto, and B was used to indicate that the person was a Negro.

7. Profession, occupation, or trade of each person, male or female over 15 years of age.

8. Value of real estate/ Value of personal estate.

9. Place of birth, naming the state, territory, or country. Here, in addition to the familiar abbreviations for the individual states of the U.S.A., the following abbreviations have been used to indicate the foreign countries, provinces or cities listed by the enumerator:

Als.	Alsace	Hes.	Hesse
Aus.	Austria	Hol.	Holland
Bad.	Baden	Ire.	Ireland
Bav.	Bavaria	Mos.	Moselle
Bas.	Basel	N.B.	New Brunswick
Boh.	Bohemia	Old.	Oldenburg
Bre.	Bremen	Pol.	Poland
Brun.	Brunswick	Pr.	Prussia
Byron	Bavaria (?)	Rhein	Rheinbyron (?)
Can.	Canada	R.F.	Republic of
D.G.	Dutch Guiana		Frankford
Dar.	Darmstadt	Sax.	Saxony
Eng.	England	Scot.	Scotland
Fr.	France	Sw.	Switzerland
Ger.	Germany	Tyr.	Tyrol
Ham.	Hamburg	Unk.	Unknown
Han.	Hanover	Wir.	Wirtemburg (?)
H.D.	Hesse-Darmstadt	Wit.	Wittemburg
H.K.	Hesse-Kassel	Wur.	Wurttemburg
		Zur.	Zurich

10. My last column is a combination of several with the informa-
    indicated as follows:

    M   Married within the year
    S   Attended school within the year
    I   Persons over 20 years of age who cannot read
            or write
    1   Blind
    2   Deaf
    3   Dumb
    4   Idiotic
    5   Insane
    6   Pauper

The ability to spell and to write legibly varied greatly with
each enumerator. In many cases the individual himself did not know
how his name was spelled, and if the enumerator was unfamiliar with
the name, he was forced to rely on phonetics. Occasionally accents
or even speech defects altered the sounds in the name, so that the
surname as written appears sometimes in as many forms as there were
families. In at least one instance I suspect a resident of Monroe
County had a wry sense of humor when he had the enumerator list his
wife as "Hettereogenia" Rodes. In the 1850 census she is listed
simply as "Hester" Rodes. So, in consulting the index, if you do
not find the surname you are looking for, try all varieties of spelling
it. If you still cannot find it, scan the particular township in
which the family or individual was known to have resided.

                                              Wilma S. Davis

Washington, D. C.
October, 1967

111

TABLE OF CONTENTS

1	1/1	MOOSE, Henry H.	24	m.	Teacher-Farmer	/200	O.
2		Sarah	19	f.			"
3		M. Adela	3/4	f.			"
4	2/2	DOUGHERTY, John	30	m.	Farmer	1000/704	"
5		Marie	26	f.			"
6		M. Madile	6	f.			¥ S
7		Seryna	4	f.			"
8		Jane	2	f.			"
9	3/3	ROSE, David	58	m.	Farmer	1000/475	Bav.
10		Marget	50	f.			"
11		Lewis	17	m.	Farmer		O.
12	4/4	SMITH, John Adam	31	m.	Farmer	1100/405	Bav.
13		Elisabeth	27	f.			"
14		John	8	m.			O. S
15		Jacob	6	m.			" S
16		Elisabeth	4	f.			"
17		Madelena	2	f.			"
18	5/5	TURNER, Harvey	25	m.	Farmer	800/310	"
19		Elisabeth	21	f.			"
20		Rosiallen	1	f.			"
21	6/6	BURKHART, John					
		Adam	31	m.	Farmer	300/340	Bav.
22		Katherine	29	f.			"
23		Anna Marie	6	f.			Pa.
24		Katherine	4	f.			O.
25		John	1	m.			"
26	7/7	WEBER, C. C.	37	m.	Farmer	2500/1247	Bav. I
27		Sarah	33	f.			Fr. I
28		Christian	14	m.			O. S
29		Louisa	12	f.			" S
30		Philip	10	m.			" S
31		Madelena	7	f.			" S
32		David	4	m.			"
33		Frederick	2	m.			"
34		Marget	69	f.			Bav.
35	8/8	WEBER, F. Peter	47	m.	Farmer	3000/1345	"
36		Marget	48	f.			Fr.
37		Frederick	21	m.	Farmer		Va.
38		Marget	19	f.			"
39		Louisa	16	f.			O.
40		Barbara	14	f.			"

1		Elisabeth	11	f.			O.
2		Philip	8	m.			"
3	9/9	GLASER, John	26	m.	Farmer	800/385	Bav.

4		GLASER, Madelena	22	f.			Bav.	
5		Marget	1 3/12	f.			O.	
6	10/10	BURKHART, Francis	34	m.	Laborer	/50	Bav.	
7		Marie A.	32	f.			"	
8		Mary A.	8	f.			Pa.	
9		George	6	m.			"	
10		Peter	4	m.			O.	
11		Joseph	2	m.			"	
12		Madelena	5/12	f.			"	
13	11/11	SPERY, Martin	48	m.	Farmer	1200/470	Fr.	
14		Elisabeth	48	f.			Bav.	
15		Madelena	10	f.			O.	S
16		Frederick	9	m.			"	S
17		Lewis	7	m.			"	S
18	12/12	KESTNER, Jacob	38	m.	Farmer	500/400	Bav.	
19		Barbara	36	f.			H-D.	I
20		Jacob	13	m.			Pa.	S
21		Frederick	4	m.			O.	
22		George	2	m.			"	
23	13/13	HAASE, John	71	m.	Laborer	/25	H-D.	I
24	14/14	DENBOW, Bazil	42	m.	Farmer	600/297	Md.	
25		Ruth	38	f.			O.	
26		Hana J.	14	f.			"	S
27		James	12	m.			"	S
28		Martha A.	10	f.			"	S
29		W. J.	7	m.			"	S
30		Sarah A.	4	f.			"	
31		Mary K.	4/12	f.			"	
32	15/15	McMILLEN, James	46	m.	Farmer	600/347	Ire.	
33		Marget J.	43	f.			"	I
34		Allen	19	m.			"	
35		James	17	m.	Farmer		"	
36		Elisabeth	14	f.			"	
37		John	12	m.			O.	
38		Wm.	8	m.			"	
39	16/16	DENBOW, John Jr.	28	m.	Farmer	600/362	Md.	I
40		Sarah	26	f.			O.	I

1		Mary E.	3	f.			O.	
2		J. W.	1	m.			"	
3		RILEY, Robert	6	m.	Adopted		"	
4	17/17	DENBOW, James	38	m.	Farmer	550/622	"	
5		R. A.	25	f.			"	I
6		Rachel A.	10	f.			"	
7		David A.	7	m.			"	
8		Marget S.	5	f.			"	
9		Anna M.	3	f.			"	
10		Francis O.	1	m.			"	

11	18/18	NASER, C. C.	29	m.	Merchant	350/700	Bav. M
12		Louisa	24	f.			Pa..M
13	19/19	BAKIO, George	33	m.	Grocer	600/100	Bav.
14		Charlotte	29	f.			
15		Frederick	4	m.			O.
16		(Marie	2	f.			"
17		(Henry	2	m.			
18	20/20	BRISTOR, James	49	m.	Farmer	6000/1422	"
19		Marget	50	f.			"
20		Wm. Samuel	16	m.			"
21		Nancy T.	12	f.			"
22	21/21	WEBER, Christian	33	m.	Merchant	5000/2494	Bav.
23		Caroline	35	f.			O.
24	22/22	BILLMAN, F. C.	31	m.	Clerk	/300	Sw. M
25		Hanna Jane	22	f.			O. M
26	23/23	KESTNER, George L.	27	m.	Saw-miller	/500	Bav.
27		Elisabeth	25	f.			"
28		George L.	4	m.			Pa.
29		Elisabeth	2	f.			O.
30	24/24	WITTENBROCK, Fred	42	m.	Farmer	2500/1468	Pr.
31		Elisabeth	35	f.			Bav.
32		Henry	14	m.			Va. S
33		Frederick	12	m.			O. S
34		William	10	m.			" S
35		Madelena	8	f.			" S
36		John	6	m.			" S
37		Charles	4	m.			"
38		Lewis	3	m.			"
39		George	1 6/12	m.			
40	25/25	DENBOW, William	21	m.		/150	"

1		Anna	21	f.			O.
2		Thomas	2	m.			"
3		Hamilton	6/12	m.			"
4		BIDENHARN, William					
		J.	19	m.	Clerk		"
5	26/26	POGGENBURG, George	25	m.	Merchant	600/1500	Han.
6		Maria	21	f.			O.
7		Mina	6/12	f.			"
8		PIERSON, Josiah	21	m.	Teacher	1200/50	"
9	27/27	BUTT, Michael	49	m.	Laborer	310/	Bav.
10		Elisabeth	16	f.			O.
11		Jacob	19	m.	Cordwainer		"
12	28/28	FISHER, John	49	m.	Blacksmith	600/50	"
13		Mary J.	49	f.			Ire.
14		William	18	m.	Blacksmith		O.

15		FISHER, Joseph	16	m.			O.
16		Isaac	14	m.			"
17		Garison	12	m.			"
18		Hanna Jane	10	f.			"
19	29/29	WATSON, George W.	42	m.	Cabinetmaker	300/200	Va.
20		Mary A.	45	f.			O.
21		Charles D.	17	m.	Laborer		" S
22		John W.	14	m.			" S
23		Theoder E.	12	m.			" S
24		Mary R.	10	f.			" S
25		Martin P.	8	m.			" S
26		James A.	6	m.			" S
27		Lucy J.	4	f.			"
28	30/30	FISHER, Jesse	39	m.	Carpenter	500/200	"
29		Martha W.	38	f.			"
30		John R.	15	m.			"
31		Katura J.	13	f.			" S
32		Spencer S.	10	m.			" S
33		Mary K.	7	f.			"
34		Albert H.	5	m.			"
35		Boean W.	3	m.			"
36	31/31	BENDER, Mary Elisa-beth	43	f.		2000/	Bav.
37		Henry T.	22	m.	Cabinetmaker	/100	Pa.
38		Lewis	18	m.	Cabinetmaker		"
39		Christian J.	15	m.			O.S
40		Dorotha	11	f.			" S

1		Lucinda B.	9	f.			O.S
2	32/32	WOODARD, John M.	38	m.	Minister	/50	"
3		Mary	46	f.			Pa.
4		Sarah J.	17	f.			O.S
5		Stephen P.	16	m.	Student		" S
6		George H.	14	m.			" S
7		Henry R.	12	m.			" S
8		Mary A.	10	f.			" S
9		John S.	8	m.			" S
10	33/33	JOHANY, Henry	39	m.	Wagonmaker	1000/50	Han.
11		Sarah	27	f.			O.I
12		Mary A.	11	f.			" S
13		Adelina	6	f.			"
14		Henry	3	m.			"
15		William	1	m.			"
16		JOHANY, Bernhard	32	m.	Wagonmaker		Han.
17	34/34	WEBER, Philip	34	m.	Tailor	300/	Bav.
18		Christina	29	f.			"
19		Madelena	9	f.			O.S
20		Elisabeth	7	f.			" S
21		Albert	5	m.			"
22		George W.	2	m.			"

23	35/35	REED, G. W.	42	m.	Physician	600/300	Md.
24		Mary E.	38	f.			Va.
25		Marget E.	18	f.			O. S
26		John	16	m.			" S
27		Hiram	14	m.			" S
28		Theodor	12	m.			" S
29		Charles	8	m.			" S
30		L. J.	5	f.			"
31		G. W.	1 3/12	m.			"
32	36/36	SHIMP, Henry	35	m.	Cigarmaker	600/100	Bav.
33		Caroline	31	f.			O.
34		Katherine	10	f.			" S
35		Martin	9	m.			" S
36		Sarah M.	6	f.			"
37		Mary M.	3	f.			"
38		Henry	1	m.			"
							"
39	37/37	BUCHANAN, Alex.	38	m.	Farmer	3000/653	" I
40		Sarah	28	f.			

Page 6   10 July 1860   Sheet 3 verso

1		Clelland	14	m.			O. S
2		James	5	m.			"
3		Jacob M.	2	m.			"
4		Hyade	6/12	f.			
5	38/38	NEUHART, Lawrence	48	m.	Farmer	1200/800	Bav.
6		Elisabeth	37	f.			H-D.
7		Mary	17	f.			O.
8		Elisabeth	16	f.			"
9		Niclas	11	m.			Pa. S
10		Barbara	9	f.			O. S
11		Lawrence	7	m.			" S
12		Jacob	5	m.			"
13		Marget	10/12	f.			"
14	39/39	BUTT, Baltzer	28	m.	Wagoner	/300	Bav.
15		Marget	27	f.			"
16		Louisa	9	f.			O. S
17		Madelena	6	f.			" S
18		John J.	4	m.			"
19		John	2	m.			"
20	40/40	WEBER, Phillip	38	m.	Farmer	3000/2240	Bav.
21		Cassey	34	f.			Pa. I
22		Madelena	14	f.			Va. S
23		Christian	9	m.			O. S
24		George	3	m.			"
25		Jacob	8/12	m.			"
26		Peter	79	m.	Farmer	/500	Bav.
27		HANDSHUMACHER,					
		Phillip	23	m.	Carpenter		O.
28	41/41	STAIN, Henry J.	52	m.	Shoemaker	1000/100	Bav.
29		Madelena	49	f.			"
30		Frederick	22	m.	Carpenter	1500/300	"

31		STAIN, Lewis	18	m.	Cabinetmaker		Bav. S
32	42/42	STAIN, Jacob	25	m.	Blacksmith	300/100	"
33		Mary A.	24	f.			Pa.
34		John	9	m.	Adopted		O.
35	43/43	MOORE, William	52	m.	Tailor	/100	Bav.
36		Katherine	60	f.			" I
37	44/44	JOUNG, Michael	54	m.	Farmer	1000/481	"
38		Marget	53	f.			"
39		Sarah	22	f.			"
40	45/45	JOUNG, Frederick	30	m.	Laborer	/150	"

1		Eva	22	f.			O. I
2	46/46	BUTT, Baltzer Sr.	65	m.	Farmer	1800/524	Bav.
3		Barbara	63	f.			"
4	47/47	BUTT, Marx	26	m.	Laborer		O.
5		Caroline	23	f.			"
6		Jacob	4	m.			"
7		Katharina	2	f.			"
8		Louisa	4/12	f.			"
9	48/48	NEUHART, Jacob	26	m.	Farmer	800/760	Bav.
10		Marie	26	f.			O.
11		Ephraim	5	m.			"
12		David	2	m.			"
13	49/49	HAASE, John G.	30	m.	Shoemaker	/50	Wur.
14		Anna M.	25	f.			Bav.
15		Johanna M.	1	f.			O.
16	50/50	KENNEDY, Wm	56	m.	Farmer	2800/880	Ire.
17		Martha J.	42	f.			N.Y.
18		Mary	18	f.			O. S
19		James	16	m.			" S
20		Thomas	14	m.			" S
21		Elisabeth	12	f.			" S
22		Feeba J.	10	f.			" S
23		Wm.	8	m.			" S
24		John A.	6	m.			" S
25		Arthur	3	m.			"
26	51/51	EYERS, John H.	42	m.	Farmer	2500/892	"
27		Susan	27	f.			"
28		Marget A.	22	f.	Domestic		"
29		Mary E.	8	f.			" S
30	52/52	SLAP, Christian	31	m.	Tailor		H-D.
31		Mary	32	f.			Bav.
32		Katharine	8	f.			Pa. S
33		FLAMM, Lewis	7	m.	Adopted		" S

34		SLAP, Charles	2	m.			Pa.	
35		Elisabeth	2	f.			"	
36		Mary	9	f.	Adopted		"	
37	53/53	DEARTH, Barnabas	41	m.	Farmer	1000/1127	O.	
38		Mary Jane	33	f.			Md.	
39		Sarah A.	15	f.			O.	S
40		F.	12	f.			"	S

Page 8			10 July 1860				Sheet 4 verso	
1		B.	10	m.			"	S
2		Wm.	8	m.			"	S
3		Nancy J.	2	f.			"	
4	54/54	KOCHERT, Fred	34	m.	Blacksmith	800/300	Bav.	
5		Elisabeth	34	f.			"	
6		Katherine	14	f.			"	S
7		Jacob	11	m.			"	S
8		Elisabeth	7	f.			O.	S
9		Mary A.	3	f.			"	
10		Louisa	6/12	f.				
11	55/55	SHENK, Fred	62	m.	Laborer		Bav.	
12		Barbara	58	f.			"	
13		Eva	18	f.			"	
14		NEEP, Jacob	61	m.	Laborer	/100	"	I
15	56/56	HARBIN, Darling	38	m.	Laborer	/100	O.	
16		Elisa	42	f.			Va.	
17		John W.	18	m.	Laborer		O.	
18		G. W.	12	m.			"	S
19		Martha A.	14	f.			"	S
20		Mary A.	10	f.			"	S
21	57/57	FISHER, Joseph	56	m.	Laborer	/50	Va.	
22		Elisabeth	35	f.			O.	
23		Susanah	9	f.			"	
24		Benjamin	13	m.			"	
25		Levi	3	m.			"	
26	58/58	DENBOW, John Sr.	63	m.	Laborer	600/	Md.	
27		Mahaley	48	f.			O.	
28	59/59	BROWN, Josiah Sr.	57	m.	Farmer	3000/1217	Va.	
29		Mary	50	f.			O.	
30		Ruth	24	f.			"	
31		Josiah Jr.	20	m.	Farmer	/100	"	
32		John	18	m.	Farmer		"	S
33		James	16	m.			"	S
34		Wilbert	14	m.			"	S
35		Absolon	12	m.			"	S
36		Vincent	6	m.			"	S
37		Sarah	11	f.			"	S
38	60/60	CAMPELL, David	45	m.	Teacher-Farmer 1800/825		Ire.	
39		Mary	40	f.			O.	

40		CAMPELL, Andrew	17	m.	Farmer		Va.	S

1		Mary A.	15	f.			O.	S
2		Fanny J.	13	f.			"	S
3		Wm. David	4	m.			"	
4	61/61	FLEMING, Wm.	72	m.	Farmer	1600/205	Ire.	
5		Mary	78	f.			"	I
6		GIFFIN, Mary Jane	20	f.	Domestic		O.	
7	62/62	BECKER, Joseph	34	m.	Farmer	2000/1230	Bav.	
8		Christina	34	f.			"	
9		Barbara	12	f.			O.	S
10		Marget	10	f.			"	S
11		John	8	m.			"	S
12		Theobald	6	m.			"	S
13		George	4	m.			"	
14		Mary	2	f.			"	
15		George	69	m.	Laborer	/725	Bav.	
16		HELBLING, Mary A.	69	f.			"	
17	63/63	FISHER, John R.	31	m.	Farmer	2000/950	O.	
18		Marget A.	27	f.			"	
19		James M.	7	m.			"	S
20		Charles F.	5	m.			"	
21		Martha Jane	1 7/12	f.			"	
22	64/64	BACHT, Adam	70	m.	Farmer	2000/550	Pa.	I
23		Susanah	60	f.			"	I
24		Emanuel	24	m.	Farmer		O.	
25		Henry	30	m.	Farmer		"	I
26		Joseph	19	m.	Farmer		"	
27		Mary A.	35	f.			"	I
28		Backey	15	f.			"	S
29		FISHER, Hariette	8	f.	Adopted		"	
30	65/65	STARKEY, Gabriel	71	m.	Farmer	600/370	Va.	
31		Mary	45	f.			Pa.	
32		Sarah A.	10	f.			O.	S
33		Marget	7	f.			"	S
34	66/66	HUNTER, Anthony	55	m.	Farmer	2400/742	Ire.	
35		Jane	54	f.			"	
36		Samuel	19	m.			O.	
37		John	14	m.			"	
38		Amalie	12	f.			"	S
39		Sarah A.	10	f.			"	S
40	67/67	DAILY, Robert	40	m.	Laborer	/50	"	

1		Hanna	35	f.			O. I
2		Rachel	15	f.			"
3		Sarah	13	f.			"

4		DAILY, Christian	11	m.			O.
5		Nancy	6	f.			"
6		Bathie	4	f.			"
7		George	3	m.			"
8		Pauly	1 6/12	f.			"
9	68/68	PICKENS, Martha	22	f.	Domestic		"
10		Marget	24	f.	Domestic		"
11		Nancy	30	f.	Domestic	2000/200	"
12		James C.	11	m.			" S
13		Rebecca J.	7	f.			" S
14		Wm. J.	4	m.			"
15		Thomas A.	2	m.			"
16	69/69	PICKENS, Wm.	26	m.	Laborer	/200	"
17	70/70	HUNTER, Anthony Jr.	26	m.	Laborer	/150	"
18		Mary	20	f.			"
19		(Samuel	3	m.			"
20		(Vincent	3	m.			"
21		John W.	1	m.			"
22		PICKENS, Ross	1	m.			"
23		Anna M.	2	f.			"
24	71/71	WEBER, George	35	m.	Day Laborer	/100	Fr.
25		Elisabeth	27	f.			Bav.
26		George	12	m.			Fr. S
27		Caroline	5	f.			Bav.
28		Elisa	2	f.			Pa.
29	72/72	EGGER, Jacob	41	m.	Farmer	2000/1800	N.J.
30		Marget	30	f.			Fr.
31		Emilia	9	f.			O. S
32		George J.	8	m.			" S
33		Fred W.	6	m.			" S
34		Elisa	4	f.			"
35		Louisa	2	f.			"
36		John Henry	3/12	m.			"
37	73/73	SAGESER, Jacob	34	m.	Farmer	1500/970	Sw.
38		Elisabeth	46	f.			"
39		Elisa	6	f.			O.
40	74/74	SHEETS, Henry	58	m.	Farmer		Bav.

Page 11			11 July 1860				Sheet 6
1		Mary	57	f.			Bav.
2		George	17	m.			O. 4
3	75/75	WAHL, Mary K.	42	f.		3000/717	Fr. I
4		George	20	m.	Farmer		O.
5		Mary	19	f.			"
6		Madelena	17	f.			" S
7		Barbara	15	f.			" S
8		John	13	m.			" S

9		WAHL, Peter	6	m.			O.	
10		Adam	10	m.			"	S
11		Hanna	5	f.			"	
12		Phelomina	3	f.			"	
13	76/76	JACKEY, Jacob	52	m.	Farmer	2000/350	Bav.	
14		Madelena	56	f.			"	
15		Philip	23	m.	Farmer		O.	
16		Henry	21	m.	Farmer		"	
17		Christian	14	m.	Farmer		"	S
18	77/77	ROSE, Jacob	60	m.	Farmer	1500/970	Bav.	
19		Marget	50	f.			"	
20		Jacob Jr.	23	m.	Blacksmith		"	
21		Fred	21	m.	Laborer		"	
22		Mary	11	f.			O.	S
23		Katherina	8	f.			"	S
24	78/78	JONES, John	45	m.	Farmer	2000/752	Pa.	I
25		Marget	41	f.			O.	
26		William H.	18	m.	Farmer		"	
27		Elisabeth	16	f.			"	S
28		Jacob	13	m.			"	S
29		Mary F.	11	f.			"	S
30		Macinda	9	f.			"	S
31		Wilson S.	7	m.			"	S
32		James S.	6/12	m.			"	
33	79/79	BUTT, John	22	m.	Grocer	400/75	"	
34		SMITH, Xavier	63	m.	Laborer	/600	Bav.	
35	80/80	WISE, William	30	m.	Farmer	1800/750	O.	
36		Mary	27	f.			Va.	I
37		Lucinda	10	f.			O.	S
38		Ruth	9	f.			"	S
39		Elisabeth	7	f.			"	S
40		Rachel	5	f.			"	

Page 12   12 July 1860   Sheet 6 verso

1		Peter L.	6/12	m.			"	
2	81/81	WISE, John C.	34	m.	Farmer	1500/620	"	
3		Louisa M.	31	f.			"	
4		Theodor B.	9	m.			"	S
5		Charles W.	7	m.			"	S
6	82/82	WISE, Julie A.	37	f.		500/490	"	
7		Jacob	13	m.			"	S
8		Elisa	13	f.			"	S
9		Sarah A.	10	f.			"	S
10	83/83	WILSON, John	50	m.	Laborer	/25	O.	
11		Nancy	44	f.			Mass.	
12		Jane	15	f.			O.	
13		Assey	13	f.			"	S
14		Mary A.	10	f.			"	S

15	84/84	WISE, Samuel	25	m.	Farmer	2500/650	O.	I
16		Elisabeth	25	f.			"	
17		M. A.	3	f.			"	
18		Charles W.	1	m.			"	
19		James	21	m.	Laborer		"	
20	85/85	WISE, Mary A.	47	f.		/200	"	I
21		Robert B.	18	m.	Farmer		"	
22		Marget	14	f.			"	
23		Mary Elisabeth	7	f.			"	
24		Mary	87	f.			Md.	I
25	86/86	DEARTH, John	37	m.	Farmer	1250/745	O.	
26		Elisabeth	30	f.			Pa.	I
27		Elias	14	m.			O.	S
28		Nancy	13	f.			"	S
29		Edward	9	m.			"	S
30		Mary E.	5	f.			"	
31		Mary J.	3	f.			"	
32	87/87	LIGHT, Jacob	55	m.	Laborer		Va.	I
33		Rachel	42	f.			O.	I
34		Mathias J.	22	m.	Laborer		"	I
35		James	18	m.	Laborer		"	
36		Mary A.	14	f.			"	
37		Martin	11	m.			"	
38		Thomas	5	m.			"	
39		Robert	1	m.			"	
40	88/88	HOGUE, Nelson	46	m.	Farmer	8750/4525Va.		

Page 13   12 July 1860   Sheet 7

1		Susan A.	44	f.			O.	
2		William	23	m.	Farmer		"	
3		Luvina	20	f.			"	
4		Jacob	19	m.	Farmer		"	
5		Mary	17	f.			"	S
6		Stephen	16	m.			"	S
7		Lydlie	14	f.			"	S
8		John	12	m.			"	S
9		Martha	10	f.			"	S
10		James	8	m.			"	S
11	89/89	BROWN, Edward	22	m.	Farmer	1900/700	"	
12		Marget	22	f.			"	
13	90/90	BOBST, Anthony	54	m.	Farmer	1200/350	Fr.	I
14		Regina	51	f.			"	
15		Phelomina	15	f.			Pa.	S
16		Emma	8	f.			"	S
17	91/91	BURKHART, John Adam	27	m.	Farmer	1200/750	Bav.	
18		Anny Mary	28	f.			"	
19		Katharine	5	f.			Pa.	
20		HUFFMAN, Jacob	18	m.	Cordwainer		O.	

21		SOOTER, Elisabeth	64	f.			Sw.	
22	92/92	SOOTER, David F.	30	m.	Cordwainer	600/100	"	
23		Louisa	23	f.			Bav.	
24		Frederick	1 1/2	m.			O.	
25		WAGENFIELD, Fred	23	m.	Clerk	/940	Bre.	
26		ZWICK, Martin	35	m.	Day Laborer		Bav.	
27		HODGE, Robert	30	m.	Day Laborer		Va.	
28		STEEL, Christian	25	m.	Day Laborer		O.	
29	93/93	HAMILTON, Jacob H.	42	m.	Merchant	8280/3140	Pa.	
30		Mary	40	f.			Ire.	
31		Marget J.	17	f.			O.	
32		Elisabeth	15	f.			"	S
33		Adeline	13	f.			"	S
34		M. N.	11	m.			"	S
35		John C.	9	m.			"	S
36		G. W.	7	m.			"	S
37		Ibenella	5	f.			"	
38		Oliver	3	m.			"	
39		ROBINSON, John	15	m.	Adopted		"	S
40	94/94	HARBIN, Starkey	24	m.	Carpenter	/50	"	

Page 14			12 July 1860				Sheet 7 verso	
1		Louisa	20	f.			O.	
2		John	1	m.			"	
3	95/95	POLES, Edward	27	m.	Carpenter	/150	Pa.	
4		Sarah	25	f.			"	
5		William	7	m.			"	
6		Maria	3	f.			"	
7	96/96	PEGGIN, Francis	26	m.	Laborer	/25	"	
8		A. W.	25	f.			"	
9		William	6	m.			"	
10		Jinsie	5	f.			"	
11		Thomas W.	3	m.			"	
12		Jamenan	1	f.			"	
13		HOGUE, Mary J.	18	f.	Domestic		"	
14	97/97	MYER, Bernhard	62	m.	Farmer	225/150	Wur.	
15		Anna J.	45	f.			H-D.	I
16		HAASE, Henry	14	m.	Adopted		"	S
17	98/98	METZ, Leonhard	62	m.	Farmer	1200/700	Bav.	
18		Magdalena	52	f.			"	
19		William	18	m.	Farmer		"	
20		Adam	16	m.	Farmer		"	
21	99/99	FYOCK, George	35	m.	Farmer	2000/925	Bav.	
22		Katharine	27	f.			N.Y.	
23		Jacob	12	m.			O.	S
24		Mary	7	f.			"	
25		Louisa	5	f.			"	
26		George	3	m.			"	
27		Henry	1	m.			"	

28	100/100	SMELZENBAUGH, Joseph	45	m.	Stonemason		Tyr.
29		Fransica	34	f.			Sw. I
30		William	4	m.			O.
31		Bernhard	2	m.			"
32	101/101	PAUL, Peter	68	m.	Farmer	1500/680	Bav.
33		Doretha	51	f.			Fr.
34		John	19	m.	Farmer		O.
35	102/102	RUCKER, Ephraim	61	m.	Farmer	3000/950	"
36		Martha M.	17	f.			"
37	103/103	RUCKER, Mathias	25	m.	Farmer	/200	"
38		Elisabeth	29	f.			"
39		William L.	4	m.			"
40		Martha	2	f.			"

Page 15   13 July 1860   Sheet 8

1		Backey	24	f.	Domestic		O.	
2		A. Jane	19	f.	Domestic		"	
3	104/104	RUCKER, Landy	44	m.	Farmer	/150	"	
4		Anny	37	f.			"	
5		Hubert	17	m.	Laborer		"	
6		B. Thomas	15	m.			"	S
7		Acey	7	f.			"	S
8	105/105	RUCKER, Jackson	40	m.	Laborer		"	
9		Assbey	21	f.			"	
10		Edward L.	3	m.			"	
11		R. A.	1	f.			"	
12		James J.	2	m.			"	
13		John	1	m.			"	
14	106/106	DEARTH, Ephraim	60	m.	Farmer	1500/800	"	I
15		Pauly M.	54	f.			Pa.	I
16		Lewis	21	m.	Farmer		O.	
17		Marget	19	f.			"	
18		Maria	16	f.			"	
19	107/107	GIBBINS, Charles	40	m.	Farmer	1500/350	"	
20		D.	44	f.			Pa.	I
21		Benjamin	21	m.	Laborer		O.	
22		Elisa	16	f.			"	S
23		William	14	m.			"	S
24		George	4	m.			"	
25		Marget	3/4	f.			"	
26	108/108	SCOTT, Samuel	38	m.	Farmer	1500/600	Pa.	I
27		Elisabeth	26	f.			O.	I
28		Nancy J.	2	f.			"	
29		William Thom.	3/4	m.			"	
30		Anna	72	f.			Md.	I
31	109/109	SCOTT, John	44	m.	Farmer	1000/560	Pa.	
32		Jane	34	f.			Va.	
33		Isaac	16	m.			O.	S

34		SCOTT, Mary	13	f.			O. S
35		BARNES, Wm. Andrew	5	m.	Adopted		"
36	110/110	BURKHART, Vantal	60	m.	Farmer	1500/930	Bav.
37		Katherine	24	f.			"
38		Francis J.	6/12	m.			O.
39		John	21	m.	Laborer		Bav.
40		STEUERNACHEL, Marget	54	f.	Domestic		"

1	111/111	SPANGLER, Michael	54	m.	Farmer	4000/1350	Bav.
2		Mary A.	45	f.			Fr.
3		John	19	m.	Farmer		O.
4		Simon	17	m.	Farmer		"
5		Joseph	15	m.			" S
6		Theobald	13	m.			" S
7		Anna M.	11	f.			" S
8		Francis M.	9	m.			" S
9		Uttilia	7	f.			" S
10		Philomina	4	f.			"
11	112/112	SWALLY, John	32	m.	Farmer	1200/780	Fr.
12		Barbara	31	f.			"
13		BROONER, Francis L.	11	m.	Adopted		O.
14		August	2	m.	Adopted		"
15		ANTHONY, Koontz	38	m.	Weaver		Fr.
16	113/113	NEUHARD, Philip	36	m.	Farmer	2000/730	Bav.
17		Maria	26	f.			Pr.
18		Jacob J.	11	m.			O.
19		Gottlieb	9	m.			" S
20		Ernest	7	m.			"
21		Philip	5	m.			"
22		Maria	2	f.			"
23	114/114	DEMUTH, Peter	41	m.	Farmer	800/300	Pr.
24		Katharine	33	f.			Fr. I
25		Mary	14	f.			Pa.
26		Joseph	12	m.			"
27		Peter	10	m.			O. S
28		John	8	m.			" S
29		Magdelana	6	f.			"
30		Katharine	4	f.			"
31		Barbara	2	f.			"
32		George	1/2	m.			"
33	115/115	KARG, Gottlieb	63	m.	Farmer	1200/700	Sax.
34		Elisa	52	f.			Bav.
35		Caroline	17	f.			O.
36		Lewis	12	m.			" S
37		Marget	10	f.			" S
38	116/116	BURKHART, Sebastian	37	m.	Farmer	1000/500	Bav.
39		Katharine	18	f.			" I
40	117/117	NAUER, George	37	m.	Farmer	1200/675	Bav.

Page 17		13, 14 July 1860					Sheet 9

1		NAUER, Mary A.	35	f.			Bav.
2		Mary Anna	12	f.			O.
3		Philip	10	m.			"
4		John	8	m.			"
5		George	6	m.			"
6		Katharine	4	f.			"
7		Sebastian	2	m.			

8	118/118	ZWICK, John	45	m.	Laborer	/25	Bav.
9		Veronica	44	f.			"
10		John	10	m.			"
11		Katharina	4	f.			

12	119/119	BURKHART, Thomas	46	m.	Farmer	2000/850	Bav.
13		Mary	40	f.			"
14		Magdelena	16	f.			O.
15		Sebastian	14	m.			" S
16		John	12	m.			" S
17		Michael	10	m.			" S
18		George	8	m.			" S
19		Mary A.	6	f.			" S
20		F. Joseph	4	m.			"

21	120/120	KINELBERGER,					
		Frederick	23	m.	Laborer	/150	Bav.
22		Christina	25	f.			O.
23		Barbara	2	f.			"
24		Jacob	1/2	m.			"

25	121/121	FRYDAY, Conrad	35	m.	Farmer	1500/840	Hes.
26		A. Mary	28	f.			"
27		Mary	10	f.			O. S
28		Henry	7	m.			" S
29		John	5	m.			"
30		Dina	2	f.			"
31		Sarah	1/2	f.			
32		WISEBORN, Katharine					
		E.	70	f.			Hes.
33		LONG, William	37	m.	Laborer		"

34	122/122	ROSE, Frederick	40	m.	Farmer	3000/980	Bav.
35		Elisa	39	f.			"
36		Elisa	10	f.			Va. S
37		George W.	8	m.			O. S
38		Lewis	6	m.			" S
39		Emilie	4	f.			"
40		Henry	2	m.			"

Page 18		14 July 1860					Sheet 9 verso

| 1 | | Henry J. | 65 | m. | Laborer | | Bav. |
| 2 | | STINEHOFF, Charles | 24 | m. | Laborer | | Brun. |

3	123/123	BAKER, Jacob	53	m.	Farmer	2000/740	Bav.
4		Katherine	33	f.			Hes.
5		Frederick	18	m.	Farmer		O.

6		BAKER, Doretha	14	f.			O.	S
7		Jacob	17	m.	Farmer		"	S
8		Anna M.	2	f.			"	
9		Caspar	10/12	m.			"	
10		BACH, John	12	m.	Adopted		"	S
11		Dina	8	f.	Adopted		"	S
12		BAKER, Mary	6	f.			"	S

13	124/124	KROHNHART, John	26	m.	Cordwainer	600/65	Hes.
14		Barbara	21	f.			O.
15		Jacob	3	m.			"
16		Frederick	1	m.			"

17	125/125	LANTZ, John	41	m.	Carpenter	250/50	H-D.
18		Mary A.	28	f.			
19		Caroline	6/12	f.			O.

20	126/126	WISE, Washington	36	m.	Farmer	7000/3921	Va.	I
21		Elisabeth	35	f.			O.	
22		William	18	m.	Farmer		"	
23		Madaile	13	f.			"	S
24		Nancy J.	11	f.			"	S
25		Janette	9	f.			"	S
26		James	7	m.			"	
27		Mary C.	5	f.			"	
28		Isabelle	3	f.			"	
29		Huldy	2	f.			"	

30	127/127	DECEMBER, John	49	m.	Farmer	1900/695	Bav.
31		Anna	59	f.			"
32		Barbara	20	f.			"
33		Veronicka	16	f.			"
34		George	13	m.			O.	S

35	128/128	HAMILTON, Joseph	34	m.	Farmer	1500/345	"
36		Susanah	25	f.			"
37		James	10	m.			"
38		Jane	5	f.			"
39		Elisa	3	f.			"
40		Marget R.	2	f.			"

Page 19   16 July 1860   Sheet 10

1	129/129	WUCHENER, Wm. F. A.	54	m.	Minister		Wur.

2	130/130	KENNEDY, Alexander	39	m.	Farmer	3000/1400	Ire.
3		Mary	29	f.			O.
4		James	6	m.			"
5		Robert	4	m.			"
6		Thomas	2	m.			"

7	131/131	STARKEY, Sydnor	39	m.	Farmer	2000/604	Va.
8		Elisa A.	38	f.			O.
9		Lucindy	16	f.			"
10		Benjamin	14	m.			"	S
11		James	8	m.			"	S
12		Theodor	1	m.			"

13	132/132	SEBAUGH, John	29	m.	Farmer	3000/1590	Bav.
14		Katherine	20	f.			"
15		Henry	2	m.			O.
16		Jacob	10/12	m.			"
17	133/133	SEBAUGH, Henry	22	m.	Farmer	/300	"
18		Elisabeth	22	f.			Bav.
19		Marget	52	f.			"
20	134/134	SEBAUGH, Elisabeth	31	f.			"
21		John	9	m.			O. S
22		Elisabeth	11	f.			" S
23		Louisa	6	f.			Pa.
24		WOOLBERT, John	21	m.	Laborer		Bav.
25	135/135	BOWMAN, Fred	32	m.	Farmer	3000/1520	"
26		Katharine	31	f.			"
27		John	9	m.			O. S
28		Charles	6	m.			" S
29		William	4	m.			"
30		Elisabeth	2	f.			"
31		SLAP, Mary	8	f.	Adopted		"
32	136/136	BAKER, Mary	40	m.	Farmer	2000/630	Bav.
33		Elisabeth	26	f.			Pa.
34		Lewis	8	m.			O. S
35		Anna M.	5	f.			"
36		George	3	m.			"
37		John	4/12	m.			
38	137/137	HUFFMAN, Conrad	48	m.	Farmer	1000/450	Bav.
39		Elisabeth	47	f.			"
40		Henry	15	m.	Farmer		O. S

Page 20			18 July 1860				Sheet 10 verso
1		Frederick	13	m.			O. S
2		Lewis	9	m.			" S
3		Elisabeth	12	f.			" S
4		Katherine	7	f.			" S
5	138/138	BRUBAUGH, David	55	m.	Farmer	1500/650	Bav.
6		Philipina	54	f.			"
7		Jacob	14	m.			O.
8		Charles	10	m.			"
9	139/139	FRYDAY, Wm.	38	m.	Farmer	1700/620	Hes.
10		Doretha E.	32	f.			"
11		Conrad	13	m.			O. S
12		Caspar	11	m.			" S
13		Henry	9	m.			" S
14		Katherine	7	f.			" S
15		John	5	m.			"
16		George	3	m.			"
17	140/140	BAKER, Michael	55	m.	Farmer	800/590	Bav.
18		Katherine	43	f.			"
19		Katherine	14	f.			" S

20	141/141	SHANK, David	38	m.	Farmer	2000/620	Bav.
21		Marget	32	f.			Hes.
22		Katherine	11	f.			O. S
23		Lewis	5	m.			"
24		Mary	2	f.			"
25		Caroline	1	f.			"
26	142/142	FAELAND, Henry	27	m.	Laborer	/100	Hes.
27		Christina	21	f.			O.
28		Elisabeth	1/2	f.			" 1
29	143/143	CLEGG, Rachel	53	m.		1800/550	Va.
30		Rachel	20	f.			O.
31		Elisa J.	18	f.			" S
32		Maria	16	f.			" S
33		Sarah A.	14	f.			" S
34		Mathilda	13	f.			" S
35	144/144	WISE, Swaze	22	m.	Laborer	/50	"
36		Rebecca	23	f.			"
37	145/145	BARNEHOUSE,					
		Michael	42	m.	Farmer	2000/670	Pa.
38		Nancy	38	f.			"
39		Nancy	21	f.			O.
40		William	20	m.	Farmer		"

Page 21   18 July 1860   Sheet 11

1		Shephard	17	m.	Laborer		O.
2		Orphey	16	m.	Laborer		"
3		Elisabeth	5	f.			"
4		Mathias	14	m.			" S
5		John	11	m.			" S
6		Isaac	7	m.			" S
7		Hamilton	3	m.			"
8		Mary	84	f.			Pa.
9	146/146	DEARTH, Ruben	34	m.	Farmer	1100/490	O.
10		Ester A.	30	f.			"
11		Emilie	12	f.			" S
12		Mary	10	f.			" S
13	147/147	MAHRLE, Valentine	28	m.	Laborer	/100	"
14		Lucynde	25	f.			"
15		Louisa Jane	4	f.			"
16		Rachel A.	5/12	f.			"
17	148/148	SHOUB, Michael	57	m.	Farmer	2000/1050	Bav.
18		Katherine	59	f.			"
19		David	24	m.	Laborer		O.
20		Marget	20	f.			"
21		Elisabeth	18	f.			"
22		Henry	16	m.			" S
23	149/149	CLUND, Jacob	58	m.	Farmer	1700/400	Bav.
24		Doretha	50	f.			"
25		GAERTLER, Louisa	16	f.	Domestic		O.

26		LONG, Herrman	24	m.	Laborer		O.
27	150/150	SHELL, Andrew	51	m.	Farmer	5500/3200	Pa.
28		Elisabeth	38	f.			RF.
29		Lucynde	17	f.			O.
30		Mahale	15	f.			"
31		Henry	17	m.	Farmer		
32		WISE, Charles	16	m.	Laborer		Bav.
33		SHELL, George	76	m.	Laborer		Pa.
34	151/151	NEUHART, John M.	39	m.	Farmer	3000/780	Bav.
35		Katherine	37	f.			Pr.
36		Elisabeth	16	f.			O.
37		Philip	14	m.			" S
38		Henry	12	m.			" S
39		John	10	m.			" S
40		Mary	6	f.			" S

1		Ernestine	4	f.			O.
2		Jacob	2	m.			"
3		Katherine	9/12	f.			"
4	152/152	SHOUB, Philip	52	m.	Farmer	2000/640	Bav.
5		Katherine	55	f.			
6		Philip	21	m.	Laborer		O.
7		Caroline	18	f.			"
8		Doretha	12	f.			"
9	153/153	BARNHARD, Isaac	52	m.	Farmer	6000/8700	Pa.
10		Permillia	51	f.			Va.
11		Hariette	21	f.			O.
12		Leddy A.	19	f.			"
13		Louisa	14	f.			"
14	154/154	SHOUB, John Jr.	31	m.	Farmer	2000/535	Pr.
15		Hanna J.	22	f.			O.
16		Henry	3	m.			"
17		George	2	m.			"
18		Andrew	6/12	m.			
19	155/155	STINEHOFF, Henry	42	m.	Farmer	4000/1050	Brun.
20		Julie	38	f.			"
21		Johanna	15	f.			" S
22		Henry	14	m.			" S
23		Louisa	12	f.			" S
24		Mina	10	f.			" S
25		Julie	8	f.			O. S
26		Charles	6	m.			" S
27		Augusta	4	f.			"
28		George	2	m.			"
29	156/156	ARYS, Rebecca	70	f.		2000/250	Pa.
30		RODGERS, Mary A.	8	f.	Adopted		O. S
31	157/157	NEUHART, Frederick J.	46	m.	Farmer	800/350	Bav.

32		NEUHART, Elisabeth	40	f.			Bav.
33		Frederick	19	m.	Farmer		"
34		Philip	14	m.			" S
35		Lewis	5	m.			O.
36		William	6/12	m.			"
37	158/158	JOUNG, Philip	52	m.	Farmer	1500/610	Bav.
38		Katherine	40	f.			"
39		Henry	22	m.	Laborer		O.
40		Katherine	18	f.			Bav.

Page 23   19 July 1860   Sheet 12

1		Barbara	15	f.			O.
2		Frederick	13	m.			"
3		Michael	10	m.			"
4	159/159	LONG, William	30	m.	Farmer	2000/480	"
5		Rebecca	30	f.			"
6		Susanah	2	f.			"
7		(Daniel Nelson	1	m.			"
8		(Nancy E.	1	f.			"
9		HEADLEY, Theodor	14	m.	Adopted		" S
10	160/160	FLEHMAN, Jacob	46	m.	Farmer	800/410	Bav.
11		Sophia	39	f.			"
12		Philipina	13	f.			O.
13		Jacob	10	m.			"
14		Philip	7	m.			"
15		Marget	5	f.			"
16		Frederick	2	m.			"
17	161/161	FELDNER, Jacob	47	m.	Farmer	600/490	Bav.
18		Marget	46	f.			"
19		Jacob	13	m.			" S
20		Philip	9	m.			" S
21	162/162	HILLOCK, Gottlieb	51	m.	Farmer	2500/1070	Sax.
22		Christina	48	f.			"
23		Frederick	22	m.	Laborer		"
24		Fredericka	20	f.			"
25		Caroline	16	f.			O.
26		Louisa	14	f.			" S
27		Mary	10	f.			" S
28		Henry	8	m.			" S
29	163/163	PAINE, James	28	m.	Farmer	/200	"
30		Elisa	24	f.			"
31		Robert H.	5	m.			"
32		Isaac McFaden	2	m.			"
33		Joseph C.	6/12	m.			"
34		E. B.	80	m.	Retired	1000/480	Va. 1
35	164/164	PAINE, Aaron	34	m.	Laborer	/150	O.
36		Marget A.	25	f.			"
37		Charles M.	3	m.			"
38	165/165	ATTEL, Gottlieb	73	m.	Laborer		Sax.

39		ATTEL, Christina	73	f.			Sax.
40	165/165	SHOUB, Mary E.	48	f.		600/230	Bav.

Page 24   19 July 1860   Sheet 12 verso

1		Katherine	15	f.			Bav.	
2		Elisabeth	9	f.			"	
3	167/167	WHEELER, William	26	m.	Cooper	/100	Bad.	M
4		Caroline	21	f.			Bav.	M
5	168/168	SHOUB, Frederick	24	m.	Cabinetmaker	/100	"	
6		Philipina	23	f.			O.	
7	169/169	REESBECK, Adam	47	m.	Farmer	1800/750	Bav.	
8		Mary	36	f.			Hes.	
9		Katherine	24	f.	Domestic		O.	
10		Maria	17	f.			"	
11		Marcus	14	m.			"	
12		Martin	12	m.			"	
13		Magdelena	7	f.			"	
14		George	5	m.			"	
15		Anna A.	4	f.			"	
16		Elisabeth	2	f.			"	
17		Charles	6/12	m.			Bav.	
18		Anna M.	83	f.				
19	170/170	SMITH, Reuben	71	m.	Farmer	1500/300	Pa.	
20		Anna C.	65	f.			"	
21		McCAMON, Philip	18	m.	Adopted		O.	
22	171/171	NEUHARD, Michael	43	m.	Farmer	3000/790	Bav.	
23		Johanna	41	f.			Sax.	
24		Elisabeth	15	f.			O.	S
25		Johanna	13	f.			"	S
26		Louisa	11	f.			"	S
27		Katherine	9	f.			"	S
28		Christina	7	f.			"	S
29		Frederick	3	m.			"	
30	172/172	SHOUB, John Sr.	55	m.	Farmer	3500/910	Pr.	
31		Mary	53	f.			"	
32		George	23	m.	Laborer		"	
33		Elisabeth	28	f.			"	
34	173/173	STEIGNER, Michael	38	m.	Farmer	1500/760	Bav.	
35		Johanna	20	f.			Brun.	
36		Mary	4/12	f.			O.	
37		Katherine	77	f.			Bav.	
38	174/174	HANDSHUMACHER, Frederick	28	m.	Farmer	1000/430	"	
39		Caroline	26	f.			"	
40		Christian	7	m.			O.	S

1		HANDSHUMACHER, Louis P.	2	m.			O.
2	175/175	REEVS, Thomas H.	21	m.	Laborer		"
3		John W.	18	m.	Laborer		"
4		Elisabeth	12	f.			"
5		H. Lisette	4	f.			"
6		Amilie	33	f.			"
7		Benjamin L.	45	m.	Laborer		"
8	176/176	DIEHL, Cristian	37	m.	Farmer	7600/3325	Fr.
9		Barbara	36	f.			Bav.
10		Jacob	17	m.	Laborer		O.
11		Christian	15	m.			" S
12		Rossina	14	f.			" S
13		Elisabeth	12	f.			" S
14		John	4	m.			"
15		Lewis	1 1/2	m.			"
16	177/177	DENBOW, Levi	28	m.	Laborer	/75	"
17		Rachel	24	f.			"
18		James M.	1	m.			"
19	178/178	HAMILTON, John W.	25	m.	Farmer	2900/750	"
20		M. M.	25	f.			"
21		Wm. F.	3	m.			"
22		DILLON, Rachel	12	f.	Adopted		"
23	179/179	ALLEN, James	28	m.	Farmer	2000/860	"
24		Mary	23	f.			"
25		Josephine C.	4	f.			"
26		McCIDRICK, Elizabeth	9	f.	Adopted		"
27	180/180	ALLEN, Francis	52	m.	Farmer	3200/845	Eng.
28		Martha Jane	48	f.			O.
29		Mary	17	f.			" S
30		Martha Mary	12	f.			" S
31		Katherine E.	9	f.			" S
32		Hariette L.	6	f.			" S
33	181/181	WILLARD, John	28	m.	Carpenter	/120	Pa.
34		Isabella	25	f.			O.
35		Francis	4	m.			"
36		Allen S.	2	m.			"
37		A. Jane	5/12	f.			"
38	182/182	DEVOE, John A.	25	m.	Laborer	/250	"
39		Susanah	19	f.			"
40		John A.	3/12	m.			"

1	183/183	WISE, Shephard	24	m.	Laborer	/105	O.
2		Jane S.	22	f.			"
3		Mary J.	4/12	f.			"

4	184/184	GREENBANK, William	77	m.	Farmer	1800/1180	Eng.
5		Rebecca	60	f.			O.
6		Rodger	24	m.	Laborer		"
7		John	20	m.	Laborer		"
8		George	18	m.	Laborer		"
9		Thomas	15	m.			" S
10		Nancy A.	12	f.			" S
11		Elisa S.	10	f.			" S
12	185/185	XAVIER, Michal	41	m.	Farmer	1400/630	Bav.
13		Marget	46	f.			"
14		Elisabeth	16	f.			O.
15		BOWER, Joseph	11	m.	Adopted		" S
16		XAVIER, George	9	m.			" S
17		Mary	5	f.			"
18		John	3	m.			"
19	186/186	BROWN, Isaac	39	m.	Farmer	1800/470	"
20		Hanna	25	f.			"
21		Alexander	7	m.			" S
22		Mathilda	5/12	f.			"
23		Elihu	21	m.	Laborer		"
24		Elisabeth	60	f.			Va.
25		WITTEM, James	18	m.	Laborer		O.
26	187/187	SMITH, William	56	m.	Farmer	2500/730	Va.
27		Sarah	43	f.			Pa.
28		James	19	m.	Laborer		O.
29		Katherine	15	f.			"
30		William Jr.	13	m.			"
31		Lewis	7	m.			
32		WISE, Mary Elisa-beth	14	f.	Domestic		"
33		MARTIN, Elisabeth	17	f.	Domestic		"
34	188/188	BUCHANAN, Wm.	61	m.	Farmer	3625/800	Pa.
35		Mary	40	f.			"
36		Malicey	5	f.			O.
37		Albert R.	2	m.			"
38		McVAY, Sinclair	16	m.	Laborer		"
39		Eli	11	m.	Adopted		"
40	189/189	SMITH, Thomas	56	m.	Farmer	2500/690	Va.

Page 27			20 July 1860				Sheet 14
1		Helena	45	f.			O.
2		Marget	26	f.			"
3		Jane	22	f.			"
4		Simpson	21	m.	Laborer		"
5		Robert	18	m.	Laborer		"
6		Bloomy	14	f.			" S
7		Peter	12	m.			" S
8		Thomas	10	m.			" S
9		Henry	7	m.			" S
10	190/190	RISE, George	57	m.	Blacksmith	600/100	Bav.

P. O. Woodsfield   Summit Township

11		RISE, Christina	36	f.			Hes.	
12		George W.	18	m.	Laborer		O.	
13		Rinehard	16	m.	Blacksmith		"	
14		John	15	m.	Laborer		"	
15		Lewis	7	m.			"	S
16		Julie	13	f.			"	S
17		Mary	5	f.			"	
18		Sarah	2	f.			"	
19	191/191	BELL, John	39	m.	Physician	/1400	Pa.	
20		Sarah	38	f.				
21		E. W. E.	11	f.			O.	S
22		C. M.	8	m.			"	S
23		M. E.	6	f.			"	
24		A. C. F.	4	m.			"	
25		J. J.	1 6/12	m.			Ia.	
26	192/192	BURKHART, Joseph	24	m.	Laborer	/100	Bav.	M
27		Marget	21	f.			"	M
28	193/193	STEMPERT, Jacob	23	m.	Farmer	1600/430	"	
29		Fredericka	22	f.			Sax.	
30		Philip	1 1/2	m.			O.	

Sheet 14 verso

The State of Ohio, Monroe County:

    I the undersigned Deputy Marshall for Summit
Township County and State aforsaid, so make solemn oth
that the within set of returns were by me made according
to my oth and the instructions, to the best of my knowledge
and belief.

                    Michael Haeffler, Deputy Marshall
                    of Summit Township

Sworn to before me and by the said
Michael Haeffler subscribed in my
presence this 16th day of August
A. D. 1860.

D. Walton, Clerk.

               * * *

P. O. Antioch   Perry Township

Page 1   17 July 1860   Sheet 15

1	1/1	MARTIN, Absolom	44	m.	Farmer	4000/600	O.	
2		Hester	42	f.	Domestic		"	
3		Elaron	17	m.	Farmer		"	S
4		William	13	m.			"	S
5		Albert	10	m.			"	S
6		Daniel	7	m.			"	S
7		Isabel	15	f.	Domestic		"	S

8	2/2	MARTIN, Enoch	25	m.	Teacher		O.
9		Nancy	23	f.	Domestic		"
10		Silvester	3	m.			"
11		George	1	m.			
							"
12	3/3	WEDDLE, Daniel	25	m.	Farmer		"
13		Sarah A.	26	f.	Domestic		"
14		George W.	1	m.			
15	4/4	SHEPHERD, Newten	39	m.	Broom-peddler	1200/300	"
16		Margaret	29	f.	Domestic		Pa.
17		Petter	13	m.			O. S
18		Leander W.	7	m.			"
19		Margaret J.	5	f.			"
20		John F.	4/12	m.			
21	5/5	SMITH, Wm. H.	48	m.	Farmer	/50	N.Y.
22		Mary E.	39	f.	Domestic		N.J.
23		William H.	16	m.			N.Y.
24		Elizabeth	14	f.			" S
25		Orba	11	m.			" S
26		Orrin	9	m.			" S
27		George	6	m.			O.
28		Charles	4	m.			"
29		Margaret A.	2/12	f.			::
30		Ophela	86	f.			Con.
31	6/6	TRUAX, Benjamin	48	m.	Farmer		O.
32		Elizabeth	48	f.	Domestic		Md.
33		Christopher	17	m.	Farmer		O.
34		Mary E.	11	f.			" S
35		Elizabeth J.	8	f.			" S
36		SEILE, Nancy	82	f.			Md. I
37	7/7	TWADDLE, Thomas	27	m.	Farmer	1400/100	O.
38		Luvina	29	f.	Domestic		::
39		Florenzo T.	9/12	f.			"

Page 2			17 July 1860			Sheet 15 verso	
1	8/8	SHEPHERD, James	35	m.	Farmer	3600/350	O.
2		Martha M. H.	31	f.	Domestic		"
3		Silvester F. W.	8	m.			" S
4		Suvana S. E.	6	f.			"
5		Irma S. E.	4	f.			"
5		LUCK, Virginia	19	f.			
							"
6	9/9	MOFFETT, Jacob	55	m.	Farmer		
7		Evans	54	f.			Pa. I
8		William	32	m.	Farmer		O. I
9		Thomas	32	m.	Farmer		"
10		Eldridge	28	m.	Farmer		" I
11		Perry	26	m.	Farmer		:
12		Elizabeth	22	f.	Domestic		"
13		Catharine	18	f.	Domestic		"

14	10/10	DIXSON, Andrew	67	m.	Farmer	2000/200	Ire.	
15		Margaret	50	f.	Domestic		"	
16		Catharine	18	f.	Domestic		O.	
17	11/11	DIXSON, Wm.	31	m.	Farmer	/70	Pa.	
18		Mary J.	22	f.			"	
19		Albert F.	2/12	m.			O.	
20	12/12	HOFFMAN, Urismus	31	m.	Farmer	2000/300	"	
21		Elizabeth	28	f.	Domestic		"	
22		Joseph N.	3	m.			"	
23		Mary J.	1	f.			"	
24		HILL, Thomas	9	m.			"	S
25	13/13	BRUCE, Samuel	38	m.	Farmer	/100	"	
26		Mary A.	27	f.			"	
27		Thomas R.	7	m.			"	S
28		William H.	5	m.			"	
29		Mary L.	2	f.			"	
30		John	5/12	m.			"	
31	14/14	GERRETT, Joseph	41	m.	Farmer	2500/555	Va.	
32		Mary J.	45	f.	Domestic		"	I
33		Alexander	15	m.	Farmer		O.	
34		Hetty J.	12	f.			"	S
35		Joseph W.	10	m.			"	S
36		HAMMILTON, Patrick	25	m.	Farm Laborer		"	
37	15/15	McWILLIAMS, Alex-						
		ander	25	m.	Farmer	760/400	"	
38		Harriet	23	f.			"	

1	16/16	GILMOORE, Samuel	27	m.	Farmer	2000/500	O.	
2		Sarah	26	f.	Domestic		"	
3		William W.	2	m.			"	
4	17/17	HAMMILTON, Ben-						
		jamin	63	f.?	Farmer	1900/200	Pa.	
5		Israel L.	13	m.			O.	S
6		Noah	9	m.			"	S
7	18/18	WRIGHT, Jonathan	34	m.	Carpenter	600/50	Pa.	
8		Margaret	22	f.	Domestic		O.	
9		Isaac R.	4	m.			"	
10		William A.	1	m.			"	
11	19/19	BRYANT, Josiah P.	44	m.	Farmer	2500/100	"	
12		Mary	46	f.	Domestic		Va.	I
13		Barbara L.	18	f.	Domestic		O.	
14		Thebath A.	12	f.			"	S
15		Thelida J.	12	f.			"	S
16	20/20	BRYANT, Joseph W.	24	m.	Farmer	/100	"	M
17		Elsey A.	20	f.			N.Y.	M
18		Mary A.	8/12	f.			O.	

19	21/21	BRYANT, Joseph	54	m.	Farmer	600/200	O.
20		Mary	52	f.			"
21		Richard B.	15	m.	Farmer		"
22		Margaret M.	12	f.			" S
23		JARVIS, James A.	6	m.			"
24	22/22	GERRITT, Charles	32	m.	Farmer	/75	Va.
25		Cassander	33	f.	Domestic		Pa.
26		John A.	13	m.			O. S
27		Joseph E.	11	m.			" S
28		Hannah L.	8	f.			" S
29		Heathy E.	6	f.			"
30		Samuel H.	3	m.			"
31		Melindy J.	8/12	f.			"
32	23/23	ATHERTON, Richard	36	m.	Farmer	1030/700	"
33		Elizabeth	31	f.			"
34		WALTERS, Joseph H.	23	m.			"
35	24/24	BRUCE, Thomas	77	m.	Farmer	1500/50	Va. I
36		Mary	62	f.			Pa. I
37	25/25	EDDY, Petter	45	m.	Farmer	1675/100	Va. I
38		Elizabeth	40	f.	Domestic		" I
39		Eliza J.	16	f.	Domestic		O. S

Page 4   17 July 1860   Sheet 16 verso

1		Enos P.	9	m.			O.
2		Martha E.	2	f.			"
3		Simon P.	5/12	m.			
4		HAUTT, Elizabeth	80	f.			Va.
5	26/26	BEILS, Fleming	44	m.	Shoemaker		Pa.
6		Ledoci	44	f.	Domestic		" I
7		Leander	20	m.	Farm laborer		"
8		Elizabeth	18	f.	Domestic		"
9		Nancy	14	f.			"
10		Mary M.	12	f.			" S
11		Alexander	10	m.			O. S
12		Fleming	2/12	m.			"
13	27/27	ABBOTT, Joseph S.	37	m.	Farmer	1500/100	Pa.
14		Maria	34	f.	Domestic		O.
15		Catharine	16	f.	Domestic		"
16		Nancy A.	10	f.			" S
17		Susan M.	3	f.			"
18		Mary C.	1	f.			"
19	28/28	BROOKS, Shilds *	68	m.	Farmer	500/100	Md.
20		Mary	60	f.			"
21	29/29	BROOKS, William	37	m.	Carpenter		O.
22		Martha N. L.	28	f.	Domestic		"

* The given name "Shilds" should read "Giles". Editor's note.

23		BROOKS, Annera N.	5	m.			O.	
24		Shilds (Giles) W.	2	m.			"	
25		Shilds (Giles) M.	25	m.	Artist		"	
26	30/30	FOX Joseph	38	m.	Farmer	2000/100	Pa.	
27		Me ᵤa	41	f.			O.	
28		James W.	12	m.			"	S
29		William R.	11	m.			"	S
30		John A.	8	m.			"	S
31		Isaac N.	6	m.			"	
32		Thomas J.	4	m.			"	
33		Nancy M.	3	f.			"	
34		Catharine	3/12	f.			"	
35	31/31	STEINE, John	38	m.	Farmer	2000/50	Pa.	
36		Elizabeth	34	f.	Domestic		O.	I
37		Jesse M.	15	m.	Farmer		"	
38		Isaac E.	10	m.			"	S
39		Rebecca J.	12	f.			"	S

Page 5   17 July 1860   Sheet 17

1		David L.	7	m.			O.	
2		Hannah L.	5	f.			"	
3		William H.	1	m.			"	
4		MILLNER, Elizabeth A.	16	f.	Domestic		"	
5	32/32	WINDAL, John	36	m.	Farmer	/50	"	I
6		Sarah	40	f.	Domestic		Va.	I
7		Susan	13	f.			O.	
8		Charity	10	f.			"	
9		Lucy	8	f.			"	
10		Mary J.	6	f.			"	
11		Sarah	3	f.			"	
12		Brueda	1	f.			"	
13	33/33	PITTMAN, Elias	46	m.	Farmer	500/25	"	I
14		Rebecca	35	f.			Pa.	I
15		Jacob	18	m.	Farm laborer		O.	
16		Hannah	16	f.			"	
17		Feeby	13	f.			"	S
18		Thimoty	12	m.			"	S
19		Elizabeth J.	7	f.			"	
20		Isaac	5	m.			"	
21		Lovina	4	f.			"	
22		Jonathan B.	2	m.			"	
23	34/34	ECKELBERY, Abraham	69	m.	Farmer	2500/75	Pa.	I
24		Hannah	61	f.	Domestic		"	
25		Abraham	17	m.	Farmer		O.	S
26	35/35	TRUAX, John	67	m.	Farmer	2200/125	Pa.	
27		Susan	58	f.			"	
28	36/36	WRIGHT, Nathan	34	m.	Farmer	/200	O.	

29		WRIGHT, Hannah	30	f.		O.	
30		Susan	13	f.		Ill.	
31		Livi	11	m.		O.	
32		Andrew J.	6	m.		Ind.	
33		Martha L.	2	f.		O.	
34		MAULSON, Andrew C.	17	m.	Farm laborer	"	
35	37/37	PITTMAN, William	43	m.	Farmer	"	I
36		Lyda	34	f.	Domestic	Va.	I
37		David	15	m.	Farm laborer	O.	
38		Alexander	13	m.		"	S
39		Alsy	12	f.		"	S

Page 6	18 July 1860	Sheet 17 verso

1		Christy	6	f.		O.	
2	38/38	LANTZ, Alexander	47	m.	Farmer	4250/200 Pa.	
3		Alsey	46	f.	Domestic	Va.	I
4		Delilay	18	f.	Domestic	O.	
5		Elizabeth	12	f.		"	S
6	39/39	MAULSON, George	64	m.	Farmer	Pa.	I
7		Rachel	40	f.		O.	I
8	40/40	WRIGHT, Thomas	50	m.	Farmer	3000/200 Md.	
9		Josiah	24	m.	Farmer	O.	
10		William	21	m.	Farmer	"	
11		Nelson	20	m.	Farmer	"	
12		Clauranda	23	f.	Domestic	"	
13		Ellis	18	m.	Farmer	"	S
14		Elizabeth	15	f.		"	S
15		Margaret	13	f.		"	S
16		Thomas	12	m.		"	S
17		Harvy A.	7	m.		"	
18		Robert	5	m.			
19	41/41	ECKELBERRY, Henry	41	m.	Carpenter	800/25 Pa.	
20		Catherine	30	f.	Domestic	O.	I
21		William E.	10	m.		"	S
22		Ellen	8	f.		"	S
23		Alexander	4	m.		"	
24		George W.	1	m.		"	
25	42/42	PRICE, Henry	32	m.	Farmer	/75	"	I
26		Lyda A.	28	f.		"	I
27		Isaac	10	m.		"	S
28		Charles	7	m.		"	S
29		Ruben N.	6	m.		"	
30		Sarah E.	3	f.		"	
31		John	1	m.		"	
32	43/43	STEWART, Michael	39	m.	Farmer	/100 Pa.	
33		Sarah	29	f.		"	I
34		Abraham	10	m.		O.	S
35		Eliza J.	8	f.		"	S
36		Nancy	7	f.		"	S

37		STEWART, Mary E.	5	f.			O.
38		Jacob M.	5/12	m.			"
39	44/44	HENDERSON, Thomas	64	m.	Farmer	/100	Pa. I

1		Susan	65	f.	Domestic		Pa.
2	45/45	HENTHORN, Eliza	38	f.	Domestic		" I
3		Martha	16	f.	Domestic		O.
4		Susan	14	f.			" S
5		Sarah	12	f.			" S
6		Lyda	10	f.			" S
7		Holda	6	f.			"
8		Ann E.	2	f.			"
9	46/46	CHURCH, William	40	m.	Farmer	6000/2000	Pa.
10		Susan	40	f.	Domestic		"
11		David S.	19	m.	Farmer		"
12		Lucy	16	f.	Domestic		" S
13		Ruth	13	f.			" S
14		Asa M.	10	m.			" S
15		William H.	5	m.			"
16		Henry	26	m.	Carpenter		"
17	47/47	REINHARD, Adam	37	m.	Mason	500/200	Bad.
18		Caroline	29	f.			Wur.
19		Willemine	3	f.			Pa.
20		Rebecca	1	f.			O.
21		William C.	1/12	m.			"
22	48/48	MAULSON, Livi	23	m.	Farm laborer	/50	" I
23		Nancy	20	f.			" I
24		Delila A.	5/12	f.			"
25	49/49	BARKUS, Archibal	30	m.	Farmer	/25	" I
26		Elizabeth	25	f.			" I
27		William	6	m.			"
28		Jesse	3	m.			"
29	50/50	MARECAL, Jesse	65	m.	Farmer	1000/100	"
30		Jemima	65	f.	Domestic		Pa. I
31		Francis	23	f.	Domestic		O.
32	51/51	WILLIAMS, Martha	30	f.	Domestic		" I
33		Martha	5	f.			"
34		James	3	m.			"
35	52/52	MARECAL, John	40	m.	Farmer	500/100	"
36		Mary	40	f.	Domestic		"
37		Jemima	21	f.	Domestic		"
38		Luvisa	17	f.	Domestic		"
39		Jesse	15	m.	Farm laborer		" S

1		James	13	m.			O. S

2	53/53	MARECAL, Nicholas	39	m.	Farmer	/50	O.
3		Elizabeth	29	f.			"
4		William	9	m.			" S

5	54/54	MYERS, William	40	m.	Farmer	1000/50	"
6		Susanah I.	32	f.			"
7		Hannah J.	11	f.			" S
8		Jacob	8	m.			" S
9		Mary	6	f.			"
10		Washington	3	m.			"
11		Lyda A.	3	f.			"
12		Susanah	1	f.			

13	55/55	McMOLLAN, Assra	43	m.	Farmer	1200/100	" I
14		Martha	39	f.			Va.
15		Richard	20	m.	Farm laborer		O.
16		Livi	18	m.	Farm laborer		" S
17		Elizabeth	15	f.	Domestic		" S
18		Uriah	11	m.			" S
19		Barbara	10	f.			" S
20		Joseph	6	m.			" S
21		Josiah	3	m.			

22	56/56	HAYTHORN, John	31	m.	Farmer	2000/275	"
23		Mary A.	28	f.			"
24		Elizabeth	4	f.			"
25		Catharine	3	f.			"
26		James	1	m.			"
27		Rachel	9	f.			

28	57/57	HOBURG, William	34	m.	Glass-maker	900/75	Han.
29		Johana	32	f.	Domestic		"
30		Willemine	7	f.			N.Y. S
31		Henryyettey	3	f.			Pa.

32	58/58	WALTERS, Caspar	69	m.	Farmer	700/100	Wur.
33		Mary B.	54	f.			"
34		Christopher A.	23	m.	Farmer		O.
35		Martina C.	17	f.	Domestic		"
36		John N.	11	m.			" S

37	59/59	DREEKS, Mary	60	f.	Domestic		Md.
38		James	27	m.	Lawyer		O.
39		Samuel	24	m.	Farmer		"

Page 9	18 July 1860	Sheet 19

1		Alexander	21	m.	School teacher		O.

2	60/60	YUNG, Isaac	40	m.	Miller	/500	Pa.
3		Mary	43	f.			"
4		Silas	18	m.	Farm laborer		O.
5		David	16	m.			" S
6		Mary F.	13	f.			" S
7		Sarah	11	f.			" S
8		Margaret	9	f.			" S
9		Harriet	6	f.			"
10		Ann	2	f.			

11	60/61	DYE, Enoch	21	m.	Farmer	3000/100	O.		
12	61/62	NEAL, Thomas	42	m.	Farmer	6500/1000	Pa.		
13		Clarissa	41	f.	Domestic		"		
14		Mary	17	f.	Domestic		"		
15		Clarissa	13	f.			O.	S	
16		Lussinda	13	f.			"	S	
17		Nancy	11	f.			"	S	
18		Joseph	9	m.			"	S	
19		Martin	6	m.			"		
20		Thomas	3	m.			"		
21		DYNES, David	20	m.	Servant		Ire.		
22	62/63	WOOLUM, William	31	m.	Farmer	/300	O.		
23		Elenor	29	f.			"		
24		Franklin	10	m.			"	S	
25		Thomas	8	m.			"	S	
26		Elizabeth S.	7	f.			"	S	
27		Harvey	6	m.			"	S	
28		George	4	m.			"		
29		Lussinda I.	3	f.			"		
30		Mary E.	1	f.			"		
31		Nancy A.	1/12	f.			"		
32		HENDERSON, Mary A.	30	f.	Servant		"		
33	63/64	HEARREN, Granville	30	m.	Farmer	/25	"		
34		Susanah	23	f.			"		
35		Rachel	6	f.			"	S	
36		Thomas	3	m.			"		
37	64/65	WILLIAMSON, Isaac	53	m.	Farmer	/100	Va.		
38		Susanah	27	f.	Domestic		O.		
39		Hammilton	18	m.	Farmer				

1		Moses	14	m.			O.	S	
2		William	12	m.			"	S	
3		Maria E.	10	f.			"	S	
4		Barbara C.	7	f.			"	S	
5		John P.	5	m.			"		
6		Hannah J.	3	f.			"		
7		Mary L.	6/12	f.			"		
8	65/66	MILLER, Andrew	32	m.	Farmer	/25	Pa.		
9		Letty	25	f.			O.		
10		Caroline	7	f.			"		
11		Catharine A.	4/12	f.			"		
12	66/67	ALLMAN, Jacob	56	m.	Shoemaker	200/100	Wur.		
13		Alfona	59	f.			"		
14		Lazarus	14	m.			Pa.	S	
15	67/68	HAMMILTON, John	60	m.	Farmer	1000/100	"		
16		Serina	24	f.	Domestic		O.		
17		Andrew J.	20	m.	Farmer		"		

18	68/69	LENTZ, Jonathan	31	m.	Farmer	/100	O.
19		Elizabeth	26	f.			"
20		Allmine	6	f.			"
21		Joseph W.	5	m.			"
22		George F.	2	m.			"
23	69/70	LENTZ, Israel	56	m.	Tanner	2500/2300	Wur.
24		Catharine	60	f.	Domestic		"
25		Elizabeth	25	f.	Domestic		O.
26		David	23	m.	Tanner		"
27		BATZENHARD, Bern-					
		hard	65	m.	Tanner		Wur.
28	70/71	CLITHERO, John D.	56	m.	Farmer	2500/200	Del.
29		Jemima	54	f.			Pa.
30		Isaac N.	27	m.	Farmer		O.
31		Edward	21	m.	Farmer		"
32		Jemima M.	19	f.	Domestic		"
33		Jane	17	f.	Domestic		"
34		Benton C.	14	m.			" S
35		Sirus W.	12	m.			" S
36	71/72	MOORE, Hammilton	31	m.	Farmer	1050/50	Pa.
37		Mary N.	31	f.			" 5
38		John	5	m.			"
39		Thomas	3	m.			O.

1		Mary	11/12	f.			O.
2		John	66	m.	Farmer		Ire.
3		Elizabeth	25	f.	Dressmaker		Pa.
4	72/73	EDDY, Alexander	40	m.	Farmer	1400/200	Va.
5		Elizabeth	33	f.			Pa.
6		Jemima	11	f.			O. S
7		Franklin	9	m.			" S
8		Silvester	7	m.			" S
9		John H.	5	m.			"
10		Sarah I.	3	f.			
11		WITTLATCH, Barna	28	m.	Laborer		Va. I
12	73/74	LANDIES, Daniel F.	33	m.	Farmer	1800/100	O.
13		Margaret J.	24	f.	Domestic		Pa.
14		Sarah E.	9	f.			O. S
15		John D.	7	m.			" S
16		Charles L.	5	m.			"
17		Joseph	1	m.			"
18	74/75	HOFFMAN, Jacob	63	m.	Farmer	5000/100	Va. I
19		Nancy	61	f.	Domestic		O.
20		Rossberry	25	m.	Carpenter		"
21		ELROD, Mary E.	21	f.	Domestic		"
22		David A.	1	m.			"
23	75/76	CHURCH, Reinhard	38	m.	Farmer	/300	Pa.
24		Charlote	35	f.	Domestic		"
25		Elizabeth S.	16	f.	Domestic		" S

26		CHURCH, Delila A.	14	f.			Pa.	S
27		Silas C.	11	m.			"	S
28		William H.	9	m.			"	S
29		Susan A.	7	f.			"	S
30		John S.	4	m.			"	S
31		Mandy	1	f.			"	
32		Cephas G.	1	m.			"	
33	77/78	BOYD, Jeremiah	48	m.	Farmer	3500/100	"	
34		MORTON, Thomas	44	m.	Farmer		"	
35		Hannah	81	f.	Domestic		"	
36		WIDOWRO, Mary	74	f.	Domestic		"	
37		MANSFIELD, Ann	47	f.	Domestic		"	
38		MORTON, Hannah	38	f.	Domestic		"	
39		YUNG, Ammila	10	f.			"	S

Page 12   19 July 1860   Sheet 20 verso

Town of Antioch

1	78/79	ELROD, Susannah	58	f.	Domestic		Pa.	I
2		Joseph	33	m.	Shoemaker		"	
3		Hannah	35	f.	Domestic		"	
4		Susan	26	f.	Domestic		"	
5		Martha	18	f.	Domestic		"	
6		Jane F.	1	f.			O.	
7		William H.	6/12	m.			"	
8	79/80	ELROD, James	28	m.	Farmer		Pa.	M
9		Elen	19	f.	Domestic		O.	M
10	80/81	BEAVER, William	54	m.	Farmer	300/100	Unk.	I
11		Eliza	45	f.	Domestic		Pa.	I
12		Joseph P.	25	m.	Laborer		O.	I
13		John	18	m.	Laborer		"	
14		Martha	16	f.			"	
15		Petter	15	m.			"	S
16		Amstreet	10	m.			"	S
17		Madison	7	m.			"	S
18		Thomas E.	1	m.			"	
19	81/82	BROWN, Francies	37	m.	Carpenter	300/175	Pa.	
20		Maria	24	f.	Domestic		"	
21		Catherine J.	4	f.			O.	
22		Richard T.	2	m.			"	
23	82/83	LYNCH, George	42	m.		300/100	Pa.	
24		Margaret J.	39	f.	Domestic		Md.	
25		Mandy J.	17	f.	Domestic		O.	
26		Margaret	15	f.	Domestic		"	S
27		Elias	13	m.			"	S
28		Mary E.	11	f.			"	S
29		Caroline M.	8	f.			"	S
30		Nancy E.	6	f.			"	
31		Susan E.	4	f.			"	
32		ULLOM, Silvenus	18	m.	Wagon-maker		"	
33	83/84	DAVIS, Absalon N.	45	m.	Carpenter	400/100	Va.	

34	DAVIS, Marie J.	45	f.	Domestic	Va.
35	Louisa E.	20	f.		"
36	Lovanna A.	18	f.		"
37	David W.	15	m.		"
38	George A.	12	m.		O. S
39	Casswell	8	m.		" S

Page 13   19 July 1860   Sheet 21

1	83/84	COVERT, A. B.	44	m.	Doctor	1000/4000	Pa.
2		Pheeby M.	45	f.	Domestic		N.Y.
3		Samuel N.	14	m.			O. S
4		Mary J.	12	f.			" S
5		Morris A.	6	m.			" S
6		Catharine C.	4	f.			"
7		Nancy M.	2	f.			"
8		HOFFMAN, Elias	23	m.	Farm laborer		"
9		HERRET, Winsteat	23	m.	Farm laborer		" I
10		ULLOM, Morris	19	m.	Farm laborer		"

11	84/85	BLASOR, M.	36	m.	Blacksmith	"
12		Aba	26	f.	Domestic	" I
13		Sarah E.	8	f.		" S
14		James D.	7	m.		" S
15		George B.	4	m.		"
16		Catharine	5/12	f.		"

17	85/86	PENN, William	36	m.	Wagon-maker	350/50	Md.
18		Armendy	22	f.	Domestic		O.
19		BENADIS, Elizabeth	50	f.	Domestic		Va.

20	86/87	BEAVER, William	28	m.	Laborer	Pa.
21		Elizabeth	21	f.	Domestic	O. I
22		Cornelius	6	m.		" S
23		Isabel	1	f.		"

24	87/88	BOWMAN, Isaac	60	m.	Chairmaker	300/50	Md.
25		Ann J.	60	f.	Domestic		"

26	87/88	SCHROOVAMAN, Hughe	55	m.	Shoemaker	Pa.
27		Sarah	54	f.	Domestic	O.
28		Elizabeth	17	f.	Domestic	" S

29	88/89	WALTER, Isarel	21	m.	Shoemaker	/50	"
30		Catharine	18	f.	Domestic		"
31		Henry	1	m.			"

32	89/90	PENN, John W.	48	m.	Wagon-maker	Md.
33		Catharine A.	58	f.	Domestic	Pa.
34		Elizabeth	18	f.	Domestic	O.

35	90/91	PENN, Thomas	44	m.	Merchant	5000/6000	Md.
36		Nancy	24	f.	Domestic		O. I
37		Sarah A.	16	f.	Domestic		"
38		Elizabeth	15	f.	Domestic		" S
39		William	13	m.			" S

1		PENN, Jeremiah	11	m.			O.	S
2		Mary E.	11/12	f.			"	
3		Caroline	38	f.	Domestic		Md.	I
4	91/92	BOTTENFIELD, Isaac	37	m.	Merchant	700/100	Pa.	M
5		Mary E.	19	f.	Domestic		O.	M
6		Franklin	11	m.			"	S
7		William T.	10	m.			"	S
8	92/93	BOTTENFIELD, William	35	m.	Merchant	1200/600	Pa.	
9		Meledy	27	f.	Domestic		O.	
10		Florenzo T.	5	f.			"	
11	93/94	DABBY, Charles D.	29	m.	Doctor	1000/400	Pa.	
12		Mary S.	19	f.	Domestic		"	
13	94/95	HOFFMAN, Thomas	40	m.			O.	
14		Ruth	43	f.			N.Y.	I
15		Thomas	11	m.			O.	S
16		Nancy E.	10	f.			"	S
17		William	8	m.			"	S
18		Mary	5	f.			"	
19		SHOTWELL, Alban	34	m.	Merchant	1500/1500	"	
20		SHANEY, Richard T.	21	m.			Md.	M
21	95/96	BARNES, Wm. C.	29	m.	Carpenter	/150	O.	
22		Susannah	26	f.			"	
23		Angeline	5	f.			"	
24		Elizabeth	3	f.			"	
25		Theodre M.	1	m.			"	
26		JACOBS, Mary	18	f.	Domestic		"	
27	96/97	PENN, Owen	42	m.	Blacksmith	500/400	Md.	
28		Emmelyna	42	f.	Domestic		"	
29		Columbus	17	m.			"	
30		Ann R.	14	f.			"	S
31		Elizabeth	13	f.			"	S
32		Thomas F.	10	m.			O.	S
33		Ruth	7	f.			"	S
34		Eliza	4	f.			"	
35	97/98	FREEMAN, George	21	m.	Farmer	2500/150	"	
36		Jane	22	f.			"	
37	98/99	MITCHEL, Jacob	42	m.	Merchant	4500/150	"	
38		Charlote	42	f.			Pa.	
39		Anny	15	f.			O.	S

1	Joseph	14	m.			O.	S
2	Henry	7	m.			"	S
3	John	2	f.			"	
4	GRIFFET, Alvina	20	f.	Milliner		"	

5	99/100	PEAIRS, Isaac	79	m.	Merchant	500/150	Del.	
6		Lyda	45	f.	Domestic		Pa.	
7		MARTIN, Rachel J.	37	f.	School Teacher		O.	S
8		John D.	6	m.			"	
9	100/101	DAWELL, Wm. N.	39	m.	Doctor	500/200	"	
10		Isabel	31	f.	Domestic		Va.	
11		Mary E.	13	f.			O.	S
12		John W.	7	m.			"	S
13		James N.	5	m.			"	
14		William H.	3	m.			"	
15		Isabel M.	1	f.			"	
16		Dolly	67	f.			Va.	I
17	101/102	BROOKS, John	31	m.	Carpenter	1500/200	O.	
18		Nomancy J.	22	f.	Domestic		Va.	
19		Billy J. B.	2	m.			O.	
20		Pereekathes	4/12	m.			"	
21	102/103	KINCADE, Joseph	34	m.	Merchant	300/200	Pa.	
22		Sarah J.	34	f.	Domestic		O.	
23		Leander M.	12	m.			"	S
24		Loretty	6	f.			"	S
25		Francies V.	2	f.			"	
26		Lorenzo L.	2	f.			"	
27		MORING, John B.	25	m.	Merchant		"	
28	103/104	GATTIN, Henry S.	44	m.	Mason	/75	Pa.	
29		Mary	37	f.	Domestic		O.	
30		Robert	20	m.			"	
31		Rachel	18	f.			"	S
32		Joseph	9	m.			"	S
33		Thomas	4	m.			"	
34	104/105	SLOAN, John	43	m.	Hotel Keeper	6000/1000	Pa.	M
35		Caroline	18	f.	Domestic		O.	M
36		William	17	m.			"	S
37		Mary J.	12	f.			"	S
38		John	10	m.			"	S
39		Aslomathilda	7	f.			"	S

Page 16   19 July 1860   Sheet 22 verso

1		Susan	4	f.			O.	
2		ELROD, Elizabeth	70	f.			Pa.	I

End of Town of Antioch

3	105/106	BOWMAN, Franzis	38	m.	Farmer	400/150	O.	
4		Charlote	36	f.	Domestic		Pa.	
5		Mary E.	11	f.			O.	S
6		Thomas L.	9	m.			"	S
7		Joseph F.	7	m.			"	S
8		Josiah D.	11/12	m.			"	
9	106/107	MORGAN, Thomas	45	m.	Miller		Va.	

10		MORGAN, Roda	37	f.	Domestic		Pa.
11		Frank M.	17	m.			O.	S
12		Jane	15	f.			"	S
13		John C.	12	m.			"	S
14		James H.	9	m.			"	S
15		William	4	m.			"	
16		Seladius	1	m.			"	
17	107/108	McCELSTER, Wm.	57	m.	Wool-carder	/150	Pa.
18		Julia	37	f.	Domestic		O.
19		Henryyetty	20	f.	Domestic		Pa.
20		James W.	18	m.	Wool-carder		"
21		Jerusha M.	15	f.			"	S
22		Matha L.	12	f.			"	S
23		Isabel C.	9	f.			O.	S
24	108/109	MORGAN, Samuel	43	m.	Farmer	1500/100	Va.
25		Louisa D.	41	f.	Domestic		O.
26		Paula	19	f.	Domestic		"
27		James	17	m.				S
28		Augustus	12	f.				S
29		Catharine	14	f.				S
30		Corbaly	10	m.				S
31		Elizabeth	7	f.				S
32		Amenoy	5	f.				S
33		Nathan	1	m.				
34	109/110	HOFFMAN, Henry	35	m.	Farmer	/500	Pa.
35		Maria	33	f.			O.
36		Lucia A.	13	f.			"	S
37		William J.	11	m.			"	S
38		Anngenora	7	f.			"	S
39		Rubena	5	f.			"	

1	110/111	HOFFMAN, George	27	m.	Farmer	1000/50	O.
2		Lyda	23	f.	Domestic		"
3		Elma A.	7	f.			"
4		James W.	4	m.			"	S
5		Lusinda	2	f.			"
6		Morris H.	1	m.			"
7	111/112	McWRIGHT, James D.	49	m.	Farmer	4000/200	Pa.
8		Ruth	32	f.			O.
9		Andrew D.	6	m.			"
10		Margaret E.	4	f.			"
11		Sarah E.	2	f.			"
12		STAFFORD, James	21	m.	Laborer		Ire.
13		DYE, Nancy	20	f.	Servant		O.
14	112/113	AYRES, James F.	32	m.	Farmer	/300	"
15		Syrena	22	f.			"
16		Mary A.	4	f.			"
17		Hanly	3	m.			"
18		Martha J.	1	f.			"
19		McBRIED, Daniel H.	18	m.	Farm laborer		"

20	113/114	AYRES, James	64	m.	Farmer		Md.
21		Martha	59	f.			N.C.
22		Alsy A.	18	f.			O.
23	114/115	MILLER, Samuel Sr.	59	m.	Farmer	3000/50	Pa. M
24		Rachel	30	f.			" M
25	115/116	MILLER, Samuel Jr.	37	m.	Farmer	/100	"
26		Charlote	25	f.			O.
27		Henry	12	m.			" S
28		Samuel	10	m.			" S
29		Cleray	9	f.			" S
30		Simon	7	m.			" S
31		Alles	5	f.			" S
32		Runinda	4	f.			"
33		Flora	2	f.			":
34	116/117	COVERT, Morris	44	m.	Farmer	3000/100	"
35		Catharine	33	f.			Va.
36		Charles	18	m.	Farmer		O.
37		Mandy C.	10	f.			" S
38		Clieressa	8	f.			" S
39		Morris	6	m.			" S

Page 18   19 July 1860   Sheet 23 verso

1		James O.	4	m.			O.
2		Susan A.	1	f.			"
3	117/118	NEAL, Barnad	67	m.	Blacksmith		Pa.
4		Mary	65	f.	Domestic		"
5		Lusenda	44	f.			"
6		Caroline	10	f.			O. S
7	118/119	STEWART, James	66	m.	Farmer	/200	Pa.
8		Susannah	35	f.	Domestic		" I
9		Elizabeth	17	f.	Domestic		O.
10		Hannah	16	f.			"
11	119/120	HENDERSHOT, Harvy	25	m.	Farmer	/100	"
12		Elizabeth	21	f.			"
13		Sarah M.	4	f.			"
14		Mary R.	1	f.			"
15	120/121	ECKELBERY, Wm.	42	m.	Miller	2000/75	Pa.
16		Nancy	41	f.	Domestic		O.
17		Hannah J.	16	f.	Domestic		" S
18		Isaac	15	m.			" S
19		Henry	12	m.			" S
20		Thomas	10	m.			" S
21		James W.	7	m.			" S
22		Margaret	6	f.			" S
23		Ally	2	m.			"
24	121/122	STEWART, Basal	31	m.	Blacksmith	2000/1000	Pa.
25		Elizabeth	35	f.			O.
26		Ammly M.	4	f.			"
27		Lanzo L.	8/12	m.			"

28		SHREIVERS, James	19	m.	Blacksmith appren-			
29		Merenda	14	f.	tice		O.	
							"	
30	122/123	DYE, George	46	m.	Farmer	4000/200	"	
31		Jane	41	f.			Pa.	
32		Mathias	21	m.	Farmer		O.	
33		Sarah	19	f.			"	
34		Amilia	17	f.			"	
35		Enoch	15	m.			*	S
36		Elizabeth	13	f.			"	S
37		Harvey	10	m.			"	S
38		Emey	8	f.			"	S
39		Friend	7	m.			"	S

1		Rosetty	4	f.			O.		
2	123/124	BROWN, Jesse	46	m.	Farmer	1200/100	Pa.	I	
3		Elizabeth	45	f.			O.		
4		Sarah	18	f.			"		
5		James W.	16	m.			"	S	
6		Angeline	11	f.			"	S	
7		Luther	9	m.			"	S	
8		Mary J.	5	f.			"	S	
9	124/125	ULLOM, Job S.	23	m.	Farmer	/75	"		
10		Mary	19	f.			"		
11		Elirusha M.	20	m.	Blacksmith		"		
12	125/126	MOORE, Jane	61	f.	Domestic	700/100	Pa.		
13		Sophia	36	f.	Domestic		"		
14		John	34	m.	School Teacher		"		
15		Nancy	21	f.	Domestic		"		
16		BROWN, Alexander	38	m.	Farm laborer		O.		
17	126/127	BROWNFIELD, Enoch	82	m.	Farmer	4000/100	Pa.		
18	127/128	WINDAL, Isaac	44	m.	Farmer	/150	O.		
19		Lusinda	44	f.			"	I	
20		Jesse	19	m.	Farm laborer		"		
21		John	18	m.	Farm laborer		"		
22		Margaret	16	f.			"		
23		Jacob	14	m.			"	S	
24		Josiah	12	m.			"	S	
25		William	10	m.			"	S	
26		Jamens	7	m.			"	S	
27		Isaac	6	m.			"		
28		Juliann	1	f.			"		
29	128/129	SNEIDER, Fredrick	26	m.	Farmer	/300	"		
30		Mary J.	20	f.			"		
31		Lusinda J.	5/12	f.			"		
32	129/130	COOTER, James	30	m.	Farmer	500/75	Va.	I	
33		Amilia	24	f.	Domestic		O.		

34		COOTER, Sarah	4	f.			O.	
35		George N.	1	m.			"	
36		TWELL, Franzis	15	m.	Farm laborer		Va.	
37	130/131	BOYD, James	50	m.	Farmer	1500/50	Pa.	
38		Nancy	49	f.	Domestic		"	
39		Mary J.	16	f.	Domestic		"	S

Page 20   20 July 1860   Sheet 24 verso

1		Nancy	14	f.			Pa.	S
2		Elizabeth	12	f.			"	S
3		McRAIZE, John	18	m.	Farm laborer		"	
4	131/132	KINCAID, Robert	40	m.	Farmer	1000/50	"	
5		Junus	30	f.			O.	
6		John L.	12	m.			"	S
7		William C.	10	m.			"	S
8		Mary C.	6	f.			"	
9		Samuel	4	m.			"	
10		Emmly J.	1	f.			"	
11	132/133	JARRIET, Mary	76	f.	Domestic		Pa.	I
12	132/133	HENCEL, Nathaniel	40	m.	Farmer	5000/150	Va.	
13		Emly	39	f.			O.	
14		John N.	18	m.	Farmer		"	
15		Ery	12	f.			"	S
16		Mary J.	8	f.			"	S
17		Ann M.	7	f.			"	
18		Emly	3	f.			"	
19		DYE, Wm. H.	18	m.	Farm laborer		"	
20	133/134	DYE, Ary	55	f.	Domestic	3000/100	"	I
21		Elam	19	m.	Farmer		"	
22		Mahlon	15	m.	Farmer		"	S
23		STEINE, Margaret A.	13	f.			"	S
24	134/135	SALSBERY, Jackson	22	m.	Farmer	/100	"	I
25		Lusinda	17	f.			"	
26		Thomas	1	m.			"	
27		Nathaniel	15	m.	Farm laborer		"	
28	135/136	DYE, Daniel	54	m.	Farmer	500/100	Pa.	
29		Ann	48	f.	Domestic		Md.	
30		Nancy E.	19	f.			O.	S
31		Elizabeth	12	f.			"	S
32		Abbagieal	35	f.			"	I
33	136/137	KINCADE, James	31	m.	Farmer	1000/100	"	I
34		Nancy	23	f.			"	I
35		Ann	3	f.			"	
36		Samuel	1	m.			"	
37		Nancy	76	f.			Md.	I
38	137/138	SHRIEVES, James	38	m.	Miner		Pa.	
39		Letty	30	f.			O.	

1		SHRIEVES, Jane	13	f.			O.	S
2		Franklin	7	m.			"	S
3		Sarah A.	6	f.			"	
4		Ann B.	4	f.			"	
5		Nancy	1	f.			"	
6	138/139	STEINE, Benjamin	50	m.	Farmer	2700/100	Pa.	
7		Margaret	38	f.			Va.	I
8		Isaac B.	20	m.	Farmer		O.	
9		Manorva	16	f.			"	S
10		Evendor	14	m.			"	S
11		Jusphine	12	f.			"	S
12		William	10	m.			"	S
13		Lusinda	8	f.			"	S
14		Meichal	6	m.			"	
15		Harriet	1	f.			"	
16	139/140	SALSBERY, Daniel	47	m.	Farmer	1500/100	"	I
17		Rachel	40	f.			Va.	
18		Moses D.	18	m.			O.	
19		Elizabeth	13	f.			"	S
20		George	12	m.			"	S
21		John	9	m.			"	S
22		Henry	7	m.			"	
23		James A.	1	m.			"	
24		Luvisa	1/12	f.			"	
25		STEWART, Elizabeth	23	f.			"	I
26	140/141	CISNE, Emanuel	52	m.	Farmer	2000/200	Pa.	
27		Sarah	51	f.	Domestic		"	I
28		Nancy J.	19	f.	Domestic		O.	
29		Henry G.	16	m.	Farmer		"	S
30		Sarah C.	11	f.			"	S
31		Junus A.	14	f.			"	S
32		SHEPHARD, Heniede	20	m.	Farm laborer		"	
33	141/142	JARARD, Livi	42	m.	Farmer	2000/400	Pa.	
34		Sarah	42	f.	Domestic		"	I
35		Joseph	16	m.	Farmer		O.	
36		Mary J.	10	f.			"	S
37	142/143	ACKLY, Wesly	35	m.	Farmer		"	I
38		Rachel	30	f.			"	I
39		Mary	8	f.				

1		Dosty	6	f.			O.	
2		Sendey E.	4	f.			"	
3	143/144	CLINE, Elias	38	m.	Farmer	/150	"	
4		Nancy	36	f.			"	I
5		McVAY, John	13	m.			"	S
6		CLINE, Alsenda	9	f.			"	S

7	144/145	WEDDLE, Mary	56	f.	Domestic	600/50	Pa.	I
8		Abneor	24	m.			O.	
9		John	21	m.	Farmer		"	
10		Mahalay	19	f.			"	
11		Rue	13	m.			"	S

12	145/146	DYE, Basal	32	m.	Farmer	1800/100	"	
13		Adaline	26	f.			"	
14		Franzis M.	8	m.			"	
15		William H.	7	m.			"	
16		Ary	3	f.			"	
17		Martha	4/12	f.			"	
18		BROWN, John	22	m.	Farm laborer		"	
19		CLINE, Alvina	12	f.			"	S
20		Josuha	25	m.	Farmer		"	

21	146/147	CLINE, Jacob B.	40	m.	Farmer		"	
22		Sarah	34	f.			"	
23		Calvin R.	18	m.	Farmer		"	
24		Thomas O.	16	m.	Farmer		"	S
25		Lyda	14	f.			"	S
26		Sarah J.	8	f.			"	S
27		Elias	6	m.			"	S

28	147/148	CLINE, Joseph	42	m.	Farmer	2000/100	"	
29		Maria	40	f.	Domestic		"	
30		Jasper A.	16	m.	Farmer		"	S
31		Mary J.	14	f.			"	S
32		Angeline	12	f.			"	S

33	148/149	STATES, Samuel	37	m.	Farmer	3000/200	Pa.	
34		Francies	40	f.			O.	
35		David	15	m.			"	S
36		Sarah	13	f.			"	S

37	149/150	STATES, Margaret	30	f.	Domestic	1200/100	"	
38		Franzis	12	m.			"	S
39		Sarah E.	10	f.			"	

Page 23   20 July 1860   Sheet 26

| 1 | | Mary E. | 5 | f. | | | O. | |
| 2 | | Archibal | 3 | m. | | | " | |

3	150/151	SMITH, Jonathan	28	m.	Farmer	1500/200	Pa.	
4		Sarah J.	30	f.			"	
5		William A.	7	m.			O.	
6		Emily M.	4	f.			"	
7		Sarah C.	2	f.			"	

| 8 | 151/152 | WARD, Joseph | 45 | m. | Farmer | 800/100 | Va. | I |
| 9 | | Sarah | 66 | f. | | | " | I |

| 10 | 152/153 | ROACH, Lorenzo | 79 | m. | Farmer | | Pa. | I |
| 11 | | Elizabeth | 75 | f. | | | " | I |

| 12 | 153/154 | HAUT, Petter | 41 | m. | Farmer | 300/50 | Va. | |

13		HAUT, Elizabeth	45	f.			O.
14		Enos	18	m.	Farmer		" S
15		Lorenz	16	m.	Farmer		" S
16		Margaret	14	f.			" S
17		Nancy	10	f.			" S
18		James	8	m.			"
19		William	5	m.			"
20	154/155	HAUT, James	43	m.	Farmer	800/75	Va. I
21		Nancy	47	f.			O. I
22		Clarkson	17	m.	Farmer		"
23		Evan	15	m.			"
24		Elizabeth A.	13	f.			" S
25		Astern	10	f.			" S
26		Petter	8	m.			" S
27		Nancy	5	f.			"
28		Hannah J.	2	f.			"
29	155/156	SHRIVER, Alexander	22	m.	Farmer	/100	"
30		Mary	28	f.			"
31		Catherine	2	f.			"
32		Lyda	10/12	f.			"
33	156/157	SHRIVER, George	63	m.	Farmer	800/50	Pa. I
34		Mary	20	f.	Domestic		O. I
35		Sarah J.	13	f.			S
36		Mathailda	10	f.			S
37		George	7	m.			S
38		Maria J.	5	f.			
39	157/158	DILLON, John	40	m.	Farmer	800/500	O.

Page 24			20 July 1860			Sheet 26 verso	
1		Margaret	40	f.			N.Y. I
2		Henry	19	m.	Farmer		O. S
3		Ursula	17	f.			"
4		Elen	15	f.			"
5		Sarah	13	f.			" S
6		Martin	10	m.			" S
7		Susannah	8	f.			"
8		Sephinier	5	f.			"
9		Jonathan	3	m.			"
10	158/159	BOOTH, John	40	m.	Farmer	5000/250	Eng. I
11		Mary J.	38	f.			O.
12		George W.	17	m.	Farmer		"
13		William H.	15	m.	Farmer		" S
14		Hannah J.	13	f.			" S
15		Thomas H.	12	m.			" S
16		Isaac M.	10	m.			" S
17		Elizabeth E.	8	f.			" S
18		Lorinda	6	f.			" S
19		John F.	4	m.			"
20		Samuel A.	1	m.			"
21	159/160	ACKLY, Jane	59	f.	Domestic	200/75	Pa. I

22		ACKLY, Mary J.	21	f.	Domestic		O.	
23		CURENS, Joel	30	m.	Farmer		"	
24	160/161	SLAY, Elisha	46	m.	Farmer	/100	"	
25		Ellonor	37	f.			Pa.	
26		Davidson	18	m.	Farmer		O.	
27		John	16	m.	Farmer		"	
28		Edward	14	m.			"	S
29		Lyda A.	13	f.			"	S
30		Isabel	11	f.			"	S
31		Elisuha W.	10	m.			"	S
32		Owen	7	m.			"	S
33		Selvanus	6	m.			"	
34		Susanah	4	f.			"	
35		Franklin	2	m.			"	
36	161/162	WILLIAMS, Richard	37	m.	Farmer	/100	Md.	I
37		Sarah J.	36	f.			O.	
38		Emma J.	10	f.			"	
39	162/163	ADAMS, Richard	28	m.	Farmer	/100	"	

1		Sarah J.	27	f.			O.	
2		Ellen J.	26	f.			"	I
3		Albert M.	3	m.			"	
4	163/164	ADAMS, Henry	51	m.	Farmer		"	I
5		Elizabeth	49	f.			"	I
6		Joseph M.	15	m.			"	
7		Isaac N.	11	m.			"	S
8	164/165	DRUM, John	43	m.	Farmer		"	
9		Nancy	45	f.			Va.	
10		STEWART, Elizabeth	36	f.	Servant		O.	I
11		RUTLER, Wm.	16	m.	Farm laborer		"	
12	165/166	DUNN, Dilly	50	f.	Domestic	1200/150	Pa.	
13		Mary	30	f.	Domestic		O.	
14		Josiah	22	m.	Farmer		"	
15		Silvester	19	m.	Farmer		"	
16		William	10	m.			"	S
17		Franzis M.	1	m.			"	
18	166/167	STEWART, Richard	55	m.	Farmer	4000/700	Pa.	
19		Catharine	52	f.	Domestic		"	
20		Thomas B.	21	m.	Farmer		"	
21		James N.	18	m.	Farmer		"	S
22		Catharine	15	f.	Domestic		"	S
23		John F.	12	m.			"	S
24		Mary O.	10	f.			"	
25	167/168	STEINE, David M.	30	m.	Farmer	800/200	"	
26		Mary	23	f.			"	
27		Lucy A.	4	f.			"	

28		STEINE, Melissey	2	f.		O.
29		Sarah E.	2	f.		"
30		Rubarty	1/12	f.		"
31	168/169	SHOTWELL, Thomas M.	43	m.	Farmer 3500/500	"
32		Nancy R.	40	f.	Domestic	"
33		Susan	28	f.	Domestic	"
34		CHANE, Susan M.	17	f.	Domestic	" M
35		HOFFMAN, Martin	21	m.	Farmer	"
36		DOWELL, Mary J.	3	f.		Iowa
37	169/170	DAVIDSON, Alferd A.	31	m.	Farmer	O.
38		Catherine	28	f.		"
39		Abraham	8	m.		S

1		John S.	5	m.		O.
2	170/171	RUNGAN, Samuel	47	m.	Farmer 3000/100	"
3		Sarah J.	35	f.		" I
4		Nancy C.	13	f.		" S
5		MYERS, Adam	19	m.	Farm laborer /300	"
6	171/172	TRUAX, Phillip	46	m.	Farmer 2500/100	"
7		Ruth	46	f.		" I
8		Silas	22	m.	Farmer	"
9		Emily	18	f.	Domestic	"
10		Fanny	16	f.		" S
11		Samuel	14	m.		" S
12		Henry	9	m.		" S
13		Phillip	7	m.		" S
14		Samuel	74	m.	Farmer	Pa. I
15	172/173	YOST, Petter	33	m.	Farmer 600/100	O.
16		Angelina	27	f.		"
17		John R.	11	m.		" S
18		Mary E.	9	f.		" S
19		Sarah C.	6	f.		" S
20		Martha J.	1	f.		"
21	173/174	YOST, John	77	m.	Cooper	N.J.
22		Mary	68	f.		Md. I
23		MARTIN, James	65	m.	Farmer	Eng. I
24	174/175	BEAVER, Isaac	25	m.	Farmer	O. I
25		Elizabeth	32	f.		" I
26		William H.	4	m.		"
27		George W.	2	m.		"
28		Julean	3/12	f.		"
29		WINDAL, Mary	16	f.		"
30	175/176	YOST, Jesse	47	m.	Farmer 2000/100	Md.
31		Barbara	24	f.		Pa. I
32		James	3	m.		O.

33		YOST, John	11/12 m.			O.
34	176/177	CRISTY, John	35 m.	Farmer	1800/150	"
35		Rachel	35 f.			"
36		Emannual	13 m.			" S
37		Lasly F.	10 m.			" S
38		Mary M.	6 f.			"
39		David J.	3 m.			"

Page 27   23 July 1860   Sheet 28

1		Elizabeth	10/12 f.			O.
2		WHEITE, Juleann	13 f.			" S
3	177/178	ANSLY, James	55 m.	Farmer	600/100	Pa. I
4		Elen	57 f.			Va. I
5		Rachel	27 f.			" I
6		John	26 m.	Farmer		"
7		Livi	23 m.	Farmer		"
8		Thomas	19 m.	Farmer		"
9		Emily	18 f.			"
10		Mary	16 f.			
11		MOUNT JOY, Mary A.	28 f.	Milliner		Va.
12	178/179	BEAVER, Solomon	42 m.	Farmer	1200/200	"
13		Elila	42 f.			"
14		Abraham	21 m.	Farmer		"
15		Missurie	19 f.	Domestic		"
16		Misse	17 f.	Domestic		" S
17		Nancy	15 f.	Domestic		" S
18		Eliza J.	13 f.			O. S
19		Elizabeth	11 f.			" S
20		Martin	7 m.			" S
21		Markus	4 m.			"
22		Semandy	1 f.			"
23		Henry	9 m.			" S
24	179/180	DRUM, Jacob	40 m.	Farmer	3000/400	"
25		Elen	38 f.			"
26		Mathias	9 m.			" S
27		Assra	7 m.			" S
28		Mathilda	3 f.			"
29		John	1 m.			"
30		SEE, Sarah S.	15 f.			"
31		Eliza A.	13 f.			" S
32		Catharine	10 f.			" S
33		GRIFFEN, Alben	19 m.	Farm laborer		"
34	180/181	THOMSON, John	65 m.	Farmer	1500/100	Ire.
35		Margaret	56 f.	Domestic		" I
36		Eliza A.	26 f.	Domestic		N.Y.
37		Mary J.	23 f.	Domestic		Va.
38		Margaret	22 f.	Domestic		"
39		Hughe	20 m.	Farmer		O.

Page 28   23 July 1860   Sheet 28 verso

1		Fanny	14 f.			O. S

2	181/182	HARIAN, Thomas	39	m.	Farmer	2500/200	Va.	
3		Catharine	39	f.			O.	
4		Margaret	14	f.			"	S
5		John	12	m.			"	S
6		Rebacca	9	f.			"	S
7		Jacob G.	3	m.			"	
8		Stephen D.	5/12	m.			"	
9		McMENNEMY, Thomas	15	m.	Farmer		"	
10		PERKINS, Henry	21	m.	Farmer		"	
11	182/183	ULLOM, Enoch H.	35	m.	Carpenter	/100	Pa.	
12		Minorva	32	f.			Va.	I
13		Delilah	11	f.			"	S
14		Elizha	9	m.			"	S
15		Francies L.	7	f.			"	S
16		Daniel	4	m.			"	
17		Israel F.	1	m.			"	
18	183/184	COX, Andrew	60	m.	Miller		"	I
19		Martha	60	f.			Pa.	I
20		Andrew J.	22	m.	Farmer		Va.	
21		Josephus	18	m.	Farmer		"	
22		Daniel	15	m.	Farmer		"	S
23		Landora	10	f.			"	S
24	184/185	BARNARD, James	25	m.	Farmer	1000/100	O.	I
25		Maria	24	f.			"	
26		Henry	2	m.				
27		Elizabeth	64	f.			Va.	I
28	185/186	BARNARD, Henry	32	m.	Farmer	1100/75	Md.	
29		Delila	33	f.			Va.	I
30		Solomon	13	m.			O.	S
31		Susan	8	f.			"	S
32		Catharine	7	f.			"	S
33		William	3	m.			"	
34		Elizabeth	1	f.			"	
35	186/187	JOHNES, Petter	24	m.	Farmer	/100	"	
36		Ross	23	f.			"	
37		Emily	3	f.			"	
38		Mary	1	f.			"	

1	187/188	JOHNS, Armstrong	22	m.	Farmer	/100	O.	
2		Catharine	18	f.			"	
3		Melisse	9/12	f.			"	
4	188/189	PIATT, John	62	m.	Farmer	3100/200	Va.	
5		Elizabeth	56	f.			"	
6		John	28	m.	Farmer		O.	
7		Robert	19	m.	Farmer		"	S
8		Rebacca J.	17	f.			"	S
9		Mille	13	f.			"	S
10		George	7	m.			"	S

11	189/190	PIATT, James	39	m.	Farmer	500/100	O. I
12		Sarah	32	f.			N.Y. I
13		Mary J.	7	f.			O. S
14		Elizabeth	5	f.			"
15		John	2	m.			"
16		MOTT, Jane	20	f.	Servant		"
17	190/191	FORACKER, Wm.	42	m.	Farmer	7536/500	Pa.
18		Elizabeth A.	41	f.			Va.
19		George S.	20	m.			O.
20		William	17	m.			" S
21		James	10	m.			" S
22		Elemuel S.	8	m.			" S
23		John W.	6	m.			"
24		Charles W.	4	m.			"
25		Alferd P.	1	m.			"
26	191/192	EDGE, William	28	m.	Farmer	/200	" I
27		Dina	27	f.			" I
28		Orrenda	4	f.			"
29		James F.	2	m.			"
30		John H.	2	m.			"
31		Julia Ann	1/12	f.			"
32		DUNFEE, Andrew	12	m.			" S
33		JOY, Nancy	18	f.	Servant		"
34	192/193	HAUT, Alfus	30	m.	Farmer	/100	" I
35		Feeby	33	f.			" I
36		Hannah	13	f.			" S
37		Delila	14	f.			" S
38		Henry	10	m.			" S
39		John	7	m.			" S

Page 30   24 July 1860   Sheet 29 verso

1		Elisha	5	m.			O.
2		Delyas	1	m.			"
3	193/194	RICE, Richard	41	m.	Farmer	6000/500	"
4		Mary	40	f.	Domestic		Pa.
5		Elizabeth	17	f.	Domestic		O.
6		Rachel A.	15	f.	Domestic		" S
7		John W.	13	m.			" S
8		Henry A.	4	m.			"
9		Charity	2	f.			"
10		MASON, Marion	20	m.	Farmer		"
11	194/195	PORTER, Abraham	43	m.	Farmer	/100	Pa.
12		Dolly	39	f.	Domestic		O. I
13		Mary	20	f.	Domestic		"
14		Jehu	17	m.	Farm laborer		"
15		Selona	14	f.			" S
16		Isaac M.	11	m.			" S
17		Joshua	9	m.			" S
18		Abraham C.	6	m.			"
19		Samuel C.	3	m.			"
20		Robert E.	5/12	m.			"

21		PORTER, Susannah	85	f.			Pa.	I
22	195/196	DAUGHERTY, Wm.	43	m.	Farmer	5000/600	Ire.	
23		Margaret	22	f.	Domestic		O.	
24		Ellenor	21	f.	Domestic		"	
25		Patrick	19	m.	Farm laborer		"	
26		Henry	17	m.			"	
27		John	15	m.			"	
28		Mathias	11	m.			"	S
29		George	7	m.			"	S
30		Nathan	5	m.			"	S
31		Catharine	3	f.			"	S
32		Mary E.	1	f.			"	
33		McMENIAMA, Rebecca	14	f.			"	
34		LEECK, Margaret	68	f.			Md.	
35	196/197	WEST, Thomas	40	m.	Farmer	1800/100	Pa.	
36		Elizabeth	36	f.	Domestic		"	
37		Margaret	12	f.				S
38		Eliza J.	10	f.				S
39		George	8	m.				S

Page 31   24 July 1860   Sheet 30

1		Oliver	2	m.			O.	
2	197/198	STATES, Archer	59	m.	Farmer	1000/100	Pa.	
3		Mary	40	f.	Domestic		Md.	I
4		Nathaniel	15	m.	Farm laborer		O.	S
5		Nancy T.	18	f.	Domestic		"	
6		NEIGTUNEL, Emly R.	18	f.			"	
7		Benjamin F.	15	m.	Farm laborer		"	
8		Martha	11	f.			"	S
9	198/199	DETWEILER, Robert	28	m.	Farmer	1500/100	Pa.	
10		Margaret	23	f.	Domestic		O.	
11		John A.	2	m.			"	
12	199/200	MASON, James	28	m.	Farmer	2500/150	"	
13		Jesstine	34	f.	Domestic		"	
14		Mary M.	6	f.			"	
15		William H.	4	m.			"	
16		Alferd N.	3	m.			"	
17		Malisse E.	2	f.			"	
18		ANDREWS, John	13	m.			"	
19	200/201	HOFFMAN, George H.	37	m.	Blacksmith	1042/100	Pa.	
20		Rolly M.	34	f.	Domestic		"	
21		Jacob L.	13	m.			O.	S
22		Barnard A.	11	m.			"	S
23		Isabel	9	f.			"	
24		George H.	7	m.			"	
25		BROWN, Petter	84	m.	Blacksmith		Sea	
26	201/202	MASON, Elisaha	41	m.	Farmer	3000/130	Pa.	
27		Rebecca	41	f.	Domestic		Va.	
28		Andrew D.	21	m.	Farmer		O.	

29		MASON, Orsula A.	18	f.	Domestic		O. S
30		William A.	16	m.	Farm laborer		" S
31		Maria	14	f.			" S
32		Mathielda	11	f.			" S
33		James	9	m.			" S
34	202/203	CRAWFORD, John	47	m.	Farmer	1200/150	Pa. I
35		Vermila	50	f.	Domestic		Eng.
36		George H.	22	m.	Farm laborer		O.
37		Elizabeth	19	f.	Domestic		"
38		Alban A.	17	m.	Farm laborer		" S
39		William C.	15	m.	Farm laborer		" S

Page 32   24 July 1860   Sheet 30 verso

1		SHULE, Elizabeth	18	f.	Servant		O.
2	203/204	HAWKINS, William	47	m.	Farmer	2500/200	Va.
3		Lovina	45	f.	Domestic		"
4		Mary J.	21	f.	Domestic		O.
5		Josuha	19	m.	Farm laborer		"
6		Rawly J.	18	m.	Farm laborer		"
7		William	16	m.	Farm laborer		"
8		James	14	m.			" S
9		Catharine	12	f.			" S
10		Clarinda	10	f.			" S
11		Sarah	7	f.			" S
12		Nancy E.	3	f.			"
13	204/205	HALL, Jacob	32	m.	Farmer	900/100	"
14		Sarah	34	f.	Domestic		"
15		Josiah	9	m.			" S
16		Oliver	6	m.			"
17		Cassandy	3	f.			"
18		BRIDGES, Eden	15	m.	Farm laborer		"
19		STEPHENS, Eliza-beth	25	f.	Domestic		"
20	205/206	WEDDLE, Petter	64	m.	Carpenter	/100	Pa.
21		Margaret	54	f.	Domestic		O. I
22		John	27	m.	Farm laborer		"
23		James	22	m.	Carpenter		" I
24		George	19	m.	Farm laborer		"
25		Feeby	32	f.	Domestic		" I
26		Susan	19	f.	Domestic		"
27	206/107	PHILLIPS, Isaac	49	m.	Farmer	4000/300	Pa.
28		Nancy	58	f.	Domestic		Va. I
29		Catharine	24	f.	Domestic		O.
30		Elizabeth	23	f.	Domestic		"
31		Joseph M.	21	m.	Farm laborer		"
32		Martha J.	17	f.	Domestic		"
33		Nancy M.	15	f.	Domestic		"
34		COX, Albert W.	5	m.			"
35		STEWART, Abraham	18	m.	Farm laborer		
36		HAYS, James	60	m.			Va. I6

37	207/208	ECKELBERY, Catharine	56	f.	Domestic	400/75	Pa. I
38		Mille	9	f.			O. S
39	208/209	ECKELBERY, Isaac	34	m.	Farmer	/200	Pa. I

Page 33   25 July 1860   Sheet 31

1		Mary J.	30	f.	Domestic		O.
2		Valentine	10	m.			" S
3		Rebacca	8	f.			"
4		Dabby	6	f.			"
5		Catharine	3	f.			"
6		Settue	12	m.			" S
7	209/210	ELROD, John	41	m.	Farmer	/300	Pa.
8		Margaret	37	f.	Domestic		"
9		Thomas	15	m.			"
10		David	12	m.			" S
11		John	9	m.			" S
12		Mary J.	7	f.			"
13		Addason	2	m.			O.
14	210/211	HUBBS, Solomon	37	m.	Farmer	4000/300	Pa.
15		Elizabeth	18	f.	Domestic		"
16		WHEITE, George	11	m.			O.
17	211/212	TRUAX, John A.	23	m.	Farmer	/150	O. I
18		Mary	24	f.	Domestic		"
19		William A.	10/12	m.			"
20	212/213	STEINE, Isaac	30	m.	Farmer	700/100	" I
21		Catharine	32	f.	Domestic		" I
22		Mary E.	14	f.			"
23		Calvin	11	m.			" S
24		Wilferd	10	m.			" S
25		Franzis M.	7	m.			"
26		John H.	2	m.			"
27		Lyda	5/12	f.			"
28	214/215	PHILLIPS, Issra	28	m.	Farmer	/100	"
29		Mary E.	24	f.	Domestic		"
30		Sarah J.	2	f.			"
31		Charles N.	2/12	m.			"
32	215/216	HERREN, Rebecca	71	f.	Domestic	2500/100	N.J.
33		LENN, Barney	18	m.	Farm laborer		O.
34	216/217	HUPP, Elisaha	25	m.	Farmer	/75	" I
35		Catharine	21	f.	Domestic		" I
36		Rachel A.	1	f.			"
37	217/218	STEINE, Rufus	36	m.	Farmer	2400/200	Pa.
38		Nancy	36	f.	Domestic		Va.
39		William	15	m.	Farmer		O. S

		Name	Age	Sex	Occupation	Value		
1		STEINE, James	13	m.			O.	S
2		Mandy J.	12	f.			"	S
3		Mary C.	8	f.			"	
4		Hannah	6	f.			"	
5		Thomas	3	m.			"	
6		John	1	m.				
							"	
7	218/219	HUPP, Rins	36	m.	Farmer		"	
8		Julette	23	f.	Domestic		"	
9		Mary J.	3	f.			"	
10		Daniel	1	m.				
11	219/220	STEINE. Michael	77	m.	Farmer	4000/200	Pa.	
12		Harrit	48	f.	Domestic		Va.	
13		HILL, Sofia	18	f.			"	S
14		Minorva	15	f.			"	S
15		Maria	8	f.				
16	220/221	JOHNSON, John	38	m.	Farm laborer		Pa.	
17		Mary A.	42	f.	Domestic		O.	
18		Mary J.	15	f.	Domestic		"	S
19		William P.	14	m.			"	S
20		Junaty A.	7	f.			"	
21		Franklin	4	m.			"	
22		Mandy	2	f.				
23	221/222	HOFFMAN, Mitchel	32	m.	Farmer	/150	"	
24		Isabel	28	f.	Domestic		"	
25		Edward	11	m.			"	S
26		Elizabeth J.	10	f.			"	S
27		Lusinda J.	8	f.			"	S
28		John D.	5	m.			"	
29		William A.	3	m.				

223 Dwelling houses.
224 Families. I
made a mistake in
numbers.

I do hereby certify that this is therty four (34) Pages of
Schedule No. 1 and that the were made by me acording to my oath and
instructions to the best of my knowledge and believe. Calais, Monroe
County, Ohio, August 13, 1860.   William Henning A.M.

Sworn to and subscribed before me the undersigned Justice of the
Peace for Seneca Township, Monroe County, Ohio. August 28, 1860.

     J. P. Spriggs J. P.

Page 1 4 June 1860 Sheet 33

1	1/1	RICHARDSON, William P.	36	m.	Lawyer	2000/300	Pa.	
2		Sarah E.	36	f.			Va.	
3		Emma H.	11	f.			O.	S
4		Mary E.	8	f.			"	S
5		Adelia	5	f.			"	S
6		Charles	3	m.			"	
7		Ada	1	f.			"	
8	2/2	THOMAS, Daniel	44	m.	Shoemaker	1000/150	N.Y.	
9		Mary	20	f.			O.	
10		Sarah	18	f.			"	
11		Melinda	15	f.			"	S
12		George	14	m.			"	S
13		Theodore	10	m.			"	S
14		William	4	m.			"	S
15	3/3	HADEN, Nathaneial	31	m.	Tailor	/100	Pa.	
16		Martha	27	f.			"	
17		Albert	10	m.			O.	S
18		Robert	8	m.			"	S
19		William	6	m.			"	
20		Charles	3	m.			"	
21	4/4	MORRIS, Adam	34	m.	Teamster	400/200	"	
22		Elisabeth	29	f.			"	
23		Eliza	6	f.			"	S
24		Lucinda	4	f.			"	
25	5/5	MORROW, Marshall	45	m.	Bricklayer	1000/800	Pa.	
26		Sarah	43	f.			"	
27		John C.	20	m.			O.	
28		Morten	18	m.			"	
29		James	15	m.			"	S
30		Mary	13	f.			"	S
31		Thomas	10	m.			"	S
32		Otis	4	m.			"	
33		Maclus	1	m.			"	
34	6/6	MORROW, Morten C.	40	m.	Carpenter	4000/300	"	
35		Jane	32	f.			Md.	
36		Martha	13	f.			O.	S
37		Sarah	11	f.			"	S
38	Jail	Anne	8	f.			"	S
39		Mary	4	f.			"	
40		Rachel	1	f.			"	

Page 2 4 June 1860 Sheet 33 verso

1	7/7	READ, William	42	m.	Carpenter	1500/300	Eng.	
2		Hariet	38	f.			O.	
3		Mary L.	19	f.			"	
4		Lucetta	17	f.			"	S
5		Nancy	15	f.			"	S
6		Elizabeth	13	f.			"	S

7		READ, John	10	m.		O. S
8		Sophia	8	f.		" S
9		Susann	6	f.		"
10		Hariet	5	f.		"
11		Charles	2	m.		
12	8/8	KEEPER, Jacob	24	m.	Shoemaker	/100 Ger.
13		Rhoda	24	f.		O.
14		Caroline	2	f.		"
15	9/9	BROCK, Jacob B.	51	m.	Teamster	/100 "
16		Susey	50	f.		Va.
17		Thomas	17	m.		O.
18		Rachel	14	f.		"
19	10/10	HELBLING, Chris-			Cabinet-maker	
		tian	31	m.	600/100	Fr.
20		Barbary	25	f.		Ger.
21		Augustas	2	m.		O.
22		Elisabeth	1	f.		"
23	11/11	HAFFLER, Michel	37	m.	Cabinet-maker	
					800/200	Ger.
24		Louisa	36	f.		Fr.
25		Maria A.	9	f.		Ger. S
26		Lewis	11	m.		" S
27		Barbary	5	f.		O.
28		Charles W.	3	m.		"
29		Louisa	1	f.		"
30	12/12	NUHART, Daniel	30	m.	Stone-mason 700/250	Bay.
31		Catharine	29	f.		"
32		Daniel	9	m.		
33		Louisa	5	f.		O.
34		Elizabeth	3	f.		"
35		Amelia	1	f.		"
36	13/13	NUHART, Lawrence	61	m.	Laborer 400/100	Bay.
37		Solom	56	f.		"
38		Adam	18	m.	Cooper	
39		DRIGGS, Mary	75	f.		Conn.
40		McMILLEN, Ellen	18	f.		Ire.

Page 3		4 June 1860			Sheet 34

1	14/14	WAGOHAMER, Nich-			Stone-mason	/75 Fr.
		olas	24	m.		Pa.
2		Elisabeth	23	f.		O.
3		Luly	1	f.		"
4		SPRING, Jacob	18	m.	Cooper	
5	15/15	LONG, Michel	42	m.	Cooper	1500/1000 Ger.
6		Elisabeth	38	f.		"
7		John	16	m.	Cooper	O. S
8		Ann	13	f.		" S
9		William	11	m.		" S
10		Lousa	9	f.		" S

11		LONG, Charlotte	5	f.			O.	
12		Catharine	1	f.			"	
13	16/16	SINCLAIR, Mary	43	f.		1500/300	Pa.	
14		Alexander	27	m.	Dentist		O.	
15		William	25	m.			"	
16		Western	21	m.			"	
17		Mary E.	19	f.			"	S
18		Josiah	18	m.			"	S
19		John	17	m.			"	S
20		Catharine	14	f.			"	S
21		Henry	9	m.			"	S
22		Catham	2	m.			"	
23	17/17	MOTTS, Marcus	33	m.	Stone-mason	/100	Ger.	
24		Rachel	25	f.			"	
25		Fredarick	6	m.			"	
26		Louis	4	m.				
27		Christena	2	f.			O.	
28		Jacob	1	m.			"	
29	18/18	RICHNER, George	27	m.	Millwright	700/150	Pa.	
30		Margaret	23	f.			O.	
31		Albert	1	m.			"	
32	19/19	PUGH, Aaron	28	m.	Carpenter	/150	Pa.	
33		Mary	30	f.			"	
34		John	1	m.			O.	
35	20/20	ROSENBERGH, An-drew	35	m.	Carpenter	200/250	Ger.	
36		Elizabeth	23	f.			"	
37		Charles	3	m.			O.	
38		GLOVER, John	25	m.	Tobacconist		"	
39		JUDKINS, Joel	27	m.	Druggist	/800	"	
40		Christena	1	f.			"	

1	21/21	AKERS, Daniel	50	m.	Carpenter	300/150	Pa.	
2		Sally	46	f.			O.	
3		Eliza J.	24	f.			"	
4		William	20	m.	Cordwainer		"	
5		Menerva	18	f.			"	S
6		John	15	m.			"	S
7		Alen	9	m.			"	S
8		Ada	1	f.			"	
9	22/22	BROCK, Elias G.	24	m.	Tobacconist	500/50	"	
10		Elisabeth	17	f.			"	
11		Gulia	1	f.			"	
12	23/23	BLOOR, James	71	m.	Carpenter	700/100	Md.	
13		Mary	61	f.			"	
14	24/24	RICHNER, Samuel	25	m.	Carpenter	/75	Pa.	
15		Catharine	21	f.			"	
16		Clientona	1	f.			O.	

17	25/25	SHAFER, Henry	29	m.	Tobacconist	350/75	Ger.
18		Gulia	23	f.			"
19		Michel	3	m.			O.
20		Barbary	1	f.			"
21	26/26	HENTHORN, David	26	m.	Carpenter	300/150	"
22		Jane	22	f.			"
23		John	1	m.			"
24	27/27	WAGONHAM, Philip	29	m.	Teamster	200/150	Fr.
25		Mary	23	f.			Ger.
26		Mary	4	f.			O. S
27		Amelia	1	f.			"
28	28/28	GROVE, Thomas A.	28	m.	Presb. Minister 600/150		Pa.
29		Eliza	22	f.			Md.
30		Mary	1	f.			O.
31	29/29	NUHART, George	30	m.	Laborer	275/75	Ger.
32		Williany	26	f.			O.
33		Amelia	1	f.			
34	30/30	HENTHORN, John	28	m.	Laborer	350/100	"
35		Mary	25	f.			Va.
36		Washington	4	m.			O.
37		Miles	2	m.			"
38		RICHNER, William P.	22	m.	Carpenter		"
39		HAINES, Balser	23	m.	Laborer		"
40		CAUFMAN, J. D.	21	m.	Carpenter		

Page 5   5 June 1860   Sheet 35

1	31/31	PATTON, Milton	27	m.	Carpenter	300/100	O.
2		Melisa	24	f.			"
3		Laura	4	f.			" S
4		Mary	2	f.			"
5		Violetta	1	f.			"
6	32/32	CUNNINGHAM, Jocephas	24	m.	Saddler	/150	"
7		Sarah	20	f.			"
8		Deborah	1	f.			"
9	33/33	RICHNER, William	45	m.	Miller	6000/100	Pa.
10		Rachel	32	f.			O.
11		Hannah	11	f.			" S
12		Roda	7	f.			" S
13		Washington	5	m.			"
14		Margarett	2	f.			"
15		TAGG, Margaret	16	f.	Domestic		"
16		BECK, John	20	m.	Blacksmith		Ger.
17	34/34	GADD, John	26	m.	Carpenter	200/95	O.
18		Milly	23	f.			"
19		Giles	2	m.			"
20		Charles	1	m.			"

21	35/35	BECK, Emanuel	31	m.	Plasterer	/150	Pa.
22		Fanny	22	f.			"
23		Emma	3	f.			"
24		Amanda	1	f.			"
25	36/36	SALISBERY, Edward	58	m.	Farmer	1500/200	N.Y.
26		Maria	56	f.			Conn.
27		McKEE, Seve	75	f.			"
28	37/37	YOUNG, George	30	m.	Tailor		Ger.
29		Caroline	30	f.			"
30		Mary	4	f.			O.
31		Caroline	1	f.			" S
32	38/38	SIMMENS, James N.	45	m.	Teamster	600/300	Md.
33		Lucretia	42	f.			O.
34		William	20	m.			" S
35		Joseph	17	m.			" S
36		Elisabeth	2	f.			"
37	39/39	BROCK, Martin	29	m.	Laborer		"
38		Susan	25	f.			"
39		Sarah	6	f.			" S
40		FOGLE, W. W.	23	m.			Va.

1		Elias	3	m.			Va.
2		Soloman	1	m.			"
3	40/40	DAVIS, Elias	33	m.		1200/1500	Pa.
4		Alsena	32	f.			O.
5		William	8	m.			" S
6		Robert	5	m.			" S
7		John	3	m.			"
8		Hariet	1	f.			"
9		Robert	74	m.			Md.
10		Mahala	37	f.			Pa.
11	41/41	SINCLAIR, F. M.	23	m.	Lawyer	/100	O.
12		Alvira	19	f.			"
13		Oto	1	m.			"
14	42/42	ROSE, William	28	m.	Tinner	450/100	Bav.
15		Elisabeth	18	f.			Pa.
16		William	1	m.			O.
17	43/43	BAKER, Martin	42	m.	Druggist	1000/2400	"
18		Eliza	41	f.			"
19		Mahala E.	20	f.			"
20		James	18	m.			"
21		Mary	16	f.			"
22		John	14	m.			" S
23		George	12	m.			" S
24		Elen	10	f.			" S
25		Francis	7	f.			"
26		Western	4	m.			"
27		Alexander	2	m.			"

28	44/44	HALL, Thos. J.	34	m.	Clerk	400/150	O.	
29		Margaret	36	f.			"	
30		Jane	16	f.			"	S
31		William	14	m.			"	S
32		John	12	m.			"	S
33		Mary	9	f.			"	S
34		Auther	7	m.			"	S
35		Joseph	5	m.			"	
36		BACON, May	84	f.		/500	Pa.	
37	45/45	NOLL, John B.	43	m.	Carpenter	3000/400	"	
38		Elisabeth	43	f.			Sw.	
39		Elisabeth A.	14	f.			O.	
40		BUTLER, Calvin	25	m.	Miller		"	

Page 7   5 June 1860   Sheet 36

1	46/46	RANDOLPH, Joel P.	66	m.	Lawyer	2000/300	N.J.	
2		Elisabeth	52	f.			Va.	
3		Mary V.	26	f.			O.	
4		Elisabeth	20	f.			"	
5	47/47	BENINGHAUS, Mary	32	f.		/50,000	Pa.	
6		Luzetta	10	f.			O.	S
7		Anna	9	f.			"	S
8		Author	7	m.			"	S
9	48/48	ADAMS, Thos. J.	40	m.	Silversmith	250/100	Pa.	
10		Ellenor	29	f.			O.	
11		William	11	m.			"	S
12		Archbold	9	m.			"	S
13		Olevia	5	f.			"	
14		James	3	m.			"	
15		Charles	1	m.				
16	49/49	DIEHL, Peter	33	m.	Merchant	3000/3000	Fr.	
17		T.	28	f.			Ger.	
18		Hariet	5	f.			O.	
19		F. W.	2	m.			"	
20		Miss	1	f.				
21	50/50	COOPER, Mahla	38	f.		800/100	"	
22		James C.	14	m.			"	S
23		John D.	12	m.			"	S
24		Western T.	6	m.			"	
25		Leanore E.	1	f.			"	
26	51/51	DRUMM, Alexander	23	m.	Carpenter	/600	"	
27		Ellen	23	f.			"	
28		Mary	1	f.			"	
29		Elisabeth	12	f.			"	S
30	52/52	KIRKBRIDE, Jno. M.	39	m.	Merchant	9000/2000	"	
31		Gulia	35	f.			"	
32		David M.	13	m.			"	S
33		Hariet R.	11	f.			"	S
34		Pluma A.	7	f.			"	S

35	53/53	KIRKBRIDE, David	70	m.	Clerk	2500/15,000	Md.
36		Pluma	63	f.			Conn.
37	54/54	BROCK, Slater	22	m.	Carpenter	/150	O.
38		Gulia	20	f.			"
39		REA, enry	20	m.			" S
40		BECK, Daniel	25	m.	Plasterer		Pa.

Page 8   5 June 1860   Sheet 36 verso

1	55/55	WILLIAMS, Pery	25	m.	Editor	800/	Va.
2		Flora A.	24	f.			O.
3		WEST, Henry B.	20	m.			"
4		Adalaide	18	f.			"
5		WILLIAMS, John B.	21	m.	Printer		Va.
6		WIER, Jed H.	21	m.	Printer		"
7		OKEY, Sopha J.	35	f.			O.
8		Josephine	4	f.			Md. S
9	56/56	DAVIS, Thomas K.	33	m.	Hotel-keeper	2500/300	O.
10		Jane	28	f.			"
11		Elisabeth	3	f.			"
12		Henry	1	m.			"
13		STEWARD, Ruth	40	f.	Domestic		Pa.
14		HILBERT, Henry	60	m.	Laborer		Ger.
15	57/57	MINSTERMAN, Henry	36	m.			"
16		Margaret	30	f.			"
17		John	12	m.			Mich. S
18		William	11	m.			" S
19		MARSHALL, Fred.	24	m.	Laborer		Ger.
20		KETTLE, Louisa	15	f.			" S
21	58/58	KOONTZ, Frederick	30	m.	Cordwainer	350/100	"
22		Barbary	30	f.			"
23		Louisa	8	f.			O. S
24		Edmond	7	m.			" S
25		Isabell	4	f.			"
26		William	2	m.			"
27	59/59	HUNTER, William	51	m.	Lawyer	5500/2000	D.C.
28		Mary	50	f.			Pa.
29		Ann	20	f.			O.
30		William T.	21	m.	Lawyer		"
31	60/60	SINCLAIR & BAKER	(not proper)				
32		WAY, John S.	26	m.	Lawyer	1800/3000	"
33		MANNING, N. J.	23	m.	Lawyer	400/500	Ill.
34	61/61	HENDERSON, James	42	m.	M.E.C. Minister	/300	O.
35		Elisabeth	36	f.			"
36		Thomas W.	11	m.			"
37		Jane	8	f.			" S
38		Mary C.	4	f.			"
39		DAVIS, Alice	68	f.			Conn.
40		PEARSON, Alen	22	m.			O.

1	62/62	PEARSON, Henry	29	m.	Physician	800/300	O.
2	63/63	WELLS, Milton	31	m.	Teacher	/150	Va.
3		Mary	26	f.			"
4		Josephine	10	f.			" S
5		Franklin	7	m.			" S
6		Charlotte	4	f.			" S
7	64/64	OKEY, Henry	45	m.	Carpenter	100/300	O.
8		Anne E.	39	f.			"
9		Mary	19	f.			" S
10		Milly	11	f.			" S
11		Adelaide	8	f.			" S
12		Henry	5	m.			" S
							"
13	65/65	LONGLEY, John B.	23	m.	Editor		
14	66/66	EVANS, Jesse	42	m.	Blacksmith	800/150	"
15		Caroline	41	f.			"
16		Isabell	6	f.			" S
17		COLE, Benton	20	m.	Blacksmith		"
18		STONER, Alexander	35	m.	Blacksmith		"
19	67/67	HOLLISTER, Pery	64	m.	Farmer	6000/1200	Conn.
20		Sally	65	f.			N.Y.
21		SONSBERGER, Louie	17	m.	Laborer		Ger.
22		WALTERS, Lydia	24	f.	Domestic		O.
23	68/68	SMITH, Jacob	24	m.	Painter	500/100	Ger.
24		Mary A.	30	f.			O.
25		Amanda	6	f.			" S
26		Nancy	2	f.			"
27	69/69	BAKER, N. S.	29	m.	Printer	/100	Pa.
28		Rachel A.	20	f.			O.
29		Mary Lee	2	f.			"
30	70/70	BONSER, M. L.	45	m.	Cabinet-maker	900/600	Pa.
							O.
31		Mary	35	f.			" S
32		Flora	14	f.			" S
33		Nancy	13	f.			" S
34		Cleora	11	f.			" S
35		Virgil	9	m.			" S
36		Homar	8	m.			"
37		Laura	6	f.			"
38		Ada	5	f.			"
39		Martin	3	m.			"
40		William	1	m.			

1	71/71	LITTLE, Thomas	52	m.	Farmer	1500/150	O.
2		Rebecca	54	f.			Pa.
3		Thomas O.	22	m.	Tobacco packer		O.

4		LITTLE, Oscar F.	21	m.	Tobacco packer 600/	O.	
5		Matilda	17	f.		"	S
6		Houstan B.	14	m.		"	S
7	72/72	HILL, Hugh B.	45	m.	Clerk	1200/500	Md.
8		Mary A.	44	f.		N.Y.	
9		John E.	19	m.		O.	S
10		Mary A.	17	f.		"	S
11		Terza E.	15	f.		"	S
12		Susann V.	14	f.		"	S
13		Allen E.	12	m.		"	S
14		Leora D.	8	f.		"	
15		William B.	6	m.		"	
16		Hariet B.	2	f.		"	
17	73/73	ARCHBOLD, Edward	54	m.	Lawyer	6000/2000	D.C.
18		Rachel	56	f.		Va.	
19		Alston C.	24	m.	Lawyer	"	
20		Elisabeth N.	21	f.			
21		John O.	19	m.		O.	
22		Mary A.	14	f.		"	S
								S
23	74/74	SMITH, James	44	m.	Physician 8000/2500	"	
24		Amanda J.	42	f.		"	
25		John D.	16	m.		"	S
26		Melville C.	14	m.		"	S
27		Ida A.	4	f.		"	
28	75/75	PATTON, William D.	49	m.	(Do nothing) 500/150	"	
29		Elisabeth	32	f.		"	
30		Henritta	15	f.		"	S
31		Susana	9	f.		"	S
32		Mary E.	6	f.		"	S
33		John C. C.	3	m.		"	
34		Ophelia A.	2	f.		"	
35		Rosa A.	1	f.		"	
36	76/76	SINCLAIR, Western					
		T.	40	m.	Physician 1500/2000	"	
37		Terza	23	f.		"	
38		Sarah A.	6	f.		"	S
39		Mary J.	4	f.		"	
40		Alfred H.	1	m.		"	

1	77/77	WALTON, Sidney	56	f.		1500/250	Va.
2		John	19	m.	Printer	O.	
3		Thomas	15	m.		"	S
4		Walter	13	m.		"	S
5	78/78	WALTON, Daniel	27	m.	Court Clerk 1500/2600	"	
6		Elisabeth	24	f.		"	
7		Caroline	4	f.		"	
8		William C.	2	m.		"	
9	79/79	DRIGGS, Alfred	49	m.	Merchant 5000/4000 Conn.		

10		DRIGGS, Elisabeth	43	f.			O.
11		James A.	20	m.			"
12		Sarah M.	11	f.			" S
13		Oleta Oceola	8	f.			" S
14	80/80	SMITH, James R.	46	m.	Saddler	1200/250	Pa.
15		Mary J.	43	f.			Md.
16		Narsisa J.	16	f.			O. S
17		Adaline	14	f.			" S
18		Elisabeth E.	12	f.			" S
19		Catharine	10	f.			" S
20		James H.	6	m.			" S
21		Richard R.	3	m.			
22	81/81	STAURER, J. D.	25	m.	Silversmith	/600	Boh.
23		Elisabeth	19	f.			O.
24	82/82	KOEHLER, Fredaric	44	m.	Merchant	3000/3000	Ger.
25		Mary J.	29	f.			Ire.
26		John W.	9	m.			O. S
27		Fredarick	7	m.			" S
28		Sarah	4	f.			"
29		Robbert P.	1	m.			
30	83/83	KOEHLER, Nicholas	37	m.	Merchant	400/3000	Ger.
31		Martha	37	f.			O.
32		Marie E.	6	f.			"
33	84/84	JONES, Samuel P.	53	m.	Merchant	2200/4000	N.Y.
34		Mary	51	f.			Va.
35		Isaac	31	m.	Teamster		O.
36		Charles	27	m.	Clerk		"
37		Mary	18	f.			" S
38		Francis	16	f.			" S
39		Ruberta	11	f.			" S
40		A. Delbert	8	m.			" S

1	85/85	MORRIS, Thomas	26	m.	Clerk	/500	O.
2		Hellen V.	21	f.			"
3		Everett	2	m.			"
4		Ella	1	f.			
5	86/86	RINAS, Frederick	25	m.	Cordwainer	1600/600	Ger.
6		Alena	21	f.			Va.
7		Christian	3	m.			O.
8		John	1	m.			"
9		SHOUP, Michel	21	m.	Cordwainer		"
10		BUTT, Jacob	18	m.	Cordwainer		"
11		SULTZER, W. B.	24	m.	Jailer		"
12	87/87	SHUFLE, William	24	m.	Barber	/125	Ger.
13		Louisa	16	f.			O.
14	88/88	DAVIS, William	43	m.	Hotel-keeper	2500/300	Pa.
15		Elisabeth	33	f.			O.

16		DAVIS, Henry	13	m.			O. S
17		Ruth A.	11	f.			" S
18		Robert M.	6	m.			" S
19		JONES, Elisabeth	18	f.	Domestic		"
20	89/89	CUNNINGHAM, James	63	m.	Saddler	3000/150	Va.
21		Margaret A.	57	f.			"
22		Margaret	22	f.			O.
23		Thomas C.	17	m.			"
24		Joseph	13	m.			"
25		LEWIS, Benjamin	25	m.	Cordwainer		"
26		Susann M.	20	f.			"
27		Flora M.	2	f.			"
28		James T.	1	m.			"
29	90/90	BURGHBACHER,					
		Mathias	37	m.	Tailor	2000/300	Ger.
30		Catharine	30	f.			O.
31		James H.	8	m.			"
32		Martha	6	f.			"
33		Mary	4	f.			"
34		Charles	1	m.			"
35	91/91	HENTHORN, William	37	m.	Cabinet-maker		
						400/150	O.
36		Margaret O.	32	f.			Pa.
37		Ruth A.	16	f.			O. S
38		John G.	15	m.			" S
39		Joseph H.	6	m.			"
40		Adam F.	2	m.			"

Page 13   6 June 1860   Sheet 39

1	92/92	HENTHORN, John	64	m.			Pa.
2		GONDEY, Adam	28	m.	Laborer	350/100	"
3		Elisabeth	20	f.			O.
4	93/93	VICKERS, John	50	m.	Wagon-maker	1500/150	Pa.
5		Ann	48	f.			Va.
6		Robert M.	23	m.	Wagon-maker		O.
7		John	19	m.			"
8		Ebenezer	17	m.			"
9		Mary S.	11	f.			"
10		Ida V.	2	f.			"
11	94/94	HUTCHINSON,					
		Robbert	35	m.	Printer	450/120	"
12		Esther	27	f.			"
13		Sidney J.	8	f.			"
14		Mary E.	4	f.			" S
15		Margaret	2	f.			"
16		Rebecca	77	f.			Pa.
17	95/95	SHEBLE, George	60	m.		500/2500	Ger.
18		Sophia	58	f.			"
19	96/96	KIRKWOOD, William	57	m.	Wagon-maker	1000/300	Md.
20		Jane	57	f.			"

21		KIRKWOOD, William					
		C.	22	m.	Teacher		O.
22		Samuel	19	m.	Teacher		"
23		STUERT, Margaret	13	f.			"
24	97/97	SINCLAIR, Alexander	55	m.	Butcher	900/150	Ire.
25		Jane	46	f.			Pa.
26		Sarah	23	f.			O.
27		Margaret	22	f.			"
28		James	20	m.			" S
29		Nancy E.	15	f.			" S
30		Mary O.	12	f.			" S
31		Selesta	10	f.			" S
32		Charles	7	m.			" S
33	98/98	BURGHBACHER, Jacob	32	m.	Wagon-maker	/100	Ger.
34		Elisabeth	24	f.			"
35		Emely	1	f.			O.
36	99/99	SPANGLER, Soloman	45	m.	Pedlar	/160	Pa.
37		Margaret	27	f.			"
38		Mary E.	2	f.			O.
39	100/100	SMITH, Ann	62	f.		2000/500	Pa.
40		Emla D.	11	f.			O.

Page 14   6 June 1860   Sheet 39 verso

1		Charles	9	m.			O. S
2	101/101	RICHNER, Isaac	34	m.		540/580	Pa.
3		Hannah	34	f.			O.
4		Mary J.	9	f.			" S
5		Catharine A.	7	f.			" S
6		Susann R.	3	f.			"
7		John M.	1	m.			"
8	102/102	DENNIS, Henry	36	m.	Farmer	/150	"
9		Catharine	34	f.			"
10		Elisabeth	16	f.			" S
11		Adam	13	m.			" S
12		Susann	12	f.			" S
13		James	4	m.			"
14	103/103	SHORT, Mary	29	f.			Ger.
15		Barbary	14	f.			" S
16		Jacob	9	m.			O. S
17		Henry	6	m.			"
18	104/104	McMAHON, Catharine	28	f.			"
19		Mary E.	15	f.		1400/250	" S
20	105/105	CUNNINGHAM, James	25	m.	Saddler		"
21		Mary	23	f.			"
22	106/106	OKEY, William	50	m.	Lawyer	11,000/2000	"
23		Lucinda	38	f.			Ind.

24		OKEY, Mary C.	13	f.			O. S
25		William F.	11	m.			" S
26		Sarah M.	7	f.			"
27		MOFFETT, Louisa	16	f.			"
28		SULIVAN, Eliza	20	f.			"
29		LYNCH, Mary	61	f.			N.Y.
30	107/107	MORRIS, James R.	40	m.	Farmer	8000/2000	Pa.
31		Temperance	31	f.			O.
32		Ewart	14	m.			" S
33		Sarah J.	7	f.			" S
34		Mary F.	4	f.			"
35		Sarah	65	f.			Pa.
36		STRANIGAN, Sarah	18	f.			Ire.
37	108/108	O'CONNOR, Daniel	62	m.		/150	"
38		Hannah	60	f.			Pa.
39		Loran	11	m.			O. S
40		Eliza	9	f.			" S

Page 15   6 June 1860   Sheet 40

1	109/109	MYERS, William	51	m.	Farmer	13,000/1000	Va.
2		Hannah	48	f.			Pa.
3		Minerva	23	f.			O.
4		William H.	14	m.			" S
5		OKEY, A. C.	2	m.			"
6		LEDGETT, Mary	40	f.	Domestic		Pa.
7		PRICE, Isaac	28	m.			O.
8	110/110	SCHUMAKER, Philip	38	m.	Baker	3000/300	Ger.
9		Elisabeth	37	f.			"
10		Philip	14	m.			" S
11		John	12	m.			" S
12		Lena	7	f.			O. S
13		Rosena	5	f.			" S
14		Lewis	3	m.			"
15		Frances	1	f.			"
16	111/111	DAVENPORT, Geo. H.	35	m.	Merchant	4000/600	"
17		John R.	8	m.			" S
18		Elisabeth	4	f.			"
19		MERRYMAN, Mary	44	f.			Va.
20		FURGESON, Isabell	45	f.			O.
21	112/112	PATTON, David	29	m.	Carpenter	1700/250	"
22		Mary	30	f.			"
23		Abby villa	6	f.			"
24		Henry H.	1	m.			"
25		John L.	17	m.			" S
26		SHAW, Sarah	30	f.	Domestic		"
27	113/113	BURKHEAD, John	36	m.		/200	"
28		Harriet	31	f.			"
29		Nancy	14	f.			" S
30		Henry F.	10	m.			" S

31		BURKHEAD, Ruth E.	6	f.		O. S
32		McGONIGAL, Hugh	20	m.	Laborer	Ire. S
33	114/114	HENTHORN, Jesse B.	33	m.	Engineer	/250 O.
34		Rachel	34	f.		"
35		Margaret	12	f.		" S
36		Thomas	10	m.		" S
37		David	9	m.		" S
38		Sarah	8	f.		" S
39		John	6	m.		" S
40		Cecelia	4	f.		"

Page 16   6 June 1860   Sheet 40 verso

1	115/115	POOL, Joseph	43	m.	Laborer	O.
2		Gulia	42	f.		Pa.
3		Richard C.	14	m.		O. S
4		Ann	12	f.		" S
5		John C.	10	m.		" S
6		DONLEY, Elisabeth	18	f.	Domestic	"
7		Minerva	6/12	f.		"
8		James	65	m.	Miller	/1500 Pa.
9		MERINER, Robert	51	m.	Laborer	Va.
10		James	18	m.	Laborer	"
11	116/116	FORD, Thomas	42	m.	Miller	2350/6267 O.
12		Clarinda	39	f.		"
13		Lucetta	12	f.		" S
14		Milton C.	9	m.		" S
15		Stephen D.	7	m.		" S
16		Forrest	3	m.		"
17	117/117	SMITH, Samuel	45	m.	Carpenter	2700/200 Pa.
18		Nancy	33	f.		O.
19		John H.	20	m.		" S
20		Susann F.	16	f.		" S
21		Thomas	14	m.		" S
22		Henritta J.	12	f.		" S
23		Charles W.	9	m.		" S
24		Milton D.	6	m.		" S
25		Henry G.	3	m.		"
26		HUFFMAN, John	22	m.		"
27		YOKEY, Edward	21	m.		
28	118/118	FORD, Stephen	45	m.	/600	"
29		Elisabeth	40	f.		"
30		Henry Y.	20	m.		" S
31		Hariet M.	18	f.		" S
32		Thomas O.	16	m.		" S
33		Ruthanne	12	f.		" S
34	119/119	HAMILTON, Menerva	29	f.	175/	"
35		Sylvester	10	m.		" S
36	120/120	JACKSON, Andrew	37	m.	Blacksmith 500/200	"
37		Mary	35	f.		"
38		Eugene	2	m.		"

39		JACKSON, Ann	1	f.		O.
40		PENN, Caroline	35	f.	Domestic	"

1	121/121	WASHBURN, James	39	m.	Carpenter	/150	N.Y.
2		Eliza M.	34	f.			Mass.
3		Florence	10	f.			N.Y. S
4		Louisa R.	8	f.			" S
5		Isabell M.	5	f.			O.
6		Mary E.	3	f.			"
7	122/122	LLOYD, Wilson	44	m.	Brick-moulder		
						300/150	Pa.
8		Margaret	37	f.			O.
9		John	19	m.			"
10		Lucinda	11	f.			" S
11		Mary A.	9	f.			" S
12		Ann C.	6	f.			"
13		James W.	4	m.			"
14		Franklin	1	m.			"
15	123/123	SNIDER, Adam	28	m.	Farmer		Ger.
16		Mary	29	f.			"
17		Mary	7	f.			"
18		Sophia	3	f.			O.
19	124/124	JORDAN, William W.	35	m.	Tinner	1500/500	Pa.
20		Laura A.	20	f.			O.
21		Ellenor H.	9	f.			" S
22		George W.	1	m.			"
23		Sarah	18	f.	Domestic		Pa.
24		Alex	17	m.	Apprentice		O.
25	125/125	PATTERSON, Sanson	30	m.	Tanner	2000/300	Pa.
26		Sarah J.	28	f.			"
27		LLOYD, Jackson	24	m.	Tanner	/200	"
28	126/126	OKEY, F. G.	31	m.	Merchant	3900/1000	O.
29		CARY, Alerison	2	m.			"
30	127/127	PATTERSON, Daniel	35	m.	Tanner	/500	Pa.
31		Dorthy	30	f.			O.
32	128/128	PASSMORE, Heman	26	m.	Blacksmith	/150	Pa.
33		Elisabeth	22	f.			O.
34	129/129	OKEY, Author	37	m.	Carpenter	350/150	"
35		Nancy	30	f.			Md.
36		Robbert	8	m.			O. S
37		Harrit R.	1	f.			"
38	130/130	EDNEY, Robbert	31	m.	Livery Stable		
						400/300	O.
39		Jane	28	f.			Eng.
40		Frank	3	m.			O.

1	131/131 PATTERSON, James	37	m.	Farmer	1700/500	Pa.
2	Sophia S.	26	f.			O.
3	Jacob D.	8	m.			" S
4	Wilmer	1	m.			"
5	132/132 REDDIN, Joel	64	m.	Laborer		N.J.
6	Sarah	61	f.			Pa.
7	Milton	23	m.	Teamster	500/150	O.
8	133/133 REDDIN, Uriah	33	m.	Laborer		"
9	Isabell	23	f.			N.Y.
10	Joseph	2	m.			Ill.
11	134/134 NEISWANGER, Wilson	32	m.	Painter	200/100	Pa.
12	Hellen	25	f.			O.
13	James	2	m.			"
14	135/135 EBERLINE, Permelia	32	f.			"
15	Ferdinie	15	m.			" S
16	Melinda	11	f.			" S
17	Eugene	8	f.			" S
18	Charles	7	m.			"
19	136/136 HOLLIDAY, John	42	m.			"
20	Antnett	32	f.			N.Y.
21	Mary M.	11	f.			O. S
22	Rebecca M.	3	f.			"
23	137/137 KALLENBAUGH,					
	Charles	35	m.	Butcher		Ger.
24	Ann	35	f.			Sw.
25	Lucetta	12	f.			O. S
26	Elisabeth	2	f.			"
27	Barbary	1	f.			"
28	138/138 GADD, Emly	34	f.	Milliner		"
29	LESSLY, Amanda	20	f.			"
30	139/139 GUTHRIE, Louisa	55	f.			Pa.
31	Mary A.	16	f.			O. S
32	140/140 STRICKLING, Joseph	29	m.	Teamster	/200	Va.
33	Rebecca	21	f.			O.
34	Barthenia	3	f.			"
35	Joseph W.	2	m.			"
36	141/141 HOLLISTER, Warren	38	m.		3000/500	"
37	Elisabeth	28	f.			"
38	Charles	1	m.			"
39	142/142 SHIPLEY, Lewis	50	m.		1200/800	Pa.
40	Elisabeth	46	f.			"

1	Mary A.	18	f.			O. S

2	143/143	MORFBERG, Maranda	35	f.	Milliner		O.	
3		Leonora	10	f.			"	
4		Cora B.	4	f.			"	
5	144/144	HINES, John	32	m.	Blacksmith		Ger.	
6		Catharine	24	f.			"	
7		Elisabeth	5	f.				
8		John	3	m.			O.	
9		Mary	1	f.			"	
							"	
10	145/145	CRAIG, William	62	m.	Farmer	6000/600	Pa.	
11		Elisabeth	52	f.			O.	
12		Joseph	29	m.			"	
13		Ezra	22	m.			"	S
14		Margrett	19	f.			"	S
15		Mary	12	f.			"	S
16		Elisabeth A.	10	f.			"	S
17	146/146	AMOS, James O.	27	m.		/250	"	
18		Nancy J.	24	f.			"	
19		Mary	2	f.			"	
20	147/147	MITCHELL, James	36	m.			"	
21		Lucy	35	f.			"	
22		James K.	10	m.			"	
23	148/148	POPE, Alexander	61	m.	Stone-cutter			
						6000/1208	Eng.	
24		Mary	52	f.			Ire.	
25		Robert	17	m.			O.	S
26		Jane	17	f.	Adopted		"	S
27	149/149	PARSONS, Joseph	33	m.		/150	"	
28		Mary	26	f.			"	
29		Frisby	6	m.			"	S
30		Mely	2	f.			"	
31	150/150	DAVENPORT, Jno. A.	41	m.	Merchant	3500/20,000	"	
32		Margrett	30	f.			"	
33		Martha S.	13	f.			"	S
34		Mary A.	4	f.			"	
35		Ella	3	f.			"	
36		Jno. A.	1	m.			"	
37		MERYMAN, Jno. D.	22	m.	Clerk		"	
38		VARNER, Fanny	12	f.			"	
39		SOUTH, Penina	19	f.	Domestic		"	
40		Elisabeth	5	f.			"	

Page 20   6 June 1860   Sheet 42 verso

1	151/151	DAVENPORT, Martha	71	f.			Md.	
2		SMITH, Anne	62	f.			Va.	
3	152/152	FLEMING, Hannah	45	f.		700/200	"	
4		James H.	14	m.			O.	S
5		Charles	12	m.			"	S

6	153/153	FLEEMAN, John	31	m.	Laborer	500/120	Ger.	
7		Laney	26	f.			"	
8		John	9	m.			O.	
9		George	7	m.			"	S
10		Charles	5	m.			"	S
11		James L.	2	m.			"	
12		Lewisa	65	f.			Ger.	
13	154/154	OKEY, John W.	33	m.	Lawyer	1000/250	O.	
14		Mary J.	33	f.			"	
15		George	10	m.			"	S
16		Isadore	8	f.			"	S
17		William F.	6	m.			"	S
18	155/155	HOLLISTER, Simpson	30	m.	Lawyer	1500/300	"	
19		Mary	29	f.			"	
20		William S.	4	m.			"	
21		Lucinda A.	3	f.			"	
22		Jeremiah J.	1	m.			"	
23	156/156	ULLOM, Stephen	45	m.	Farmer		Pa.	
24		Ellenor	44	f.			"	
25		Mahala	18	f.			O.	
26		Elisabeth	16	f.			"	
27		Rachel	12	f.			"	S
28		Margarit	10	f.			"	S
29		Mary A.	6	f.			"	
30		Laura	3	f.			"	
31	157/157	HOLLISTER, Nathan	40	m.	Lawyer	15,000/18,000	"	
32		Eliza	36	f.			"	
33		Isadore	16	f.			"	S
34		Adelaide	14	f.			"	S
35		Jeferson	12	m.			"	S
36		James N.	9	m.			"	S
37		DILLON, John E.	25	m.	Physician		"	S
38		Margaret	18	f.	Domestic			
39		OTTLE, Fredarick	30	m.			Ger.	
40		WOODS, Hannah	40	f.			Va.	

(End of Woodsfield)

1	158/158	HAWKINS, Levi	34	m.	Tobacco-packer	/200	Va.	
2		Margaret	33	f.			Pa.	I
3		Elisabeth	13	f.			O.	S
4		Sarah A.	10	f.			"	
5		James E.	6	m.			"	
6		Francis	4	m.			"	
7		Lydia E.	2	f.				
8	159/159	SHELL, Jacob	30	m.	Farmer	/800	Fr.	
9		Ann	25	f.			O.	
10		William D.	7	m.			"	
11		John H.	5	m.			"	
12		Alvy	3	f.				

13		SHELL, Laura	7/12	f.			O.
14		BYERS, Charles	30	m.	Laborer		"
15	160/160	RAPP, Charles	36	m.	Weaver		Wur.
16		Catharine	37	f.			"
17		Christian	7	m.			"
18		Sophia	3	f.			O.
19		Jacob	4/12	m.			"
20	161/161	SHELL, William	66	m.	Farmer	3000/400	Fr.
21		Lana	57	f.			"
22		Thersa S.	4	f.			O.
23	162/162	JOHNSON, William	64	m.	Farmer	2300/700	Pa.
24		Esther	56	f.			"
25		William Jr.	20	m.	Farmer		O.
26	163/163	JOHNSON, Robert	53	m.	Farmer	2500/600	"
27		Mary	54	f.			"
28		Elisabeth	26	f.			"
29		William V.	24	m.			"
30		Emly	22	f.			"
31		Washington	19	m.			"
32		Eliza	17	f.			"
33		James	14	m.			"
34	164/164	KEOHLER, Goshua	41	m.	Farmer	2200/500	Pa. I
35		Emly	35	f.			O. I
36		Isaac	17	m.			" S
37		Catharine	15	f.			" S
38		Sevila	14	f.			" S
39		Mary	10	f.			" S
40		Joseph	8	m.			" S

Page 22   8 June 1860   Sheet 43 verso

1		Eliza	7	f.			O. S
2		Jane	5				"
3	165/165	KOEHLER, Daniel	76	m.	Farmer	/200	Pa.
4		Sylvena	70	f.			Bav.
5		Margaret	47	f.			"
6		Philip	22	m.			O.
7	166/166	WEBBER, Henry	58	m.	Farmer	1800/750	Bav.
8		Fredarick	13	m.	Farmer		O.
9	167/167	RODECKER, Frederick	29	m.	Farmer	1700/250	Pa.
10		Susan	24	f.			O.
11		Mary A.	4	f.			"
12	168/168	BURKHEAD, Nelson H.	32	m.	Farmer	4000/600	"
13		Elisabeth	32	f.			"
14		John W.	9	m.			" S
15		Catharine	1/12	f.			"

16		BURKHEAD, Emma	6	f.			O.	
17		HEADLEY, James	16	m.	Laborer		"	S
18	169/169	BURKHEAD, Patience	69	f.			Md.	
19		Deborah	38	f.			O.	
20	170/170	LONG, John	32	m.	Farmer	1600/350	"	
21		Jane	32	f.			"	
22		Ausbern	2	m.			"	
23	171/171	RODECKER, Philip	56	m.	Farmer	1200/285	Pa.	
24		Ragmena	56	f.			"	
25		Ann C.	18	f.			"	
26		William	20	m.			"	
27	172/172	PRESHAW, William	35	m.	Merchant	800/2000	Va.	
28		Sophia	36	f.			O.	
29		John L.	10	m.			"	S
30		William	6	m.			"	S
31	173/173	HAYDEN, John	75	m.	Farmer	4000/400	Md.	
32		Ann	65	f.			Va.	
33	174/174	BECKETT, George	48	m.	Farmer	6000/200	O.	
34		Margaret	39	f.			"	
35		John C.	17	m.			"	S
36		CLINGHAN, Margaret	68	f.			Ire.	
37	175/175	LESLY, Johnson	56	m.	Wagon-maker	500/150	Md.	
38		Margaret	18	f.			O.	S
39		Therisa	15	f.			"	S
40		Forest	3	m.			"	

Page 23			8 June 1860				Sheet 44	
1		Mary	41	f.			O.	
2		Margaret	13	f.			"	S
3		Mary	9	f.			"	
4		William S.	6	m.			"	
5		Nancy E.	4	f.			"	
6		Slantha L.	2	f.			"	
7		Robbert	21	m.	Laborer		"	
8		ROUSE, William	82	m.			Md.	
9	176/176	McDIVITT, Robbert	50	m.	Cordwainer	/150	Pa.	
10		Eliza	49	f.			N.J.	
11		Sarah E.	22	f.			O.	
12		James	18	m.	Laborer		"	S
13		Mary A.	16	f.			"	S
14		Carr	14	m.			"	S
15		Burr	11	m.			"	S
16		India	6	f.			"	
17	177/177	ROUSE, Benjamin	48	m.	Farmer	3000/550	"	
18		Francis	47	f.			"	
19		Nancy A.	22	f.			"	
20		James G.	20	m.			"	

```
21              ROUSE, John W.    11   m.                            O.  S
22              William C.         5   m.                            "
23              Thomas B.          3   m.                            "
24              Mary E.            8   f.                            "   S

25  178/178 CONGER, Daniel        29   m.    Laborer    /100         "
26              Margaret          35   f.                            "
27              Hannah E.          6   f.                            "

28  179/179 McKEOWN, Elisa-
                beth              55   f.               2500/240 Ire.
29              James             29   m.                         O.
30              Daniel            19   m.                            "
31              Ellenor           23   f.                         "   3

32  180/180 FORD, Henry          66   m.    Farmer    9600/700  Md.
33              Abigail           45   f.                         O.
34              Matilda A.        19   f.                         "   S
35              Hulda F.          16   f.                         "   S
36              Menerva           11   f.                         "   S

37  181/181 FORD, William        26   m.    Merchant   /1500        "
38              HEADLEY, Catharine 50  f.                            "

39  182/182 FORD, Henry Jr.      23   m.    Merchant  4000/150       "
40              BEARD, Edward     18   m.    Laborer                 "
```

Page 24   8 June 1860   Sheet 44 verso

```
1   183/183 PRATT, William       25   m.    Miller              Pa.
2               Rebecca          28   f.                        O.
3               Louisa            4   f.                           "

4   184/184 FINEGAN, George      38   m.    Miller                "
5               Lydia A.         35   f.                        Pa.  I
6               Thomas           12   m.                        O.  S
7               Amos W.          11   m.                        "   S
8               Ellen E.          8   f.                           "
9               Tobitha J.        6   f.                           "
10              Mary E.           2   f.                           "

11  185/185 STINE, Henry         68   m.    Farmer   1100/400  Pa.  I
12              Deborah          51   f.                        "   I
13              William H.       20   m.    Farmer             O.  S
14              Malin P.         14   m.                        "   S
15              Michel S.        11   m.                        "   S
16              Mary             19   f.                        "   S
17              Ellenor J.       10   f.                           "
18              Hester A.        11   f.                           "

19  186/186 PRATT, John          48   m.    Farmer    /200    Pa.  I
20              Therisa A.       38   f.                        O.  I
21              Lilly J.         51   f.
22              Eliza             3   f.
23              John H.           2   m.
24              Nancy            70   f.                        Pa.  I
25              DONLEY, Yonry    56   f.                        Va.  I
```

26		PRATT, Samuel M.	16	m.			O.
27	187/187	PATTON, Thomas W.	49	m.	Farmer	2000/250	Pa.
28		Mary	47	f.			Va.
29		Sarah L.	19	f.			Pa. S
30		Elisabeth	16	f.			" S
31		Noah	12	m.			" S
32	188/188	ENGLISH, G. W.	31	m.		/60	O.
33		Gulia A.	18	f.			"
34		William	5/12	m.			"
35	189/189	ULLOM, Nichlan	23	m.	Farmer	/290	"
36		Margaret	18	f.			"
37		Malcom	3	m.			"
38		Lenora	1	f.			"
39	190/190	GAITS, David	39	m.		1600/300	"
40		Nancy	36	f.			"

1		Margaret J.	18	f.			O. S
2		Lewis	14	m.			" S
3		Clarinda	12	f.			" S
4		Mahala	6	f.			"
5	191/191	GAITS, George	42	m.	Farmer	900/240	" I
6		Ellenor	44	f.			"
7		William H.	16	m.	Farmer		" S
8		Lydia J.	13	f.			" S
9		Volentine	10	m.			" S
10	192/192	HESS, George	28	m.	Farmer	/150	"
11		Sarah	24	f.			"
12		Jane	2	f.			"
13		Michel	7/12	m.			"
14		BRUM, Edward	27	m.	Plasterer		" M
15		Nancy	18	f.			" M
16	193/193	HESS, Michel	83	m.	Farmer	2000/450	Pa.
17		Mary	73	f.			"
18		WRIGHT, Mary J.	13	f.	Servant		O. S
19		SOUTH, George	13	m.			"
20	194/194	GUTHRIE, Robt.	33	m.	Teamster	/300	"
21		Ann	31	f.			Pa.
22		John H.	10	m.			O.
23		Elisabeth A.	9	f.			"
24		Clara L.	5	f.			"
25		HOY, Samuel	33	m.	Laborer		Pa.
26	195/195	COATS, Eunice	67	f.		800/263	"
27		Mary A.	26	f.			"
28		Sarah J.	23	f.			O.
29	196/196	MORRIS, Thomas	75	m.	Farmer	4000/500	Pa.
30		Ann	50	f.			Md.

31		MORRIS, John D.	14	m.			O. S
32		Elisabeth	10	f.			" S
33		LAINGS, Ruth A.	4	f.			"
34	197/197	OKEY, Woodman	41	m.	Farmer	2500/500	"
35		Eliza	35	f.			"
36		Martha	10	f.			" S
37		Emely A.	8	f.			" S
38		Guly	6	f.			"
39		Cely	4	m.			"
40		Alfred	4/12	m.			"

Page 26   9 June 1860   Sheet 45 verso

1	198/198	MORRIS, David	35	m.	Farmer	2500/428	O.
2		Elisabeth	27	f.			"
3		George H.	4	m.			"
4		Thomas	3	m.			"
5		Winfield	2	m.			"
6		James	7/12	m.			"
7	199/199	TRUAX, William	40	m.	Farmer	1350/300	Pa.
8		Rebecca	38	f.			O.
9		Charlotte	15	f.			" S
10		Pict J.	14	f.			" S
11		Nancy	12	f.			" S
12		Lucind	9	f.			" S
13		Ura	7	f.			" S
14		Susan	5	f.			"
15		Barbary	3	f.			"
16		Elias	4/12	m.			"
17	200/200	MORRIS, William	50	m.	Farmer	1600/200	"
18		Elisabeth	45	f.			Pa.
19		Susan	17	f.			O.
20		Penelope	15	f.			"
21		William	13	m.			" S
22		Aaron	10	m.			" S
23		Stephen	8	m.			"
24		Gulita	6	m.			"
25		Thomas	2	m.			"
26		George W.	15	m.			"
27	201/201	DUVALL, Ephram	37	m.	Farmer	/250	Md.
28		Mary J.	33	f.			Pa.
29		Elisabeth A.	13	f.			O.
30		John T.	11	m.			"
31		Sarah J.	9	f.			"
32		Margaret C.	7	f.			"
33		Aron K.	5	m.			"
34		James F.	3	m.			"
35		John	84	m.			Md.
36	202/202	EDDY, Michel	62	m.	Farmer	4000/475	Va.
37		Mary J.	19	f.			O.
38		ECKELBERRY, Eliza	17	f.			" S

39	203/203	EDDY, John	23	m.	Farmer	/200	O.
40		Dela H.	22	f.			"

1		David	2/12	m.			O.	
2		POWELL, John	17	m.	Laborer		"	
3	204/204	COFFEE, John	56	m.	Farmer	3000/192	Ire.	
4		Mary	46	f.			Pa.	
5		Edward	24	m.	Farmer		"	
6		James	18	m.			O.	S
7		Maria	16	f.			"	S
8		Thomas	14	m.			"	S
9		John	12	m.			"	S
10		Lydia	10	f.			"	S
11		Tacy	8	f.			"	
12		William	6	m.				
13	205/205	BYERS, Jesse	36	m.	Farmer	1500/200	"	
14		Catharine	28	f.			"	
15		Hannah J.	13	f.			"	S
16		Thier	11	f.			"	S
17		Esther	8	f.			"	S
18		George S.	3/12	m.			"	
19		David	27	m.	Laborer		"	I
20		MANN, Rachel	22	f.	Domestic		"	
21		Dianner	21	f.			"	
22		BYERS, Lorenza	21	m.	Laborer			
23	206/206	BROWN, William	27	m.	Farmer	3000/170	"	
24		Sarah E.	18	f.			"	
25		Terza	2	f.			"	
26		Erza	1/12	m.			"	
27		GRANS, Simpson	24	m.	Laborer			
28	207/207	McBEE, Sidney	41	f.		/75	Md.	
29		Robbert B.	19	m.	Laborer		Pa.	S
30		Lorenza	17	m.	Laborer		"	S
31		Rebecca J.	16	f.			Va.	S
32		Ezra T.	12	m.			Pa.	S
33		G. W.	10	m.			"	S
34		Mary B.	5	f.			Va.	
35		Sarah	1	f.			O.	
36	208/208	BARRETT, Margaret	64	f.		/50	Pa.	
37		Isabell	36	f.			O.	
38	209/209	BARRETT, Calvin	40	m.	Farmer	2500/300	"	
39		Margarett	32	f.			"	
40		Wellington	10	m.			"	S

1		John	8	m.		O. S
2		Sarah	5	f.		"
3		Melinda	2	f.		"
4		Isaac	7/12	m.		"

5	210/210	EDY, Silais	30	m.	Farmer	/200	Va.
6		Susan	32	f.			O.
7		Thomas	18	m.	Farmer	"	S
8		Rebecca	16	f.		"	S
9		Clarinda	14	f.		"	S
10		Sarah	6	f.		"	
11		Pardelia	6	f.		"	
12		Albert	4	m.		"	
13		Alferd	4	m.		"	
14		Pheoba	2	f.		"	
15	211/211	FRIEND, George	46	m.	Farmer	/150	Pa.
16		Catharine	18	f.			"
17		Mary E.	16	f.			"
18		Sarah V.	11	f.			"
19		George	5	m.			"
20		John	3	m.			"
21		Lydia	1/12	f.			"
22	212/212	OKEY, Walker	37	m.	Farmer	4000/700	O.
23		Jane	32	f.			"
24		Hannah	12	f.			" S
25		Milton	9	m.			" S
26		Sinclair	7	m.			" S
27		John	5	m.			" S
28		Archbold	2	m.			"
29		Sophia	73	f.			N.Y.
30		BROWN, Joseph	23	m.	Laborer		O.
31	213/213	EDDY, Isaac	41	m.	Farmer	700/240	"
32		Nancy	42	f.			" I
33		George W.	13	m.			" S
34		Mary E.	8	f.			" S
35		Vandilia	8	f.			" S
36		Abraham	6	m.			"
37	214/214	PRUETT, Robert	56	m.	Farmer	4200/720	Md.
38		Catharine	56	f.			"
39		Wesley	24	m.			"
40		Elisabeth	26	f.			"

Page 29   10 June 1860   Sheet 47

1		Robert	18	m.			O. S
2		Mary M.	15	f.			" S
3		Catharine	13	f.			" S
4		Daniel N.	12	m.			" S
5	215/215	DUNN, Milton	45	m.	Farmer	2500/600	Va.
6		Sarah	39	f.			O.
7		Amanda J.	20	f.			" S
8		John	17	m.			" S
9		Susan	15	f.			" S
10		Albert W.	12	m.			" S
11		Sebastian C.	10	m.			" S
12		Eliza L.	5	f.			"
13		James M.	2	m.			"

14	216/216	WILLIAMS, Absolom	35	m.	Farmer	/140	0. I
15		Arthamer	30	f.			" I
16		Arkemidns	14	m.			" S
17		Nancy E.	11	f.			" S
18		Nancy J.	6	f.			"
19		Margaret	3	f.			"
20		Mary	1	f.			"
21	217/217	STONEBREAKER, Sam-uel	21	m.	Farmer	/125	" M
22		Merinda	19	f.			" M
23	218/218	HOWELL, Harrison	30	m.	Farmer	/328	"
24		Matilda	29	f.			"
25		William H.	7	m.			"
26		Mary J.	5	f.			"
27		Susan S.	3	f.			"
28		Leander J.	4/12	m.			
29	219/219	PASCOE, Mary	40	f.		/100	"
30		William	20	m.	Laborer		"
31		Soliman	18	m.	Laborer		"
32		Manuel	16	m.	Laborer		"
33		Francis M.	10	m.			"
34		Jasper N.	8	m.			"
35		Xavida M.	6	m.			"
36		Theodocio	3	f.			
37	220/220	CAATES, Benjamin	40	m.	Farmer	2000/348	"
38		Louisa E.	37	f.			"
39		Maria	16	f.			"
40		G. W.	10	m.			

Page 30   10 June 1860   Sheet 47 verso

1		Elizabeth	7	f.			0.
2		John W.	5	m.			"
3	221/221	HOWELL, Aaron	67	m.	Farmer	3500/200	"
4		Margaret	64	f.			"
5	222/222	KEEPER, Charles	26	m.	Farmer	300/150	Bav.
6		Nancy	23	f.			0.
7		Margaret A.	2	f.			"
8		Mary	1	f.			"
9	223/223	HOWELL, James	41	m.	Farmer	400/200	"
10		Barbary	40	f.			"
11		Emely	15	f.			"
12		Mary	12	f.			"
13		Margaret	10	f.			"
14		Angeline	7	f.			"
15		John E.	3	m.			"
16	224/224	HOWELL, John	46	m.	Farmer	860/500	"
17		Elizabeth	43	f.			"
18		William	21	m.	Farmer		"
19		Hannah	20	f.			" S

20		HOWELL, David	18	m.			O.	S
21		John	16	m.			"	S
22		Lucinda	14	f.			"	
23		Abner	12	m.			"	S
24		Margaret	10	f.			"	
25		Ranna	8	f.			"	
26		Mary	6	f.			"	
27		Rhoda	4	f.			"	
28		Sarah	2	f.			"	

29	225/225	TILLET, R. W.	34	m.	Miller	1000/150	"	
30		Harriet	24	f.			"	
31		Clorance	4	f.			"	
32		Pleasant A.	2	f.			"	
33		WINDLAND, Hannah	60	f.		/1000	Pa.	

34	226/226	WINDLAND, Isah	37	m.	Miller	900/400	O.	
35		Catharine	38	f.			"	
36		Isaac	18	m.			"	
37		Elisabeth	13	f.			"	
38		John W.	9	m.			"	
39		Catharine	7	f.			"	
40		Sarah	6	f.			"	

Page 31			10 June 1860				Sheet 48	
1		Henry	3	m.			O.	

| 2 | 227/227 | WINDLAND, John | 75 | m. | Farmer | 4000/600 | Pa.| |
| 3 | | Catharine | 78 | f. | | | " | |

4	228/228	WINDLAND, Henry	28	m.	Farmer		O.	
5		Mary A.	23	f.			"	
6		Susanah	3	f.			"	
7		Jesse	8/12	m.			"	
8		John	18	m.	Laborer		"	S

9	229/229	XAVIER, Jacob	48	m.	Farmer	2000/800	Wur.	
10		Barbary	49	f.			Darm.	
11		George	15	m.			O.	S
12		Jacob	12	m.			"	S
13		John	6	m.			"	S

14	230/230	BELT, Middleton	48	m.	Farmer	770/220	Md.	
15		Nancy	46	f.			O.	
16		William	19	m.			"	S
17		Cornelius	17	m.			"	S
18		Sarah	12	f.			"	S

19	231/231	BEARD, Francis	25	m.	Farmer	/150	"	
20		Elisabeth J.	28	f.			"	
21		Mary C.	1	f.			"	
22		OKEY, Henry	45	f.			"	
23		Sophia	40	f.			"	

24	232/232	MURPHY, G. W.	27	m.	Farmer	/155	"	
25		Cordelia	29	f.			"	
26		Forrest W.	3	m.			"	

27		MURPHY, Flora J.	8/12	f.			O.	
28	233/233	SMITH, Harison	38	m.	Carpenter	2500/750	Pa.	
29		Eliza J.	32	f.			O.	
30		Emely	10	f.			"	S
31		Maria K.	9	f.			"	S
32		Gulia	7	f.			"	S
33		Sabina H.	5	f.			"	S
34		George M.	3	m.			"	
35		Mary P.	1	f.			"	
36	234/234	TRIMLEY, Abraham D.	21	m.	Farmer	/100	"	M
37		Catharine E.	22	f.			"	M
38	235/235	SHUMACHER, Joseph	46	m.	Farmer	1000/600	Bav.	
39		Margaret	44	f.			"	
40		George	20	m.			"	

Page 32   11 June 1860   Sheet 48 verso

1		Joseph	19	m.			Bav.	
2		Franklin	17	m.			"	
3		Lewis	16	m.			"	
4		Michel	14	m.			"	S
5		Charles	10	m.			"	S
6		Daniel	10	m.			"	S
7		Philip	8	m.			"	S
8		John	4	m.			O.	
9		Henry	3	m.			"	
10	236/236	SNIDER, Jacob	31	m.	Farmer	1400/300	Bav.	
11		Eve	28	f.			O.	
12		Fredaric	7	m.			"	S
13		Jacob	3	m.			"	
14	237/237	BARNETT, William	86	m.		/200	"	
15		Hannah	67	f.			Pa.	
16		Sarah L.	20	f.			O.	
17		Eveline	13	f.			"	
18	238/238	FELTNER, Jacob	23	m.	Farmer	700/200	"	
19		Barbary	28	f.			Bav.	
20		Fredarick	6/12	m.			"	
21	239/239	SHOUP, Henry	26	m.	Farmer	600/150	O.	
22		Margaret	26	f.			Darm.	
23		Gayhart	2	m.			"	
24		Amelia	1/12	f.			O.	
25	240/240	RICHNER, Claudus	78	m.	Farmer	/150	Pr.	
26		Margaret	66	f.			Pa.	
27		Elisabeth	44	f.			"	
28		Robbert	24	m.			"	
29	241/241	DREW, Nathaniel	65	m.		/200	N.H.	
30		Sally	55	f.			N.Y.	

31		DREW, John	13	m.		Pa.
32		Charles	37	m.		N.Y.
33		Gulia A.	22	f.		"
34		Amelia	7/12	f.		O.
35	242/242	RICHNER, Levi	38	m.	Millwright 4000/350	Pa.
36		Sarah	28	f.		O.
37		John	8	m.		" S
38		George	6	m.		" S
39		William	3	m.		"
40		Mary	7/12	f.		"

Page 33   11 June 1860   Sheet 49

1	243/243	SOUTHERS, Sidney	60	m.		/100	Del.
2		Benjamin	27	m.			O.
3		Samuel	23	m.			"
4		CONGER, Enos	20	m.			" M
5		Emely	18	f.			" M
6		Samuel	8/12	m.			"
7	244/244	BONHAM, Aaron	42	m.		/75	"
8		Martha	42	f.			Va.
9		William	19	m.			O.
10		Malin	17	m.			" S
11		Kesiah	16	m.			" S
12		Ruben	12	m.			" S
13		James	10	m.			" S
14		Archbold	2	m.			"
15	245/245	NALLY, Joseph	25	m.	Farmer	/60	"
16		Amanda	22	f.			"
17		John	3	m.			"
18		Aaron	5/12	m.			"
19	246/246	WINDLAND, Jacob	41	m.	Carpenter	/125	O.
20		Hannah	34	f.			"
21		John	14	m.			" S
22		Rachel	12	f.			" S
23		Hannah	4	f.			"
24	247/247	FLEMMING, Joseph	31	m.	Farmer	/132	"
25		Sarah	28	f.			"
26		Mary	6	f.			"
27		Catharine	4	f.			"
28		Samuel	2	m.			"
29		John	4/12	m.			"
30	248/248	ROUSE, Abram	50	m.	Farmer	/200	"
31		Nancy	50	f.			"
32		William	29	m.	Farmer		" I
33		George	27	m.	Farmer		"
34		Benjamin	25	m.	Farmer	/210	"
35		Mary	20	f.			"
36		Hannah	14	f.			" S
37	249/249	MOOSE, Ithamer	28	m.	Farmer		"
38		Nancy	28	f.			"

39		MOOSE, Loretta	8	f.			O.	S
40		Samuel	4	m.			"	

Page 34   11 June 1860   Sheet 49 verso

1	250/250	SOUTHERS, Ensly	33	m.		/150	O.	
2		Sarah	26	f.			"	
3		Amanda	11	f.			"	S
4		Sarah	9	f.			"	S
5		Siydia	2	f.			"	
6		Samuel	2/12	m.			"	

7	251/251	POTTS, Samuel	84	m.	Farmer	3000/155	Va.	
8		Arvilia	76	f.			"	
9		Emely	50	f.			O.	

10	252/252	POTTS, Hanson	47	m.	Farmer	/300	Va.	
11		Sarah	31	f.			O.	
12		James	23	m.	Farmer		"	
13		Elisabeth	22	f.			"	
14		Samuel	20	m.	Farmer		"	S
15		Sarah	18	f.			"	S
16		William	17	m.	Farmer		"	S
17		Mary	15	f.			"	S
18		Martha	14	f.			"	S
19		Thomas	11	m.			"	S
20		Emely	8	f.			"	S
21		John	7	m.			"	

22	253/253	POTTS, William	38	m.	Farmer	/200	"	
23		Mary	33	f.			"	
24		John	16	m.			"	S
25		Joseph	7	m.			"	S
26		Menerva	6	f.			"	S
27		Harriet	3	f.			"	S
28		Clarinda	2	f.			"	

29	254/254	McCAMMON, George	38	m.	Farmer	500/150	Ire.	
30		Catharine	28	f.			O.	
31		John	6	m.			"	
32		Mary	5	f.			"	
33		Susanah	2	f.			"	
34		Eliza	1	f.			"	

35	255/255	WOODRING, Susan	48	f.		400/100	"	
36		PRATT, John	23	m.	Laborer		"	

37	256/256	POTTS, David	44	m.	Farmer	3000/750	"	
38		Mary	19	f.			"	
39		George	1	m.			"	
40		Maletha	4/12	f.			"	

Page 35   12 June 1860   Sheet 50

1	257/257	WOODRING, William	28	m.	Laborer	/75	O.	
2		Sarah	22	f.			"	
3		David	8	m.			"	

4		WOODRING, Henry	2	m.			O.
5		Mary	1	f.			"
6	258/258	McFADDIN, Martha	64	f.		1500/136	Ire.
7	259/259	McFADDIN, Joseph	26	m.		/150	O.
8		Catharine	25	f.			"
9		Hannah	4	f.			"
10		Henry	2	m.			"
11	260/260	HAYDEN, Thomas	27	m.	Farmer	/240	"
12		Mary E.	21	f.			"
13		Stephen F.	3	m.			"
14		John	2/12	m.			"
15	261/261	YOST, Edward	32	m.	Farmer	2500/200	Han.
16		Louisa	30	f.			O. I
17		Peter	7	m.			" S
18		Theodore	4	m.			"
19		Hulda	1	f.			"
20	262/262	KERR, John	52	m.	Farmer	6000/1100	Scot.
21		Jennett	53	f.			"
22		Mary	26	f.			"
23		Elisabeth	24	f.			O.
24		Isabell	22	f.			" S
25		William	20	m.	Farmer		" S
26		John	18	m.	Farmer		" S
27		George	16	m.			" S
28		Jennett	14	f.			" S
29	263/263	FARENBAUGH, Adam	31	m.	Farmer	/100	Bav.
30		Ann	34	f.			"
31		Jacob	9	m.			O.
32		Ann M.	7	f.			"
33	264/264	NICH, Andrew	39	m.	Farmer	650/180	Fr.
34		Therisa	36	f.			"
35		Louis	14	m.			O. S
36		Barbary	12	f.			" S
37		Mary	10	f.			" S
38		Louisa	8	f.			" S
39		Philepena	4	f.			"
40		Bettecia	2	f.			"

1	265/265	EGGAR, Adam	48	m.	Farmer	600/300	Wit.
2		Christian	48	f.			"
3		Louis	14	m.			O. S
4		Barbary	12	f.			" S
5		Mary	10	f.			" S
6		Louisa	8	f.			" S
7		Philepina	4	f.			"
8		Bettsa	2	f.			"
9	266/266	ATTLE, Fredarick	30	m.	Farmer	2500/420	Bav.
10		Rosana	29	f.			"

11		ATTLE, Henry	5	m.			O.
12		Louis	2	m.			"
13		Fredarick	2/12	m.			"
14	267/267	COCHRAN, John	38	m.	Farmer	2000/340	Ire.
15		Ann	40	f.			"
16		Sarah	8	f.			O.
17		KEELBOUGH, Jackson	15	m.	Laborer		Va.
18	268/268	PRESHAW, Alex.	67	m.	Farmer	5000/1000	Ire.
19		Elisabeth	63	f.			"
20		Elisabeth Jr.	27	f.			O.
21		James	16	m.			" S
22		Mary E.	4	f.			"
23		ROSE, Louisa	25	f.	Domestic		"
24	269/269	TIDD, Wm.	74	m.	Farmer	800/320	N.J.
25		Emily A.	44	f.			Pa.
26		William	14	m.			O. S
27		Sarah	8	f.			" S
28	270/270	McCAMMON, James	52	m.	Farmer	650/439	Ire.
29		Susann	38	f.			Pa.
30		Margaret	21	f.			O. S
31		Alexander	16	m.			" S
32		Mary J.	14	f.			" S
33		Martha	12	f.			" S
34		Caloline	8	f.			" S
35		Sarah	8	f.			" S
36		Eliza	5	f.			"
37		John	45	m.	Laborer		Ire.
38	271/271	SMITH, John	44	m.	Farmer	1400/700	"
39		Elisabeth	34	f.			O.
40		Elisa J.	19	f.			"

Page 37   12 June 1860   Sheet 51

1		Joseph	17	m.			O.
2		Robbert	16	m.			"
3		Mary	17	f.			"
4		George	14	m.			" S
5		John	12	m.			" S
6		Margaret	10	m.			" S
7		Harriet	8	f.			" S
8		George	6	m.			" S
9		Mahala	4/12	f.			"
10	272/272	KEYLOR, Samuel	36	m.	Farmer	/165	Pa.
11		Pluma	35	f.			O. I
12		Jacob C.	17	m.	Farmer		"
13		Sevia	14	f.			" S
14		Melinda	12	f.			" S
15		Martha	9	f.			" S
16		Susann	7	f.			" S
17		Franklin	5	m.			"
18		Samuel	4	m.			"
19		Sinclair	1	m.			"

20	273/273	YOHO, Peter	73	m.	Farmer	4000/429	Va.	
21		Sarah	72	f.			"	
22		Lucinda	19	f.			O.	
23		Malin	2	m.			"	
24	274/274	YOHO, Jacob	34	m.	Farmer	/300	"	
25		Elisabeth	27	f.			"	
26		Ruben	8	m.			"	S
27		Eliza J.	6	f.			"	S
28		Peter	2	m.			"	
29	275/275	CRAWFORD, Hugh	58	m.	Farmer	2400/600	Ire.	
30		Elisabeth	60	f.			"	
31		William	28	m.	Saddler		"	
32		Thomas	26	m.	Farmer		"	
33		Hugh	24	m.	Farmer		"	
34		Elisa	22	f.			"	
35		David	19	m.	Farmer		"	S
36		Andrew	16	m.	Farmer		"	S
37	276/276	MARTIN, James	61	m.	Laborer	/50	O.	
38		Catharine	60	f.			"	
39		Isaac	18	m.			"	I
40		Jeremiah	2	m.			"	

Page 38   12 June 1860   Sheet 51 verso

1		Rebecca	24	f.			O.	I
2	277/277	SMITH, Henry	31	m.	Farmer	2500/400	Bav.	
3		Hariet	30	f.			"	
4		Catharine	9	f.			O.	S
5		Jacob	7	m.			"	S
6		Elisabeth	3	f.			"	
7		Caroline	2	f.			"	
8		Mary	6/12	f.			"	
9	278/278	PALLSCRAFT, Jacob	27	m.	Miller	2500/250	"	
10		Catharine	23	f.			"	
11		Lydia	10	f.			"	
12		Louisa	4	f.			"	
13		Lewis	3	m.			"	
14		George	1	m.			"	
15		WHITMAN, Peter	22	m.	Laborer		"	
16	279/279	SMITH, William	24	m.	Farmer	700/350	"	
17		Nancy	28	f.			"	
18		Samuel	7	m.			"	S
19		Sophia	5	f.			"	S
20		George	3	m.			"	
21		William	1	m.			"	
22	280/280	SMITH, Robert	67	m.	Farmer	6000/700	Ire.	
23		Jane	69	f.			Pa.	
24		TIDD, Samuel	18	m.	Laborer		O.	
25	281/281	ZANGER, John	41	m.	Farmer	3000/500	Ger.	
26		Lydia	45	f.			Pa.	

27		ZANGER, Samuel	23	m.			O.
28		Emanuel	19	m.			"
29		Elisabeth	13	f.			"
30		Sevilla	11	f.			"
31		Rosana	7	f.			"
32		John	3	m.			"
33		Isaac	8/12	m.			"
34	282/282	BACH, Daniel	32	m.	Farmer	1300/190	"
35		Margaret	32	f.			"
36		Jacob S.	9	m.			"
37		Ann C.	1	f.			"
38		PICKENS, Rebecca	65	f.			Pa.
39	283/283	EDGAR, Samuel	36	m.		2750/540	O.
40		Magdalena	30	f.			"

Page 39   13 June 1860   Sheet 52

1		Jacob	9	m.			O.	S
2		Rosana	7	f.			"	S
3		William H.	5	m.			"	
4		Samuel	3	m.			"	
5		John	1	m.			"	
6		EBERLY, Christian	22	m.	Laborer			
7	283/283	REISBECK, Sebastian	50	m.	Farmer	1800/435	Bav.	
8		Catherine	49	f.			"	
9		Mary	22	f.			Pa.	
10		John	17	m.			"	
11		Elisabeth	15	f.			"	S
12		Peter	13	m.			"	S
13		Joseph	11	m.			"	S
14		Catharine	8	f.				
15	284/284	BOWMAN, Philip	48	m.		1600/438	"	
16		Catharine	49	f.			"	
17		Elisabeth	18	f.			"	
18		George	13	m.			"	
19	285/285	JONES, Amos B.	69	m.	Farmer	3000/260	Conn.	
20		Sterling	26	m.			O.	
21	286/286	BONAR, Isaac	36	m.	Teacher	/150	"	
22		Ellenor	28	f.			"	
23		Olevia	8/12	f.			"	
24	287/287	McDONALD, Archbold	69	m.	Farmer	2000/350	Ire.	
25		Jane	27	f.			O.	
26		Susan	21	f.			"	
27		Agnes	19	f.			"	
28		Margaret	17	f.			"	
29		Samuel F.	14	m.			"	S
30	288/288	MINOR, Solomon	32	m.	Farmer	3000/250	Pa.	
31		Levina J.	25	f.			O.	

32		MINOR, Sarah	7	f.			O. S
33		Margaret	6	f.			" S
34		Thomas	4	m.			"
35		Joseph	2	m.			"
36	289/289	ROSS, Isaac	35	m.	Farmer	/125	"
37		Christina	32	f.			Pa.
38		Sarah J.	12	f.			O. S
39		James	10	m.			" S
40		Mary	8	f.			" S

Page 40   13 June 1860   Sheet 52 verso

1		Rachel	5	f.			O.
2		Margaret	2	f.			"
3	290/290	McANDLESS, Ann	45	f.			Pa.
4	291/291	GRAY, Elisabeth	88	f.		3000/200	"
5		Jane E.	48	f.			"
6		JONES, Maria B.	45	f.			"
7		Newton E.	16	m.			O. S
8		Martha J.	13	f.			" S
9		Jane E.	11	f.			" S
10		Leigh	9	m.			" S
11		William	6	m.			" S
12	292/292	GRAY, Alexander	68	m.	Carpenter		Pa.
13		Melinda	34	f.			O.
14		Ellen J.	2	f.			"
15		John	3/12	m.			"
16	293/293	McMAHON, James	70	m.	Farmer	700/50	"
17	294/294	MOBLEY, William	28	m.	Farmer	600/150	"
18		Rebecca J.	27	f.			"
19	295/295	MOBLEY, Leaven	55	m.	Farmer	600/135	Md.
20		Hulda	33	f.			O.
21		Margaret	21	f.			"
22		Joel R.	5	m.			"
23	296/296	CARRICK, Thomas	61	m.	Blacksmith	1500/150	Md.
24		Rachel	52	f.			Va.
25		DARNELL, Thomas	22	m.	Blacksmith		O.
26	297/297	VOHN, James	30	m.	Blacksmith	/100	"
27		Deborah	29	f.			"
28		James M.	8	m.			" S
29		Martha J.	6	f.			" S
30		Elias M.	4	m.			"
31		Deborah L.	2	f.			"
32	298/298	CLEGG, Leve	38	m.	Laborer		"
33		Susan	32	f.			"
34		Hannah J.	13	f.			"
35		Margaret	10	f.			"

36		CLEGG, Sarah A.	7	f.			O.
37		Armstrong	5	m.			"
38		Theodore	2	m.			"
39		George W.	1	m.			"
40	299/299	JESHSON, William	40	m.	Physician		"

Page 41   13 June 1860

1	300/300	JEFFRIES, Elias	67	m.	Farmer	3000/500	Pa.
2		Deborah	63	f.			"
3	301/301	JEFFRIES, Abraham	32	m.		900/413	O.
4		Margaret	31	f.			"
5		Christina	14	f.			" S
6		Elisabet A.	9	f.			" S
7		Thomas	7	m.			" S
8		Deborah	2	f.			"
9	302/302	MASON, George	60	m.	Farmer	3000/468	Pa.
10		Mary	30	f.			O.
11	303/303	HOLMES, William W.	60	m.	Farmer	2000/385	Pa.
12		Rebecca	41	f.			"
13		Catharine	7	f.			" S
14		Eliza	5	f.			"
15		Ruth	2	f.			"
16		Nancy E.	1	f.			O.
17		HELDEN, Thomas	17	m.	Laborer		"
18	304/304	EDDY, Robert	30	m.	Farmer	/260	"
19		Mary J.	29	f.			Pa.
20		Albert	11	m.			O. S
21		Sarah E.	5	f.			"
22		Michel	2	m.			"
23		Social	3/12	f.			"
24		MONTGOMERY, Ada-line	17	f.	Domestic		"
25	305/305	HIXENBAUGH, Henry B.	24	m.	Farmer	600/211	Pa.
26		Sarah A.	24	f.			O.
27		Margaret A.	3	f.			"
28		Charloott	1	f.			"
29		SHIPMAN, John	47	m.	Laborer	/100	Sw.
30	306/306	PIRTLER, Fredarick	47	m.	Farmer	1300/600	Rhein.
31		Barbary	46	f.			"
32		George	19	m.	Farmer		"
33		Fredarick	16	m.	Farmer		"
34		Catharine	8	f.			" S
35	307/307	METTS, Henry	38	m.		1400/217	Ger. I
36		Catharine	33	f.			" I
37		Catharine	8	f.			Pa. S
38		Elisabeth	6	f.			O.
39		Jacob	3	m.			"
40		Adam	1	m.			"

	Page 42		June 1860			Sheet 53 verso	
1	308/308	SHAFLER, Nicholas	44	m.	Farmer	1300/220	Ba♥.
2		Fredaricka	41	f.			Wit.
3		Elisabeth	11	f.			O. S
4		John	6	m.			" S
5		Margaret	3	f.			"
6	309/309	BRACY, John	42	m.	Miller	/1000	"
7		Therisa	39	f.			"
8		Ann	19	f.			"
9		Hannah J.	15	f.			"
10		Catharine	11	f.			" S
11		James M.	8	m.			" S
12		Sarah	6	f.			"
13		Mary	1	f.			"
14		George	3	m.			"
15	310/310	GOUDY, David	50	m.	Farmer	1000/200	Pa.
16		Frances A.	47	f.			Md.
17		Margaret	22	f.			O.
18		Francis A.	16	f.			" S
19		WARFIELD, Henry	85	m.			Md.
20	311/311	FISHER, George	23	m.	Farmer	/237	O.
21		Margaret M.	22	f.			"
22		Elisabeth A.	1	f.			"
23	312/312	BROUN, Anthony	27	m.	Farmer	1500/231	Ger.
24		Mary A.	22	f.			O. I
25		Mary V.	5	f.			"
26		John	3	m.			"
27		Jacob	2	m.			"
28		CARRICK, Comedill	10	f.			" S
29	313/313	EMMONS, George	27	m.	Farmer	/75	"
30		Mary	24	f.			"
31		Philip	2	m.			"
32	314/314	GRANT, John	32	m.	Farmer	1600/350	Pa.
33		Maria J.	33	f.			O.
34		Mary A.	8	f.			" S
35		Robbert	6	m.			" S
36		Sarah E.	4	f.			"
37		Menerva	2	f.			"
38		Mary M.	3/12	f.			"
39		CARRICK, John	16	m.	Laborer		" S
40		Maurice	45	m.	Laborer		"

	Page 43		June 1860			Sheet 54	
1	315/315	GRANT, Mary	56	f.		/400	Pa.
2		EDDY, Mary J.	22	f.			"
3		Moses	2	m.			O.
4		GRANT, Susan	15	f.			"
5	316/316	JEFFERIES, Taylor	41	m.	Farmer	2000/500	Pa.
6		Lydia	30	f.			O.

```
7          JEFFERIES, Abraham  16   m.                         O.  S
8            Lydia J.          15   f.                          "  S
9            Soloman           12   m.                          "  S
10           John H.           10   m.                          "  S
11           Deborah            8   f.                          "  S
12           Mary A.            6   f.                          "  S
13           Elias              4   m.                          "
14           Levana          1/12   f.                          "

15 317/317  WALTERS, Adam       30   m.   Farmer   300/200       "
16           Lucinda           30   f.                          "
17           James N.           2   m.                          "
18           Henritta           1   f.                          "

19 318/318  WALTERS, Jonah      38   m.            600/300   Pa. M
20           Mary J.           28   f.                      O.  M
21           Perry             14   m.                       "  S
22           Alfred            12   m.                       "  S
23           Elisabeth         10   f.                       "  S
24           Joseph            65   m.                      Pa.
25           Rachel            63   f.                       "

26 319/319  DUVALL, Perry       38   m.   Farmer   1200/261  Md.
27           Mary A.           25   f.                      Pa.
28           Morrison V.        9   m.                      O.  S
29           Abert W.           7   m.                       "  S
30           Levina J.          1   f.                       "

31 320/320  JEFFRIES, Joel      36   m.   Farmer   1500/235   "
32           Ruth              34   f.                       "
33           George M.          7   m.                       "  S
34           Sarah A.           2   f.                       "

35 321/321  BLOWERS, Samuel     51   m.   Farmer   4000/600  Md.
36           Susan             48   f.                       "
37           Mary E.           15   f.                      O.  S
38           Martha            12   f.                       "  S
39           Samuel             9   m.                       "  S
40           James              6   m.                       "  S
```

Page 44   June 1860   Sheet 54 verso

```
1  322/322  STEPHENS, Rebecca   67   f.            700/260   Pa. I
2           William           40   m.   Farmer              O.

3  323/323  GRIFFITH, Jackson   41   m.   Farmer   2000/429  Pa.
4           Mary              42   f.                      O.
5           Hannah             8   f.                       "
6           BRIGHT, James      27   m.                       "

7  324/324  POLAND, Nancy       56   f.            2000/400   "
8           Hannah            35   f.                       "
9           James             18   m.                       "
10          George            13   m.                       "

11 325/325  LUKE, William       62   m.   Farmer   300/125   Ire.
12           Margaret          50   f.                         "
13           Eliza J.          22   f.                      O.
```

14		LUKE, Hannah	20	f.			O.	
15		Jenny	19	f.			"	
16		Margaret	18	f.			"	
17		John A.	15	m.			"	S
18		William	13	m.			"	S
19	326/326	STARR, Moses F.	32	m.	Farmer	1000/248	"	
20		Elisabeth	33	f.			"	
21		Gemima	8	f.			"	S
22		John W.	6	m.			"	S
23		Samuel W.	1	m.			"	
24	327/327	STEPHENS, Evan	52	m.		400/163	"	I
25		Nancy	41	f.			"	
26		Elisabeth	21	f.			"	
27		Evan	21	m.			"	S
28		Deborah	19	f.			"	S
29		Rebecca J.	15	f.			"	S
30		Mary	13	f.			"	S
31		Elias	8	m.			"	S
32		David	6	m.			"	S
33		Taylor	3	m.			"	
34	328/328	STEPHENS, Marion	26	m.	Farmer	300/125	"	
35		Rachel A.	23	f.			"	
36		Peter H.	8	m.			"	
37	329/329	STEPHENS, Jesse	50	m.	Farmer	1500/320	"	I
38		Hannah	38	f.			"	
39		David	14	m.			"	
40		Sarah	13	f.			"	

<u>Page 45</u>   June 1860   <u>Sheet 55</u>

1		Hezakiah	2	m.			O.	
2	330/330	STEPHENS, Abraham	44	m.	Farmer	3000/500	Pa.	
3		Mary	34	f.			O.	
4		Sarah A.	16	f.			"	S
5		John D.	14	m.			"	S
6		Jane	12	f.			"	S
7		Martha C.	7	f.			"	S
8	331/331	GRIFFITH, Mary	70	f.		/120	Pa.	
9		Elisabeth	40	f.			O.	
10		JACKSON, Louis	16	m.	Laborer		"	
11	332/332	GRIFFITH, David	38	m.		1500/362	"	
12		Sarah A.	35	f.			"	
13		Robbert	7	m.			"	S
14		Mary O.	4	f.			"	S
15		John W.	2	m.			"	
16		CARRICK, Sarah	14	f.			"	
17	333/333	GRIFFITH, Ann	44	f.		1500/360	"	
18		William D.	22	m.	Farmer		"	
19		Abram J.	21	m.	Farmer		"	S

20		GRIFFITH, Joseph	N.18	m.			O.	S
21		George W.	16	m.			"	S
22		Elias J.	14	m.			"	S

23	334/334	STEPHENS, David	45	m.	Farmer	2400/700	"	
24		Hulda	42	f.			"	I
25		Hannah	17	f.			"	S
26		Louis	15	m.			"	S
27		JACKSON, Jane	73	f.			Pa.	

28	335/335	MASON, Henry	64	m.	Farmer	2400/265	"	
29		Deborah	58	f.			"	
30		Clara	16	f.			O.	S
31		BLOWERS, McGruder	20	m.	Farmer		"	

32	336/336	MASON, Rusell	26	m.	Farmer	/400	"	
33		Mary W.	27	f.			"	
34		Bellvidard	3	f.			"	
35		Olevicora	7/12	f.			"	

36	337/337	DAVIS, William	36	m.	Farmer	1800/258	"	
37		Louisa	35	f.			"	
38		Frank	12	m.			"	
39		Gulia	4	f.			"	
40		Grace	2	f.			"	

Page 46   June 1860   Sheet 55 verso

1	338/338	JOHNSON, Lewis	37	m.	Cordwainer	500/100	O.	
2		Margaret	37	f.			"	
3		Therisa J.	16	f.			"	S
4		Isaac A.	14	m.			"	S
5		Esther A.	13	f.			"	S
6		Sarah W.	11	f.			"	S
7		William H.	9	m.			"	S
8		Lewis E.	7	m.			"	S
9		Margaret E.	5	f.			"	S
10		Elizabeth	3	f.			"	
11		Abraham F.	11/12	m.			"	

| 12 | 339/339 | DUNN, John | 39 | m. | Farmer | 3500/220 | Pa. | |

13	340/340	NUHART, Christain	30	m.	Farmer	1500/255	Bav.	
14		Rachel	38	f.			O.	
15		Milten	17	m.			"	S
16		Mary C.	16	f.			"	S
17		Henry	8	m.			"	S
18		James L.	7	m.			"	S
19		Thomas F.	6	m.			"	S
20		Sophia	2	f.			"	

21	341/341	NUHART, Henry	23	m.	Farmer	/140	Bav.	
22		Margaret	19	f.			O.	
23		CLOGGUS, Fredarick	17	m.			"	

| 24 | 342/342 | NUHART, Leonard | 60 | m. | Farmer | 3500/600 | Bav. | |
| 25 | | Sarah | 55 | f. | | | " | |

26		NUHART, John	19	m.			O.	S
27		Sophia	16	f.			"	S
28	343/343	NORRIS, Robbert	66	m.	Farmer	3000/700	Va.	
29		Ann	64	f.			Md.	
30		Mary	32	f.			O.	
31		Ann	30	f.			"	
32		George	24	m.	Farmer	/208	"	
33	344/344	MILLER, Paxton	30	m.	Miller	2500/150	"	
34		Sarah	26	f.			"	
35		Elisabeth E.	6/12	f.			"	
36	345/345	JACKSON, Leonard	37	m.	Farmer	2000/500	"	
37		Hannah	36	f.			"	
38		John	14	m.			"	S
39		Nancy J.	13	f.			"	S
40		William	9	m.			"	S

Page 47			June 1860				Sheet 56	
1		Mary	6	f.			O.	
2	346/346	MILLER, Robert	70	m.	Miller	/150	Pa.	
3		Hannah	68	f.			"	
4	347/347	SCHALL, Jacob	61	m.	Farmer	700/100	Leinster	
5		Catharine	36	f.			"	
6		Esther	9	f.			"	S
7		Elisabeth	7	f.			O.	S
8		Jacob	4	m.			"	
9		Franklin	1	m.			"	
10	348/348	HAY, John	57	m.	Farmer	300/160	Pa.	
11		Elisabeth	56	f.			"	
12	349/349	HAY, Elisabeth J.	25	f.		/120	O.	
13		Joseph	3	m.			"	
14		Rachel L.	1	f.			"	
15	350/350	NORRIS, Aquilla	23	m.	Farmer	/261	"	
16		Martha	22	f.			"	
17	351/351	NORRIS, John	34	m.	Farmer	2500/360	"	
18		Catharine	26	f.			"	
19		Clarrisa J.	6	f.			"	S
20		Isaac N.	3	m.			"	S
21		Mary A.	2	f.			"	
22		Robbert	8/12	m.			"	
23	352/352	POULES, Ignitus	63	m.	Farmer	2500/800	Fr.	
24		Catharine	61	f.			"	
25		Anthony	32	m.			"	
26		Joseph	24	m.			"	
27		Caroline	20	f.			"	
28	353/353	STIFLE, George	48	m.	Farmer	800/250	Fr.	
29		Barbary	48	f.			"	

30		STIFLE, Mary	20	f.		Fr.
31		Catharine	18	f.		" S
32		Elisabeth	15	f.		" S
33	354/354	KEYSER, Jacob	26	m.	Farmer	O.
34		Martha J.	24	f.		"
35		Albert	3	m.		"
36		Isaac W.	2	m.		"
37		Joseph N.	9/12	m.		
38	355/355	KEYSER, Reason	34	m.	Farmer	"
39		Mary	64	f.		"
40		Susann	14	f.		"

Page 48   June 1860   Sheet 56 verso

1	356/356	TRUAX, Obediah	42	m.	Farmer	/200 Pa.
2		Mary	44	f.		O.
3	357/357	HENDERSHOT, Benjamin	35	m.	Laborer	/100 "
4		Charlotte	33	f.		"
5		Margaret	12	f.		"
6		Samuel K.	10	m.		"
7		Western	8	m.		"
8		Emma J.	5	f.		"
9		Mary R.	3	f.		"
10	358/358	KETTLE, Christin	45	m.	Farmer	1500/246 Byron
11		Catharine	43	f.		"
12		Michel	11	m.		"
13		Catharin	15	f.		" S
14		Mary A.	9	f.		" S
15		John	7	m.		" S
16		Elisabeth	1	f.		O.
17	359/359	NORRIS, Jacob	49	m.	Farmer	2500/250 Pa.
18		Nancy	48	f.		O.
19		John	23	m.	Laborer	" I
20		William	17	m.	Laborer	"
21		Abby J.	15	f.		" S
22		Lucinda	13	f.		" S
23		Robbert A.	8	m.		" S
24		David	5	m.		"
25	360/360	RISER, Francis	53	m.	Farmer	1400/200 Bav.
26		Caroline	41	f.		"
27		Jacob	20	m.	Farmer	" S
28		Lewis	18	m.	Farmer	" S
29		Anthony	16	m.		O. S
30		Fredarick	14	m.		" S
31		Caroline	11	f.		" S
32		Charles	8	m.		" S
33		Catharine	6	f.		" S
34	361/361	DESELL, Jacob	34	m.	Farmer	1800/150 Byron
35		Eve	30	f.		"
36		Jacob	7	m.		

37		DESELL, Elisabeth	4	f.			O.	
38		Mary	4/12	f.			"	
39	362/362	MARTIN, Joseph	21	m.	Laborer		"	M
40		Maria	17	f.			"I	M

Page 49   June 1860   Sheet 57

1	363/363	DICKS, John	60	m.	Farmer	450/300	O.	
2		Mary	51	f.			Del.	
3	364/364	FURNACE, Wesley	28	m.		400/200	N.J.	
4		Pheoba	23	f.			N.Y.	
5		Thomas T.	2	m.			O.	
6		Mary E.	1	f.			"	
7	365/365	TWADDLE, Philip	57	m.	Farmer	2000/550	"	
8		Mary	52	f.			"	
9		John	30	m.			"	
10		Elisabeth J.	18	f.			"	S
11		Samuel	16	m.			"	S
12		Mary E.	12	f.			"	S
13		Diana	10	f.			"	S
14	366/366	BRADY, Ebenezer	43	m.	Farmer	3000/170	Pa.	
15		Margaret	36	f.			O.	
16		Mary J.	18	f.			"	S
17		James	16	m.			"	S
18		David	14	m.			"	S
19		William	12	m.			"	S
20		Jacob	4	m.			"	
21	367/367	McDONELL, Elza	42	m.	Farmer	1600/600	"	
22		Mary	43	f.			Va.	
23		Margaret	18	f.			O.	S
24		Hannah	16	f.			"	S
25		Joseph	13	m.			"	S
26		Amanda	11	f.			"	S
27	368/368	DRUMM, John B.	33	m.	Carpenter	500/400	"	
28		Sarah	32	f.			"	
29		Philip H.	8	m.			"	S
30		David M.	4	m.			"	S
31		Eugene M.	2	m.			"	
32	369/369	DRIGGS, Wm.	48	m.	Farmer	7000/900	Conn.	
33		Sarah L.	38	f.			O.	
34		James E.	20	m.	Farmer		"	
35		John B.	17	m.	Farmer		"	S
36		Henry E.	9	m.			"	S
37		Estila	7	f.			"	S
38		William A.	5	m.			"	S
39		Sophia	3	f.			"	
40		Augustas L.	4/12	m.			"	

Page 50   June 1860   Sheet 57 verso

1	370/370	BROWN, Alex	49	m.	Farmer	2500/1100	Va.

2		BROWN, Margaret	43	f.			Pa.
3		Margaret Jr.	24	f.			O.
4		John	22	m.	Farmer		"
5		James	20	m.	Farmer		" S
6		Bengga	18	m.			" S
7		Mary A.	12	f.			" S
8		Daniel	8	m.			" S
9		Ebenezer	4	m.			"
10	371/371	RUTTER, John	53	m.	Farmer	800/300	N.J.
11		Susanah	52	f.			O.
12		Hester	18	f.			"
13		Rachel	15	f.			" S
14		John F.	14	m.			" S
15		Talbert	6	m.			" S
16	372/372	ORSBERR, Gideon	47	m.	Farmer	2000/500	Pa.
17		Elisabeth	46	f.			"
18		John	24	m.	Farmer		O.
19		Gideon A.	11	m.			"
20		James	4	m.			" S
21		Clarinda	2	f.			"
22	373/373	McFADDIN, Isaac	32	m.	Farmer	/120	"
23		Christena	33	f.			"
24		Willie	10	m.			"
25		Joseph	4	m.			"
26		Margaret	2	f.			"
27		Isaac F.	6/12	m.			"
28	374/374	JACKSON, Robert	44	m.	Farmer	1800/500	"
29		Mary	49	f.			"
30		Casa	23	f.			"
31		Sylvester	20	m.	Farmer		"
32		William P.	16	m.	Farmer		"
33		Mary	14	f.			"
34		Martha	11	f.			"
35		Albert R.	6	m.			"
36	375/375	McCOMAS, Augustas	40	m.	Farmer	1600/1000	"
37		Delilah	35	f.			"
38		James	17	m.	Farmer		" S
39		Sarah J.	14	f.			"
40		John W.	11	m.			

Page 51			June 1860				Sheet 58
1		Aquilla	8	m.			O.
2		Franklin	6	m.			"
3		Augustas	4	m.			"
4		John	8/12	m.			
5	376/376	MOOSE, Jacob	53	m.	Farmer	16,000/1200	Va.
6		Catharine	47	f.			O.
7		Emely	19	f.			" S
8		Jacob	15	m.	Farmer		" S
9		Louisa C.	12	f.			" S
10		Melisa J.	4	f.			

11	377/377	CHRISMAN, Louis	32	m.	Farmer	1000/250	Fr.	
12		Martha	29	f.			Pa.	
13		Christena	8	f.			O.	S
14		John	6	m.			"	
15		Jacob	6	m.			"	
16		Fredarick	5	m.			"	
17		Henry	6/12	m.			"	
18	378/378	MOOSE, Iseral	25	m.	Farmer	/550	"	
19		Sarah J.	17	f.			"	S
20		Mary L.	3/12	f.			"	
21		HUFFMAN, Franklin	14	m.			"	
22	379/379	KEYSER, Moses	23	m.	Laborer	/50.	"	
23		Margaret	24	f.			"	
24		Amanda J.	4	f.			"	
25		James	2	m.			"	
26	380/380	(BUCHANAN, C. S.)	32	m.		4000/700	"	
27		Mary A.	30	f.			"	
28		William H.	7	m.			"	S
29		John A.	5	m.			"	
30		James M.	3	m.			"	
31		Nancy	2	f.			"	
32	381/381	GADD, Stephen	33	m.		400/175	"	
33		Mary	25	f.			"	
34		George F.	10	m.			"	
35	382/382	HAWKINS, Jared	47	m.		2500/600	Pa.	
36		Isabell	33	f.			Va.	
37		Barbary E.	11	f.			O.	S
38		Martha C.	10	f.			"	S
39		John W.	8	m.			"	S
40		Andrew	3	m.			"	

Page 52   June 1860   Sheet 58 verso

1		Nancy J.	6	f.			O.	S
2		Comfort R.	4	f.			"	
3		Terry W.	2	m.			"	
4		Mary E.	8/12	f.			"	
5	383/383	SMITH, John	24	m.	Farmer	/120	"	
6		Susan	18	f.			"	
7	384/384	CARROTHERS, G. W.	43	m.	Farmer	4000/700	"	
8		Mary	43	f.			"	
9		Ann	20	f.	Teacher		"	S
10		Percila	8	f.			"	
11		Abby	8/12	f.			"	
12		TIDD, William	14	m.			"	S
13	385/385	WOODRING, James	20	m.	Farmer	/100	"	M
14		Jane	18	f.			"	M
15	386/386	WINDLAND, Charles	52	m.	Farmer	/100	Pa.	
16		Nancy	46	f.			"	

17		WINDLAND, Elisa-					
		beth	17	f.		O.	
18		James	15	m.		"	S
19		Joseph	13	m.		"	S
20		Susan	10	f.		"	S
21	387/387	METTS, Jacob	29	m.	Farmer	600/100	Bav.
22		Elisabeth	26	f.			Fr.
23		GOODERALL, Chris-					
		tina	34	f.	Domestic		"
24	388/388	MORTES, Jacob	33	m.	Farmer	1300/200	Sw.
25		Elisabeth	30	f.			"
26		Caroline	5	f.			O.
27	389/389	CROUSE, Jacob	56	m.	Farmer	800/125	Rhein.
28		Menia	47	f.			"
29		Christene	17	f.			" S
30		Manerva	16	f.			" S
31		Henry	11	m.			" S
32	390/390	NUHART, Soloman	23	m.	Farmer		Pa.
33		Menia	23	f.			"
34	391/391	BAKER, Henry	26	m.	Laborer	/210	O.
35		Mary	20	f.			"
36		SINCLAIR, A. W.	16	m.	Laborer		" S
37	392/392	BAKER, Martin	23	m.	Laborer	/60	"
38		Mary A.	18	f.			"
39	393/393	BAKER, Henry	36	m.	Laborer	260/100	"
40		Mary L.	1	f.			"

Page 54			June 1860				Sheet 59
1		Emily J.	32	f.			O.
2		Vincent	16	m.			"
3		Lucinda	15	f.			" S
4		Samuel	13	m.			" S
5		Sarah E.	11	f.			" S
6		Mary	9	f.			" S
7		David	7	m.			"
8		William	5	m.			"
9		Martin	2	m.			"
10	394/394	KEYSER, David	26	m.	Farmer		"
11		Juda J.	32	f.			"
12		John H.	4	m.			"
13		Mary E.	2	f.			"
14		Susan M.	1	f.			"
15		Susan	62	f.			"
16	395/395	BAKER, John F.	27	m.	Farmer	/150	"
17		Mary A.	20	f.			"
18		Margaret	4	f.			" S
19		Martin	3	m.			"
20		Garison	3/12	m.			"

21		POLAND, Jacob	18	m.	Cooper	/65	o.
22	396/396	POLAND, Samuel	23	m.		/75	"
23		Sarah E.	21	f.			"
24		Cecilia J.	1	f.			"
25	397/397	STEED, John	49	m.	Farmer	2500/300	"
26		Elisabeth	44	f.			"
27		John W.	22	m.	Farmer		"
28		James	20	m.			"
29		George W.	17	m.			"
30		William	15	m.			" S
31		Elisabeth	14	f.			" S
32		Menerva	12	f.			" S
33		Martha	7	f.			" S
34	398/398	LOUTHERS, George	33	m.	Shoemaker	500/125	Va.
35		Margaret	31	f.			O.
36		Celestia	10	f.			"
37		JENNINGS, Elias	62	m.			Md.
38		Elisabeth	55	f.			Va.
39		Sarah E.	15	f.			O.
40		MOFFETT, Benjamin	41	m.			"

Page 55			June 1860			Sheet 59 verso	
1	399/399	PIATT, William	34	m.	Farmer	1200/125	O.
2		Pricias	33	f.			"
3		James	12	m.			" S
4		Lorenza D.	10	m.			" S
5		Benjamin	8	m.			"
6		John H.	5	m.			"
7		Richard H.	3	m.			"
8		Catharine	1/12	f.			"
9		MOFFETT, Sarah	15	f.	Domestic		"
10	400/400	MOFFETT, Mary	39	f.		700/200	"
11		Lucinda	13	f.			" S
12		Susann	11	f.			" S
13		Winfield S.	9	m.			" S
14		Elisabeth	86	f.			"
15	401/401	JACKSON, Simon	41	m.	Blacksmith	1200/120	"
16		Sidney	44	f.			"
17		Aaron	21	m.	Blacksmith		"
18		Abram	20	m.	Blacksmith		"
19		John	18	m.	Blacksmith		" S
20		Hulda	16	f.			" S
21		Samuel	14	m.			" S
22		Joshua	12	m.			" S
23		Taylor W.	11	m.			" S
24		Nathan	9	m.			" S
25		Simon P.	6	m.			" S
26	402/402	JACKSON, Abraham	33	m.	Farmer	600/200	"
27		Jane	32	f.			"
28		Jesse	15	m.			" S
29		Oliver	11	m.			" S

30		JACKSON, Rebecca	9	f.			O. S
31		Jefferson	7	m.			" S
32		Alcinda	5	f.			"
33		Vincent	3	m.			"
34		Margaret	1	f.			"
35	403/403	JACKSON, Isaac	23	m.	Farmer		"
36		Ellenor	21	f.			"
37	404/404	CRAIG, Margaret	45	f.		2500/700	"
38		Abraham	29	m.	Farmer		"
39		Mary A.	27	f.			"
40		John	25	m.	Farmer		"

Page 56			June 1860				Sheet 60
1		Enoch	19	m.	Farmer		O. S
2		Robbert	15	m.			" S
3	405/405	MOFFETT, John	61	m.	Farmer	3200/350	Va.
4		Sarah	60	f.			Md.
5		PIERCE, Lasria	33	f.			"
6		Isaac N.	8	m.			" S
7		Emely	7	f.			" S
8		Elisabeth	3	f.			"
9		Hester R.	14	f.			" S
10	406/406	MOFFETT, Harvy	26	m.	Farmer	700/200	"
11		Sarah A.	25	f.			"
12		Leaides S.	3	m.			"
13		Francis S.	1	f.			"
14	307/307	MOFFETT, Nathaniel	27	m.	Farmer	700/300	"
15		Elisa	24	f.			Ire.
16		Adaline E.	2	f.			O.
17	408/408	DRUMM, James	31	m.	Farmer	/250	"
18		Rachel	28	f.			"
19		Henry	9	m.			" S
20		Lenerd	7	m.			" S
21		Hannah J.	5	f.			" S
22		Mary E.	3	f.			"
23		Sarah F.	1	f.			"
24	409/409	HAGEN, David	44	m.	Farmer	2600/430	"
25		Susann	43	f.			"
26		Elisabeth	16	f.			" S
27		John	14	m.			" S
28		Mary	12	f.			" S
29		Louis	11	m.			" S
30		Jeremiah	9	m.			" S
31		Isaih	7	m.			" S
32		Hannah	4	f.			"
33		Naome	3	f.			"
34	410/410	DRUMM, Philip	60	m.	Farmer	4000/850	"
35		Mary	57	f.			"

36		DRUMM, William	35	m.	Carpenter		O.	
37		Emly J.	20	f.			"	S
38		Martha A.	11	f.			"	S
39	411/411	KEENE, James	30	m.	Farmer	1500/240	"	
40		Susann	60	f.			Pa.	

Page 57   June 1860   Sheet 60 verso

1		Benjamin	21	m.	Farmer		O.	
2		Martha A.	17	f.			"	S
3		James M.	15	m.			"	S
4	412/412	GRIFFETH, Naomie	45	f.		400/560	Pa.	I
5		William	17	m.	Farmer		O.	S
6		Henry	15	m.	Farmer		"	S
7		Elisabeth	12	f.			"	S
8		Asher	10	m.			"	
9		MOWDER, Elisabeth	72	f.			"	
10		Sarah	25	f.			"	
11	413/413	MOWDER, Henry	33	m.	Farmer	1600/546	"	
12		Catharine	34	f.			"	
13		William	8	m.			"	S
14		David	6	m.			"	S
15		Neomia J.	5	f.			"	S
16		Elisabeth	4	f.			"	
17		Mary C.	2	f.			"	
18	414/414	PENNINGTON, Thomas	57	m.	Farmer	4200/297	Del.	
19		Sarah	57	f.			Pa.	
20		Elisabeth	30	f.			O.	
21		Amanda	24	f.			"	S
22		Maria J.	21	f.			"	S
23		Lydia A.	18	f.			"	S
24	415/415	MOFFETT, James	53	m.	Farmer	1300/418	"	
25		Melinda	35	f.			Pa.	
26		Martha	19	f.			O.	S
27		Louisa	16	f.			"	S
28		Mary J.	11	f.			"	S
29		John W.	2	m.			"	
30	416/416	PENNINGTON, John R.	33	m.	Farmer	800/317	"	
31		Catharine J.	30	f.			"	
32		James T.	5	m.			"	
33		Ann E.	3	f.			"	
34	417/417	GADD, Giles	64	m.	Farmer	1500/140	Pa.	
35		Elisabeth	57	f.			"	
36		Ida J.	18	f.			O.	S
37		Catharine	20	f.			"	
38	418/418	DETWILER, James	24	m.	Farmer	350/200	"	
39		Margaret	20	f.			"	

40	419/419	BURGBACHER, John	26	m.	Farmer	900/725	Bad.	

1		John W.	8/12	m.			Bad.	
2	420/420	JACKSON, Bryson	22	m.	Farmer	/200	O.	
3		Hannah J.	22	f.			"	
4	421/421	JACKSON, Silais	50	m.	Farmer	3000/325	"	
5		Eliza	43	f.			"	
6		W. S.	18	m.	Farmer		"	S
7		George	11	m.			"	S
8		Jery	9	m.			"	S
9		Jane	14	f.			"	S
10		Margaret	7	f.			"	
11		Andrew	9	m.			"	
12	422/422	TRUAX, John	23	m.	Farmer	/100	"	
13		Ann	21	f.			"	
14		James	1	m.			"	
15	423/423	DETWILER, Samuel	57	m.	Farmer	2500/460	"	
16		Lutecia	45	f.			"	
17		William	16	m.			"	S
18		Taylor	13	m.			"	S
19	424/424	DETWILER, John	28	m.	Farmer		"	
20		Martha	17	f.			"	
21		Franklin	8/12	m.			"	
22	425/425	WINDLAND, Jacob	47	m.	Farmer	500/200	"	
23		Elisabeth	48	f.			"	
24		James	19	m.			"	S
25		Henry	14	m.			"	S
26		Obadiah	11	m.			"	S
27		Gemima	9	f.			"	S
28	426/426	WINDLAND, William	24	m.	Farmer	/162	"	
29		Gulia	24	f.			"	
30		Nelson	3	m.			"	
31		Miller	1	m.			"	
32	427/427	WINDLAND, Isaac	17	m.		/50	"	
33		Louisa	22	f.			"	
34		William H.	1/12	m.			"	
35		WIDDOWS, Luther M.	13	m.	Laborer		"	
36	428/428	BRUCE, H. W.	40	m.	Farmer	500/130	"	
37	429/429	MOFFETT, Samuel P.	26	m.	Farmer	800/300	"	
38		Martha A.	25	f.			"	
39		Thomas H.	4	m.			"	
40		Dellmore	2	m.				

1		BRUCE, Catharine	37	m.			O.	

2		BRUCE, Martha E.	15	f.			O.	S
3		Eliza J.	12	f.			"	S
4		Theodore	10	m.			"	S
5		Hariet	9	f.			"	S
6		Mary C.	5	f.			"	S
7		Margaret A.	3	f.			"	
8	430/430	DENT, John P.	58	m.	Farmer	1500/328	Md.	
9		George	23	m.	Farmer		O.	
10		Mary E.	19	f.			"	
11		Sarah A.	17	f.			"	S
12		Susan L.	14	f.			"	S
13		Lucy A.	12	f.			"	S
14	431/431	DENT, John Q.	31	m.	Farmer	1800/230	"	
15		Elisabeth	29	f.			"	
16		Louisa	5	f.			"	
17		John M.	1	m.			"	
18		HUCLE, Stanton	16	m.	Laborer		"	
19	432/432	COOPER, Robbert	60	m.	Farmer	600/160	Eng.	
20	433/433	SHEPHARD, Peter	80	m.	Farmer	500/240	Ire.	
21		Nancy	60	f.			Md.	
22		MOFFETT, Lucinda	14	f.	Domestic		Ire.	
23	434/434	BOTHWELL, Thomas	41	m.	Farmer	3000/700	O.	
24		Mary A.	40	f.			"	
25		Gulia A.	12	f.			"	S
26		George	9	m.			"	S
27		Mary J.	7	f.			"	S
28		John	6	m.			"	S
29		Christena	5	f.			"	
30		Ensley	3	m.			"	
31		James W.	10/12	m.			"	
32	435/435	MARTIN, Edward	33	m.	Farmer	500/232	"	
33		Eliza	36	f.			"	
34		Hannah E.	7	f.			"	
35		Laura J.	6	f.			"	
36		Ruth A.	3	f.			"	
37		Mary	1	f.			"	
38		CARPENTER, Rebecca	25	f.			"	
39	436/436	HALL, William	58	m.	Farmer	2300/600	Va.	
40		Mary	56	f.			Pa.	

1		John	18	m.	Farmer		Pa.	S
2		Asa	15	m.			"	S
3		Lydia J.	12	f.			"	S
4	437/437	HALL, Ephraim J.	21	m.	Farmer	/225	"	
5		Mary S.	16	f.			"	
6	438/438	DIXON, Scott	25	m.	Farmer	2000/150	Pa.	
7		Hannah J.	23	f.			O.	

8		DIXON, Samuel N.	1	m.			O.	
9	439/439	TRUAX, John	67	m.	Farmer	2000/320	"	
10		Margaret	65	f.			"	
11	440/440	TRUAX, Alen	45	m.	Farmer		"	
12		Susana	39	f.			"	
13		Jane	12	f.			"	
14	441/441	STATES, William	47	m.	Farmer		Pa.	
15		Margaret	45	f.			O.	
16		Martha A.	22	f.			Pa.	
17		Joseph E.	19	m.			"	S
18		Lucinda	16	f.			"	S
19		Thomas	13	m.			O.	S
20		Rebecca E.	10	f.			"	S
21		Sarah F.	5	f.			"	
22	442/442	WILSON, John	41	m.	Farmer	2500/350	"	
23		Martha J.	21	f.			"	
24		Matilda	3	f.			"	
25		Mary L.	2	f.			"	
26		Amanda C.	2/12	f.			"	
27		SHOUP, Elisabeth	18	f.	Servant		"	
28		HIXEN, John	20	m.	Laborer		"	
29	443/443	TWINUM, Thomas	65	m.	Farmer	2000/	Ire.	
30		Charles	29	m.	Farmer			
31		Thomas	17	m.			O.	
32		John M.	14	m.			"	
33		Margaret L.	10	f.			"	
34		William E.	7	m.			"	
35		OKEY, Nancy	27	f.	Servant		Ire.	
36		Asher	4	m.			O.	
37	444/444	GRAY, Arthur	54	m.	Farmer	4000/900	"	
38		Margaret	40	f.			Pa.	
39		William R.	23	m.	Farmer		O.	
40		TWINUM, Mary A.	50	f.			Ire.	

Page 60			June 1860			Sheet 62 verso		
1		Louisa	20	f.			O.	
2		Mary B.	18	f.			"	S
3		Elisabeth	17	f.			"	S
4		Nancy	16	f.			"	S
5		Robbert	13	m.			"	S
6		HAWKINS, Franklin	25	m.	Laborer		"	
7	445/445	HAWKINS, John	33	m.	Farmer	700/120	"	
8		Semantha E.	23	f.			"	
9		William P.	3	m.			"	
10		Catharine	2	f.			"	
11		Benjamin F.	4/12	m.			"	
12	446/446	BRADY, Daniel	33	m.	Farmer	/120	Pa.	
13		Mary	66	f.			"	
14		John	8	m.			O.	S

15		BRADY, Sarah	6	f.			O.	S
16		William	4	m.			"	
17		Margaret	6/12	f.			"	
18	447/447	BROWN, William	26	m.	Farmer	1000/236	"	I
19		Eliza J.	26	f.			"	I
20		Sarah L.	2	f.			"	
21	448/448	STARKEY, Henry	43	m.	Farmer	1500/200	"	M
22		Hannah	23	f.			"	M
23		Thomas E.	19	m.	Farmer		"	S
24		John W.	15	m.			"	S
25		Margaret J.	12	f.			"	S
26		Alexander P.	11	m.			"	S
27		Caroline M.	10	f.			"	S
28		Jane M.	8	f.			"	S
29		Mary E.	4	f.			"	
30	449/449	DYER, Philip	29	m.	Farmer	/300	"	
31		Adelia A.	26	f.			"	
32		William C.	2	m.			"	
33		John G.	11/12	m.			"	
34	450/450	DYER, John	56	m.	Farmer	3000/325	Md.	
35		Amelia	57	f.			Va.	
36		John	22	m.	Farmer		O.	
37		Sarah E.	18	f.			"	
38		Robbert H.	15	m.			"	
39	451/451	RUTTER, George	32	m.	Farmer	500/218	"	
40		Amelia A.	32	f.			"	

Page 62			June 1860				Sheet 63	
1		Wilber M.	7	m.			O.	S
2		John A.	3	m.			"	
3	452/452	HAWKINS, James	39	m.	Farmer	2000/550	Va.	
4		Isabell	29	f.			"	
5		Sarah J.	9	f.			O.	
6		Clarrisa M.	8	f.			"	
7		Mary A.	6	f.			"	
8		Western A.	5	m.			"	
9		Robbert	2	m.			"	
10		James M.	5/12	m.			"	
11		BROWN, Francis	16	m.	Laborer		"	
12		BRON, Dakes	18	f.	Domestic		"	
13	453/453	CRAIG, Elias	24	m.	Farmer	500/120	"	
14		Francis	19	f.			"	
15		Leander W.	1	m.			"	
16	454/454	BROWN, Benjamin	32	m.	Farmer	1500/318	"	
17		Nancy	21	f.			"	
18		James A.	11	m.			"	S
19		Josiah	7	m.			"	S
20		Richard H.	5	m.			"	

21		BROWN, Daniel	2	m.			O.
22		Ruth	1	f.			"
23	455/455	JACKSON, Jesse	38	m.	Farmer	600/346	"
24		Rebecca	34	f.			"
25		John M.	14	m.			" S
26		Hellen M.	9	f.			" S
27		David D.	1/12	m.			"
28	456/456	HAMILTON, John	48	m.	Farmer	3000/500	"
29		Rachel	47	f.			"
30		David	23	m.	Farmer		"
31		William R.	19	m.	Farmer		" S
32		John	13	m.			" S
33		Sinclair	9	m.			" S
34	457/457	JACKSON, Abraham	73	m.	Farmer	2000/278	Pa.
35		Barbary	59	f.			"
36		Sarah	9	f.			O. S
37	458/458	HIXENBAUGH, George	22	m.	Farmer	/100	" M
38		Rebecca	21	f.			" M
39	459/459	DEITER, Andrew	36	m.	Stone-cutter	300/125	Bav.
40		Louisa	45	f.			"

Page 63   June 1860   Sheet 63 verso

1		Andrew	10	m.			Bav.
2	460/460	CLINGHAN, Robbert	43	m.	Miller	10,000/1200	Pa.
3		Elisabeth A.	39	f.			O.
4		George	19	m.	Miller		" S
5		Louisa A.	18	f.			" S
6		Sarah H.	15	f.			" S
7		Mary	13	f.			" S
8		Margaret V.	5	f.			"
9		BERTNER, Noah	25	m.	Miller	/400	Pa.
10	461/461	ANDERSON, Andrew	55	m.	Miner	/100	"
11		Joseph	30	m.	Miner		"
12		Nathaniel	16	m.	Miner		"
13		Margaret	13	f.			"
14		Simeon	12	m.			"
15		William	10	m.			"
16	462/462	SMITH, Author	62	m.	Farmer	4900/1200	Ire.
17		Nancy	49	f.			Pa.
18		Dorthy	22	f.			O.
19		Margaret	20	f.			"
20		Mary L.	18	f.			" S
21		Agnes	15	f.			" S
22		Eliza	14	f.			" S
23		Gennett	12	f.			" S
24		Manerva	9	f.			" S
25	463/463	CRONIN, Henson	35	m.	Laborer	/75	"
26		Martha A.	33	f.			"

27		CRONIN, Catharine	14	f.			O.
28		Sarah M.	12	f.			"
29		Margaret	9	f.			"
30		James N.	5	m.			"
31		Mary E.	2	f.			"

32	464/464	ALFORD, Charles	38	m.	Farmer	4000/700	Conn.
33		Mary J.	39	f.			O.
34		Samuel	18	m.			"
35		Melissa	15	f.			" S
36		Elisabeth J.	13	f.			" S
37		James R.	10	m.			" S
38		Emma S.	8	f.			" S
39		May A.	6	f.			" S
40		John M.	3	m.			"

Page 64   June 1860   Sheet 64

| 1 | | Thankful | 81 | f. | | | Conn. |

2	465/465	TRUAX, Amos	44	m.	Farmer	1500/337	O.
3		Mary	30	f.			"
4		Leander	8	m.			" S
5		Anderson	5	m.			" S
6		Nancy	3	f.			"
7		FERILL, Matilda	16	f.	Servant		"
8		TRUAX, Elishae	28	m.	Laborer		"

9	466/466	TRUAX, Henry	36	m.	Farmer	400/100	"
10		Siphrona	29	f.			"
11		Oliver	6	m.			"
12		Henry	3	m.			"
13		William O.	3/12	m.			"

14	467/467	ROTH, Nicholas	80	m.	Farmer	3000/321	Ger.
15		Ann	60	f.			O.
16		Susann	30	f.			
17		Henry	18	m.			
18		Harrit	15	f.			

19	468/468	STIMPER, Jacob	52	m.	Farmer	3500/700	Ger.
20		Louisa	51	f.			"
21		Daniel	13	m.			O.
22		Thabolt	11	m.			"

23	469/469	MONROE COUNTY INFIRMARY					
24		FULTON, John	86	m.	Insane		Ire.
25		McVEY, Benjamin	29	m.	Insane		O.
26		CHARLTON, Matilda	50	f.	Insane		"
27		WILLIAMS, Baxter	27	m.	Insane		"
28		BARKER, Isaac	16	m.	Deformed		"
29		BENNETT, Elisabeth	21	f.	Idiot		"
30		BUCKINGHAM, Jared	60	m.	Insane		Pa.
31		DAVIS, Abraham	72	m.	Infirm		"
32		CLINE, Rachel	67	f.	Infirm		Md.
33		SUTTON, David	60	m.	Idiot		O.
34		FRENCH, George	57	m.	Cripple		Pa.
35		PEGGS, Samuel	109	m.	Blind		"

36	CONNER, Adam	79	m.	Infirm	O.
37	FALLWELL, Joseph	70	m.	Cripple	"
38	CRAIG, Enoch	55	m.	Insane	"
39	ENGLISH, Rachel	27	f.	Insane	"
40	KEEPER, Leonard	35	m.	Insane	Ger.

Page 65   June 1860   Sheet 64 verso

1	SOLAND, Henry	73	m.	Infirm	Sw.
2	GRIMM, Eliza	84	f.	Infirm	Pa.
3	KIMBLE, Harvy	85	m.	Infirm	Ger.
4	MENTI, J. L.	41	m.	Insane	Pol.
5	OSSBURN, James	28	m.	Insane	O.
6	HAYES, James	59	m.	Cripple	Va.
7	SUTER, Martha	34	f.	Idiot	Sw.
8	Alexander	2	m.	Pauper	O.
9	CONGER, John	26	m.	Insane	"
10	SMITH, Menerva	16	f.	Pauper	"
11	THOMAS, Joel	22	m.	Pauper	"
12	Elisabeth	21	f.	Insane	"
13	Alonzo	4	m.	Pauper	"
14	Josiah	32	m.	Infirm	"

I do hereby certify that the within contais a true
statement of the census of Center Township taken by me in
pursuance of the Law and Instrutions Received by me for the
purpose that the same is truly taken as I verily believe.
August 29, 1860.

Thomas Little A. M.
For Center and Malaga Tps.

Sworn to and subscribed before me this 29th day of
August 1860.

D. Walton, Clerk
of Monroe County Com. Pleas

* * *

Malaga Township   P. O. Woodsfield

Page 66   9 July 1860   Sheet 65

1	445/445 MORE, William T.	28	m.	Farmer	1600/200 Ire.	
2	Mary V.	24	f.		O.	
3	William	6	m.		"	S
4	Mary C.	3	f.		"	
5	Elisabeth J.	4/12	f.		"	
6	446/446 MORRIS, Daniel	72	m.	Farmer	1600/200 Md.	
7	Hanah	64	f.		Va.	
8	Artsmaca	40	f.		"	
9	447/447 HAGERMAN, Powell	26	m.	Farmer	250/100 Hes.	
10	Catharina	26	f.		"	

11		HAGERMAN, William	3	m.			O.
12		Coonrod	2	m.			"
13	448/448	TILLOTT, Samuel	71	m.	Farmer	1000/150	Va.
14		Pleasant	65	f.			"
15		James	35	m.	Miller		O.
16		Delila	22	f.			"
17		Thomas	33	m.	Farmer		"
18		Lucy E.	18	f.			" S
19	449/449	MOORE, William	62	m.	Farmer	3000/700	Ire.
20		Elisabeth	64	f.			"
21		John	24	m.	Farm laborer		O.
22		Mathew	20	m.			" S
23	450/450	LUPTON, David	65	m.	Farmer	6000/2000	Va.
24		Margrett	65	f.			Del.
25		Rachell A.	40	f.			O.
26		John	30	m.	Farm laborer		"
27		Margrett	17	f.	Domestic		" S
28		HINDMAN, John	12	m.			" S
29	451/451	MINOR, Jane	73	f.			Pa.
30		Matilda	16	f.			O.
31	452/452	BOOTHE, Hannah	77	f.		2000/700	Eng.
32		LOW, Caroline	16	f.			O. S
33		Western	10	m.			" S
34	453/453	BOOTHE, John A.	22	m.	Farmer		"
35		Drusilla	22	f.			"
36		Nancy E.	4/12	f.			"
37	454/454	BROWN, Stephen	33	m.	Farmer	2500/350	Md.
38		Filenia	28	f.			O.
39		Isaac	8	m.			" S
40		Lydia J.	5	f.			" S

1	455/455	CLARK, James	73	m.	Farmer	2000/220	Pa.
2		Anne	52	f.			"
3		Hanah	20	f.			"
4	456/456	FLOWERS, George	47	m.	Farmer	1800/400	"
5		Susan	38	f.			Va.
6		Amanda	10	f.			O. S
7		James A.	9	m.			" S
8		John F.	6	m.			" S
9	457/457	LAWARANCE, Jacob	50	m.	Farmer	2500/300	"
10		Rebeca	37	f.			Va.
11		John W.	23	m.	Farm laborer		O.
12	458/458	CLARK, Lewis	44	m.	Blacksmith	/150	Pa.
13		Lydia A.	42	f.			"
14		Jefferice	19	m.	Farm laborer		O. S
15		Lara	5	f.			" S

16	459/459	FOSSETT, Sitha	33	f.		/100	O.	
17		Mary S.	13	f.			"	
18		Martha E.	7	f.			"	S
19		John A.	4	m.			"	S
20		Thomas A.	2	m.			"	

21	460/460	CARLTON, Samuel	56	m.	Farmer	2500/600	Pa.	
22		Nancy	49	f.			"	
23		Martha	21	f.			O.	
24		David	16	m.			"	S
25		Thomas C.	15	m.			"	S
26		Isaac B.	10	m.			"	S

27	461/461	GARTSON, Isaac P.	42	m.	Farmer	1700/200	Va.	
28		Sophia	40	f.			Md.	
29		John	13	m.			O.	S
30		Lewis W.	12	m.			"	S
31		Henry E.	10	m.			"	S
32		Hanah	6	f.			"	S

33	462/462	BONNER, Joseph	52	m.	Farmer	4000/350	Pa.	
34		Hetty D.	48	f.			"	
35		Marime C.	20	f.			O.	
36		Mary	17	f.			"	S
37		Eliza	16	f.			"	S
38		John	13	m.			"	S
39		David	11	m.			"	S
40		Sarah	9	f.			"	S

Page 68   9 July 1860   Sheet 66

1	463/463	GATCHELL, Robert	41	m.	Merchant	600/250	Pa.	
2		Mary A.	39	f.			"	
3		James C.	18	m.			O.	S
4		Mary J.	14	f.			"	S
5		Debora E.	10	f.			"	S
6		Elias P.	8	m.			"	S
7		Hanah E.	6	f.			"	S

8	464/464	THOMAS, Mordica	43	m.	Farmer		Pa.	
9		Caroline	35	f.			"	
10		Sodna C.	13	f.			O.	S
11		Isaac	7	m.			"	S
12		Sarah	3	f.			"	

13	465/465	LARANCE, William	22	m.	Farmer	"
14		ELLER, James H.	22	m.		"
15		TIPTON, Hannah	40	f.		"
16		Pheby	30	f.		"
17		Susan P.	42	f.		"

18	466/466	PIPTON, Elihu	42	m.	Teamster	1200/700	Md.	
19		Sarah	41	f.			O.	
20		Anne E.	19	f.			"	S
21		Rachell	17	f.			"	S
22		Lewisa K.	14	f.			"	S
23		MACHETT, Sarah E.	5	f.			"	S

24		ADAMS, C. W.	21	m.	Laborer		O.	
25	467/467	MORRIS, Robert L.	38	m.	Teacher	900/150	"	
26		Susan J.	38	f.			Md.	
27		Elisabeth	15	f.			O.	S
28		Almerian	13	m.			"	S
29		Alvin	8	m.			"	S
30		Levi	5	m.			"	S
31		Lucinda J.	3	f.			"	
32		MOORE, Benjamin	63	m.	Farmer			
33		Elisabeth	62	f.			N.C.	
34	468/468	LUPTON, Levi	38	m.	Tanner	1500/500	Md.	
35		Elisabeth	32	f.			O.	
36		Margrett J.	11	f.			"	S
37		Lora E.	9	f.			"	S
38		William O.	6	m.			"	S
39		Irena	1	m.			"	
40		HANSON, J. S.	33	m.	Shoemaker	600/150	"	

Page 69			9 July 1860			Sheet 66 verso	
1		McCOY, Joseph	55	m.	Day laborer		Md.	
2	469/469	THOMAS, Isaac	66	m.	Farmer	825/220	Pa.	
3		Martha	63	f.			Md.	
4		Jane	30	f.			O.	
5		DAVIS, Miles	14	m.			"	S
6		EATON, Isaac	25	m.	Blacksmith		"	
7	470/470	LARANCE, John	55	m.	Carpenter	450/125	Pa.	
8		Catharine	52	f.			Va.	
9		Emly	18	f.			O.	S
10		Meryman	14	m.			"	S
11		Hulda	11	f.			"	S
12		HARIS, Jerimiah	22	m.	Teacher		"	
13	471/471	ADAMS, N. P.	45	m.	Merchant	800/360	Pa.	
14		Rachel	44	f.			Md.	
15		Clarkson	21	m.			O.	
16		Lydiane	20	f.			"	
17		David	9	m.			"	S
18	472/472	BARNES, William	30	m.	Laborer		Md.	
19		Lydia	67	f.		700/150	"	
20		Rachel M.	23	f.			"	
21	473/473	THOMAS, Thomas W.	40	m.	Farmer	3000/600	Md.	
22		Martha A.	40	f.			"	
23		Lucetta	15	f.			O.	S
24		Jeramiah	13	m.			"	S
25		Rachell	12	f.			"	S
26		Joseph	11	m.			"	S
27		Elizabeth	9	f.			"	S
28		Anthony	6	m.			"	S
29		William	4	m.			"	S
30		Ruhamme	1	f.			"	

31		BROOKS, James	45	m.	Carder	Eng.
32	474/474	GRAHAM, Robert	36	m.	Farmer	/225 O.
33		Mahala	36	f.		" S
34		Nathen	11	m.		" S
35		William	9	m.		" S
36		Mary E.	7	f.		" S
37		Sarah C.	7	f.		" S
38		James	4	m.		" S
39		Charles	3	m.		"
40		John	1	m.		

Page 70   9 July 1860   Sheet 67

1	475/475	PROBASCO, William	11	m.		O. S
2		Elisa	9	f.		" S
3	476/476	TARBET, William D.	37	m.	Farmer	300/375 Pa.
4		Amanda	25	f.		"
5		Elihu T.	3	m.		O.
6		Andrew B.	2	m.		"
7		Amos D.	7/12	m.		"
8	477/477	MERSER, Washington	56	m.	Farmer	300/200 Pa.
9		Martha	42	f.		"
10	478/478	PERKINS, Mary	55	f.		Va.
11		Fanny	53	f.		"
12	479/479	POWELL, John	63	m.	Farmer	4000/650 Pa.
13		Hanah	49	f.		"
14		Nelson	27	m.	Farm laborer	O.
15		Mary J.	20	f.		" S
16		Sivena	18	f.		" S
17	480/480	THORNBERY, William	59	m.	Farmer	4000/540 Pa.
18		Elisa J.	26	f.		O.
19		Alexander	22	m.	Farm laborer	"
20		James M.	14	m.		" S
21		Elisabeth	12	f.		"
22	481/481	KENNEY, Thomas E.	42	m.		3000/700 Ire.
23		Matilda	48	f.		Va.
24		William H.	19	m.		O. S
25		Malisa	17	f.		" S
26		Alvira	15	f.		O. S
27		Erwin C.	13	m.		" S
28		Amanda	10	f.		" S
29	482/482	HENDERSON, John	59	m.	Farmer	3000/500 Pa.
30		Mary	65	f.		"
31		Simpson	23	m.	Farm laborer	O.
32		HINDS, Nancy E.	17	f.		"
33	483/483	KOOK, William	34	m.	Farmer	3000/800 "
34		Anne	33	f.		Pa.
35		Maryanne	14	f.		" S
36		John W.	12	m.		" S

37		KOOK, Martha	9	f.			Pa.	S
38		James D.	7	m.			"	S
39		Hanah J.	5	f.			"	S
40		Charles	3	m.			"	

Page 71   9 July 1860   Sheet 67 verso

1		George W.	5/12	m.			O.	
2	484/484	HECK, Jacob	51	m.	Butcher	/200	Pa.	
3		Sarah	46	f.			"	
4		Mary	25	f.			O.	
5		Osweld	23	m.			"	
6		Catharine	22	f.			"	
7		Lydia	18	f.			"	
8		Jacob	16	m.	Farm laborer		"	S
9		John	16	m.	Farm laborer		"	S
10		David	14	m.			"	S
11		William	12	m.			"	S
12		Margrett	11	f.			"	S
13		Elisabeth	10	f.			"	S
14		Harvy	7	m.			"	S
15		Emly J.	5	f.			"	S
16	485/485	LIGHTFOOT, Isaac	54	m.	Farmer	1060/400	Pa.	
17		Emma	49	f.			O.	
18		Mary	24	f.			"	
19		William	19	m.			"	S
20		Hannah	19	f.			"	S
21		Samuel	13	m.			"	S
22		Sarah	8	f.			"	S
23		Thomas	5	m.			"	
24	486/486	TURNLISTON, John F.	23	m.	Farmer		"	
25		Jane	25	f.			"	
26	487/487	BEARDMORE, Elloner	64	f.		4000/1000	"	
27		Emma	17	f.			Pa.	
28		OBLINGER, John	11	m.			O.	S
29		SMITH, Malilda	17	f.			"	
30		Hanah E.	14	f.			"	
31	488/488	McCOULAHS, William	37	m.	Farmer		"	
32		Isabella	27	f.			"	
33		Martin L.	9	m.			"	
34		James T.	7	m.			"	S
35		Larabell	5	f.			"	S
36		William A.	2	m.			"	S
37	489/489	BOOTH, Isaac	46	m.	Farmer	1100/600	Eng.	
38		Mary	19	f.			Pa.	
39		William	19	m.	Farm laborer		O.	S
40		Milton	18	m.			"	S

Page 72			9 July 1860				Sheet 68
1		BOOTH, Emly	17	f.			O. S
2		Lewisa	12	f.			" S
3		John	9	m.			" S
4		Elloner	5	f.			"
5	490/490	GRISELL, Edward	39	m.	Farmer	4160/700	Pa.
6		Emly	34	f.			O.
7		Jesse B.	14	m.			" S
8		Sharlotta	10	f.			" S
9		Anne E.	8	f.			" S
10		Semeon L.	6	m.			" S
11		George N.	3	m.			"
12		Lewisa A.	1	f.			"
13		TREWAX, Lewisa	19	f.			Pa.
14		GRISSELL, Elmyra	23	f.			O.
15	491/491	GRAY, Elgha	56	m.	Farmer	300/150	"
16		Elisabeth	61	f.			"
17		Lydia	19	f.			" S
18		John	10	m.			" S
19	492/492	THOMAS, Jonah	44	m.	Farmer	1300/300	Md.
20		Pheby	38	f.			Pa.
21		Martha M.	13	f.			O. S
22		Lewis B.	12	m.			"
23		Levi L.	6	m.			" S
24	493/493	FRAME, Thomas L.	40	m.	Farmer	4200/800	"
25		Elisabeth	38	f.			"
26		Mary A.	15	f.			" S
27		Rebeca J.	13	f.			" S
28		Lydia G.	11	f.			" S
29		Hannah T.	9	f.			" S
30		Margrett	7	f.			" S
31		Atlantica L.	5	f.			" S
32		William T.	4	m.			"
33		Pheby A.	1	f.			"
34		MIDLEN, Benjamin	17	m.	Farm laborer		"
35	494/494	GRISSELL, Simon	33	m.	Farmer	900/250	"
36		Rebeca J.	22	f.			Pa.
37		Alonzo	8	m.			" S
38		Edward C.	6	m.			" S
39		Almanda J.	4	f.			" S
40		John	1	m.			"
Page 73			10 July 1860				Sheet 68 verso
1	495/495	VANHORN, Charles	29	m.	Farmer	/150	O.
2		Jane	28	f.			"
3		William F.	5	m.			" S
4		George N.	3	m.			" S
5		Howard	1	m.			"
6		GIVONS, Tacy	12	f.			" S
7	496/496	GRISSELL, Thomas	68	m.	Farmer	1500/300	Pa.

8		GRISSELL, Elisa-beth	65	f.		Pa.	
9		Mary	30	f.		O.	
10		Sarah D.	25	f.		"	
11		Elmyra	23	f.		"	
12		Thomas S.	20	m.	Farm laborer	"	S
13		BRYANT, Thomas	11	m.	Adopted	"	S
14	497/497	BRIANT, Elisabeth	37	f.		"	
15		Emly	4	f.		"	S
16		Francis H.	3	m.		"	
17	498/498	TIPTON, John	41	m.	Blacksmith 2700/350	Md.	
18		Hannah A.	42	f.		Pa.	
19		Stephen	20	m.	Farm laborer	O.	
20		Thomas L.	16	m.	Farm laborer	"	S
21		Precilla	15	f.		"	S
22		Simeon G.	14	m.		"	S
23		Lorenca L.	11	m.		"	S
24		Mary L.	8	f.		"	S
25		David A.	6	m.		"	S
26		Elmyra	5	f.		"	S
27		Samuel L.	3	m.		"	
28	499/499	MARTIN, Henry	40	m.	Farmer 5460/700	Pa.	
29		Pheby	37	f.		"	
30		Ruth	15	f.		"	S
31		Silas S.	13	m.		"	S
32		Henry P.	11	m.		"	S
33		Maryanne	9	f.		"	S
34		Isaac	7	m.		O.	S
35		William	5	m.		"	S
36		Margrett	2	f.		"	
37	500/500	GRAHAM, James H.	37	m.	Teacher 1200/450	"	
38		Elisa	54	f.		"	
39		COEN, Nancy	78	f.		Pa.	
40		POLAND, John F.	40	m.		O.	

1	501/501	BROWN, Elihu	41	m.	Farmer 2000/350	Md.	
2		Nancy	33	f.		O.	
3		Agnes	14	f.		"	S
4		John H.	8	m.		"	S
5		Nancy E.	4	f.		"	
6		Thomas C.	2	m.		"	
7	502/502	FRED, James	38	m.	Farmer 2500/500	"	
8		Sarah Anna	44	f.		"	
9		John D.	15	m.	Farm laborer	"	S
10		Mary E.	13	f.		"	S
11		Henry E.	11	m.		"	S
12		Uly C.	7	f.		"	S
13	503/503	COEN, Thomas J.	43	m.	Farmer 3750/1100	Pa.	
14		Elisabeth	25	f.		O.	
15		John H.	20	m.	Farm laborer	"	S

16		COEN, Nancy Anne	18	f.		O. S
17		Mary Ann	16	f.		" S
18		Robbert L.	14	m.		" S
19		Thomas L.	12	m.		" S
20		Susanah	11	f.		" S
21		Tacy Jane	7	f.		" S
22		Catharine	5	f.		"

23	504/504	TILLETT, E. J.	40	m.	Miller	"
24		Martha E.	30	f.		"
25		Delilah A.	13	f.		" S
26		Lucy E.	11	f.		" S
27		Samuel H.	7	m.		" S
28		John T.	1	m.		"

29	505/505	BROWN, William	45	m.	Farmer	5800/1700	Md.
30		Hester	45	f.			Pa.
31		Achsah	19	f.			O. S
32		David L.	17	m.	Farm laborer		" S
33		Mary J.	15	f.			" S
34		Rachell	13	f.			" S
35		Pheoba	10	f.			" S
36		Hannah	4	f.			"
37		TOWNSEND, Mark	10	m.			" S

38	506/506	CARLTON, Aner	63	m.	Farmer	5000/800	Pa.
39		Elisabeth G.	55	f.			"
40		Abener G.	22	m.	Blacksmith		O.

Page 75		10 July 1860				Sheet 69 verso
1		John	21	m.	Farmer	" S
2		Thomas	18	m.	Farmer	" S
3		Mark	16	m.	Farmer	" S
4		Agnes	14	f.		" S
5		Lewis	24	m.	Carpenter	"

6	507/507	LANDIS, Abram	69	m.	Millwright	1000/300	Pa.
7		Sarah	68	f.			"
8		Benjamin	40	m.	Farm laborer		O.
9		Sarah Anne	25	m.			"
10		Abram	9	m.			" S
11		Mary	4	f.			"

12	508/508	CLARK, Margaret	43	f.		"
13		John	14	■.		" S
14		Mary	13	f.		" S
15		Isaac	11	m.		" S
16		William	8	m.		" S
17		Olevia	7	f.		" S
18		Anne M.	1	f.		"
19		BYERS, Margaret	29	f.		Pa.
20		Lucinda	2	f.		O.

21	509/509	TRUAX, Jane	40	f.	2500/250	"
22		Margaret E.	16	f.		" S
23		Mary C.	14	f.		" S

24		TRUAX, Martin L.	12	m.			O.	S
25		Sarah V.	10	f.			"	S
26		George F.	8	m.			"	S
27		David N.	6	m.			"	
28	510/510	TRUAX, Cornelius	46	m.	Farmer	4000/365	Pa.	
29		Delilah	22	f.			O.	
30		Nathaniel	18	m.	Farmer		"	S
31		Matilda	16	f.			"	S
32		Nathan	8	m.			"	S
33		Isaac	6	m.			"	S
34	511/511	GAITS, Elisabeth	36	f.			Md.	
35		May F.	15	f.			O.	S
36		Nancy J.	13	f.			"	S
37		Louisa D.	10	f.			"	S
38		James S.	7	m.			"	S
39		George W.	6	m.			"	
40		Madison V.	3	m.			"	

1	512/512	ANDREWS, Robert	34	m.	Farmer	4400/950	Pa.	
2		Martha L.	22	f.			O.	
3		William F.	4	m.			"	
4		Rosale R.	1	f.			"	
5		HESS, Rebecca	12	f.			"	S
6	513/513	MONTGOMERY, Will-						
		iam	29	m.	Farmer	/100	Pa.	
7		Mary Anne	27	f.			O.	
8		Sada C.	5	f.			"	
9		Anne M.	3	f.			"	
10		Laura	2	f.			"	
11		LEWIS, Francis A.	10	m.			"	S
12	514/514	GAITS, Valentine	38	m.	Farmer	2500/250	"	
13		Pheoba	36	f.			"	
14		CROSBY, Mary M.	10	f.			"	S
15		GAITS, Valentine	74	m.			"	
16	515/515	ELLOTT, Thomas	38	m.	Farmer	3000/500	Pa.	
17		Margaret	30	f.			O.	
18		Adaline	10	f.			"	S
19		Montarey	7	m.			"	S
20		Raymond	5	m.			"	
21		Arelius	2	f.			"	
22		Arettas	2	f.			"	
23		Samuel	6/12	m.			"	
24	516/516	STEWART, James	28	m.	Farmer	2500/240	Pa.	
25		Elisabeth	26	f.			O.	
26		Sementha	10	f.			"	S
27		Camsedel	8	f.			"	S
28		Vilena	6	f.			"	S
29		Clinton	4	m.			"	
30		William E.	2/12	m.			"	

```
31 517/517 JOHNSON, John        40   m.    Farmer        1600/400   O.
32          Elisabeth            35   f.                             "
33          Ezra                 12   m.                             "    S
34          Jobe                  4   m.                             "
35          HAYS, Elisabeth A.   13   f.                             "    S

36 518/518 GRAVES, R. C.         24   m.                            Va.
37          Martha               22   f.                            Pa.
38          Anne                  1   f.                            O.

39 519/519 LACKER, John          50   m.    Tobacco packer
                                                          800/200   Md.
40          Gulia A.             50   f.                             "
```

Page 77   10 July 1860   Sheet 70 verso

```
1          John H.              18   m.    Farm laborer          O.  S
2          Walter               16   m.    Farm laborer          "   S
3          David                14   m.                          "   S
4          Sarah A.             12   f.                          "   S

5 520/520 MANN, William G.      43   m.    Farmer      4000/1200  "
6          Pheoba               39   f.                           "
7          Mary L.              20   f.                           "
8          Alfred A.            19   m.    Farm laborer           "   S
9          Lydia J.             14   f.                           "   S
10         Hannah E.            12   f.                           "   S
11         Barnett G.           10   m.                           "   S
12         Thomas D.             8   m.                           "   S
13         Hester G.             5   f.                           "
14         Margaret A.           2   f.                           "

15 521/521 MANN, David          75   m.    Farmer                Pa.
16         Delilah              52   f.                          O.

17 522/522 MANN, Peter          80   m.    Farmer      4000/800  Pa.
18         Elisabeth            67   f.                           "
19         Jackson              28   m.    Farm laborer          O.
20         Mary Ann             26   f.                           "
21         Joseph               25   m.    Farm laborer          "
22         Elisabeth             1   f.                          "

23 523/523 DETLING, George      36   m.    Farmer     4000/1200  Fr.
24         Mary E.              20   f.                          O.
25         Matilda L.            5   f.                           "   S
26         William T.            3   m.                           "
27         Frederick            76   m.                           "
28         HARRIS, Sarah        84   f.                           "

29 524/524 MANN, Peter          30   m.    Farmer        300/500  "
30         Susanah              28   f.                           "
31         Mary V.               7   f.                           "   S
32         Sarah S.              5   f.                           "   S
33         Nancy E.              2   f.                           "
34         Isaac              6/12   m.

35 525/525 HARDESTY, William    27   m.    Farmer                 "
```

36		HARDESTY, Rachell	25	f.		O.	
37		Arattes L.	4	f.		"	
38		MORRIS, Lucinda	27	f.		"	
39		FOULER, Cornelia	30	f.		Md.	
40		MOOSE, Samuel	7	m.		O.	S

Page 78   10 July 1860   Sheet 71

1	526/526	SMITH, Ezra	49	m.	Stone mason	300/150	Pa.	
2		Nancy	39	f.			"	
3		Luceta	18	f.			O.	
4		Eli	16	m.	Farm laborer		"	S
5		Stephen	14	m.			"	S
6		Samuel	12	m.			"	S
7		Lavina	10	f.			"	S
8		Mary	8	f.			"	S
9		Sidna	14	f.			"	

10	527/527	SILL, John	34	m.	Carpenter	125/100	"	
11		Elisabeth	30	f.			"	
12		Elmira	11	f.			"	S
13		William	9	m.			"	S
14		Fredrick	7	m.			"	S
15		Thomas	5	m.			"	S
16		Emma	1	f.			"	
17		Philip	68	m.			"	

18	528/528	HARDISTY, Joseph	45	m.	Tobacco packer 400/150	Md.	
19		Maria	40	f.		"	
20		William	24	m.	Apprentice	O.	
21		Almond	20	m.	Farm laborer	"	
22		Walter	18	m.		"	S
23		Webster	11	m.		"	

24	529/529	JUDKINS, Hiram G.	37	m.	Physician	900/200	"	
25		Mary	28	f.			Va.	
26		Adarana	4	f.			O.	
27		Cullen	3	m.			"	
28		Wallace	1	m.			"	
29		Mary	63	f.			"	

30	530/530	MACHETT, J. B.	36	m.	Blacksmith 4840/350	"	
31		Mary	37	f.		"	
32		Stephen	12	m.		"	S
33		Francis	8	m.		"	S
34		Sarah E.	5	f.		"	S
35		Elsa E.	2	f.		"	

36	531/531	THORNBERY, James M.	31	m.	Shoemaker	1000/150	Pa.	
37		Elisabeth	23	f.			O.	
38		Lana	6	f.			"	S
39		Cecilia	4	f.			"	
40		Lewis N.	1	m.			"	

Page 79   10 July 1860   Sheet 71 verso

1	532/532	HANLON, P. P.	31	m.	Clerk	1500/150	O.	

2		HANLON, Mary E.	23	f.			O.
3		William	5	m.			" S
4		Oliver	1	m.			"
5	533/533	KOTZBULE, H. C.	35	m.	Merchant	3650/7000	"
6		Luisa	29	f.			"
7		Charles	10	m.			" S
8		Lewisa	8	f.			" S
9		William	5	m.			" S
10	534/534	MOONEY, Eli	29	m.	Saddler	400/150	Pa.
11		Mary	25	f.			"
12		Lucinda	3	f.			O.
13		Enmeta	1	f.			"
14	535/535	LUDWICK, Daniel	27	m.	Farmer		Pa.
15		Lewisa	23	f.			O.
16		Nicholis	3	m.			"
17		Lewis	2	m.			"
18		Lewisa	9/12	f.			"
19	536/537	FORD, Simon	50	m.	Carpenter		"
20		Mary	47	f.			Va.
21		Amanda	21	f.			O.
22		Elisa P.	16	f.			" S
23		William	9	f.			" S
24	537/537	VANHORN, Nathaniel	74	m.	Farmer	4000/1300	Md.
25		Margaret	65	f.			"
26		Catharine	28	f.			O.
27	538/538	VANHORN, Edman	40	m.	Farmer		"
28		Sarah A.	38	f.			"
29	539/539	HILL, Eli H.	33	m.	Farmer		"
30		Margrett	27	f.			"
31		William	8	m.			" S
32		Edward	5	m.			" S
33		Abigal P.	3	f.			"
34		Rachell A.	6/12	f.			"
35	540/540	SLUSHER, John	31	m.	Farmer	400/150	"
36		Rosanah	38	f.			"
37		Lydia	7	f.			" S
38		Loretta	6	f.			" S
39		William	3	m.			"
40		Thomas R.	2	m.			"

1	541/541	MOORE, Elija	42	m.	Tobacco packer		
						300/150	Va.
2		Rebeca	40	f.			Md.
3		Elisabeth	17	f.			" S
4		Amanda	15	f.			O. S
5		Mary	13	f.			" S
6		William	10	m.			" S
7		Anne	7	f.			" S

8	542/542	WHEETEN, William	25	m.	Farmer		Pa.
9		Levina	24	f.			O.
10		John M.	1	m.			"
11		THORNBERY, Rily	22	m.	Farm laborer		"
12	543/543	WELING, Assa	57	m.	Farmer		Va.
13		Aceneth	58	f.			"
14		George D.	21	m.			O.
15		Lydia L.	15	f.			" S
16	544/544	LOGAN, James	30	m.	Minister, Cumberl. Presbyterian		"
17		Caroline	25	f.			Pa.
18		Eliza H.	2	f.			"
19		Morice S.	1	f.			O.
20		BURLEY, Sarah E.	15	f.	Domestic		"
21	545/545	MANN, Sinclair	39	m.	Farmer	1500/400	"
22		Hester A.	37	f.			"
23		Allen	17	m.	Farmer		"
24		Charles	15	m.	Farmer		" S
25		Nathen	13	m.			" S
26		Simpson	11	m.			" S
27		Margrett	9	f.			" S
28		James	7	m.			" S
29		Eliza	5	f.			" S
30		Mary	3	f.			"
31	546/546	MANN, Barnett	52	m.	Farmer	6000/850	Pa.
32		Mary	47	f.			Eng.
33		John	23	m.	Farm laborer		O.
34		David	20	m.	Farm laborer		" S
35		Wilson	18	m.	Farm laborer		" S
36		Sinclair	16	m.	Farm laborer		" S
37		Harriott	6	f.			" S
38		Peter	4	m.			"
39	547/547	BYERS, Nancy	66	f.		1200/300	Pa.
40		Emanuel	23	m.	Farmer		O.

Page 81   10 July 1860   Sheet 72 verso

1		Catharine	48	f.			O.
2		John	13	m.			"
3		Hugh	10	m.			" S
4		Catharine	8	f.			" S
5	548/548	OBLINGER, Amelia	42	f.		1000/150	Pa.
6		Clarinda	23	f.			O.
7		Maria	22	f.			"
8		Elisebeth	22	f.			"
9		Sarah	17	f.			" S
10		Emly	15	f.			" S
11		Lewis	14	m.			" S
12		John	12	m.			" S
13		Henry	10	m.			" S

14		OBLINGER, Solamon	7	m.			O. S
15		Washington	5	m.			"
16	549/549	SLUSHER, Demas	45	m.	Farmer	2000/400	Pa.
17		Hanah	42	f.			"
18		Martin	19	m.	Farmer		O. S
19		John D.	14	m.			" S
20		Mary L.	12	f.			" S
21		Giles E.	8	m.			" S
22		Elisabeth A.	5	f.			"
23		Sarah	7/12	f.			"
24	550/550	GRAHAM, Thoms	57	m.	Farmer	900/300	Ire.
25		Mary	47	f.			Va.
26		William	23	m.	Farm laborer		O.
27		Elisabeth	12	f.			" S
28		Susan	10	f.			" S
29		Levina	9	f.			" S
30		Thomas	7	m.			" S
31		Johnston	5	m.			"
32	551/551	MACKELFRESH, James	27	m.	Farmer		Pa.
33		Sarah	30	f.			O.
34		Amanda J.	8	f.			"
35		John N.	4	m.			"
36		Henry	9/12	m.			
37		SMITH, Elisabeth A.	36	f.			"
38	552/552	STEEL, John L.	28	m.	Farmer	5000/1000	"
39		Hanah	25	f.			"
40		Julia	7	f.			"

Page 82   10 July 1860   Sheet 73

1		Mary S.	4	f.			O.
2		Emma	2	f.			"
3	552/552	TAGGART, James	25	m.	Teacher	450/200	"
4		Elisabeth E.	31	f.			"
5		Sarah J.	4	f.			"
6		Samuel J. T.	2	m.			"
7		Thomas J.	6/12	m.			"
8	553/553	GRAHAM, John S.	38	m.	Farmer		"
9		Mary Anne	34	f.			"
10		Margaret T.	3	f.			"
11		Sarah B.	2	f.			"
12		TAGGART, Barbara	30	f.			"
13	554/554	FLEEMAN, Jerry J.	29	m.	Farmer		Bav.
14		Elisabeth	23	f.			O.
15		George	2	m.			"
16	555/555	FOULER, Thomas	39	m.	Tailor	750/200	Md.
17		Sarah	34	f.			O.
18		Mary E.	33	f.			"

19		FOULER, Ella May	4	f.			O.	
20		Valentine A.	29	m.			"	
21	556/556	LONG, Henry	70	m.	Farmer	3000/800	Bad.	
22		Hannah	58	f.			Pa.	
23		Jane	25	f.			O.	
24		Lydia A.	14	f.			"	S
25		MOOSE, Barbara	15	f.			"	S
26	557/557	EGGAR, John	30	m.	Farmer		"	
27		Ruth	22	f.			"	
28		Jane	10	f.			"	S
29		George	5	m.			"	S
30		Andrew	1	m.			"	
31	558/558	LEACH, Joel	55	m.	Farmer	/350	N.J.	
32		Margaret	51	f.			Pa.	
33		Elisabeth A.	18	f.			"	S
34		Abram	15	m.			"	S
35		Albert	13	m.			"	S
36		William H.	10	m.			"	S
37		John	5	m.			"	S
38	559/559	ERICKSON, John	59	m.	Farmer	4000/600	Del.	
39		Rachell	54	f.			Va.	
40		Mary E.	30	f.			Pa.	

Page 83			11 July 1860				Sheet 73 verso	
1		Samuel	27	m.	Farmer		Pa.	
2	560/560	MANN, William C.	23	m.	Farmer	1500/250	O.	
3		Rachell J.	25	f.			"	
4	561/561	EGGAR, Daniel	27	m.	Carpenter		"	
5		Catharine	27	f.			"	
6	562/562	STEEL, Dolly	48	f.		2000/300	Ire.	
7		GRAHAM, Dolly	19	f.			O.	S
8		Margaret	18	f.			"	S
9		Thomas	17	f.			"	S
10	563/563	JOHNSON, Nancy	32	f.			"	
11		Mary L.	11	f.			"	S
12		Dolly	9	f.			"	S
13		Lydia J.	8	f.			"	S
14		Gulia A.	6	f.			"	S
15		Eliza	5	f.			"	S
16		Adam	4	m.			"	
17	564/564	BRUCE, Joshua	35	m.	Farmer	600/150	"	
18		Lucetta A.	35	f.			Va.	
19		Nathaniel D.	14	m.			"	S
20		John W.	13	m.			"	S
21		William H.	12	m.			"	S
22		Mary C.	9	f.			"	S
23		Loretta	5	f.			"	

24		BRUCE, Charles	2	m.			O.
25	565/565	STEEL, John	61	m.	Farmer	5000/1000	Pa.
26		Mary	58	f.			O.
27		Nancy	24	f.			"
28		Mary	21	f.			"
29		Adam	19	m.			" S
30		Sevilla J.	15	f.			" S
31		CARICK, Andrew	18	m.			" S
32		STEEL, Wesly	5	m.			"
33		Sophia	4	f.			"
34	566/566	DORR, Simon	48	m.	Farmer	5000/900	Fr.
35		Ellenor	44	f.			Ire.
36		Francis	22	m.	Farmer		O.
37		Catharine	20	f.			" S
38		John T.	19	m.	Farmer		" S
39		George B.	17	m.	Farmer		" S
40		Mary Ann	15	f.			" S

Page 84   11 July 1860   Sheet 74

1		William	14	m.			O. S
2		Charles P.	11	m.			" S
3		Anthony	10	m.			" S
4		James	8	m.			" S
5		Gertrude	6	f.			"
6		Harietta E.	4	f.			"
7		Sebastian	2	m.			"
8	567/567	MANN, Andrew	40	m.	Farmer	110/100	Pa.
9		Nancy	32	f.			"
10		Hester A.	15	f.			" S
11		William J.	13	m.			" S
12		Elisabeth	11	f.			" S
13		Catharine	9	f.			" S
14		Gabis	6	m.			⊙.
15		Rosetta	2	f.			"
16	568/568	HUTH, John	38	m.	Farmer	1500/400	Pa.
17		Margarett	36	f.			"
18		William	12	m.			Va. S
19		Elisabeth	10	f.			" S
20		John	8	m.			O. S
21		Catharine	5	f.			"
22		Eva	3	f.			"
23		Mary	1	f.			"
24		Henry	43	m.	Laborer		"
25		NOLL, John	68	m.	Laborer		"
26	569/569	SHADOCK, Richard	54	m.	Farmer	2800/900	Md.
27		Eliza	50	f.			"
28		Elisabeth	16	f.			O. S
29		Mary	14	f.			" S
30		Martha S.	12	f.			" S
31		Caroline	10	f.			" S
32		Oliver	8	m.			" S

33	570/570	HARPER, Daniel	48	m.	Farmer	/600	Pa.
34		Rachell	48	f.			"
35		Harison	23	m.	Farmer		O. S
36		Nelson	21	m.	Farmer		" S
37		Madison	14	m.			" S
38		Elias	12	m.			" S
39		David	9	m.			" S
40		Lydia	8	f.			" S

Page 85   11 July 1860   Sheet 74 verso

1		William	6	m.			O. S
2		Marion E.	1	m.			"
3	571/571	THOMPSON, Rebecca	43	f.			"
4		Lewis	23	m.			"
5		Charles	21	m.			" S
6		James	19	m.			" S
7		Stillwell	13	m.			" S
8		Rachell J.	10	f.			" S
9		Henry	7	m.			" S
10	572/572	BENNETT, George W.	39	m.	Farmer	4750/1200	Pa.
11		Olivia P.	32	f.			O.
12		Seawell E.	10	m.			" S
13		Leroy C.	9	m.			" S
14		William M.	7	m.			" S
15		Melinda A.	4	f.			"
16		Casnick L.	3	m.			"
17		TRUAX, David	26	m.			"
18		William	21	m.			" S
19	573/573	BIDENHARN, George H.	34	m.	Merchant	2500/3000	Han.
20		Amelia	23	f.			Pr.
21		Otto	2	m.			O.
22		Permelia	6/12	f.			"
23		ASKENOE, F. H.	23	m.			Pr.
24		HEYLMANN, Tracy	59	m.			"
25		JOHANING, Elijah	19	m.			Pa. S
26	574/574	MANN, Hughs	46	m.	Farmer	4000/800	O.
27		Margarett	43	f.			"
28		Susann	25	f.			"
29		William	23	m.	Farmer		"
30		James	21	m.	Farmer		" S
31		Milly	19	f.			" S
32		Sarah	17	f.			" S
33		Lyman	14	m.			" S
34		Amanda	11	f.			" S
35		Lauretta	9	f.			" S
36		Anchless	5	f.			"
37		Alemeda	1	f.			"
38		Hughs	8	m.			" S
39		Abigal	1	f.			"
40	575/575	MANN, Catharine	57	f.		1500/150	Va.

Page 86			12 July 1860				Sheet 75	
1		MANN, Margaret E.	64	f.			Pa.	
2	576/576	NEPTUNE, John H.	45	m.	Farmer	1000/850	Va.	
3		Catharine	44	f.			Pa.	
4		Margaret	18	f.			O.	S
5		Fredarick F.	16	m.	Farmer		"	S
6		Samuel	14	m.			"	S
7		Elisabeth	14	f.			"	S
8		Martha E.	10	f.			"	S
9		Ruth J.	8	f.			"	S
10		Sarah N.	5	f.			"	
11	577/577	VANCE, William	66	m.	Farmer	4800/725	Pa.	
12		John	44	m.	Farmer		"	
13		Rhoda	30	f.			"	
14		Sarah	25	f.			"	
15		SQUIRES, Milford	10	m.			"	S
16	578/578	MOOSE, Jacob	31	m.	Farmer		"	
17		Elisabeth	34	f.			O.	
18		Selestial V.	4	f.			"	
19		Charles L.	1	m.			"	
20	579/579	FOGLE, John P.	39	m.	Farmer	5000/1000	"	
21		Margaret A.	38	f.			"	
22		Mary C.	14	f.			"	S
23		Asenath	12	f.			"	S
24		George W.	9	m.			"	S
25		Martin L.	5	m.			"	
26		RICH, Michel	25	m.			"	
27		SLACK, Houston	49	m.			"	
28		FOGLE, Sarah	28	f.			"	
29		Nancy	26	f.			"	
30	580/580	TRUAX, Jobe	45	m.	Farmer		Pa.	
31		Ellenor	40	f.			"	
32		William	26	m.	Farmer		"	
33		Jasper	22	m.	Farmer		"	S
34		Franklin	21	m.	Farmer		"	S
35		Wesly	18	m.	Farmer		"	S
36		Fletcher	18	m.	Farmer		"	S
37		Lewis	17	m.			O.	S
38		John	12	m.			"	S
39		Savilian	7	m.			"	S
40		Mary E.	15	f.			"	

Page 87			12 July 1860				Sheet 75 verso	
1	581/581	MILLER, Frank	30	m.	Carpenter	300/150	Bav.	
2		Catharine	22	f.			O.	
3		Louisa	2	f.			"	
4	582/582	HUNGLER, Michel	51	m.	Farmer	2000/900	Fr.	
5		Mary	53	f.			"	
6		Magdaline	19	f.			O.	S

7		HUNGLER, John	17	m.		O.	S
8		Michel	15	m.		"	S
9		Elisabeth	12	f.		"	S
10	583/583	BURKHEART, Fred.					
		J.	38	m.	Farmer	3000/700 Bav.	
11		Margaret	32	f.		Pr.	
12		Barbary	10	f.		O.	S
13		Jacob	8	m.		"	S
14		Nicholas	5	m.		"	
15		Mary M.	3	f.		"	
16		Catharine	1	f.		"	
17		WISENT, George	15	m.	Laborer	"	S
18		SHORT, Catharine	75	f.		Pr.	
19	586/586	HULLER, David	59	m.	Farmer	Bav.	
20		Catharine	61	f.		Fr.	
21		Elisabeth	19	f.		O.	S
22		Joseph	16	m.		"	S
23	585/585	WEST, David	60	m.	Shoemaker	1000/250 Del.	
24		Mary	40	f.		Va.	
25		Martha	4	f.		O.	
26	586/586	VALTON, John	47	m.	Farmer	Va.	
27		Elisabeth	42	f.		O.	
28		Adrian	20	m.	Laborer	"	S
29		William	18	m.	Laborer	"	S
30		Oswalld	16	m.	Laborer	"	S
31		John W.	14	m.		"	S
32		Sarah E.	12	f.		"	S
33		Michell	10	m.		"	S
34		Henry	6	m.		"	S
35		George T.	4	m.		"	
36		Mary W.	2	f.		"	
37	587/587	PATTON, Joshua	25	m.	Laborer	2400/550 "	
38		Eliza J.	22	f.		"	
39		Sarah A.	2	f.		"	
40		John	3/12	m.		"	

1	588/588	HUGHS, Francis	56	m.	Farmer	Md.	
2		Nancy	50	f.		O.	
3		Robert H.	23	m.	Farmer	"	
4		Reece	21	m.	Farmer	"	
5		James F.	18	m.	Farmer	"	S
6		Alfred P.	9	m.		"	S
7	589/589	SINGER, Enos	28	m. B.	Farmer	"	
8		Rhoda	32	f. B.		"	
9		William W.	13	m. B.		"	S
10		Benjamin	11	m. B.		"	S
11		George W.	8	m. B.		"	S
12		John W.	6	m. B.		"	S
13		Joseph H.	4	m. B.		"	

14		SINGER, Rodgers	3	m.	B.		O.
15		Silka A.	1	f.	B.		"
16	590/590	GAMPS, Nicholas	51	m.		Farmer	500/700	Fr.
17		Mary	47	f.				"
18		Mary	13	f.				"
19		Peter	17	m.				"
20		Pcwell	11	m.				" S
21		Lana	9	f.				" S
22		John N.	4	m.				O.
23	591/591	BOWEN, Rachell	58	f.			1500/350	Ger.
24		Margaret	18	f.				O. S
25		Adam	17	m.				Ger.
26		POWER, Adam F.	76	m.				"
27	592/592	MILLER, Samuel	50	m.		Farmer	600/3C0	O.
28		Lana	30	f.				"
29		John	16	m.				" S
30	593/593	MATCHETT, James M.	29	m.		Farmer	/300	"
31		Elisabeth	25	f.				"
32		George W.	4	m.				"
33		Mary E.	3	f.				"
34		John	5/12	m.				"
35	594/594	MATCHETT, George	36	m.		Farmer	/350	"
36		Rachell	23	f.				"
37		Martha E.	12	f.				" S
38		Sarah E.	10	f.				" S
39		Lydia J.	6	f.				" S
40		William E.	4	m.				"

Page 89			13 July 1860				Sheet 76 verso
1		Thomas L.	2	m.			"
2		Joseph W.	1/12	m.			"
3	595/595	MATCHETT, William	74	m.		Farmer	3000/400	Ire.
4		Elisabeth	71	f.				"
5	596/596	HINDMAN, James	48	m.		Farmer	2430/1100	Pa.
6		Susanah	50	f.				"
7		Elisabeth	18	f.				O. S
8		John	15	m.				" S
9		GIVENS, Susanah	10	f.				" S
10		MANN, Nathan	11	m.				" S
11	597/597	SLCAN, William	37	m.		Farmer	3600/700	"
12		Eliza C.	33	f.				Md.
13		Elisabeth	10	f.				O. S
14		James M.	5	m.				"
15		George W.	1	m.				"
16	598/598	SAMPSON, David	65	m.		Farmer	2700/1000	Pa.
17		Anne	47	f.				"
18		Prudence A.	15	f.				O. S
19		BONMAN, David	16	m.				" S

20	599/599 GILBERT, Johnithan	30	m.	Farmer		Pa.
21	Mary A.	33	f.			O.
22	Nancy J.	6	f.			"
23	Margarett	1	f.			"

24	600/600 SPALDING, George					
	W.	32	m.	Farmer	1700/400	"
25	Lydia	29	f.			"
26	David L.	7	m.			" S
27	Mary E.	5	f.			"
28	Marilda J.	2	f.			"
29	William V.	10/12	m.			"

30	601/601 WATT, Joseph	51	m.	Farmer	4000/525	"
31	Maria	40	f.			Pa.
32	Sarah M.	22	f.			O. S
33	James H.	20	m.			" S
34	Rosanah	18	f.			" S
35	John W.	16	m.			" S
36	Steward	14	m.			" S
37	Lena	10	f.			" S
38	Jane	8	f.			" S
39	WHEATON, Jacob	43	m.	Laborer		"
40	(line is blank)					

1	602/602 ARMSTRONG, James	42	m.	Farmer	1500/500	O.
2	Julia A.	37	f.			"
3	Mary L.	16	f.			" S
4	Elisa J.	14	f.			" S
5	Emma	9	f.			" S
6	William	6	m.			" S
7	Ida	4	f.			"
8	Lena	2	f.			"

9	603/603 JOHNSON, Ezra	54	m.	Farmer	5000/1000	Va.
10	Catharine	50	f.			"
11	Mary	23	f.			O. S
12	Joseph	20	m.			" S
13	Sarah A.	16	f.			" S
14	Rosanah O.	9	f.			" S

15	604/604 JOHNSON, Benjamin	22	m.	Farmer		"
16	Mary J.	20	f.			"
17	Infant	2/12	f.			"

18	605/605 HOWILER, Jacob	29	m.	Farmer	4000/1000	Ger.
19	Margarett	25	f.			"
20	John	8	m.			O. S
21	Lana	7	f.			" S

22	606/606 SMITH, Henry	35	m.	Farmer		"
23	Mary A.	26	f.			"
24	Henry	9/12	m.			"
25	HENING, Margarett	5	f.			" S

26	607/607	COOLEY, Samuel	26	m.	Farmer	1200/350	O.
27		Margarett	30	f.			"
28		BROWN, George	10	m.			"

29	608/608	SMITH, Jacob	32	m.	Farmer	1600/500	Bav.
30		Mary	25	f.			Md.
31		Henry	3	m.			O.
32		Catharine	1	f.			"

33	609/609	SMITH, Henry	63	m.	Farmer		Bav.
34		Dolly	65	f.			"
35		HIND, John	11	m.			O. S

36	610/610	WALTER, Henry	35	m.	Farmer	1500/450	Bav.
37		Mary	26	f.			"
38		Jacob	7	m.			O. S
39		Henry	5	m.			" S
40		George	3	m.			"

Page 91   13 July 1860   Sheet 77 verso

1		Fredrick	4/12	m.			O.
2		ARNET, Mary	10	f.			"

3	611/611	MILLER, John	35	m.	Farmer	1600/300	Darm.
4		Mary	28	f.			"
5		Elisebeth	10	f.			O. S
6		Catharine	8	f.			" S
7		Margarett	6	f.			" S
8		Mary	4	f.			"
9		Emmy	2	f.			"

10	612/612	WALTER, Lewis	40	m.	Farmer	1800/200	Bav.
11		Cristena	38	f.			Darm.
12		Catharine	11	f.			O. S
13		George	9	m.			" S
14		Lenna	7	f.			" S
15		Eewis	5	m.			" S
16		Abraham	2	m.			"
17		Barbary	6/12	f.			"
18		GRONEHART, Anna	65	f.			"

19	613/613	BURKHART, John G.	24	m.	Farmer	2000/250	Bav.
20		Mary A.	20	f.			"
21		Mary A.	6/12	f.			O.
22		SRIVER, Charles	40	m.			Hes.

23	614/614	RICEMAN, Adam	23	m.	Farmer	1400/200	Bav.
24		Lena	24	f.			"
25		Mary	5	f.			O. S
26		Joseph	3	m.			"
27		Jacob	2	m.			"

28	615/615	HORN, Peter	63	m.	Farmer	3000/800	Fr.
29		Catharine	53	f.			"
30		Jacob	25	m.			O.
31		Adam	12	m.			" S
32		Michell	18	m.			" S

33		HORN, Barbary	15	f.			O. S
34		John	11	m.			" S
35	616/616	BURKHART, Michel	28	m.	Farmer	4000/700	Byron
36		Matilda	25	f.			"
37		Barbary	3	f.			O.
38		Martin	2	m.			"
39		Mary	4/12	f.			"
40		John	17	m.	Laborer		Byron

Page 92   13 July 1860   Sheet 78

1	617/617	HORN, Peter Jr.	30	m.	Farmer	1120/600	Fr.
2		Catharine	26	f.			"
3		Mary	3	f.			O.
4		George	1	m.			"
5		Franklin	5/12	m.			"
6	618/618	REMENSNIDER, J. P.	25	m.	Shoemaker		Hes.
7		Catharine	24	f.			"
8		PEPLE, Casper	60	m.	Farm laborer		"
9	619/619	MORRIS, Henry G.	61	m.	Farmer	1240/900	D.C.
10		Mary	56	f.			Pa.
11		Henry G.	25	m.	Farm laborer		O.
12		Mary J.	22	f.			"
13		Pheby	21	f.			"
14		Thomas J.	15	m.	Farm laborer		" S
15		Sarah	12	f.			" S
16		Nancy	9/12	f.			"
17	620/620	BARE, Lewis	25	m.	Farmer		Pa.
18		Sidny A.	9	f.			O. I
19		John E.	7	m.			" S
20		George S.	4	m.			" S
21		Mary J.	3	f.			"
22		Albert W.	3	m.			"
23		Charles U.	9/12	m.			"
24	621/621	BROWNFIELD, William	49	m.	Farmer	2000/650	Pa.
25		Elisabeth	40	f.			O.
26		Alexander	17	m.	Farm laborer		" S
27		Lydia	14	f.			" S
28		Margrett	10	f.			" S
29		Enos	9	m.			" S
30		Mary	7	f.			" S
31		Romuless	5	m.			"
32		Stephen	3	m.			"
33		Sarah	2	f.			"
34	622/622	HORN, Fredric	28	m.	Farmer	3000/450	Fr.
35		Barbary	25	f.			Byron
36		Tobald	5	m.			O.
37		Simon	2	m.			"
38		Catharine	1	f.			"
39		Ferdinand	16	m.	Farm laborer		" S
40		Lana	11	f.			" S

Page 93   13 July 1860   Sheet 78 verso

1	623/623	RUBLE, Daniel	45	m.	Farmer	800/350	Byron
2		Catharine	59	f.			"
3		Fredric	15	m.			O.

4	624/624	REMANSNIDER, John	46	m.	Farmer	1200/400	Hes.
5		Catharine	48	f.			"
6		Elisabeth	20	f.			" S
7		Catharine	18	f.			" S
8		John	12	m.			O. S
9		Nicholis	7	m.			"
10		Fredrick	4	m.			"

11	625/625	RICEMAN, Jacob	49	m.	Farm laborer	1500/500	Rhein.
12		Mary	40	f.			"
13		Jacob	20	m.			"
14		Michel	16	m.			"
15		Mathews	14	m.			" S
16		John	12	m.			" S
17		Mary	6	f.			O. S

18	626/626	SNIDER, Philip	30	m.	Farmer		Byron
19		Catharine	30	f.			Wit.
20		Philip	6	m.			O.
21		Henry	4	m.			"
22		Mary	3	f.			"
23		John	3/12	m.			"
24		Philipenia	60	f.			Wit.

25	627/627	CLOUSE, Nicholas	48	m.	Farmer	1600/700	Hes.
26		Catharine	44	f.			"
27		William	18	m.			O. S
28		Mary	16	f.			" S
29		Margrett	13	f.			" S
30		John	10	m.			" S
31		Adolp	7	m.			" S
32		Charles	4	m.			"

33	628/628	CLOUSE, William	45	m.	Farmer	2300/750	Hes.
34		Margrett	51	f.			"
35		Catharine	17	f.			O.
36		POTTER, Michel	22	m.			Fr.
37		Catharine	8/12	f.			O.
38		WAGONER, Frederic	22	m.	Farm laborer		Byron

| 39 | 629/629 | EBERLY, Adam | 22 | m. | Farm laborer | | Wit. |
| 40 | | Catharine | 18 | f. | | | Byron |

Page 94   13 July 1860   Sheet 79

1	630/630	HIND, John	36	m.	Blacksmith	1200/250	Darm.
2		Elisabeth	32	f.			"
3		Elisabeth	12	f.			O.
4		John	11	m.			" S
5		Cristena	9	f.			" S

6		HIND, William	6	m.			O. S
7		Catharine	3	f.			" S
8	631/631	DEST, John	27	m.	Farmer	1000/150	Hes.
9		Elisebeth	31	f.			Pa.
10		Mary C.	1	f.			O.
11		Catharine	3/12	f.			"
12		DEIST, Coonrad	65	m.	Farm laborer		Hes.
13		Cary	58	f.			"
14	632/632	EGGER, Jaha C. P.	48	m.	Farmer	2700/450	Sw.
15		Lewisa	51	f.			Wit.
16		John S.	16	m.			O. S
17		Matilda	9	f.			" S
18	633/633	GRINER, Jacob	34	m.	Farmer	3000/500	Fr.
19		Marymagdelena	33	f.			"
20		John	14	m.			O. S
21		Francis	13	m.			" S
22		Joseph	9	m.			" S
23		Rosanah	8	f.			" S
24		Emly	7	f.			" S
25		Jacob	5	m.			"
26		Edward	3	m.			"
27		Lucetta	2	f.			"
28		Benjamin	4/12	m.			"
29	634/634	WILSON, Johnston	63	m.	Farmer	3000/800	Pa.
30		Eliza	52	f.			O.
31		William	30	m.			"
32		Alexander	26	m.			"
33		Susan	20	f.			"
34		Elisabeth	15	f.			" S
35		Josiah	9	m.			" S
36	635/635	YOCKEY, Philip	43	m.	Farm laborer 3000/560		Bav.
37		Marymagdelena	39	f.			"
38		Christena	18	m.			O. S
39		Augusta	15	f.			" S
40		John L.	13	m.			" S

1		Lewisa	11	f.			" S
2		Philip O.	8	m.			" S
3		Mary J. C.	3	f.			"
4	636/636	YOCKEY, Casper	75	m.	Farmer		Bav.
5		Sharlotta	67	f.			"
6		Larance	23	m.			O.
7	637/637	SMITH, George	56	m.	Farmer	2500/400	Byron
8		Cristena	56	f.			"
9		Cristena	13	f.			O.
10	638/638	WALTER, Lewis	54	m.	Farmer	2000/600	Bav.

| 11 | | WALTER, Mary | 55 | f. | | | Bav. | |
| 12 | | Lewis | 20 | m. | | | " | |

13	639/639	SHEETS, Jacob	40	m.	Farmer	3000/700	Byron	
14		Margrett	39	f.			Hes.	
15		Mary	7	f.			O.	S
16		Catharine	5	f.			"	S
17		Elisabeth	3	f.			"	
18		Lewisa	1	f.			"	
19		HAFT, Fredrick	30	m.			Byron	

20	640/640	EMMETT, John	45	m.	Farmer	/150	Bav.	
21		Anna	35	f.			"	
22		Eve	14	f.			O.	
23		Barbary	12	f.			"	S
24		Mary	11	f.			"	S
25		John	8	m.			"	S
26		Philepena	5	f.			"	S
27		Matilda	3	f.			"	
28		Franklin	1	m.			"	

29	641/641	WAGONER, George	39	m.	Farmer	/150	Bav.	
30		Casy	38	f.			"	
31		Caspar	12	m.			O.	S
32		Catharine	8	f.			"	S
33		George	6	m.			"	S
34		Magdlene	4	f.			"	
35		Elisa	4	f.			"	
36		Barbary	2	f.			"	
37		Mary	2/12	f.			"	

38	642/642	ALTER, Augusta	49	m.	Farmer	/160	Fr.	
39		Barbary	47	f.			"	
40		Emley	5	f.			O.	S

Page 96   13 July 1860   Sheet 80

1	643/643	YONKIS, Maria	44	f.			Fr.	
2		Mary	16	f.			O.	
3		Benjamin	12	m.			"	

4	644/644	BURKHART, John	38	m.	Farmer	2500/600	Byron	
5		Barbary	35	f.			"	
6		Adam	16	m.			O.	S
7		Philip	13	m.			"	S
8		Mariah	11	f.			"	S
9		Mary R.	8	f.			"	S
10		Joseph	7	m.			"	S
11		John	7	m.			"	S
12		Charles	5	m.			"	
13		Lana	2	f.			"	

14	445/445	BURKHART, Adam	47	m.	Farmer	4000/250	Byron	
15		Barbary	46	f.			"	
16		Mary	19	f.			O.	S
17		John	17	m.			"	S
18		George	14	m.			"	S

19		BURKHART, Cath-						
		arine	12	f.			O.	S
20		Barbary	9	f.			"	S
21		Adam	6	m.			"	S
22		Nicholis	4	m.			"	
23	646/646	STANSLE, Fredrick	48	m.	Brewer	1500/300	Fr.	
24		Barbary	38	f.			"	
25		Elisabeth	17	f.			O.	
26		John	15	m.			"	S
27		Caroline	13	f.			"	S
28		Charles	8	m.			"	S
29		Jacob	7	m.			"	S
30		Emaline	3	f.			"	
31		Lucetta	5/12	f.			"	
32	647/647	OBLINGER, J. B.	50	m.	Merchant	1500/1000	Fr.	
33		Dina	45	f.			Bav.	
34		Ottilia	19	f.			O.	
35		Lisette B.	17	f.			"	
36		Frank B.	16	m.	Clerk		"	
37		Josephine	14	f.			"	S
38		Charles L.	12	m.			"	S
39		Mary Virginia	10	f.			"	S
40		John B.	7	m.			"	

Page 97   14 July 1860   Sheet 80 verso

1		Clement L.	5	m.			O.	S
2	648/648	JOHNSTON, William						
		L.	32	m.	Teamster		"	
3		Eve	24	f.			"	
4		Martha	7	f.			"	S
5		Margrett E.	5	f.			"	
6		Richard C.	2	m.			"	
7	649/649	GIBBENS, William	43	m.	Laborer		Md.	
8		Ruth A.	35	f.			O.	
9		Sarah E.	12	f.			"	S
10		Elisa J.	9	f.			"	S
11		Nancy E.	6	f.			"	S
12		Susan A.	3	f.			"	
13	650/650	STUMP, Larance	60	m.	Basketmaker	300/150	Wit.	
14		Magdlena	50	f.			Fr.	
15		Larance	25	m.	Day laborer		Pa.	
16	651/651	WINGERT, Philip	33	m.	Shoemaker		Bav.	
17		Magedelana	26	f.			O.	
18		Mary E.	5	f.			"	S
19		John F.	1	m.			"	
20	652/652	MENCE, John	32	m.	Carpenter	300/150	Bad.	
21		Lewisa	32	f.			Sax.	
22		John	6	m.			Va.	S
23		Benjamin	3	m.			O.	

24		MENCE, Lewisa	1	f.			O.
25	653/653	HANT, George	26	m.	Carpenter	200/150	Han.
26		JOHANING, Joseph	65	m.			"
27		Mary	14	f.			"
28	654/654	FOX, Charles	27	m.	Laborer		Bad.
29		Mary A.	21	f.			Pa.
30	655/655	COONRAD, George	33	m.	Brewer		Pr.
31		Cristena	28	f.			Wit.
32	656/656	MENKLE, Henry	37	m.	Carpenter	700/200	Pr.
33		Caroline	34	f.			Byron
34		Caroline	11	f.			Va. S
35		Henry	9	m.			O. S
36		Charles	5	m.			" S
37		Philip	2	m.			"
38		Julia	6/12	f.			"
39	637/637	LUDWIC, Nicholis	32	m.	Shoemaker	400/150	Byron
40		Catharine	32	f.			"

Page 98			14 July 1860				Sheet 81
1		Charles	7	m.			Pa. S
2		Nicholis	6	m.			" S
3		Caroline	4	f.			O.
4		Louisa	2	f.			"
5		Mary	10/12	f.			"
6		KROUSE, Henry	16	m.	Apprentice		" S
7	658/658	STOUT, Nicholas	50	m.	Stone mason	2700/700	Byron
8		Eve	44	f.			"
9		Francis	19	m.	Blacksmith		O. S
10		Jacob	17	m.	Farmer		" S
11		John	13	m.			" S
12	659/659	JOHNSON, Vance	60	m.	Postmaster	300/150	"
13		Caroline	60	f.			N.J.
14		John	30	m.	Carpenter		O.
15		Thomas	22	m.	Tobacco packer		"
16	660/660	FRISELL, Christian	58	m.	Tailor	1000/200	Sax.
17		Elisabeth	38	f.			Byron
18		Catharine	16	f.			O. S
19		Louisa	11	f.			" S
20		John	8	m.			" S
21		Lewis	5	m.			" S
22	661/661	YOCKEY, Lewis	31	m.	Blacksmith	600/400	Byron
23		Barbary	25	f.			
24		William H.	6	m.			O. S
25		James M.	3	m.			"
26		BAKER, John	64	m.	Farmer		Byron

27	662/662	MOOSE, Coonrad	29	m.	Farmer	400/200	O.	
28		Mary	30	f.			"	
29		John	4	m.			"	
30		Louisa	3/12	f.			"	
31	663/663	SHELL, George	47	m.	Farmer		Pa.	
32		Margarett	45	f.			"	
33		Elisabeth	20	f.			O.	S
34		Lydia Anne	17	f.			"	S
35		John	15	m.			"	S
36		George	13	m.			"	S
37		Charles	11	m.			"	S
38		Francis	9	m.			"	S
39		Joseph	5	m.			"	S
40		Camaline	2	f.			"	

Page 99   14 July 1860   Sheet 81 verso

1		Infant	3/12	m.			O.	
2	664/664	KROUSE, Coonrad	49	m.	Evang. Minister		Ger.	
3		Rosetta	43	f.			Wer.	
4		Henry	16	m.			"	S
5		Adolph	14	m.			"	S
6		Mary	8	f.			O.	S
7		Conrad	6	m.			"	S
8		Hannah	4	f.			"	
9		Caroline	2	f.			"	
10	665/665	KISER, Mary	32	f.		300/150	Fr.	
11		Lana	11	f.			O.	S
12		Mary Anne	13	f.			"	S
13		Filmena	11	f.			"	S
14		George	9	m.			"	S
15		Adam	7	m.			"	S
16		Fredarick	4	m.			"	
17		John	2	m.			"	
18		Elisabeth	3/12	f.			"	
19	666/666	MILLEMAN, Lukes	40	m.	Laborer		Sw.	
20		Caroline	26	f.			Swope	
21	667/667	GEHONA, William	85	m.		150/100	Han.	
22		Geerhart	26	m.	Laborer		"	
23		Mary	14	f.			"	S
24	668/668	LETZLER, Michel	51	m.	Wagon maker		Eyron	
25	669/669	BLOCKER, Gottlieb	36	m.	Brewer	1000/250	Wit.	
26		Mary	34	f.			Darm.	
27		Catharine	8	f.			O.	S
28		Mary	7	f.			"	S
29		Christena	4	f.			"	
30		John W.	2	m.			"	
31	670/670	WALTERS, Helena	60	f.		3500/200	Byron	
32		Jacob	21	m.	Merchant		O.	

33	671/671	BACH, Henry	67	m.		700/200 Darm.
34		Mary	66	f.		"
35	672/672	DORR, Peter	32	m.	Merchant	1500/2000 Fr.
36		Catharine	18	f.		O. S
37	673/673	GREENLY, Christopher	50	m.	Saddler	200/160 Wit.
38		Rachell	42	f.		"
39		Elisabeth	22	f.		O. S
40		John	20	m.		" S

1		Ellenor	18	f.		O. S
2		Henrietta	14	f.		" S
3		William	11	m.		" S
4		Emma	9	f.		" S
5		Benjamin	6	m.		" S
6		Charles	3	m.		"
7	674/674	FEIOK, George	29	m.	Blacksmith	250/160 Byron
8		Adolphene	21	f.		Hes.
9		George	3	m.		O.
10		Louisa	2	f.		"
11		Infant	6/12	m.		"
12		NEEPS, Fredarick	17	m.	Laborer	" S
13	675/675	RETLER, Michel	32	m.	Blacksmith	900/250 Byron
14		Mary	24	f.		Darm.
15		John	4	m.		"
16		Henry	2	m.		O.
17		Charles	5/12	m.		"
18	676/676	KELLER, Charles	50	m.	Physician	"
19		Charles	13	m.		Darm.S
20		Lena	10	f.		" S
21		George	8	m.		" S
22	677/677	KRELERS, Andrew	41	m.	Tobacco packer 1000/300	"
23		Barbary	31	f.		Bav.
24		Margaret	13	f.		Fr. S
25		John P.	11	m.		O. S
26		Anne	8	f.		" S
27		Philepina	7	f.		" S
28		George W.	4	m.		"
29		Jacob F.	3	m.		"
30	678/678	WISENT, Jacob	82	m.	Laborer	500/400 Byron
31		Margaret	75	f.		"
32	679/679	CRAMER, Philip	36	m.	Farmer	700/150 Hes.
33		Margaret	30	f.		O.
34		Abert	9	m.		" S
35		Catharine	5	f.		"
36		Philip	3	m.		"
37		George	1	m.		"

38	680/680	LUBY, S. B.	25	m.	Tinner	250/150	O.
39		Michel	77	m.			Darm.
40		Barbara	59	f.			"

Page 101   16 July 1860   Sheet 82 verso

1	681/681	SCHWEB, J. A.	29	m.	Cabinet-maker			
						600/100	Fr.	
2		Wilhelmina	31	f.			Byron	
3		William	6	m.			O.	
4		Amelia	4	f.			"	
5		Eliza	1	f.			"	
6	682/682	READ, Benjamin	65	m.	Hotel-keeper			
						700/200	"	
7		Nancy	55	f.			"	
8		Benjamin F.	32	m.	Laborer		"	
9	683/683	HOBAUGH, William	40	m.	Tanner	2500/300	Pa.	
10		Martha A.	36	f.			O.	
11		James M.	15	m.			"	S
12		Charles B.	12	m.			"	S
13		Eliza C.	6	f.			"	S
14		Emma F.	1	f.			"	
15	684/684	KETTER, Fredarick	34	m.	Farmer	4000/800	"	
16		Rachell	34	f.			"	
17		John	12	m.			"	S
18		Charles	19	m.			"	S
19		Louisa	7	f.			"	S
20		Amelia	4	f.			"	
21		Mary	9/12	f.			"	
22	685/685	YOCKEY, Lewis	29	m.	Farmer	/400	"	
23		Rebecca A.	23	f.			"	
24		Lucetta M.	2	f.			"	
25		John M.	8/12	m.			"	
26	686/686	MILLER, Samuel	59	m.	Farmer	4000/1500	Sw.	
27		Barbary	60	f.			"	
28		Samuel	23	m.	Farmer		O.	
29		Elisabeth	21	f.			"	
30		John	15	m.			"	S
31	687/687	BURKHEART, John	29	m.	Farmer	1500/600	Byron	
32		Martin	70	m.			"	
33		Elisabeth	68	f.			"	
34		Mary	23	f.			"	
35	688/688	STEEL, Samuel	44	m.	Farmer	1200/800	O.	
36		Julia A.	40	f.			"	
37		David C.	20	m.			"	S
38		Mary C.	18	f.			"	S
39		Elisabeth	16	f.			"	S
40		Harriet R.	14	f.			"	S

1		STEEL, John H.	12	m.			O. S
2		William J.	10	m.			" S
3		Hannah J.	8	f.			" S
4		James S.	6	m.			" S
5		Sylvester	5	m.			"
6		Emely E.	3	f.			"
7		Vance	1	m.			"
8	689/689	SNIDER, Fredarick J.	47	m.	Farmer	1400/620	Rhein.
9		Elisabeth	40	f.			"
10		BETRAM, Elisabeth	60	f.			"
11	690/690	YOCKEY, Lawrence	65	m.	Farmer	3500/400	Byron
12		Elisabeth	63	f.			"
13		Lydia	14	f.			O. S
14		Charles	12	m.			" S
15		Casper	21	m.	Tinner		" S
16	691/691	CROPP, Labolt	45	m.	Carpenter		Aus.
17		Mary	38	f.			Byron
18		Labolt	2	m.			O.
19	692/692	HUFFMAN, George	66	m.	Farmer	1400/350	O.
20		Charles	18	m.	Laborer		" S
21		Mary	16	f.			" S
22		Christian	14	m.			" S
23		Fredarick	12	m.			" S
24	693/693	SHELL, Daniel	32	m.	Farmer	1800/500	Pa.
25		Ann M.	26	f.			Sw.
26		Louisa	7	f.			O. S
27		Melinda	6	f.			" S
28		Anne	5	f.			"
29		Emely	4	f.			"
30		Levina	2	f.			"
31		William	7/12	m.			"
32		MARTY, Jacob	63	m.	Laborer		Sw.
33		Menne	50	f.			"
34	694/694	STEEL, Christopher	67	m.	Farmer	1700/430	Pa.
35		Catharine	44	f.			"
36		Julia A.	18	f.			" S
37		Lydia A.	17	f.			" S
38		Nancy	16	f.			" S
39		William	12	m.			O. S
40		George	10	m.			" S

1	695/695	KEYSER, John	37	m.	Farmer	1600/500	Fr.
2		Amelia	35	f.			Ger.
3		Elisabeth	10	f.			O. S
4		Barbary	8	f.			" S
5		Emly	6	f.			" S
6		Mary	4	f.			"

7		KEYSER, John	8/12	m.			O.	
8		Emly	70	f.			Fr.	

9	696/696	RAPP, Jacob	55	m.	Farmer	1000/350	Bav.	
10		Agnes	45	f.			"	

11	697/697	FABER, Henry	44	m.	Farmer	3500/700	Fr.	
12		Sophia	37	f.			Sax.	
13		Caroline	16	f.			O.	S
14		Louisa	14	f.			"	S
15		John	12	m.			"	S
16		Mary	10	f.			"	S
17		Jacob	8	m.			"	S
18		Henry	6	m.			"	S
19		Elisabeth	4	f.			"	
20		Willphelen	1	f.			"	
21		Henry	82	m.			Fr.	
22		Christena	80	f.			Byron	

23	698/698	KOONTZ, Andrew	48	m.	Farmer	1500/600	Byron	
24		Barbary	41	f.			O.	
25		Mary	17	f.			"	S
26		Elisabeth	15	f.			"	S
27		Joseph	13	m.			"	S
28		Adam	12	m.			"	S
29		John	7	m.			"	S
30		Barbary	5	f.			"	
31		Christena	3	f.			"	
32		Jacob	11/12	m.			"	
33		BROUN, Jacob	79	m.			Pa.	

34	699/699	FURGENSON, Robert	77	m.	Farmer	170/100	O.	
35		Elisabeth	34	f.			"	
36		HOPPER, Samuel	21	m.			Fr.	

37	700/700	PETERS, John	55	m.	Farmer	1500/500	Fr.	
38		Elisabeth	64	f.			O.	
39		Charles	17	m.			"	S
40		DETLING, Catharine	14	f.			"	S

Page 104			16 July 1860				Sheet 84	

1	701/701	GRAHAM, James	81	m.	Farmer	5000/620	Pa.	
2		Jane	56	f.			Md.	
3		Sarah N.	32	f.			O.	
4		Lucinda	29	f.			"	
5		Samuel	27	m.	Farmer		"	
6		Joseph H.	23	m.	Farmer		"	
7		Edward	13	m.			"	S
8		Catharine	11	f.			"	S

9	702/702	BEARDMORE, William	55	m.	Farmer	7000/2500	Eng.	
10		Mary	55	f.			"	
11		Elisabeth	25	f.			O.	
12		Isaac	23	m.	Farmer		"	
13		John	21	m.	Farmer		"	
14		Anne	20	f.			"	S

15		BEARDMORE, Ellenor	18	f.			O.	S
16		Jane	16	f.			"	S
17		Thomas	14	m.			"	S
18		James	12	m.			"	S
19		Louisa	8	f.			"	S
20	703/703	LATSHAW, William	26	m.	Laborer		"	
21	704/704	FEUBLE, George	26	m.	Farmer		Hes.	
22		Anne	27	f.			Han.	
23		Louisa	3	f.			O.	
24		John H.	1	m.			"	
25		BAKER, Nicholas	62	m.			Han.	
26		Margaret	56	f.			"	
27		Catharine	86	f.			"	
28		Julia	7	f.			Va.	S
29	705/705	SHROEDER, Adam	40	m.	Farmer	1600/500	Bav.	
30		Louisa	18	f.			Pa.	S
31	706/706	SNIDER, George	29	m.	Farmer	800/175	Bad.	
32		Elisabeth	31	f.			"	
33		Catharine	8	f.			O.	S
34		Louisa	5	f.			"	
35		George	3	m.			"	
36	707/707	PRUTZ, George J.	56	m.	Farmer	1300/340	Bav.	
37		Mary E.	50	f.			"	
38	708/708	SIMERLY, Adam	61	m.	Farmer	1400/160	Byron	
39		Pheoba	63	f.			"	
40		Margarett	19	f.			Pa.	S

Page 105			16 July 1860			Sheet 84 verso		
1		Rachell	18	f.			O.	S
2		SINK, John	36	m.	Farmer		Hes.	
3		Pheby	22	f.			Pa.	
4		Mary	1	f.			O.	
5	709/709	CLOUCE, Henry	41	m.	Farmer	1200/400	Hes.	
6		Elisabeth	40	f.			"	
7		Justice	16	m.	Farm laborer		"	S
8		Elisabeth	12	f.			O.	S
9		Henry	10	m.			"	S
10		Adolph	8	m.			"	S
11		Fredric	5	m.			"	S
12	710/710	SIMERLY, Jacob	27	m.	Farmer	600/200	Byron	
13		Caroline	26	f.			"	
14		Jacob	3	m.			O.	
15		Henry	2	m.			"	
16	711/711	HINDS, William	23	m.	Farmer	3000/700	"	
17		Elisabeth	18	f.			"	
18		Aron	62	m.	Farm laborer		Han.	
19		Catharine	63	f.			"	

20	712/712	MARTY, Fredrick	25	m.	Farmer		Sw.	
21		Rosanah	22	f.			Va.	
22		Mary	2	f.			O.	
23	713/713	SMITH, Margrett	53	f.		1700/400	Byron	
24		Philip	15	m.			O.	
25		Caroline	12	f.			"	S
26		Barbary	8	f.			"	S
27	714/714	NEECE, John	46	m.	Farmer	2500/500	Darm.	
28		Christina	45	f.			"	
29		Mary	17	f.			O.	S
30		Catharine	15	f.			"	S
31		John	10	m.			"	S
32		Henry	8	m.			"	S
33		Christina	5	f.			"	S
34	715/715	EBERLY, Godlip	28	m.	Carpenter	900/150	Wit.	
35		Elisabeth	22	f.			O.	
36		Magdelina	1	f.			"	
37	716/716	BARTRAM, Fredric	34	m.	Farmer	1200/400	Byron	
38		Mary	36	f.			"	
39		Ludwic	10	m.			"	S
40		Jacob	2	m.			O.	

Page 106   17 July 1860   Sheet 85

1		Elisabeth	1	f.			O.	
2	717/717	WISENT, Michell	40	m.	Farmer	3000/900	Byron	
3		Barbary	40	f.			"	
4		Elisabeth	18	f.			O.	S
5		Barbary	17	f.			"	S
6		Mary	15	f.			"	S
7		George	14	m.			"	S
8		Michell	12	m.			"	S
9		Joseph	8	m.			"	S
10		Catharine	6	f.			"	S
11		John	4	m.			"	
12		Matilda	2	f.			"	
13	718/718	WILLIAMS, John	65	m.	Farmer	1000/250	"	
14		Elisabeth	40	f.			Byron	
15		Powell W.	12	m.			"	S
16		Anna	11	f.			O.	S
17	719/719	FELTNER, Philip	65	m.	Farmer	800/200	"	
18		Elisabeth	62	f.			Byron	
19		Caroline	19	f.			"	
20		HUFFMAN, Lewis	12	m.			O.	
21	720/720	HOUK, Jacob	62	m.	Farmer	600/500	"	
22		Caroline	62	f.			Byron	
23		David	20	m.	Farm laborer		"	
24	721/721	NIPS, John	40	m.	Farmer	1500/700	"	

25		NIPS, Elisabeth	43	f.		Brussel
26		Fredrick	18	m.	Farm laborer	Byron
27		Philip	17	m.	Farm laborer	O. S
28		Caroline	10	f.		" S
29		John	5	m.		" S
30		George	2	m.		"
31	722/722	PINTZ, David	30	m.	Farmer	1800/600 Byron
32		Magdlena	26	f.		Fr.
33		Magdelena	5	f.		O. S
34		George J.	3	m.		"
35		Lewis	1	m.		"
36	723/723	SHOUB, David	58	m.	Farmer	1500/40 Byron
37		Catharine	61	f.		"
38		SHOUB, David D.	58	m.		"
39		Filena	61	f.		"
40		Catharine	22	f.		"

1	724/724	SHOUB, George	87	m.	Farmer	Rhein.
2		MEHL, Andrew	33	m.	Farm laborer	Fr.
3		Elisabeth	33	f.		"
4		George	9	m.		O. S
5		John	6	m.		" S
6		Mary C. E.	3	f.		"
7		Anne	4	f.		"
8		MEHEL, Mary	10/12	f.		"
9	725/725	LUDWIC, Jacob	39	m.	Farmer	2000/400 Byron
10		Mary	28	f.		"
11		Jacob	10	m.		O. S
12		Caroline	8	f.		" S
13		Charles	7	m.		" S
14		Lewis	5	m.		"
15		Lewisa	2	f.		"
16		George J.	3/12	m.		"
17	726/726	COOPPER, Robert	60	m.	Farmer	8000/950 Pa.
18		Mary G.	60	f.		"
19		GRAHAM, Mary J.	30	f.		O.
20		COOPPER, Robert	21	m.		"
21		CROSEN, Delilah	8	f.		"
22	727/727	COOPPER, James	26	m.	Farmer	8000/1500 "
23		Mary A.	29	f.		"
24		John	24	m.	Farm laborer	"
25		Margrett	20	f.		" S
26		William	18	m.	Farm laborer	" S
27		Nancy J.	16	f.		" S
28		Archabeld	14	m.		" S
29		David	12	m.		" S
30		Francis F.	10	m.		" S
31		Lydia L.	8	f.		" S
32		Lydia	51	f.		

33	728/728	STAKLETHE, Elisa-						
		beth	57	f.		1500/600	Byron	
34		Eve	23	f.			"	
35		Elisabeth	21	f.			O.	
36		Barbary	17	f.			"	S
37		John	15	m.			"	S
38		Catharine	12	f.			"	S
39		William	10	m.			"	S
40		James	8	m.			"	S

Sheet 86 verso

I do hereby Certify that the within contains a true
Statement of the Census of Malaga Township taken by me in
pursuance of the Law and Instructions Received by me for
that purpose that that the same is truly taken as I Verily
Believe this 29th day of August 1860.

Thos. Little A. M.
For Malaga & Center Tps.

Sworn to and Subscribed before me this 29 day of August
1860.

D. Walton Clerk
Of Monroe Co. Com. Pleas

* * *

	P. O. Ozark			Sunsberry Township

1	1/1	COSS, John	78	m.	Farmer	15,000/200	Md.	
2		Margaret	43	f.			Pa.	
3		PARKER, Amanda	41	f.	Servant		"	
4	2/2	HENDERSHOT, Chan-						
		cey	47	m.	Farmer	450/234	O.	
5		Deborah	37	f.			Pa.	
6		Adam C.	22	m.			O.	
7		Lorenza D.	20	m.			"	
8		Iceline	17	f.			"	S
9		Oscar T.	16	m.			"	S
10		Zelotes	14	m.			"	S
11		Roxenia	12	f.			"	S
12		Johnson L.	10	m.			"	S
13		Asbury G.	3	m.			"	
14		Joseph D.	1	m.			"	
15	3/3	CARTER, Enos P.	49	m.	Farmer	1400/210	Md.	
16		Philena	47	f.			Pa.	
17		Lydia	23	f.			Md.	
18		Julia	19	f.			O.	S
19		William	17	m.			"	S
20		Mary	15	f.			"	S
21		Sarah	13	f.			"	S
22		Isabell	10	f.			"	S
23		Elizabeth P.	4	f.			"	

24	4/4	HAYDEN, Abraham	44	m.	Carpenter	1500/215	O.
25		Maria	35	f.			Eng.
26		Elizabeth A.	10	f.			O. S
27		Mary E.	6	f.			" S
28	5/5	LOWE, William	28	m.	Farmer		"
29		Margaret	21	f.			"
30		Amanda J.	7/12	f.			"
31		JOHNSON, Isaac A.	15	m.	Laborer		"
32	6/6	WILLIAMSON, John	47	m.	Farmer	2000/400	Md.
33		Terza	36	f.			O.
34		DRIGGS, Susan A.	15	f.	Adopted		" S
35	7/7	ADAMS, Ira	39	m.	Farmer	2000/425	"
36		Amanda	34	f.			"
37		Sarah E.	19	f.			"
38		Lydia	17	f.			" S
39		Thomas	15	m.			" S
40		Mary A.	12	f.			" S

Page 2   9 July 1860   Sheet 87 verso

1		Susan	10	f.			O. S
2		Isaac	8	m.			" S
3		Milton	5	m.			"
4		Bizara	3	f.			"
5	8/8	KELCH, George	24	m.	Farmer	4500/320	"
6		Julia A.	21	f.			"
7		Hulda A.	9/12	f.			"
8	9/9	MILLER, George W.	20	m.	Farmer	2500/650	"
9		Ruth A.	25	f.			"
10		Mary A.	2	f.			"
11		Eliza P.	11/12	f.			"
12	10/10	HAINS, John	30	m.	Farmer		"
13		Rebecca	29	f.			"
14		William M.	1	m.			"
15	11/11	BARNES, Josiah	48	m.	Farmer	8000/1200	"
16		Mary E.	25	f.			"
17		William W.	20	m.			"
18		Abel B.	18	m.			" S
19		Mary E.	16	f.			" S
20		Lydia	12	f.			" S
21		Benjamin	4	m.			"
22		Milton	2	m.			"
23	12/12	WILEY, Nathaniel	44	m.	Farmer	2000/380	Md.
24		Nancy A.	53	f.			O.
25		Margaret	19	f.			"
26		Leander	17	m.			" S
27		Wilson	12	m.			" S
28		BURKHEAD, Aurelia	17	f.	Teacher		"

29	13/13	WILLIAMS, John	40	m.	Carpenter	300/90	O.	
30		Desdemona	35	f.			"	
31		Cordelia	16	f.			"	S
32		Seabery	14	m.			"	S
33		Lenor	10	m.			"	S
34		Casius C.	6	m.			"	S
35		Caroline	3	f.			"	
36	14/14	WILEY, John	60	m.	Farmer	6000/1600	Pa.	
37		Sarah	60	f.			Md.	
38		Andrew	23	m.			O.	
39		Joseph	22	m.			"	
40		William	21	m.			"	

Page 3   10 July 1860   Sheet 88

1		Sarah E.	17	f.			O.	S
2		Emely	15	f.			"	S
3	15/15	AMOS, Joshua	55	m.	Farmer	4000/1700	Pa.	
4		Orpah	44	f.			Md.	
5		Sarah C.	22	f.			O.	S
6		Elisabeth J.	20	f.			"	S
7		McONAS, Aquilla	17	m.			"	S
8		Benjamin F.	13	m.			"	S
9		Ann M.	8	f.			"	S
10		DUVALL, Samuel N.	20	m.	Laborer		"	S
11	16/16	WILEY, Nathaniel	33	m.	Farmer	600/300	Md.	
12		Elisabeth	33	f.			Pa.	
13		John L.	10	m.			O.	S
14		William F.	5	m.			"	
15		Mary C.	3	f.			"	
16		Francis J.	1	m.			"	
17	17/17	DRIGGS, Benjamin	53	m.	Farmer	3000/1400	Conn.	
18		Margaret	48	f.			Eng.	
19		William D.	19	m.			O.	S
20		John	17	m.			"	S
21		Clara S.	11	f.			"	S
22		Benjamin R.	9	m.			"	
23		Alfred B.	5	m.			"	
24	18/18	DRIGGS, Harison	24	m.	Farmer	/200	O.	M
25		Sarah J.	22	f.			"	M
26	19/19	EVANS, Joel	46	m.	Farmer	3000/1100	Va.	
27		Merinda	41	f.			O.	
28		Simpson	24	m.			"	I
29		Craven	23	m.			"	S
30		Pleasi	19	f.			"	
31		Stephen	16	m.			"	S
32		Hulda	15	f.			"	
33	20/20	BLACKLEGE, David	35	m.		/180	"	
34		Caroline	27	f.			"	
35		Hannah E.	8	f.			Ind.	S
36		Asa	5	m.			"	S

37	21/21	BLACKLEGE, Robert	27	m.	Shoemaker	300/158	O.
38		Rebecca	31	f.			"
39		Hannah F.	5	f.			" S
40		Sarah A.	7	f.			" S

Page 4   10 July 1860   Sheet 88 verso

1		Mary Ellen	4	f.			O.
2		Martha J.	10/12	f.			"
3	22/22	MERADETH, Robbert	31	m.	Wagon-maker	200/150	"
4		Sarah J.	32	f.			"
5		Elnora E.	8	f.			"
6		Mary E.	5	f.			"
7		Alphosa A.	11/12	m.			
8	23/23	THOMAS, Benjamin	39	m.	Farmer	1300/225	Md.
9		Rachel	37	f.			O.
10	24/24	THOMAS, Elwood	30	m.	Farmer	/240	"
11		Elisabeth	32	f.			"
12		Samuel B.	7	m.			"
13	25/25	SIMERAL, William	34	m.	Laborer	/140	"
14		Rachel A.	24	f.			"
15		Johnson O.	3	m.			"
16		Laura	6/12	f.			"
17	26/26	BLACKLEGE, Sarah	45	f.		2500/425	Pa.
18		Ann	22	f.			O.
19		Susan	19	f.			" S
20		Rachel	14	f.			" S
21		Tacy	9	f.			"
22		GRAY, Ensly	13	m.	Adopted		
23		BLACKLEGE, Sarah	60	f.			Pa.
24	27/27	BLACKLEGE, William	31	m.	Farmer	1100/216	O.
25		Lydia A.	27	f.			"
26		Tacy J.	5	f.			"
27		SPENCER, Thomas	2	m.			
28	28/28	BLACKLEGE, Samuel	60	m.	Farmer	1500/200	Pa.
29		Anne	44	f.			O.
30		Cyrus	11	m.			"
31		Sarah P.	8	f.			
32	29/29	DUVALL, Jeptha	57	m.	Farmer	5000/900	Pa.
33		Mary	56	f.			Va.
34		Elias	25	m.			O. S
35		Jeptha	20	m.			" S
36		Lydia	17	f.			" S
37		Marguaret	15	f.			" S
38		HOGUE, Granville	10	m.	Adopted		" S
39	30/30	BARNES, Rachel	33	f.			"
40		Mary E.	5	f.			"

1	31/31	PEEPER, William	49	m.	Farmer	3000/400	N.J.
2		Rachel	50	f.			Pa.
3		Isaac	20	m.			O.
4		Sidney	17	f.			"
5		Lydia	13	f.			"
6		William	10	m.			"
7		James	6	m.			"
8	32/32	LAMBOURN, Pheoba	76	f.			Pa.
9	33/33	ADAIR, James	50	m.	Farmer	1800/465	"
10		Elisabethe	39	f.			O.
11		Joseph M.	13	m.			" S
12		Robbert E.	12	m.			" S
13		Martha A.	10	f.			"
14		William J.	1	m.			"
15	34/34	PATTERSON, Robert	27	m.	Farmer	1600/400	Pa.
16		Hannah	25	f.			O.
17		Margaret P.	4	f.			"
18		Mary E.	1	f.			"
19		SURGESON, William	15	m.	Laborer		Pa.
20		PEEPER, Mary	14	f.	Domestic		O.
21	35/35	STREET, Emery	28	m.	Farmer	1200/146	"
22		Catharine	21	f.			"
23		Elisabeth A.	6	f.			"
24		Menerva	3	f.			"
25	36/36	LAWRENCE, William	65	m.	Farmer	1300/285	Pa.
26		Catharine	54	f.			"
27		Mary	21	f.			O.
28		Gulia A.	18	f.			" S
29		Louis A.	13	m.			"
30	37/37	EATON, George W.	28	m.	Farmer	2500/800	"
31		Mary E.	21	f.			"
32		HARRIS, Isaac	14	m.	Laborer		"
33	38/38	GRIFFETH, John	61	m.	Farmer	3500/1000	Pa.
34		Susan	46	f.			"
35		Jonna A.	27	f.			"
36		SLAY, Milton B.	20	m.	Laborer		O.
37		NELSON, Susanah	15	f.	Domestic		"
38		HUTCHINSON, A. C.	6	m.	Adopted		"
39	39/39	GRIFFETH, George W.	45	m.	Farmer	3000/500	Pa.
40		Charlott	36	f.			O.

1		Mary C.	15	f.			O. S
2		Rebecca E.	13	f.			" S
3		Roswell P.	10	m.			" S

4		GRIFFETH, Henry U.	7	m.			O. S
5		Clara	3	f.			"
6	40/40	MELLOTT, Fred-					
		arick	37	m.	Farmer	1600/420	"
7		Elisabeth	35	f.			Pa.
8		Ann E.	12	f.			O. S
9		William H.	9	m.			" S
10		Wilson W.	7	m.			" S
11		Mary J.	3	f.			"
12		STEWART, James	17	m.	Laborer		"
13	41/41	NELSON, John	79	m.	Farmer	3000/300	Pa.
14	42/42	NELSON, Washington	40	m.	Farmer	400/500	"
15		LESLEY, Sarah A.	27	f.			O.
16	43/43	HENDERSON, John	30	m.	Farmer	2075/700	Pa.
17		Deborah	30	f.			O.
18		George	11	m.			" S
19		Mary V.	8	f.			"
20		John	5	m.			"
21		William	1	m.			"
22	44/44	ELY, Elisabeth	70	f.		3000/500	Pa.
23		Ruth E.	30	f.			O.
24		SMITH, Nathan	20	m.	Laborer		"
25		THOMAS, Elisabeth	7	f.			"
26	45/45	NELSON, Thomas	51	m.	Farmer	3990/700	Pa.
27		Gemima	40	f.			O.
28		Vance	19	m.			" S
29		Washington	17	m.			" S
30		Grier	8	m.			" S
31		Emma D.	6	f.			" S
32		Adda	4	f.			"
33		COX, Martha J.	14	f.	Domestic		" S
34	46/46	STEEL, Jacob	34	m.	Farmer		"
35		Elisabeth	30	f.			"
36		Eliza J.	8	f.			"
37		William D.	8/12	m.			"
38	47/47	TIPTON, Mary K.	39	f.		1700/375	"
39		William	23	m.	Farmer		"
40		Tacy A.	21	f.			"

Page 7   10 July 1860   Sheet 90

1		Luke	20	m.			O.
2		Hannah P.	15	f.			"
3		Pheoba J.	13	f.			"
4		Joseph	11	m.			"
5	48/48	FLOWERS, James	59	m.	Farmer	800/400	Md.
6		Mary	55	f.			O.
7		Benjamin	29	m.			"

8		FLOWERS, Caroline	31	f.			O.
9		Sarah	23	f.			"
10		Charity A.	20	f.			"
11		Mary E. L. P.	9	f.			"
12	49/49	EVANS, Eli	34	m.	Farmer	800/350	"
13		Rebecca	32	f.			"
14		John A.	16	m.			" S
15		Sarah A.	14	f.			" S
16		Lemuel	11	m.			" S
17		Mary E.	9	f.			" S
18		Susan V.	4	f.			"
19		David L.	3	m.			"
20		William C.	11/12	m.			"
21	50/50	DAVIS, Alfred	54	m.	Farmer	2000/600	Pa.
22		Jane	23	f.			O.
23		James	21	m.			"
24		Ellen	19	f.			"
25		Ruth A.	15	f.			"
26		Isaih	8	m.			"
27		GRIZZLE, Sarah	25	f.	Teacher		"
28	51/51	HUTCHINSON, Alex.	45	m.	Farmer	3000/900	Pa.
29		Elenor	27	f.			O.
30		Mary J.	19	f.			"
31		John	15	m.			" S
32		Ross L.	2	m.			"
33		Clara O.	8/12	f.			"
34		STEEL, Richard	23	m.	Laborer		"
35		CRAIG, William	22	m.	Laborer		"
36	52/52	STEWARD, David	44	m.	Farmer	2500/600	"
37		Hannah	22	f.			"
38		Eugene	18	f.			" S
39		William M.	16	m.			" S
40		George E.	14	m.			" S

Page 8		11 July 1860				Sheet 90 verso	
1		Mary E.	12	f.			O. S
2		Eveline	9	f.			" S
3		Asbery	6	m.			"
4		Oliver	4	m.			"
5		Elmyra	1	f.			"
6	53/53	TAYLOR, Nimrod	42	m.	Farmer	2000/400	Va.
7		Rachel	37	f.			O.
8		Melinda J.	18	f.			" S
9		Mary E.	17	f.			" S
10		Asbery	15	m.			" S
11		James M.	13	m.			" S
12		John H.	11	m.			" S
13		Spencer R.	9	m.			" S
14		Amanda J.	7	f.			"
15		Ruth E.	5	f.			"
16		Menerva	3	f.			"

17		TAYLOR, Adison R.	10/12	m.			0.	
18	54/54	HUDSON, Thomas	44	m.	Farmer	1600/360	Pa.	
19		Sidney	44	f.			"	
20		William E.	19	m.			0.	
21		Samuel	17	m.			"	S
22		Harriet E.	14	f.			"	S
23		Emeline	8	f.			"	S
24		Asbery	6	m.			"	
25	55/55	ELOTT, Thomas	70	m.	Farmer	900/240	Pa.	
26		Caroline	28	f.			0.	
27		Lewis	8	m.			"	
28	56/56	MILLER, Henry	27	m.	Farmer	1500/500	"	
29		Sarah J.	27	f.			"	
30		John A.	6	m.			"	
31		Gemima	3	f.			"	
32		MOSBERG, William	13	m.	Adopted		"	
33	57/57	STEWARD, George	69	m.	Farmer	4500/455	Md.	
34		Nancy	65	f.			Pa.	
35		George W.	12	m.			0.	
36		Samuel L.	11	m.			"	
37	58/58	MARSHALL, John	42	m.	Cooper	350/175	Pa.	
38		Rhoda	40	f.			"	
39		William	17	m.			0.	S
40		Mary	18	f.			"	S

Page 9			11 July 1860				Sheet 91	
1		Margaret	12	f.			0.	S
2	59/59	GRIFFETH, Ephram	47	m.	Farmer	2500/400	Pa.	
3		Amanda J.	15	f.			0.	
4		Ruthvin	10	m.			"	
5		Geraldine	13	f.			"	
6		EVANS, Aaron	40	m.			"	
7	60/60	ARMSTRONG, Thomas	48	m.	Farmer	2500/500	Ire.	
8		Louisa	45	f.			0.	
9		Emeline	18	f.			"	S
10		Caloline	15	f.			"	S
11		Lorretta	14	f.			"	S
12		McDOUGLE, Jennett	31	f.	Domestic		"	
13	61/61	SCOOT, James	38	m.	Farmer	/150	Pa.	
14		Catharine	33	f.			0.	
15		Elisabeth	11	f.			"	S
16		James	8	m.			"	S
17		Jess	6	m.			"	
18		Sarah	4	f.			"	
19		David	2	m.			"	
20	62/62	GRIFFETH, Thomas	63	m.	Farmer	3800/600	Md.	
21		Elisabeth	37	f.			Ire.	

22		GRIFFETH, Franklin					
		C.	17	m.			O. S
23		Menerva J.	19	f.			" S
24		Gerge W.	12	m.			"
25		Mary C.	9	f.			"
26	63/63	GRIFFETH, Samuel	59	m.	Farmer	1900/400	Pa.
27		Mary	58	f.			N.J.
28		Thomas J.	28	m.			O.
29		Alexander	19	m.			"
30		WHITNEY, Elsy R.	16	f.	Domestic		Va.
31	64/64	HARPER, Harrison	42	m.	Farmer	3000/420	O.
32		Mortica	20	m.			" S
33		Stillwell	19	m.			" S
34		Gideon	17	m.			" S
35		Alexander	15	m.			" S
36		Mary C.	12	f.			" S
37		Byron E.	5	f.			"
38		Margaret	5/12	f.			"
39		CRAIG, Ellen	58	f.	Domestic		Ire.
40		Sally A.	17	f.	Domestic		Pa.

Page 10			**11 July 1860**			**Sheet 91 verso**	
1	65/65	SIMERAL, Citizen	34	m.	Farmer	1500/360	O.
2		Mary A.	27	f.			"
3		John L.	5	m.			"
4		Mary J.	3	f.			"
5		William H.	1	m.			"
6	66/66	RILEY, Barthaniel	40	m.	Farmer	3000/700	Va.
7		Rachel	36	f.			"
8		Crawford W.	16	m.			O. S
9		John W.	15	m.			" S
10		Eliza A.	13	f.			" S
11		Charles W.	11	m.			" S
12		James T.	9	m.			" S
13		Druzilla J.	11	f.			" S
14		May V.	7	f.			" S
15		Emeline E.	4	m.			"
16		Theodore A.	1	m.			"
17	67/67	HECKLER, Joseph	39	m.	Farmer	450/160	"
18		Nancy	28	f.			"
19		William F.	12	m.			" S
20		Helbery	9	m.			" S
21		Mary C.	6	f.			"
22		Nancy M.	2	f.			"
23	68/68	TRUAX, Daniel	38	m.	Farmer	1800/422	"
24		Margaret	29	f.			"
25		Cyrus L.	9	m.			"
26		Elwood W.	6	m.			"
27	69/69	HESS, Ann	47	f.			"
28		Margaret	17	f.			"
29		Susan	15	f.			"

30		HESS, Rebecca	12	f.			O.
31		Mary	10	f.			"
32		Robbert	7	m.			"
33		Terzza E.	5	f.			"
34		William	3	m.			"
35	70/70	PATTERSON, Daniel	71	m.	Farmer	2000/225	Ire.
36		Margaret	69	f.			"
37		Margaret	22	f.			O.
38	71/71	KEYSER, Levi	32	m.	Farmer	1500/350	"
39		Rosana	29	f.			"
40		Luther	8	m.			"

Page 11   **11 July 1860**   **Sheet 92**

1		Adaline	7	f.			O.	
2		Sansann	4	m.			"	
3		Francis E.	1	m.			"	
4	72/72	HILYMAN, Mary	60	f.		1200/200	Pa.	
5		LLOYD, Deborah	83	f.			"	
6	73/73	BAKER, William	40	m.	Farmer	300/120	Md.	
7		Nancy	35	f.			O.	
8		Sarah	13	f.			"	S
9		Rhoda J.	11	f.			"	S
10		William A.	7	m.			"	S
11		Mary E.	5	f.			"	
12		Rebecca A.	3	f.			"	
13		Albert R.	2	m.			"	
14	74/74	PICKENS, Thomas	31	m.	Laborer	/50	Pa.	
15		Nancy	28	f.			"	
16		William	5	m.			O.	
17		Mary	3	f.			"	
18		George	2/12	m.			"	
19	75/75	SOUTH, Sarah	35	f.		/25	"	
20		Samuel	13	m.			"	S
21		Benjamin T.	10	m.			"	S
22		Alfred J.	3	m.			"	
23		John W.	3	m.			"	
24	76/76	COX, William	78	m.	Farmer	2500/220	N.J.	
25		Catharine	69	f.			Pa.	
26		Dolly	34	f.			O.	
27	77/77	MOOSE, Jess	60	m.	Farmer	500/155	Pa.	
28		Susanah	50	f.			O.	
29		Isaac	16	m.			"	S
30		David	14	m.			"	S
31	78/78	MORRIS, Andrew	50	m.	Farmer	4000/800	"	
32		Mary A.	46	f.			"	
33		Wesley J.	19	m.			"	
34		Andrew J.	19	m.			"	S

35		MORRIS, Mary A.	17	f.			O.	S
36		Louisa	12	f.			"	S
37		Lucinda	11	f.			"	S
38		John	9	m.			"	S
39		Asbery S.	5	m.			"	
40	79/79	BOOTH, Thomas	48	m.	Farmer	2000/500	Eng.	

Page 12   12 July 1860   Sheet 92 verso

1		Sarah	47	f.			O.	
2		Mary E.	23	f.			"	
3		Hannah	21	f.			"	S
4		Thomas C.	18	m.	Farm laborer		"	S
5		Francis M.	14	m.			"	S
6		Isaac N.	6	m.			"	S
7		George G.	4	f.			"	S
8		LOWE, Mary J.	13	f.	Domestic		"	S
9	80/80	MILLER, Jacob	38	m.	Farmer	2500/400	Pa.	
10		Hannah	28	f.			O.	
11		Mary A.	2	m.			"	
12		Laura	5/12	f.			"	
13	81/81	MILLER, John	75	m.	Farmer	6000/800	Pa.	
14		Mary	72	f.			"	
15		Mary B.	35	f.			"	
16	82/82	PICKENS, Louis	37	m.	Laborer	/150	"	
17		Clarissa	26	f.			O.	
18		Amanda E.	4	f.			"	
19	83/83	EVANS, William	48	f.	Farmer	2500/425	"	
20		Catharine	45	f.			Pa.	
21		John	21	m.	Farm laborer		O.	
22		Zedic	18	m.	Farm laborer		"	S
23		Albert	14	m.			"	S
24		Albin	14	m.			"	S
25		William J.	7	m.			"	S
26	84/84	EVANS, John	74	m.	Farmer	4000/200	Va.	
27		Sarah	71	f.			"	
28	85/85	HILL, Isaac	22	m.	Farmer	1200/200	O.	
29		Hannah	22	f.			"	
30		Mary J.	1	f.			"	
31	86/86	YOUNG, Isaac	60	m.	Miller	1000/210	Pa.	
32		Catharine	39	f.			O.	
33		Hannible W.	13	m.			"	S
34		Albert G.	11	m.			"	S
35		Malangthon	9	m.			"	S
36		Isadore	7	m.			"	S
37		Maria T.	5	f.			"	S
38		Velva T.	4/12	f.			"	
39	87/87	MARTIN, Johnithan	52	m.	Farmer	1500/220	Ire.	

| 40 | | MARTIN, Jane | 43 | f. | | | Ire. |

1	88/88	TRIMLEY, David	25	m.	Farmer	1000/300	O.
2		Sarah A.	23	f.			"
3		Virginia J.	2	f.			Va.
4		BOSTON, Mary	12	f.			O. S
5		MARTIN, John	24	m.	Laborer		"
6	89/89	TRIMLEY, Gemima	30	f.			"
7		Elisabeth	23	f.			"
8	90/90	SLACK, John	25	m.	Farmer	2000/250	"
9		George	73	m.			Va.
10		Mary	37	f.			O.
11		Margaret	22	f.			"
12		Diantha L.	13	f.			" S
13	91/91	TRUAX, Benjamin	73	m.	Farmer	1000/150	"
14		Pheoba	68	f.			"
15	92/92	DECKER, Isaac	27	m.	Farmer	1200/300	"
16		Lydia A.	22	f.			"
17		Clark C.	3	m.			"
18		Milton	1	m.			"
19		WATTERS, Adaline	13	f.			" S
20	93/93	DECKER, George	46	m.	Farmer	2500/420	Pa.
21		Jerusha	46	f.			"
22		David	22	m.			O.
23		Jacob	19	m.			" S
24		Melinda	18	f.			" S
25		Amos	13	m.			" S
26		Eliza J.	10	f.			" S
27		George H.	6	m.			" S
28	94/94	WRIGHT, Thomas	38	m.	Farmer	5000/700	Md.
29		Sarah	36	f.			N.C.
30		William J.	14	m.			Md. S
31		Sarah O.	13	f.			" S
32		Oliva	10	f.			" S
33		Aurila W.	3	f.			O.
34		Millard L.	4/12	m.			"
35		HESS, Robbert A.	6	m.			"
36		MOOSE, Ann	21	f.	Servant		"
37		CUNNINGHAM, Samuel	24	m.	Laborer		"
38	95/95	MILLER, John	52	m.	Farmer	6000/840	Pa.
39		Mary	50	f.			O.
40		Sarah A.	19	f.			"

1		Cyrus	12	m.			O. S
2		Hannah	10	f.			" S
3		George E.	4	m.			"

4		MANN, William E.	18	m.	Laborer		O.	
5		WILSON, Abel	38	m.	Laborer		"	
6	96/96	DUNN, Johnithan	32	m.	Farmer	/150	Pa.	
7		Jane A.	25	f.			O.	
8		Sar﹒ ﹐ E.	7	f.			"	
9		Milton	4	m.			"	
10		Johnithan Jr.	1	m.			"	
11	97/97	DENT, A. Y.	45	m.	Tanner	700/600	"	
12		Jane	40	f.			"	
13		John H.	14	m.			"	S
14		Alexander E.	11	m.			"	S
15		Zdrani	5	f.			"	
16		Millard	3	m.			"	
17		SLACK, Martha	14	f.	Servant		"	
18	98/98	FORSHY, Henry	40	m.	Tanner		Pa.	
19	99/99	SIMERAL, John	36	m.	Tobacco packer			
						600/150	O.	
20		Lucretia	31	f.			Md.	
21		John S.	18	m.			O.	S
22		Susan C.	6	f.			"	S
23		Catharine	4	f.			"	
24	100/100	IMES, Isaac	31	m.	Teacher	600/240	"	
25		Lucind	30	f.			"	
26		Byron	5	m.			"	
27		Olvie	4	f.			"	
28		Caroline	3	f.			"	
29		Marion	10/12	m.			"	
30	101/101	THORNBERY, Eliza-beth	39	f.		300/145	Pa.	
31		Mary J.	8	f.			O.	
32		Galveston	3	m.			"	
33	102/102	MARSHALL, John R.	42	m.	Cooper	300/150	Pa.	
34		Rhoda	38	f.			O.	
35		William	17	m.			"	
36		Mary E.	15	f.			"	
37		Margaret A.	13	f.			"	
38	103/103	ARMSTRONG, Jas. W.	38	m.	Merchant	3000/1000	"	
39		Sarah E.	32	f.			"	
40		Eusebius	14	m.			"	S

Page 15			13 July 1860			Sheet 94	
1		Leonidas H.	12	m.			"	S
2		Wilber F.	10	m.			"	S
3		Martha A.	8	f.			"	S
4		Alice C.	6	f.			"	S
5		Ruth E.	4	f.			"	
6		Elisabeth	1	f.			"	

```
7   104/104  THORNBERY, Joseph    25   m.    Merchant     1000/150   O.

8   105/105  MOONEY, Samuel L.    30   m.    Merchant     500/       "
9            Martha               28   f.                            Pa.
10           William C.            5   m.                            O.
11           Salena                2   f.                            "

12  106/106  JACKSON, Henry Y.    39   m.    Shoemaker    400/200    N.H.
13           Mary A.              22   f.                            Ire.
14           Harvey                3   m.                            O.
15           Margaret              1   f.                            "

16  107/107  JACKSON, Samuel      24   m.    Shoemaker    /150       "
17           Mary J.              22   f.                            "
18           Mary               1/12   f.                            "

19  108/108  GADD, John           71   m.                 /100      Pa.

20  109/109  GAITS, Mary          52   f.                 300/150   Va.
21           Rebecca              45   f.                            "

22  110/110  KING, Sarah          40   f.                 250/140   O.
23           Margaret             16   f.                            "     S
24           Alfred               11   m.                            "     S
25           Arabelle              4   f.                            "

26  111/111  READ, Samuel         59   m.    Farmer       1500/300   "
27           Margaret             52   f.                            Pa.
28           James                16   m.                            O.   S
29           Samuel               18   m.                            "    S
30           Mary                 14   f.                            "    S
31           Sarah                11   f.                            "    S

32  112/112  LOHMIRE, Marion      39   m.                 300/150   "
33           Martin L.            15   m.                            "    S
34           Lucetta L.           14   f.                            "    S
35           Laonidas              9   m.                            "    S
36           Amelia                6   f.                            "    S
37           Alexander C.          4   m.                            "
38           Mary A.            11/12   f.                            "

39  113/113  CARPENTER, George    20   m.    Blacksmith   /140      "
40           Emma                 21   f.                            "
```

```
1   114/114  WOLLENWEBER, Louis   46   m.    Tailor       600/400   Brun.
2            Wilmyna              42   f.                            "
3            SMITH, Lowisa        18   f.    Domestic                O. S

4   115/115  McELROY, A.          22   m.                 /150      "
5            Martha L.            17   f.                            "
6            Martha             5/12   f.                            "

7   116/116  KING, George W.      28   m.    Blacksmith   500/160   "
8            Susan R.             22   f.                            "
```

9		KING, Amanda J.	8	f.			O. S
10		William	2	m.			"
11	117/117	LANE, A. P.	32	m.	Minister	300/160	Pa.
12		Margaret P.	24	f.			"
13		Thomas W.	4	m.			"
14		Camden F.	3	m.			O.
15	118/118	GIFFINS, George	32	m.	Laborer	250/175	"
16		Elisabeth	23	f.			"
17		Mary A.	4	f.			"
18	119/119	THORNBERY, Joseph	33	m.	Tailor	1000/100	Pa.
19		Sarah	28	f.			O.
20		Evaline	10	f.			" S
21		Lowis O.	7	m.			" S
22		Josephen	4	f.			"
23		William C.	1	m.			"
24	120/120	WILSON, William S.	57	m.	Tailor	200/135	Pa.
25		Rachel	58	f.			"
26		Ann E.	16	f.			O.
27	121/121	BROWN, John	55	m.	Farmer	3500/140	"
28		Mary	36	f.			Md.
29		John	2	m.			O.
30		CLINE, Hannah	20	f.	Domestic		"
31		Caroline	2	f.			"
32	122/122	WEBB, John A.	46	m.	Saddler	300/163	Va.
33		William G.	23	m.			"
34		Charles	18	m.			" S
35		Elisabeth	13	f.			" S
36		Thomas	10	m.			O. S
37	123/123	KIMPTON, Jane	65	f.		300/100	"
38	124/124	THORNBERY, G. W.	31	m.	Hotel-keeper	800/250	Pa.
39		Pheoba J.	21	f.			Va.
40		Virginia	5	f.			O.

Page 17			13 July 1860				Sheet 95
1		Isabell	9/12	f.			O.
2	125/125	THORNBERY, Johnson	25	m.	Tailor	450/150	"
3		Rebecca J.	23	f.			"
4		Wellington	3	m.			"
5		Emit L.	1	m.			"
6	126/126	SMITH, S. B.	37	m.	Tobacconist	500/135	"
7		Adaline	19	f.			" S
8		Millard	9/12	m.			"
9	127/127	HUFFMAN, Stephen	29	m.	Blacksmith	700/165	"
10		Louisa	18	f.			" S

11	128/128	WRIGHT, John	71	m.	Farmer	800/200	Md.	
12		Francis	65	f.			Va.	
13		Amanda	18	f.			O.	
14		GAYHART, Ellen	31	f.	Domestic		"	
15		Alonzo R.	8	m.			"	S
16	129/129	GRATIGNY, Lewis	65	m.	Physician	1000/375	Eng.	
17		Desdemonia	63	f.			Me.	
18	130/130	JOHNSON, John	36	m.	Saddler	/100	O.	
19		Anne E.	32	f.			"	
20		Eunice A.	7	f.			"	S
21		Mary C.	5	f.			"	S
22		James M.	2	m.			"	
23	131/131	GRATIGNY, Louis	33	m.	Saddler	/185	"	
24		Susanah	31	f.			"	
25		Olevia	9	f.			"	S
26		Desdemonia	7	f.			"	S
27		Caroline	3	f.			"	
28	132/132	MARSHALL, Jesse	43	m.	Farmer	1500/250	Pa.	
29		Sarah	45	f.			"	
30		William	14	m.			O.	S
31		Caroline E.	12	f.			"	S
32		ARMSTRONG, Rachel	93	f.			Md.	
33	133/133	CLINE, Mary	47	f.		/100	Va.	
34		Berthenia	16	f.			O.	S
35		Andrew J.	14	m.			"	S
36		Rachel	66	f.			Va.	
37	134/134	BEALL, Citizen	60	m.	Farmer	500/220	Md.	
38		BEBOUT, Iseral	13	m.			O.	S
39		MICHEM, Mary	65	f.	Servant		Md.	
40	135/135	GRATIGNY, Thadius	36	m.	Tanner	1000/300	O.	

Page 18		13 July 1860				Sheet 95 verso	
1		Indiana	28	f.			O.
2		Jerome	3	m.			"
3		Ida E.	1	f.			"
4		FRENDORFF, Julius	29	m.	Tanner		Ger.
5		STEWARD, Martha	18	f.	Domestic		O.
6	136/136	MORRIS, William R.	32	m.	Cabinet-maker	300/200	"
7		Rachel A.	24	f.			Pa.
8		Howard	9	m.			O. S
9		Emaline	6	f.			" S
10		Alvira	1	f.			"
11	137/137	ARNOLD, James	30	m.	Carpenter	100/125	"
12		Maria J.	23	f.			"
13		Martha	5	f.			" S
14		William	3	m.			"
15		Frank	1	m.			"

16	138/138	DANFORD, Charles						
		H.	36	m.	Farmer	900/200	O.	
17		Elisabeth	35	f.			"	
18		Mary M.	16	f.			"	S
19		Milton T.	13	m.			"	S
20		Alonzo P.	10	m.			"	S
21	139/139	LOWE, C. W.	27	m.	Tinsmith	/300	"	
22		Ellen	20	f.			"	
23		Mary E.	2	f.			"	
24	140/140	VOLENTINE, Michel	67	m.	Wagon-maker	/135	Va.	
25		Sarah	67	f.			"	
26		McDOUGLE, Carolin	14	f.	Servant		Pa.	
27	141/141	BROWN, Henry	40	m.	Drover	400/900	O.	
28		Mary J.	36	f.			"	
29		McCONELL, Martha	41	f.	Servant		"	
30		HENDERSHOT, Ice-						
		line	14	f.	Servant		"	
31	142/142	PEARSON, William	36	m.	Carpenter	400/165	Va.	
32		Mary A.	35	f.			O.	
33		Albert	14	m.			"	S
34		William	12	m.			"	S
35		George	10	m.			"	S
36		Samuel	7	m.			"	S
37		Josephene	5	f.			"	
38		Jonna L.	2	f.			"	
39		Elisabeth J.	17	f.			"	S
40	143/143	STEWARD, Noah	51	m.	Farmer	175/120	Pa.	

Page 19   13 July 1860   Sheet 96

1		Margaret	40	f.			O.	
2		Maria	20	f.			"	
3		George	18	m.			"	S
4		Desdemonia	9	f.			"	S
5	144/144	THORNBEY, Madison	46	m.	Farmer	1200/150	"	
6		Lydia	30	f.			"	
7		Shannon	22	m.			"	
8		Shanklin	20	m.			"	
9		Menerva	18	f.			"	S
10	145/145	ARMSTRONG, Ruth	70	f.		600/100	"	
11		BRENS, Charlott	21	f.	Servant		"	
12		SEWART, Mary	21	f.	Servant		"	
13	146/146	McDONELL, George	35	m.	Physician	700/380	"	
14		Alexander	8	m.			"	S
15		Winfield	6	m.			"	S
16		Elisabeth	60	f.			"	
17	147/147	JAMES, Hamilton	30	m.	Clerk	800/175	Pa.	
18		Sarah A.	26	f.			O.	

19		JAMES, Mary	5	f.			O. S
20		Edith	3	f.			"
21		Milton N.	1	m.			"
22		STEWART, Adaline	15	f.	Servant		"
23		JAMES, Oloff	9	m.			" S
24	148/148	LILLY, John	26	m.	Shoemaker	/100	Va.
25		Rebecca A.	22	f.			Pa.
26	149/149	FLETCHER, William	42	m.	Shoemaker		O.
27	150/150	EVANS, Aaron S.	42	m.	Carpenter	400/100	"
28		Nancy	41	f.			"
29		Josephena	12	f.			" S
30	151/151	THOMAS, J. K.	38	m.	Physician	300/100	Md. S
31		Almyra	28	f.			O.
32		Sarah S.	12	f.			" S
33		Mary E.	7	f.			" S
34	152/152	BLACK, John	35	m.	Wagon-maker	450/125	"
35		Emely	30	f.			"
36		Oscar C.	16	m.			" S
37		Charles	14	m.			" S
38		Lenora	7	f.			" S
39		William	3	m.			"
40	153/153	HUTCHINSON, W. H.	35	m.	Merchant	1200/800	Pa.

Page 20   13 July 1860   Sheet 96 verso

1		Mary K.	22	f.			Pa.
2		John M.	4	m.			"
3		Daniel	37	m.	Merchant	600/700	"
4		PRICE, Martha	13	f.	Domestic		O. S
5	154/154	STEWARD, Nancy	77	f.		/100	Ire.
6		Sarah	32	f.			Pa.
7	155/155	WISNER, Isaac	46	m.	Merchant	2500/3000	"
8		Roby	46	f.			Mass.
9		John H.	19	m.			O. S
10		Amanda J.	16	f.			" S
11		Adaline	9	f.			" S
12	156/156	WISNER, John	41	m.	Merchant	2000/2500	Pa.
13		Mary	38	f.			O.
14		George	16	m.			" S
15		Amanda	11	f.			" S
16		Virginia	9	f.			" S
17		Isaac	7	m.			" S
18		John	3	m.			"
19	157/157	CUMMINGS, Thomas	63	m.	Farmer	6000/2000	Md.
20		Ann	47	f.			Pa.
21		NOFFSINGER, Lu-					
		cinda	23	f.	Servant		O.

22		THORNBERY, David	17	m.		O.
23		Thomas	20	m.		"
24	158/158	HUDSON, Elija	70	m.	Farmer	"
25		ARNOLD, Adam	31	m.	Farmer	2500/500 Ger.
26		Barbary	29	f.		"
27		Mary E.	9	f.		O. S
28		John B.	5	m.		" S
29		Christopher	4	m.		" S
30		Peter	2	m.		"
31	159/159	FLETCHER, Thomas	26	m.	Farmer	600/250 "
32		Lydia A.	21	f.		"
33		Susanah	54	f.		"
34		Henretta	21	f.		"
35	160/160	WILLIAMS, Elliam	37	m.	Farmer	1600/200 "
36		Elisabeth	37	f.		"
37		Lyman	13	m.		" S
38		Martha J.	11	f.		" S
39		William A.	6	m.		" S
40	161/161	ANDREWS, John	37	m.	Farmer	/100 "

Page 21   14 July 1860   Sheet 97

1		Margaret	31	f.		O.
2		John M.	5	m.		" S
3		Mary	2	f.		"
4		Louisa	8/12	f.		"
5	162/162	ANDREWS, Charles	75	m.	Farmer	1200/140 Md.
6		Harriet	76	f.		"
7	163/163	KING, Hiram	38	m.	Farmer	1800/200 O.
8		Martha	18	f.		"
9		Elisabeth A.	15	f.		" S
10		Sarah A.	13	f.		" S
11		George W.	8	m.		" S
12	164/164	HUDSON, Elijah	40	m.	Farmer	900/160 "
13		Elisabeth	35	f.		"
14		McDonald	9	m.		" S
15		Martha	7	f.		" S
16		Maywood	2	m.		"
17	165/165	TAYLOR, John	35	m.	Farmer	1100/200 "
18		Gulia	21	f.		"
19		Lucy E.	8/12	f.		"
20	166/166	WILLIAMS, John	29	m.	Farmer	2000/500 "
21		Rebecca	23	f.		"
22		George E.	3	m.		"
23		Grammar E.	1	m.		"
24	167/167	RILEY, William	23	m.	Miller	/120 "
25		Brida S.	21	f.		"

26	168/168	ORN, Prudence	72	f.		/50	N.J.
27	169/169	WILLIAMS, Benjamin	53	m.	Farmer	/280	O.
28		Susanah	47	f.			"
29		Elisabeth J.	18	f.			" S
30		Ruhama	15	f.			" S
31		Franklin	13	m.			" S
32		Thomas M.	11	m.			" S
33		Morgan	9	m.			" S
34		Martha J.	6	f.			" S
35	170/170	MORRISON, David	43	m.	Farmer	1400/220	"
36		Mary A.	45	f.			"
37		Roena J.	14	f.			" S
38		Charles R.	12	m.			" S
39	171/171	KING, Madison	24	m.	Farmer	/165	"
40		Elisabeth	22	f.			"

Page 22			14 July 1860			Sheet 97 verso

1		Merryman L.	2	m.			O.
2	172/172	ORN, William	52	m.	Farmer	1500/500	"
3		Mary	42	f.			Va.
4		Francis M.	11	m.			O. S
5		Mary J.	7	f.			" S
6		Johnson	3	m.			"
7		Margaret	41	f.	Servant		"
8	173/173	MORRIS, Elijah	51	m.	Farmer	1600/600	"
9		Nancy	47	f.			Va.
10		Louis S.	18	m.			" S
11		William H.	16	m.			O. S
12		James W.	12	m.			" S
13		John	10	m.			" S
14		Mary E. A.	7	f.			"
15	174/174	McKIRAHAN, Joseph	28	m.	Farmer	2000/220	"
16		Mary J.	28	f.			"
17		John A.	7	m.			" S
18		William T.	6	m.			" S
19		Isaac F.	4	m.			"
20		Mary J.	3	f.			"
21		Chalmer N.	6/12	m.			"
22		DAVIS, George	17	m.	Laborer		"
23	175/175	GRATIGNY, Cyrus	38	m.	Farmer	2000/365	"
24		Elisabeth	34	f.			"
25		Caroline	15	f.			" S
26		Mary	12	f.			" S
27		Louis D.	7	m.			" S
28		Lizzy	3	f.			"
29		THORNBERRY, Marion	21	m.	Laborer		"
30	176/176	ARMSTRONG, Henry	50	m.		2700/400	Pa.
31		Margaret	42	f.			"

32	ARMSTRONG, Andrew	20	m.			O.	S
33	Francis	18	m.			"	S
34	Josiah	15	m.			"	S
35	Alfred	12	m.			"	S
36	Johnson	8	m.			"	S
37	177/177 MORRISS, Jesse	56	m.	Cabinet-maker			
				800/237		"	
38	Emely P.	57	f.			Mass.	
39	Margaret E.	17	f.			O.	S
40	Rhuben	14	m.			"	S

Page 23   17 July 1860   Sheet 98

1	178/178 KEYSER, John	45	m.	Farmer	6000/800	O.	
2	Menerva	35	f.			"	
3	William	26	m.			"	
4	Jesse	18	m.			"	S
5	John L.	8	m.			"	S
6	Joshua	6	m.			"	S
7	Rachel	4	f.			"	
8	179/179 MALLORY, Nelson	48	m.	Farmer	1800/300	"	
9	Jane	48	f.			"	
10	Harriet	18	f.			"	S
11	Jane A.	15	f.			"	S
12	Jenett	12	f.			"	S
13	180/180 RILEY, Iseral D.	47	m.	Farmer	10,000/2200	"	
14	Massa	48	f.			"	
15	Samuel	20	m.			"	S
16	Elisabeth	18	f.			"	S
17	Isabell	17	f.			"	S
18	Mary J.	14	f.			"	S
19	Richard	12	m.			"	S
20	Iseral	10	m.			"	S
21	Alfred J.	8	m.			"	S
22	George W.	5	m.			"	
23	181/181 PHILIPS, John	42	m.	Farmer	2000/300	"	
24	Rachel	42	f.			"	
25	William	21	m.			"	
26	Fanny	16	f.			"	S
27	Lydia A.	12	f.			"	S
28	George	7	m.			"	
29	John P.	9/12	m.			"	
30	182/182 STUKEY, John	38	m.	Farmer	1800/400	"	
31	Mary A.	33	f.			"	
32	Catharine	11	f.			"	
33	Hannah	61	f.			"	
34	Daniel	58	m.			"	3
35	GATTON, John	13	m.			"	S
36	183/183 STUKEY, Jacob	69	m.	Farmer	1000/225	N.J.	
37	Abigal	63	f.			Pa.	
38	Asbery	16	m.			O.	S

39	184/184	BARCUS, George	47	m.	Farmer	1000/240	O.
40		Delilah	36	f.			"

Page 24   17 July 1860   Sheet 98 verso

1	David	16	m.	O. S
2	Joseph	14	m.	" S
3	Isaac	6	m.	" S
4	Hannah	5	f.	" S
5	John	1	m.	"
6	Elisabeth	73	f.	Pa.

7	185/185	GATTEN, R. E.	47	m.	Farmer	900/240	"
8		Hannah	43	f.			"
9		Catharine J.	16	f.			O. S
10		John A.	14	m.			" S
11		Margaret	12	f.			" S
12		Mary E.	10	f.			" S
13		Eli	7	m.			" S
14		Amanda M.	4	f.			"

15	186/186	STUKEY, Isaac	35	m.	Farmer	/125	"
16		Charlott	34	f.			"

17	187/187	GAITS, James	50	m.	Tanner	/500	"
18		Mary	48	f.			Md.
19		Laben	18	m.			O. S
20		Albert	15	m.			" S
21		James P.	12	m.			" S
22		Madison C.	7	m.			" S
23		Matilda	10	f.			" S
24		Nancy	20	f.			"
25		Mary	4	f.			"
26		WATSON, Lydia	15	f.	Servant		"
27		REEDER, John	24	m.	Laborer		"
28		LEONARD, John	60	m.	Tanner		Sw.
29		GAITS, Mary	80	f.			Pa.

30	188/188	GALL, Z.	26	m.	Farmer	/300	O.
31		Harriet	24	f.			"

32	189/189	GAITS, Daniel	74	m.	Farmer	3500/400	Pa.
33		Nancy	68	f.			O.
34		Elisabeth	10	f.			"
35		Alexander	11	m.			"

36	190/190	ALBERT, Mark	38	m.	Farmer	4000/600	Ger.
37		Melissa	35	f.			O.
38		Daniel	8	m.			" S
39		Jacob	10	m.			" S
40		Samuel	6	m.			" S

Page 25   17 July 1860   Sheet 99

1	Amos	4	m.	O.
2	Lewis	2	m.	"
3	Caroline	3/12	f.	"

4		HARMIN, Lany	13	f.	Servant		O.
5	191/191	BUTLER, Susan	60	f.		/75	Pa.
6		Rachel	35	f.			O.
7		Nimrod	25	m.	Laborer		"
8		Beal	20	m.	Laborer		"
9		Thomas	19	m.	Laborer		"
10	192/192	GAITS, Mathias	37	m.	Farmer	/200	"
11		Lydia	36	f.			"
12		Henry	12	m.			" S
13		Melinda	13	f.			" S
14		Zepana	8	m.			" S
15		Simon	4	m.			"
16		Clark	1	m.			"
17	193/193	BARCUS, Daniel	36	m.	Farmer	1500/150	"
18		Elisabeth	40	f.			"
19	194/194	GAITS, Henry	44	m.	Farmer	2500/500	"
20		Louisa	38	f.			"
21		Samuel	17	m.			" S
22		Percilia	14	f.			" S
23		Elisabeth	10	f.			" S
24		Nancy	8	f.			" S
25		Pearson	6	m.			" S
26		Tenty	2	f.			"
27		Douglass	8/12	m.			"
28	195/195	BEBOUT, Pearson	28	m.	Farmer	/100	"
29		Catharine	22	f.			"
30		George W.	1	m.			"
31		Samuel	7	m.			" S
32	196/196	PITTMAN, John	37	m.	Farmer	2000/225	"
33		Margaret J.	38	f.			Va.
34		Mary	15	f.			O. S
35		Elisabeth	13	f.			" S
36		David E.	11	m.			" S
37		Grier	9	m.			" S
38		Ira	6	m.			"
39		Isora	3	f.			"
40		Margaret	6/12	f.			"

Page 26   17 July 1860   Sheet 99 verso

1		EARLYWINE, Mary	86	f.			Md.
2	197/197	DECKER, John	50	m.	Farmer	2500/200	Pa.
3		Pheoba	48	f.			"
4		William	18	m.			O. S
5		David	16	m.			" S
6	198/198	DECKER, George	22	m.	Farmer	500/250	"
7		Lydia	20	f.			"
8		Pheoba A.	3	f.			"

9	199/199	WORKMAN, William	40	m.	Farmer	2000/400	O.	
10		Elisabeth	37	f.			"	
11		Sarah J.	17	f.			"	S
12		Martha J.	15	f.			"	S
13		Robbert	12	m.			"	S
14		Elisabeth J.	7	f.			"	S
15		David G.	1	m.			"	
16		STEWART, John	10	m.	Adopted		"	S
17	200/200	HEADLEY, Isaac	27	m.	Farmer	2500/238	"	
18		Deborah	25	f.			"	
19		WHEELER, Margaret	48	f.	Servant		Md.	
20		Elisabeth	11	f.			O.	
21	201/201	HEADLEY, Silais	55	m.	Farmer	3500/400	Va.	
22		Seville	56	f.			"	
23		Barbary	17	f.			O.	S
24		SHEPARD, Andrew	12	m.	Adopted		"	S
25	202/202	PITTMAN, Theodore	40	m.	Farmer	600/230	"	
26		Eliza A.	36	f.			"	5
27		Ida	17	f.			"	S
28		Matilda	16	f.			"	S
29		David	13	m.			"	S
30		Louis	11	m.			"	S
31		John	9	m.			"	S
32		Theodore	6	m.			"	S
33		William	3	m.			"	
34	203/203	AULT, Peter	40	m.	Farmer	1000/184	"	
35		Catharine	35	f.			"	
36		Volentine	16	m.			"	S
37		Mary C.	14	f.			"	S
38		William	12	m.			"	S
39		David	10	m.			"	S
40		Melvin	4	m.			"	

Page 27			17 July 1860				Sheet 100
1		Sarah J.	8	f.			O. S
2	204/204	WHEELER, Henry	30	m.	Farmer	1200/240	"
3		Nancy	28	f.			"
4		Mary J.	6	f.			" S
5		Robbert	4	m.			"
6		Clark S.	2	m.			"
7	205/205	SMITH, James	53	m.	Farmer	400/200	"
8		Dorothy A.	43	f.			"
9		George	20	m.			" S
10		Matilda	17	f.			" S
11		Clark	13	m.			" S
12		Sarah A.	10	f.			" S
13		Amanda E.	5	f.			
14	206/206	HEADLEY, John	32	m.	Farmer	1400/200	"
15		Susanah	25	f.			"

16	207/207	MELLOTT, James	33	m.	Miller	1800/500	O.	
17		Louisa J.	30	f.			"	
18		William H.	12	m.			"	S
19		Elisabeth A.	11	f.			"	S
20		Reason	9	m.			"	S
21		Greer	8	m.			"	S
22		Lafayette	6	m.			"	
23		Clark	2	m.			"	
24		Hulda J.	3/12	f.			"	
25	208/208	POOL, Samuel	60	m.	Farmer	1800/462	Md.	
26		Sarah	43	f.			O.	
27		Catharine	19	f.			"	S
28		Mathias	17	m.			"	S
29		George	13	m.			"	S
30		Margaret	4	f.			"	
31		William S.	7	m.			"	S
32		Sarah E.	2	f.			"	
33	209/209	MELOTT, William	47	m.	Farmer	1900/248	"	
34		Ruth	47	f.			"	
35		Gilbert	22	m.	Farmer		"	
36		Sarah	16	f.			"	S
37		Henry	18	m.	Farmer		"	S
38		Peter	12	m.			"	S
39		Hester	10	f.			"	S
40		Abert	7	m.			"	S

Page 28			**17 July 1860**				**Sheet 100 verso**	
1		Isabell	2	f.			O.	
2	210/210	SLACK, Houston	39	m.	Farmer	/110	"	
3		Susann	38	f.			"	
4		Elisabeth A.	10	f.			"	S
5		Hamilton	6	m.			"	S
6		George	2	m.			"	
7	211/211	WILLIAMS, Joseph	51	m.	Farmer	350/180	Pa.	
8		Susanah	47	f.			"	
9		Mary E.	18	f.			Va.	S
10		Thomas	13	m.			"	S
11	212/212	DAKEN, John	42	m.	Farmer	400/100	"	
12		Jane	40	f.			O.	
13		Henophin	16	m.			"	S
14		Ebenezar	14	m.			"	S
15		Mary	12	f.			"	S
16		Catharine	10	f.			"	S
17		Sarah	4	f.			"	
18		Peter	1	m.			"	
19	213/213	BUSH, Richard	40	m.	Farmer	600/165	"	
20		Mary A.	37	f.			Va.	
21		Isaac	20	m.	Farmer		O.	S
22		Nancy J.	18	f.			"	S

23		BUSH, Salathiel	16	m.			O. S
24		Adaline	14	f.			" S
25		Albina	11	f.			" S
26		Caroline	7	f.			" S
27		William E.	5	m.			"
28		Lilly A.	4	f.			"
29		Semantha	4/12	f.			"
30	214/214	AULT, Joseph	19	m.	Laborer	/100	"
31		Nancy	18	f.			"
32		Henry N.	1/12	m.			"
33	215/215	MELLOTT, Levi	42	m.	Farmer	2500/400	"
34		Elisabeth	32	f.			"
35		John	12	m.			" S
36		Theodore	11	m.			" S
37		Margaret	8	f.			" S
38		Sarah E.	6	f.			" S
39		David N.	4	m.			"
40		Amanda A.	1	f.			"

1	216/216	MELOTT, Peter	42	m.	Farmer	3000/900	O.
2		Catharine	39	f.			"
3		Thomas	18	m.			" S
4		Huma J.	12	f.			" S
5		William	6	m.			"
6		Milly A.	2	f.			"
7		Peter	83	m.			Pa.
8		Hester	79	f.			"
9	217/217	MOOSE, Isaac	30	m.	Farmer	250/100	O.
10		Marcila	22	f.			"
11		John W.	12	m.			" S
12		Anna	6	f.			"
13		Daniel	4	m.			"
14	218/218	SINGLEDECKER, John	70	m.	Farmer	/100	Pa.
15		Mary	62	f.			"
16		Isaac	15	m.			O. S
17	219/219	SINGLEDECKER,					
		George	30	m.	Farmer	300/145	"
18		Mary	35	f.			"
19		Peter	15	m.			" S
20		William	7	m.			" S
21		Alexander	5	m.			"
22		Amanda J.	3	f.			"
23		George	1	m.			"
24	220/220	PITTMAN, Johnson	64	m.	Farmer	500/100	Pa.
25		Mary	65	f.			"
26	221/221	PITTMAN, Moses	24	m.	Laborer	/125	O.
27		Lydia	34	f.			"
28		David B.	1	m.			"

29	222/222	TENER, David	60	m.	Farmer	1500/350	Md.	
30		Elisabeth	52	f.			"	
31		David B.	27	m.			O.	
32		Elisabeth	23	f.			"	S
33		TOWNSEND, Evenas	11	m.			"	S
34	223/223	POULSON, Mortimore	50	m.	Laborer	/100	Va.	
35		Olevia	48	f.			"	
36		Hannah L.	20	f.			O.	S
37		Franklin	17	m.			"	S
38		John W.	14	m.			"	
39	224/224	JEFFRIES, James	28	m.	Farmer	1000/200	"	
40		Agnes	24	f.			"	

Page 30　　　　　　　18 July 1860　　　　Sheet 101 verso

1	225/225	BONAR, David	40	m.	Farmer	2000/420	Pa.	
2		Elisabeth	36	f.			O.	
3		Hester	15	f.			Pa.	S
4		Elisabeth	14	f.			O.	S
5		Samuel N.	13	m.			"	S
6		Joseph	10	m.			"	S
7		William	9	m.			"	S
8		Newton	8	m.			"	S
9		Martha A.	6	f.			"	S
10		David	5	m.			"	
11		Barnett	3	m.			"	
12		Pheoba V.	1	f.			"	
13	226/226	KING, G. W.	26	m.	Farmer	2500/220	"	
14		Elisabeth	27	f.			"	
15		Oscar B.	6/12	m.			"	
16	227/227	KING, David	47	m.	Farmer	/350	"	
17		Fanny	48	f.			"	
18		Jackson	22	m.	Farmer		"	
19		Thomas J.	18	m.			"	S
20		Gulia A.	20	f.			"	S
21		Isabell	16	f.			"	S
22		Adam J.	13	m.			"	S
23		Franklin P.	10	m.			"	S
24	228/228	JEFFRIES, William	60	m.	Farmer	7000/700	Ire.	
25		Mary	46	f.			O.	
26		Isabell	19	f.			"	S
27		Benjamin	18	m.	Farmer		"	S
28		Pheoba	16	f.			"	S
29		William	15	m.			"	S
30		Robbert	14	m.			"	S
31		Marria	12	f.			"	S
32		Joseph	10	m.			"	S
33		Isaac	8	m.			"	
34		McPLYAR, Andrew	6	m.			"	
35	229/229	MYERS, William	45	m.	Farmer	3000/600	"	

36		MYERS, Sarah	42	f.			O.
37		David	21	m.	Farmer		"
38		James	18	m.	Farmer		" S
39		Abraham	15	m.			" S
40		Sarah	11	f.			" S

Page 31   18 July 1860   Sheet 102

1		Massy L.	9	f.			O. S
2		Pheoba	7	f.			" S
3	230/230	SMITH, Joseph	39	m.	Farmer	2500/375	Pa.
4		Eda	37	f.			"
5		Johnson	18	m.			O. S
6		Matilda	15	f.			" S
7		Margaret J.	11	f.			" S
8		Eda	7/12	f.			"
9	231/231	TRIMBLY, John C.	23	m.	Laborer	/200	"
10		Catharine	20	f.			" S
11		Clara	1	f.			"
12	232/232	SMITH, David	35	m.	Farmer	3000/400	"
13		Melinda	28	f.			"
14		Menerva C.	11	f.			" S
15		Joshua T.	10	m.			" S
16		Mary E.	8	f.			" S
17		Elisabeth A.	6	f.			"
18		Shedarick A.	5	m.			"
19		Jacob V.	2	m.			"
20	233/233	McELROY, Jess	40	m.	Farmer	800/189	"
21		Louisa	32	f.			"
22		Johnson	14	m.			" S
23		Jesse	12	m.			" S
24		Elisabeth	8	f.			" S
25		John	6	m.			" S
26		Oliver	2	m.			"
27	234/234	SMITH, Joel	28	m.	Farmer	1800/309	"
28		Hannah	24	f.			"
29		Rosa	2	f.			"
30	235/235	SMITH, Rebecca	60	f.			Pa.
31		Elisabeth A.	13	f.			O. S
32	236/236	HOOD, Sylvenas	28	m.	Farmer	1000/305	"
33		Elisabeth	20	f.			"
34		Martha J.	3	f.			"
35		William J.	6/12	m.			"
36	237/237	McELROY, Allen	50	m.	Farmer	1000/300	Pa.
37		Elisabeth	49	f.			"
38		William	19	m.	Farmer		O. S
39		Albert	16	m.			" S
40		Sarah	13	f.			" S

| Page 32 | | | | | 18 July 1860 | | | Sheet 102 verso |

1		McELROY, Isaac	12	m.			O.	S
2	238/238	McDOUGLE, Theadore	49	m.	Blacksmith	100/225	"	
3		Mary	48	f.			Md.	
4		William	21	m.	Blacksmith		O.	
5		Mary J.	17	f.			"	S
6		Barbary	15	f.			"	S
7		Thomas	13	m.			"	S
8		Amanda	5	f.			"	
9	239/239	ANDERSON, James	58	m.	Farmer	765/238	Md.	
10		Hannah	49	f.			O.	
11		Charles	23	m.	Farmer		"	
12		John T.	21	m.	Farmer		"	
13		Wilber H.	19	m.	Farmer		"	S
14		James H.	16	m.	Farmer		"	S
15		Garwood	11	m.			"	S
16		Benjamin F.	8	m.			"	S
17		Sylvester	5	m.			"	
18	240/240	MELOTT, Benjamin	45	m.	Farmer	2000/400	"	
19		Mary	30	f.			"	
20		Abby	13	f.			"	S
21		Rebecca	11	f.			"	S
22		Charles	9	m.			"	S
23		Franklin	7	m.			"	S
24		Clarisa	5	f.			"	
25		George	3	m.			"	
26	241/241	MEAK, George	40	m.	Farmer	1800/346	Pa.	
27		Newton	18	m.			O.	S
28		Elisabeth A.	11	f.			"	S
29		Robbert F.	6	m.			"	S
30		William N.	3	m.			"	
31		DENT, Mary A.	39	f.	Domestic		"	
32		CRAMER, Cyntha	23	f.	Domestic		"	
33	242/242	JONES, Jesse	77	m.	Farmer	1200/239	Va.	
34		Rachel	70	f.			"	
35	243/243	PITTMAN, Benjamin	45	m.	Farmer	/168	O.	
36		Margaret	40	f.			"	
37		Peter	11	m.			"	S
38		James	9	m.			"	S
39		John W.	6	m.			"	
40		William H.	4	m.			"	

| Page 33 | | | | | 18 July 1860 | | | Sheet 103 |

1	244/244	MEEKS, William	47	m.	Farmer	4000/380	Pa.	
2		Jane	41	f.			"	
3		Martha	16	f.			O.	S
4		Sarah	12	f.			"	S
5		Margaret	11	f.			"	S
6		Henry H.	8	m.			"	S

7		MEEKS, McPlyar	6	m.		O.
8		Angeline	4	f.		"
9		Louisa	2	f.		"
10		WHITTEM, Margaret	90	f.		Pa.
11	245/245	HUBBS, George	65	m.	Farmer	3000/600 Eng.
12		Martha	62	f.		"
13		Martha	38	f.		
14		James	21	m.	Farmer	O.
15	246/246	HUBBS, John	25	m.	Farmer	/195 Va.
16		Nancy	19	f.		O. S
17		Abner	2	m.		"
18		Western	6/12	m.		"
19	247/247	MORRIS, Richard	42	m.	Farmer	/100 "
20		Martha	37	f.		"
21		Caroline	14	f.		" S
22		BARCUS, Thomas	14	m.		" S
23	248/248	PARMER, Jacob	42	m.	Farmer	/125 "
24		Barthenia	26	f.		"
25		Peter	1	m.		"
26		TIDEMORE, Merinora	10	f.		"
27	249/249	PARMER, Peter	71	m.	Farmer	4000/400 Pa.
28		Mary	65	f.		"
29	250/250	PARMER, William	31	m.	Farmer	/300 O.
30		Margaret	27	f.		"
31		Anne J.	12	f.		" S
32		Mary E.	8	f.		" S
33		Sarah E.	6	f.		" S
34		Gulia A.	3	f.		"
35		Martha	5/12	f.		"
36	251/251	KEYSER, Jacob	24	m.	Farmer	/200 "
37		Mary L.	22	f.		"
38		Pheoba J.	1	f.		"
39	252/252	SNIDER, Levi	35	m.	Farmer	1000/300 "
40		Mary	30	f.		"

Page 34		18 July 1860				Sheet 103 verso
1		Gulia E.	15	f.		O. S
2		William	13	m.		" S
3		Oswell	10	m.		" S
4		Jesse W.	7	m.		" S
5		Anne J.	2	f.		"
6	253/253	TRUAX, Edward	34	m.	Farmer	/100 "
7		Mary	26	f.		"
8		John S.	11	m.		"
9		Geo. W.	9	m.		"
10		Nathan G.	7	m.		"
11		William M.	1	m.		

12	254/254	HESS, John C.	47	m.	Blacksmith	4000/500	Pa.	
13		Sarah A.	39	f.			O.	
14		Louisa A.	18	f.			"	S
15		Adrian	17	m.			"	S
16		Martha E.	15	f.			"	S
17		Eliza	5	f.			"	S
18		John W.	1	m.			"	

19	255/255	LINDSY, Abraham	31	m.	Farmer	2000/400	"
20		Susann	30	f.			"
21		HUDSON, William	19	m.	Laborer		"

22	256/256	KIPTON, David	25	m.	Farmer	2000/350	"
23		Rachel	24	f.			"
24		John L.	3	m.			"
25		Elisabeth	1	f.			"

26	257/257	COULTER, Andrew	52	m.	Farmer	/160	Pa.	
27		Pheoba	47	f.			O.	
28		William	28	m.	Farmer		"	
29		Jesse	19	m.	Farmer		"	S
30		Abraham	18	m.	Farmer		"	S
31		Harison	15	m.			"	S
32		Sarah	14	f.			"	S
33		Pheoba	11	f.			"	S
34		Margaret	10	f.			"	S
35		John H.	7	m.			"	S
36		Amos	5	m.			"	
37		Nancy	4	f.			"	
38		Elisabeth	75	f.			Del.	

39	258/258	SMITH, Henry	68	m.	Farmer	2000/400	Pa.
40		Effamy	60	f.			"

Page 35   18 July 1860   Sheet 104

1		John	21	m.	Laborer		Pa.	

2	259/259	THORNBEY, Yearsley	55	m.	Farmer	3000/500	Pa.	
3		Alice	49	f.			"	
4		John	21	m.	Farmer		O.	S
5		Albert	17	m.	Farmer		"	S
6		Wilberforce	9	m.			"	S
7		Desdemonia	6	f.			"	S
8		SLACK, Agnes	35	f.	Domestic		"	
9		Losetta	6	f.			"	

Page 36   Sheet 104 verso

I do Certify that the within Contains a true statement
of the Census of Sunsbery Township taken by me in pursuance
of the Law and Instructions received by me for that purpose
that the same is truly taken as I verily believe August 23rd
1860 and the number of pages of Schedule 1 is thirty-five and
a fraction over.

Thomas O. Little, A. M.
For Sunsbery Township, M. C. O.

Sworn to and subscribed before me this 23rd day of
August 1860.

Daniel Walton, Clerk
Of Monroe Co. Com. Pleas

* * *

Ohio Township   P. O. Hannibal

Page 1					16 July 1860			Sheet 105	
1	1/1	WINKLER, Joseph	39	m.	Farmer	1000/400	Sw.		
2		Elisabeth	40	f.			"		
3		Rudolph	13	m.			"		
4		Joseph	12	m.			"		
5		Mary Ann	11	f.			"		
6		Godfrey	9	m.			"		
7		John	7	m.			"		
8		Sophia	3	f.			O.		
9	2/2	RODOCKER, Fred	27	m.	Farmer	1600/470	Sw.		
10		Anna	30	f.			O.		
11		John	25	m.	Farmer		Sw.		
12		Emma	3	f.			O.		
13		William J.	1	m.			"		
14	3/3	BEAR, Jacob	44	m.	Carpenter	600/100	Pa.		
15		Rachel	52	f.			"		
16	4/4	LEHMAN, Jacob Jr.	35	m.	Farmer	1800/1300	Sw.		
17		Barbary	33	f.			"		
18		Thoffield	11	m.			O.	S
19		Daniel	9	m.			"	S
20		Edward	7	m.			"	
21		Louisa	5	f.			"	
22		Barbary	3	f.			"	
23		Jacob	2	m.				
24	5/5	LEHMAN, Jacob Sr.	55	m.	Farmer	800/325	Sw.		
25		Mary	67	f.			"		
26	6/6	INGOLD, Jacob	55	m.	Farmer	1600/800	"		
27		Barbary	50	f.			"		
28		John	25	m.			"		
29		Jacob	16	m.			"		
30		Joseph	13	m.			O.	S
31		Mary Ann	20	f.			Sw.	
32		Rosean	18	f.			"	
33		Caroline	10	f.			O.	S
34		Louisa	6	f.			"	S
35	7/7	KERNOW, Saml.	47	m.	Farmer	600/250	Sw.		
36		Sarah	46	f.			"		
37		Mary	17	f.			"	S
38		Jacob	15	m.			"	S
39		Saml.	11	m.			"	S
40		David	10	m.			O.	S

1		KERNOW, John	7	m.			O. S
2	8/8	LUTHY, John Sr.	57	m.	Farmer	2000/900	Sw.
3		Mary	62	f.			"
4		Louisa	27	f.			O.
5		Samuel	23	m.	Teacher		"
6		Christian	22	m.	Farmer		"
7	9/9	SPRING, David	32	m.	Farmer	400/200	Sw.
8		Elisabeth	33	f.			"
9		Elisabeth	6	f.			N.Y. S
10		Augustus	5	m.			" S
11		Roseana	3	f.			" S
12		Mary	1/2	f.			"
13	10/10	SNIDER, J. G.	47	m.	Farmer	400/125	Bad.
14		Magdalena	41	f.			"
15		Gustaves	15	m.			" S
16		Pius	12	m.			Pa. S
17		John	10	m.			" S
18		Oswald	8	m.			O. S
19		Godfrey	6	m.			"
20		Elisabeth) Twins	4	f.			"
21		Louisa)	4	f.			"
22		Augustus	2	m.			"
23	11/11	KERPER, Theopolis	40	m.	Farmer	800/160	Sw.
24		Elisabeth	30	f.			"
25		Barnabus	12	m.			O. S
26		Batula	11	f.			" S
27		Elisamo	9	m.			" S
28		Arelia	7	f.			" S
29		Elisabeth	6	f.			" S
30		Jemima	4	f.			"
31		Gotleip	1	m.			"
32	12/12	NISPERLEY, Jacob	60	m.	Miller-Farmer 3000/1000		Sw.
33		Frances	55	f. M.			Va.
34		David	32	m.	Sawyer		O.
35		John	25	m.	Miller		"
36		Lewis	23	m.	Miller		"
37		Martin	18	m.	Farmer		"
38		Mary	30	f.			"
39		Emily	21	f.			"
40		Elisabeth	16	f.			" S

1		Caroline	13	f.			O. S
2		Catherine	10	f.			" S
3	13/13	DERKES, Charles	39	m.	Farmer	500/200	Ger.
4		Elisabeth	35	f.			Sw.
5		Christena	4	f.			O.
6		Fred	2	f.			"

7		DERKES, Ann E.	1/4	f.			O.	
8	14/14	TISHER, Nicholas	46	m.	Farmer	2500/800	Sw.	
9		Roseanna	40	f.			"	
10		Elisabeth	18	f.			O.	
11		John	16	m.			"	S
12		Mary Ann	14	f.			"	S
13		Susan	10	f.			"	S
14		Louisa	4	f.			"	S
15		Rosana	2	f.			"	
16	15/15	HOMELL, Andrew	26	m.	Farmer	500/100	H-D.	
17		Elisabeth	22	f.			O.	
18		Catherine	1	f.			"	
19	16/16	ZEH, Fred	65	m.	Farmer	800/270	Wur.	
20		Elisabeth	56	f.			"	
21		Frederic	28	m.	Farmer		"	
22		John	20	m.	Farmer		O.	
23		Geo.	19	m.	Farmer		"	
24		Mary	11	f.			"	S
25	17/17	ANDERICKS, Fred	54	m.	Farmer	300/100	Sw.	
26		Anna	54	f.			"	
27		John	18	m.	Farmer		"	
28		Rosean	12	f.			"	
29	18/18	TALBOTT, Upton	52	m.	Miller	3000/500	Md.	
30		Mary	45	f.			Pa.	
31		John	25	m.			O.	
32		Cornelia	21	f.			"	
33		Nancy E.	19	f.			"	S
34		Roderic	15	m.			"	S
35		Mary F.	10	f.			"	S
36		Alberta	7	f.			"	S
37		Stella	4	f.			"	
38	19/19	MOBBERLY, William	25	m.	Laborer	/100	"	
39		Jane	22	f.			"	
40		John W.	5	m.			"	

Page 4			17 July 1860			Sheet 106 verso		
1		Chas. W.	2	m.			O.	
2		Henry T.	1/2	m.			"	
3	20/20	LUDI, Geo.	58	m.	Physician	/100	Wur.	
4		Catherine	56	f.			Sw.	
5	21/21	LUDE, Geo. Jr.	34	m.	Farmer	1500/400	Wur.	
6		Mary Ann	30	f.			"	
7		John C.	10	m.			O.	S
8		J. Ludwic	9	m.			"	S
9		J. George	7	m.			"	S
10		J. Micheal	5	m.			"	
11		Mary A.	4	f.			"	
12		William C.	1	m.			"	

13	22/22	LUDE, Michael	30	m.	Farmer	900/450	Wur.	
14		Sarah	28	f.			O.	
15		Roseana	7	f.			"	S
16		George	4	m.			"	
17		Matilda	2	f.			"	
18	23/23	SNIVELY, Benj.	59	m.	Farmer	800/100	Pa.	
19		Mary Ann	41	f.			O.	I
20		James	19	m.			"	S
21		John	16	m.			"	S
22		Charles	13	m.			"	S
23		Marion	10	m.			"	
24		Eliza J.	6	f.			"	
25		Mary A.	3	f.			"	
26	24/24	BAUR, John C.	60	m.	Tanner-Farmer			
						1000/800	Sw.	
27		Catherine	47	f.			Pr.	
28		John	20	m.	Farmer		O.	S
29		Catherine	15	f.			"	S
30		Frederic	5	m.			"	
31	25/25	TAYLOR, John W.	31	m.	Farmer	3000/600	"	
32		Hannah	28	f.			"	
33		Sarah A.	6	f.			"	
34		Jas. H.	5	m.			"	
35		Thos. W.	3	m.			"	
36		Mary J.	1/2	f.			"	
37	26/26	SHILLING, Jacob	41	m.	Farmer	1000/100	Ger.	
38		Martha E.	37	f.			"	
39		Philip	12	m.			"	
40		Henry	10	m.			"	

Page 5   17 July 1860   Sheet 107

1		Catherine	7	f.			Ger.	
2		Margaret	5	f.			O.	
3		Augustus	4	m.			"	
4		Charles	2	m.			"	
5	27/27	MENGUS, Eve	55	f.	Widow	/600	Pa.	
6		Andrew	21	m.	Farmer		O.	
7		James	17	m.	Farmer		"	S
8	28/28	SHAW, William	24	m.	Farmer	3000/700	Va.	I
9		Rebecca	32	f.			O.	
10		James	12	m.			"	S
11		Ruth	6	m.			"	
12		John A.	4	m.			"	
13		Joseph	1	m.			"	
14	29/29	GOTHERD, Charles	30	m.	Farmer	800/400	Ger.	
15		Frederica	26	f.			"	
16		William	6	m.			O.	
17		Amelia	3	f.			"	
18		Henry	1/2	m.			"	

19	30/30	GOTHERD, Henry	64	m.	Farmer	500/200	Ger.
20		Frederica	60	f.			"
21	31/31	GOTHERD, Augustus	58	m.	Farmer	/100	"
22		Wilhelamina	56	f.			"
23	32/32	HILLER, Nicholas	48	m.	Laborer		H-C.
24		Catherine	43	f.			"
25		Lorence	12	m.			"
26		Anne E.	7	f.			"
27		Louisa	3	f.			"
28	33/33	THOMAS, Jacob	33	m.	Farmer	500/200	Pa.
29		Mary	21	f.			O.
30		Nancy	1	f.			"
31	34/34	HEGERSTON, Henry	54	m.	Farmer	1000/200	Ger.
32		Elisabeth	40	f.			"
33		Mary	4	f.			O.
34		Amelia	1	f.			"
35	35/35	THOMAS, Micheal	67	m.	Farmer	800/350	Pa.
36		Rachel	64	f.			"	I
37	36/36	THOMAS, Micheal Jr.	35	m.	Farmer	/100	"
38		Elisabeth	33	f.			O.
39		Mary L.	7	f.			"
40		Rachel J.	2	f.			"

Page (6)   17 July 1860   Sheet 107 verso

1	37/37	WETTER, David	42	m.	Farmer	800/500	Sw.
2		Catherine	38	f.			"
3		John	15	m.	Farmer		O. S
4		Elisabeth	13	f.			" S
5		David	10	m.			" S
6		Catherine	7	f.			" S
7		Mary	5	f.			"
8		Magdulena	2	f.			"
9	38/38	BRUNY, Magdulena	67	f.	Widow	500/150	Sw.
10	39/39	KASSEMIAN, Stephen	62	m.	Farmer	1500/450	"
11		Ann Elis	64	f.			"
12		Jacob	18	m.	Farmer		"
13	40/40	BRUNEY, John	58	m.	Farmer	2200/550	"
14		Mary A.	55	f.			"
15		Charlotte L.	24	f.			O.
16		John	18	m.	Farmer		"
17		Mary M.	14	f.			" S
18		FISHER, August	26	m.	Laborer		
19	41/41	WALTER, Jacob	28	m.	Shoemaker	/100	Sw.
20		Anna	25	f.			"
21		Louisa	6	f.			O.
22		Mary	4	f.			"

23		WALTER, Caroline	2	f.			O.	
24		Jacob	1/4	m.			"	
25	42/42	THOMEN, David	62	m.	Farmer	2000/530	Sw.	
26		Mary	57	f.			"	
27		David	17	m.	Farmer		O.	
28		Rosean	15	f.			"	
29		Elisabeth	14	f.			"	S
30	43/43	RUBY, John	25	m.	Farmer	2500/700	"	M
31		Caroline	20	f.			"	M
32	44/44	NEARGART, John	50	m.	Carpenter	/100	Sw.	
33		GISSER, John	8	m.			O.	
34	45/45	MITTENDORF, Fred-						
		erica	59	f.	Widow	1800/225	Wur.	
35		George	25	m.	Farmer		O.	
36		Sophia	19	f.			"	
37		Roseana	16	f.			"	
38		Mary	14	f.			"	S
39	--/46	MITENDORF, Ben	32	m.	Farmer	/100	Han.	
40		Susan	26	f.			O.	

Page 7   17 July 1860   Sheet 108

1		Caroline	9	f.			O.	S
2		John	6	m.			"	S
3		Louisa	3	f.			"	
4	46/47	ENSINGER, Adam	49	m.	Farmer	800/250	Wur.	
5		Elisabeth	31	f.			Sw.	
6		John	9	m.			O.	S
7		Christian	7	m.			"	S
8		Lydia	5	f.			"	
9		Amelia	1/12	f.			"	
10		Caroline	3	f.			"	
11	47/48	HICKS, Joseph	43	m.	Farmer	600/200	"	
12		Mary	48	f.			Va.	
13		John	22	m.	Boatman		O.	
14		Wm.	20	m.	Farmer		"	
15		Isaac	18	m.	Farmer		"	
16		Araminta	12	f.			"	S
17		Roseana	10	f.			"	S
18		Joseph	8	m.			"	S
19	48/49	CESHES, Christian	43	m.	Farmer	2800/900	Sw.	
20		Barbary	30	f.			"	
21		Godfrey	16	m.	Farmer		O.	S
22		Eliza	4	f.			"	
23		Anna	2	f.			"	
24		Amy	5/12	f.			"	
25	49/50	DENNIS, David	44	m.	Farmer	800/175	"	I
26		Mary	46	f.			"	I
27		Henry	18	m.	Farmer		"	S

28		DENNIS, John	15	m.	Farmer		O.	S
29		Elisabeth	13	f.			"	S
30		Leander	9	m.			"	S
31		James	4	m.			"	
32	50/51	HOWELL, Martha	48	f.	Widow	2500/400	"	
33		Jacob	27	m.	Farmer		"	
34		Benj.	18	m.	Farmer		"	
35		Mary A.	12	f.			"	
36		Margaret	7	f.			"	
37	51/52	HOWELL, Freeman	29	m.	Farmer	/100	"	
38		Sophia	31	f.			"	
39		Sarah J.	7	f.			"	
40		Madison	5	m.			"	

Page 8			18 July 1860				Sheet 108 verso	
1		Elisabeth	3	f.			O.	
2	52/53	SMITH, Jacob	58	m.	Farmer	2000/600	Pa.	
3		Ruth	55	f.			"	I
4	53/54	LITMAN, Isaac	39	m.	Laborer	/200	O.	
5		Abigail	32	f.			"	
6		Kissiah	15	f.			"	S
7		Job	14	m.			"	S
8		Jacob	11	m.			"	S
9		Edmund	7	m.			"	S
10		Luel	5	m.			"	
11		Isaac	3	m.			"	
12		Anna	1	f.			"	
13	54/55	WANKE, Joseph	37	m.	Farmer	400/200	Aus.	
14		Terrisa	39	f.			"	
15		Cesillia	12	f.			"	S
16		Martha	10	f.			"	S
17		Sarah	6	f.			O.	S
18		Louisa	3	f.			"	
19		Joseph	3/4	m.			"	
20		KAMMERMAN, C.	45	m.	Laborer		Sw.	
21	55/56	HARRISON, Fleming	30	m.	Farmer	800/300	O.	
22		Mary	24	f.			"	
23		Amanda	3	f.			"	
24		Emma	1/2	f.			"	
25	56/57	MOSENEY, Lewis	71	m.	Farmer	500/350	Conn.	
26		Roseanna	66	f.			Va.	
27		Lewis	21	m.	Farmer		O.	
28		Joseph	32	m.	Farmer		"	
29		Melissa	19	f.			"	
30		Angelia	17	f.			"	
31	57/58	MESSERLY, Abram	49	m.	Farmer	800/450	Sw.	
32		Ann	54	f.			"	
33		William	23	m.	Farmer		N.Y.	

```
34          MESSERLY, Anthoney  21    m.    Farmer              N.Y.

35   58/59  HONISA, Fred        46    m.    Farmer      1600/500 Wur.
36          Christena           44    f.                         Sw.
37          Mary                15    f.                         O. S
38          Elis                13    f.                         "  S
39          Sarah                9    f.                         "

40   59/60  WALTER, Jacob       25    m.                1200/300 Bav.
```

Page 9   18 July 1860   Sheet 109

```
1           Margaret            24    f.                         Fr.
2           Amelia               3    f.                         O.
3           Geo. W.              2    m.                         "
4           Mary S.           4/12    f.                         "

5    60/61  KOON, Micheal       72    m.    Laborer             Fr.

6    60/61  BRENZEKOFFER, Chris-
            tian                36    m.    Farmer       500/300 Sw.
7           Susan               31    f.                         "
8           Edward               8    m.                         O. S
9           Caroline             7    f.                         "  S
10          Charles L          1/2    m.                         "
11          Peter               32    m.    Laborer             Sw.
12          GERBER, C.          60    m.    Laborer             "

13   61/62  NITCHE, Micheal     49    m.    Farmer       400/150 Aus.
14          Barbary             45    f.                        Wur.
15          Charles             16    m.    Farmer              "
16          Catherine           10    f.                         O. S
17          Mary                 7    f.                         "  S
18          Mariah               3    f.                         "
19          Rosean               2    f.                         "

20   62/63  GEHRIG, Christ      37    m.    Farmer      2000/500 Sw.
21          Mariah              35    f.                         "
22          Serah                6    f.                         O. S
23          John H.              4    m.                         "
24          Rebecca              2    f.                         "

25   63/64  SINGENWALD, Chas.   35    m.    Farmer       500/200 Sax.
26          Barbary             30    f.                        Wur.
27          Mary                 9    f.                         Va.
28          Dorathea             5    f.                         "

29   64/65  PEARSOLL, Jesse     29    m.    Farmer         /200  O.
30          Mary J.             28    f.                         "
31          Irwin                7    m.                         "
32          Mary E.              4    f.                         "
33          Ruth V.              1    f.                         "

34   65/66  PEARSOLL, Job       72    m.    Farmer      1000/100 Pa. I
35          Nathan              44    m.    Cripple             "  I
```

36	66/67	HOWELL, Job	38	m.	Farmer	300/700	O. I
37		Christena	38	f.			"
38		Anthoney	16	m.	Farmer		"
39		Isaac	15	m.	Farmer		"
40		James	11	m.			"

1		Eliza	9	f.			O.
2		Wm. Henry	7	m.			"
3		Harriet	6	f.			"
4		Pheoba	5	f.			"
5		Ruth A.	3	f.			"
6		not named	1	f.			"
7	67/68	BOWERY, Sabastian	60	m.	Farmer	2500/550	Ger.
8		Elisabeth	53	f.			Pa.
9		Sabastian	32	m.	Farmer		"
10		Robt.	24	m.	Farmer		O.
11		Isaac	18	m.	Farmer		"
12		Elisabeth	20	f.			"
13		Geo.	16	m.	Farmer		" S
14		Caroline	14	f.			" S
15		Abba J.	12	f.			" S
16	68/69	CRIST, Wm.	32	m.	Farmer	700/150	" I
17		Rebecca	22	f.			"
18		Abba J.	3	f.			"
19		Cammilla	1	f.			"
20	69/70	HOSKINS, Sarah	82	f.	Widow	/50	Pa. I
21		STEENROD, Nancy	48	f.	Widow		O.
22		Mary	4	f.			"
23	70/71	STEENROD, Wm.	27	m.	Farmer	2000/200	"
24		Eliza A.	23	f.			"
25		Mary E.	4	f.			"
26		Sarah	2	f.			"
27	71/72	CRAIGE, John	50	m.	Laborer	/50	"
28		Elisabeth	58	f.			"
29		Jerome	26	m.	Laborer		"
30	72/73	RUBLE, Micheal	52	m.	Farmer	300/175	Wur.
31		Fredericka	39	f.			"
32	73/74	ESTENHORSH, Detrich	53	m.	Carpenter	/100	Han.
33		Roseana	40	f.			Sw.
34		Louisa	14	f.			O.
35		John	12	m.			"
36		Christian	9	m.			"
37		Detrich	5	m.			"
38		Fred	2	m.			"
39	74/75	KASSERMAN, Fred	33	m.	Farmer	1200/350	Sw.
40		Catherine	32	f.			"

Page 11   18 July 1860   Sheet 110

1		KASSERMAN, Louisa	4	f.			O.
2		Stephen	3	m.			"
3		Edward	2	m.			"
4		FRICK, Geo.	16	m.	Laborer	/500	Pa. S
5		KASSERMAN, Mary	18	f.	Domestic		O.
6	75/76	LEUKART, John	52	m.	Farmer	400/250	Sw.
7		Mary Ann	33	f.			O. I
8		Catherine	14	f.			" S
9		Elisabeth	12	f.			" S
10		John	10	m.			" S
11		David	8	m.			" S
12		Christian	7	m.			"
13		Peter	3	m.			"
14		Saml.	2	m.			"
15	76/77	CRIST, John	55	m.	Farmer	300/200	Pa. I
16		Polly	64	f.			" I
17		Samuel	57	m.	Laborer	/200	" I
18	77/78	OLIVER, Giles	22	m.	Laborer		O.
19		Elisabeth	22	f.			" I
20		John	3	m.			"
21		Job	3/4	m.			"
22	78/79	SALTZER, Geo.	58	m.	Farmer	400/200	Wur.
23		Catherine	51	f.			"
24		Loenard	16	m.	Farmer		" S
25	79/80	ROACH, Adam	55	m.	Laborer		O.
26		Julian	46	f.			"
27		James	20	m.	Laborer		"
28		Vandusan	19	m.	Laborer		" S
29		Joseph	17	m.	Laborer		"
30		Sarah	15	f.			"
31		Julian	10	f.			"
32		Barbary	7	f.			"
33	80/81	YONLY, John J.	33	m.	Farmer	300/100	Wur.
34		Catherine	43	f.			"
35		John J.	4	m.			O.
36	81/82	ENTERMAN, Chris-					
		tian	41	m.	Farmer	500/250	Wur.
37		Mary M.	42	f.			"
38		Christian F.	13	m.			"
39		Jacob T.	12	m.			"
40		Mary M.	11	f.			"

Page 12   18 July 1860   Sheet 110 verso

1		Gotleip	9	m.			Wur.
2		Christian C.	5	m.			O.
3		Catherine D.	3	f.			"
4		John F.	1 1/2	m.			"

5	82/83	PUGH, Jesse	45	m.	Farmer	800/350	O.	
6		Angeline	40	f.			"	I
7		Ruth A.	19	f.			"	
8		David	18	m.	Farmer		"	
9		Herculas	14	m.			"	S
10		John	12	m.			"	S
11		Susan	10	f.			"	S
12		Mariah	8	f.			"	S
13		Terissa	5	f.			"	
14		Delia	2	f.			"	
15	83/84	MILLER, Samuel	29	m.	Farmer	500/125	Sw.	
16		J. S.	50	m.	Farmer		"	
17		Elisabeth	34	f.			"	
18	84/85	MOSER, John	48	m.	Carpenter	/300	"	
19		Elisabeth	17	f.			"	
20		John	15	m.			"	S
21		Mary	13	f.			"	S
22		Eliza	11	f.			"	S
23		Fred	6	m.			O.	
24		Charlotte	3	f.			"	
25	85/86	SHAFER, Fred	48	m.	Farmer	1000/350	Wur.	
26		Christeena	47	f.			"	
27		Catherine	18	f.			O.	
28		Adam	15	m.			"	S
29		Roseana	13	f.			"	S
30		Barbary	11	f.			"	S
31		Frederic	8	m.			"	S
32		Fredericka	6	f.			"	
33		John	4	m.			"	
34	86/87	STETSON, Geo. H.	34	m.	Farmer	1000/200	"	
35		Sarah	37	f.			"	
36		Joseph	13	m.			"	S
37		Franklin	1C	m.			"	S
38		Mary J.	9	f.			"	S
39		Eliza A.	7	f.			"	S
40		James L.	4	m.			"	

Page 13   19 July 1860   Sheet 111

1		Sarah A.	2	f.			O.	
2	87/88	VOGLE, Joseph	48	m.	Farmer	500/200	Aus.	
3		Terrissa	38	f.			"	
4		Joseph	13	m.			"	S
5		Mary A.	15	f.			"	
6		John	11	m.			"	S
7		Francisco	9	f.			"	S
8		Frantz	7	m.			"	S
9		Terissa	5	f.			"	
10		Frederick	3	m.			"	
11		Wilhelamina	1	f.			O.	
12	88/89	HOWELL, Hamilton	50	m.	Farmer	700/300	"	

13		HOWELL, Mary S.	12	f.			O.
14		Louisa	10	f.			"
15		Joseph	8	m.			"
16	89/90	HENTHORN, Richard	23	m.	Blacksmith		"
17		Kis. ah	24	f.			"
18		Jacoo	3/4	m.			"
19	90/91	COULTER, Mary	51	f.	Widow	400/100	Md.
20		Geo. M.	21	m.	Farmer		O.
21	91/92	PALMER, Andrew	35	m.	Farmer	400/100	Pa.
22		Sarah	42	f.			O. I
23		Amanda J.	13	f.			"
24		Grandason) twins	11	m.			" S
25		Joseph)	11	m.			" S
26		Wm.	8	m.			"
27		Saml.	3	m.			"
28		Lewis W.	1	m.			"
29	92/93	MASER, Benedict	56	m.	Farmer	500/100	Sw.
30		Mary	50	f.			"
31	93/94	HARISON, Martin	45	m.	Farmer	1500/500	O.
32		Catherine	38	f.			"
33		Emaline	15	f.			" S
34		Pheoba	13	f.			" S
35		Jesse	12	m.			" S
36		Martha	8	f.			" S
37		Elisabeth	6	f.			"
38		Mary	3	f.			"
39		Ruth	1	f.			"
40	94/95	KREIGE, John	53	m.		500/275	Wur.

Page 14			19 July 1860			Sheet 111 verso	
1		Elisabeth	60	f.			Wur.
2		Catherine	18	f.			O.
3		Elisabeth	12	f.			" S
4	95/96	KEIDASH, Geo.	45	m.	Farmer	1200/600	Wur.
5		Rosean	42	f.			"
6		John	16	m.			" S
7		George	14	m.			" S
8		Roseana	12	f.			O. S
9		Adam	10	m.			" S
10		Christena	8	f.			" S
11		Anna M.	6	f.			" S
12		Alexander	2	m.			"
13	96/97	LITMAN, John W.	43	m.	Farmer	2000/700	"
14		Ruth	41	f.			"
15		Adaline	20	f.			" S
16		Mary	18	f.			" S
17		Edward	16	m.			" S

18		LITMAN, John W.	14	m.			O.	S
19		Rheuhama	12	f.			"	S
20		George	9	m.			"	S
21		Walker	8	m.			"	S
22		MOSENEY, Isaiah	21	m.	Laborer		"	

23	97/98	SKINNER, Wm.	35	m.	Laborer		"	
24		Naomi	23	f.			"	I
25		Martha J.	4	f.			"	
26		Dennis	1	m.			"	

27	98/99	MUHLEMAN, John Esq.	56	m.	Farmer	8000/1200	Sw.	
28		Mary	39	f.			"	
29		Charles T.	26	m.	Clk. on Boat		C.	
30		Godfrey	24	m.	Clk. on Boat		"	
31		Julius	17	m.	Clk. on Boat		"	
32		Louisa	12	f.			"	S
33		Augustus	10	m.			"	S
34		Emly	5	f.			"	S
35		Wilhelamina	4	f.			"	
36		CAUFMAN, Joseph	35	m.	Laborer		Sw.	
37		SUTER, John	18	m.	Laborer		Pa.	
38		Margaret	16	f.	House maid		"	

| 39 | 99/100 | MOSENEY, Cornelius | 44 | m. | Farmer | 1500/600 | O. | |
| 40 | | Nancy | 38 | f. | | | " | |

Page 15   19 July 1860   Sheet 112

1		Milton	17	m.	Farmer		O.	S
2		Roseana	15	f.			"	S
3		George	14	m.			"	S
4		Jane	12	f.			"	S
5		Fleming	10	m.			"	S
6		Ruth	4	f.			"	
7		Cornelia	1/2	f.			"	

| 8 | 100/101 | MOSENEY, Alex. | 25 | m. | Laborer | | " | M |
| 9 | | Amy | 23 | f. | | | Va. | M |

10	101/102	HENDERSON, Ber-thaniel	30	m.	Cooper	/100	O.	I
11		Rachel	32	f.			"	I
12		John	12	m.			"	S
13		Hiram	8	m.			"	S
14		Mary	6	f.			"	S
15		William	4	m.			"	
16		no name	2/12	m.			"	

17	102/103	MARTIN, Adam	57	m.	Farmer	1200/600	Sw.	
18		Magdelena	55	f.			"	
19		John	29	m.	Farmer		"	
20		Jacob	27	m.	Farmer		"	
21		Adam	25	m.	Farmer		"	
22		Randolph	18	.n.	Farmer		"	
23		Barbary	20	f.			"	

24	103/104	THOMPSON, Isaac	55	m.	Ship carpenter		O.
						3000/300	
25		Mary Ann	44	f.			Va.
26		Adaline	23	f.			O.
27		Mary E.	15	f.			" S
28		Virginia	11	f.			" S
29		Adaline	2	f.			"
30		REID, James	33	m.	Farmer		Va.
31	104/105	BARE, John	50	m.	Farmer	2000/500	Pa.
32		Sarah	48	f.			O.
33		Franklin	17	m.			" S
34		Alfred	15	m.			" S
35		George	13	m.			" S
36		Sarah F.	12	f.			" S
37		Virginia	10	f.			" S
38		John	8	m.			" S
39		Jane	1	f.			"
40	105/106	JONES, Jacob T.	46	m.	Wagoner	200/300	Pa. I

1		Mary	46	f.			Pa.
2		Amanda	22	f.			"
3		James	2	m.			O.
4	106/107	TISHER, John	50	m.	Farmer	4000/1000	Sw.
5		Pheoba	48	f.			"
5		Abram	24	m.	Carpenter		O.
6		John	22	m.	Carpenter		"
7		Alex	17	m.	Farmer		" S
8		William	15	m.	Farmer		" S
9		Geo.	12	m.			" S
10		Saml.	8	m.			" S
11		Mary Ann	14	f.			" S
12	107/108	FRY, Peter	59	m.	Laborer	/50	Pa.
13		Sarah	56	f.			"
14		Jacob	22	m.	Laborer		O.
15		Joshua	19	m.	Laborer		"
16	108/109	TISHER, Samuel	37	m.	Farmer	1600/500	"
17		Louisa	30	f.			"
18		Helen J.	12	f.			" S
19		Caroline	8	f.			" S
20		Elisabeth	4	f.			"
21		Emma	3	f.			"
22		Charles A.	3/4	m.			"
23		SUTER, Saml.	12	m.			Pa. S
24	109/110	ANGUS, Wm.	26	m.	Teacher	/125	O.
25		Mary C.	20	f.			"
26		Isadore E.	2	f.			"
27		Margaret	3/4	f.			"
28	110/111	OBER, David	67	m.	Laborer	/100	Pa.
29		Elisabeth	58	f.			"

30		WATERS, Jas.	10	m.			Va.	
31	111/112	SUTER, Ann	54	f.	Widow	300/	Sw.	I
32		Jacob	33	m.	Laborer		O.	I
33		Elisabeth	19	f.			"	
34		Nancy J.	10	f.			"	S
35	112/113	GEHRING, John M.	56	m.	Farmer	400/200	Sax.	
36		Roseana	39	f.			"	
37		Henry	21	m.	Farmer		"	
38		Lewis	11	m.			"	S
39		Emma	4	f.			O.	
40		Betta	2	f.			"	

Page 17   20 July 1860   Sheet 113

Baresville

1	113/114	BARE, Ann	60	f.	Widow	6000/300	Va.	
2		Wm.	15	m.	Farmer		O.	S
3		CNEILL, Charles	14	m.			"	S
4	114/115	ONEILL, Nancy	45	f.	Widow	400/100	"	
5		Benson	21	m.	Carpenter		"	
6		Cornelia	19	f.			"	S
7	115/116	WILLIAMS, Robt.	50	m.	Millwright	1500/300	"	
8		Sarah	40	f.			Pa.	
9		Jane E.	21	f.			O.	
10		Hannah	19	f.			"	S
11		Mary L.	16	f.			"	S
12		Benj. F.	14	m.			"	S
13		Roseana	10	f.			"	S
14		Sarah	8	f.			"	S
15		Seth O.	5	m.			"	S
16		Harriet	3	f.			"	
17	116/117	WILLIAMS, Saml.	33	m.	Millwright	1500/300	"	
18		Ruth A.	33	f.			"	
19		Emma	7	f.			"	S
20		Sarah	4	f.			"	
21	117/118	KEYSER, William	34	m.	Laborer	/100	"	
22		Elisabeth	32	f.			"	
23		Araminta	8	f.			"	S
24		Mary E.	6	f.			"	S
25		Margaret	4	f.			"	
26		Juliet	2	f.			"	
27	118/119	LLOYD, Humphrey	45	m.	Plasterer	1200/200	Pa.	
28		Christena	39	f.			Va.	
29		Isaac	20	m.	Plasterer		O.	S
30		Edward	16	m.	Plasterer		"	S
31		Winfield	13	m.			"	S
32		Arthur	7	m.			"	S
33		Humphrey	3	m.			"	
34	119/120	REIMER, William	25	m.	Physician	/100	Pa.	

35		REIMER, Agnes	2C	f.		Va.	
36		Ella	1	f.		"	
37		BARE, Mary	16	f.	Domestic	Pa.	
38	120/121	RAY, W. T.	37	m.	Mate on Boat /100	"	
39		Mary	25	f.		O.	
40		John	5	m.		"	

Page 18   20 July 1860   Sheet 113 versi

1		Thomas	3	m.		O.	
2		Elisabeth	2/12	f.		"	
3	121/122	HENTHORN, Adam	42	m.	Watchman on boat /200	Va.	
4		Cassy A.	40	f.		O.	
5		Alonzo F.	18	m.	Scholar	"	S
6		Nimrod E.	16	m.	Scholar	"	S
7		Charles	14	m.		"	S
8		Mary V.	12	f.		"	S
9		Martha	10	f.		"	S
10		Sarah	8	f.		"	S
11		Elisabeth	4	f.		"	
12		Mary	75	f.	Widow	Md.	
13	122/123	HOFFER, John	23	m.	Miller /100	Pa.	
14		Susanah	23	f.		O.	
15	123/124	KREPS, Ben	27	m.	Wagon-maker	Sw.	
16		Elizabeth	25	f.		O.	
17		John	4	m.		"	
18		Alexander	3	m.		"	
19	124/125	NOLL, S. W.	43	m.	Post Master 4200/600	Pa.	
20		Mary A.	33	f.		O.	
21		John	14	m.		"	S
22		Syrus	12	m.		"	S
23		Elisabeth	7	f.		"	S
24		Martin	10	m.		"	S
25		Mary Etta	3	f.		"	
26		nct named	1/2	f.		"	
27		BORTMAN, Martha	20	f.	Domestic	"	
28	125/126	NOLL, David P.	35	m.	Blacksmith 1600/2000	Sw.	
29		Rebecca	27	f.		Pa.	
30		James P.	5	m.		Ky.	
31		Geo. W.	4	m.		O.	
32		Wm. H.	2	m.		"	
33	126/127	KAST, Wm.	25	m.	Merchant /1600	Pa.	
34		Mary	28	f.		O.	
35	127/128	KAST, Geo.	63	m.	2500/300	Wur.	
36		Barbary	57	f.		"	
37		Joseph	17	m.		Pa.	
38	128/129	HARISON, Andrew	35	m.	500/300	O.	

```
39            HARISON, Lathana    31    f.                          O.
40            Charles              4    m.                          "
```

Page 19   20 July 1860   Sheet 114

```
1             Ann B.               2    f.                          O.

2             ISANBARTH, Casper   48    m.    Shoemaker  1200/700  Wur.
3             Mary                40    f.                          "
4             Christian           13    m.    Shoemaker            O.  S
5             Roseman             16    f.                          "   S
6             Isaac               14    m.                          "   S
7             Catherine           12    f.                          "   S
8             Barbary             10    f.                          "   S
9             Sarah                8    f.                          "   S
10            John                 6    m.                          "
11            Eve                  4    f.                          "
12            Margaret             2    f.                          "

13  130/131  TISHER, Isaac        29    m.    Mate on Boat
                                                        1200/400   "
14            Helen               27    f.                          "
15            Sarah               10    f.                          "   S
16            Almedia              8    f.                          "   S
17            Isaac                2    m.                          "
18            VARNER, Jane        18    f.    Domestic              "

19  131/132  CLINE, Perry        40    m.    Cooper     1500/600   "
20            Elisabeth           39    f.                         Va.
21            Lucy F.             13    f.                          O.  S
22            Rebecca             11    f.                          "   S
23            Worth                9    m.                          "
24            Adam                 3    m.                          "   S
25            Mary               1/2    f.                          "

26  132/133  NOLL, Mary A.       34    f.               400/      Va.
27            Saml.               13    m.                          O.  S
28            Elisabeth           11    f.                          "   S
29            Franklin             9    m.                          "   S
30            John                 6    m.                          "   S

31  133/134  NISPERLY, Lewis Sr. 57   m.    Engineer   1000/200   Sw.
32            Margaret            49    f.                          "
33            Roseana             22    f.                          O.
34            Saml.               20    m.                          "
35            Elisabeth           17    f.                          "   S
36            Sarah               12    f.                          "   S
37            Rebecca              4    f.                          "

38  134/135  LANKERD, Jno.  A.   49    m.                          Pa.
39            Sarah A.            31    f.                          O.
```

Page 20   20 July 1860   Sheet 114 verso

```
1             Eliza J.             8    f.                          O.  S
2             Margaret             6    f.                          "   S
3             Mary                 5    f.                          "
```

4		LANKERD, Saml. R.	3	m.			O.
5		Jno. A.	2	m.			"
6	135/136	BOICE, John A.	40	m.	Physician	1200/900	Pa.
7		Sarah M.	21	f.			O.
8		Jno. M.	4	m.			"
9		Jesse V.	2	m.			"
10	136/137	VOEGTLY, Martin	54	m.	Merchant	5000/3500	Sw.
11		Elisabeth	43	f.			
12		Alex	18	m.			Pa. S
13		Albert	16	m.			O. S
14		John	13	m.			" S
15		Josephine	9	f.			" S
16		Jacob	5	m.			"
17		LUEKART, Rosana	19	f.			"
18		HEDINGER, Susan	17	f.			Sw.
19		Emma	14	f.			O.
20		MILLER, John F.	54	m.			Sw. 5
21	137/138	RIST, Andrew	29	m.		1100/200	Bad.
22		Julian	30	f.			Bav.
23		Anne	5	f.			O.
24		Emmil	3	m.			"
25		Julian	1	f.			"
26	138/139	HINDMAN, John	43	m.			Va.
27		Christena	18	f.			"
28		Accles	4	f.			"
29	139/140	RIST, Paul	38	m.		1000/300	Ger.
30		MEYER, Susan	21	f.			Sw.
31	140/141	REITHMILLER, John G.	30	m.		800/300	Wur.
32		Regenia	28	f.			"
33		Alexander	5	m.			O.
34		Hermon	1/2	m.			"
35		AMWEIGH, Henry	26	m.	Apprentice		Sw.
36		MATELY, Fred	23	m.	Blacksmith		"
37	141/142	GRIFFIN, Geo.	57	m.	Carpenter	/300	Va.
38		Elisabeth	55	f.			"
39		Elisabeth J.	22	f.			"

Page 21   20 July 1860   Sheet 115

1		Catherine	20	f.			Va. S
2		Wm.	14	m.			" S
3		Mary B.	1	f.			O.
4	142/143	NOLL, John Sr.	73	m.	Gunsmith	/100	Pa.
5		Elisabeth	72	f.			"
6	143/144	DUNLAP, John R.	46	m.	Miller	4000/1100	Pa.
7		Catherine	47	f.			Md.

8		DUNLAP, Absclom	21	m.		O.	
9		Susanah	16	f.		"	S
10		Catherine	14	f.		"	S
11		John	9	m.		"	S
12	144/145	HOFFER, Samuel	43	m.	Miller	4000/1100 Pa.	
13		Mary	41	f.		"	
14		Martin	20	m.	Miller	O.	S
15		Sarah	18	f.		"	S
16		Margaret	16	f.		"	S
17		Adam H.	14	m.		"	S
18		Susan	10	f.		"	S
19		Hester A.	7	f.		"	S
20		Rebecca	2	f.		Mo.	S
21		Susan	64	f.	Widow	Pa.	
22	145/146	SHUMAKER, Henry	32	m.	Cabinet-maker	/200 Ger.	
23		Christena	30	f.		Sax.	
24		Caroline	6	f.		Va.	
25		John	4	m.		O.	
26		Charles	2	m.		Va.	
27	146/147	SUTER, John	36	m.	Tavern keeper	/500 O.	
28		Sarah	35	f.		"	
29		Geo. C.	8	m.		"	S
30		Mary V.	7	f.		"	S
31		Anne E.	5	f.		"	
32		Westley	3	m.		"	
33		Gilbert M.	1/3	m.		"	
34		STRAIN, J. T.	36	m.	Boat builder	"	
35		NOLL, Joseph	22	m.	Blacksmith	Pa.	
36		HARRISON, Jesse	64	m.	Hostler	Md.	
37		Anna	22	f.	Domestic	O.	
38		HARTER, Margaret	57	f.	Widow-Seamstress		
						300/	N.Y.
39		Mary	28	f.	Seamstress	O.	

Page 22   20 July 1860   Sheet 115 verso

1	147/148	NISPERLY, Lewis					
		Jr.	24	m.	Blacksmith	/200 O.	
2		Sarah J.	20	f.		"	
3		John L.	1/12	m.		"	
4	148/149	THOMPSON, Geo.	53	m.	Ship carpenter		
						1800/500	"
5		Margaret	47	f.		Ire.	
6		Edward B.	18	m.		O.	S
7		Mary J.	16	f.		"	S
8		Sarah	14	f.		"	S
9		Martha	12	f.		"	S
10		Geo.	10	m.		"	S
11		Wm.	8	m.		"	S
12		Margaret	6	f.		"	
13	149/150	MONROE, John	25	m.	Tinner	/800	"
14		Malinda	22	f.			"
15		James H.	3/4	m.			"

16   HENDERSON, Lucinda 22   f.   O.

23   Baresville contains 213 inhabitants.

Page 23		26 July 1860			Sheet 116	
1	150/151 MUHLEMAN, Fred	47	m.	Farmer	7000/6000	Sw.
2	Elisabeth	40	f.			"
3	Edward	16	m.			O. S
4	Mary	15	f.			" S
5	Caroline	13	f.			" S
6	Henry	12	m.			" S
7	Sarah	10	f.			" S
8	Emma	8	f.			" S
9	Robert	7	m.			" S
10	Charles	6	m.			" S
11	REITS, John	30	m.	Stone-mason		Sw.
12	MUHLEMAN, John	86	m.	Retired		"
13	151/152 MUHLEMAN, Barbary	74	f.	Widow	/5000	"
14	152/153 MUHLEMAN, Albert	52	m.	Farmer	4000/800	"
15	Anna	41	f.			
16	Josephine	19	f.			O. S
17	Eliza	17	f.			" S
18	Samuel	15	m.			" S
19	Augustus	13	m.			" S
20	Sophia	11	f.			" S
21	Albert	10	m.			" S
22	Salome	8	f.			" S
23	Joanna	1/3	f.			"
24	153/154 HARRISON, Jackson	29	m.	Captain of S. Boat	3000/2000	"
25	Louisa	24	f.			Va.
26	Josephine	17	f.			"
27	John R.	13	m.			"
28	154/155 ANSHUTTS, Margaret	55	f.	Widow	4000/1000	Fr.
29	Phillip	21	m.			O.
30	Louisa	18	f.			"
31	Rebecca	14	f.			"
32	155/156 MOSENEY, Andrew	54	m.	Farmer	/300	Va.
33	Sarah	44	f.			O.
34	Mary J.	22	f.			"
35	Phoeba	21	f.			"
36	Dennis	20	m.			"
37	Anna	19	f.			"
38	Sophia	18	f.			"
39	Washington	17	m.			" S

Page 24		26 July 1860			Sheet 116 verso	
1	Wm. Henry	14	m.			O. S
2	Nancy	13	f.			" S

3		MOSENEY, John	12	m.			O.	S
4		Julia	3	f.			"
5		Charles	2	m.			"
6	156/157	STETSON, Jane	64	f.	Widow		Pa.
7		Mary	25	f.			O.
8	157/158	MUHLEMAN, John	56	m.	Farmer	10,000/1000	Sw.
9		Susan	45	f.			"
10		Fred	20	m.			O.
11		John	17	m.			"	S
12		Joseph	17	m.			"	S
13		Henry	14	m.			"	S
14		Caroline	9	f.			"	S
15	/159	CUTLER, William	27	m.	Steward on boat		Va.
16		Mary	27	f.			O.
17		Juliett	4	f.			"
18		Louisa	2	f.			"
19	158/160	MUHLEMAN, Jacob	58	m.	Farmer	8000/800	Sw.
20		Catherine	56	f.			"
21		Jacob	26	m.	Farmer		O.
22		Rudolph	23	m.	Farmer		"
23		J. L.	21	m.	Farmer		"
24		Roseana	17	f.			"	S
25		Caroline	16	f.			"	S
26	159/161	MUHLEMAN, Godfrey	32	m.	Carpenter	/500	"
27		Margaret	29	f.			Pa.
28		John A.	5	m.			O.
29		Mary	2	f.			"
30		ANSHUTTS, Phillip	18	m.	Apprentice		"
31	160/162	PORTER, Wm.	50	m.	Farmer	/500	Pa.
32		Amelia A.	40	f.			N.Y.
33		Marinda	17	f.			O.
34		Perrine	12	m.			"
35		Winfield	10	m.			"
36		Franklin	8	m.			"
37		William	3	m.			Va.
38		Edward	1/2	m.			O.
39	161/163	PERRINE, Mary	80	f.	Widow	4000/300	N.Y.

Page 25   26 July 1860   Sheet 117

1	162/163	GLASFORD, Margaret	83	f.	Widow		Pa.
2		Alexander	40	m.	Laborer		"
3	163/165	FISHER, Charles	44	m.	Tanner	500/400	Wur.
4		Elisabeth	40	f.			Ger.
5		Charles	19	m.			O.
6		Roseana	17	f.			"
7		Mary	15	f.			"	S
8		John F.	12	m.			"	S

9		FISHER, Christian	10	m.			O.	S
10		Margaret J.	7	f.			"	S
11		Sarah E.	6	f.			"	S
12		Isaac	4	m.			"	
13		William	3	m.			"	
14		Elisabeth	1	f.			"	
15	164/166	COULTER, John	29	m.	Laborer	/100	"	
16		Eliza J.	22	f.			"	
17		Julian	3	f.			"	
18		Wm. M.	1/4	m.			"	
19	165/167	HENTHORN, N. E.	49	m.	Physician	/500	Va.	
20		Nancy	43	f.			Mass.	
21		Matilda	21	f.			O.	
22		John W.	19	m.			"	
23		James	17	m.			"	
24		Demming	15	m.			"	S
25		Adam	11	m.			"	S
26		Geo.	7	m.			"	S
27		Nimrod	5	m.			"	
28		Charles	2	m.			"	
29	x	DURKEE, Benj.	77	m.	Retired		Conn.	
30	166/168	COULTER, Edward	27	m.	Cooper	/100	O.	
31		Lydia J.	23	f.			"	
32		Nimrod M.	5	f.			"	
33		Allice J.	2	f.			"	
34		x HENTHORN, Margaret						
		B.	2	f.			"	
		(x should be at 30)						
35	167/169	FRY, Geo.	25	m.	Laborer		"	
36		Nancy	36	f.			Pa.	
37		Mary A.	17	m.			O.	
38		Wm. Henry	14	m.			"	S
39		Geo. D.	10	m.			"	S

Page 26   26 July 1860   Sheet 117 verso

1		Martin V.	8	m.			O.	
2		Sampson T.	4	m.			"	
3		Sarah E.	3	f.			"	
4	168/170	STEWARD, Uriah	42	m.	Laborer		Pa.	I
5		Elisabeth	36	f.			O.	
6		Penelpe	18	f.			"	
7		Leomy	16	f.			"	
8		Mary	14	f.			"	S
9		Acel	12	m.			"	S
10		Chas. W.	9	m.			"	S
11		Wm. T.	5	m.			"	
12		Nimrod	1	m.			"	
13	169/171	ATKINS, Asail Jr.	28	m.	Laborer		O.	I
14		Lucretia	28	f.			"	I
15		Wm. P.	10	m.			"	S

16		ATKINS, Mary	7	f.			O.	S
17		John W.	4	m.			"	
18		Samuel	1	m.			"	
19	/172	ATKINS, Asail Sr.	65	m.	Laborer		Vt.	
20		Mary	58	f.			Va.	I
21	170/173	GEORGE, Chris-						
		topher	79	m.	Laborer		Wur.	
22		Heunetta	77	f.			"	
23	171/174	THOMPSON, Sarah	85	m.	Widow		Pa.	
24		Jacob	38	m.	Farmer		O.	
25		BOOTH, Susan	45	f.	Widow		"	
26		Victoria	20	f.			"	S
27	172/175	MONTIETH, James	33	m.	Farmer	2000/300	Pa.	
28		Susan	28	f.			O.	
29		Barbary E.	4	f.			"	
30		Anna	2	f.			"	
31	173/176	HARTER, John	57	m.	Farmer	2500/400	Pa.	
32		Vina	43	f.			O.	
33		Henry F.	24	m.	Farmer		"	
34		Ann	22	f.			"	
35		John	20	m.	Farmer		"	
36		James	18	m.	Farmer		"	
37		Charles	14	m.			"	S
38		Geo.	12	m.			"	S
39		Isaac	10	m.			"	S

1		Nancy	8	f.			O.	
2		Joseph	6	m.			"	
3		Mary	4	f.			"	
4		Martha	1	f.			"	
5	174/176	MOSENEY, Lewis Sr.	45	m.	Boat builder	/100	"	
6		Martha J.	39	f.			"	
7		Eveline	19	f.			"	
8		Rachel	17	f.			"	S
9		Minerva	15	f.			"	S
10		Dennis	13	m.			"	S
11		Wm. H.	11	m.			"	S
12		Mary J.	9	f.			"	S
13		Louella	7	f.			"	S
14		Clara B.	5	f.			"	
15		Marshall	3	m.			"	
16	175/177	SUTER, Wm.	60	m.	Laborer		Sw.	
17		Mrs.	35	f.			"	
18		Elisabeth	4	f.			Pa.	
19		Rosean	2	f.			"	
20	/178	SPEDLEBOUGH, ----	59	m.	Butcher		Wur.	

21		WALTER, L.	24	m.	Pedlar	/100	Wur.	
22		YOST, Micheal	58	m.	Shoemaker		Ger.	
23	176/179	SUTER, Nicholas	27	m.	Laborer	/100	O.	
24		Catherine	24	f.			"	
25		Isaac	4	m.			"	
26		Adelia	1	f.			"	
27	177/178	GERBER, Ulerich	46	m.	Farmer	1000/800	Sw.	
28		Elisabeth	42	f.			"	
29		Frederic	18	m.			"	
30		Elisabeth	16	f.			"	
31		Christeena	13	f.			"	S
32		Ulerich	11	m.			"	S
33		John	7	m.			O.	S
34		Mary	5	f.			"	
35		Joseph	2	m.			"	
36	178/181	MEYER, John	40	m.	Farmer	1800/500	Sw.	
37		Elisabeth	39	f.			"	
38		do	13	f.			"	S
39		John	9	m.			"	

Page 28		27 July 1860				Sheet 118 verso		
1		Mary	6	f.			Sw.	S
2		Rosana	3	f.			O.	
3		SHAAR, Nicholas	18	m.	Laborer		Sw.	
4		WECKLEY, Anna	40	f.			"	
5		SHAAR, John	25	m.	Laborer		"	
6		Mary	63	f.			"	
7	179/182	UETTCHEY, Henry	46	m.	Tanner	1800/600	"	
8		Elisabeth	13	f.			O.	S
9		Adolph	25	f.	Farmer		Sw.	
10		Mary	21	f.			Wur.	
11		Rosana	1/4	f.			O.	
12	180/183	LARMCRE, William	27	m.	Laborer		"	
13		Mary	20	f.			"	
14		Anna	1	f.			"	
15	181/184	LUCAS, Wm.	35	m.	Merchant	/900	Va.	
16		Sarah	24	f.			"	
17		WILSON, Nancy	20	f.	Domestic		O.	
18	182/185	THOENEN, Martin	29	m.	Farmer	700/200	Sw.	
19		Louisa	20	f.			O.	
20		Albert	3/4	m.			"	
21	183/186	MELOTT, Wm.	36	m.	Farmer	3000/700	"	
22		Nancy	36	f.			"	
23		Elisabeth	13	f.			"	S
24		Julian	11	f.			"	S
25		Margaret	9	f.			"	S
26		James	6	m.			"	S
27		Isabel	4	f.			"	

28		MELOTT, Lucinda	1	f.			O.
29	184/187	SCHRIEVES, John	41	m.	Coal digger	400/100	"
30		Rebecca	33	f.			Va.
31		Sarah J.	9	f.			O. S
32		Joseph M.	7	m.			" S
33		Emma	5	f.			"
34		Pheoba	1/2	f.			"
35	185/188	HICKMAN, Lewis	53	m.	Farmer	/300	Pa. I
36		Fanny	51	f.			"
37		Polly	21	f.			O.
38		Catherine	20	f.			"
39		Margaret	18	f.			"

Page 29   27 July 1860   Sheet 119

1		John	14	m.	Farmer		O. S
2		Thos.	12	m.			" S
3	186/189	SCHAFROTH, John	49	m.	Farmer	500/250	Sw.
4		Elisabeth	44	f.			"
5		Fred	19	m.	Farmer		"
6		Mary	17	f.			"
7		Gotleip	16	m.			" S
8		Catherine	14	f.			" S
9		Louisa	11	f.			" S
10		Caroline	7	f.			O. S
11		Edward	4	m.			"
12		Lewis	1 1/2	m.			"
13	187/190	FLOGERCE, Anna	48	f.	Widow	600/150	Sw.
14		Solomon	19	m.	Farmer		O.
15		David	20	m.	Farmer		"
16		Abram	17	m.	Farmer		"
17		Josephine	9	f.			" S
18		Julia	7	f.			" S
19		Daniel	5	m.			"
20	188/191	SUTER, Adam	59	m.	Farmer	1500/300	Sw.
21		Christena	43	f.			Ger.
22		John	26	m.	Farmer		O.
23		Emly	21	f.			"
24		David	14	m.			" S
25		Adam	10	m.			" S
26		Abram	8	m.			" S
27		Jacob	6	m.			"
28		Geo.	4	m.			"
29		Susan	2	f.			"
30	189/192	NEIMAN, Henry	48	m.	Farmer	1000/200	Han.
31		Mary	37	f.			"
32		Henry)	12	m.			O. S
33		Anna)	12	f.			" S
34		Geo.	8	m.			" S
35		Sophia	6	f.			" S
36		Louisa	3	f.			"

37	190/193	RAPKING, Chris	64	m.	Farmer	1200/300	Han.	
38		Lucy	45	f.			"	
39		Benj.	23	m.			"	

Page 30   27 July 1860   Sheet 119 verso

1		Henry	10	m.			O.	S
2		Mary	8	f.			"	S
3		Jetta	6	f.			"	S
4	191/194	KNURST, Henry	52	m.	Farmer	800/250	Han.	
5		Margaret	49	f.			"	
6		Henry	15	m.			"	G
7	192/193	MEYER, Charles	43	m.	Farmer	1200/300	Han.	
8		Sophia	45	f.			"	
9		Henry	13	m.			O.	S
10		Geo.	11	m.			"	S
11		Susan	9	f.			"	S
12		Jetta	7	f.			"	
13		Caroline	2	f.			"	
14	193/196	MOSER, Mathias	35	m.	Farmer	300/100	Sw.	
15		Anna B.	25	f.				
16		John	4	m.			O.	
17		Elisabeth	2	f.			"	
18		BAUMGARTENER, John	21	m.	Farmer		Sw.	
19	194/197	DOUGLE, Catherine	61	f.	Widow	1200/200	Wur.	
20		Jacob	26	f.	Farmer		"	M
21		Magdeline	28	f.			"	M
22		John	18	m.	Farmer		O.	
23	195/198	RENTZ, Jacob	62	m.	Farmer	200/	Wur.	
24		Barbary	60	f.			"	
25	196/199	DOUGLE, Christian	33	m.	Farmer	2000/500	"	
26		Susan	31	f.			Sw.	
27		Cecelia	6	f.			Va.	S
28		Edward	4	m.			"	
29		Helen	1/12	f.			O.	
30	197/200	LOLADIN, John	43	m.	Laborer	/100	Wur.	
31		Caroline	38	f.			"	
32		Frederic	12	m.			O.	S
33		Micheal	11	f.			"	S
34		John	9	m.			"	S
35		Conrad	8	m.			"	S
36		Christian	6	m.			"	S
37		Catherine	5	f.			"	
38		William	2	m.			Ill.	

Page 31   27 July 1860   Sheet 120

1	198/201	FUCHS, Gotleip	44	m.	Farmer	1000/300	Wur.	
2		Frederica	25	f.			O.	
3		John	9	m.			"	S

4		FUCHS, Elisabeth	7	f.			O. S
5		Mary)	4	f.			"
6		Catherine) twins	4	f.			"
7		Gotleip	3	m.			"
8		not named	1/3	f.			"
9	199/202	LUIKART, Jacob A.	48	m.	Farmer	1500/600	Wur.
10		Barbary	50	f.			"
11		Frederic	20	m.			" S
12		Jacob	18	m.			" S
13		Catherine	17	f.			" S
14		John	14	m.			O. S
15		Gottleip	11	m.			" S
16		William	6	m.			"
17	200/203	HULPH, Jacob	38	m.	Farmer	800/200	Wur.
18		Sophia	26	f.			Als.
19		Peter	5	m.			O.
20		Evea	3	f.			"
21		Adam	1	m.			"
22	201/204	HENGER, Henry	48	m.	Minister	/300	Han.
23		Margaret	38	f.			Als.
24		Mary	14	f.			Va. S
25		John	12	m.			O. S
26		Caroline	10	f.			Va. S
27		Geo.	7	m.			Pa. S
28		Samuel	2	m.			O.
29	202/205	PHINDER, Micheal	33	m.	Farmer	2000/700	Wur.
30		Mary	50	f.			"
31		MEATING, Barbary	71	f.			
32	203/206	WALTER, Jacob	31	m.	Farmer	600/250	Sw.
33		Susan	40	f.			"
34	204/207	SHAFER, Adam	38	m.	Farmer	2500/600	Wur.
35		Wilhelamina	39	f.			Sax.
36		John	19	m.			O.
37		Mary	16	f.			" S
38		William	14	m.			" S
39		Wilhelamina	12	f.			" S

Page 32   27 July 1860   Sheet 120 verso

1		Adam	10	m.			O. S
2		Barbary	8	f.			" S
3		Rosean	6	f.			" S
4		Charles	4	m.			"
5		Adolph	2	m.			"
6		Caroline	1/2	f.			"
7	205/208	MARTIN, John J.	41	m.	Tailor	250/50	Sw.
8		Anna B.	38	f.			"
9		Elisabeth	11	f.			" S
10		Adolph	4	m.			O.
11		Godfrey	2	m.			"

12	206/209	ABBUHL, Jacob	45	m.	Farmer	800/250	Sw.	
13		Elisabeth	42	f.			"	
14	207/210	SNETZLER, Henry	34	m.	Shoemaker	400/500	"	
15		Barbary	40	f.			"	
16		Nicholas	15	m.	Farmer		"	S
17		Henry	4	m.			C.	
18		Joseph	2	m.			"	
19	208/211	ENGLE, Rudolp	61	m.	Farmer	300/100	Sw.	
20		Barbary	58	f.			"	
21	209/212	WELCHLY, John	60	m.	Farmer	300/100	"	
22		Anna	63	f.			"	
23		John	30	m.			"	
24		Fred	28	m.			"	
25	210/213	RESECKER, Martin	27	m.	Farmer	/100	O.	
26		Elisabeth	27	f.			"	
27		Elias	4	m.			"	
28		Julian	2	f.			"	
29	210/213	RESECKER, Levi	37	m.	Farmer	1200/400	"	
30		Elisabeth	32	f.			"	
31		James	4	m.			"	
32	211/214	LUIKART, Jacob	53	m.	Farmer	1200/300	Wur.	
33		Elisabeth	52	f.			Sw.	
34		Wilhelamina	18	f.			O.	S
35		Louisa	15	f.			"	S
36		John	12	m.			"	S
37	212/215	BACHMAN, Louisa	66	f.	Widow	100/400	Han.	
38		Hermon	21	m.	Farmer		"	
39		Fred	23	m.	Farmer		"	

1	213/216	BLATTER, Christian	40	m.	Grocery	800/450	Sw.	
2		Susan	36	f.			"	
3		Sarah	2	f.			O.	
4		Mary	1	f.			"	
5	214/217	BRUNEY, Christian	55	m.	Farmer	2000/700	Sw.	
6		Anna	53	f.			"	
7		Anna	18	f.			O.	S
8		David	16	m.			"	S
9		Magdelana	14	f.			"	S
10		Christian	12	m.			"	S
11		Catherine	10	f.			"	S
12	215/218	BRUNEY, Saml.	26	m.	Mason	/200	"	
13		Barbary	24	f.			Sw.	
14		John	2	m.			O.	
15		Fred	3/4	m.			"	
16	216/219	YOUSICH, Daniel	55	m.	Farmer	1500/400	Sw.	
17		Mary	55	f.			"	

| 18 | | YOUSICH, Saml. | 26 | m. | Farmer | | Sw. | |
| 19 | | John | 23 | m. | Carpenter | | " | |

20	217/220	RUBY, John Sr.	56	m.	Farmer	1800/600	"	
21		Barbary	51	f.			"	
22		Rosean	24	f.			O.	
23		Barbary	20	f.			"	
24		Elisabeth	18	f.			"	S

25	218/221	GEORGE, Gotliep	52	m.	Farmer	400/100	Wur.	
26		Mary	53	f.			"	
27		Elisabeth	16	f.			O.	S
28		Catherine	13	f.			"	S
29		John	9	m.			"	S

30	219/222	HARTLEY, John	40	m.	Minister	/100	Wur.
31		Louisa	25	f.			Pr.
32		Emmil	4	m.			Tex.
33		Paulina	2	f.			Pa.
34		Matilda	1/2	f.			O.
35		WAGNER, Amelia	50	f.			Pr.

| 36 | 220/223 | MEYER, John | 66 | m. | Cheese-maker | | Sw. |
| 37 | | Elisabeth | 63 | f. | | | " |

| 38 | 221/224 | RESECKER, Saml. | 48 | m. | Farmer | 2000/500 | Sw. |
| 39 | | Mary | 38 | f. | | | " |

| Page 34 | | | 27 July 1860 | | | Sheet 121 verso |

1		John	16	m.	Farmer		O.	
2		Margaret	18	f.			"	
3		Elisabeth	13	f.			"	S
4		Susan	11	f.			"	S
5		Mary	9	f.			"	S

6	222/225	MAUER, Jacob	36	m.	Farmer	/100	Sw.
7		Mary	27	f.			"
8		Jacob	10	m.			"
9		Gotfrey	1	m.			O.

10	223/226	KOONTS, John	43	m.	Farmer	600/300	Sw.	
11		Barbary	42	f.			"	
12		Jacob	14	m.			"	S
13		Fred	12	m.			"	S
14		John	10	m.			"	S
15		Rudolph	7	m.			"	S
16		Louisa	5	f.			O.	
17		David	2	m.			"	

18	224/227	YOUSICH, Christian	36	m.	Farmer	1200/550	Sw.	
19		Elisabeth	40	f.			"	
2C		Elisabeth	11	f.			O.	S
21		Godfrey	9	m.			"	S
22		Caroline	7	f.			"	S
23		John	4	m.			"	
24		Edward	1	m.			"	

25		YOUSICH, Roseana	16	f.	Domestic		Sw.
26		KERNOW, Jacob	62	m.	Laborer	/300	"
27	225/228	MOSER, Christian	59	m.	Farmer	1800/500	"
28		France	47	f.			"
29		John	17	m.			"
30		Mary	15	f.			"
31	226/229	SHEIVELY, John	35	m.	Farmer	3000/400	Wur.
32		Joanna	34	f.			"
33		William	6	m.			O. S
34		Caroline	4	f.			"
35		Roseana	2	f.			"
36		LUDE, Roseana	14	f.			Sw. S
37		SNIDER, Lewis	12	m.			O. S
38	227/230	THOENEN, Alexander	26	m.	Farmer	1000/350	"
39		Elisabeth	22	f.			Sw.

1		John	23	m.	Carpenter		O.
2		Louisa	4	f.			"
3		Fred	2	m.			"
4		Mary A.	1/2	f.			"
5		MINDER, Elisabeth	12	f.			"
6	228/231	WOLF, Henry	44	m.	Shoemaker	500/200	Fr.
7		Christena	39	f.			Wur.
8		Henry	18	m.	Shoemaker		O.
9		Geo.	16	m.	Farmer		" S
10		Lewis	12	m.			" S
11		Mary	6	f.			" S
12		Elisabeth	4	f.			"
13		John W.	1	m.			"
14	229/232	MELOTT, Theodore	58	m.	Farmer	3000/600	Pa.
15		Catherine	55	f.			Va.
16		Henry	26	m.	Farmer		O.
17		Margaret	23	f.			"
18		Amos	21	m.	Farmer		"
19		Sarena	18	f.			"
20	230/233	BRAUN, Casper	53	m.	Farmer	/1000	Sw.
21		Frances	64	f.			"
22	231/234	BRAUN, Fred	26	m.	Farmer	1800/600	" M
23		Elisabeth	20	f.			" M
24		STOUFFER, Nicholas	52	m.	Retired		"
25		MUHLEMAN, Jacob	37	m.	Laborer	/572	"
26		Mary	32	f.	Domestic	/343	"
27	232/235	RUFFNER, Saml.	43	m.	Carpenter	500/250	"
28		Anna	48	f.			"
29		Samuel	19	m.	Farmer		"
30		Christian	17	m.	Farmer		"
31		Madaline	12	f.			"

32	233/236	POTTS, Frank	26	m.	Farmer	2500/300	O.
33		Mary	23	f.			Va.
34		Whetsel	7	m.			O.
35		Eliza J.	4	f.			"
36		John	2	m.			"
37	234/237	BERRY, James	35	m.	Farmer	/150	Ire.
38		Ruth	30	f.			Va.

Page 36   28 July 1860   Sheet 122 verso

1	235/238	STEWARD, John	37	m.	Farmer	/100	Pa.	
2		Prissilla	31	f.			O.	
3		Bazil	12	m.			"	S
4		Nancy J.	7	f.			"	S
5		Elias	6	m.			"	
6		Eugene	5	m.			"	
7	236/239	MONROE, Nicholas	50	m.	Laborer	/100	Del.	
8		Amanda	50	f.			O.	
9		Charlotte	15	f.			"	S
10		James W.	12	m.			"	S
11		William	10	m.			"	S
12	237/240	DIXON, Wm.	25	m.	Farmer	800/100	Ire.	
13		Margaret	27	f.			"	
14		Mary	4	f.			"	
15		Sarah	2	f.			O.	
16	238/241	SUTER, Jacob	25	m.	Farmer	1800/150	"	
17		Martha	28	f.			"	
18		John D.	6	m.			"	
19		Alonzo	4	m.			"	
20		William	1 1/2	m.			"	
21		RESECKER, William	16	m.	Laborer		"	
22	239/242	CLITZLY, John	29	m.	Farmer	/100	Sw.	
23		Catherine	26	f.			"	
24		Caroline	1	f.			O.	
25		GASSET, Jacob	10	m.			Sw.	
26	240/243	RAHM, Peter	33	m.	Farmer	1200/275	"	
27		Elisabeth	29	f.			"	
28		Caroline	2	f.			O.	
29	241/244	GIGGLER, Fred	52	m.	Farmer	800/200	Wur.	
30		Barbary	54	f.			"	
31		George	14	m.			"	S
32		Fredericka	12	f.			"	S
33	242/245	DARE, John M.	63	m.	Farmer	800/350	"	
34		Catherine	48	f.			"	
35		William	19	m.	Farmer		O.	S
36		Rosean	17	f.			"	S
37		Frederick	13	m.			"	S
38		Catherine	10	f.			"	S
39		Micheal	8	m.			"	S

P. O. Hanibal   Ohio Township

40   DARE, Elisabeth   4   f.   O.

1	243/246	NIPPART, Godfrey	48	m.	Farmer	1500/600 Als.
2		Saloma	43	f.		"
3		Godfrey	19	m.	Farmer	O. S
4		Eve	17	f.		" S
5		Louisa	15	f.		" S
6		George	12	m.		" S
7		Henry	9	m.		" S
8		Mary	7	f.		" S
9		Margaret	5	f.		"
10		John W.	3	m.		"

11	244/247	BLACK, Conrad	40	m.	Tanner	1000/800 Wur.
12		Caroline	38	f.		Sax.
13		Christopher	17	m.	Farmer	O.
14		Margaret	15	f.		" S
15		David	13	m.		" S
16		Thomas	11	m.		" S
17		Susan	9	f.		" S
18		John	7	m.		" S
19		Jonathan	5	m.		"
20		Elisabeth	2	f.		"

21	245/248	MOORMAN, William	45	m.	Farmer	800/300 Han.
22		Mary	48	f.		"
23		Caroline	15	f.		"
24		Louisa	12	f.		O. S
25		Henry	10	m.		" S
26		John	8	m.		" S

27	246/249	RAMSIER, John	33	m.	Carpenter	300/200 Sw.
28		Elisabeth	33	f.		"
29		John	4	m.		O.
30		Mary	2	f.		"
31		Saml.	2/12	m.		"

32	247/250	BLAUR, John	40	m.	Farmer	300/150 Sw.
33		Anna	36	f.		"
34		Mary	15	f.		"
35		John	10	m.		"
36		Jacob	8	m.		O.
37		David	6	m.		"
38		Joseph	1	m.		"

1	248/251	SUTER, Mary	31	f.	Widow	800/100 Sw.
2		Roseana	8	f.		O. S
3		Jacob	6	m.		" S
4		Mary	4	f.		"
5		Nancy	2	f.		"

6	249/252	SCHUMACHER, Henry	37	m.	Farmer	800/300 Sw.
7		Anna	34	f.		"
8		Anna	7	f.		O. S

9		SCHUMACHER, Henry	5	m.		O.
10		Isaac	3	m.		"
11		Saml.	1	m.		"
12		GOSSER, John	19	m.	Laborer	Sw.
13	250/253	BLUNIER, Peter	27	m.	Farmer	700/250	"
14		Anna	24	f.		"
15		Mary	4	f.		O.
16		Peter	2	m.		"
17		Casper	1/2	m.		"
18		REITER, Mary	42	f.		Sw.
19	251/254	MATHIAS, N.	30	m.	Farmer	300/100	"
20		Christena	25	f.		"
21		Mary	23	f.		"
22		Martha	20	f.		"
23		Frederic	10	m.		"
24	252/255	BRUE, John	48	m.	Cheese-maker	/100	"
25		Caroline	24	f.		Bad.
26		John	3	m.		O.
27		Caroline	1	f.		"

28	253/256	BAUMGARTEN, Bene-dict	54	m.	Farmer	1500/700	Sw.
29		Anna	38	f.			"
30		Mary	9	f.			"	S
31		John	8	m.			"	S
32		Simon	7	m.			"	S
33		Rosean	6	f.			"	S
34		Anna	5	f.			O.	S
35		Eliza	3	f.			"
36		Joseph	1 1/2	m.			"
37		Samuel	13	m.			Sw.

38	254/257	SHINDLER, Elisa-beth	56	f.	Widow	500/	"

Beginning of Sardis.

1	255/258	RAMSIER, John	53	m.	Farmer	200/100	Sw.
2		Magdalena	52	f.			"
3		Caroline	7	f.			"	S
4	256/259	GEHRING, Isaac	41	m.	Farmer	1800/1500	"
5		Margaret	50	f.			"
6		Isaac	12	m.			O.
7		Margaret	9	f.			"
8		MILLER, Jacob	24	m.	Laborer		Sw.
9		BELLER, Joseph	48	m.	Watchmaker	/200	Aus.
10		BACKODA, John	31	m.	Watchmaker		"
11		BURI, Jacob	43	m.	Shoemaker	/100	Sw.
12	257/260	NEISWANDER, Ulrich	60	m.	Farmer	2000/900	"
13		Susanah	53	f.			"

14		NEISWANDER, Mary	15	f.			Sw.	S
15		Susan	13	f.			"	S
16		Roseana	11	f.			"	S
17		Nanetta	9	f.			"	S
18		BAUMGARTNER, Peter	19	m.	Farm hand		"	
19		Christian	23	m.	Farm hand		"	
20	258/261	GOSSER, Elisabeth	54	f.	Widow	200/	"	
21		Nicholas	17	m.	Farmer		"	S
22		Elisabeth	13	f.			"	S
23		Saml.	8	m.			"	S
24		Margaret	6	f.			"	S
25		Fred	4	m.			"	
26	259/262	LONGWELL, Rebecca	53	f.	Widow		Va.	
27		Joseph	23	m.	Laborer		O.	
28		Robt.	21	m.	Laborer		"	
29		Benton	18	m.	Laborer		"	
30		Martha	16	f.			"	
31		Nancy	14	f.			"	S
32	260/263	HERIGAN, Micheal	30	m.	Miner		Ire.	
33		Rebecca	28	f.			Va.	
34		Nancy	12	f.			"	
35		Julia	9	f.			"	
36		Wm.	8	m.			O.	
37		John	5	m.			"	
38		Ruth	1	f.			"	
39		NOLAND, Nancy	45	f.	Widow		Va.	

Page 40   28 July 1860   Sheet 124 verso

1	261/264	HOSKINS, Jefferson	54	m.	Laborer		O.	
2		Grace	29	f.	Child		"	
3		Rebecca	24	f.	Child		"	
4		Susan	21	f.	Child		"	
5		John	19	m.	Laborer		"	
6		Joseph	18	m.	Laborer		"	
7		Elisabeth	13	f.			"	
8	262/265	BERGER, Peter	38	m.	Farmer	/300	Sw.	
9		Magdalena	32	f.			"	
10		Christian	10	m.			"	S
11		Gottleip	9	m.			"	S
12		Elisabeth	7	f.			"	S
13		Magdalena	5	f.			O.	
14		Caroline	3	f.			"	
15		Roseana	1	f.			"	
16	263/266	BOWMAN, Mary	37	f.	Widow	8000/3000	Sw.	
17		John	18	m.	Farmer		"	
18		Godfrey	14	m.			"	S
19		Levi	12	m.			"	S
20		Robt.	11	m.			"	S
21		Emmil	2	m.			O.	
22		Elisabeth	54	f.			Sw.	
23	264/267	WITEMER, John	49	m.	Farmer	/250	"	
24		Elisabeth	36	f.			"	

25		WITEMER, Elis--	15	f.			Sw. S
26		Albert	13	m.			" S
27		Roseana	11	f.			" S
28		John	9	m.			O. S
29		Mary	3	f.			"
30	265/268	WITCHER, Jacob	38	m.	Farmer	/200	Sw.
31		Ann	36	f.			"
32		Roseana	4	f.			O.
33	266/269	BARE, William	55	m.	Farmer	2500/700	Pa.
34		Mary	49	f.			O.
35		Leander	26	m.	Teacher		"
36		George	24	m.	Farmer		"
37		John	22	m.	Millwright		"
38		Wm.	20	m.	Farmer		" S
39		Sansom	18	m.	Farmer		" S

Page 41   30 July 1860   Sheet 125

1		Edward	16	m.	Farmer		O. S
2		Sarah	14	f.			" S
3		Susanah	12	f.			" S
4		Mary	9	f.			" S
5		Jacob H.	6	m.			" S
6	267/270	HOWARD, Arnold	62	m.	Hermit	150/	Sw.
7	268/271	BOWERY, John	25	m.	Farmer	400/100	O.
8		Emly	25	f.			"
9		Mary F.	1/4	f.			"
10	269/272	DINGER, David	56	m.	Farmer	2700/500	Sax.
11		Mary R.	53	f.			Old.
12		Franklin	17	m.			Sax.
13	270/273	BRAMLICH, Geo.	28	m.	Farmer		Sax.
14		Hanah S.	26	f.			"
15		Mary	6	f.			O. S
16		Charles	4	m.			"
17		Saml.	1	m.			"
18	271/274	HENTHORN, John	53	m.	Farmer	1500/400	Pa.
19		Persia	50	f.			Conn.
20		Nimrod J.	27	m.	Mate on boat		O.
21		Jno. B.	24	m.	Mate on boat		"
22		Wm. S.	22	m.	Farmer		"
23		Elisabeth	20	f.			" S
24		Lafayette	18	m.	Farmer		" S
25		Martha J.	16	f.			" S
26		James	14	m.			" S
27		Charles	12	m.			" S
28		Washington	9	m.			" S
29	272/275	SCHRODER, John	56	m.	Laborer		D.C. S
30		Elisabeth	41	f.			Va.
31		Saml.	25	m.	River		"
32		Wm.	23	m.	River		"

33		SCHRODER, Caroline	19	f.		Va.
34		Thos.	14	m.		0. S
35		Danl.	12	m.		" S
36		Mary J.	10	f.		"
37		Susan	6	f.		"
38		Sarah	5	f.		"

Page 42   30 July 1860   Sheet 125 verso

1	273/276	GEHRIG, John	56	m.	Farmer	800/200	Sax.
2		Rosean	40	f.			"
3		Lewis	11	m.			" S
4		Emly	4	f.			0.
5		Mary E.	2	f.			"
6	274/277	GEHRIG, Augustus	24	m.	Farmer		Sax.
7		Louisa	20	f.			0.
8		Mary	3/4	f.			"
9	275/278	HARMON, Benj.	43	m.	Farmer	500/150	Pa.
10		Mary	43	f.			0.
11		Joseph	14	m.			" S
12		Melvina	11	f.			" S
13		Cornelius	9	m.			" S
14		Benjamin	7	m.			" S
15		James D.	5	m.			"
16	276/279	HARMON, Samuel	39	m.	Grocery	500/500	Pa.
17		Mary	37	f.			0.
18		Savillah	18	f.			"
19		Joseph	16	m.			" S
20		Mary E.	14	f.			" S
21		Caroline	8	f.			" S
22		Martha A.	5	f.			"
23		Geo. H.	3	m.			"
24		Emma J.	1/12	f.			"
25		GEHRING, Henry	20	m.	River		Sax.
26		HARMON, Lydia J.	10	f.			0.
27	277/280	THOMAS, Samuel	24	m.	Laborer-Bachelor		"
28	278/281	SUTER, Samuel	26	m.	River		"
29		Hannah	24	f.			"
30	279/282	LIVELY, David	27	m.	Tavern-keeper and ferry	1000/500	Va.
31		Mary	23	f.			0.
32		Philip	2	m.			"
33	280/283	BROWN, Smith	37	m.	Laborer		"
34		Nancy	34	f.			"
35		Jane	13	f.			" S
36		Mary	11	f.			" S
37		John	10	m.			" S
38		Adaline	8	f.			" S
39		LARMORE, Margaret	16	f.			"

1	281/284	LARMORE, Joseph	28	m.	Laborer		O.
2		Catherine	26	f.			"
3		David)	6	m.			"
4		John) twins	6	m.			"
5		Mary E.	1/4	f.			"
6	282/285	POTTS, Jackson	35	m.	Laborer	400/200	"
7		Maria	33	f.			"
8		James	13	m.			" S
9		Saml.	10	m.			" S
10		Roseana	7	f.			" S
11		Savilla	1	f.			"
12	283/286	HURLEY, Washington	32	m.	Cooper	300/200	"
13		Sarah	27	f.			"
14		Mary C.	12	f.			" S
15		Maria	9	f.			" S
16		James W.	6	m.			" S
17		MONROE, Lidia	17	f.	Domestic		"
18	284/287	ALLEN, Mahlon	43	m.	Farmer	/300	Va.
19		Adaline	8	f.			"
20		Mary	5	f.			" S
21		CLARK, Sarah J.	25	f.	Housekeeper		"
22		Amanda	15	f.			" S
23		HUGHES, Kinsey	12	m.			" S
24	285/288	THISTLE, George S.	46	m.	Farmer	5000/800	Va.
25		Sarah	54	f.			"
26		SCOTT, Elisa	19	f.	Domestic		Ill.
27		Henry	18	m.			" S
28	286/289	CHURCH, Henry	35	m.	Farmer	/500	Va.
29		Rebecca	36	f.			O.
30		Wm. H.	12	m.			" S
31		Robt.	8	m.			" S
32		Martha	6	f.			" S
33		George	2	m.			"
34	287/290	POOL, Phillip	55	m.	Farmer	8000/1000	Pa.
35		Ann M.	56	f.			Va.
36		George W.	20	m.	Farmer		O.

1	288/291	McCAMMICK, Isaac	35	m.	Laborer	/100	O.
2		Sarah	33	f.			"
3		Mary A.	12	f.			" S
4		Eliza J.	10	f.			" S
5		Nathan	8	m.			" S
6		Josephine	6	f.			"
7		Charles	4	m.			"
8		Edward	1/4	m.			

P. O. Sardis   Ohio Township

30 July 1860   Sheet 127

Beginning of Sardis.

1	289/292	KNIGHT, Wm.	37	m.	Carpenter	/200	O.	
2		Elisabeth	28	f.			Pa.	
3		John L.	13	m.			O.	S
4		Sarah J.	11	f.			"	S
5		Ella	6	f.			"	S
6		Isadore	4	f.			"	
7	290/293	NEISWANDER, John	48	m.	Grocer	/250	Sw.	
8		Susanah	28	f.			Bad.	
9		Anna	12	f.			Sw.	S
10		Henry	4	m.			O.	
11		Ferdinand	2	m.			"	
12	291/294	SHAUB, J. J.	48	m.	Physician	/300	Fr.	
13		Elisabeth	34	f.			O.	
14		Jacob	21	m.	River		"	
15		Frederic	17	m.			"	S
16		Catherine	11	f.			"	S
17	/295	BUCHWALD, J. F.	29	m.	Silversmith	/200	Ger.	
18		Mary	25	f.			"	
19		Charles	3	m.			O.	
20		Mary	3/4	f.			"	
21	292/296	RICKABOUGH, Adam	33	m.	Laborer	/200	Sw.	
22		Anna M.	34	f.			Ger.	
23		Mary	8	f.			"	S
24	293/297	IRWIN, James	55	m.	Farmer	700/700	Ire.	
25		Jno. B.	24	m.	Farmer		O.	
26		Hugh	22	m.	Farmer		"	
27		James C.	21	m.	Farmer		"	
28	/298	QUIN, Margaret	34	f.			"	
29		John	13	m.			"	S
30		Quiltilla	18	f.			Va.	S
31		Jesse	1/12	m.			O.	
32	294/298	GOODIN, Jno. M.	30	m.	Merchant	1200/2500	Ind.	
33		Nancy J.	19	f.			O.	
34		Geo. P.	2	m.			"	
35		RESECKER, Margaret	18	f.	Domestic		"	
36	295/299	BRIDGMAN, Augustus	34	m.	Farmer	5000/1000	"	
37		MARLING, Eliza	48	f.	Housekeeper	2500/	Pa.	
38		MOBLEY, Amy	18	f.	Domestic		O.	

30 July 1860   Sheet 127 verso

1	296/300	BARKES, Nelson	54	m.	Carpenter		O.
2		Rebecca	44	f.			Va.
3	297/301	WILSON, Saml.	51	m.	Cooper	/100	Pa.
4		Anna	55	f.			Va.

5		WILSON, Jas. Alex.	16	m.			O.
6		Saml. S.	14	m.			Tenn.S
7	298/302	DETWILER, Henry	31	m.	Carpenter	/700	Pa.
8		Elisabeth	25	f.			O.
9		Lillia	5	f.			Ind.
10		May	3	f.			"
11		Samuel	22	m.	Carpenter		Pa.
12	299/303	GILMORE, James	23	m.	Boatman		O. M
13		Elisabeth	21	f.			" M
14	300/304	THOMPSON, John	42	m.	Cooper	/200	Va.
15		Catherine	41	f.			"
16		Peter	18	m.			O.
17		Levi	14	m.			" S
18		Wm.	11	m.			" C
19		Mary E.	8	f.			" S
20		Charles	6	m.			" S
21		Ceo.	3	m.			"
22	301/305	SULIVAN, Wm.	27	m.	Laborer	/100	"
23		Elisabeth	22	f.			"
24		Jas. H.	4	m.			"
25		Pheoba	2	f.			
26	302/306	CHAPMAN, Gideon	76	m.	Shoemaker	300/100	Conn.
27		Mary	40	f.			O.
28		KINKAID, Sarah	21	f.	Domestic		"
29	303/307	BRENAN, Martin	39	m.	Merchant	1200/2000	Ire.
30		Elisabeth	39	f.			Md.
31		Mary	9	f.			O. S
32		Sarah	7	f.			" S
33		Catharine	5	f.			" S
34		Douglas	3	m.			"
35		KERNS, Rhuhama	17	f.	Domestic		
36	304/308	McMAHON, Stanton	37	m.	Physician	500/300	"
37		Sarah	31	f.			"
38		Juliet	4	f.			"
39		Virginia	3	f.			

Page 47   30 July 1860   Sheet 128

1	305/309	FOWLER, Richard	43	m.	Carpenter	400/200	O.
2		Rachel	35	f.			Va. I
3		John	17	m.			O.
4		Sarah	14	f.			" S
5		Resin	11	m.			" S
6		Cater	9	m.			" S
7	306/310	MARTIN, Wilson	43	m.	Postmaster	500/200	O.
8		Mary	24	f.			"
9		Thomas	19	m.	River		"
10		Bishop	17	m.	School		" S
11		Absolom	16	m.	School		" S

12		MARTIN, Josiah	13	m.			O.	S
13		Eliza	11	f.			"	S
14		Rebecca	3	f.			"	
15		Elisabeth	1/2	f.			"	
16	307/311	THOMAS, Adam	35	m.	Tailor	/100	Bav.	
17		Elisabeth	30	f.			Sw.	
18		Elis	11	f.			Va.	S
19		Frederic P.	9	m.			O.	S
20		Ernest	8	m.			"	S
21		Jno. W.	6	m.			"	S
22		Jacob J.	4	m.			"	
23		Mary E.	2	f.			Va.	
24		Adam	3/4	m.			O.	
25	308/312	DUNN, John	31	m.	Mate		"	M
26		Rebecca	20	f.			"	M
27	309/313	TAYLOR, Elis	52	f.	Widow		Va.	I
28		Alford	21	m.	River		"	
29		John	18	m.	River		Md.	
30	310/314	HORNBROOK, Edwin	35	m.	Miller	10,000/6000	Va.	
31		Eliza	34	f.			"	
32		Jacob	12	m.			O.	S
33		Eugene	10	m.			"	S
34		Charles	7	m.			"	S
35		Edward	4	m.			"	
36		TREMBLE, R. D.	24	m.	Engineer		Va.	
37		GARL, Z.	63	m.	Miller		Md.	
38		TREMBLE, John	28	m.	Engineer	2000/	Va.	
39		WILLIAMSON, C.	20	f.	Domestic		O.	

End of Sardis. Contains 116.

Page 48			31 July 1860			Sheet 128 verso	
1	311/315	HEDINGER, Rudolph	48	m.	Farmer	900/450	Sw.	
2		Mary	49	f.			"	
3		John	24	m.	Farmer		"	
4		Rudolph	22	m.	Farmer		"	
5		Gotleip	21	m.	Farmer		"	
6		Mary	19	f.			"	
7		Frederic	17	m.	Farmer		"	S
8		Susan	15	f.			"	S
9		Elisabeth	13	f.			"	S
10		Jacob	11	m.			"	S
11		Alexander	9	m.			"	S
12		RODOCKER, C.	40	m.	Laborer		"	
13	312/316	NESBITT, James	41	m.	Farmer	5000/2000	Va.	
14		Caroline	35	f.			"	
15		Martha	14	f.			O.	
16		Elisabeth	12	f.			"	S
17		Susan	10	f.			"	S
18		Ella	6	f.			"	S
19		Parthena	3	f.			"	S

20		NESBITT, James					
		Douglas	1/12	m.		O.	
21		DILLON, Geo.	26	m.	Sawyer	N.Y.	
22		McMAHON, Jno.	24	m.	Laborer	O.	
23	313/317	NESBITT, Elisabeth	62	f.	Widow	6000/600	Pa.
24		Margaret	35	f.		2000/	Va.
25		Mary	37	f.		500/	"
26		PATTON, Johnathon	21	m.	Merchant	300/1500	O.
27		Marinda	18	f.	Scholar	/1400	" S
28		William	15	m.	Scholar	2000/1400	" S
29	314/318	SHIPBOUGH, Fred	28	m.	Farmer	3500/1200	Sw.
30		Elisabeth	40	f.			"
31		John	17	m.	Farmer		"
32		Fred	14	m.			" S
33		Christian	10	m.			" S
34		Adolph	7	m.			O.
35		Caroline	2	f.			"
36		Elisabeth	1/2	f.			"
37		GROEBACHER, Samuel	16	m.	Laborer		Sw.
38	315/319	HAVELY, Wm. D.	41	m.	Farmer	12,000/6000	Pa.
39		Jane	48	f.			Va.

Page 49   31 July 1860   Sheet 129

1		Robt.	17	m.			O. S
2		James	15	m.			" S
3		Nancy	13	f.			" S
4		John	11	m.			" S
5		Owen	8	m.			" S
6		George	6	m.			Va. S
7	316/320	ELLIOT, Samuel	41	m.	Laborer	/200	O.
8		Susan	40	f.			Pa.
9		John	18	m.	Laborer		O.
10		Micheal	16	m.			" S
11		Peter	12	m.			" S
12		Minerva	11	f.			" S
13		Arthur	8	m.			" S
14		Jacob	4	m.			"
15		John	86	m.	Retired		Va.
16	317/321	KELLER, Nicholas	29	m.	Grocer	400/500	Sw.
17		Mary	35	f.			"
18		John	10	m.			"
19		STEIBLEY, John	30	m.	Shoemaker	/100	"
20	318/322	SAGERSEMAN, Elis	54	f.	Widow		Sw.
21	319/323	STALDER, Nicholas	56	m.	Farmer	700/250	"
22		Magedelana	45	f.			"
23		" "	24	f.			"
24		Nicholas	21	m.	Farmer		"
25		Roseana	18	f.			"
26		John	11	m.			" S
27		Christian	8	m.			" S

28		STALDER, Fred	3	m.			O.
29	320/324	KERNOW, John	62	m.	Farmer	600/200	Sw.
30		Mary	40	f.			"
31		Amelia	4	f.			O.
32	321/325	SPRING, Michael	30	m.	Farmer	/100	Sw.
33		Catherine	46	f.			"
34		Margaret	10	f.			" S
35		Alberta	8	f.			O. S
36		Caroline	2	f.			"
37	322/326	GROUX, Samuel	25	m.	Farmer	1000/200	Sw.
38		Anna	22	f.			"
39		BAHN, Elisabeth	33	f.	Domestic		"
40		Peter	40	m.	Laborer		"

Page 50   31 July 1860   Sheet 129 verso

1	323/327	KERNOW, John	43	m.	Farmer	500/200	Sw.
2		Susan	51	f.			"
3		John	20	m.	Farmer		"
4		Susan	18	f.			"
5		MAUR, Jacob	9	m.			"
6	324/328	WINKLER, Peter	40	m.	Farmer	/150	"
7		Mary	32	f.			"
8		Roseana	5	f.			N.Y.
9		Caroline	4	f.			O.
10		Lewis	3	m.			"
11		Louisa	2	f.			"
12		Emma	1/2	f.			"
13	325/329	SHOTT, Gotleip	47	m.	Wagon-maker	400/200	Wur.
14		Mary	37	f.			"
15		Philip	20	m.	Farmer		"
16		Mary	15	f.			" S
17		Gotleip	10	m.			" S
18		Barbary	5	f.			O.
19		John	2	m.			"
20		Sophia	1	f.			"
21	326/330	RICKABOUGH, John	54	m.	Farmer	1000/600	Bas.
22		Ursilla	54	f.			"
23		Sabastian	21	m.	Farmer		"
24		John	19	m.	Farmer		"
25	327/331	PINDLE, Chris♀.	38	m.	Farmer	1200/600	Wur.
26		Christina	36	f.			"
27		John	14	m.			O. S
28		Christopher	12	m.			" S
29		Mary	7	f.			" S
30		Catherine	5	f.			"
31		Roseanna	2	f.			"
32		KREIGE, Mary A.	81	f.	Retired		Wur.
33	328/332	ICE, Uriah	48	m.	Tanner	800/375	Va.

34	ICE, Lucinda	48	f.			O.
35	Elam	21	m.	Tanner		"
36	Geo.	19	m.	Tanner		"
37	Caroline	17	f.			"
38	Almira	15	f.			"
39	Matilda	13	f.			"

Page 51   31 July 1860   Sheet 130

1		Arche	11	m.			O. S
2		Rebecca	7	f.			" S
3		John	6	m.			" S
4	329/333	HOSKINS, Azriah	24	m.	Farmer	/100	"
5		Elisabeth	23	f.			"
6		Thos.	5	m.			"
7		Geo.	3	m.			"
8		Lucinda	1	f.			Va.
9	330/334	BADER, Martin	60	m.	Farmer	500/250	Wur.
10		Magdelena	60	f.			"
11		Anna	17	f.			"
12	331/335	DUKE, Wm.	40	m.	Farmer	500/150	O. I
13		Hannah	29	f.			"
14		Mary J.	10	f.			" S
15		Rebecca	5	f.			"
16		Margaret	3	f.			"
17		John	1	m.			"
18	332/336	GLUSENKAUF, Chris-					
		tian	71	m.	Retired	400/750	Han.
19		Mary	72	f.			"
20	333/337	GAUDING, Henry	46	m.	Farmer	1000/650	"
21		Mary	38	f.			"
22		Sophia	16	f.			O. S
23		William	14	m.			" S
24		Mary	11	f.			" S
25		Caroline	9	f.			" S
26		Louisa	7	f.			" S
27		John	6	m.			" S
28		Charles	3	m.			"
29		Elisabeth	3/4	f.			"
30	334/338	STORRER, Conrad	47	m.	Farmer	300/100	Sw.
31		Elisabeth	35	f.			"
32		Fred	14	m.			" S
33		Alfred	12	m.			" S
34		Mary	10	f.			" S
35		George) Twins	8	m.			" S
36		John)	8	m.			" S
37		Jacob	4	m.			"
38		Elisabeth	1	f.			O.

Page 52   31 July 1860   Sheet 130 verso

1 334/339 BEY, William   54   m.   Farmer   300/100 Wur.

2		BEY, Shilla	52	f.			Wur.
3		Emma	10	f.			"
4	335/340	MAUR, John	51	m.	Farmer		Wur.
5		Christena	42	f.			Sw.
6		Christian	18	m.			"
7		Ann	13	f.			" S
8		Martha	11	f.			" S
9		Benedict	10	m.			" S
10		Susan	6	f.			O. S
11		Eliza	4	f.			"
12		Roseanna	2	f.			"
13	336/341	MOSERMAN, Chris-					
		tian	57	m.	Farmer	1300/450	Sw.
14		Catherine	42	f.			"
15		MENGER, Godfrey	8	m.			O.
16	337/342	GEHRING, Isaac Jr.	25	m.	Farmer		Sw.
17		Mary	25	f.			"
18		child	2/12	m.			O.
19	338/343	FARMER, S. W.	71	m.	Farmer	1400/600	Md.
20		Mary A.	62	f.			"
21		Garie	30	m.	Farmer		O.
22		Elisabeth	25	f.			"
23		Marion	19	m.	Farmer		"
24		Mariah	16	f.			"
25	339/344	MARTIN, Ebenezer	28	m.	Tanner	500/300	O.
26		Mary Ann	25	f.			"
27		Missouri Bell	2/12	f.			"
28	340/345	MARTIN, Absolom	56	m.	Farmer	1200/450	Va.
29		Jane	56	f.			O.
30		Geo. M.	20	m.	Farmer		"
31		James T.	14	m.			" S
32		UMMENSETER, Sarah	14	f.			" S
33		LONGWELL, Thos.	54	m.			" 23
34	341/346	HOSKINS, John	43	m.	Farmer	600/200	"
35		Dorathy	40	f.			"
36		Walter H.	18	m.	Farmer		"
37		Josephus	16	m.	Farmer		"
38		Margaret	14	f.			" S
39		Dudley	12	m.			" S

1		Elisabeth	8	f.			O.
2		John	2	m.			"
3	342/347	HOSKINS, David	49	m.	Farmer	700/250	"
4		Elisabeth	44	f.			Va.
5		John	24	m.	Farmer		O.
6		Rachel	19	f.			"
7		Azariah	18	m.	Farmer		"

8		HOSKINS, Caroline	16	f.			O.	
9		Robt.	11	m.			"	S
10		David	8	m.			"	S
11		Sandford	6	m.			"	S
12		Perry	3	m.			"	
13	343/348	MOSEMAN, Christian	50	m.	Farmer	800/300	Sw.	
14		Magdelana	41	f.			"	
15		Roseana	5	f.			O.	
16	344/349	OTTO, Mary	65	f.	Widow		Sw.	
17	345/350	TOMMY, Jacob	50	m.	Farmer	2000/800	"	
18		Christena	44	f.			"	
19		Elisabeth	22	f.			"	
20		Roseana	19	f.			"	
21		Mary	25	f.			"	
22		Anna	17	f.			"	
23		Catherine	15	f.			"	S
24		John	12	m.			"	S
25		Jacob	9	m.			O.	S
26		Henry	7	m.			"	S
27		OTTO, John	23	m.	Farmer		Sw.	
28	346/351	GROSERBACHER,						
		Jacob	60	m.	Farmer	1000/850	"	
29		Elisabeth	48	f.			"	
30		John	12	m.			"	S
31	347/352	TISHER, Joseph	33	m.	Boat watchman	/200	O.	
32		Gemima	31	f.			"	
33		Isaac	5	m.			"	
34		Slater B.	2	m.			"	
35	348/353	TISHER, David	30	m.	Farmer	800/200	"	
36		Ellen	27	f.			"	
37		Julian	6	f.			"	
38		Mary	4	f.			"	
39		Joseph	2	m.			"	

Page 54		1 August 1860					Sheet 131 verso	
1	349/354	BERGER, John	34	m.	Farmer	500/300	Ger.	
2		Elisabeth	32	f.			"	S
3		Margaret	12	f.			"	S
4		Jacob	6	m.			"	
5		John	4	m.			"	
6		Elisabeth	2	f.			"	
7		Saml.	1/2	m.				
8	350/355	BLACK, Christopher	38	m.	Farmer	2000/600	Wur.	
9		Catherine	28	f.			Han.	
10		Conrad	14	m.			O.	
11		Jacob	10	m.			"	S
12		William	8	m.			"	S
13		Saml.	6	m.			"	S
14		Isaac	4	m.			"	

15	351/356	TUBAUGH, Ann	27	m.	Widow	500/100	Sw.
16		Frederic	9	m.			O.
17		Louisa	7	f.			"
18		Christian	5	m.			"
19		Amelia	3	f.			"
20		John C.	2	m.			"
					(deced.)		
21	352/357	LUTHY, John Jr.	36	m.	Carpenter/	900/300	Sw.
22		Mary	25	f.			O.
23		Simon P.	5	m.			"
24		David	3	m.			"
25		Albert	1	m.			"
26	353/358	FANKHOUSER, John	45	m.	Farmer	1600/650	Sw.
27		Elisabeth	34	f.			"
28		John	6	m.			O. S
29		Eliza	5	f.			"
30		Rosetta	3	f.			"
31		William	2	m.			"
32		Caroline	1/4	f.			"
33		SOLOBERGER, Jacob	25	m.	Laborer		Sw.
34		TEBAY, Benj.	45	m.	Laborer		"
35	354/359	DANDLER, John	46	m.	Weaver	/100	"
36		Magdelena	38	f.			"
37		Margaret	10	f.			" S
38	355/360	DANNER, John W.	63	m.	Farmer	500/200	"
39		Anna	60	f.			"

Page 55   1 August 1860   Sheet 132

1	356/361	HICKMAN, Wm.	29	m.	Farmer	800/300	O.
2		Mary	29	f.			Pa.
3		Charles	4	m.			O.
4		Joseph	1½	m.			"
5		not named	1/12	f.			"
6	357/362	KAUFMAN, Saml.	59	m.	Farmer	1500/600	Sw.
7		Catherine	35	f.			"
8		Mary	25	f.			"
9		John	21	m.	Farmer		"
10		Elizabeth	19	f.			"
11		Margaret	18	f.			"
12		Augustus	8	m.			O. S
13		Louisa	4	f.			"
14		Fred	2	m.			"
15	358/363	BACHMAN, Christian	45	m.	Farmer	1600/550	Sw.
16		Anna	43	f.			"
17		Anna) twins	21	f.			"
18		Christena)	21	f.			"
19		Fred	19	m.	Farmer		"
20		Elisabeth	17	f.			"
21		Catherine	15	f.			" S
22		Roseanna	13	f.			" S
23		John	9	m.			O. S

24		BACHMAN, Ann	7	f.			O.	S
25		Alex.	3	m.			"	
26	359/364	JOSS, Jacob	51	m.	Farmer	800/600	Sw.	
27		Elisabeth	50	f.			"	
28		Jacob	24	m.	Farmer		"	
29		Mary	23	f.			"	
30		Elisabeth	19	f.			"	
31		Fred	17	m.	Farmer		"	
32		Mary Ann	15	f.			"	S
33		Annetta	14	f.			"	S
34		Simon	11	m.			O.	S
35		Martha	8	f.			"	S
36	360/365	STALDER, Nicholas	52	m.	Cheese-maker	/100	Sw.	
37	361/366	KING, Peter	52	m.	Farmer	2500/1000	Pa.	
38		Sarah	49	f.			"	
39		John	20	m.	Farmer		O.	

Page 56			1 August 1860				Sheet 132 verso	
1		Henry	16	m.			O.	
2		HENTHORN, Susan	11	f.			"	
3	362/367	KING, William	29	m.	Farmer	/100	"	
4		Nancy	18	f.			"	
5		Peter	1	m.			"	
6	363/368	BACHMAN, Fred	44	m.	Farmer	1800/600	Sw.	
7		Magdelana	42	f.			"	
8		Godfrey	18	m.	Farmer		"	
9		Magdalena	14	f.			"	S
10		Anna	12	f.			"	S
11		Rosetta	5	f.			O.	
12		Rudolph	3	m.			"	
13		Simon Peter	1/2	m.				
14		John	41	m.	Laborer		Sw.	
15	364/369	ROTHENBUHLE, Saml.	26	m.	Shoemaker	/100	"	
16	365/370	MARTEE, Jacob	50	m.	Farmer	1000/300	"	
17		Anna	41	f.			At sea	
18		Saml.	20	m.	Farmer		O.	
19		Rosean	18	f.			"	S
20		Caroline	16	f.			"	S
21		Louisa	14	f.			"	S
22		Sarah	12	f.			"	S
23		Mary	10	f.			"	S
24		Barbary	8	f.			"	S
25		William	7	m.			"	
26		Elisabeth	5	f.			"	
27		Alexander	3	m.			"	
28		Margaret	2	f.				
29	366/371	YOST, John	39	m.	Carpenter	400/100	Sw.	
30	367/372	WYSS, Simon	34	m.	Saddler	1500/300	"	

31	368/373	GROCERBACHER, Stephen	57	m.	Farmer	500/100	Sw.

32	369/374	BRUNEY, John	32	m.	Farmer	800/200	O.
33		Catherine	25	f.			"
34		Henry	1	m.			"
35		MAUR, Chris	20	m.	Laborer		Sw.

36	370/375	HALDEMAN, Fred	32	m.	Farmer	1000/500	"
37		Elis	27	f.			"
38		Bertha	6	f.			O. S
39		Ludwic	4	m.			"

Page 57   1 August 1860   Sheet 133

1		Sophia	3	f.			O.
2		John	1/2	m.			"
3		ARNDRICKS, John	35	m.	Cheese-maker		Sw.

4	371/376	STEWARD, James	28	m.	Blacksmith	/100	O.
5		Mary	24	f.			"
6		Emaline	3	f.			"

7	372/377	RUFNER, John	36	m.	Farmer	400/150	Zur.
8		Mary	28	f.			"
9		Rosean	10	f.			O. S
10		John	8	m.			" S
11		Jacob	6	m.			" S
12		Mary	1	f.			"

13	373/378	ROTH, Frances	38	m.	Farmer	400/350	Sw.
14		Anna	40	f.			"
15		France	18	m.	Farmer		"
16		Eliza	14	f.			"
17		Saml.	12	m.			"
18		Mary	9	f.			"
19		Fred	5	m.			O.
20		John	3	m.			"
21		Caroline	1/2	f.			"

22	374/379	SHAMBOUGH, Henry	55	m.	Farmer	500/200	Sax.
23		Mary	53	f.			"
24		Emmill	15	m.			"
25		George	13	m.			" S

26	375/380	KASSERMAN, Ursis	65	m.	Farmer	/700	Sw.
27							
28		JONES, J. L.	23	m.	Minister	/100	O.
29		PEARSOLL, Lemuel	40	m.	Laborer		Pa.
30		KASSERMAN, Mary	25	f.	Seamstress		O.
31							
32		Total 2172 in Ohio Township.					

                                             (Jno. B. Noll)

* * *

Page 1					4 June 1860			Sheet 135	

1	1/1	DANIEL, Joseph	46	m.	Farmer	1600/600	Va.		
2		Rebecca	38	f.	Domestic		O.		
3		Alexander	16	m.	Farmer		"	S	
4		Samuel W.	15	m.	Farmer		"	S	
5		Sarah E.	13	f.			"	S	
6		Anne O.	3	f.			"		
7	2/2	RILEY, Robert	39	m.	Farmer	2250/417	Va.	I	
8		Hannah	39	f.	Domestic		O.		
9		Sarah J.	18	f.	Domestic		"	S	
10		Celia A.	16	f.	Domestic		"	S	
11		Joshua	14	m.			"	S	
12		Margaret A.	13	f.			"	S	
13		Mary A.	12	f.			"	S	
14		Hannah M.	8	f.			"	S	
15		Nancy E.	7	f.			"	S	
16		Susanna S.	4	f.			"	S	
17		Martha	2	f.			"		
18		John W.	7/12	m.			"		
19	3/3	JOY, Levi	54	m.	Farmer	125/100	Pa.		
20		Nancy	50	f.	Domestic		Va.	I	
21		Warren	16	m.	Day laborer		O.	S	
22		Harvey	15	m.	Day laborer		"	S	
23		Cornelius	13	m.			"	S	
24		Mary	12	f.			"	S	
25		Adaline	8	f.			"	S	
26		Clarissa	3	f.			"		
27		Elizabeth	1	f.			"		
28		Nancy	83	f.	Retired		Va.	I	
29	4/4	JOHNSON, Joseph	40	m.	Carpenter	300/200	O.		
30		Nancy	30	f.			"		
31		Russell	14	m.			"	S	
32		Henry	12	m.			"	S	
33		James	10	m.			"	S	
34		Harriet	6	f.			"		
35		Enos	3	m.			"		
36		Wm.	1	m.			"		
37	5/5	CLINE, David	42	m.	Farmer	/250	"	M	
38		Harriet	26	f.	Domestic		"	M	

Page 2					4 June 1860			Sheet 135 verso	

1		Rufus E.	14	m.			O.	S	
2	6/6	RING, Lewis C.	30	m.	Farmer	400/100	"		
3		Hannah	30	f.	Domestic		"		
4		Margaret E.	7	f.			"		
5		Mary E.	4	f.			"		
6		Walter	2	m.			"		
7		Nancy	3/12	f.			"		
8	7/7	HILL, Hezekiah	32	m.	Farmer	1500/200	"		

9		HILL, Catherine	30	f.	Domestic		O.	
10		James H.	9	m.			"	S
11		Mary E.	8	f.			"	S
12		Simeon T.	6	m.			"	S
13		Nancy E.	3	f.			"	
14		Sarah F.	1	f.			"	
15	8/8	CLINE, Samuel	35	m.	Farmer	/100	"	
16		Margaret	35	f.	Domestic		Pa.	
17		Daniel	13	m.			O.	S
18		Roseberry	12	m.			"	S
19		Gemima A.	10	f.			"	S
20		John	8	m.			"	S
21		William W.	4	m.			"	
22		Mary E.	2	f.			"	
23		Eunice M.	6/12	f.			"	
24	9/9	MILLS, John	52	m.	Farmer	/40	"	
25		Mary	47	f.	Domestic		"	I
26		Drusilla	22	f.	Domestic		"	
27		David	14	m.			"	S
28		Nancy J.	10	f.			"	S
29		Mary E.	3	f.			"	
30	10/10	CLINE, Jacob Sr.	62	m.	Farmer	400/300	"	
31		Nancy	64	f.	Domestic		Va.	
32		Samuel H.	37	m.	Farm laborer		O.	
33		Susannah	19	f.	Domestic		"	
34		MILLS, Jacob	18	m.	Farm laborer		"	S
35	11/11	CLINE, John	42	m.	Farmer	2500/178	"	
36		Nancy	42	f.	Domestic		"	
37		Malinda	16	f.	Domestic		"	S
38		Ruth A.	9	f.			"	S
39		Theadore P.	12	m.			"	S

Page 3   4 June 1860   Sheet 136

1		Jacob N.	8	m.			O.	S
2		Josiah	6	m.			"	S
3		Susannah	3	f.			"	
4	12/12	RING, George Jr.	37	m.	Farmer	3800/700	"	
5		Drusilla	24	f.	Domestic		"	
6		Julia A.	2	f.			"	
7		Elmore	7/12	f.			"	
8	13/13	HILL, Mary	54	f.	Domestic	4500/300	Pa.	
9		Cornelius	22	m.	Farmer	/50	O.	
10		Sarah	20	f.	Domestic		"	
11		Mary	18	f.	Domestic		"	S
12		Simeon	18	m.	Farmer		"	S
13		GROVES, Sarah	50	f.	Servant		Pa.	
14		Sylvester	15	m.			O.	S
15	14/14	KEESY, Jacob	86	m.	Retired	/50	Pa.	
16		Nancy	80	f.	Domestic		"	

17	15/15	FERGUSON, John	49	m.	Farmer	/75	O.	
18		Rebecca	49	f.	Domestic		"	
19		James K.	16	m.	Farm laborer		"	S
20		Samuel W.	14	m.			"	S
21		John G.	12	m.			"	S
22		Martha J.	9	f.			"	S
23	16/16	WILLIAMSON, Thomas	47	m.	Farmer	400/200	Va.	
24		Susanna	44	f.	Domestic		O.	I
25		LAMBERSON, Eliza-beth	22	f.	Servant		Pa.	
26		GRAY, Walter	16	m.	Farm laborer		O.	
27		DAVIS, James	7	m.			"	S
28	17/17	RING, Benjamin	33	m.	Farmer	/50	"	
29		Eveline	25	f.	Domestic		Va.	
30		Thomas C.	7	m.			O.	
31		George	5	m.			"	
32		David·	4	m.			"	
33		Margaret F.	3	f.			Va.	
34		Nancy	2	f.			O.	
35	18/18	CLINE, Thomas	40	m.	Farmer	1200/400	"	
36		Mary	35	f.	Domestic		"	I
37		Marshall	16	m.			"	S
38		James	14	m.			"	S
39		Nancy	11	f.			"	S

Page 4   5 June 1860   Sheet 136 verso

1		Hannah M.	6	f.			O.	
2		Ary	2	f.			"	
3	19/19	CLINE, Joseph	42	m.	Farmer	1600/500	"	
4		Mary	41	f.			"	
5		Harvey	20	m.			"	S
6		Elizabeth	18	f.			"	
7		Zepheniah	11	m.			"	S
8		Sarah	7	f.			"	
9		Louisa J.	5	f.			"	
10		Margaret K.	3	f.			"	
11	20/20	TEBAY, James M.	27	m.	Farmer	/400	Pa.	
12		Catharine E.	23	f.			O.	
13		Isabel M.	2	f.			"	
14	21/21	HUFFMAN, Casper	53	m.	Farmer	400/70	Pr.	M
15		Mary	16	f.	Domestic		"	S
16		Elizabeth	12	f.			"	S
17	22/22	BEYMOUR, Frederick	31	m.	Farmer	600/140	"	
18		Sophia	27	f.	Domestic		Ger.	
19		William	5	m.			O.	
20		John	4	m.			"	
21		Emily	2	f.			"	
22	23/23	MURPHEY, William	70	m.	Farmer	2400/250	Pa.	
23		Jane	65	f.	Domestic		"	

24		MURPHEY, Elizabeth	34	f.	Domestic		O.
25		Samuel	11	m.			" S
26	24/24	BEYMOUR, Henry	36	m.	Farmer	600/80	Pr.
27		Mary	36	f.			"
28		Charles	6	m.			O.
29		Mena	5	f.			"
30		Charlota	3	f.			"
31		William	1	m.			"
32	25/25	TEGTMIRE, Chris-					
		tian	33	m.	Farmer	1400/150	Ger.
33		Luisa	33	f.			Hes.
34		Charles	8	m.			O. S
35		Wilmira	7	f.			" S
36		Frederick	2	m.			"
37	26/26	BOYD, James	47	m.	Farmer	2000/400	Pa.
38		Elisabeth	46	f.			"
39		Henry	21	m.	Farmer		"

Page 5			5 June 1860				Sheet 137
1		Joseph	20	m.	Farmer		Pa. S
2		Nancy Jane	18	f.			" S
3		William C.	16	m.			" S
4		Albert N.	14	m.			" S
5		Elisabeth	12	f.			" S
6		Andrew C.	12	m.			" S
7		Abagail	10	f.			" S
8		Margaret	8	f.			" S
9		James	6	m.			" S
10	27/27	JOHNSON, James	32	m.	Farmer	600/75	O.
11		Lavina	30	f.			"
12		Alice D.	3	f.			"
13		James W.	2	m.			Ia.
14	28/28	BROWN, Michael	44	m.	Farmer	1000/150	Pa.
15		Christena	35	f.			"
16		Pheobe	17	f.			O. S
17		Elisabeth	15	f.			" S
18		James	14	m.			" S
19		Mary J.	12	f.			" S
20		Margaret	11	f.			" S
21		Rachel	9	f.			" S
22		George	7	m.			" S
23		Susanah	5	f.			"
24		Henry S.	3	m.			"
25		Eliza	1	f.			"
26	29/29	RING, Jacob	32	m.	Farmer	400/40	"
27		Walter	7	m.			"
28		Margaret	6	f.			"
29		Samuel	4	m.			"
30	30/30	RING, Walter	66	m.	Miller	6000/1211	N.Y.
31		Margaret	57	f.			Va.

32		OKEY, Margaret	6	f.			O.
33	31/31	FAUCETT, Benjamin	53	m.	Farmer	2000/1000	"
34		Lydia A.	53	f			Md.
35		Amy E.	21	f.			O.
36		Lydia J.	19	f.			" S
37	32/32	FERGUSON, Thomas	22	m.	Farm laborer		"
38		Rachel E.	20	f.			"

Page 6   6 June 1860   Sheet 137 verso

1	33/33	DYE, Benjamin	26	m.	Farmer	500/100	O.
2		Martha A.	22	f.	Domestic		"
3		Amons	10/12	m.			"
4	34/34	CLEVICE, Conrad	47	m.	Farm laborer	/50	Han.
5		Eugusta	30	f.	Domestic		Hes.
6		Charles	10	m.			Va.
7		John	8	m.			"
8		Lien	5	m.			"
9		Theadore	3	m.			"
10		Julia	4/12	f.			
11	35/35	SWARTZ, Peter	56	m.	Farmer	600/150	Ger.
12		Mary M.	53	f.	Domestic		"
13		Henry	22	m.	Farm laborer	/85	Pa.
14		Bonyvant	15	m.			" S
15	36/36	McWILLIAMS, James	46	m.	Farmer	500/150	O.
16		Hannah	45	f.	Domestic		"
17		Jamima	11	f.			" S
18	37/37	BAGEL, Frederick	59	m.	Farmer	1500/300	Ger.
19		Emeli	67	f.	Domestic		" I
20		Charles	27	m.	Farmer	/60	"
21		William	25	m.	Farmer		"
22		Carolina	13	f.			Pa.
23	38/38	ADAMS, Robert	33	m.	Carpenter	/150	"
24		Mary E.	27	f.	Domestic		O.
25		Thomas	16	m.	Farmer	/60	" S
26		Anjoline	6	f.			" S
27		Ruth E.	5	f.			"
28		Margaret	78	f.			Ire.
29	39/39	HILL, John M.	34	m.	Farmer	100/360	O.
30		Vilinda	33	f.	Domestic		"
31		Vachel	11	f.			" S
32		Avery	9	m.			" S
33		Jacob	7	m.			" S
34		Josiah	5	m.			" S
35		Ruth	3	f.			"
36		Martha	1	f.			"
37	40/40	BLACK, James	27	m.	Farmer	1200/1000	Pa.
38		Susanah	24	f.	Domestic		O.

39   BLACK, Margaret E.   6   f.   O. S

1   Amandy E.   4   f.   O. S
2   Henry H.   2   m.   "
3   LAPORT, James M. 11   m.   "   S
4   NEWEL, Sarah E. 19   f.   Servant   "

5   41/41   MERPHY, Thomas   37   m.   Carpenter 1000/200   "
6   Attila   33   f.   Domestic   "
7   Samuel   11   m.   "   S
8   Luisa   9   f.   "   S
9   John A.   7   m.   "   S
10   James   4   m.   "
11   William   2   m.   "
12   Avery   4/12 m.   "
13   RIPPLE, Mary   50   f.   Servant   Pa.

14   42/42   THOMPSON, James A. 31 m.   R. P. Minister
                                                           300/200   O.
15   Sarah M.   29   f.   Domestic   "
16   William A. J.   3   m.   "
17   James J.   1   m.   "
18   Martha M.   4/12 f.   "

19   43/43   CLINE, G. W.   31   m.   Farmer   /200   "
20   Elisabeth   29   f.   Domestic   Va.
21   James W. W.   2   m.   O.
22   Sarah J.   1   f.   "

23   44/44   MASON, Thompson 73   m.   Farmer   800/100   Pa.
24   Elisabeth   53   f.   Domestic   O.
25   NEWEL, Salome H. 18   f.   Servant   "

26   45/45   TEEMAN, John D. 32   m.   Farmer   5000/700 Ger.
27   Amee A.   20   f.   Domestic   O.
28   Wm. F.   3   m.   "
29   Mary   1   f.   "

30   46/46   ROWAN, Matthew   52   m.   Farmer   1500/500 Pa.
31   Jane   33   f.   Domestic   Scot.

32   47/47   TEBAY, Isaac   57   m.   Farmer   2000/500 Eng.
33   Isabella   53   f.   Ire.
34   Joseph   25   m.   Farmer   /200 Pa.

35   48/48   CLINE, George   64   m.   Farmer   1800/500 Va.
36   Nancy   61   f.   Domestic   O. I
37   David   17   m.   Farmer   "   S
38   Madama   12   f.   "   S
39   Philip   11   m.   "   S

1   49/49   TEEMAN, Lewis   23   m.   Farm laborer   /50   Pa.
2   Catharine   23   f.   Domestic   O.

3		TEEMAN, Ann C.	2	f.			O.	
4		Eunice J.	2/12	f.			"	
5	50/50	TEEMAN, Henry H.	37	m.	Farmer	5000/700	Pr.	
6		Eunice	25	f.	Domestic		O.	
7		Eliza	4	f.			"	
8		John W.	2	m.			"	
9		William H.	1	m.			"	
10	51/51	BOYD, Saml.	57	m.	Farmer	4000/600	Pa.	
11		Elizabeth	53	f.	Domestic		"	
12		James A.	24	m.	Farmer		"	S
13		Matthew	18	m.	Farmer		"	S
14		Nancy	13	f.			"	S
15		Mary E.	11	f.			"	S
16		Deborah A.	9	f.			O.	S
17		William	25	m.	Student (?)		Pa.	
18	52/52	CLINE, John Sr.	60	m.	Farmer	5000/1000	Va.	
19		Elvira	57	f.	Domestic		°O.	I
20		Lydia	22	f.	Domestic		"	
21		Rosebery	20	m.	Farmer		"	S
22		Harvy	18	m.	Farmer		"	S
23		Elvíra	15	f.			"	S
24		John M.	13	m.			"	S
25		William H.	13	m.			"	S
26		Elvira	11	f.			"	S
27		McVEY, Mary E.	6	f.			"	S
28		CLINE, Elisabeth	5	f.			"	
29		Martha	3	f.			"	
30		Mary	3	f.				
31	53/53	CLINE, George Sr.	72	m.	Farmer	5000/620	Pa.	
32		Christena	71	f.	Domestic		"	I
33		Isaac	29	m.	Farmer		O.	
34		Narcissa	32	f.	Domestic		"	
35		Levina	15	f.			"	S
36		Catharine	19	f.			"	S
37		Malissa	17	f.			"	S
38		Christena	1/12	f.			"	

1	54/54	MINDER, Samuel	37	m.	Day laborer	/50	Bern	
2		Catharine	25	f.	Domestic		Md.	
3		Margaret E.	5	f.			O.	
4		John W.	3	m.			"	
5		Merryman	4/12	m.				
6	55/55	HILLEBROUGH,			Cabinet-maker			
		William	35	m.		300/200	Pr.	
7		Wilemana	27	f.	Domestic		"	I
8		Henry	11	m.			Pa.	S
9		Willemany	8	f.			O.	S
10		Julia	4	f.			"	
11		Frederick	5/12	m.				
12	56/56	TEEMAN, Scharlota	64	f.	Domestic	1500/2000	Ger.	

13	57/57	JOHNSON, William	51	m.	M.E.P. Minister/290	O.	
14		Elisabeth	25	f.	Domestic	"	
15		Aloritta	2	f.		"	
16	58/58	KOONTZ, Anne	33	f.	3000/200	Md.	
17		William	9	m.		O.	S
18		Martha	8	f.		"	S
19		Samuel	6	m.		"	S
20		Adalade	4	f.		"	S
21	59/59	SMYTH, George	40	m.	Shoemaker	250/50	Pr.
22		Heneritta	39	f.	Domestic	"	I
23		Heneritta	13	f.		"	S
24		William	10	m.		"	S
25		Henry	7	m.		"	S
26		Matilda	4	f.		Pa.	
27		George	2	m.		O.	
28	60/60	SWARTZER, Henry	53	m.	Blacksmith	500/60	Hes.
29		Jacob	11	m.		O.	S
30	61/61	BARNS, Ruth	49	f.	Domestic	300/150	Md.
31		Mary E.	21	f.	Domestic		O.
32		Emily	20	f.	Domestic		"
33		Luisa	16	f.	Domestic		"
34		Marinda	14	f.			"
35		Robert A.	12	m.			"
36		Margaret C.	9	f.			"
37	62/62	BARNS, Israel	58	m.	Farmer	/280	Md.
38		Sarah	57	f.	Domestic		Va.
39		Susanah	23	f.	Domestic		O.

Page 10			7 June 1860			Sheet 139 verso	
1		Grifeth C.	20	m.	Tobacco packer	O.	
2		Sarah	18	f.	Domestic	"	
3		Hariet	14	f.		"	
4		CAMPBELL, Margaret	23	f.	Milliner	"	
5	63/63	BROWN, Enoch	33	m.	Indianier (?) /25	"	
6		Mary A.	32	f.	Domestic	"	
7		Joseph N.	11	m.		"	S
8		Sarah J.	6	f.		"	S
9		James A.	4	m.		"	
10		William	2	m.		"	
11	64/64	ANDERSON, A. R.	44	m.	Physician	500/165	Pa.
12		Mary H.	33	f.	Domestic		N.J.
13		Sarah R.	5	f.			Pa.	S
14		Margaret E.	3	f.			O.
15		BELL, E. R.	19	m.	Teacher		"
16	65/65	WILEY, Isabella	33	f.	Teacher	500/100	Pa.
17		Ann M.	12	f.		"	S
18		John P.	6	m.		"	S
19		Oliver	3	m.		O.	S

20	66/66	WILSON, Josiah	40	m.	Physician	2000/3000	O.
21		Ruth	29	f.	Domestic	3500/	"
22		Alonzo	8	m.			" S
23		Gertrude	6	f.			" S
24		Isadora	4	f.			" S
25		Vilinda J.	2	f.			"
26		Anne A.	9/12	f.			"
27	67/67	SANDAR, Christian	35	m.	Tinner	/500	Bav.
28		Mary E.	33	f.	Domestic		"
29		George W.	12	m.			N.Y. S
30		Christian	5	m.			O. S
31		Margaret E.	2	f.			"
32	68/68	ALGEO, George S.	32	m.	Merchant	/8000	Pa.
33		Anne	25	f.	Domestic		O.
34		Adam	2	m.			"
35		SOUTH, G. S.	21	m.	Clerk	/100	Pa.
36	69/69	BONELL, George W.	49	m.	Tobacco-packer	700/600	Va.
37		Levina	35	f.	Domestic		Del.
38		Ruth A.	17	f.	Domestic		O. S
39		Hariet E.	15	f.	Domestic		" S

Page 11	7 June 1860	Sheet 140

1		Sarah J.	13	f.			O. S
2		George W.	12	m.			" S
3		Vachel T.	11	m.			" S
4		James	2	m.			"
5		Philo P.	5/12	m.			
6	70/70	VANZANT, Samuel	59	m.	Tobacco-packer	/170	Pa.
7		Mary A.	61	f.	Domestic		Md.
8		Mary	23	f.	Teacher		O.
9		Susanna	19	f.			" S
10		Emily	17	f.			" S
11	71/71	HILL, John	58	m.	Farmer	300/225	Del.
12		Elisabeth	52	f.	Domestic		"
13		Hellen	17	f.	Domestic		Va. S
14		Elisabeth	17	f.	Domestic		" S
15		George B.	13	m.			" S
16		COPELAND, Jose-phene	10	f.			" S
17	72/72	AMOS, Corbon	50	m.	Merchant	2500/3000	Md.
18		Juliana	40	f.	Domestic		Va.
19		Sarah L. C.	10	f.			O. S
20	73/73	ALLEN, Arthur	32	m.	Wool-carder	/100	Scot.
21		Agnes	31	f.	Domestic		Ire.
22		John W.	9	m.			Pa. S
23		Elisabeth W.	8	f.			" S
24		Robert	6	m.			" S
25	74/74	SCHWARTZER, Catharine	45	f.		250/75	Hes. I

26		SCHWARTZER, Fred-					
		erick	22	m.	Blacksmith	/25	Pa. S
27		Charles	20	m.	Blacksmith		Va. S
28		Gunderman	17	f.			Pa. S
29		Mary E.	5	f.			O. S
30	75/75	COURTNEY, Wm. F.	48	m.	Wagon-maker	100/100	Va.
31		Temperence	34	f.	Domestic		"
32		Benjamin J.	9	m.			" S
33		James S.	5	m.			" S
34		Jeremiah B.	2	m.			"
35		Not named	2/12	m.			O.

Page 12   7 June 1860   Sheet 140 verso

1	76/76	GROATHENS, Geo. H.	27	m.	Tanner & currier		
						/100	O.
2		Levina	21	f.	Domestic		"
3		#Sophiah	1	f.			"
4	77/77	HILL, Avery	62	m.	Farmer	1500/200	N.Y.
5		Levina	55	f.	Domestic		O.
6		Simeon	25	m.	Farmer	/70	"
7		Emily	19	f.	Domestic		" S
8		Harvy	17	m.	Farmer		" S
9		Elisabeth	12	f.			" S
10	78/78	LIST, Nicholas	57	m.	Farmer	2000/300	Va.
11		Mary ann	32	f.	Domestic		O.
12		Susanna	16	f.	Domestic		"
13		Nicholas	14	m.			" S
14		Elisabeth	14	f.			" S
15		Jasper	24	m.	Teacher	800/350	"
16	79/79	SNIDER, James	26	m.	Farmer	/250	"
17		Magdalina	25	f.	Domestic		Sw. I
18		Elisebeth	9	f.			O. S
19		Luisa	8	f.			" S
20		Matilda	6	f.			" S
21		Nathaniel	4	m.			" S
22		Margaret E.	10/12	f.			Ill.
23	80/80	LIST, Saml.	32	m.	Farmer	1300/300	Va.
24		Catharine J.	48	f.	Domestic		O.
25		Mary A.	19	f.	Domestic		"
26		Eliza J.	18	f.	Domestic		"
27		James E.	15	m.			"
28		Lucretia	13	f.			" S
29		Alexandria	12	m.			" S
30		Amandy	6	f.			" S
31		John W.	3	m.			"
32		Mariah L.	1	f.			"
33	81/81	POWELL, William	65	m.	Farmer	2000/250	Va.
34		Hannah	48	f.	Domestic		N.J.
35		Catharine	16	f.	Domestic		O. S
36		George W.	14	m.			" S
37	82/82	DOWELL, Jessee	48	m.	Farmer	/60	Pa. I

38		DOWELL, Elisabeth	40	f.	Domestic		Pa.
39		Charity	14	f.			O. S

Page 13			11 June 1860				Sheet 141

1		Jefferson	11	m.			O. S
2		Rebecca	10	f.			" S
3		Marthy	7	f.			" S
4		Samuel	6	m.			" S
5	83/83	McKNIGHT, David R.	26	m.	Tanner	/175	"
6		Hester Anne	26	f.	Domestic		" I
7		Thomas	4	m.			"
8		Otho	1	m.			"
9	84/84	THOMPSON, George	27	m.	Farmer	/300	N.Y.
10		Ame Jane	20	f.	Domestic		O.
11		James W.	1	m.			"
12	85/85	DOTT, George	50	m.	Farmer		H.-D.
13		Charlotty	41	f.		1000/300	"
14		Mary	18	f.	Domestic		"
15		William	15	m.			" S
16		Catharine	13	f.			" S
17		Margaret	10	f.			O. S
18		Peter	6	m.			"
19		Charles	4	m.			"
20		Magadlena	1	f.			"
21		VREH, Christenah	69	f.	Retired		Han.
22	86/86	HILL, Ed	50	m.	Farmer	/50	N.Y.
23		Malissa	48	f.	Domestic		Pa.
24		Jane	22	f.			O.
25		Elisabeth	16	f.			" S
26		Nancy	7	f.			" S
27		John	11	m.			" 4
28		Margaret	6	f.			"
29		Emily	5	f.			"
30	87/87	McKASLIN, Jas.	28	m.	Farmer	/300	"
31		Mary	22	f.	Domestic		Pa.
32		Thomas	1	m.			O.
33	88/88	DON, Johnathon	60	m.	Farmer	1200/800	Md.
34		Margaret	28	f.			O. I
35		Mary J.	13	f.			"
36		Ephram	1	m.			Ind.
37		Robinson	6	m.			Ill.
38		TURNER, Marthy	72	f.	Servant		Pa. I
39	89/89	HARRISON, Thomas A.	40	m.	Day laborer	/100	Va.

Page 14			11 June 1860				Sheet 141 verso

1		Rebecky	30	f.	Domestic	O. I
2		Austi.ı A.	6	m.		"
3		Sarah L. A.	3	f.		"

4		HARRISON, Laury B.	2	f.			O.	
5	90/90	SWARTWOOD, Levi	25	m.	Carpenter (?)	/100	"	
6		Sarah	24	f.	Domestic		"	
7		Abagail J.	4	f.			"	
8		James W.	1	m.			"	
9	91/91	SWALLOW, James	36	m.	Farmer	3600/1000	Va.	
10		Susanna	26	f.	Domestic		O.	
11		Rebecky Anne	7	f.			"	S
12		Zilly	5	f.			"	
13		Amanda J.	2	f.			"	
14		Sarah	2/12	f.			"	
15	92/92	SWALLOW, Joseph	47	m.	Farmer	2160/600	Va.	
16		Mary	43	f.	Domestic		Pa.	
17		John W.	19	m.	Farmer		O.	S
18		Martha E.	14	f.			"	S
19		Serepta	12	f.			"	S
20		Arbola S.	9	f.			"	S
21		Wm. J.	9	m.			"	S
22		James M.	6	m.			"	S
23		Mary C.	3	f.			"	
24	93/93	ROBINSON, Sarah A.	49	f.	Domestic	350/75	"	
25		William	15	m.	Farmer		"	S
26		James	13	m.			"	S
27		Robert	11	m.			"	S
28		POOL, Permelia A.	11	f.			"	S
29		Mary E.	10	f.			"	S
30		ROBINSON, John R.	21	m.	Student (?)		"	
31	94/94	ROBINSON, David	23	m.	Farm laborer	/60	Pa.	
32		Catharine	28	f.	Domestic		O.	
33		DONN, Mariah	9	f.			"	S
34	95/95	ALGOE, Charles	65	m.	Farmer	7000/2000	Ire.	
35		Elisa	64	f.	Domestic		"	
36		Joseph	26	m.	Farmer	800/50	O.	
37		Anne	18	f.	Domestic		"	
38		CALDERBRAUGH,						
		Charles	12	m.			Ger.	

Page 15			12 June 1860				Sheet 142	
1	96/96	POOL, Charles	65	m.	Farmer	1000/50	Va.	I
2		Margaret	54	f.	Domestic	/20	Pa.	
3		Adaline	23	f.	Domestic	/20	O.	
4		Isaac	24	m.	Farmer	/60	"	
5		Margaret	19	f.	Domestic		"	
6		James	18	m.	Farmer		"	
7		William	16	m.	Farmer		"	
8	97/97	CHALK, Leonard	55	m.	Shoemaker	800/100	Md.	
9		Julianna	30	f.	Domestic		O.	
10	98/98	POOL, William	57	m.	Farmer	8000/1000	"	
11		Jane	42	f.	Domestic		Pa.	

12		POOL, Leonard	22	m.	Farmer		O.	
13		Zilla	17	f.	Domestic		"	
14		Elisabeth J.	16	f.	Domestic		"	S
15		William C.	15	m.			"	S
16		Mary E.	13	f.			"	S
17		Emma	9	f.			"	S
18		John M.	3	m.			"	
19		Anna C.	1	f.			"	
20		HUFFMAN, Martha	17	f.	Servant		"	
21	99/99	JACOBS, Elisabeth	51	f.	Domestic	/60	Pa.	
22		Mataias	24	m.	Farm laborer	/55	O.	
23		Roseberry	22	m.	Farm laborer		"	
24		Mary	18	f.	Domestic		"	
25		Elisabeth	16	f.	Domestic		"	S
26		HARTHORN, Hachel	9	f.			"	S
27	100/100	WELLS, Warren	48	m.	Farmer	2500/400	Va.	
28		Actious	46	f.	Domestic		O.	
29		James H.	24	m.	Farmer & broom-maker /100		"	
30		Emasa	22	f.	Domestic		"	
31		Mordica	15	m.			"	S
32		John M.	12	m.			"	S
33		Emma	10	f.			"	S
34		Wilber F.	8	m.			"	S
35		Ella R.	6	f.			"	S
36	101/101	WINOH, John	51	m.	Farmer	5000/100	Eng.	
37		Elisabeth	51	f.	Domestic		"	
38		Nicholas	27	m.	Farmer	/600	"	
39		Mary E.	21	f.			Pa.	4

Page 16   12 June 1860   Sheet 142 verso

1		John	20	m.	Farmer		Pa.	S
2		Cordelia	18	f.	Domestic		O.	S
3		Sarah	15	f.			"	S
4		William H.	11	m.			"	S
5		Samuel P.	8	m.			"	S
6		Theabal	6	m.			"	S
7	102/102	EDDY, Eli	40	m.	Farmer	1600/300	Va.	
8		Nancy	33	f.	Domestic		"	
9		Samuel	17	m.	Farmer		O.	S
10		Irema	13	f.			"	S
11		Marthy E.	12	f.			"	S
12		Augustus	10	m.			"	S
13		Albert	8	m.			"	S
14		Francis	7	f.			"	
15		James F.	5	m.			"	
16		Harmon R.	4	m.			"	
17		Mary E.	5/12	f.				
18	103/103	RIGG, Nathaniel	54	m.	Teacher	600/150	Pa.	
19		Mancy	49	f.	Domestic	/80	O.	
20	104/104	CALHOON, James	59	m.	Steamboat builder 200/80		"	

21		CALHOON, Eliza	51	f.	Domestic		Va.
22		Mary J.	14	f.			Pa. S
23		Arvilla	12	f.			" S
24	105/105	BARTON, Enos	57	m.	Farmer	800/60	" I
25		Sarah	37	f.	Domestic		Va. I
26		Jeremiah	16	m.	Farmer		O.
27	106/106	BARTON, Enos	26	m.	Farm laborer	300/50	" I
28	107/107	WILLIS, James	32	m.	Day laborer	/50	Va.
29		Syntha	25	f.	Domestic		Pa.
30		Henson	11	m.			O. S
31		Sophia	9	f.			" S
32		John	8	m.			Pa. S
33		Thomas	6	m.			"
34		Joseph	3	m.			O.
35	108/108	PATERSON, Robert A.	25	m.	Farmer	200/150	Pa.
36		Catharine	23	f.	Domestic		"
37		George W.	7/12	m.			O.
38	109/109	FERGISON, Saml.	34	m.	Farmer	2000/200	Ire.
39		Susanna	32	f.	Domestic		O.

Page 17   13 June 1860   Sheet 143

1		Rachael	4	f.			O.
2		Mary J.	3	f.			"
3		Henry	11/12	m.			
4		FERGUSON, Grace	64	f.	Retired		Ire.
5	110/110	BRADFIELD, Jas.	42	m.	Farmer	3000/250	Md.
6		Lusinda	46	f.	Domestic		Ky.
7		Ephraim	19	m.	Farmer		O. S
8		Jacob	15	m.	Farmer		" S
9		Mary	12	f.			" S
10		Harvey	10	m.			" S
11		Lewis C.	8	m.			" S
12		Corben	4	m.			" S
13		Sarah E.	4/12	f.			"
14	111/111	JUDGE, Saml.	30	m.	Farmer	1300/300	"
15		Jane	25	f.	Domestic		" I
16		James	4	m.			"
17		William	1	m.			"
18		DELAWN, Nancy	18	f.	Servant		"
19		JUDGE, John	16	m.	Farm laborer		Ark.
20		DELONG, William	9	m.			O.
21		JUDGE, Sarah	72	f.	Retired		Conn.1
22	112/112	BURNFIELD, Mathias	52	m.	Farmer	400/300	Pa.
23		Mary	46	f.	Domestic		"
24		Lusindia	27	f.	Domestic		"
25		John	25	m.	Farm laborer	350/	"
26		Abij	23	m.			" I4
27		Mary J.	21	f.	Domestic		"

28		BURNFIELD, Thomas	18	m.	Farmer	Pa.	S
29		Catharine	16	f.	Domestic	O.	S
30		Eliza J.	11	f.		"	S
31		Maria E.	8	f.		"	S
32		Robert	3	m.		"	
33		Lucretia J.	3	f.		"	
34		Elisabeth J.	4/12	f.		"	

35	113/113	CALDERBAUGH, Charles	50	m.	Farmer	/100 Ger.
36		Laury	40	f.	Domestic	"
37		John	18	m.	Farmer	" S
38		Philip	16	m.	Farmer	" S
39		Charles	14	m.		" S

Page 18   13 June 1860   Sheet 143 verso

1		Catharine	11	f.		Ger. S
2		Coonrad	5	m.		O. S
3		Mary M.	3	f.		"
4		GRAFT, Catharine	74	f.	Domestic	Ger.

5	114/114	LARCOMBEL, John	55	m.	Tanner & currier	/50 Eng.
6		Mary	49	f.	Domestic	
7		Charles	21	m.	Farm laborer	O.
8		Sarah V.	18	f.	Domestic	"
9		Geo. W.	15	m.		" S
10		Levi A.	13	m.		" S
11		Deborah	11	f.		" S
12		Dorcas	10	f.		" S
13		James C.	5	m.		"

14	115/115	HOTT, Saml.	32	m.	Farmer	400/150 Va.
15		Susanna	32	f.	Domestic	"
16		Tobias	12	m.		O. S
17		Nancy A.	11	f.		" S
18		Catharine	9	f.		" S
19		Enos N.	6	m.		"
20		Saml. J.	4	m.		

21	116/116	HUTCHINSON, William	42	m.	Farmer	2000/300 Pa.
22		Caroline	26	f.	Domestic	O.
23		Luisa	4	f.		"

24	117/117	SELLERS, Pheobe	58	f.	Domestic	800/399 Pa.
25		Leonard	21	m.	Farmer	/45 O.
26		John J.	19	m.	Farmer	/30 "

27	118/118	HOYL, John	44	m.	Farmer	1000/300 Ger.
28		Mene	44	f.	Domestic	Hes.
29		John	13	m.		" S
30		Charlotta	12	f.		" S
31		Mena	9	f.		Pa.
32		Margaret	2	f.		O.
33		Deborah	6/12	f.		"

```
34 119/119 BUSH, Charles      41   m.   Farmer       700/350  Ger.
35          Meni              30   f.   Domestic              "
36          Charles            5   m.                         Ky.
37          Henry              3   m.                         O.
38          CROFT, Margaret   51   f.   Servant               Pr.
```

Page 19   13 June 1860   Sheet 144

```
1  120/120 BUSH, Frederick    40   m.   Farmer       900/150  Pr.
2          Charloty           40   f.   Domestic              "
3          Harman              4   m.                         O.
4          Frederick           2   m.                         "
5          Christian        3/12   m.                         "

6  121/121 HENSEL, John F.    25   m.   Farmer       400/      "
7          Martha             22   f.   Domestic              Pa.

8  122/122 HENSEL, Saml.      50   m.   Farmer      6000/500  Va.
9          Rue Ann            44   f.   Domestic              Pa.
10         Philip H. K.       24   m.   Farmer        /150    O.
11         Mary E.            19   f.   Domestic       /40    "   S
12         Rue Ann            17   f.   Domestic               "   S
13         Anne N.            16   f.   Domestic               "   S

14 123/123 DYE, Enoch Sr.     73   m.   Farmer        /60     N.J.
15         Mary A.            65   f.   Domestic              Md. I

16 124/124 HOTT, Jesse        40   m.   Farmer        /100    Va.
17         Sarah              40   f.   Domestic              Pa.
18         Rachel             17   f.   Domestic              O.
19         John               12   m.                         "
20         Sarah A.            7   f.                         "
21         Levi                4   m.                         "
22         Tobias              1   m.

23 125/125 MORE, James        27   m.   Carpenter     /200    Pa.
24         Sarah A.           20   f.   Domestic              "

25 126/126 WATTANBAUGH, John  62   m.   Farmer       600/200  "
26         Hannah             60   f.   Domestic              "
27         Hannah             26   f.   Domestic              "
28         Therisa            15   f.   Domestic              "   S
29         GRAHAM, Jas.       39   m.   Boatman               "
30         Margaret           39   f.   Domestic              "
31         Hannah             12   f.                         "   S
32         Floretta            8   f.                         "   S
33         Anna E.             6   f.                         "   S
34         Margaret C.         2   f.                         "
35         Eldervima        9/12   m.                         "

36 127/127 HENSEL, John       48   m.   Farmer      3000/1000 Va.
37         Prisilla           32   f.   Domestic              O.
38         John W.            13   m.                         "
39         Emily J.           11   f.                         "
```

Page 20   14 June 1860   Sheet 144 verso

```
1          Mary A.             6   f.                         O.
```

2		HENSEL, Arye E.	3	f.			O.
3		Julianne	9/12	f.			"
4	128/128	HOTT, Joseph	28	m.	Farmer	/100	Va.
5		Mary	30	f.	Domestic		O.
6		Hannah J.	4	f.			"
7		John W.	1	m.			"
8	129/129	HOTT, Tobias	70	m.	Farmer	200/200	Pa.
9		Catharine	63	f.	Domestic		" I
10		Hencel	21	m.	Farmer		O.
11	130/130	HOTT, Benjamin	26	m.	Farmer		"
12		Mariah M.	20	f.	Domestic	/100	" I
13		Benjamin T.	2	m.			"
14	131/131	HOTT, Jesse	34	m.	Farmer	/200	Va. I
15		Anne	30	f.	Domestic		" I
16		Catharine	9	f.			O.
17		William J.	1	m.			"
18	132/132	DORNBUSH, John J.	50	m.	Farmer	3000/800	Ger.
19		Mine M.	47	f.	Domestic		"
20		Mary C.	20	f.	Domestic		Va.
21		William	19	m.	Farmer		" S
22		John J.	14	m.			O. S
23		Maria S.	13	f.			" S
24		Christopher	11	m.			" S
25		Frederick	8	m.			" S
26	133/133	WHITNEY, Eliza	40	f.	Domestic	4000/500	"
27		Reuben W.	16	m.	Farmer	/150	" S
28		Thomas	14	m.			" S
29	134/134	PETTY, Saml. H.	49	m.	Wagon-maker	2500/500	Pa.
30		Margaret	48	f.	Domestic		"
31		Samuel	23	m.	Farmer		"
32		Daniel	21	m.	Farmer		"
33		Margaret	20	f.	Domestic		" S
34		Mary Anne	12	f.			" S
35		Rebecca J.	10	f.			" S
36		Jemima	7	f.			O. S
37		WALTONBOUGH,					
		Israel	30	m.	Farm laborer		Pa.
38	135/135	McUGH, David	25	m.	Farmer	/450	O.
39		Elzina N.	22	f.	Domestic		Pa.

Page 21			14 June 1860				Sheet 145
1		William H.	10/12	m.			O.
2	136/136	CLINE, Peter	34	m.	Farmer	/60	"
3		Dorcas	30	f.	Domestic		" I
4		Etholinda	12	f.			" S
5		Josiah	10	m.			" S
6		Vincent	8	m.			" S
7		Emelia	6	f.			" S

8		CLINE, Nancy	4	f.			O.	
9		Sally	1	f.			"	
10	137/137	MASON, John	49	m.	Farmer	6000/600	"	
11		Elisabeth	49	f.	Domestic		Va.	
12		Lewis G.	24	m.	Student	/40	O.	
13		William	21	m.	Farmer	/30	"	
14		James Harvy	20	m.	Farmer		"	
15		Elisabeth	17	f.	Domestic		"	S
16		John W.	16	m.	Farmer		"	S
17		Vachel B.	14	m.			"	S
18		Mariah E.	12	f.			"	S
19		Daniel W.	11	m.			"	S
20		Ruth A.	9	f.			"	S
21		Manervy	8	f.			"	S
22		COX, William	36	m.	Farm laborer		"	
23	138/138	RIGWAY, James	47	m.	Farmer	2300/650	"	
24		Catharine	48	f.	Domestic		Pa.	
25		Samuel	23	m.	Farmer	/125	O.	
26		Elisabeth	21	f.	Domestic		"	
27		Joseph	18	m.	Farmer		"	S
28		Benjamin	18	m.	Farmer		"	S
29		Emily	15 •	f.	Domestic		"	S
30	139/139	MILLER, Samuel	47	m.	Farmer	600/300	Va.	
31		Abigail	45	f.	Domestic		Pa.	
32		James G.	19	m.	Student		"	S
33		Margaret B.	17	f.	Domestic		"	S
34		William A.	15	m.	Farmer		"	S
35		Robert E.	11	m.			"	S
36		Joseph A.	9	m.			"	S
37		Silas	6	m.			O.	S
38		Sarah L.	3	f.			"	
39		John G.	1	m.			"	

Page 22   14 June 1860   Sheet 145 verso

1	140/140	EATMAN, William	56	m.	Farmer	500/350	Pa.	
2		Charlotta	56	f.	Domestic		"	
3		Joseph	19	m.	Day laborer		"	S
4		Smith	18	m.	Day laborer		"	S
5		Mary J.	16	f.	Domestic		"	S
6	141/141	BARLOW, James	48	m.	Farmer	/125	Md.	
7		Mariah	37	f.	Domestic		O.	
8		Margaret	18	f.	Domestic		"	S
9		Mary E.	16	f.	Domestic		"	S
10		Martha A.	14	f.			"	S
11		John E.	11	m.			"	S
12		Benjamin S.	7	m.			"	
13		Hannah F.	4	f.			"	
14		Rhoda C.	2	f.			"	
15		Amelia J.	3/12	f.			"	
16	142/142	STARKEY, Benjamin	26	m.	Farmer	/200	O.	
17		Emily	23	f.	Domestic		"	
18		Sarah A.	1	f.			"	

```
19 143/143 DENNIS, Hue           34    m.   Farmer      1200/400 Ire.
20         Isabella             30    f.   Domestic             Pa.
21         Elisabeth J.          6    f.                       "    S
22         Isabella            2/12   f.                       O.

23 144/144 McCUTHAN, Mary        25    f.   Domestic    1000/50  Ire.
24         Hugh                  7    m.                        Pa.
25         Anne J.               5    f.                        "
26         James                 3    m.                        "
27         Mary E.               1    f.                        "

28 145/145 McCASLEN, Thomas      56    m.   Farmer      1500/500 Ire.
29         Isabella             61    f.   Domestic             "
30         David                23    m.   Farmer      /100 · O.
31         Margaret A.          26    f.   Domestic     /75     "

32 146/146 AMONS, Robert         42    m.   Farmer      200/400  Md.
33         Elisabeth            36    f.   Domestic             O.
34         Francis M.           13    m.                       "    S
35         Manervey              9    f.                       "    S
36         Elam                  8    m.                       "    S
37         James L.              6    m.                       "    S
38         George                2    m.                       "
39         Elisabeth A.        7/12   f.                       "
```

Page 23   15 June 1860   Sheet 146

```
 1 147/147 HILL, Joseph         30    m.   Farmer      3700/300 Va.
 2         Hannah               20    f.   Domestic             O.
 3         Eliza P.              3    f.                        "
 4         Roberta               1    f.                        "
 5         STACA, Mary          14    f.   Servant              "

 6 148/148 HICKMAN, John        43    m.   Farmer      1400/400 Pa.
 7         Susania              43    f.   Domestic             O.   I
 8         Elisabeth            19    f.   Domestic             "    S
 9         Mary                 17    f.   Domestic             "    S
10         Henry                15    m.                        "    S
11         William              10    m.                        "

12 149/149 GATES, Judson        48    m.   Shoemaker   /100     Va.
13         Mary F.              51    f.   Domestic             "
14         Eliza                17    f.   Domestic             O.

15 150/150 LONG, Richard        24    m.   Farmer               "
16         McELHANY, Martha     28    f.   Domestic    /250     "
17         HUFMAN, Matilda      13    f.                        "    S

18 151/151 LONG, Levi           49    m.   Farmer      3000/100 Va.
19         Kesiah               50    f.   Domestic             Pa.
20         Franklin             19    m.   Farmer               O.
21         Henryetta            16    f.   Domestic             "
22         Elihu                12    m.                        "    S
23         Levi J.               9    m.                        "    S
24         Lucretia E.           5    f.                        "    S
25         James G.              1    m.                        "
26         SMITH, Henretta      86    f.   Retired              Md.
```

27	152/152	RAGEL, Christopher	39	m.	Wagon-maker	400/300	Ger.
28		Frances	37	f.	Domestic		"
29		Adam	10	m.			O. S
30		John	10	m.			" S
31		Joseph	8	m.			" S
32		Martin	5	m.			"
33		Elisabeth	2	f.			"

34	153/153	SCIPP, George	28	m.	Farmer	1000/400	Bav.
35		Luisa	38	f.	Domestic		
36		SANDER, Augustus	12	m.			" S
37		Luisa	10	f.			"
38		Robert	6	m.			O.
39		Catherine	2	f.			"

Page 24   15 June 1860   Sheet 146 verso

1		Elisabeth	3/12	f.			O.

2	154/154	POPE, Lucas	45	m.	Farmer	/100	Bad.
3		Barbary	37	f.	Domestic		"
4		Peter	11	m.			O. S

5	155/155	PHAGEL, Philip	71	m.	Farmer	/100	Ger.
6		Margaret	75	f.	Domestic		" I
7		Philip	33	m.	Farmer		"

8	156/156	KYGER, Henry	43	m.	Farmer	600/250	"
9		Catharine	39	f.	Domestic		"
10		Magdalena	15	f.	Domestic		"
11		Charles	9	m.			O. S
12		William	7	m.			" S
13		August	5	m.			"
14		Philip	3	m.			"
15		Catherine	3/12	f.			"

16	157/157	LOHER, Eve	61	f.	Domestic	/50	Ger.

17	158/158	LOWER, John	30	m.	Farmer	100/300	"
18		Carolina	25	f.	Domestic		"
19		George M.	6	m.			O.
20		John M.	4	m.			"
21		Louisa C.	2	f.			"
22		Carolina E.	1	f.			"

23	159/159	DEGAL, Bartholomy	64	m.	Farmer	300/100	Ger.
24		Anne C.	63	f.	Domestic		"

25	160/160	BYERS, Coonrod	51	m.	Carpenter	400/300	"
26		Eliza	54	f.	Domestic		" I
27		George	21	m.	Farmer		"
28		Elisabeth	16	f.	Domestic		O. S
29		Daniel	14	m.			" S

30	161/161	WILBERT, Peter	35	m.	Farmer	900/300	Ger.
31		Catharine	35	f.	Domestic		"
32		Catharine	12	f.			Pa. S
33		Elisabeth	10	f.			" S

34		WILBERT, Peter	6	m.			Pa.	S
35		John	3/12	m.			O.	
36	162/162	HILEY, Peter	66	m.	Farmer	500/200	Va.	
37		Margaret	58	f.	Domestic		"	
38		Abraham	21	m.	Farmer	400/150	O.	
39		John	35	m.	Farmer	450/180	Va.	

Page 25			15 June 1860				Sheet 147	
1		Robert	6	m.			O.	
2		Peter	3	m.			"	
3		Sarah J.	1	f.			"	
4	163/163	FULMER, James	35	m.	Farmer	300/100	"	
5		Catharine	31	f.	Domestic		"	
6		John W.	12	m.			"	S
7		James F.	10	m.			"	S
8		William J.	7	m.			"	S
9		Mary M.	5	f.			"	
10		Hannah	6/12	f.			"	
11	164/164	JONES, Margaret	24	f.	Domestic	800/100	Ger.	
12		Saphire	3	f.			Pa.	
13		Isabella	2	f.			"	
14		Henry	6/12	m.			O.	
15	165/165	ZIPP, Andrew	49	m.	Farmer	900/250	Ger.	
16		Elisabeth	40	f.	Domestic		"	
17		Louisa	14	f.			Pa.	
18		Mary	9	f.			"	S
19		Elisabeth	7	f.			"	S
20		George	4	m.			"	
21		John	1	m.			O.	
22	166/166	HINDLAN, Adam	47	m.	Farmer	/200	Ger.	
23		Elisabeth	44	f.	Domestic		"	
24		Margaret	8	f.			"	S
25	167/167	STACY, Richard	58	m.	Farmer	1400/250	Eng.	
26		Sarah	60	f.	Domestic		"	
27		Hannah	20	f.	Domestic		O.	
28		Thomas	18	m.	Farmer		"	
29		John	16	m.	Farmer		"	
30		Catharine	14	f.			"	
31		Mary Anna	12	f.			"	
32		Rachel	9	f.			"	
33		Richard	7	m.			"	
34		George	5	m.			"	
35		Sarah E.	3	f.			"	
36	168/168	CULP, Martin	28	m.	Farmer	/200	Pa.	I
37		Charlotta A.	29	f.	Domestic		"	
38		Oliva	7	f.			"	
39		Isabella	5	f.			"	

Page 26			15 June 1860				Sheet 147 verso	
1		John	1	m.			O.	

2	169/169	DENIST, Levi	41	m.	Farmer	/350	Pa.	
3		Susanna	16	f.	Domestic		O.	
4		Sarah	14	f.			"	
5		John	11	m.			"	
6		Martha	8	f.			"	
7		Elisabeth	4	f.			"	
8	170/170	HOWELL, Andrien	41	m.	Farmer	/125	"	I
9		Anna	43	f.	Domestic		Pa.	I
10		Levi	18	m.	Farmer		O.	
11		Elisabeth	16	f.	Domestic		"	
12		Henry	13	m.			"	
13		Freeman	10	m.			"	
14		William	7	m.			"	
15		John	4	m.			"	
16	171/171	HUFMAN, Sarah	55	f.	Domestic	/50	Pa.	
17		Roseberry	21	m.	Farm laborer		O.	
18	172/172	DICKEY, Saml. N.	38	m.	Farmer	1500/300	"	
19		Mary Anne	28	f.	Domestic		"	
20		Arabella	8	f.			"	
21		Julius L.	6	m.			"	S
22		William A.	5	m.			"	S
23		Hiram H.	1	m.			"	
24	173/173	MORGAN, Willoughby	41	m.	Miller		Va.	
25		Rebecca	32	f.	Domestic		O.	
26		James L.	9	m.			"	S
27		Nancy J.	4	f.			"	
28		Asa C.	1	m.			"	
29	174/171	OLEM, Elijah	56	m.	Farmer	6700/600	Pa.	
30		Elisabeth	65	f.	Domestic		"	
31		Shadrach	24	m.	Farm laborer		"	
32		Isaac	20	m.	Farm laborer		"	S
33		Mary	17	f.	Domestic		"	
34		Nancy	13	f.			O.	S
35	175/175	CIMS, John	39	m.	Farmer	800/200	"	
36		Elisabeth	36	f.	Domestic		"	S
37		Sarah	15	f.	Domestic		"	S
38		Jacob	11	m.			"	S

Page 27   16 June 1860   Sheet 148

1	176/176	DENNIS, Jacob	75	m.	Retired		Pa.	I
2		Elisabeth	76	f.	Retired		"	I
3	177/177	BUDD, William G.	23	m.	Farmer	2000/270	Pa.	
4		Lidia anne	23	f.	Domestic		O.	
5		Joseph C.	5/12	m.			"	
6	178/178	HANDLAY, William	26	m.	Farmer	/150	Pa.	
7		Hannah	21	f.	Domestic		"	
8		~~Still-born~~ not named	1/12	m.			O.	

9	179/179	GRAHAM, John W.	55	m.	Carpenter	800/400	Pa.
10		Luisa	48	f.	Domestic		N.Y.
11		Lorain	23	m.	Farmer		Pa.
12		Sarah J.	21	f.	Domestic		"
13		Luisa	19	f.	Domestic		" S
14		John A.	15	m.	Farmer		" S
15		Hariet S.	12	f.			" S
16		Olive M.	6	f.			" S
17		HALL, John M.	13	m.			O. S
18	180/180	ALLEN, Robert	60	m.	Farmer	1860/600	Scot.
19		Anne	56	f.	Domestic		"
20		Mary	21	f.	Domestic		Pa.
21		Thomas	20	m.	Farm laborer		"
22		John	18	m.	Farm laborer		"
23		Robert	16	m.	Farm laborer		"
24	181/181	GIVENS, Daniel	25	m.	Farmer	/40	O.
25		Mary Anne	24	f.	Domestic		Va.
26		Thomas W.	3	m.			O.
27		Charlotta	9/12	f.			"
28	182/182	GIVENS, William	53	m.	Farmer	1200/150	Pa.
29		Elisabeth	50	f.	Domestic		"
30		Charlotta	20	f.	Domestic		O.
31		Lida Anne	18	f.	Domestic		"
32		Saml.	15	m.	Farm laborer		"
33		Charles	13	m.			"
34		Leander	10	m.			"
35	183/183	GIVENS, Enos J.	27	m.	Farmer	/100	"
36		Martha A.	21	f.	Domestic		" I
37		William T.	5	m.			"
38		Joseph A.	3	m.			"
39		Henry H.	1	m.			"

Page 28			16 June 1860			Sheet 148 verso	
1	184/184	CLINE, Leonard	19	m.	Farmer	/80	O. I
2		Elisabeth	22	f.	Domestic		"
3		Marion	1	m.			"
4	185/185	MALSON, Geo.	38	m.	Farmer	500/150	Pa.
5		Elisabeth	43	f.	Domestic		Va.
6		Drusilla	12	f.			O.
7		James W.	9	m.			"
8		Anne E.	8	f.			"
9		Martin V.	2	m.			
10		Mary	28	f.	Domestic		Va. I
11	186/186	MALSON, John	47	m.	Farmer	/600	Pa.
12		Rebecca	37	f.	Domestic		O.
13		Atkinson	7	m.			"
14		Rachel	2	f.			"
15		Axsah	12	f.			N.Y.
16	187/187	HOSKINS, Jeremiah	23	m.	Farmer	/50	O.
17		Sarah	20	f.	Domestic		" I

P. O. Antioch   Benton Township

```
18          HOSKINS, Geo. B.    1   m.

19 188/188  EAKELBERRY, Wil-
              liam            36   m.    Farmer        600/140  Pa. I
20            Sarah A.        336  f.    Domestic               O.

21 189/189  CLINE, Henry M.    25   m.    Farmer        600/200   "
22            Amanda           24   f.    Domestic                "   I
23            Edward J.         3   m.                            "
24            James M.          2   m.                            "

25 190/190  WEDDLE, Neomi      26   f.    Domestic      350/120  Pa.
26            Elisabeth E.      6   f.                            O.
27            William J.        5   m.                            "
28            Mary              3   f.                            "
29            Manerva        3/12   f.                            "
```

                    (Benton Township Concluded)   (Jas. Okey, A. M.)

                                    * * *

                              P. O. Laings   Green Township

Page 29   18 June 1860   Sheet 149

```
 1 191/191  AGIN, Jacob        49   m.    M. Tanner &
                                          Currier      700/350  Pa.
 2            Phebe            48   f.    Domestic               N.Y.
 3            Catharine        16   f.    Domestic               O.  S
 4            Sarah J.         12   f.                            "  S
 5          PRICE, Isaac       35   m.    Apprentice     /325    "

 6 196/192  AGIN, James        22   m.    Farmer         /150    "
 7            Margaret         22   f.    Domestic                "

 8 193/193  DENT, William Z.   33   m.    Farmer       800/1300   "
 9            Elisabeth        32   f.    Domestic                "
10            Loretta           9   f.                            "  S
11            Oscar B.          5   m.                            "  S
12            Nancy             4   f.                            "  S
13            Madison M.        2   m.                            "

14 194/194  AGAIN, Asher       26   m.    Carpenter    900/253    "
15            Caroline         22   f.    Domestic                "
16            Wm. V.            1   m.                            "

17 195/195  GOUDY, Robert      36   m.    Farmer         /150    Pa.
18            Hariet J.        30   f.    Domestic               O.
19            Lavine J.        12   f.                            "  S
20            Mary A.           8   f.                            "  S
21            Josiah            6   m.                            "  S
22            John              4   m.                            "
23            Martha        11/12   f.                            "

24 196/196  ROTH, Christian    36   m.    Farmer       3800/723  Ger.
25            Nancy            27   f.    Domestic               Pa.
```

26		ROTH, Nicholas	7	m.			O. S
27		Mary	5	f.			" S
28		Elisabeth	2	f.			"
29	197/197	SEALS, James	42	m.	Farmer	300/550	Pa.
30		Mahala	37	f.	Domestic		Va.
31		Rachel	14	f.			O. S
32		James E.	12	m.			" S
33		Jasper M.	9	m.			" S
34		William M.	6	m.			" S
35		John M.	4	m.			"
36	198/198	FISHER, Jacob	46	m.	Farmer	5000/700	O.
37		Elisabeth	44	f.	Domestic		Md. I
38		John W.	20	m.	Farm laborer		O.
39		Ruth A.	18	f.	Domestic		"

Page 30			18 June 1860				Sheet 149 verso
1		Samuel	16	m.	Farmer		O. S
2		Mitchell L.	13	m.			" S
3		Leanna	11	f.			" S
4		Sarah E.	10	f.			" S
5		Matilda A.	7	f.			" S
6		James	4	m.			" S
7		Loretta	2	f.			"
8		Mary E.	3	f.			"
9	199/199	ALEXANDRIA, William	28	m.	Farmer	700/210	"
10		Emeline	18	f.	Domestic		Pa.
11		Jane	9/12	f.			O.
12	200/200	EDDY, Isaac	59	m.	Farmer	6000/700	Va.
13		Lucretia	57	f.	Domestic		N.Y.
14		Leander	19	m.	Farm laborer		O.
15		Lucretia J.	17	f.	Domestic		"
16		Mary N.	8	f.			" S
17		Leander A.	4	m.			"
18	201/201	EDDY, Elisabeth	28	f.	Domestic	230/200	"
19		Lucretia M.	6	f.			" S
20		Rachel	1	f.			"
21	202/202	EDDY, Alphus	35	m.	Farmer	3100/600	Va.
22		Elisabeth	35	f.	Domestic		O.
23		Cyrena	12	f.			" S
24		Elias J.	10	m.			" S
25		Isaac W.	8	m.			" S
26		Asberry A.	1	m.			"
27	203/203	THORNTON, Joseph	49	m.	Farmer	/250	Md. I
28		Sophena	40	f.	Domestic		Va. I
29		Emily A.	19	f.	Domestic		O. S
30		James	15	m.	Farmer		" S
31		Joseph A.	12	m.			" S
32		Wm. O.	5	m.			" S
33		Alphonzo	3	m.			"

34	204/204	PENINGTON, Richard	27	m.	Carpenter	700/461	O.	
35		Rebecca	25	f.	Domestic		"	
36	205/205	WORKMAN, John	25	m.	Shoemaker	/150	"	
37		Mary	21	f.	Domestic		"	
38		Isaac	4	m.			"	
39		Elisabeth	3	f.			"	

Page 31   19 June 1860   Sheet 150

1		Permelia	1	f.			O.	
2	206/206	DOWELL, Thomas	51	m.	Farmer	600/164	Va.	
3		Hannah	38	f.	Domestic		"	I
4		Adam S.	17	m.	Farm laborer		O.	S
5		Elisabeth	12	f.			"	
6		Margaret A.	9	f.			"	
7		Christena	7	f.			"	
8		John T.	4	m.			"	
9		Mercy J.	2	f.			"	
10	207/207	EDGAR, Cyrus	33	m.	Farmer	1000/523	"	
11		Nancy M.	29	f.	Domestic		"	
12		Elijah G.	9	m.			"	
13		Eleanor	6	f.			"	
14		Benjamin H.	5	m.			"	
15		Nancy E.	3	f.			"	
16		Charity M.	1	f.			"	
17		HAMILTON, Saml. B.	18	m.	Farm laborer		"	
18	208/208	RICKEY, Wm.	38	m.	Farmer	700/200	"	
19		Elisabeth J.	28	f.	Domestic		"	
20		Sarah D.	10	f.			"	S
21		Rachel J.	8	f.			"	S
22		Benjamin F.	6	m.			"	S
23		MOFFATT, Martha	19	f.	Servant		"	
24	209/209	EDGAR, Adam	35	m.	Farmer	1800/360	"	
25		Margaret E.	32	f.	Domestic		"	I
26		Wm. F.	7	m.			"	
27		Charles N.	3	m.			"	
28		James A.	1	m.			"	
29	210/210	SRIVER, Elisabeth	57	f.	Domestic	3500/260	Pa.	
30		Margaret J.	23	f.	Domestic	/10	"	
31		Isabella	20	f.		/8	O.	
32	211/211	SHRIVER, John	33	m.	Farmer	575/325	Va.	
33		Elisabeth	30	f.	Domestic		O.	I
34		Wm. M.	9	m.			"	S
35		Adam L.	5	m.			"	
36		Mary E.	3	f.			"	
37		Margaret A.	1	f.			"	
38	212/212	ADAMSON, Barnet	65	m.	Farmer	5000/350	Pa.	
39		Isabella	58	f.	Domestic		"	

1	213/213	ADAMSON, Wm. J.	32	m.	Farmer	/350	Pa.
2		Mary	31	f.	Domestic		Va.
3		Elisabeth J.	3	f.			O.
4		Isabella C.	3/12	f.			"
5	214/214	BARACKMAN, John	45	m.	Farmer	1500/250	Pa.
6		Christena	36	f.	Domestic		Va.
7		John A.	17	m.	Farmer		O. S
8		Elisabeth J.	13	f.			" S
9		Sarah R.	10	f.			" S
10		Adam S.	8	m.			" S
11		Margaret D.	6	f.			" S
12		Samuel P.	2	m.			"
13	215/215	ADAMSON, Wm. S.	33	m.	Farmer	/100	Pa.
14		Mary	35	f.	Domestic		O.
15		Nancy J.	11	f.			" S
16		Mary Anne	7	f.			"
17		Mariah C.	5	f.			Pa.
18		Lettecia	3	f.			"
19		Eunice	5/12	f.			O.
20	216/216	LEMONS, Christenia	52	f.	Domestic	4000/175	Del. I
21		Salatia	18	m.	Farmer		O. S
22		Mary	15	f.	Domestic		" S
23		Martha A.	14	f.			" S
24	217/217	LEMONS, Ezery M.	30	m.	Farmer	/220	Pa.
25		Mary	28	f.	Domestic		O.
26		Vinciedore Anne	4	f.			"
27		Wm. G.	6/12	m.			"
28	218/218	McELROY, Pery	25	m.	Farmer	/65	" I
29		Martha A.	21	f.	Domestic		" I
30		George H.	3	m.			"
31		Sarah J.	1	f.			"
32	219/219	EDDY, Nathaniel	21	m.	Farmer	120/225	" M
33		Margaret	24	f.	Domestic		Pa. M
34	220/220	KNIGHT, Stephen	66	m.	Farmer	1600/260	"
35		MITCHEL, Dilila	35	f.	Domestic		O.
36		John M.	14	m.			" S
37		Wm. F.	13	m.			" S
38		Cascy	9	f.			" S
39		AGNAS, Elisa J.	16	f.	Domestic		"

1	221/221	COEN, Ezry	41	m.	Farmer	1900/642	Pa.
2		Mary	36	f.	Domestic		" I
3		Benit	12	m.			O. S
4		Randolph	2/12	m.			"
5		KNIGHT, Stephen	15	m.	Farm laborer		" S
6		FERMAL, Rebecca J.	6	f.			Va. S
7		Frances	4	f.			"

```
8  222/222 MITCHEL, Andrew   44  m.   Farmer      3000/400  O.
9          Anne M.           37  f.   Domestic              Pa.
10         Wm. H.            17  m.   Farmer                Va. S
11         Andrew J.         15  m.                         "  S
12         John C.            9  m.                         La. S
13         Thec ore J.        2  m.                         O.

14 223/223 BARACKMAN, Kinnard 27 m.   Blacksmith    /500    Pa.
15         Mary              24  f.   Domestic              O.
16         John P.            2  m.                         "
17         Jacob V.         9/12 m.                         "
18         BATTON, Charity    5  f.                         "
19         Aaron             13  m.                         "  S

20 224/224 OTT, Jacob        35  m.   Farmer      190/500    "
21         Sarah             32  f.   Domestic              Pa.
22         John M.           10  m.                         O. S
23         Leander            9  m.                         "  S

24 225/225 PIATT, John       28  m.   Farmer      800/250    "
25         Elisabeth         27  f.   Domestic               "
26         Margaret E.        1  f.                          "

27 226/226 CULVERHOUSE, John
           J.                32  m.   Farmer      2600/675   "
28         Rachel            30  f.   Domestic              Va.
29         Mary E.            5  f.                         O. S
30         Ethilinda          3  f.                          "
31         Francis           71  f.   Retired               Va.

32 227/227 SHEPHERD, George H.37 m.   Sawyer-Farmer
                                                  2600/1000  O.
33         Belinda           33  f.   Domestic               "

34 228/228 FERRELL, Thomas   41  m.   Farmer      500/364    "
35         Elisabeth         41  f.   Domestic               "
36         Wm. A.            19  m.   Farm laborer           "
37         Jas. D.           17  m.   Farm laborer           "
38         Rebecky J.        16  f.   Domestic               "
39         John H.            6  m.                          "
```

Page 34   20 June 1860   Sheet 151

```
1          McGONE, Elisabeth 22  f.   Servant               O.

2  229/229 SHEPHERD, John    33  m.   Farmer      1200/150   "
3          Delila            28  f.   Domestic               "
4          Jas. P.            7  m.                          "
5          Geo. A.            4  m.                          "
6          John W.            2  m.                          "
7          Mary J.         5/12 f.                           "

8  230/230 WORKMAN, Isaac    50  m.   Farmer      1200/50    "
9          Catharine         45  f.   Domestic               "
10         Finley            21  m.   Farmer                 "
11         Archabald         19  m.   Farmer                 "
12         Solomon           17  m.   Farmer                 "
```

13		WORKMAN, Mary E.	15	f.			O.	S
14		Sally M.	12	f.			"	
15		David	9	m.			"	S
16		Pracilla	6	f.			"	
17		Narcisy	8	f.			"	S
18	231/231	NIXON, Ed	59	m.	Farmer	/280	Pa.	
19		Margaret	49	f.	Domestic		"	
20		John	27	m.	Farmer	/150	"	
21		Bulford	21	m.	Farmer		"	
22		Rebecca	19	f.	Domestic		"	
23		Joshua	16	m.	Farmer		"	S
24		Nancy	14	f.			O.	S
25		MIERS, Catharine	29	f.	Domestic	/75	Pa.	
26		Catharine	6	f.			O.	
27		Wm.	4	m.			"	
28	232/232	CONGER, Benoni	47	m.	Farmer	5000/1000	Pa.	
29		Catharine	50	f.	Domestic		"	I
30		Samuel	24	m.	Farmer		O.	
31		Enos	23	m.	Farmer		"	
32		Nancy	19	f.	Domestic		"	
33		Elisabeth	17	f.	Domestic		"	
34		Catharine	15	f.	Domestic		"	
35		John W.	12	m.			"	
36		Rebecca J.	10	f.			"	
37		Noble	8	m.			"	
38	233/233	MITCHELL, Isaac Sr.	82	m.	Retired		Pa.	
39		Margaret A.	73	f.	Retired		"	I

1	234/234	MITCHELL, Isaac Jr.	42	m.	Farmer	50,000/1000	Pa.	
2		Margaret	41	f.	Domestic		O.	
3		James	18	m.	Farmer		"	S
4		Nancy	17	f.	Domestic		"	S
5		Isaac	15	m.	Farmer		"	S
6		Lusinda	14	f.			"	S
7		Elsabeth J.	10	f.			"	S
8		Margaret J.	7	f.			"	
9	235/235	MAHONEY, James	52	m.	Cabinet-maker	200/150	Va.	I
10		Phebe	39	f.	Domestic		O.	I
11		Richard	18	m.	Farmer		"	S
12		Wm.	16	m.	Farmer		"	S
13		Hariet	11	f.			"	S
14		Harvy	8	m.			"	S
15		Samuel	6	m.			"	S
16		Alonzo	2	m.			"	
17		Mary	2/12	f.			"	
18	236/236	MITCHEL, S. B.	36	m.	Farmer	2800/500	Pa.	
19	237/237	CURBY, Cyrus	21	m.	Blacksmith	/200	O.	M

20		CURBY, Lucy H.	22	f.	Domestic		Pa.	M
21	238/238	DICKSON, Alex	35	m.	Teacher	1200/400	Pa.	
22		Rachel	35	f.	Domestic		O.	
23		James	11	m.			"	S
24		Nancy J.	10	f.			"	S
25		Robert S.	8	m.			"	S
26		David	4	m.			"	
27		William R.	7/12	m.			"	
28	239/239	BERRY, Jas. A.	30	m.	Wagon-maker	400/175	Va.	
29		Deborah	25	f.	Domestic		O.	
30		Jno. W.	5	m.			"	S
31		Adamson R.	3	m.			"	
32		Robert J.	4/12	m.			"	
33	240/240	JACKSON, Jesse	46	m.	Farmer	/1500	Pa.	
34		Levina	44	f.	Domestic		O.	I
35		Hannah	22	f.	Domestic		"	
36		Lenard	18	m.	Farmer		"	S
37		Mary	14	f.			"	S
38		Jane	14	f.			"	S
39		Marthy H.	11	f.			"	S

Page 36			20 June 1860				Sheet 152 verso	
1		Nathaniel	7	m.			O.	S
2		Thomas J.	2	m.			"	
3	241/241	PEPPERS, Geo.	35	m.	Carpenter	150/300	Va.	
4		Dianna	35	f.	Domestic		Pa.	
5		Earnast	6	m.			O.	S
6		Mary E.	3	f.			"	
7		Francis M.	8/12	f.			"	
8		DAUGHERTY, Catharine	69	f.	Retired		Pa.	
9		J. W.	16	m.	Day laborer		O.	S
10	242/242	DAVENPORT, Geo.	65	m.	Store clerk	600/450	Va.	
11		Louisa	55	f.	Domestic		O.	
12		Lucretia	18	f.	Domestic		"	
13		Martha	17	f.	Domestic		"	S
14		Frances	13	f.			"	S
15	243/243	CLARK, Jacob	51	m.	Carpenter	650/250	O.	
16		Margaret	50	f.	Domestic		"	
17		Elizabeth A.	22	f.	Domestic		"	
18		David	17	m.	Day laborer		"	S
19		Larence	15	m.	Day laborer		"	S
20		Allan	14	m.			"	S
21		Margaret	9	f.			"	S
22		Eliza E.	2	f.			"	
24	244/244	HOPTON, Ed	62	m.	Tavern-keeper	600/100	Pa.	
25		Elisabeth	68	f.	Domestic		N.J.	
26		YAGER, Mary Ann	22	f.	Servant		Pa.	

27	245/245	GRIMSHAW, Samuel	52	m.	Physician	1000/300	Eng.
28		McFARLAN, Cath-					
		arine	66	f.	Domestic		Ire.
29		WALTON, Wm.	25	m.	Physician	/300	O. M
30		Mary	19	f.	Domestic		N.Br.M
31	246/246	OKEY, Jeremiah	45	m.	Merchant		O.
32		J. S.	22	m.	Merchant	1500/2000	"
33		Mervil G.	14	m.			" S
34	247/247	MASILIET, Augustus	31	m.	Merchant	/4000	"
35		Catharine	26	f.	Domestic		"
36		Hariet L.	3	f.			"
37		Mary	5/12	f.			"
38	248/248	JONES, Saml.	25	m.	Farm laborer	/50	"
39		Elisabeth	25	f.	Domestic		"

Page 37			**20 June 1860**			**Sheet 153**
1		Thomas H.	4	m.			O.
2		Randolph L.	3	m.			"
3		Saml. D.	1	m.			"
4	249/249	DAUGHERTY, John	31	m.	Tobacco-packer		
						700/100	Pa.
5		Mary J.	26	f.	Domestic		O.
6		Windfield S.	7	m.			" S
7		Balford B.	5	m.			" S
8		John F.	3	m.			"
9		Wm. M.	2	m.			"
10		MIRES, Matilda	19	f.	Servant		"
11	250/250	SPERE, Sylvester	27	m.	Shoemaker	/100	"
12		Mary Anne	32	f.	Domestic		Eng. I
13		Franklin A.	1	m.			O.
14		SMITH, Lidda	17	f.	Servant		" S
15		Mortimer	15	m.	Day laborer		" S
16		Edward	12	m.			" S
17		Mary Anne	10	f.			" S
18	251/251	COEN, Isiah	36	m.	Farmer-Teacher		
						500/100	Pa.
19		Eleanor	32	f.	Domestic		Va.
20		Alexandria	14	m.			O. S
21		Juliane	12	f.			" S
22		Waren C.	11	m.			" S
23		John F.	8	m.			" S
24		Thos. W.	6	m.			" S
25		Bennet	3	m.			"
26		Jas. W.	11/12	m.			"
27	252/252	BERDETT, William	42	m.	Blacksmith	1500/400	"
28		Mary	34	f.	Domestic		"
29		Hester A.	17	f.	Domestic		" S
30		Seda E.	15	f.	Domestic		" S
31		Wm. J.	13	m.			" S

32		BERDETT, Sophia J.	11	f.			O. S
33		Mary L.	9	f.			" S
34		Miller S.	7	m.			" S
35		John M.	4	m.			"
36		Robert M.	2	m.			"
37	253/253	FENER, Jon E.	28	m.	Farmer	/200	"
38		Violetta	20	f.	Domestic		"
39	254/254	OKEY, John	39	m.	Farmer	/2000	"

Page 38			21 June 1860			Sheet 153 verso	
1		Mariah	36	f.	Domestic		O.
2		Theadore G.	14	m.			" S
3		Leanora	12	f.			" S
4		Sophiah	9	f.			" S
5		Lusinda	8	f.			" S
6		Barbary	6	f.			" S
7		Frederick	3	m.			"
8		Sally	1	f.			"
9	255/255	GOUDY, John	60	m.	Farmer	/375	Pa.
10		Mary	56	f.	Domestic		"
11		James W.	23	m.	Farmer		O.
12		Micajah	20	m.	Farmer		"
13		Mary J.	19	f.	Domestic		"
14		Sarah A.	15	f.	Domestic		"
15		Ruth A.	30	f.	Servant		Pa.
16		HENTHORN, Ophala	6	f.	Servant		O.
17	256/256	NORAS, Ed	38	m.	Farmer	3500/950	Pa.
18		Jane	39	f.	Domestic		O.
19		Wm. L.	17	m.	Farmer		" S
20		Martha A.	13	f.			" S
21		John W.	9	m.			" S
22		Isaac H.	7	m.			" S
23		Geo. T.	4	m.			"
24		Mary E.	1	f.			"
25	257/257	DENT, Wm. B.	48	m.	Farmer	/400	"
26		Elisabeth	52	f.	Domestic		Eng.
27		Geo. E.	23	m.	Farmer	/100	O.
28		Hannah J.	21	f.	Domestic		"
29		JACKSON, James A.	9	m.			" S
30		STACKHOUSE, Mary J.	4	f.			"
31	258/258	WRIGHT, Robert	77	m.	Farmer	750/150	Md. I
32		Elisabeth	75	f.	Domestic		"
33		HENTHORN, Huhamma	16	f.	Domestic		O.
34	259/259	BRYAN, Wm.	43	m.	Farmer	/400	"
35		Malinda	41	f.	Domestic		" I
36		Washington	20	m.	Farmer		" S
37		Mary P.	2	f.			"
38	260/260	CONN, Stephen	32	m.	Farmer	2000/521	"
39		Rhoda	26	f.	Domestic		"

1		CONN, Simon	4	m.			O.	
2		Ezry	2	m.			"	
3		John C.	1	m.			"	
4	261/261	RIGHT, John	31	m.	Farmer	450/140	"	
5		Louisa	27	f.	Domestic		Pa.	
6		Wm. T.	9	m.			O.	S
7		Eva A.	4	f.			"	
8		Ellis	2	m.			"	
9		Margaret J.	6/12	f.			"	
10	262/262	HICKMAN, Henry	37	m.	Farmer	1400/400	Pa.	
11		Susanna	29	f.	Domestic		O.	
12		John M.	10	m.			"	S
13		Mary E.	9	f.			"	S
14		Rebecca J.	6	f.			"	S
15		Manervy	4	f.			"	
16		Louisa	2	f.			"	
17	263/263	SMITH, S.	45	m.	Day laborer	/130	Pa.	
18		Rebecca	45	f.	Domestic		Ire.	
19		Sidina Ann	19	m.	Day laborer		Pa.	
20		Hugh H.	17	m.	Day laborer		"	S
21		Margaret R.	16	f.	Domestic		O.	S
22		CUNNINGHAM, Saml.	23	m.	Farm laborer		Ire.	
23	264/264	GRAY, Lewis	27	m.	Farmer	1400/155	O.	
24		Sarah	23	f.	Domestic		"	
25	265/265	PIATT, Catharine	65	f.	Domestic	800/320	Va.	
26		Simon	28	m.	Farmer		O.	
27		Susiana	24	f.	Domestic		"	
28		Catharine	11	f.			"	S
29	266/266	PITTMAN, Peter	42	m.	Farmer	/50	"	
30		Christena	40	f.	Domestic		Pa.	I
31		Wm.	18	m.	Farm laborer		O.	S
32		Isaac	17	m.	Farm laborer		"	S
33		Isabella	15	f.	Domestic		"	S
34		Hiram	13	m.			"	S
35		John	11	m.			"	S
36		Gideon	7	m.			"	
37		Franklin	4	m.			"	
38		Nathan	2	m.			"	
39		Clarissa	2/12	f.			"	

1		PITMAN, William	69	m.	Retired		Pa.	
2	267/267	NEAL, Joseph	31	m.	Farmer	3000/700	Pa.	
3		Elisabeth	27	f.	Domestic		O.	
4		Thomas M.	6	m.			"	S
5		Barnet	4	m.			"	
6		John H.	3	m.			"	
7		Mary E.	11/12	f.			"	

8	268/268	EDDY, Adam	34	m.	Farmer	1200/320	Va.	
9		Perdila	26	f.	Domestic		"	
10		Delila J.	3	f.			O.	
11		John F.	8/12	m.			"	
12	269/269	EDDY, Asel	36	m.	Farmer		Va.	I
13		Susanna	60	f.	Domestic	/70	O.	I
14		Lucretia	25	f.	Domestic		"	I
15		Mary J.	23	f.	Domestic		"	I
16	270/270	BUCHANON, James	40	m.	Farmer	4000/850	Pa.	
17		Huldah	40	f.	Domestic		O.	
18		Wm. T.	17	m.	Farmer		"	S
19		Samuel J.	13	m.			"	S
20		Moses F.	10	m.			"	S
21		Chloe	8	f.			"	S
22		James M.	5	m.			"	
23		Jefferson	2	m.			"	
24		John	8/12	m.			"	
25	271/271	PITTMAN, Saml.	31	m.	Farmer	/85	"	
26		Frances	26	f.	Domestic		Pa.	I
27		Charity L.	6	f.			O.	S
28		Jemima J.	4	f.			"	
29		Huldah	2	f.			"	
30		Ruth R.	1/12	f.			"	
31	272/272	WRIGHT, Charity	61	f.	Domestic	1200/150	Va.	I
32		Jane	17	f.	Domestic		Pa.	
33	273/273	WRIGHT, Isaac	31	m.	Farmer	/150	"	
34		Ida	22	f.	Domestic		O.	
35		Jonathon A.	37	m.	Day laborer		"	
36	274/274	FOX, Jacob	29	m.	Farmer	/200	"	
37		Elisabeth	27	f.	Domestic		Va.	I
38		Heseciah	5	m.			"	
39		John F.	3	m.			O.	

1		Susanna C.	1/12	f.			O.	
2	275/275	FOX, James	64	m.	Farmer	4475/470	Pa.	
3		Susiana	62	f.	Domestic		Va.	
4		Matthis	21	m.	Farm laborer	/75	O.	
5		Hannah J.	18	f.	Domestic	/75	"	
6		SHANNON, Hariet	7	f.			"	
7	276/276	STRAIGHT, Jeffer-						
		son	55	m.	Farmer	2000/250	Va.	I
8		Barbary	60	f.	Domestic		"	I
9		James	22	m.	Farm laborer	/300	"	
10		Urias	19	m.	Farm laborer		O.	S
11		Alexandria	17	m.	Farm laborer		"	S
12		Elizabeth	15	f.	Domestic		"	S
13	277/277	DEVALL, Gustavus	52	m.	Farmer	1500/290	Md.	

14		DEVALL, Rossannah	40	f.	Domestic		O.	
15		John W.	17	m.	Farm laborer		"	
16		BELFORD, John	21	m.	Farm laborer		"	
17		Marthy	14	f.			"	S
18	278/278	EDDY, David	67	m.	Farmer	2500/500	Pa.	
19		Christena	63	f.	Domestic		Va.	
20		STEWART, Daniel	21	m.			O.	I
21		Frances	21	f.	Domestic	/50	"	
22		Wm.	3	m.			"	
23		Elisabeth	1	f.			"	
24		EDDY, Josephus	17	m.	Farmer		"	S
25		Sarah	15	f.	Domestic		"	S
26	279/279	EDDY, Jas.	26	m.	Farmer	/120	"	
27		Mary E.	23	f.	Domestic		"	
28		David	6	m.			"	S
29		Sylvanus	4	m.			"	
30		Delila J.	1	f.			"	
31	280/280	WOOD, Micajah	27	m.	Farmer	/550	"	
32		Lucy	23	f.	Domestic		"	
33		Thomas A.	3	m.			"	
34	281/281	HENDERSON, John	43	m.	Preacher--Christian	400/200	Pa.	
35		Luisa	22	f.	Domestic		O.	
36		Elisabeth	19	f.	Domestic		"	
37		Wm.	17	m.	Farm laborer		"	S
38		Frances	12	f.			"	S
39		Matilda	10	f.			"	S

Page 42   22 June 1860   Sheet 155 verso

1		Benjamin	4	m.			O.	
2		John	1	m.			"	
3	282/282	HENTHORN, Wm.	23	m.	Farmer	/175	"	I
4		Nancy	21	f.	Domestic		"	I
5		Ezra	5/12	m.			"	
6	283/283	WILLEY, Jon	62	m.	Farmer	875/150	Pa.	
7		Rebecca	56	f.	Domestic		Va.	
8		Wilson S.	16	m.	Farmer		O.	S
9	284/284	COX, Hiram	33	m.	Carpenter	500/100	Pa.	
10		Emeline	30	f.	Domestic		"	
11		Lusippa	12	f.			O.	S
12		Sarah	10	f.			"	S
13		Monroe	8	m.			"	S
14		Cordela	6	f.			"	S
15		Pernina E.	3	f.			"	
16		Elwood	1	m.			"	
17	285/285	BOLEN, S.	28	m.	Farmer	900/244	O.	
18		Elisabeth	21	f.	Domestic		"	
19		Letticia	3	f.			"	

20		BOLEN, Wm. G.	1	m.			O.	
21		Stewart	30	m.	Farm laborer	600/200	Md.	I
22		Elisabeth	25	f.	Domestic		O.	

23	286/286	WORTHMADE, Nicho-						
		las	57	m.	Farmer	800/500	Sw.	
24		Barbery	50	f.	Domestic		Ger.	
25		Godfrey S.	18	m.	Farm laborer		"	

26	281/281	PARKER, T.	23	m.	Farm laborer	/300	Pa.	M
27		Levina J.	22	f.			O.	M

28	282/282	PARKER, Andrew	55	m.	Farmer	3000/500	Pa.	
29		Nancy	54	f.	Domestic		Md.	I
30		Robert T.	20	m.	Farmer		O.	
31		Elisabeth E.	13	f.	Domestic		"	S
32		John M.	10	m.			"	S

33	283/283	RUTTER, Sarah	65	f.	Domestic	/50	Pa.	
34		Stephen	26	m.	Day laborer		O.	
35		John	21	m.	Day laborer		"	
36		Eve	13	f.			"	

37	284/284	PORTER, Jacob	54	m.	Farmer	1000/200	Va.	
38		Dorcas	56	f.	Domestic		Md.	I
39		James	22	m.	Farm laborer	/40	O.	

Page 43   22 June 1860   Sheet 156

1		Absolom	20	m.	Farm laborer		O.	S
2		Alvin	17	m.	Farm laborer		"	S

3	291/291	WICHEY, Fred	37	m.	Farmer	800/278	Sw.	
4		Anna	35	f.	Domestic		"	
5		Elisabeth	11	f.			"	S
6		Godfrey	9	m.			"	S
7		Rose	5	f.			O.	S
8		Siegfried	4	m.			"	

9	292/292	BONTRIGER, Jacob	42	m.	Farmer	1500/250	"	
10		Margaret	44	f.	Domestic		"	I
11		John C.	20	m.	Day laborer	/65	"	S
12		Heseciah	18	m.	Day laborer		"	S
13		Sarah A.	16	f.	Domestic		"	S
14		Adaline	15	f.	Domestic		"	S
15		Catharine	13	f.			"	S
16		Elisabeth	11	f.			"	S
17		Thomas B.	9	m.			"	S
18		Mahala	7	f.			"	S
19		Margaret L.	2	f.			"	
20		Jacob F.	4/12	m.			"	

21	293/293	RUTTER, John	60	m.	Farmer	400/150	Pa.	I
22		Patience	58	f.	Domestic		"	I
23		William	23	m.	Farmer		O.	
24		Ebenesar	18	m.	Day laborer		"	S
25		Rebecca	17	f.	Domestic		"	S

26		RUTTER, Robert	15	m.			O. S
27		Lewis	4	m.			"
28	294/294	MOBLEY, Lewis	47	m.	Farmer	2000/567	"
29		Catharine	52	f.	Domestic		"
30		Lusinda A.	5	f.			"
31		Mary L.	19	f.	Domestic		" S
32		Jas.	18	m.	Farm laborer		" S
33		Robert	17	m.	Farm laborer		" S
34	295/295	COLWELL, Geo.	33	m.	Farmer	2500/450	"
35		Mary J.	25	f.	Domestic		"
36		Oscar B.	21	m.			"
37		Penina A.	2	f.			"
38	296/296	ADAMS, Elias	30	m.	Farmer	1500/420	"
39		Hannah	28	f.	Domestic		" I

Page 44	22 June 1860				Sheet 156 versc

1		Franklin	8	m.			O. S
2		Eveline	6	f.			" S
3		Cyntha A.	4	f.			"
4		Philip E.	6/12	m.			"
5	297/297	SHRIVER, Adam	37	m.	Farmer	1600/400	"
6		Eleanor	40	f.	Domestic		Pa. I
7		DENNIS, Philip	14	m.			Ia. S
8		Richard	13	m.			Ill. S
9		Mary E.	11	f.			" S
10		Elias	7	m.			O. S
11		SHRIVER, Nancy E.	5	f.			"
12		Abreham	2	m.			"
13	298/298	MATTHEWS, Elijah	50	m.	Farmer		Pa. I
14		Hanna	63	f.	Domestic		" I
15		Abreham	23	m.	Farm laborer		O.
16		TRIMLEY, Saml.	17	m.	Farm laborer		" S
17	299/299	CONLEY, Isaac	23	m.	Farmer	425/100	" M
18		Leticia	17	f.	Domestic		Va. M
19	300/300	BERGER, Christian	32	m.	Farmer	1000/350	Sw.
20		Luisa	31	f.	Domestic		Ger.
21		Carolina	36	f.	Domestic		O.
22		Luisa	4	f.			"
23		Mary	3	f.			"
24		Charles W.	1	m.			
25	301/301	GIGLEY, Jacob	42	m.	Farmer	400/100	Sw.
26		Elisabeth	42	f.	Domestic		"
27		Samuel	9/12	m.			O.
28	302/302	STRAIGHT, William M.	22	m.	Farmer	/175	"
29		Lucinda	21	f.	Domestic		"
30		Silas J.	7/12	m.			"

31	303/303	HUFFMAN, Philip	65	m.	Farmer	1600/400	Va.	
32		Leticia	61	f.	Domestic		Pa.	
33		Nathan	23	m.	Farm laborer		O.	
34		Joseph	17	m.	Farm laborer		"	
35		Daniel	14	m.	Farm laborer		"	S
36		STEWART, Daniel	65	m.	Retired		Pa.	
37		HENDER, Frances	12	f.			O.	
38	304/304	BRACY, James	54	m.	Farmer	2600/2516	Pa.	
39		Grace	56	f.	Domestic		O.	I

Page 45   22 June 1860   Sheet 157

1	305/305	PITMAN, Timothy	42	m.	Farmer	1000/250	O.	I
2		Ruth	49	f.	Domestic		Pa.	
3		Rachel Jane	21	f.	Domestic		O.	
4		Joshua	17	m.	Farmer		"	S
5		Hester	11	f.			"	S
6		Mermela	8	f.			"	S
7		Sampson	13	m.			"	S
8		Jacob	73	m.	Retired		Va.	I
9	306/306	PITMAN, Thomas	55	m.	Farmer	500/130	Pa.	
10		Elisabeth	3-	f			Va.	I
11		Andrew	27	m.	Farm laborer		O.	
12		Harvy	21	m.	Farm laborer		"	
13		Elias	16	m.	Farm laborer		"	
14		Barbary	12	f.			"	
15		Hannah	12	f.			"	
16		Clark	8	m.			"	
17		Eli	6	m.			"	
18		Delilah	5	f.			"	
19		Perninah	4	f.			"	
20	307/307	Absolom	25	m.	Farmer	900/280	O.	
21		Sarah	23	f.	Domestic		"	
22		Wm. H.	1	m.			"	
23	308/308	Mancy	61	f.	Domestic	1000/535	"	I
24		Rachel	36	f.	Domestic		"	
25		Milliner	18	m.	Farm laborer		"	S
26	309/309	TUBAH, Peter	46	m.	Farmer	1800/600	Sw.	I
27		Roseanna	34	f.	Domestic		Ger.	
28		John	15	m.			O.	
29		Peter	13	m.			"	S
30		Elisabeth	11	f.			"	S
31		William	8	m.			"	S
32		Christopher	6	m.			"	S
33		Mary	5	f.			"	S
34		Rose anne	3	f.			"	
35		Alexandria	1	m.			"	
36	310/310	NULTY, Christian	60	m.	Farmer	/100	Sw.	
37		Elisabeth	52	f.	Domestic		"	
38		Godfrey	14	m.			"	

Page 46				23 June 1860			Sheet 157 verso		
1	311/311	WOOD, Michael S.	23	m.	Farmer	/300	O.		
2		Sarah	23	f.	Domestic		"		
3		Mary J.	4/12	f.			"		
4	312/312	WOOD, Simon P.	27	m.	Farmer	700/100	Pa.		
5		Mary Ann	24	f.	Domestic		O.		
6		Wm. T.	5	m.			"		
7		Sarah	3	f.			"		
8		James F.	6/12	m.			"		
9	313/313	MOBLEY, John	38	m.	Farmer	2000/400	O.	I	
10		Mary	27	f.	Domestic		Ger.	I	
11		Christopher	8	m.			O.	S	
12		John T.	6	m.			"	S	
13		Samuel	4	m.			"	S	
14		Margaret A.	2	f.			"		
15		Gemima	72	f.	Retired		Md.	I	
16	314/314	LAING, Randolph	65	m.	Farmer	6000/1800	Pa.		
17		James	33	m.	Carpenter	350/200	O.		
18		Mary	27	f.	Domestic		"		
19		Sarah Y.	4	f.			"	S	
20		Mary J.	7	f.			"	S	
21		Alfred R.	2	m.			"		
22		CHADNET, Malinda	16	f.	Domestic		Va.		
23		CATON, John	20	m.	Farm laborer		O.		
24	315/315	SMITH, Jacob	40	m.	Farmer	1200/345	Pa.		
25		Catharine	35	f.	Domestic		"		
26		Mary M.	14	f.			"		
27		George W.	12	m.			"	S	
28		Josephine	10	f.			"	S	
29		Emmy F.	8	f.			"	S	
30		Jacob	6	m.			"	S	
31		William	5	m.			"	S	
32		Catharine	3	f.			"		
33		Alexandria	1	m.			O.		

Page 47				25 June 1860			Sheet 158		
1	316/316	MITCHEL, Harvy T.	40	m.	Farmer	1600/500	Pa.		
2		Elisabeth	24	f.	Domestic		"	I	
3		Hannah	11	f.			O.	S	
4		RICH, Mary	52	f.	Domestic		Pa.	I	
5		JEFFERSON, Charles	16	m.	Day laborer		O.	S	
6	317/317	MYRES, Sarah	53	m.	Domestic		"	I	
7		Luisa	25	f.	Domestic		"		
8		Sarah A.	23	f.	Domestic		"		
9		Matilda	19	f.	Domestic		"		
10		Rheuhana	17	f.	Domestic		"		
11		John M.	11	m.			"	S	
12	318/318	McCASLIN, John	44	m.	Farmer	4000/675	Ire.		
13		Anna J.	44	f.	Domestic		Pa.		
14		Isabelle	20	f.	Teacher		O.		

15		McCASLIN, Rachel	18	f.	Domestic		0.	S
16		Margaret	16	f.	Domestic		"	S
17		Susanna	13	f.			"	S
18		Mary J.	11	f.			"	S
19		James	9	m.			"	S
20		Andrew	4	m.			"	
21		Nancy A.	2	f.			"	
22	319/319	BARBER, John	31	m.	Farmer	1450/325	Ire.	
23		Mary	23	f.	Domestic		"	
24		Elisabeth	4	f.			0.	
25		Joseph	2	m.			"	
26		Sarah J.	4/12	f.			"	
27		John	67	m.	Retired		Ire.	
28	320/320	HASLUM, Thomas	23	m.	Farmer	/25	Pa.	
29		Sally	24	f.	Domestic		0.	I
30		Marthy E.	6	f.			"	
31		Agnas M.	11/12	f.			"	
32	321/321	BARCUS, Thomas	36	m.	Farmer	80/	"	M
33		Mary	33	f.	Domestic		"	MI
34		Susanna	10	f.			"	
35		Timothy	7	m.			"	
36		Rachel	6	f.			"	
37		Elisabeth A.	5	f.			"	

Page 48			25 June 1860			Sheet 158 verso		
1	322/322	HICKMAN, Isaac	48	m.	Farmer	1000/260	Pa.	I
2		Nancy A.	44	f.	Domestic		Va.	I
3		Sarah	24	f.	Domestic		0.	I
4		Wm.	19	m.	Farmer		"	
5		John	21	m.	Farmer		"	I
6		David W.	16	m.			"	
7		Rebecca	13	f.			"	
8		Elizabeth	11	f.			"	
9		Joseph	8	m.			"	
10		Peter K.	4	m.			"	
11		Isaac A.	2	m.			"	
12		WRIGHT, Levi L.	6	m.			Ill.	
13	323/323	PRICE, Margaret	60	f.	Domestic	1000/250	Pa.	I
14		John	23	m.	Farm laborer		0.	
15		Jacob	20	m.	Farm laborer		"	S
16		ANDERSON, Cathar-ine	14	f.			Va.	S
17	324/324	PRICE, Daniel	22	m.	Farmer	/50	0.	I
18		Mary J.	21	f.	Domestic		"	
19		William H.	2/12	m.			"	
20	325/325	BRADFORD, Benja-min	47	m.	Day laborer	/50	"	I
21		Sally	30	f.	Domestic		"	I
22		Wm.	7	m.			"	
23	326/326	BENET, Robert	57	m.	Farmer	/250	Pa.	I

24		BENET, Christena	56	f.	Domestic		O.	I
25		Benonia	23	m.	Day laborer		"	
26		Simon	19	m.	Day laborer		"	
27		Charles W.	16	m.	Day laborer		"	
28		Sarah R.	13	f.			"	
29	327/327	HOPTON, Thomas D.	31	m.	Farmer	/165	Pa.	
30		Mary A.	28	f.	Domestic		Va.	
31		Francis M.	5	m.			"	S
32		Luisa	3	f.			"	
33		CONAWAY, Levina	12	f.			"	
34	328/328	BROWN, John	52	m.	Farmer	/150	O.	
35		Nancy	31	f.	Domestic		"	I
36		Marion	10	m.			"	
37		Angaline	8	f.			"	
38		Christian	5	m.			"	
39		Zephaniah	3	m.				

Page 49   25 June 1860   Sheet 159

1		Lida	1	f.			O.	
2	329/329	WOOD, Thomas	53	m.	Farmer	3000/2190	Pa.	
3		Mary A.	51	f.	Domestic		"	
4		Thomas P.	18	m.	Farm laborer		O.	S
5		SMITH, Hugh	15	m.	Farm laborer		"	
6	330/330	STEWART, Isaac	36	m.	Farmer	/200	"	
7		Esther	33	f.	Domestic		"	
8		Rebecca J.	6	f.			"	
9		Henry	3	m.			"	
10		Peter	1	m.				
11	331/331	STEWART, Rebecca	60	f.	Domestic	/80	Pa.	I
12		Peter	16	m.	Farmer	/50	O.	
13	332/332	CUNNINGHAM, Wm. J.	32	m.	Farmer	600/200	Ire.	
14		Mary	25	f.	Domestic		O.	I
15		Margaret	9	f.			"	S
16		Sarah E.	5	f.			"	
17		Rebecca A.	3	f.			"	
18		Isaac F.	1	m.				
19		CONLEY, Elisabeth	70	f.	Retired	300/50	Pa.	
20	333/333	HASHER, Andrew	36	m.	Farmer	200/550	O.	
21		Elisabeth	29	f.	Domestic		"	I
22		John W.	11	m.			"	S
23		George W.	9	m.			"	S
24		Wilson S.	6	m.			"	S
25	334/334	RUTTER, Geo.	25	m.	Farmer	/50	"	MI
26		Elisabeth	28	f.	Domestic		Pa.	MI
27		LEGAT, Jas. R.	2	m.			O.	
28	335/335	GROSEBAUGH, Jacob	53	m.	Farmer	/200	Sw.	I
29		Anna	48	f.	Domestic		"	

30		GROSEBAUGH, Fred-erick	16	m.			Sw.	
31		John	14	m.			"	
32	336/336	KELLER, Vernah	61	f.	Domestic	2500/600	"	I
33		Verenah	22	f.	Domestic		O.	
34	337/337	EASTON, George	26	m.	Farmer	500/100	"	
35		Mary Anne	25	f.	Domestic		"	
36		Peter	3	m.			"	
37		John	1	m.			"	

1	338/338	PATTON, Geo. W.	30	m.	Farmer	500/200	O.	
2		Mary Ann	21	f.	Domestic		Pa.	
3		Margaret	8	f.			O.	
4		John W.	1	m.			"	
5		Manervy	1/12	f.			"	
6		David	16	m.	Day laborer		"	
7	339/339	MORISON, E. A.	48	m.	Stone cutter	1000/250	Pa.	
8		Margaret	35	f.	Domestic		O.	
9		Ursila	18	f.	Domestic		"	
10		Wm. F.	14	m.			"	S
11		John W.	12	m.			"	S
12		Robert L.	10	m.			"	S
13		Benjamin L.	8	m.			"	S
14		Charloty M.	5	f.			"	
15		Linda E.	2	f.			"	
16	340/340	HICKMAN, Jas.	32	m.	Farmer	1000/300	O.	I
17		Elisabeth	26	f.	Domestic		"	I
18		Timothy	8	m.			"	S
19		Wm. H.	6	m.			"	S
20		Jas. T.	4	m.			"	
21		Hachel A.	1	f.			"	
22	341/341	MATHEWS, Pracilla	57	f.	Domestic	1800/100	Pa.	
23		Huma	30	f.	Domestic		O.	
24		Abraham	28	m.	Farm laborer		"	I
25		Benjamin	25	m.	Farm laborer		"	
26		Wm.	22	m.	Farm laborer		"	
27		Gemima A.	19	f.	Domestic		"	
28		Sarah	17	f.	Domestic		"	
29		Mahela	15	f.	Domestic		"	
30	342/342	MATHEWS, Wm.	55	m.	Farmer	/100	Pa.	
31		Mary	55	f.	Domestic		N.Y.	I
32		David	22	m.	Farm laborer		O.	I
33		Caleb	15	m.	Farm laborer		"	S
34	343/343	ANGUS, Richard	23	m.	Farmer	1000/225	"	
35		Anne M.	21	f.	Domestic		Ger.	
36		Elisabeth	11/12	f.			O.	

1	344/344	RACY, John	29	m.	Farmer	250/150	O.
2		Margaret	29	f.	Domestic		" I
3		Sarah J.	1	f.			"
4	345/345	DENT, Wm. B.	48	m.	Farmer	3400/450	"
5		Elisabeth	52	f.	Domestic		Eng.
6		George	23	m.	Farm laborer	/80	O.
7		Hannah J.	21	f.	Domestic		"
8		JACKSON, Jas. A.	10	m.			" S
9		STACKHOUSE, Mary J.	4	f.			"
10	346/346	REAFF, Frederick	45	m.	Farmer	600/211	Sw.
11		Mary ann	40	f.	Domestic		"
12		John	14	m.			O. S
13		Elisabeth	13	f.			"
14		Mary	11	f.			"
15		Levi	10	m.			"
16		Carolina	8	f.			"
17		Rose	7	f.			"
18		Jacob	5	m.			"
19		Mary Ann	4	f.			"
20		Frances	2	f.			"
21		Frederick	8/12	m.			"
22	347/347	MILLER, Jacob	43	m.	Farmer	/200	Sw.
23		Magdelena	44	f.	Domestic		" I
24		Jacob	20	m.	Farm laborer		"
25		Magdelena	21	f.	Domestic		"
26		Margaret	12	f.			"
27		Rose A.	9	f.			"
28		Anne	7	f.			"
29		Carolina	1	f.			O.
30		Elisabeth	1	f.			"
31	348/348	SMITH, Thomas	45	m.	Farmer	3000/500	Ire.
32		Mary	49	f.	Domestic		" I
33		James	22	m.	Teacher		O.
34		Allen	17	m.	Farm laborer		"
35		Rachel	14	f.			" S
36		Thomas	11	m.			" S

1	349/349	DUFF, Michael	30	m.	Well-digger and collier	3100/100	Ire. M
2		Anne	36	f.	Domestic		" M
3		William	1/2	m.			O.
4		EASTON, Wm.	24	m.	Farmer	/100	"
5	350/350	Elisabeth	21	f.	Domestic		"
6	351/351	EASTON, John	58	m.	Farmer	/300	Pa.
7		Elisabeth	58	f.	Domestic		O.
8		Jane	16	f.			"
9		John	18	m.	Farm laborer		"

10		EASTON, James	13	m.			O.
11		James	60	m.	Farm laborer		Pa.
12	352/352	WHICHNAY, Jacob	71	m.	Farmer	3000/480	Sw.
13		Magdalena	68	f.	Domestic		"
14		Elisabeth	45	f.	Domestic		"
15		John	38	m.	Farmer		" 23
16		Barbary	32	f.	Farmer		" 23
17		Nicholas	31	m.	Farmer		" 23
18		Frederick	28	m.	Farmer		" 23
19		Anne	25	f.	Domestic		" 23
20	353/353	HOWNEL, David	26	m.	Farmer	1500/200	O.
21		Roseanne	23	f.	Domestic		Sw.
22		Rose Anne	2	f.			O.
23	354/354	HOWNEL, Sarah	60	f.	Domestic	/450	Pa.
24		James R.	40	m.	Farmer	700/40	"
25		Thomas	22	m.	Farmer	800/25	O.
26		Mathias	19	m.	Farmer	800/60	"
27	355/355	FENZ, Christian	46	m.	R. L. Preacher	600/200	Sw.
28		Anne	23	f.	Domestic		"
29		Godfrey	3	m.			O.
30		Charles A.	2	m.			"
31		Abraham	5/12	m.			"
32	356/356	GILMAN, Peter	37	m.	Farmer	650/250	Sw.
33		Magdelena	35	f.	Domestic		"
34		Margaret	9	f.			O. S
35		Elisabeth	5	f.			"
36		Susanna	2	f.			"
37	357/357	DENIS, Barbary	55	f.	Domestic	/50	Pa. I

Page 53   27 June 1860   Sheet 161

1	358/358	DENAS, Michael	57	m.	Farmer	3000/375	Pa. I
2		Elcy	40	f.	Domestic		" I
3		Barbary	22	f.	Domestic		O.
4		Jacob	18	m.	Farm laborer		"
5		Henry	15	m.	Farm laborer		"
6	359/359	CONER, Joseph	23	m.	Farmer	350/150	O. M
7		Anna B.	24	f.	Domestic		Sw. M
8	360/360	HARY, John	40	m.	Farmer	100/50	"
9		Susiana	56	f.	Domestic		" I
10	361/361	HAULSCHILD, John	34	m.	Farmer	2000/403	"
11		Catharine	28	f.	Domestic		"
12		Emma E.	7	f.			Va.
13		Edward	5	m.			"
14		John W.	4	m.			O.
15		Frederick W.	3	m.			"
16		Mary Ann	7/12	f.			"
17		ROSE, Frederick	22	m.	Farm laborer		Ger.
18		RE, Mary Elisabeth	45	f.	Domestic		"

19	362/362	ANGUS, John	46	m.	Farmer	3400/560	Pa.	
20		Jane	44	f.	Domestic		O.	
21		John	22	m.	Farmer		"	
22		Isaac	17	m.	Farmer		"	S
23		James	14	m.			"	S
24		Abagail	12	f.			"	S
25		Eliza J.	10	f.			"	S
26		Marthy J.	8	f.			"	S
27		William	6	m.			"	S
28		Edward	2	m.			"	
29	363/363	ESCHE, Jacob	53	m.	Farmer	2500/700	Sw.	
30		Elisabeth	24	f.	Domestic		"	
31		Jacob	21	m.	Farmer		"	
32		Mary	15	f.			"	S
33		John	11	m.			"	S
34	364/364	ALAMAN, John	49	m.	Farmer	1000/560	"	
35		Anna	56	f.	Domestic		"	I
36		William	21	m.	Farmer		"	I
37		Anna	17	f.	Domestic		"	
38		John	16	m.			"	
39		READ, Nicholas	60	m.	Farmer	200/350	"	

Page 54   27 June 1860   Sheet 161 verso

1		SECONDAKER, Chris-tian	40	m.	Dairyman	200/	Sw.	
2	365/365	THOMAS, Alex	61	m.	Farmer	/20	Pa.	
3		Sarah	60	f.	Domestic		Va.	I
4		Alexandria	19	m.	Farmer		O.	S
5		Sarah	15	f.			"	
6	366/366	FOX, Christina	35	f.	Domestic		Sw.	
7		John	17	m.			O.	S
8	367/367	FOX, John	83	m.	Farmer		Sw.	
9		Anna	51	f.	Domestic		"	
10		Frederick	20	m.	Farmer		O.	
11	368/368	FOX, John	54	m.	Farmer	1500/250	Sw.	
12		Mary	25	f.	Domestic		"	
13		John	9	m.			O.	S
14		Christian	7	m.			"	S
15		Saml.	6	m.			"	
16		Frederick	5	m.			"	
17		Elisabeth	3/12	f.			"	
18	369/369	BOMBARGER, Samuel	39	m.	Farmer	800/200	Sw.	
19		Christena	37	f.	Domestic		"	
20		Jacob	14	m.			"	S
21		Saml. J.	13	m.			"	S
22		Caroline	11	f.			"	S
23		Mary Ann	10	f.			"	S
24		Saml. F.	8	m.			"	S
25		Polena	7	f.			O.	S
26		Louisa	3	f.			"	

27		BOMBARGER, Chris- tena	2	f.			O.	
28	370/370	SNIDER, Valentine	37	m.	Farmer	500/250	Ger.	
29		Carolina	27	f.	Domestic		"	
30		Albert	6	m.			Va.	S
31		Matilda	3	f.			Mo.	
32		Amelia	2	f.			O.	
33		Josephen	2/12	f.			"	
34	371/371	GATERMAN, Fred- erick	60	m.	Farmer	/50	Pr.	
35		Carolina	62	f.	Domestic		"	
36	372/372	THOMAS, Alexandria	72	m.	Farmer	400/175	Pa.	
37		Sally	49	f.	Domestic		"	I
38		MILLER, Catharine	63	f.	Domestic		"	I

Page 55			27 June 1860				Sheet 162	
1	373/373	PILES, David	44	m.	Farmer	1000/280	O.	
2		Mary	43	f.	Domestic		"	
3		James M.	17	m.	Farmer		"	S
4		Mary E.	2	f.			"	
5	374/374	SHEPHERD, Elzy	44	m.	Carpenter	/100	"	
6		Mily	44	f.	Domestic		"	
7		John F.	15	m.			"	S
8		Isiah	8	m.			"	S
9		Sarah A.	6	f.			"	
10		Elisabeth	1	f.			"	
11	375/---	CLEGG, Thomas	62	m.	Farmer	1200/250	Pa.	
12		Margaret	58	f.	Domestic		Va.	
13		Joseph	25	m.	Farm laborer		O.	
14		Hannah	23	f.	Domestic		"	
15		Thomas J.	21	m.	Farm laborer		"	
16		Sarah	19	f.	Domestic		"	
17		Catharine	18	f.	Domestic		"	S
18		Elisabeth	15	f.	Domestic		"	S
19		Susanah	13	f.			"	S
20	376/376	CLEGG, Moses	28	m.	Farmer	/200	"	
21		Luisa	21	f.	Domestic		"	
22		Charles W.	4	m.			"	
23		Henry W.	2	m.			"	
24	377/377	CLEGG, Saml.	30	m.	Farmer	/100	"	
25		Eliza J.	27	f.	Domestic		"	
26		David E.	6	m.			"	
27		Sarah J.	5	f.			"	
28		Andrew F.	6/12	m.			"	
29	378/378	CLEGG, Saml. Sr.	47	m.	Farmer	200/550	Pa.	
30		Catharine	44	f.	Domestic		Ger.	
31		James	18	m.	Farm laborer		O.	S
32		John	16	m.	Farm laborer		"	S

33		CLEGG, Richard	14	m.			O. S
34		Lusinda	11	f.			" S
35		Levi	9	m.			" S
36		Margaret	6	f.			" S
37		Isabella	1	f.			"
38	379/379	SAWYER, Andrew	37	m.	Farmer	2000/300	"
39		Elizabeth	33	f.	Domestic		"

Page 56   28 June 1860   Sheet 162 verso

1		Wm. H.	12	m.			O. S
2		Margaret	10	f.			" S
3		Isabell	8	f.			" S
4		Jane	6	f.			" S
5		Bunevesta	4	f.			"
6		Mary E.	1	f.			"
7		McELNAN, Henry	68	m.	Farm laborer		Ire.
8	380/380	McELVEY, Robt.	38	m.	Farmer	5000/575	O.
9		Margaret	36	f.	Domestic		"
10		Elisabeth	9	f.			"
11		Nancy	6	f.			"
12		James B.	3	m.			"
13		Augustin C.	11/12	m.			"
14		McELVER, James	67	m.	Retired	/1200	Ire.
15	381/381	WALTERS, Adam	50	m.	Farmer	2000/417	O.
16		Eve	50	f.	Domestic		Pa.
17		Wm.	20	m.	Farm laborer		O. S
18		Andrew	19	m.	Farm laborer		" S
19		Shannon	18	m.	Farm laborer		" S
20		Susanna	15	f.	Domestic		" S
21		Margaret J.	14	f.			" S
22		Albert	8	m.			"
23	382/382	IMHOOF, Jacob	30	m.	Farmer	3000/525	"
24		Elisabeth	26	f.	Domestic		"
25		Sharlotta	4	f.			"
26		John J.	2	m.			"
27		Mary J.	4/12	f.			"
28	383/383	DUTWILER, John	33	m.	Farmer	/100	Sw.
29		Elisabeth	33	f.	Domestic		"
30		Saml.	10	m.			O. S
31		Emelia	9	f.			"
32		Carolina	4	f.			"
33		Daniel	1	m.			"
34	384/384	STOFFER, John	40	m.	Farmer	200/105	Sw.
35		Margaret	30	f.	Domestic		"
36		Rose	7	f.			"
37		Wm.	4	m.			Pa.
38		Mary	1	f.			O.

Page 52   28 June 1860   Sheet 163

1	385/385	BONTY, Nicholas	53	m.	Farmer	/150	Sw. I

2		BONTY, Anna	49	f.	Domestic		Sw.	I
3		John	30	m.	Day laborer		"	
4		Mary	32	f.	Domestic		"	I
5		Nicholas	23	m.	Farm laborer		"	
6		Jacob	19	m.	Farm laborer		"	
7	386/386	CASMAN, Saml.	65	m.	Farmer	2800/600	"	
8		Magdelena	57	f.	Domestic		"	
9		Frederick	24	m.	Farm laborer		O.	
10		John	21	m.	Farm laborer		"	
11		Jacob	17	m.	Farm laborer		"	S
12		Elisabeth	15	f.			"	
13	387/387	SNELL, John H.	38	m.	Farmer	/100	Sw.	
14		Mary	34	f.	Domestic		"	
15		Charles	15	m.			"	S
16		Bourcanx	13	m.			"	S
17		Emma	11	f.			"	S
18		Elisabeth	9	f.			O.	S
19		Adolph	9	m.			"	S
20		Frederick	6	m.			"	S
21		Henry	3	m.			"	
22		Edward	3	m.			"	
23		Mary	2	f.			"	
24		Louisa	1	f.			"	
25	388/388	CLEGG, John	37	m.	Farmer	3000/503	"	
26		Mary Anne	39	f.	Domestic		Pa.	
27		Hughs	16	m.	Farmer		O.	S
28		Richard	14	m.			"	S
29		Rachel J.	12	f.			"	S
30		Margaret A.	11	f.			"	S
31		Mary E.	9	f.			"	
32		Campsadel	6	f.			"	
33		Hannah L.	4	f.			"	
34		John C.	1	m.			"	
35	389/389	GRIM, Catharine	38	f.	Domestic	800/250	Pa.	I
36		Eliza J.	16	f.			O.	S
37		Lucretia	14	f.			"	S
38		David R.	12	m.			"	S
39		Rose Anne	10	f.			"	

Page 58   28 June 1860   Sheet 163 verso

1		Margaret	9	f.			O.	
2		Sarah	3	f.			"	
3		Mathias	1	m.			"	
4	390/390	GRIM, Thomas	46	m.	Farmer	/250	Pa.	I
5		Eve	48	f.	Domestic		Va.	I
6		Armstrong	26	m.	Farm laborer		Pa.	
7		Mary	25	f.	Domestic		"	
8		Levina	23	f.	Domestic		"	
9		Frederick	19	m.	Farm laborer		O.	S
10		Charles	18	m.	Farm laborer		"	S
11		Thomas	16	m.	Farm laborer		"	S

12		GRIM, Eleanor	15	f.		O.	S
13		Carolina	12	f.		"	S
14		Wm.	10	m.		"	S
15		Catharine	8	f.		"	S

16	391/391	OFHOLDER, Jacob	35	m.	Stone-cutter 550/200	Sw.	
17		Elisabeth	40	f.	Domestic	"	
18		Susanna	14	f.		"	
19		Elisabeth	11	f.		"	S
20		Rose A.	6	f.		O.	
21		Carolina	2	f.		"	
22		Charlotta	6/12	f.		"	
23		John	20	m.	Farm laborer	Sw.	
24		Levi	18	m.	Farm laborer	"	
25		Henry	9	m.		O.	

26	392/392	GRINER, John	37	m.	Farmer 750/300	Ger.	
27		Margaret	27	f.	Domestic	O.	I
28		Thomas	7	m.		"	S
29		Margaret	5	f.		"	
30		Catharine	3	f.		"	
31		Franklin	20	m.		"	
32		Hannah	3/12	f.		"	

33	393/393	EACKLES, Saml.	40	m.	Farmer 2200/550	Pa.	
34		Elisa	37	f.	Domestic	O.	
35		Wilson S.	18	m.	Farm laborer	Va.	S
36		Marshal M.	17	m.	Farm laborer	Pa.	S
37		Wm.	15	m.		O.	S
38		Margaret	12	f.		Pa.	S
39		Anjolina A.	10	f.		Va.	S

Page 59			28 June 1860			Sheet 164	

1		Samuel	7	m.		Va.	
2		Hannah J.	3	f.		O.	
3		David J.	1	m.		"	

4	394/394	ROEMER, Jacob	34	m.	Merchant 1000/1000	Ger.	
5		Elisabeth	23	f.	Domestic	"	I
6		Harmon	10	m.		Pa.	
7		Wm.	1/12	m.		O.	

8	395/395	McILTINE, Albert	26	m.	Farmer 4000/500	"	
9		Caroline	21	f.	Domestic	"	
10		Catharine Vio-					
		laddelon	5	f.		"	S
11		Amos J.	3	m.		"	
12		WHITE, John	22	m.	Farm laborer	Sw.	

13	396/396	GATES, Geo. W.	31	m.	Farmer /285	O.	
14		Sarah E.	24	f.	Domestic	"	
15		Eunace	9	f.		"	S
16		Jasper	6	m.		"	S
17		David S.	4	m.		"	S
18		Charles E.	1	m.		"	

| 19 | 397/397 | McINTIRE, David S. | 53 | m. | Blacksmith   /150 | Va. | |

20		McINTIRE, Mary	49	f.	Domestic		O.	
21		Catharine	22	f.	Domestic		"	
22	398/398	McELVEY, Geo.	41	m.	Farmer	4000/800	Ire.	
23		Margaret J.	20	f.	Domestic		O.	
24		David	19	m.	Farm laborer		"	S
25		Mary Anne	15	f.			"	S
26		Nancy	13	f.			"	S
27		Isabelle	12	f.			"	S
28		Emily	10	f.			"	S
29		Wm.	8	m.			"	S
30		Violet	6	f.			"	S
31	399/399	SUPERS, Geo.	29	m.	Merchant	400/1000	Dar.	
32		Mary J.	29	f.	Domestic		O.	
33		Margaret S.	5	f.			"	S
34		Theadore	4	m.			"	
35		John	2	m.			"	
36	400/400	WILLIAMS, John	55	m.	Farmer	3000/3000	Va.	
37		Sarah N.	41	f.	Domestic		Pa.	
38		Malissa	22	f.	Domestic		O.	
39		Levina	20	f.	Domestic		"	

Page 60   29 June 1860   Sheet 164 verso

1		Leander	17	m.	Farmer		O.		
2		Eliza J.	16	f.			"	S	
3		Mary	13	f.			"	S	
4		Isabel	10	f.			"	S	
5		Emily	6	f.			"		
6		Wm.	4	m.			"		
7	401/401	TWINEM, Andrew	35	m.	Farmer	3000/400	O.		
8		Margaret	27	f.	Domestic		"		
9		Thomas J.	7	m.			"	S	
10		Mary L.	5	f.			"	S	
11	402/402	OFHOLDER, Jacob	35	m.	Farmer	200/225	Sw.		
12		Margaret	29	f.	Domestic		O.	I	
13		Jacob	8	m.			"	S	
14		Elisabeth	6	f.			"		
15		John	3	m.			"		
16		Mary	7/12	f.			"		
17	403/403	COLEMAN, William	38	m.	Farmer	/200	"		
18		Matilda	32	f.	Domestic		"		
19		Anderson	12	m.			"	S	
20		Wm.	9	m.			"	S	
21		David	4	m.			"		
22	404/404	HARTLINE, John C.	32	m.	Farmer	/125	"	M	
23		Harmony	18	f.	Domestic		"	M	
24		Wm. P.	10	m.			"	S	
25		Mary	9	f.			"	S	
26		Joseph	5	m.			"		
27		Thomas J.	4	m.			"		

```
28 405/405 SAWYERS, George    27  m.   Farmer      700/275  O.
29          Margaret          24  f.   Domestic             "
30          John D.            3  m.                         "
31          Albert             2  m.                         "

32 406/406 GILASPIE, Thos.    40  m.   Farmer      4500/600  "
33          Isabelle J.       37  f.   Domestic             "
34          Joseph H.         16  m.   Farm laborer         "   S
35          Geo.              14  m.                         "   S
36          Nancy J.          10  f.                         "   S
37          James              5  m.                         "   S
38          Mary J.            2  f.                         "
```

Page 61   29 June 1860   Sheet 165

```
1  407/407 GILIPSY, John      48  m.   Farmer      700/600  Pa.
2          Tamer             49  f.   Domestic             "
3          Robert B.         24  m.   Farm laborer         O.
4          Geo. L.           22  m.   Farm laborer         "
5          Mary B.           18  f.   Domestic             "   S
6          Thomas E.         15  m.                         "   S
7          John S.           13  m.                         "   S

8  408/408 TWINUM, Jas.       41  m.   Farmer      4000/500  "
9          Olevia            43  f.   Domestic             "
10         Margaret          17  f.   Domestic             "   S

11 409/409 McDONLON, Edward
            J.               27  m.   Farmer       /375    Pa.
12         Hannah            24  f.   Domestic             Ire.
13         Wm. S.             1  m.                         O.
14         Daniel F.       3/12  m.                         "
15         ELIOTT, Adaline   16  f.   Servant              Va.

16 410/410 SHAW, John         37  m.   Farmer      500/150  "   I
17         Lydia             37  f.   Domestic             O.  I
18         Thomas J.         15  m.   Farmer       /100    "
19         Valentine          7  m.                         "

20 411/411 WILCOX, Geo.       31  m.   Farmer       /100    "
21         Sarah             33  f.   Domestic             "

22 412/412 WILCOX, Mary       58  f.   Domestic    1200/280 Del.
23         Lutecia           22  f.   Domestic             O.
24         Walter            19  m.   Farm laborer         "   S
25         Taylor            16  m.   Farm laborer         "   S

26 413/413 OWENS, John        48  m.   Farmer      5000/778  "
27         Mary A.           35  f.   Domestic             "   I
28         Henry             20  m.   Farm laborer         "   S
29         Pheebe J.         12  f.                         "   S
30         Jacob M.          10  m.                         "   S
31         Marinda McK.       7  f.                         "   S
32         Jas. P.            5  m.                         "
33         Isiah              2  m.                         "

34 414/414 WILKISON, John     45  m.   Farmer       /85     "   I
35         Sarah A.          37  f.   Domestic             "   I
```

36		WILKISON, Jane	71	f.	Retired	/320	Pa. I
37	415/415	McELVY, James	32	m.	Farmer	3500/500	O.
38		Elisabeth	36	f.	Domestic		"
39		FISHER, Ruth	14	f.			" S

Page 62   29 June 1860   Sheet 165 verso

1	416/416	ECKELS, Wm.	42	m.	Farmer	/100	Pa.
2		Mary	40	f.	Domestic		O.
3		Anne	17	f.	Domestic		"
4		Jesse	16	m.	Farm laborer		" S
5		Margaret J.	14	f.			" S
6		Frances	12	f.			" S
7		Isabel	11	f.			" S
8		Robert	9	m.			"
9		Hariet	7	f.			"
10		Mary E.	3	f.			"
11	417/417	McELVY, Edward	28	m.	Farmer	/345	"
12		Elisabeth	26	f.	Domestic		"
13		Milton	3	m.			"
14		Mary L.	1	f.			"
15	418/418	FISHER, Simon	24	m.	Farmer	/225	"
16		Rebecca A.	22	f.	Domestic		"
17		Mary E.	2	f.			"
18		Amanda A.	4/12	f.			"
19		William	12	m.			"
20	419/419	KINEY, Timothy	57	m.	Farmer	1800/400	Pa.
21		Rachel	49	f.	Domestic		O.
22		McELROY, Rachel	12	f.			"
23		NOLAND, Aaron	20	m.	Farm laborer		"
24		FISHER, John B.	7	m.			"
25		DAVIS, Mary	80	f.	Retired	/20	Md.
26	420/420	PENNEL, Wm. D.	56	m.	Farmer	2400/542	Pa.
27		Susanna	49	f.	Domestic		O.
28		Geo.	25	m.	Farm laborer		"
29		Margaret J.	23	f.	Domestic		"
30		Samuel	20	m.	Farm laborer		"
31		Wm.	18	m.	Farm laborer		"
32		Hannah M.	14	f.			" S
33		Susanna	11	f.			" S
34		John A.	9	m.			"
35	421/421	GOUDY, Robert	54	m.	Farmer	800/425	Pa.
36		Averilla	51	f.	Domestic		Md.
37		Francis A.	23	f.	Domestic		O.
38		Margaret	21	f.	Domestic		"
39		John J.	19	m.	Farm laborer		" S

Page 63   29 June 1860   Sheet 166

1		Robt. F.	15	m.	Farm laborer		O. S
2	422/422	DEVAL, James	36	m.	Farmer	2000/225	"

3		DEVAL, Sarah	31	f.	Domestic		O.	
4		Simon P.	9	m.			"	S
5		Semantha A.	4	f.			"	
6		Kisiah	2	f.			"	
7	423/423	KING, David	57	m.	Farmer	/150	Md.	I
8		Evaline	50	f.	Domestic		Va.	I
9		Wm. H.	21	m.	Farm laborer		O.	I
10		Jacob L.	18	m.	Farm laborer		"	
11		Marthy E.	15	f.			"	
12		Jesse L.	12	m.			"	
13		David F.	9	m.				
14	424/424	BROWN, Philip	56	m.	Farmer	1200/300	Ger.	
15		Mary A.	50	f.	Domestic		"	I
16		John	21	m.	Farmer		"	
17		Barbary	18	f.	Domestic		O.	
18		Markus	16	m.	Farmer		"	S
19	425/425	GOUDY, Isaac	51	m.	Farmer	800/400	"	
20		Mary	48	f.	Domestic		Md.	
21		David P.	20	m.	Farm laborer		O.	S
22		Isaac L.	18	m.	Farm laborer		"	S
23		John M.	15	m.	Farm laborer		"	S
24		Saml. P.	12	m.			"	S
25		McMAN, Sarah	11	f.			"	S
26	426/426	CAMPBELL, Joshua	45	m.	Potter	500/550	Ire.	
27		Isabella	31	f.	Domestic		O.	
28		Mary	14	f.			Va.	
29		Eliza	10	f.			"	S
30		Alexander	7	m.			"	S
31		Archibald	4	m.			O.	
32		Frances J.	2	f.			"	
33	427/427	CAMPBELL, Mary	88	f.	Retired		Ire.	
34		Frances M.	47	f.	Domestic	/75	"	
35	428/428	FERNASH, Elijah	32	m.	Farmer	/225	O.	I
36		Lusinda	35	f.	Domestic		"	
37		John W.	3	m.			"	
38		Samuel G.	1	m.			"	
39		DEVOL, Conrad	65	m.	Farmer	500/40	Pa.	

1	429/429	MORE, Lewis	57	m.	Farmer	/125	Pa.	
2		Rebecca	53	f.	Domestic		O.	
3		McCASLIN, Jane C.	27	f.	Teacher	/150	"	
4		John	5	m.			"	
5		Henry	22	m.	Farmer		"	
6		Elias	19	m.	Farmer		"	
7		Edward	17	m.	Farmer		"	
8		Sarah	9	f.			"	
9	430/430	WILISON, Isaac	25	m.	Farmer	/160	"	I
10		Jane	30	f.	Domestic		"	I
11		James B.	3	m.			"	

12		WILISON, Susiana	2	f.			0.	
13		McELROY, Harriet A.	7	f.			"	S
14		Margaret	11	f.			"	

15	431/431	DEVOL, Coonrad	21	m.	Farmer	/75	"	
16		Frances	18	f.	Domestic		"	
17		HENTHORN, Hulda	6	f.			"	

18	432/432	JONES, Daniel O.						
		C.	32	m.	Farmer	/260	"	
19		Sarah	27	f.	Domestic		"	
20		James H.	9	m.			"	S
21		Joel	7	m.			"	S
22		Catharine J.	5	f.			"	
23		Mary E.	3	f.			"	
24		Samuel G.	1	m.			"	

25	433/433	DEVOL, John	47	m.	Farmer	5000/794	Pa.	
26		Elisabeth	35	f.	Domestic		0.	
27		Simon	12	m.			"	S
28		CONLAH, Hannah	9	f.	Servant		"	

29	434/434	DEVOL, James	20	m.	Farmer		"	M
30		Jane	16	f.	Domestic		"	

31	435/435	CEILS, James	73	m.	Farmer	1500/225	Pa.
32		Catharine	68	f.	Domestic		"

Page 65   30 June 1860   Sheet 167

1	436/436	DAUGHERTY, Frank	37	m.	Farmer	225/100	Pa.	
2		Nancy	24	f.	Domestic		0.	
3		Josephine	7	f.			"	S
4		Mathena	5	f.			"	S
5		Lafyett	3	m.			"	
6		Sarah	2/12	f.			"	

7	437/437	WAYT, Allen	48	m.	Farmer	4500/478	"	I
8		Margaret	46	f.	Domestic		"	
9		Henry	16	m.	Farm laborer		"	S
10		Abraham	14	m.	Farm laborer		"	S
11		Geo. W.	11	m.			"	S
12		Quintilla	9	f.			"	S
13		Allen S.	5	m.			"	

14	438/438	MIRES, Joseph	45	m.	Farmer	6750/2209	Va.	
15		Eleanor	33	f.	Domestic		0.	
16		Mary	10	f.			"	S
17		Manervy	7	f.			"	S
18		Lauretta	6	f.			"	S
19		Marinda	4	f.			"	S
20		Eleanor	2	f.			"	
21		Joseph W.	4/12	m.			"	
22		Frederick	84	m.	Retired		Pa.	

23	437/437	WATE, Wm. T.	21	m.	Farmer	/100	0.
24		Frances	19	f.	Domestic		"
25		Allen	1/12	m.			"

(Green Township Concluded)

(Jas. Okey, Asst. Marshall)

* * *

Adams Township   P. O. Cameron

Page 66   2 July 1860   Sheet 167 verso

1	440/440 WADKINS, Wm.	38	m.	Farmer	3500/680	O.	
2	Mary J.	28	f.	Domestic		"	
3	Wm. T.	13	m.			"	S
4	Hariet	9	f.			"	S
5	Isabel	7	f.			"	S
6	Margaret	5	f.			"	S
7	Mary R.	1	f.			"	
8	Wm.	81	m.	Retired		Eng.	
9	KING, John	17	m.	Farm laborer		O.	S
10	441/441 COX, Joseph	27	m.	Farmer	2000/650	Pa.	
11	Catharine	25	f.	Domestic		O.	
12	Martha	3	f.			"	
13	Thomas C.	1	m.			"	
14	442/442 ALEXANDRIA, William	59	m.	Farmer	3000/553	Ire.	
15	Mary	57	f.	Domestic		"	
16	James	21	m.	Farmer		O.	S
17	443/443 TRACY, Jeremiah	46	m.	Farmer	1800/600	"	
18	Piety	47	f.	Domestic		"	
19	Joshua F.	26	m.	Farm laborer		"	
20	Thomas W.	22	m.	Farm laborer		"	
21	Sarah O.	20	f.	Domestic		"	
22	Marshal J.	15	m.			"	S
23	Nancy J.	9	f.			"	S
24	Elijah M.	9	m.			"	S
25	444/444 HART, Thomas	69	m.	Farmer	/200	Pa.	
26	Margaret	65	f.	Domestic		"	
27	Thomas J.	28	m.	Farm laborer		O.	
28	PARKER, Elisabeth	12	f.			"	S
29	445/445 HART, Corydon	36	m.	Farmer	1600/325	Pa.	
30	Nancy J.	29	f.	Domestic		O.	I
31	Wm.	10	m.			"	S
32	Thos.	6	m.			"	S
33	Margaret J.	3	f.			"	
34	446/446 DUFFY, John	44	m.	Cloth factory	1800/340	N.Y.	
35	Jane	44	f.	Domestic			
36	John	16	m.	Farm laborer		Pa.	S
37	Gilbert	12	m.			"	S
38	Catharine	10	f.			O.	S
39	Wm.	4	m.			"	

Page 67		2 July 1860					Sheet 168	
1	447/447	FULTON, Wm.	55	m.	Farmer	1600/350	Ire.	
2		Jane	50	f.	Domestic		Pa.	I
3		John	22	m.	Farmer		O.	
4		Margaret A.	18	f.	Domestic		"	S
5		Charles	16	m.	Farmer		"	S
6		Sarah A.	15	f.			"	S
7	448/448	GASTON, John	48	m.	Carpenter	300/200	Pa.	
8		Oliver	22	m.	Carpenter		O.	
9		James	19	m.	Farmer		"	
10		Caroline	18	f.	Domestic		"	
11		Susanna	16	f.	Domestic		"	
12	449/449	DUFFY, Charles	23	m.	Farmer	/157	Pa.	
13		Hannah	23	f.	Domestic		O.	
14		John	1	m.			"	
15	450/450	McFARLAN, Thomas J.	31	m.	Farmer	1800/350	"	
16		Sarah	30	f.	Domestic		Pa.	
17		David S.	9	m.			O.	S
18		John G.	8	m.			"	S
19		George W.	7	m.			"	S
20		Elisa S.	5	f.			"	S
21		Milton E.	3	m.			"	
22		Ruth E.	2	m.			"	
23	451/451	ALEXANDRIA, Thomas	30	m.	Farmer	1500/300	"	
24		Sarah E.	25	f.	Domestic		"	
25		Mary J.	5	f.			"	S
26		John W.	2	m.			"	
27	452/452	ANDREWS, Reuben	53	m.	Physician	1700/500	Pa.	
28		Temperance	51	f.	Domestic		"	
29		Roseann	23	f.	Domestic		O.	
30		Lida E.	19	f.	Domestic		"	S
31		Alto S.	14	f.			"	S
32		Eldorado	10	f.			Pa.	S
33		HALE, David	18	m.	Farm laborer		"	S
34	453/453	SAWYERS, John	33	m.	Farmer	1600/403	O.	
35		Francis	27	f.	Domestic		"	I
36		Mary E.	6	f.			"	
37		Sarah	4	f.			"	
38		Saml.	2	m.			"	
39		Letha A.	7/12	f.			"	
Page 68		3 July 1860					Sheet 168 verso	
1	454/454	HART, Cephus	43	m.	Farmer	2300/500	Pa.	
2		Sarah	39	f.	Domestic		O.	
3		Margaret A.	18	f.	Domestic		"	
4		John	16	m.	Farmer		"	S
5		David	14	m.			"	S
6		Thos.	12	m.			"	S
7		Jas.	10	m.			"	S

8		HART, Nancy J.	7	f.			O.	S
9		Franklin	6	m.			"	S
10		Mary E.	4	f.			"	
11		Lewis	7/12	m.			"	

12	455/455	ENLOW, Michael	46	m.	Farmer	1000/275	Pa.	
13		Lydia A.	38	f.	Domestic		O.	
14		Joseph	13	m.			"	S
15		Jas.	11	m.			"	S
16		Mary	9	f.			"	S
17		Jane	7	f.			"	S
18		Amos	4	m.			"	
19		Jesse	2	m.			"	
20		MINER, Mary	65	f.	Domestic		Pa.	
21		ENLOW, Jesse	48	m.	Day laborer		"	

22	456/456	McMAN, Isaac	30	m.	Farmer	/125	O.	
23		Jennetta	28	f.	Domestic		"	
24		Mary A.	10	f.			"	S
25		Daniel	8	m.			"	S
26		Emily	5	f.			"	
27		Rue eny	2	f.			"	

28	457/457	McMAN, Elijah	26	m.	Farmer	1100/180	"	
29		Elisabeth	19	f.	Domestic		"	
30		Sarah A.	4/12	f.			"	
31		TAGG, Geo.	11	m.			"	S

32	458/458	McMAN, John	30	m.	Farmer	1100/300	"	
33		Sarah	59	f.	Domestic		Md.	
34		Albert	3	m.			O.	

35	459/459	TAYLOR, Alexandria	25	m.	Farmer	/100	"	
36		Jane A.	21	f.	Domestic		Pa.	
37		Isabella	5	f.			O.	
38		Julian	3	f.			"	
39		John	6/12	m.			"	

| Page 69 | | | 4 July 1860 | | | | Sheet 169 | |

1	460/460	McMAN, Elijah	49	m.	Farmer	6500/800	Va.	
2		Jane	48	f.	Domestic		O.	
3		Wm. H.	12	m.			"	S
4		HASE, Lida J.	25	f.	Servant		"	

5	461/461	TRACY, Shirden B.	25	m.	Farmer	1000/150	"	
6		Sarah A.	22	f.	Domestic		"	
7		Idella	4/12	f.			"	

8	462/462	McMAN, Thomas	54	m.	Farmer	3000/517	Pa.	
9		Sarah	54	f.	Domestic		"	
10		Elisabeth	23	f.	Domestic		O.	
11		Hannah	15	f.	Domestic		"	S
12		Martha	12	f.			"	S
13		Eliza	9	f.			"	S

| 14 | 463/463 | LOPER, John | 40 | m. | Farmer | 1400/1477 | N.Y. | |
| 15 | | Jane | 46 | f. | Domestic | | Pa. | |

16		LOPER, Alexandria				
		S.	19	m.	Farm laborer	Pa.	S
17		Jonathan Mc.	16	m.		"	S
18		Geo. W.	13	m.		"	S
19		Mary E.	8	f.		"	S
20		Jane S.	7	f.		".	S
21		John G.	2	m.		O.	
22	464/464	TRACY, Rachel	50	f.	Domestic 700/100	"	
23		Rebecca	27	f.	Domestic	"	
24		Nancy	25	f.	Domestic	"	
25		Kesiah	22	m.	Farm laborer	"	
26		Saml. W.	18	m.		"	S
27		Basel A.	12	m.		"	S
28	465/465	HENTHORN, Abram	27	m.	Well-digger 325/50	"	I
29		Rebecca	27	f.		"	I
30		Menerva	7	f.		"	
31		William	4	m.		"	
32		Eliza J.	1	f.		"	
33	466/466	HENTHORN, Isaac	28	m.	Farm laborer /50	"	
34		Rachel	26	f.	Domestic	"	
35		John H.	4/12	m.		"	
36		Margaret	14	f.		"	
37	467/467	GILIPSY, Geo.	53	m.	Farmer 3500/781	Pa.	
38		Elisabeth	46	f.	Domestic	O.	

Page 70   4 July 1860   Sheet 169 verso

1		Thomas	26	m.	Farmer	O.	
2		Wm.	22	f.	Farmer	"	
3		Jane	19	f.	Domestic	"	
4		John	16	m.	Farm laborer	"	S
5		George	14	m.		"	S
6		Nancy	11	f.		"	S
7		Elizabeth	9	f.		"	S
8		Obediah	5	m.		"	S
9		Jas. H.	2	m.		"	
10	468/468	SOFFELL, John	32	m.	Farmer 1600/325	"	
11		Mary E.	26	f.	Domestic	"	
12		Mary E.	12	f.		"	S
13		Eliza J.	9	f.		"	S
14		Sophronia	2	f.		"	
15		Thomas A.	1	m.		"	
16		MOBLEY, Hezikiah	21	m.	Farm laborer	"	
17	469/469	ROSS, Hirum	58	m.	Farm laborer /175	"	I
18		Sarah	56	f.	Domestic	Va.	I
19		John	21	m.	Farm laborer	O.	I
20		Elisabeth	17	f.	Domestic	"	
21	470/470	FULTON, Anda Ruth	42	m.	Farmer 3000/350	"	
22		Margaret	36	f.	Domestic	"	
23		Wm.	15	m.	Farmer	"	S
24		Isabell	13	f.		"	S

25		FULTON, Andrew	9	m.			O.	S
26		Samuel	7	m.			"	S
27		Mary E.	4	f.			"	
28		John	2	m.			"	
29		James	1/12	m.			"	
30	471/471	McCAIN, Jas.	51	m.	Farmer	300/	"	I
31	472/472	MARROW, Jchn Sr.	75	m.	Farmer		Ire.	
32		John	27	m.	Farmer	700/300	O.	
33		Anne J.	24	f.	Domestic		"	
34		Ruth E.	20	f.	Milliner		"	
35		Sarah	16	f.	Domestic		"	
36	473/473	MONAHAN, Elijah	33	m.	Blacksmith	400/400	"	
37		Julian	32	f.	Domestic		"	
38		Hannah	8	f.			"	

Page 71   5 July 1860   Sheet 170

1		Elisabeth	7	f.			"	S
2		David	3	m.			"	
3		Amanda J.	1	f.			"	
4	474/474	WILLIAMS, Sulves-ter	28	m.	Farmer	/160	"	
5		Catharine	26	f.	Domestic		"	
6		Alonzo C.	2	m.			"	
7		Allice	9/12	f.			"	
8	475/475	McFARLEN, John	66	m.	Farmer	4000/500	Ire.	
9		Isabel	56	f.	Domestic		Pa.	
10		Jas.	27	m.	Farmer		O.	
11		Geo. L.	24	m.	Farmer		"	
12		Wm. D.	22	m.	Farmer		"	
13		John	19	m.	Farmer		"	
14		Catharine	13	f.			"	
15		Margaret	11	f.			"	
16		Olea	9	f.			"	
17	476/476	WILLIAMS, Moses	52	m.	Farmer	3000/300	Pa.	
18		Rebecca	48	f.	Domestic		O.	I
19		John G.	26	m.	Farm laborer		"	
20		Amanda	22	f.	Domestic		"	
21		Mary	21	f.	Domestic		"	
22		Ephram	18	m.	Farm laborer		"	
23		Margaret	14	f.			"	
24		Clenning A.	3	m.			"	
25	477/477	MARROW, Thomas	32	m.	Farmer	1200/800	"	
26		Sarah	37	f.	Domestic		Eng.	
27		Elisabeth	9	f.			O.	S
28		Margaret A.	7	f.			"	S
29		Wm. J.	5	m.			"	S
30		Thomas H.	2	m.			"	
31		THOMAS, Leander	15	m.	Farm laborer		"	
32	478/478	SAWYERS, Henry	64	m.	Farmer	3200/200	Ire.	

33		SAWYERS, Wm.	30	m.	Farmer		O.
34		Nancy	21	f.	Domestic		Ire.
35		Henry	1	m.			O.
36	479/479	SAWYERS, Jas.	27	m.	Farmer	/180	O. M
37		Margaret	26	f.	Domestic		" M
38		Saml.	25	m.	Farm laborer	/125	"

Page 72   5 July 1860   Sheet 170 verso

1	480/480	TWINAM, Leonard	37	m.	Farmer	7000/980	O.
2		Marthy L.	39	f.	Domestic		"
3		Martha	11	f.			"
4		Isabel	6	f.			"
5		Sarah J.	4	f.			"
6		Margaret A.	2	f.			"
7		DISART, Andrew A.	19	m.	Farmer		"
8		Wm.	17	m.	Farmer		"
9		John B.	15	m.	Farmer		"
10	481/481	WILLIAMSON, Dan-iel	23	m.	Carpenter	/120	"
11		Rebecca	27	f.	Domestic		Pa.
12	482/482	HENTHORN, Elijah	52	m.	Farmer	/100	Va.
13		Mary A.	45	f.	Domestic		"
14		Clarisa P.	18	f.	Domestic		O.
15		Susianna	13	f.			"
16		Wm.	11	m.			" S
17	483/483	FRANK, John	47	m.	Farmer	3000/450	Ger.
18		Mary	36	f.	Domestic		" I
19		Anne	10	f.			Va. S
20		Eliza	6	f.			O. S
21		Margaret	3	f.			"
22		SPARGROVE , Joseph	55	m.	Day laborer		Md.
23	484/484	BUSKIRK, Oliphant	32	m.	Physician	/400	O.
24		Sarah A.	42	f.	Domestic		Va.
25		Joseph	20	m.	Farmer		O. S
26		Stephen	18	m.	Farmer		"
27		Noah	15	m.	Farmer		" S
28		Marthy	13	f.			" S
29		Harvy	11	m.			" S
30		Denice	8	m.			" S
31	485/485	BERSKERK, Saml. S.	63	m.	Farmer	4000/510	Pa.
32		Marthy	57	f.	Domestic		Va.
33		Wilson S.	19	m.	Shoemaker		O. S
34		Marthy A.	12	f.			" S
35	486/486	BROTHERS, Stephen	49	m.	Farmer	2000/465	"
36		Levina	49	f.	Domestic		" I
37		Benjamin F.	17	m.	Farm laborer		" S
38		James	14	m.	Farm laborer		" S
39		Emily	12	f.			" S

Page 73   5 July 1860   Sheet 171

1		BROTHERS, John W.	9	m.			O. S
2	487/487	HATHORN, Jno. W.	35	m.	Farmer	3500/687	"
3		Mary A.	25	f.	Domestic		"
4		Lutellus	8	m.			" S
5		Randolph	7	m.			" S
6		Alta	5	f.			" S
7		Anne	4	f.			"
8		Hannah	2	f.			"
9	488/488	GREEN, Saml.	30	m.	Farmer	1300/265	"
10		Elisabeth	26	f.	Domestic		Pa.
11		Henry H.	4	m.			O.
12		Jas. A.	3	m.			"
13		Sarah A.	1	f.			"
14	489/489	ABERSOLD, John Jr.	29	m.	Farmer	800/225	"
15		Mary Ann	21	f.	Domestic		Md.
16		Wm. H.	5	m.			O.
17		John	3	m.			"
18		Elisabeth	2	f.			"
19	490/490	KENNER, Jas.	65	m.	Farmer	1600/200	Eng.
20		Sarah	65	f.	Domestic		Md. I
21	491/491	BONER, Samuel	21	m.	Cooper	/50	O.
22		Penelope	21	f.	Domestic		" I
23		Alice	2	f.			"
24		Mary	10/12	f.			"
25	492/492	JONES, Hamilton	37	m.	Wagon-maker	/100	"
26		Amy	44	f.	Domestic		Va.
27		Jane M.	3	f.			O.
28	493/493	THOMAS, John	58	m.	Farmer	750/105	Va.
29		Elisabeth	54	f.	Domestic		Pa.
30		Wm. H.	29	m.	Farm laborer		O.
31		John A.	27	m.	Farm laborer		"
32		Andrew J.	24	m.	Farm laborer		"
33		Haretta	19	f.	Domestic		"
34		WATSON, Roena	7	f.			"
35		MARTIN, Julian	4	f.			"
36	494/494	HARINGTON, John	35	m. m.	Cooper	300/100	Va. I
37		Susanna	44	f. m.	Domestic		" I
38		Daniel C.	11	m. m.			"
39		Geo. W.	10	m. m.			"

Page 74   6 July 1860   Sheet 171 verso

1		Joanna	9	f. m.			Va.
2	495/495	TRUAX, Jacob	36	m.	Farmer	125/100	O. I
3		Elisabeth	33	f.	Domestic		"
4		Margaret A.	10	f.			" S
5		Wm.	7	m.			" S

6		TRUAX, John M.	3	m.			O.
7		Stephen M.	11/12	m.			"
8	496/496	HERD, Saml.	54	m.	Farmer	3000/500	"
9		Louisa	41	f.	Domestic		Pa.
10		Mary	20	f.	Domestic		O.
11		Jacob	16	m.	Farmer		"
12		Manervy	13	f.			"
13		Mariah L.	3	f.			"
14	497/497	HERD, David S.	21	m.	Farmer	/75	" M
15		Rebecca	20	f.	Domestic		" M
16	498/498	PENNEL, Clark	47	m.	Farmer	/108	Pa.
17		Hariet	37	f.	Domestic	800/	N.Y.
18		Henry	21	m.	Farmer		Pa.
19		Wm.	18	m.	Farmer		O.
20		Sarah J.	16	f.	Domestic		"
21		Evander	14	m.			"
22		Adaline	12	f.			"
23		Mahaly	10	f.			"
24		Marthy	8	f.			"
25		Hariet	6	f.			"
26		Margaret	3	f.			"
27		John D.	8/12	m.			"
28	499/499	BROCK, Levi	46	m.	Farmer	1700/425	"
29		Mary Ann	31	f.	Domestic		"
30		Martha	7	f.			"
31		Mary	5	f.			"
32		Isaac	3	m.			"
33	500/500	BARCUS, Geo.	26	m.	Farmer	1000/250	"
34		Mary Ann	24	f.	Domestic		"
35		Marthy	10/12	f.			"
36		Lewis	19	m.	Farm laborer		"
37		Enoch	16	m.	Farm laborer		"

Page 75   6 July 1860   Sheet 172

1	501/501	NICOLS, Tilmon	44	m.	Day laborer	/50	Pa. I
2		Nancy A.	44	f.	Domestic		O.
3		Marion	18	m.	Day laborer		"
4		Indiana	13	f.	Domestic		"
5		Columbus	11	m.			"
6		Misouri	9	f.			"
7		Mary	6	f.			"
8	502/502	WILLAS, Daniel	44	m.	Farmer	100/420	Pa.
9		Anne	41	f.	Domestic		O.
10		Nancy J.	20	f.	Domestic		"
11		Caroline	18	f.	Domestic		"
12		Mary M.	12	f.			" S
13		Catharine	8	f.			" S
14		Lydia	5	f.			"
15		Isora J.	2	f.			"
16		Elisabeth	3/12	f.			"

```
17 503/503 IRVEN, John          44    m.    Farmer    2000/750  Va.
18         William S.            9    m.                        O.
19         Mary J.               7    f.                        "
20         Samuel G.             2    m.                        "
21         Sarah J.          11/12    f.                        "

22 504/504 HAYWARD, Rebecca     42    f.    Domestic   400/150  "   I
23         PENELL, Marthy        8    f.                        "

24 505/505 CONGER, Nelson       24    m.    Farmer       /150   "
25         Sarah                32    f.    Domestic             "   I
26         Mary Anne             4    f.                        "
27         Gresham               1    m.                        "

28 506/506 CONGER, David        36    m.    Farmer       /225   "
29         Margaret A.          34    f.    Domestic             "   I
30         Elisabeth            17    f.    Domestic             "
31         Hannah               15    f.    Domestic             "
32         John                 14    m.                        "
33         Elijah               12    m.                        "

34 507/507 CONGER, Gresham      61    m.    Farmer    3000/500  Pa.
35         Hannah               59    f.    Domestic            Va.
36         Mary                 21    f.    Domestic            O.
```

Page 76   6 July 1860   Sheet 172 verso

```
1  508/--- WALTER, Jeremiah     51    m.    Farmer    5000/2940 Pa.
2          Margaret             48    f.    Domestic            O.
3          Amanda               20    f.    Domestic            "
4          Delila               17    f.    Domestic            "
5          Wm.                  15    m.                        "
6          Jeremiah             10    m.                        "
7          Margaret              7    f.                        "
8          Mary                  4    f.                        "
9          Juliette              1    f.                        "

10 509/509 TRUAX, Ace           33    m.    Farmer       /100   "
11         Susianna             29    f.    Domestic           Md.
12         Rebecca J.            8    f.                        O.
13         Enoch                 6    m.                        "
14         Lusinda               4    f.                        "
15         Sarah E.              2    f.                        "

16 510/510 WALTON, Rickard K.   23    m.    Teacher      /100   "
17         Julian               24    f.    Domestic            "

18 511/511 HERD, Daniel C.      28    m.    Shoemaker    /100   "
19         Louisa               27    f.    Domestic            "
20         Alofton W.            1    m.                        "

21 512/512 HARTLINE, Joseph     26    m.    Farmer       /150   "
22         Elisabeth            25    f.    Domestic            "
23         Mary E.               1    f.                        "

24 513/513 TRUAX, Jacob         73    m.    Farmer    2000/250  Pa.
25         Rebecca              68    f.    Domestic            "   I
```

26		TRUAX, Rachel	45	f.	Domestic		O. I
27		Nancy J.	17	f.	Domestic		"
28		COALS, Rachel	38	f.	Servant		"
29	514/514	TRUAX, Wm.	28	m.	Farmer	/250	"
30		Mary Anne	20	f.	Domestic		"
31		Margaret A.	3/12	f.			"
32	515/515	CONGER, Elias	69	m.	Farmer	600/350	N.J.
33		Margaret	66	f.	Domestic		Pa.
34		Stephen L.	21	m.	Farm laborer	/100	O.
35		FERRY, Mary E.	14	f.			" S
36	516/516	WALTERS, Geo.	32	m.	Farmer	/150	"
37		Phebe	34	f.	Domestic		"
38		John H.	7	m.			"
39		Jas. M.	6	m.			"

| Page 77 | | 6 July 1860 | | | | | Sheet 173 |

1		Geo. N.	4	m.			O.
2		Clarinda	3	f.			"
3		Ira B.	10/12	m.			"
4	517/517	BRAGE, Ira	63	m.	Merchant	1700/1000	Conn.
5		Lethe	58	f.	Domestic		Md.
6		GASPIN, Caroline	18	f.	Servant		O.
7	518/518	NORAS, Josiah	23	m.	Well-digger	/50	" I
8	519/519	JAMES, Jas.	55	m.	Farmer	1000/180	"
9		Catharine	54	f.	Domestic		Pa.
10		Elisabeth	30	f.	Domestic		O.
11		Amanda J.	20	f.	Domestic		"
12		Stephen A.	17	m.	Farm laborer		"
13		Jas. S.	14	m.			"
14	520/520	NORAS, Wm.	70	m.	Farmer	700/100	Ire.
15		Nancy	23	f.	Domestic	/25	O.
16		Rachel	22	f.	Domestic	/25	"
17		Geo.	25	m.	Farmer	/75	"
18		Hariet	19	f.	Domestic	/25	"
19	521/521	YOUNG, Wm.	34	m.	Blacksmith	/138	Pa.
20		Sarah	32	f.	Domestic		O.
21		Ebenezar	11	m.			" S
22		Mary	9	f.			" S
23		Clarissa	6	f.			" S
24		Nathan	4	m.			" S
25		Franklin	10/12	m.			"
26	522/522	MOBLEY, Charles	27	m.	Farmer	/100	"
27		Eliza J.	28	f.	Domestic		" I
28		John L.	3	m.			"
29		Wm. W.	3/12	m.			"
30		DEVAL, Nancy	55	f.	Domestic		"
31	523/523	SANPEL, Hezekiah	43	m.	Farmer	2100/349	"

32	SANPEL, Marthy	36	f.	Domestic	O.	
33	Wm. B.	21	m.	Farmer	"	
34	Mary Anne	18	f.	Domestic	"	S
35	Sarah E.	16	f.	Domestic	"	
36	Eliza J.	15	f.	Domestic	"	S
37	Ruth E.	14	f.		"	S
38	Sinthy	12	f.		"	S
39	Wilson S.	11	m.		"	S

Page 78   7 July 1860   Sheet 173 verso

1	Luisa S.	9	f.		O.	
2	Emily C.	8	f.		"	
3	Marthy L.	7	f.		"	
4	Alexandria J.	5	m.		"	
5	Amanda	4	f.		"	
6	Nathan E.	2	m.		"	
7	Harvy W.	3/12	m.		"	
8	524/524 YOUNG, Nathan	24	m.	Miller	1200/203	Pa.
9	Mary Ann	25	f.	Domestic		"
10	Alonzo	1	m.		O.	
11	Sarah E.	4/12	f.		"	
12	Malankthaen	8	m.		"	S
13	525/525 TILER, Thomas H.	26	m.	Farmer	2000/479	"
14	Nancy	21	f.	Domestic		"
15	Layfayett	1	m.			"
16	526/526 PARKER, John	52	m.	Shoemaker	/50	Pa.
17	Sarah	38	f.	Domestic		O. I
18	Mary E.	13	f.			" S
19	Marthy L.	11	f.			" S
20	John M.	9	m.			"
21	Margaret	8	f.			"
22	Martin M.	5	m.			"
23	Jas. F.	4	m.			"
24	Geo. W.	2	m.			"
25	527/527 STEAL, Wm.	35	m.	Farmer	1100/1050	"
26	Deborah	35	f.	Domestic		"
27	Phebe E.	8	f.			"
28	Nancy L.	6	f.			"
29	Saml. B.	5	m.			"
30	Geo. W.	11/12	m.			"
31	Elisabeth E.	11/12	f.			"
32	528/528 KEEPER, Jacob	38	m.	Farmer	625/300	Ger.
33	Angaline	26	f.	Domestic		O.
34	Henry	2	m.			"
35	Geo. J.	64	m.	Farmer		Ger.
36	529/529 HICKMAN, Wm.	41	m.	Miller	3000/153	Pa.
37	Matilda	36	f.	Domestic		O.
38	Roseberry	18	m.	Farmer		" S
39	Francis	17	f.	Domestic		" S

Page 79		7 July 1860				Sheet 174	
1		HICKMAN, Mary	15	f.		O.	S
2		Nancy	14	f.		"	S
3		Elisabeth	11	f.		"	S
4		Wm. T.	9	m.		"	S
5		Eli	6	m.		"	S
6		Huldah J.	3	f.		"	
7	530/530	CENT, Samuel	35	m.	Miller	1500/100	"
8		Francis	33	f.	Domestic		"
9		Martha	13	f.			" S
10		Madison	11	m.			" S
11		Mary	9	f.			" S
12		Mathis	5	m.			"
13		Manlius	3	m.			"
14		Ira L.	1	m.			"
15	531/531	PUGH, Daniel	49	m.	Farmer	/118	Pa.
16		Elisabeth	45	f.	Domestic		" I
17		Samuel	21	m.	Miller		" S
18		Catharine	12	f.			"
19		Wilson W.	9	m.			"
20		Phebe R.	7	f.			"
21		Margaret L.	5	f.			"
22		Mary E.	2	f.			O.
23	532/532	WILSON, John	39	m.	Carpenter	1800/297	Pa.
24		Phebe	38	f.	Domestic		"
25		Nancy L.	14	f.			"
26		Saml. A.	12	m.			"
27		Geo. B.	7	m.			O.
28		Wm. T.	2	m.			"
29		PUGH, Nancy	65	f.	Domestic		Pa.
30	533/533	HOWELL, Thomas	33	m.	Day laborer	/80	O.
31		Mary Ann	32	f.	Domestic		" I
32		John M.	10	m.			"
33		Wm.	9	m.			"
34		Madison	7	m.			"
35		Susanna	1	f.			"
36	534/534	HOPTON, Edward	41	m.	Carpenter	/318	Pa.
37		Sarah W.	38	f.	Domestic		O.
38		Jas. M.	13	m.			" S
39		Isabel	12	f.			" S

Page 80		7 July 1860				Sheet 174 verso	
1		Wm.	9	m.			O. S
2		Josephus	5	m.			" S
3		Elisa L.	4	f.			"
4		Amanda	2	f.			"
5	535/535	VAUGHN, Joshua	25	m.	Farmer	/182	"
6		Elisabeth	25	f.	Domestic		"
7		Jas. H.	2	m.			"
8		Thomas	7/12	m.			"

9	536/536	HILL, William	55	m.	Farmer	5000/1656	Pa.
10		Mary	53	f.	Domestic		O.
11		John	21	m.	Farmer	/100	"
12		Mary Ann	19	f.	Domestic		"
13		Elisabeth	15	f.	Domestic		" S
14		Wm.	17	m.	Farmer		" S
15		Anderson C.	13	m.			" S
16		Josiah	9	m.			" S
17		Marinda	7	f.			" S
18	537/537	HOPTON, Isabella	72	f.	Domestic	900/200	Pa.
19		Joseph	26	m.	Farmer	800/100	"
20	538/538	CHYNOWETH, Wm.	72	m.	Farmer	5500/647	Eng.
21		Biddy	69	f.	Domestic		"
22		Joseph	40	m.	Farmer		Md.
23		Wm. J.	21	m.	Farmer		N.C.
24		Thomas B.	3	m.			O.
25	539/539	DENT, Wm.	28	m.	Carpenter	175/296	"
26		Emily J.	30	f.	Domestic		Md.
27		Albert E.	7	m.			O. S
28		Wilbert R.	5	m.			" S
29		Marthy E.	3	f.			"
30		Sarah M.	7/12	f.			"
31		Henry	21	m.	Carpenter	/100	"
32	540/540	MONTGOMERY, Alexandria	24	m.	Farmer	/245	"
33		Margaret A.	25	f.	Domestic		Pa.
34		Mellsirlle L. M.	9/12	m.			O.
35	541/541	WORKMAN, Hannah T.	36	f.	Domestic	3000/550	Pa.
36		Joseph M.	11	m.			O. S
37		Wm. B.	10	m.			" S
38		David	8	m.			" S
39		Jas. L.	7	m.			"

Page 81	9 July 1860					Sheet 175	
1		Robert A.	5	m.			O. S
2		Geo.	3	m.			"
3		Mary J.	1	f.			"
4	542/542	PRACY, Geo.	40	m.	Farmer	4500/573	"
5		Elisabeth S.	37	f.	Domestic		"
6		Jas. W.	16	m.	Farmer		" S
7		Mary Ann	14	f.			" S
8		Eunace	12	f.			" S
9		Sarah J.	9	f.			" S
10		Leander D.	7	m.			" S
11		Walter S.	2	m.			"
12	543/543	HENTHORN, David	57	m.	Farmer	800/285	Va.
13		Jane	54	f.	Domestic		Pa. I
14		Sarah	27	f.	Domestic		O.
15		Levina	20	f.	Domestic		"

16		HENTHORN, Elisa-						
		beth	18	f.	Domestic		O.	
17		Mary	18	f.	Domestic		"	
18		Clarinda	14	f.			"	
19		Julyan	12	f.			"	
20		Silvester	16	m.	Farm laborer		"	
21		WRIGHT, Robert	57	m.	Day laborer		Pa.	I
22	544/544	BRACY, Phebe	60	f.	Domestic	2000/455	"	
23		Jas.	24	m.	Farmer		O.	
24		Eveline	21	f.	Domestic		"	
25	545/545	McCLARY, Thomas	51	m.	Farmer	3200/650	Del.	
26		Agatha	24	f.	Domestic		O.	
27		Thomas D.	22	m.	Farmer		"	
28		Joanne	20	f.	Domestic		"	
29		Elisa	18	f.	Domestic		"	S
30		Caroline	15	f.			"	S
31		Sarah J.	10	f.			"	S
32		Washington	9	m.			"	S
33	546/546	HOPTON, Jacob	34	m.	Farmer	200/453	Pa.	
34		Julyanne	32	f.	Domestic		O.	
35		Wm.	13	m.			"	S
36		John	11	m.			"	S
37		Geo.	9	m.			"	S
38		Margaret P.	6	f.			"	S
39		Sarah J.	1	f.			"	

Page 82   9 July 1860   Sheet 175 verso

1	547/547	McAHON, Benjamin	37	m.	Farmer	2800/300	O.	
2		Sarah	32	f.	Domestic		"	
3		Phebe	14	f.			"	S
4		Elijah	13	m.			"	S
5		Elisabeth	7	f.			"	S
6		Mary E.	6	f.			"	S
7		Albert	1	m.			"	
8	548/548	BURRIS, Thomas	61	m.	Farmer	1600/225	Del.	
9		Persosha	57	f.	Domestic		Pa.	
10		John	25	m.	Day laborer		O.	
11	549/549	STEWART, Evan	24	m.	Farmer	/309	"	
12		Honor	24	f.	Domestic		"	
13		Sarah J.	6	f.			"	S
14		Alonzo	3	m.			"	
15		Geo. W.	2	m.			"	
16	550/550	SENDLETAKER, Jos-						
		eph	34	m.	Farmer	/160	Pa.	I
17		Ruth A.	33	f.	Domestic		O.	I
18		Aaron C.	11	m.			"	S
19		Phebe	9	f.			"	S
20		Sarah	7	f.			"	S
21		Rebecca	5	f.			"	
22		Malinda	3	f.			"	
23		Allen	1	m.			"	

24	551/551	STACKHOUSE, Jona-					
		thon	58	m.	Wheelmaker	192/138	O.
25		Rhoda	40	f.	Domestic		"
26		Caroline	5	f.			"
27		Benjamin	2	m.			"
28	552/552	BERRY, John	38	m.	Farmer	800/300	"
29		Joanna	31	f.	Domestic		Eng.
30		Marthy A.	12	f.			O. S
31		Daniel W.	9	m.			" S
32		John W.	7	m.			" S
33		Sarah E.	3	f.			"
34		Mary A.	1	f.			"
35	553/553	MEEKS, Geo. W.	23	m.	Farmer	2000/370	"
36		Mary J.	21	f.	Domestic		"
37		Emuretta	1	f.			"

Page 83   9 July 1860   Sheet 176

1	554/554	BARCUS, Cornelus	32	m.	Farmer	/185	O. I
2		Lida	32	f.	Domestic		"
3		Archabald	6	m.			" S
4		Isesene J.	2	f.			"
5		Mary E.	1	f.			"
6	555/555	RUBEL, Jacob	68	m.	Farmer	2500/488	Pa.
7		Lidda	62	f.	Domestic		Va.
8		PRIOR, Calvin	14	m.			O. S
9	556/556	TAYLOR, W.	44	m.	Farmer	800/493	Va.
10		Elisabeth	40	f.	Domestic		"
11		Alfred	16	m.	Farm laborer		O.
12		Mary A.	18	f.	Domestic		"
13		Western	14	m.			" S
14		Jonson	12	m.			" S
15		Joel	10	m.			" S
16		Jas.	8	m.			" S
17		Josiah	6	m.			"
18		Benson	4	m.			"
19		Thomas	2	m.			"
20	557/557	TAYLOR, Hampton	65	m.	Farmer	2000/220	Va.
21		Sharlotta	60	f.	Domestic		"
22	558/558	SPRAGE, Mary	56	f.	Domestic	2000/384	O.
23		Samuel	28	m.	Farmer-Carpenter		"
24		Edna J.	25	f.	Domestic		"
25		Hiram	23	m.	Farmer		"
26		John	21	m.	Farmer		"
27		Labon	20	m.	Farmer		"
28		Syras	18	m.	Farmer		"
29	559/559	MELOTT, Abraham	37	m.	Farmer	2500/322	"
30		Nancy	32	f.	Domestic		" I
31		Elisabeth	12	f.			" S
32		Mahala	8	f.			" S
33		Rebecca	5	f.			" S

34		MELOTT, Jemima	3	f.			0.	
35	560/560	WEEKLEY, Jacob	49	m.	Farmer	4500/617	"	
36		Mariah	47	f.	Domestic		Va.	
37		Mary	23	f.	Domestic		0.	
38		Aaron	20	m.	Farm laborer		"	S
39		John	14	m.			"	S

Page 84   10 July 1860   Sheet 176 verso

1		Susanna	12	f.			0.	S
2		Jane	9	f.			"	S
3	561/561	STEEL, John B.	39	m.	Farmer	300/400	"	
4		Anjaline	48	f.	Domestic		Va.	
5		Cela	17	f.	Domestic		0.	
6		Samuel	14	m.			"	S
7		Silas	7	m.			"	S
8	562/562	WEEKLY, Wm.	26	m.	Farmer	/100	"	
9		Sarah E.	18	f.	Domestic		"	
10	563/563	MOBLEY, Wm.	44	m.	Farmer	1500/400	"	
11		Ruth	44	f.	Domestic		"	
12		Archibald	16	m.	Farmer		"	S
13		Lucyanne	14	f.			"	S
14		John W.	9	m.			"	S
15		BARCUS, Susanna	67	f.	Domestic		N.J.	
16	564/564	SINDLEBECKER, John	56	m.	Farmer-Cooper	/50	Pa.	
17		Marthy A.	37	f.	Domestic		0.	I
18		Wm. J.	19	m.	Farm laborer		"	
19		Barbary E.	16	f.	Domestic		"	S
20		James	12	m.			"	S
21		Ira	8	m.			"	S
22		Bethany	3	m.			"	
23		Mary	1	f.			"	
24	565/565	McOY, Mitchel	76	m.	Farmer	2000/310	"	
25		Elisabeth	20	f.	Domestic		"	
26		Juliann	19	f.	Domestic		"	
27	566/566	ANDERSON, Wm. H.	38	m.	Farmer	/86	"	
28		Lusinda J.	31	f.	Domestic		"	
29		Hannah J.	10	f.			"	S
30		John R.	8	m.			"	S
31		Margaret	7	f.			"	S
32		Isaac	6	m.			"	
33		Samuel	4	m.			"	
34		Mary C.	4	f.			"	
35		Eve	2	f.			"	
36		James W.	4/12	m.			"	
37	567/567	EARLEYWINE, Abra-						
		ham	44	m.	Farmer	2000/411	Va.	
38		Elisabeth	39	f.	Domestic		"	

Page 85					10 July 1860		Sheet 177	
1	568/568	STEWART, Ervin	35	m.	Farmer	/135	Va.	
2		Sarah	33	f.	Domestic		"	
3		John W.	12	m.			"	S
4		Sarah F.	7	f.			"	S
5		Lewis	4	m.			"	
6		Abraham	2	m.			O.	
7	569/569	FORKER, John	30	m.	Farmer	400/550	Pa.	
8		Amanda	26	f.	Domestic		Va.	
9	570/570	PARMER, John W.	46	m.	Farmer	/120	O.	
10		Elisabeth	43	f.	Domestic		Pa.	
11		Michael	18	m.	Farmer		O.	
12		Henry	16	m.	Farmer		"	S
13		Hannah	8	f.			"	
14		Jacob	6	m.			"	
15		Hirum	4	m.			"	
16	571/571	STEEL, Saml.	65	m.	Farmer	2500/488	Md.	
17		Selia	57	f.	Domestic		"	
18		Alfred E.	27	m.	Farmer	/100	O.	
19		Richard	24	m.	Farmer		"	
20		Amos	19	m.	Farmer		"	S
21		Jesse	14	m.			"	S
22		Eleanor	23	f.	Domestic		"	
23		WATSON, Mary	74	f.	Domestic		Md.	
24		BOOKS, Saml.	12	m.			O.	S
25		Benjamin F.	10	m.			"	S
26	572/572	McINTYRE, David	32	m.	Farmer	4000/400	"	
27		Rebecca	34	f.	Domestic		"	
28		Jesse	19	m.	Farm laborer		"	
29		Gilbert	16	m.	Farm laborer		"	S
30		Sarah	5	f.			"	
31		Julian	4	f.			"	
32		Jas.	1	m.			"	
33	573/573	HENTHORN, Andrew J.	27	m.	Farmer	/100	"	
34		Jane	34	f.	Domestic		"	
35		Elisabeth	3	f.			"	
36	574/574	MEEKER, Benjamin	54	m.	Farmer	350/120	"	I
37		Catharine	47	f.	Domestic		"	I
38		William	23	m.	Farm laborer		"	
39		David	4	m.			"	

Page 86					10 July 1860		Sheet 177 verso	
1	575/575	SMITH, Philip	51	m.	Farmer	/80	Pa.	
2		Nancy	47	f.	Domestic		"	
3		Wm. T.	26	m.	Farmer		"	
4		Richard A.	17	m.	Farmer		"	S
5		Emanuel	14	m.			"	S
6		Rachel	11	f.			O.	S
7		Sarah J.	8	f.			"	S

8		SMITH, Geo. W.	6	m.			O.	
9	576/576	ARMSTRONG, Mason	50	m.	Farmer	1200/225	Va.	
10		Elisabeth	52	f.	Domestic		Md.	
11		Geo.	23	m.	Farm laborer		O.	
12		Jas. F.	22	m.	Farm laborer		"	
13	577/577	MELOTT, John	22	m.	Farmer	/75	"	
14		Lidastone	19	f.	Domestic		"	
15		Gilbert	2	m.			"	
16		Melvina	5/12	f.			"	
17	578/578	McELROY, Alfred	27	m.	Farmer	300/100	"	
18		Rhoda	26	f.	Domestic		"	
19		Wm.	7/12	m.			"	
20	579/579	VENNESS, Cornelus	43	m.	Farmer	2000/354	N.J.	
21		Permely A.	50	f.	Domestic		Pa.	
22		David	21	m.	Farmer		O.	S
23		Martin	19	m.	Farmer		"	S
24		Rachel	16	f.	Domestic		"	S
25		Jane	14	f.			"	S
26		Catharine	11	f.			"	S
27	580/580	VENESE, Peter	23	m.	Farmer-Gunsmith			
						/240	"	
28		Elisabeth	22	f.	Domestic		"	
29		Hannah	1	f.			"	
30		FRANKUS, Christian	35	m.	Master Gunsmith		Ger.	
31	581/---	MATHEWS, Andrew	27	m.	Farmer	/225	O.	
32		Mary E.	23	f.	Domestic		"	
33		ANDERSON, John	19	m.	Farm laborer		"	
34	582/582	MENATT, Abigal	64	f.	Domestic	800/100	Pa.	
35		ANDERSON, Mary	43	f.	Domestic		O.	
36	583/583	MELOTT, Michael	24	m.	Farmer	/264	"	M
37		Dilla	17	f.	Domestic		"	M
38	584/584	MELOTT, Joseph	34	m.	Farmer	/385	"	
39		Delila	24	f.	Domestic		"	

Page 87			11 July 1860				Sheet 178	
1		Luther	3	m.			O.	
2		Mary Anne	1	f.			"	
3		Willis	1/12	m.			"	
4	585/585	MELOTT, John	49	m.	Farmer	2500/500	Pa.	
5		Clarissa	37	f.	Domestic		O.	
6		John	10	m.			"	S
7		Huma	7	f.			"	S
8		Catharine	4	f.			"	
9		Abraham	2	m.			"	
10		Mary E.	14	f.			"	S
11		Wm.	12	m.			"	S

12		MELOTT, Benjamin	9	m.			O.	S
13		David	5	m.			Ind.	S
14	586/586	MELOTT, David	28	m.	Farmer	700/150	O.	
15		Mary E.	22	f.	Domestic		"	
16		Amanda	2	f.			"	
17		Dilla	4/12	f.			"	
18	587/587	MELOTT, Theadore	47	m.	Farmer	1400/330	Pa.	
19		Elisabeth	48	f.	Domestic		O.	I
20		Elisabeth	17	f.	Domestic		"	
21		Matilda	14	f.	Domestic		"	
22		Gemima	10	f.			"	
23		Elias	5	m.			"	
24	588/588	PITTMAN, Obediah	21	m.	Farmer		"	M
25		Sarah	21	f.	Domestic		"	M
26	589/589	MELOTT, Benjamin						
		T.	31	m.	Farmer	1500/368	"	
27		Margaret A.	28	f.	Domestic		"	
28		Eveline	5	f.			"	
29		Harvy	4	m.			"	
30		Nathan	2	m.			"	
31		Isaac	5/12	m.			"	
32	590/590	_____, Greenberry	51	m.	Farmer	3000/700	Md.	
33		Rebecca	53	f.	Domestic		O.	
34		Green H.	21	m.	Farmer		"	
35		Rhoda	24	f.	Domestic		"	
36		Gemima	18	f.	Domestic		"	S
37		John N.	15	m.	Farmer		"	S
38		Isaac	13	m.			"	S

1	591/591	MOBLEY, Nathan	26	m.	Farmer	3000/250	O.	
2		Jane	20	f.	Domestic		"	
3		Zenas	7/12	m.			"	
4	592/592	ABERSOLD, John	64	m.	Farmer	900/557	Sw.	
5		Marthy	58	f.	Domestic		"	
6		Christopher	37	m.	Teamster		"	
7		Phelix	27	m.	Carpenter	/50	O.	
8		Saml.	23	m.	Wagon-maker	/50	"	
9		Wm.	20	m.	Farmer		"	
10		David	14	m.			"	S
11		Nancy	39	f.	Domestic		Sw.	
12		Catharine	18	f.	Domestic		O.	
13		Mary A.	16	f.	Domestic		"	
14	593/593	MOBLEY, Nathan	49	m.	Farmer	1200/350	Md.	
15		Susanna	50	f.	Domestic		O.	
16		John	22	m.	Farmer	/80	"	
17		Gemima	16	f.	Domestic		"	
18		Nancy	13	f.			"	
19		Lusinda	10	f.			"	

20	594/594	MILLER, Elsabeth	55	f.	Domestic	900/300	Sw.
21		John	32	m.	Farmer		"
22		Frederick	15	m.	Farmer		O. S
23		PHENDER, Magdalena	30	f.	Domestic		Sw.
24		Mary E.	10	f.			O. S
25	595/595	THOMAS, Wm.	46	m.	Blacksmith	500/200	Wales
26	596/596	ATKINSON, Elisa-beth	49	f.	Domestic	/50	O.
27		Hariet	19	f.	Domestic		"
28	597/597	HEDILY, David S.	24	m.	Teacher	400/60	"
29		Susanna	25	f.	Domestic		"
30		Rebecca J.	3	f.			"
31	598/598	WATSON, Washington	26	m.	Farmer	/60	"
32		Mary J.	22	f.	Domestic		"
33		Manervy	4	f.			"
34		Clark	4/12	m.			"
35	599/599	DAVIS, Joseph	39	m.	Cabinet-maker 400/160		Del.
36		Sarah	38	f.	Domestic	"	I
37		Wm. H.	18	m.	Day laborer		O. S
38		Josephene	10	f.			" S
39		Mary V.	9	f.			" S

Page 89   11 July 1860   **Sheet 179**

1		Joseph	4	m.			O.
2		Stephen	1	m.			"
3	600/600	BONER, John	57	m.	Farmer	1800/368	Pa.
4		Mary	56	f.	Domestic		N.Y.
5		Stephen	20	m.	Teacher		O. S
6		Mary	16	f.	Domestic		" S
7		Andrew W.	13	m.			" S
8		Caroline	11	f.			" S
9		Malinda	6	f.			" S
10		HANNELS, Mary E.	9	f.			" S
11	601/601	BONER, John M.	25	m.	Farmer	/57	"
12		Joanna	29	f.	Domestic		"
13		Hilah A.	5	f.			"
14		Crawford	3	m.			"
15		Michael A.	1	m.			"
16		Benjamin F.	3/12	m.			"
17	602/602	MARSHAL, John N.	38	m.	Merchant	2400/3300	Pa.
18		Isabelle	28	f.	Domestic		O.
19		Jas. A.	8	m.			" S
20		Wm. G.	2	m.			"
21		Frances	5/12	f.			"
22	603/---	VANLAW, Reason	32	m.	Merchant	2400/3300	"
23		Elisa J.	26	f.	Domestic		"
24		E. Alice J.	4	f.			"

25		VANLAW, Sarah J.	1	f.			O.	
26		ALEXANDRIA, Jane	53	f.	Domestic	1000/	"	
27		John	32	m.	Merchant	2400/2300	"	
28		Joshua J.	22	m.	Clerk	1600/	"	
29	604/604	MATHEWS, Jesse	41	m.	Farmer	1200/300	"	
30		Sarah	42	f.	Domestic		Pa.	
31		Theadore	17	m.	Farmer		O.	S
32		Rebecca A.	15	f.	Domestic		"	S
33		Jas.	12	m.			"	S
34		Elisabeth	11	f.			"	S
35		David	8	m.			"	S
36		Gemima	7	f.			"	S
37		Nancy	6	f.			"	S
38		Catharine	1	f.			"	
39		Francis M.	15	m.			"	S

Page 90   11 July 1860   Sheet 179 verso

1	605/605	MIER, Gottlob	31	m.	Blacksmith	550/75	Ger.	
2		Catharine	23	f.	Domestic		"	
3		Geo.	9	m.			"	S
4		John	2	m.			O.	
5		Levi	3/12	m.			"	
6	606/606	FRIEDLY, Gottlob	40	m.	Shoemaker	600/50	Sw.	
7		Rose Anne	40	f.	Domestic		"	
8		Barbary	39	f.	Domestic		"	
9	607/607	HERD, Mary	69	f.	Domestic	650/75	Pa.	
10		Mary	36	f.	Domestic		O.	
11	608/608	GRITHENS, P. D.	28	m.	Physician	/800	N.J.	
12		Elisabeth	21	f.	Domestic		O.	
13		William	1/12	m.			"	
14	609/609	CLARK, Nancy	26	f.	Domestic	500/75	"	
15		Elle J.	6	f.			"	S
16	610/610	HOLTSCLAW, Wm. A.	39	m.	Miller	/100	Va.	
17		Elisabeth	30	f.	Domestic		Del.	I
18		Marthy E.	11	f.			O.	S
19		Malinda J.	8	f.			"	S
20		Laura B.	1	f.			"	
21		Martha	68	f.	Retired		Md.	
22	611/611	BOUGHNER, Michel	35	m.	Cooper-Farmer			
						600/190	O.	
23		Jane	36	f.	Domestic		"	
24		James M.	12	m.			"	S
25		John	11	m.			"	S
26		Elias	9	m.			"	S
27		Margaret	6	m.			"	S
28		Mary	4	f.			"	
29		Julyanne	2	f.			"	
30		Thomas J.	1/12	m.			"	
31	612/612	HURD, John J.	40	m.	Shoemaker	300/150	"	

32		HURD, Sarah	43	f.	Domestic		O.	
33		Owen	6	m.			"	S
34		Elmore	2	m.			"	

35	613/613	HEDILY, Eli	49	m.	Merchant	2500/6000	"	
36		Rebecca	41	f.	Domestic		"	
37		Susianna	17	f.	Domestic		"	S
38		Rachel Rebecca	9	f.			"	S
39		Margaret A.	7	f.			"	

Page 91		11 July 1860					Sheet 180	
1		Emma A.	6	f.			O.	S
2		TREMBLEY, Margaret						
		A.	13	f.			"	S

3	614/614	DILLON, Jas. M.	20	m.	Tavern-keeper	/150	"	
4		Mary L.	18	f.	Domestic		"	
5		Charles O.	4/12	m.			"	

6	615/615	HOLTSCLAW, Charles	21	m.	Tailor	150/100	"	
7		Jane	24	f.	Domestic		Ire.	
8		Martha A.	4	f.			O.	
9		Herod	2	m.			"	
10		Eliza	7/12	f.			"	

11	616/616	ROSS, Nancy	51	f.	Domestic	100/75	"	
12		Wm. A.	21	m.	Day laborer		"	
13		Vincent V.	20	m.	Day laborer		"	
14		Sebastian C.	18	m.		/30	"	S
15		Amanda	11	f.			"	S
16		George W.	15	m.			"	S

17	617/617	ATKISON, Stephen	66	m.	Farmer	7000/225	Pa.	
18		Elisabeth	51	f.	Domestic		O.	
19		Rebecca A.	33	f.	Domestic		"	
20		Louisa	24	f.	Domestic		"	
21		Stephen	20	m.	Day laborer		"	S
22		John	18	m.	Day laborer		"	S
23		Abel	16	m.	Day laborer		"	S
24		Julia	9	f.			"	S

25	618/618	ATKISON, Saml.	23	m.	Farmer	/185	"	
26		Emily	24	f.	Domestic		"	
27		Mary Elisabeth	3	f.			"	
28		Sarah L.	1	f.			"	

29	619/619	McNICHOLS, Tilmon	45	m.	Day laborer	/50	Md.	I
30		Nancy	35	f.	Domestic		O.	I
31		Sarah S.	19	f.	Domestic		"	
32		Marion	17	m.	Day laborer		"	S
33		Indiana	14	f.			"	S
34		Columbus	11	m.			"	S
35		Misouri	10	f.			"	S
36		Mary E.	7	f.			"	S

| 37 | 620/620 | PANCOST, Samuel | 22 | m. | Clerk | /100 | " | M |
| 38 | | Anne | 23 | f. | Domestic | | " | M |

#	Dwelling	Name	Age	Sex	Occupation	Value	Birthplace	
1	621/621	SWETGART, Christian	31	m.	Farmer	/200	Sw.	
2		Mary Anne	34	f.	Domestic		"	
3		John	1	m.			O.	
4	622/622	SCHWING, Geo.	40	m.	Merchant	4000/430	Ger.	
5		Sophia	37	f.	Domestic		"	
6		Theadore	11	m.			Pa.	S
7		Margaret	9	f.			O.	S
8		Charles	5	m.			"	
9		HANES, John	82	m.	Farmer	/1200	N.J.	
10	623/623	PANCOST, Stephen	45	m.	Merchant	4000/10,000	O.	
11		Mary	48	f.	Domestic		"	
12		GORDEN, Geo. C.	26	m.	Miller	1500/200	Va.	
13	624/624	LISLE, Jas.	34	m.	Miller-Farmer	4000/5000	O.	
14		Amelia	28	f.	Domestic		"	
15		Zenas M.	6	m.			"	S
16		Mary E.	4	f.			"	
17		Jas. E.	1	m.			"	
18		HENCEN, Jas.	9	m.			"	S
19	625/625	BROCK, Daniel	35	m.	Tanner	500/300	"	
20		Mariah	31	f.	Domestic		"	
21		Lisle	8	m.			"	S
22		Allen	5	m.			"	S
23		STEPHENS, Mary	11	f.			"	S
24	626/626	GRODHANS, Geo. C.	48	m.	Distiller	1950/1675	Ger.	
25		Amelia	41	f.	Domestic		Md.	
26		Bennet A.	20	f.	Domestic		O.	S
27		Margaret W.	18	f.	Domestic		"	S
28		Charles	16	m.	Farm laborer		"	S
29		Peter A.	14	m.			"	S
30		Geo. H.	12	m.			"	S
31		Valentine	9	m.			"	S
32		Amanda J.	6	f.			"	S
33		Wm. W.	1	m.			"	
34	627/627	ADY, Joshua	37	m.	Farmer-Miner	300/318	"	I
35		Catharine	27	f.	Domestic		"	I
36		Lavosier C.	13	m.			"	S
37		Nathaniel S.	12	m.			"	S
38		Rachael J.	9	f.			"	S
39		Mary L.	7	f.			"	S

#	Dwelling	Name	Age	Sex	Occupation	Value	Birthplace	
1		Mitchel B.	5	m.			O.	
2		Louisa	1	m.			"	
3	628/628	CRAIG, Wm.	25	m.	Farmer	/100	"	I
4		Eliza J.	24	f.	Domestic		"	I
5		Andrew J.	4	m.			"	S

6		CRAIG, John A.	3	m.		O.	
7		Sarah A. V.	2	f.		"	
8		Nathan	6/12	m.		"	
9		REED, Catharine	70	f.	Retired	Md.	I

10	629/629	MOBLEY, Andrew	25	m.	Farmer	/240	O.
11		Sarah E.	25	f.	Domestic		"
12		Helen V.	7	f.			" S

13	630/630	CATHEL, P.	48	m.	Farmer	600/200	Del.
14		Matilda	48	f.	Domestic		"
15		Sarah E.	21	f.	Domestic		Va. S
16		Mary J.	18	f.	Domestic		O. S
17		Jonathon W.	12	m.			" S
18		Elisabeth A.	9	f.			"
19		Geo. P.	5	m.			"

20	631/631	McCONEL, Samuel	43	m.	Farmer	/300	"
21		Mary	41	f.	Domestic		"
22		Rachel A.	18	f.	Domestic		" S
23		Isaac	14	m.			" S
24		Joshua	6	m.			"

25	632/632	KINSEY, F. A.	29	m.	Farmer	1200/400	"
26		Hannah	21	f.	Domestic		"
27		Josephene	5	f.			"
28		Asenith	3	f.			"
29		Jacob	5/12	m.			"

30	633/633	GOURLEY, Saml.	40	m.	Farmer	150/200	"
31		Mary	38	f.	Domestic		"
32		Jas.	11	m.			" S
33		Elly	8	f.			" S
34		Joseph W.	5	m.			"
35		Mary	69	f.	Retired		Ire.

36	634/634	HUTCHISON, Robert	38	m.	Farmer	900/150	O.
37		Pheobe J.	28	f.	Domestic		"
38		Marthy J.	8	f.			"
39		Saml.	7	m.			"

Page 94   12 July 1860   Sheet 181 verso

1		Emily V.	5	f.			O.
2		John L.	1/12	m.			"

3	635/635	MELOTT, Archibald	37	m.	Farmer	/80	"
4		Lydia	25	f.	Domestic		"
5		Joshua	5	m.			"
6		Hester	3	f.			"
7		Wm.	1	m.			"

8	636/636	CROFT, Melvin	27	m.	Farmer	/75	Sw.
9		Sarah E.	21	f.	Domestic		O.
10		John	1	m.			"

11	637/637	BRECK, Edward	27	m.	Farmer	500/100	Sw. M
12		Anne	21	f.	Domestic		O. M

13	638/638	BAKER, Valentine	38	m.	Farmer	500/47	Ger.
14		Mary	26	f.	Domestic		Sw.
15		July anne	16	f.	Domestic		Va.
16		Geo. H.	14	m.			" S
17		John W.	11	m.			" S
18		Samuel	6	m.			" S
19		Louisa	4	f.			O.
20		David	3	m.			"
21		Barbary	2	f.			"
22		Jacob	1/12	m.			"
23	639/639	SCOTT, Elisabeth	57	f.	Domestic	/150	"
24		Wm.	19	m.	Farmer		"
25		BURGG, Lovica	24	f.	Domestic		"
26		Wm. W.	1	m.			"
27		WORKMAN, Mary A.	28	f.	Domestic		"
28		Phebe	7	f.			" S
29	640/640	POOL, Alfred	21	m.	Day laborer	/40	" M
30		Emeline	16	f.	Domestic		" M
31		John A.	1/12	m.			"
32	641/641	HOOVER, Richard T.	35	m.	Farmer	450/297	"
33		Elisabeth	35	f.	Domestic		"
34		Avinda	13	f.			" S
35		Amanda	12	f.			" S
36		Andaline	10	f.			" S
37		David	9	m.			" S
38		Nancy J.	7	f.			" S
39		Ithamer	6	m.			" S

Page 95   12 July 1860   Sheet 182

1		Louisa	4	f.			O.
2		Caroline	2	f.			"
3		Saml.	2/12	m.			"
4	642/642	BERKEY, C.	26	m.	Farmer	/50	Ger.
5		Charlotty	21	f.	Domestic		O.
6		John W.	1/12	m.			"
7	643/643	RALSTON, Wm.	62	m.	Farmer	500/100	Ire. I
8		Perthenia	64	f.	Domestic		Pa. I
9		HARTSOOK, Mary	14	f.			Eng.
10	644/644	WARD, Moses	29	m.	Farmer	300/125	O.
11		Rachel A.	26	f.	Domestic		"
12		Jas. M.	8	m.			" S
13		Phebe J.	7	f.			" S
14		Wm. A.	4	m.			" S
15		Mary J.	2	f.			"
16	645/645	McCOY, Mary E.	45	f.	Domestic	1000/125	"
17		John	13	m.			" S
18	646/646	FREDEL, Geo.	44	m.	Farmer	600/210	Ger.
19		Catharine	42	f.	Domestic		"

20		FREDEL, Sophia	16	f.	Domestic		Ger.	
21		John	14	m.			O.	S
22		Geo.	12	m.			Va.	S
23		Elisabeth	10	f.			"	S
24		Margaret	8	f.			"	S
25		Henry	5	m.			O.	
26		Theadore	3	m.			"	
27		Wm. H.	1	m.			"	
28	647/647	EARLYWINE, Jacob						
		F.	49	m.	Farmer	1600/328	Va.	
29		Ruth	50	f.	Domestic		"	
30		Mary J.	22	f.	Domestic		O.	
31		Ruthanne	16	f.			"	
32	648/648	SAFELL, Griffith	30	m.	Day laborer		Md.	
33		Mary	24	f.	Domestic	600/100	O.	I
34		Gewis G.	5	m.			"	
35		July anne	3	f.			"	
36		Lyda A.	1	f.			"	
37		Lyda	72	f.	Retired		Md.	I
38	649/649	HARTLINE, Samuel	29	m.	Farmer	600/150	O.	
39		Elisabeth	25	f.	Domestic		"	

Page 96			12 July 1860			Sheet 182 verso		
1		Mary J.	4	f.			O.	
2		Christian	3	m.			"	
3		Ruth A.	1	f.			"	
4		Catharine A.	3/12	f.			"	
5	650/650	HARTLINE, Conrod	31	m.	Farmer	1200/536	"	
6		Eleanor	28	f.	Domestic		"	
7		Emadelia	8	f.			"	S
8		Mary A.	5	f.			"	S
9		Christian	4	m.			"	
10		Edman	1	m.			"	
11	651/651	HARTLINE, Chris-						
		tian	55	m.	Farmer	3575/1905	N.Y.	
12		Mary	67	f.	Domestic		Pa.	
13		LIPONCOTT, John	49	m.	Farm laborer		Pa.	
14		McCANE, Sarah	46	f.	Domestic		O.	
15	652/652	McCOY, Thomas	52	m.	Farmer		"	
16		Ruth	47	f.	Domestic		"	
17		Paulina	20	f.	Domestic		"	
18		Elisabeth	14	f.			"	S
19		James	7	m.			"	
20		Julia A.	1	f.			"	
21		ATKISON, Marion	20	m.	Farm laborer		"	
22		Clarinda	19	f.	Domestic		"	

(Adams Township Concluded)

(Jas. Okey, Asst. Marshall)

* * *

1	653/653	KINSEY, Frederick	44	m.	Farmer	2000/230	Sw.	
2		Catharine	45	f.	Domestic		"	
3		Frederick	16	m.	Farm laborer		"	
4		Mary A.	14	f.			"	S
5		Jacob	12	m.			"	S
6		Anne	10	f.			"	S
7		Wm.	4	m.			O.	
8		John	3	m.			"	
9	654/654	ENSINGER, Adam	36	m.	Farmer	1800/300	Ger.	
10		Mary	29	f.	Domestic		"	
11		Mary	5	f.			O.	
12		Rose A.	3	f.			"	
13		Catharine	2	f.			"	
14		Louisa	3/12	f.			"	
15	655/655	WARD, Jas.	51	m.	Farmer	1000/200	"	
16		Phebe	48	f.	Domestic		"	
17		Mary A.	19	f.	Domestic		"	S
18		Jas. W.	18	m.	Farm laborer		"	S
19		Phebe A.	16	f.	Domestic		"	S
20		Louisa	12	f.			"	S
21	656/656	WARD, Isaac	26	m.	Farmer	150/75	"	
22		Susiana	24	f.	Domestic		Sw.	
23		Wm.	1	m.			O.	
24	657/657	EARLYWINE, Jacob	30	m.	Farmer	500/	Va.	
25		Anne	31	f.	Domestic		Pa.	
26		Elisabeth	8	f.			O.	S
27		John	4	m.			"	
28		James	2	m.			"	
29		Mary J.	7/12	f.			"	
30	658/658	AMBLUHE, Jacob	50	m.	Farmer	500/	Sw.	
31		Elisabeth	51	f.	Domestic		"	
32	659/659	WARD, Joseph	56	m.	Farmer	1000/350	O.	
33		Ruth	56	f.	Domestic		"	
34	660/660	KIGER, Henry	56	m.	Farmer	700/225	Ger.	I
35		Elisabeth	42	f.	Domestic	400/	"	I
36		SWING, Catharine	18	f.	Domestic		"	
37		Sophia	12	f.			Va.	
38		Margaret	8	f.			O.	

1	661/661	WARD, Seth	34	m.	Farmer	/160	O.	
2		Catharine	34	f.	Domestic		"	
3		Caroline	13	f.			"	S
4		Josephus	11	m.			"	S
5		Ruth E.	9	f.			"	S
6		Mary J.	6	f.			"	S
7		Bently	3	m.			"	
8		Albert	8/12	m.			"	

```
9  662/662 RUBLE, David      40  m.   Farmer      1200/280   O.
10           Malissa         28  f.   Domestic               "
11          BONER, Rose       9  f.                          "

12 663/663 WHEELER, Thomas   45  m.   Farmer      2500/325   Md.
13           Elisabeth       52  f.   Domestic               O.
14           Lewis G.        18  m.   Farmer                 "
15           Elisabeth       15  f.   Domestic               "
16          SHEPHERD, Nancy  73  f.   Domestic               Va.
17          WHEELER, Philena 19  f.   Servant                O.

18 664/664 MOUGHOY, Jacob    55  m.   Farmer      5200/500   Sw.
19           Magdelena       50  f.   Domestic               "
20           John            23  m.   Farmer                 O.
21           Mary A.         21  f.   Domestic               "
22           Wm.             18  m.   Farmer                 "
23           Frederick       17  m.   Farmer                 "     S
24           Henry           15  m.                          "     S
25           Alexandria      12  m.                          "     S
26           Saml.            8  m.                          "

27 665/665 HENTHORN, Andrew  37  m.   Farmer      7000/650   "
28           Mariah          50  f.   Domestic               "
29           Matilda         21  f.   Domestic               "
30           Rolly           20  m.   Farm laborer           "
31           Jane            16  f.   Domestic               "     S
32           Franklin        14  m.                          "     S
33           Nancy           13  f.                          "     S
34           Sesington       11  m.                          "     S
35           Saml. S.         9  m.                          "     S

36 666/666 SPEARS, Joseph    25  m.   Cooper         /40     "
37           Nancy           23  f.   Domestic               "     I
38           Ephraim          2  m.                          "
39           Jas.             1  m.                          "
```

```
1  667/667 HENTHORN, Wm.     62  m.   Merchant       /200    Va.
2            Jane            55  f.   Domestic               Eng.
3            Nathaniel       14  m.                          O.    S
4            Jane            12  f.                          "     S

5  668/668 ALEXANDRIA, Andrew 50 m.  Miller-Farmer
                                                 3640/580    "
6            Marthy          43  f.   Domestic               Pa.
7            Sarah J.        21  f.   Domestic               O.
8            Robert C.       18  m.   Farmer                 "     S
9            Silas G.        16  m.   Farmer                 "     S
10           John            14  m.                          "     S
11           James           19  m.                          "     S
12           Margaret         8  f.                          "     S
13           Saml.            6  m.                          "     S
14           Andrew           1  m.                          "
15           Marthy L.        1  f.                          "

16 669/669 HAYWARD, Anthony  28  m.   Farmer         /250    "
17           Mary Anne       26  f.   Domestic               "
```

18		HAYWARD, John A.	3	m.			O.
19		Ceville	1	f.			"
20	670/670	LANP, Henry	45	m.	Farmer	/140	" I
21		Mary	35	f.	Domestic		" I
22		Ruth A.	13	f.			" S
23		Francis L.	12	m.			" S
24		Isaiah	10	m.			" S
25		Elisabeth	5	f.			"
26		Marthy J.	3	f.			"
27		Joshua	2	m.			"
28	671/671	RUTTER, John H.	52	m.	Farmer	6000/305	"
29		Nancy	45	f.	Domestic		Pa.
30		Wm.	18	m.	Farmer		O. S
31		Harvy	11	m.			" S
32		Mary E.	9	f.			"
33		Samanthy	7	f.			"
34		FREELAND, Levina	20	f.	Servant		Pa.
35	672/672	McGONAGOLL, Joseph	67	m.	Farmer		Ire.
36		Isabelle	68	f.	Domestic	2500/506	"
37		Charles	41	m.	Farmer		"
38		Isabell	30	f.	Domestic		"
39		RIKARD, Christian	25	m.	Farm laborer		Can.

1	673/673	CESIDER, John	24	m.	Farmer	/150	O.
2		Elisabeth E.	18	f.	Domestic		"
3		Lewis F.	1	m.			"
4	674/674	CESIDER, Rudolph	50	m.	Farmer	10,000/2000	Sw.
5		Mary	45	f.	Domestic		"
6		Rudolph	21	m.	Farmer		O.
7		Christian	18	m.	Farmer		"
8		Mary E.	15	f.	Domestic		" S
9		Louisa	12	f.			" S
10		Elisabeth	10	f.			" S
11		Jacob	6	m.			" S
12	675/675	HENTHORN, Elisa-beth	64	f.	Domestic		Va. I
13		Phebe	33	f.	Domestic	1000/225	O.
14		ULLOM, John	22	m.	Farm laborer		"
15	676/676	BOLDEN, Eli	43	m.	Farmer	200/500	"
16		Amee	38	f.	Domestic		"
17		Layfayette	18	m.	Farmer		"
18		Malanthon	16	m.	Farmer		" S
19		Sanford	14	m.			" S
20		Fayette	12	m.			" S
21		Nathaniel	9	m.			" S
22		Albilda	5	f.			" S
23		Alvira	1	f.			"
24	677/677	GILMORE, Levi	47	m.	Farmer	400/350	"
25		Jane	41	f.	Domestic		Pa.

26		GILMORE, Albert	21	m.	Farmer	/50	O.	S
27		Charles	18	m.	Farmer		"	S
28		Augustus	16	m.			"	S
29		Florence	12	f.			"	S
30		John	2	m.			"	
31		Isabell	1/12	f.			"	

| 32 | 678/678 | GILMORE, Ary | 66 | m. | Domestic | | Va. | |

33	679/679	COCHRAN, Wm.	64	m.	Farmer	20,000/2600	"	
34		Frances	58	f.	Domestic		"	
35		Jeremiah W.	36	m.	Clerk on Steamboat		O.	
36		Elisabeth A.	34	f.	Domestic		"	
37		Lewis	29	m.	Engineer		"	
38		Wm. M.	27	m.	Farmer		"	
39		Thos. J.	24	m.	Teacher		"	

Page 101   14 July 1860   Sheet 185

| 1 | | Mary L. | 16 | f. | | | O. | |

2	680/680	NICHOLS, Edward	43	m.	Farmer	/110	Md.	
3		Anne	31	f.	Domestic		O.	I
4		Sarah E.	11	f.			"	
5		Hannah	9	f.			"	
6		John	5	m.			"	
7		Nancy J.	4	f.			"	
8		Cassia	2	f.			"	

9	681/681	SMITH, Mariah	56	f.	Domestic	2000/100	Md.	
10		Mary	29	f.	Domestic		O.	
11		Hannah	17	f.	Domestic		"	

12	682/682	FARMER, Reuben	22	m.	Farmer	/150	"	
13		Rachel	21	f.	Domestic		"	
14		Mariah E.	9/12	f.			"	

15	683/683	CANE, Wm.	37	m.	Farmer	50/300	"	
16		Sarah	35	f.	Domestic		"	
17		Charles	13	m.			"	S
18		Eliza J.	10	f.			"	S
19		John D.	9	m.			"	S
20		Jas. W.	6	m.			"	S
21		Sarah A.	5	f.			"	
22		Amanda	3	f.			"	
23		Franklin	10/12	m.			"	

24	684/684	USELTON, Daniel	29	m.	Farmer	/50	Va.	
25		Christena	23	f.	Domestic		O.	
26		Benjamin	5	m.			"	
27		Geo. W.	3	m.			"	
28		Wm. H.	1	m.			"	

29	685/685	DERING, Frederick	28	m.	Farmer	/150	Ger.	
30		Margaret	31	f.	Domestic		"	
31		David	1/12	m.			O.	
32		RODES, C.	55	f.	Domestic		Ger.	
33		John	26	m.	Day laborer		"	I

34		RODES, Elisabeth	20	f.	Domestic		Pa.	
35	686/686	CALPFLESH, Adam	52	m.	Farmer	1200/250	Ger.	
36		Fredreche	41	f.	Domestic		"	
37		Catherine	13	f.			O.	S
38		Frederick	10	m.			"	S
39		Mary	7	f.			"	S

Page 102   14 July 1860   Sheet 185 verso

1		Conrod	25	m.	Steamboating		O.	
2		John	22	m.	Steamboating		"	
3		Adam	18	m.	Steamboating		"	
4	687/687	WISTERMAN, Samuel	44	m.	Farmer	3000/704	Sw.	
5		Margaret	42	f.	Domestic		Ger.	
6		Samuel	20	m.	Farmer		O.	
7		Mary	17	f.	Domestic		"	
8		John	15	m.			"	S
9		Lina	13	f.			"	S
10		Elisabeth	10	f.			"	S
11		Louisa	5	f.			"	S
12		Sophiah	3	f.			"	
13		Emma	10/12	f.			"	
14	688/688	WESTERMAN, Christian	47	m.	Farmer	3000/600	Sw.	
15		Elisabeth	42	f.	Domestic		"	
16		Elisabeth	19	f.	Domestic		O.	
17		Mary	17	f.	Domestic		"	S
18		Saml.	16	m.	Farm laborer		"	S
19		Caroline	14	f.	Domestic		"	S
20		Frederick	13	m.			"	S
21		Daniel	11	m.			"	S
22		Anna	10	f.			"	S
23		Jacob	8	m.			"	S
24		Christian	7	m.			"	S
25		Saloma	5	f.			"	
26		Louisa	3	f.			"	
27		Wm.	1	m.			"	
28	689/689	FOS, John	60	m.	Farmer	1000/475	Ger.	
29		Anne M.	59	f.	Domestic		"	
30		Sophiah	19	f.	Domestic			
31		Elisabeth	5	f.			Pa.	
32	690/690	FERRY, Anne	58	f.	Domestic	4000/450	Eng.	
33		John	33	m.	Farmer		O.	I
34		Geo.	31	m.	Farmer		"	I
35		Alice	26	f.	Domestic		"	I
36		Jane	21	f.	Domestic		"	
37		Abigal	11	f.			"	S
38		Samuel	5	m.			"	

Page 103   14 & 16 July 1860   Sheet 186

1	691/691	FERRY, Wm.	33	m.	Farmer	/100	O.	

2		FERRY, Hester	32	f.	Domestic		O.	
3		Robinson	8/12	m.			"	
4	692/692	FRANKHOUSER, War-						
		ren	50	m.	Farmer	2500/600	Sw.	I
5		Barbary	41	f.	Domestic		"	I
6		Wm.	21	m.	Farmer		O.	S
7		Alexander	19	m.	Farmer		"	S
8		Louisa	17	f.	Domestic		"	S
9		Lewis	15	m.	Farmer		"	S
10		David	14	m.			"	S
11		Daniel	12	m.			"	S
12		Henry	10	m.			"	S
13		Charlotta	6	f.			"	S
14		Saml.	4	m.			"	
15	693/693	MELOTT, James D.	29	m.	Farmer	3150/350	"	
16		Louisa	23	f.	Domestic		"	
17		Bertha	4	f.			"	
18		Emma	2	f.			"	
19		Jacob	23	m.	Day laborer	/50	"	
20	694/694	CAIN, Thomas	21	m.	Farmer	/50	"	
21		Catharine	22	f.			Ger.	
22		NELSON, J. M.	8/12	m.			O.	
23	695/695	CAIN, Mary	49	f.	Domestic	2000/520	N.Y.	
24		Richard L.	27	m.	Teacher	/100	O.	
25		Amanda J.	19	f.	Domestic		"	
26		John R.	15	m.	Farmer		"	S
27		Alfred L.	12	m.			"	S
28		Nancy	10	f.			"	S
29		Horatio N.	6	m.			"	S
30	696/696	BANDI, Nicholas	56	m.	Farmer	500/250	Sw.	
31		Mary	56	f.	Domestic		"	
32		Nicholas	16	m.	Farmer		"	
33	697/697	VONDI, John	33	m.	Farmer	400/100	"	
34		Mary	30	f.	Domestic		"	I
35		John	2	m.			O.	
36	698/698	EBERT, Lewis	25	m.	Farmer	2000/470	Fr.	
37		Caroline	23	f.	Domestic		O.	
38		BAKER, Geo.	13	m.			Va.	
39		ALBUS, Coonrod	64	m.	Farmer		Ger.	

Page 104			16 July 1860			Sheet 186 verso		
1	699/699	EBERT, Lewis	60	m.	Farmer	3000/550	Fr.	
2		Jacob	22	m.	Farmer		"	M
3		Elisabeth	18	f.	Domestic		O.	M
4	700/700	TRIVER, Lewis	50	m.	Farmer	2000/350	Ger.	
5		Doratha	45	f.	Domestic		"	
6		Louisa	12	f.			O.	S
7		Lewis	10	m.			"	S

8		TRIVER, Caroline	8	f.			O. S
9		Frederick	4	m.			"
10		Henry	2	m.			"
11	701/701	BURKEY, Jacob	26	m.	Farmer	/75	"
12		Nancy	21	f.	Domestic		Va.
13		John A.	1	m.			O.
14		Cemantha	1/12	f.			"
15	702/702	MARTIN, John G.	50	m.	Farmer	/125	"
16		Mary	43	f.	Domestic		"
17		Mary	19	f.	Domestic		"
18		Catharine	17	f.	Domestic		" S
19		John	17	m.	Farmer		" S
20		Lusinda	15	f.	Domestic		" S
21		Hariet	12	f.			" S
22		Mahela	10	f.			" S
23		Sarah J.	7	f.			"
24	703/703	FRANCE, Conrod	45	m.	Farmer	600/250	Ger.
25		Margaret	41	f.	Domestic		" I
26		Conrod	18	m.	Boating		"
27		Adam	12	m.			O.
28		Charles	10	m.			"
29		Margaret	7	f.			"
30		John	5	m.			"
31		Lewis	3	m.			"
32		Frederick	9/12	m.			"
33	704/704	BITNER, Henry	42	m.	Farmer	1200/200	Ger. I
34		Elisabeth	39	f.	Domestic		Sw.
35		Elisabeth A.	17	f.	Domestic		O. S
36		Catharine	15	f.	Domestic		" S
37		Augusty	13	f.			" S
38		Mary	10	f.			" S
39		Barbary	8	f.			" S

Page 105			16 July 1860				Sheet 187
1		Julia A.	6	f.			O.
2		John H.	3	m.			"
3	705/705	CORTZ, Dortha J.	72	f.	Domestic	/50	Ger.
4	706/706	SMITH, Levi	56	m.	Farmer	600/525	"
5		Rose A.	56	f.	Domestic		"
6	707/707	LONG, Abraham	38	m.	Farmer	1500/300	O.
7		Hester	37	f.	Domestic		"
8		Ebenezar	17	m.	Farmer		" S
9		Mary J.	14	f.	Domestic		" S
10		Jesse	1	m.			"
11	708/708	GILMORE, Pary	41	m.	Farmer	800/350	"
12		Nancy	32	f.	Domestic		"
13		Robert	10	m.			" S
14		Martha	6	f.			" S
15		Mary	3	f.			"

16	709/709	USELTON, Wm.	70	m.	Carpenter	100/100	N.J.
17		Elisabeth	64	f.	Domestic		"
18		Andrew J.	24	m.	Day laborer		Va.
19		MILLER, Theadore	13	m.			O.
20		Elisabeth	1	f.			"
21	710/710	THOMAS, David	39	m.	Farmer	300/550	"
22		Sydina	33	f.	Domestic	1500/	Pa.
23		Lydia	17	f.	Domestic		O.
24		Geo. W.	15	m.			" S
25		Francis M.	14	m.			"
26		Margaret A.	12	f.			" S
27		David	10	m.			" S
28		Isibell	4	f.			"
29		STERGON, Wm.	16	m.	Day laborer		" S
30		Mariah J.	14	f.			" S
31		Reuben	11	m.			" S
32		Robert	9	m.			" S
33		James	7	m.			" S
34		Charles	2/12	m.			"
35	711/711	ALBUS, Conrod	53	m.	Farmer	1500/325	Ger.
36		Elisabeth	44	f.	Domestic		" I
37		Sophia	18	f.	Domestic		"
38		John	16	m.	Farm laborer		" S
39		Frederick	12	m.			"

Page 106   16 July 1860   Sheet 187 verso

1		Charles	3	m.			O.
2		SESIKER, Louisa	3	f.			"
3	712/712	EVERHART, Nicholas	53	m.	Farmer	500/250	Ger.
4		Elisabeth	52	f.	Domestic		" I
5		VEHELLER, Philip	22	m.	Day laborer		" I
6		Augusta	19	m.	App. Carpenter		"
7		Mary	17	f.	Domestic		O.
8	713/713	PHALL, John H.	42	m.	Farmer	700/200	Ger.
9		USELTON, Mary	20	f.	Domestic		Va. I
10		SANDERS, John	13	m.			O.
11		Christopher	10	m.			" S
12		Casper	6	m.			" S
13		Rachel	4	f.			"
14		Jas.	3	m.			"
15		Anne	1/12	f.			"
16	714/714	KLAGE, Christopher	45	m.	Farmer	2000/500	Ger. I
17		Elisabeth	38	f.	Domestic		" I
18		Elisabeth	16	f.	Domestic		"
19		Christian	12	m.			Pa. S
20		Julia A.	8	f.			O. S
21		Charles	6	m.			"
22		Carolina	4	f.			"
23		Emeline	1	f.			"
24	715/715	HEATH, Thomas	55	m.	Farmer	/150	Pa.
25		Agnas	49	f.	Domestic		O.

```
26          HEATH, Samuel       27   m.    Boating                 O.
27          Ambrose             19   m.    Farmer                  "
28          John                17   m.    Farmer                  "    S
29          Daniel C.           12   m.                            "    S
30          Anjoline             8   f.                            "    S
31          Jefferson            5   m.                            "

32 716/716  MARIS, John         27   m.    Boating        700/50   "
33          Hannah              29   f.    Domestic                "
34          Agnas                5   f.                            "
35          Charity              4   f.                            "
36          Jas. F.           3/12   m.                            "

37 717/717  HEATH, Catharine    75   f.    Domestic       600/75   Ga.
38          Catharine           42   f.    Domestic                Pa.
```

Page 107   16 July 1860   Sheet 188

```
1  718/718  KNERIM, Charles     40   m.    Farmer       2000/425   Ger.
2           Margaret            31   f.    Domestic                "
3           Caroline             7   f.                            O.  S
4           Geo.                 6   m.                            "   S
5           Charles              4   m.                            "
6           Julia A.             2   f.                            "

7  719/719  FOBLE, Peter        65   m.    Day laborer             Ger.
8           Catharine E.        63   f.    Domestic                "

9  720/720  LONG, Christopher   65   m.    Farmer         800/310  "
10          Catharine           64   f.    Domestic                "

11 721/721  THOMAS, Aquilla     36   m.    Day laborer      /50    O.
12          Phebe               34   f.    Domestic                "   I

13 722/722  MARTIN, Grifeth     50   m.    Day laborer      /50    Pa.
14          Mary                35   f.    Domestic                O.
15          Mary                19   f.    Domestic                "   S
16          Catharine           17   f.    Domestic                "   S
17          John                17   m.    Farm laborer            "   S
18          Lusinda             14   f.                            "   S
19          Hariet              12   f.                            "   S
20          Mahala              10   f.                            "   S
21          Sarah J.             6   f.                            "   S

22 723/723  LANDIS, Saml.       46   m.    Farmer       5220/284   Pa.
23          Mary                50   f.    Domestic                O.
24          Elisabeth           19   f.    Domestic                "
25          Margaret            16   f.    Domestic                "   S
26          John                16   m.    Farmer                  "

27 724/724  COX, Hannah         44   f.    Domestic       275/40   "
28          Syrintha            20   f.    Domestic                "
29          Napoleon B.         12   m.                            "

30 725/725  CANE, Frances M.    27   m.    Farmer       1000/585   "
31          Mary J.             24   f.    Domestic                "
32          Elisabeth M.         3   f.                            "
33          Mary M.              3   f.                            "
```

34		CANE, Earnest O.	1	m.			O.
35	726/726	CANE, Richard	76	m.	Farmer	2500/100	Va.
36		Hannah	73	f.	Domestic		"
37	727/727	LANDIS, Reuben	24	m.	Farmer	/275	O. M
38		Jane	20	f.	Domestic		" M

Page 108   17 July 1860   Sheet 188 verso

1	728/728	AMBLER, Saml.	36	m.	Farmer	900/100	O.	
2		Rachel	29	f.	Domestic		"	
3		Alfred W.	8	m.			"	S
4		Louisa	5	f.			"	
5		Levina	5	f.			"	
6		Marinda	4/12	f.			"	
7	729/729	HENTHORN, Ruth	55	f.	Domestic	/50	"	
8		Emaline	25	f.	Domestic		"	
9		Ephram	20	m.	Day laborer		"	
10		Malinda	16	f.	Domestic		"	S
11		Maicy	13	f.			"	S
12		Cornelia E.	8	f.			"	S
13	730/730	BROOKOVER, John	70	m.	Physician	/150	Pa.	
14		Sarah	67	f.	Domestic		"	
15		MILLER, William	16	m.	Day laborer		O.	
16		JORDEN, Mary	13	f.			"	
17		DACON, Thos.	12	m.			Va.	
18	731/731	JACKSON, John W.	49	m.	Farmer	/315	Md.	
19		Sarah M.	39	f.	Domestic		O.	
20		Mary J.	20	f.	Domestic		Va.	S
21		Sarah E.	15	f.			"	S
22		Corneilus	9	m.			O.	S
23		Alice	6	f.			Va.	
24		John D.	3	m.			O.	
25		Jacob R.	8/12	m.			"	
26	732/732	MARIS, Charles H.	26	m.	Farmer	/240	"	
27		Ruth E.	19	f.	Domestic		Va.	
28		Marthy	1	f.			"	
29		NORAS, Norman	18	m.	Day laborer		O.	
30	733/733	BOOTH, John H.	37	m.	Boat Captain	6000/2500	Va.	
31		Mary	34	f.	Domestic		"	
32		Eva	10	f.			"	S
33		Eugene	8	m.			"	S
34		Earnast	6	m.			"	S
35		Catharine M.	5	f.			"	
36	734/734	BOOTH, Bethire	72	m.	Retired		Conn.	
37	735/735	BISHOP, Asten C.	40	m.	Steamboating	400/50	O.	
38		Sophia A.	36	f.	Domestic		Pa.	
39		Sarah	16	f.	Domestic		O.	

Page 109		16 July 1860				Sheet 189	
1		BISHOP, Daniel	14	m.			O. S
2		Wm.	11	m.			" S
3		Nancy A.	8	f.			" S
4		Pary	5	m.			" S
5		Lucretia	3	f.			"
6	736/736	MESSERLY, John	40	m.	Tailor	1000/50	Ger.
7		Catharine	40	f.	Domestic		Mass. I
8		Mary E.	16	f.	Domestic		N.Y. S
9		Charles	11	m.			" S
10		Anne	10	f.			O. S
11		John	8	m.			" S
12		August E.	6	m.			" S
13		Alice	3	f.			"
14	737/737	UELPMANN, Peter	33	m.	Bakery	400/500	Ger.
15		Mary	37	f.	Domestic		"
16		Mary	5	f.			Pa.
17		Geo. A.	3	m.			Va.
18	738/738	STOVER, Nicholas	36	m.	Shoemaker	/50	Ger.
19		Mary	36	f.	Domestic		" I
20		Mary A.	4	f.			Pa.
21		Elisabeth	2	f.			O.
22	739/739	McINTON, Godfrey	52	m.	Currier		Ger.
23		Mary	45	f.	Domestic		" I
24		Jacob	23	m.	Currier		"
25		Marthy	21	f.	Domestic		"
26		Elisa	19	f.	Domestic		"
27		Mary	15	f.			"
28		Louisa	13	f.			"
29		Amelia	10	f.			"
30		Edward	5	m.			"
31	740/740	GLUSON, Frederick	37	m.	Tailor	400/200	Ger.
32		Mary	30	f.	Domestic		"
33		Elisabeth	18	f.	Domestic		" S
34		Wilhemer	9	f.			" S
35		Edman	5	m.			"
36		Hulda	3	f.			O.
37		Wm.	5/12	m.			"
38	741/741	KEIHN, Herman	49	m.	Shoemaker	/50	Ger.
39		Elisabeth	39	f.	Domestic		"

Page 110		17 July 1860				Sheet 189 verso	
1	742/742	ARCHER, Dickson	35	m.	Farmer	600/150	O.
2		Eliza	28	f.	Domestic		Ger. I
3		Mary J.	8	f.			O. S
4		Alice	3	f.			"
5	743/743	MALORY, John	35	m.	Merchant	1500/1410	"
6		Susianna	35	f.	Domestic		Conn.

7		MALORY, Mary M.	15	f.	Domestic		O. S
8		Benjamin H.	11	m.			" S
9	744/744	McCARTY, Matilda	57	f.	Domestic	450/80	Md.
10		DARBY, John	8	f.			O. S
11	745/745	WENSBURGH, Levi	37	m.	Cooper	80/50	Va.
12		Nancy	37	f.	Domestic		O.
13		Calvin	11	m.			" S
14		Samuel	9	m.			" S
15		Melvina	6	f.			"
16		Mary J.	5	f.			Va.
17		Thornton W.	1	m.			O.
18	746/746	THOMAS, Reuben	46	m.	Shoemaker	900/300	N.Y.
19		Margaret	37	f.	Domestic		O.
20		Matilda J.	18	f.	Domestic		Va.
21		Wilson S.	16	m.	Farm laborer		O.
22		Geo. G.	14	m.			"
23		Mary	13	f.			" S
24		Henry	10	m.			" S
25		Martha	8	f.			" S
26		Wm.	5	m.			" S
27		Eveline	2	f.			"
28	747/747	HORNE, Geo. P.	44	m.	Merchant	/1200	Del.
29		Jane B.	44	f.	Domestic		Ire.
30		Joseph	14	m.			O. S
31		Mary A.	12	f.			" S
32		Matilda J.	9	f.			" S
33		STEED, Martha	18	f.	Servant		" S
34	748/748	BOOTH, Wm. S.	46	m.	Tavern-keeper	5000/700	Va.
35		Emily	46	f.	Domestic		"
36		Mary B.	25	f.	Domestic		O.
37		Adelia	23	f.	Domestic		"
38		Charles	19	m.	Farm laborer		" S
39		Emma J.	13	f.			" S

1		John M.	10	m.			O. S
2		JACKSON, Eliza-beth	18	f.	Servant		"
3	749/749	SANDERS, John W.	21	m.	Merchant	/4000	Pa.
4		MERSELLY, Jas.	29	m.	Merchant	/4000	N.Y.
5	750/750	SMITH, Jas. R.	41	m.	Merchant	1200/4000	O.
6		Alice	9	f.			" S
7		Eva	6	f.			" S
8		Ebith	4	f.			"
9		MAY, Mary	18	f.			"
10		WILSON, Nancy	63	f.	Domestic		Va.
11	751/751	BALDWIN, Levi	50	m.	Merchant	3400/1200	O.

12		BALDWIN, Elisabeth	28	f.	Domestic		Va.	
13		Wm. H.	12	m.			O.	S
14		Charles	9	m.			"	S
15		Alven A.	4	m.			O.	
16	752/752	DILLON, Peter	46	m.	Tavern-keeper	/350	Pa.	
17		Julia A.	22	f.	Domestic		O.	
18		Hamilton	21	m.	Hack driver		"	
19		Maizy	16	f.	Domestic		"	
20		Mark	14	m.			"	S
21		Margaret	12	f.			"	S
22		Mary L.	3	f.			"	
23		Jacob	1	m.			"	
24		James	2/12	m.			"	
25		WHITE, John	38	m.	Farm laborer		Pa.	
26		MEAD, Uriah	46	m.	Drayman		Md.	
27		Margaret	57	f.	Domestic		"	
28	754/754	COX, Edward B.	45	m.	Tailor	450/100	Va.	
29		Rebecca	35	f.	Domestic		"	
30		Albina	20	f.	Domestic		O.	
31		Isabell	15	f.	Domestic		"	S
32		Volney	9	m.			"	S
33		Wm. H.	10/12	m.			"	
34		STARKEY, Rebecca	9	f.			Ky.	S
35	755/755	EDWARDS, Charles	29	m.	E.P.M. Minister	/300	O.	
36		Marthy	23	f.	Domestic		"	
37		ROSEMAN, Eleanor	55	f.	Domestic		Va.	
38	756/756	ATKISON, Mary	59	f.	Domestic	1000/50	O.	
39		Susianna	28	f.	Domestic		"	

Page 112			17 July 1860				Sheet 190 verso	
1		Oliver	24	m.	Tinner	/50	O.	
2	757/757	BROWN, Wm. J.	58	m.	Carpenter	900/100	"	
3		Sarah A.	38	f.	Domestic		"	
4		John	26	m.	Steamboating		"	
5		Joshua	19	m.	Cigar maker		"	S
6		Virginia	7	f.			"	
7		Lizzia	4	f.			"	
8	758/758	HERD, Joshua	45	m.	Shoemaker	300/100	"	
9		Jane C.	44	f.	Domestic		Eng.	
10		Maria	24	f.	Domestic		O.	
11		William C.	23	m.	Farm laborer		"	
12		Samuel B.	21	m.	Boating		"	
13		Elisabeth	19	f.	Domestic		"	
14		Mary	17	f.	Domestic		"	S
15		Roswell	11	m.			"	S
16		John F.	6	m.			"	
17	759/759	HARTLINE, Henry S.	36	m.	Cooper	500/175	"	
18		Mary A.	31	f.	Domestic		"	
19		Saml. M.	8	m.			"	S

```
20          HARTLINE, Anna J.    4   f.                              O.
21          Dorsy L.             1   m.                              "

22 760/760  RODGERS, Joseph     38   m.   Blacksmith  450/100   Pa.
23          Charlotta           34   f.   Domestic              O.
24          Lucia               13   f.                         "    S
25          Wm.                  9   m.                         Pa.  S
26          Annabell             7   f.                         O.   S
27          Jas. A.              4   m.                         "
28          Hariet               1   f.                         "

29 761/761  HERD, Wm.           41   m.   Wagon-maker 500/100   "
30          Susiana             32   f.   Domestic              Va.
31          Wesley B.           11   m.                         O.   S

32 762/762  THOMPSON, Emery     26   m.   Steamboating   /150   "
33          Emily               24   f.                         "

34 763/763  SANFORD, Saml.      32   m.   Carpenter  200/100    "
35          Mary                32   f.   Domestic              "
36          Daniel               5   m.                         "
37          John                 2   m.                         "
38          HERD, Elisabeth     67   f.   Domestic              Pa.

39 764/764  LINEGAR, John       36   m.   Watchmaker     /100   Ger.
```

<u>Page 113</u>   <u>17 July 1860</u>   <u>Sheet 191</u>

```
1           Mary                33   f.   Domestic              O.
2           John K.              7   m.                         "    S
3           Jas. F.              4   m.                         "
4           Geo. W.              1   m.                         "

5  765/765  TROY, Martin        48   m.   Collector      /200   Pa.
6           Anna                45   f.   Domestic              "
7           Charles             20   m.   Boatman               "
8           Anjaline            18   f.   Domestic              O.
9           Nancy J.            15   f.   Domestic              "
10          Windfield S.        10   m.                         "    S
11          Geo. W.              8   m.                         "    S

12 766/766  BERTON, Henry       28   m.   Boatman        /250   Va.  I
13          Rose A.             24   f.   Domestic              Pa.  I
14          Erastus              4   m.                         O.

15 767/767  NEWHOUSE, Geo.      28   m.   Wagon-maker    /400   Va.
16          Victora             21   f.   Domestic              O.
17          Margaret             3   f.                         "
18          Adelia               1   f.                         "

19 768/768  RAY, Jas.           41   m.   Farmer         /50    Conn.
20          Abbie               41   f.   Domestic              O.
21          Josephene           18   f.                         "
22          Charles             15   m.                         "
23          Hariet              12   f.                         "    S
24          Wm.               6/12   m.                         "
25          PRESCOTT, Augustus  23   m.   Tailor                "
26          Samuel              18   m.   Farmer                "
```

```
27 769/769 MORELL, Jacob T.    37   m.    Lawyer        950/200  Me.
28         Dorintha            37   f.    Domestic               Va.
29         Elisabeth J.        17   f.    Domestic               O. S
30         Leander B.          12   m.                           "  S
31         John E.             11   m.                           "  S
32         Sarah E.             9   f.                           "  S
33         Nancy A.             7   f.                           "  S
34         Jas. C.              3   m.                           "
```

```
35 770/770 MALLORY, Jasper     76   m.    Commission   3000/100 Conn.
36         Hariet              69   f.    Domestic               "
```

```
37 771/771 MAY, Wm. H.         26   m.    Liquor dealer  /350   O.
38         Clarinda E.         24   f.    Domestic               "
39         Wm. F.               5   m.                           "
```

Page 114   17 July 1860   Sheet 191 verso

```
1          Hosea B.            10   m.                           O.
```

```
2  772/772 KYGER, F. C.        26   m.    Physician      /150   Ill.
3          Jennett C.          23   f.    Domestic               N.Y.
4          Birdsey C.        1/12   m.                           O.
```

```
5  773/773 MERSELEY, Abraham   38   m.    Farm laborer   /50    Sw.
6          Catharine S.        38   f.    Domestic               N.Y.
7          Juliaetta           16   f.    Domestic               "
8          Wm. W.              11   m.                           "  S
9          Jas. B.              6   m.                           O. S
```

```
10 774/774 FANDSEN, John       62   m.    Farmer         /60    N.Y.
11         Hannah              58   f.    Domestic               "
```

```
12 775/775 LIPENCOTT, Wm.      27   m.    Grocer         /700   O.
13         Nancy               26   f.    Domestic               "
14         Mandy J.             5   f.                           "
15         Anna A.              3   f.                           "
16         Marthy L.            1   f.                           "
```

```
17 776/776 WESTEN, Thomas      68   m.    Farm laborer   /100   Mass.
18         Martha              67   f.    Domestic               R.I.
```

```
19 777/777 LITTON, Noah        35   m.    Blacksmith    450/50  O.
20         Mary A.             31   f.    Domestic               "
21         Samanthy E.         11   f.                           "  S
22         Marthy               9   f.                           "  S
23         John W.              6   m.                           "  S
24         Wm. F.               3   m.                           "
25         Charles E.        3/12   m.                           "
26         EVERSON, Samanthy   22   f.    Seamstress             "
```

```
27 778/778 McMANN, Charles     24   m.    Merchant       /1000  Pa.
28         Harriet A.          17   f.    Domestic               "
29         Jas.                22   m.    Merchant               "
```

```
30 779/779 O'CONNER, John D.   38   m.    Physician    3000/3000 O.
31         Ruth C.             38   f.    Domestic               O.
```

32		O'CONNER, Elen J.	12	f.			O.	S
33		Juliaetta O.	14	f.			"	S
34		Marthy E.	10	f.			"	S
35		Rebecca J.	4	f.			"	
36		NEFF, Amanda J.	18	f.	Domestic		"	S
37	780/780	THOMAS, Gardner	50	m.	Shoemaker	1000/100	N.Y.	
38		Matilda	49	f.	Domestic		Va.	
39		SHINN, Ann	16	f.			O.	

1	781/781	RILEY, Motmer	23	m.	Boating	/100	O.	M
2		Delora	21	f.	Domestic		"	M
3	782/782	FULTON, Saml.	25	m.	Blacksmith	350/50	"	M
4		Margaret	21	f.	Domestic		"	M
5		Charles	18	m.	App. Blacksmith		"	
6	783/783	CUNINGHAM, G. W.	39	m.	Miller	/50	Md.	
7		Marthy	36	f.	Domestic		"	
8		Mary E.	13	f.			"	S
9		Anne E.	11	f.			"	S
10		G. W.	7	m.			"	S
11		BARTON, Joshua	88	m.	Retired		"	
12	784/784	HANLON, Peter O.	57	m.	Blacksmith	3000/50	Ire.	
13		Anne	35	f.	Domestic		O.	
14		Wm.	3	m.			"	
15	785/785	ATKISON, Mathew	29	m.	Day laborer	/50	"	
16		Amanda	20	f.	Domestic		"	
17		Orlena V.	4	f.			"	
18		Thos.	2	m.			"	
19	786/786	DENNEY, John	32	m.	Pedlar	/300	Pa.	
20		Catharine	25	f.	Domestic		O.	
21		Margaret	2	f.			"	
22		BERTON, Wm. B.	38	m.	Pedling	/270	"	
23	787/787	LACY, Jas. R.	55	m.	Bricklayer	/100	Del.	
24		Garwood P.	16	m.	Boating		O.	
25		Wilber O.	14	m.			"	
26		Lorra A.	12	f.			"	
27	788/788	CONILY, Geo.	23	m.	Day laborer	150/10	Va.	I
28		Nancy	21	f.	Domestic		Pa.	I
29		Wm.	2	m.			Va.	
30		Elisabeth	6/12	f.			O.	
31	789/789	LITTON, Wm.	36	m.	Engineer	2000/300	"	
32		Anne	35	f.	Domestic		Pa.	
33		Alice J.	12	f.			O.	S
34		Irene E.	10	f.			"	S
35		Wm. F.	8	m.			"	S
36		Saml. W.	6	m.			"	
37		Elisabeth	69	f.	Retired		Pa.	

Page 116		18 July 1860				Sheet 192 verso
1	790/790 MARSHAL, Jas.	39	m.	Tanner	/100	Pa.
2	Sarah F.	37	f.	Domestic		Va.
3	791/791 DUFFIELD, P. B.	43	m.	Merchant	1000/1000	O.
4	Lusinda	31	f.	Domestic		N.Y.
5	Nanie Rose	6	f.			Pa.
6	Emmy G.	4	f.			O.
7	Jesse B.	2	m.			"
8	Henry W.	7/12	m.			"
9	DAVIDSON, Nancy A.	60	f.	Domestic		Pa.
10	792/792 BERLT, Charles	60	m.	Wagonmaker	1100/300	Sax.
11	Mary	40	f.	Domestic		Pa.
12	Margaret	9	f.			O. S
13	Francis	7	m.			" S
14	Mary	6	f.			" S
15	Wm.	2	m.			"
16	793/793 GESSER, John	55	m.	Farmer	/150	Sw.
17	Mary	63	f.	Domestic		"
18	Mary	33	f.	Domestic		"
19	794/794 COLER, Jacob	35	m.	Farmer	/100	Sw.
20	Anne	31	f.	Domestic		"
21	Ann	1	f.			O.
22	GOSSER, Levi	20	m.	Farmer		Sw.
23	Christian	34	m.	Basket-maker		"
24	795/795 SIVERT, Polickman	62	m.	Shoemaker	300/110	Ger.
25	Mary	61	f.	Domestic		" I
26	796/796 SMITH, Elieal	36	m.	Engineer	600/100	Pa.
27	Susianna	41	f.	Domestic		O.
28	Mary E.	11	f.			" S
29	Sophia A.	9	f.			" S
30	John N.	6	m.			" S
31	Layfette	4	m.			"
32	Martha J.	2/12	f.			"
33	797/797 BOOTH, Charles H.	44	m.	Steamboat Captain 490/500		Va.
34	Hannah	44	f.	Domestic		"
35	Crawford	17	m.			O. S
36	Asael	15	m.			" S
37	Elisabeth	12	f.			" S
38	Wm. B.	11	m.			" S
39	Frank	6	m.			" S

Page 117		18 July 1860			Sheet 193
1	798/798 DURKEE, Matilda	36	f.	4800/500	O.
2	Sanford W.	11	m.		" S
3	Anne J.	6	f.		" S
4	799/799 THOMAS, Daniel	24	m.	Steamboat Pilot /700	"
5	Isabell	21	f.	Domestic	Va.

6		THOMAS, Frank D.	3	m.			Va.
7	800/800	ANDERSON, Harvy	33	m.	Cooper	1100/300	O.
8		Sarah	33	f.	Domestic		Va.
9		Elisabeth	8	f.			" S
10		Sarah L.	2	f.			O.
11	801/801	ARCHER, Dickerson	32	m.	Day laborer	500/100	" I
12		Elisa	27	f.	Domestic		Ger. I
13		Mary P.	8	f.			O.
14		Alice G.	2	f.			"
15	802/802	STEENROD, Jeremiah	34	m.	Boatman	700/100	"
16		Eleanora	34	f.	Domestic		Va.
17		Charles V.	12	m.			O. S
18		Louis F.	1	m.			"
19	803/803	HAUDENCHILD, John W.	27	m.	Shoemaker	1000/300	Sw.
20		Mary A.	26	f.	Domestic		N.Y.
21		Mary E.	5	f.			O.
22		Jas. S.	2	m.			"
23	804/804	FERRY, William F.	27	m.	Boat carpenter	500/400	"
24		Julia	26	f.	Domestic		"
25		Rosealfa J.	6	f.			"
26		Evva	4	f.			"
27	805/805	BISHOP, Camiless	25	m.	Saddler	800/500	"
28		Martha	26	f.	Domestic		Pa.
29		Hannah J.	1	f.			O.
30		THORNBER, Jefferson	33	m.	Saddler		Pa.
31	806/806	CHASE, Robt.	53	m.	Farmer	2500/150	"
32		Agnas	46	f.	Domestic	500/	"
33		Eleanor	19	f.			" S
34		Charles F.	17	m.	Farmer		" S
35		WALTER, Jacob	15	m.			Sw.
36	807/807	WETZEL, Geo.	30	m.	Cooper	300/50	Va.
37		Malinda	29	f.	Domestic		C.
38		Priscilla J.	8	f.			" S

Page 118		18 July 1860			Sheet 193 verso

1	808/808	HUBER, Andrew	23	m.	Merchant	1200/2500	Va.
2		Catharine	19	f.	Domestic		O.
3		Malinda	2	f.			"
4		Charles	7/12	m.			"
5		Philip	19	m.	Clerk		" S
6	809/809	HOWELL, Jacob W.	33	m.	Barkeeper & Steward	/150	O.
7		Mary	28	f.	Domestic		"
8		Edwin	7	m.			" S

9		HOWELL, Juliaetta	5	f.		O. S
10		Stephen C.	2	m.		"
11	810/810	POLOCK, Mortimer	37	m.	Miller-Merchant	
					7100/500	Va.
12		Amanda S.	37	f.	Domestic	O.
13		Isabelle	1	f.		"
14		BLACK, Mary	26	f.	Teacher	N.Y.
15		POLOCK, Julius	25	m.	Merchant 2500/	Va.
16		WILLIAMS, Marthy	22	f.	Servant	O.
17		SMITH, Lucia	58	f.	Domestic	Va.
18	811/811	FERRIER, James	42	m.	Merchant /200	O.
19		Flora L.	33	f.	Domestic	"
20		Saml.	18	m.	Shoemaker /250	" S
21		John W.	16	m.	Merchant /250	" S
22	812/812	LOBENSTINE, Char-				
		les	35	m.	Tanner 3000/7000	Ger.
23		Frederiche	34	f.	Domestic	"
24		Mary	6	f.		O. S
25		Clary	4	f.		"
26		Emma	1/12	f.		"
27	813/813	BRIDEGROOM, Geo.	35	m.	Tanner 700/100	Ger.
28		Catharine	32	f.	Domestic	"
29		Sopha	5	f.		O.
30		Edward	4	m.		"
31		Anne	1	f.		"
32		Elisa	1/12	f.		"
33		BRUNER, John	34	m.	Tanner	Ger.
34	814/814	HETLER, August	31	m.	Tanner-Currier /50	"
35		Dorathy	30	f.	Domestic	"
36		Catharine	4	f.		Pa.
37		Geo.	2	m.		"

Page 119   18 July 1860   Sheet 194

1	815/815	McBRIDE, Jess	26	m.	Engineer on Boat	
					600/150	O.
2		Margaret	62	f.	Domestic /125	Pa.
3		Mary	21	f.	Domestic	O.
4		Saml.	15	m.	Farm laborer	"
5	816/816	BRIDEGROOM, Chris-				
		tian	34	m.	Wagon-maker 700/100	Ger.
6		Jacolina J.	31	f.	Domestic	"
7		Caroline	6	f.		Va. S
8		Frederick W.	5	m.		"
9		John	3	m.		O.
10		Charles	1	m.		"
11		Emelia L.	1/12	f.		"
12	817/817	SCHUTTY, Henry	28	m.	Blacksmith 1100/	Ger.
13		Elisabeth	23	f.	Domestic	"
14		Elisabeth	1	f.		O.
15		THIER, Berthold	21	m.	Painter	Ger.

16	818/818	BRAGUE, Wesley	33	m.	Shoemaker	500/100	O.
17		Mary	29	f.	Domestic		"
18		Irea	5	m.			"
19		Alpha A.	3	m.			"
20		Lethe	1	f.			"
21		BANI, Jacob	18	m.	Shoemaker		Sw.
22	819/819	SPERLMAN, James	51	m.	Tailor	550/200	Md.
23		Amelia	58	f.	Domestic		Pa.
24		GAND, John M.	43	m.	Merchant	/500	O.
25	820/820	WHEELER, Solomon	62	m.	Merchant	1500/500	N.Y.
26		Eliza D.	30	f.	Domestic		"
27	821/821	BROWN, John G.	49	m.	Plasterer		Md.
28		Elisabeth	50	f.	Domestic	300/100	O.
29		Ephram	18	m.	Farmer		" S
30		Hariet	15	f.	Domestic		"
31		Wm.	13	m.			" S
32		Margaret	11	f.			" S
33		Joshua	10	m.			" S
34	822/822	BONER, Andrew	50	m.	Cooper	1500/300	Pa.
35		Mazy	44	f.	Domestic		Va.
36		Ebenezer	21	m.	Farmer		O. S
37		Marion	20	m.	Farmer		" S
38		Adaline	18	f.	Domestic		" S
39		Oregon	15	m.			" S

1		Anne A.	13	f.			O.	S
2		John M.	11	m.			"	S
3		Rebecca	8	f.			"	S
4		Mary E.	6	f.			"	S
5		Wm. H.	3	m.			"	
6		Sarah A.	7/12	f.			"	
7	823/823	FOGGIN, Rebecca J.	34	f.	Domestic	1200/100	Va.	I
8		Jas. M.	13	m.			O.	S
9		Florence V.	11	f.			"	
10		Mayzy O.	8	f.			"	S
11		Georga A.	4	f.			"	
12	824/824	ANSHULTZ, William	33	m.	Merchant	3750/4000	Pa.	
13		Gouldy	28	f.	Domestic		O.	
14		Eugene	3	m.			"	
15		KIGER, Hannah	23	f.	Servant		"	
16	825/825	HOWARD, David	32	m.	Ferryman	400/100	Va.	
17		Mary A.	27	f.	Domestic		"	
18		Sarah A.	10	f.			O.	S
19		Jas.	6	m.			"	S
20		Alinda	5	f.			"	S
21		Wm.	2	m.			"	
22		Amanda E.	1/12	f.			"	
23	826/826	THOMAS, Reuben	25	m.	Engineer	/300	"	

24		THOMAS, Elisa	22	f.	Domestic	O.
25		Charles G.	1	m.		"
26		WOODINGTON, Cate	12	f.		" S
27	827/827	BREST, John	42	m.	Stone mason	/75	Ger.
28		Louisa	23	f.	Domestic		"
29		Jzadorah	6	f.			Va.
30		Wm.	3	m.			O.
31		Louis	10/12	m.			"
32	828/828	LANTZ, Gotlip	31	m.	Carpenter	500/100	Sw.
33		Susianna	23	f.	Domestic		O.
34		Sarah J.	5	f.			"
35		Mary B.	3	f.			"
36		James W.	1	m.			"
37	829/829	MARSH, John	26	m.	Boatman	600/100	O. I
38		Hannah	29	f.	Domestic		" I
39		Agnas A.	5	f.			"

Page 121   18 July 1860   Sheet 195

1		Charity	3	f.		O.
2		Franklin	4/12	m.		"
3	830/830	CASE, Wm.	29	m.	Teamster	/400	"
4		Elsinda	22	f.	Domestic		Va.
5		Mary B.	3	f.			O.
6		John M.	1	m.			"
9	831/831	ROMERS, John	41	m.	Butcher		Ger.
10		Mary	32	f.	Domestic		"
11		Peter	8	m.			O.
12		Mary	5	f.			"
13		Julia A.	3	f.			"
14		Rose A.	1	f.			"
15	832/832	MATTHEWS, Thomas	28	m.	Steamboating	/150	"
16		Susianna	30	f.	Domestic		N.Y.
17		Sarah A.	5	f.			Ky.
18		Emmy R.	10/12	f.			"
19	833/833	BERTON, John	30	m.	Wagoner		Va.
20		Catharine	27	f.	Domestic		O.
21		Frank	6	m.			"
22		Adaline	1	f.			"
23		Emily	3	f.			"
24	834/834	WALTON, Geo.	47	m.	Cooper	/50	Pa.
25		Frances	49	f.	Domestic		N.Y.
26		Robert	25	m.	Boating		O.
27		Josiah	23	m.	Farmer		"
28		Elisabeth	21	f	Domestic		"
29		Francis	19	f.	Domestic		"
30		Cornelius	17	m.	Day laborer		"
31		Nancy	16	f.	Domestic		" S
32		Adaline	12	f.			" S

33		WALTON, Emma	3	f.			O.	
34		Geo.	5	m.			"	S
35	835/835	LITTLETON, Isaac	30	m.	Day laborer	/50	"	
36		Christena	29	f.	Domestic		"	
37		Sarah A.	5	f.			"	S

Page 122   18 July 1860   Sheet 195 verso

1		John C.	3	m.			O.	
2		Thos.	9/12	m.			"	
3	836/836	LITTLETON, John C.	33	m.	Coal digger	/65	"	I
4		Nancy	22	f.	Domestic		"	I
5		Mary E.	7	f.			"	
6		Jennet H.	2	f.			"	
7	837/837	CRAMER, Jacob	39	m.	Steamboating		Pa.	
						2000/200		
8		Mary Anne	37	f.	Domestic		Va.	
9		Lamphier	15	m.			O.	S
10		James A.	12	m.			"	S
11		Richard H.	9	m.			"	S
12		Charlie	6	m.			"	
13		Franklin	3	m.			"	
14		MILLER, Anne	55	f.	Domestic	/200	Va.	
15	838/838	HAYWARD, Ezeiel	23	m.	Day laborer	/50	O.	
16		Elisabeth	25	f.			"	I
17		Franky	2	m.			"	
18		Calvin	1/12	m.			"	
19	839/839	GOSSER, Mary	43	f.	Domestic	/60	Ger.	
20		Susianna	15	f.	Domestic		"	S
21		Mary	12	f.			"	S
22		John	9	m.			O.	S
23		Frederick	5	m.			"	S
24		Carolina	2	f.			"	
25	840/840	HACKELL, Geo. A.	42	m.	Cabinet-maker	/75	Ger.	
26		Sarah	28	f.	Domestic		O.	
27		Mary M.	11	f.			"	S
28		Nancy	9	f.			"	S
29		Thomas J.	7	m.			"	S
30		Charles	4	m.			"	
31		Emelia	1	f.			"	
32	841/841	LITTLETON, Thos.						
		A.	41	m.	Farmer	/150	"	I
33		Lucinda	35	f.	Domestic		"	I
34		Josephus	6	m.			"	S
35		Nancy	4	f.			"	S
36		Earnest	9/12	m.			"	
37		Agnas	13	f.			"	S
38		BISHOP, Michael	15	m.			"	S

Page 123   19 July 1860   Sheet 196

1	842/842	McKEY, Barbary	54	f.	Domestic	2500/360	Sw.	I
2		Christian	24	m.	Farm laborer		O.	I
3		Louisa	20	f.	Domestic		"	S
4		Caroline	18	f.	Domestic		"	S
5		John	16	m.	Farmer		"	S
6		Henry	14	m.			"	S

| 7 | 843/843 | CRAMER, Jas. | 70 | m. | Retired | /100 | Hol. | |
| 8 | | Elisabeth | 60 | f. | Domestic | | " | |

9	844/844	SIEBERT, John	37	m.	Farmer	2000/275	Ger.	
10		Margaret	31	f.	Domestic		O.	I
11		Albert	9	m.			"	S
12		Susianna	8	f.			"	S
13		Mary A.	6	f.			"	S
14		Emeline	3	f.			"	
15		Henry	2/12	m.			"	

16	845/845	LENTZ, Henry	54	m.	Farmer	1600/425	Ger.	
17		Catharine	43	f.	Domestic		"	
18		Caroline	21	f.	Domestic		"	
19		Mary	20	f.	Domestic		"	
20		Marthy	18	f.	Domestic		"	
21		Margaret	16	f.	Domestic		O.	
22		Anne	10	f.			"	S
23		Charles H.	8	m.			"	S
24		Geo. P.	6	m.			"	
25		Louisa	3	f.			"	
26		July M.	7/12	f.			"	

27	846/846	LITTLETON, Thos.	58	m.	Farmer	350/150	Md.	I
28		Esther	56	f.	Domestic		Conn.	I
29		Esther	24	f.	Servant		O.	
30		Mary	20	f.	Domestic		"	
31		Hariet M.	17	f.	Domestic		"	
32		Jennet	14	f.			Conn.	
33		Frances	12	f.			O.	

34	847/847	FARMER, Otho	55	m.	Farmer	2000/300	Md.	
35		Prudence	55	f.	Domestic		"	
36		Elisabeth	20	f.	Domestic		O.	
37		Nancy	14	f.			"	S

| 38 | 848/848 | EDWARDS, Jas. | 53 | m. | Farmer | 2000/450 | Pa. | |

Page 124   19 July 1860   Sheet 196 verso

1		Catharine	61	f.	Domestic	Md.	
2		FULK, Catharine	11	f.		O.	S
3		Mary J.	5	f.		"	
4		STURGEON, William	16	m.	Day laborer	"	S
5		Jane	14	f.		"	S
6		Reuben	12	m.		"	S
7		Robert	10	m.		"	S
8		Jas.	7	m.		"	S

9	849/849	EDWARDS, Michael	26	m.	Farmer	/275	O.	
10		Isabelle	5	f.			"	S
11		James	3	m.			"	
12		SMITH, Elisabeth	24	f.	Domestic		"	
13	850/850	CASE, John	41	m.	Farmer	1300/300	"	
14		Rose A.	34	f.	Domestic		"	
15		Levi	15	m.	Farmer		"	S
16		Nancy A.	13	f.			"	S
17		Barbary J.	10	f.			"	S
18		Frederick	4	m.			"	S
19	851/851	LANDIS, David	37	m.	Farmer	1800/533	Pa.	
20		Rose A.	36	f.	Domestic		O.	
21		Rachel A.	15	f.	Domestic		"	S
22		Catharine	14	f.			"	S
23		Barbary	12	f.			"	S
24		Susianna	11	f.			"	S
25		Henry	10	m.			"	S
26		Jas.	8	m.			"	S
27		Margaret	6	f.			"	S
28		Amanda	4	f.			"	
29		Reuben W.	10/12	m.			"	
30	852/852	RENSEG, Jacob	44	m.	Farmer	2800/220	Ger.	
31		Elisabeth	44	f.	Domestic		"	I
32		Christian	23	m.	Day laborer		O.	
33		Frederick	21	m.	Day laborer		"	
34		Jacob	13	m.			"	S
35		Samuel	12	m.			"	S
36		Elisabeth	16	f.	Domestic		"	
37		Mary	14	f.			"	S
38		Louisa	9	f.			"	S

1		Wm.	8	m.			O.	S
2		Caroline	6	f.			"	
3		Rose A.	3	f.			"	
4	853/853	YOST, Jacob	46	m.	Farmer	2500/650	Sw.	
5		Elisabeth	41	f.	Domestic		O.	
6		Christian	19	m.	Farmer		"	S
7		Rose A.	17	f.	Domestic		"	S
8		John	15	m.			"	S
9		Louisa	13	f.			"	S
10		Elisabeth	11	f.			"	S
11		Noah	9	m.			"	S
12		Jacob	6	m.			"	
13		Enoch	4	m.			"	
14		Reuben	1	m.			"	
15		Nicholas	1/12	m.			"	
16	854/854	MEAL, Nicholas	52	m.	Carpenter	700/250	Ger.	
17		Margaret	51	f.	Domestic		"	
18		Michael	24	m.	Carpenter		"	
19		Jacob	22	m.	Carpenter		"	
20		Catharine	17	f.	Domestic		"	

21		MEAL, Mary	16	f.	Domestic		Ger. S
22		Sally	13	f.			" S
23		Elisabeth	11	f.			O. S
24	855/855	WARD, Seth	37	m.	Farmer	3000/1150	"
25		Eliza	30	f.	Domestic		"
26		Stephen	13	m.			" S
27		Jas. M.	11	m.			" S
28		Seth	9	m.			" S
29		Alvira	7	f.			" S
30		Mary A.	5	f.			"
31		Eliza J.	4	f.			"
32		Simon	3	m.			"
33		Lydia	1	f.			"
34	856/856	MARTIN, Joseph	85	m.	Grocer	/50	Va.
35		Christena	87	f.	Domestic		Pa.
36	857/857	WALTON, Robt.	26	m.	Boating	/75	O.
37		Mary E.	31	f.	Domestic		"
38		Mosses	4	m.			"
39		Frances	2	f.			"

Page 126   19 July 1860   Sheet 197 verso

1	858/858	LOBENSTINE, Henry	32	m.	Farmer	1000/3000	Ger.
2		Christena	3C	f.	Domestic		"
3		Christian	2	m.			O.
4		Lewis G.	1	m.			"
5		Emmy	1/12	f.			"
6		OTTO, John	40	m.	Farmer		Hes.
7	859/859	BLAIZER, Susanna	45	f.	Domestic	100/100	Sw.
8		Christian	16	m.	Day laborer		"
9		John	11	m.			"
10	860/860	TYLOR, Gideon L.	33	m.	Farmer	8000/150	N.Y.
11		Mary	33	f.	Domestic		O.
12		Jas. W.	8	m.			" S
13		Charles A.	7	m.			" S
14	861/861	WHITE, Wm.	45	m.	Farmer	500/150	Va.
15		Sarah	43	f.	Domestic		O.
16		Manervy	23	f.	Domestic		"
17		Saul	21	m.	Farm laborer		"
18	862/862	GORDON, Louis H.	43	m.	Farmer	/250	Pa.
19		Belinda	39	f.	Domestic		"
20		Catharine	16	f.			Va. S
21		Mary J.	13	f.			O. S
22		Isaac B.	11	m.			" S
23		Wm. J.	8	m.			" S
24		Lewis	6	m.			" S
25		Belinda	3	f.			" S
26	863/863	STIDING, Theodore	50	m.	Farmer	300/250	Sax.
27		Rose	40	f.	Domestic		"

28		STIDING, Augusta	14	f.		Sax.	S
29		Louisa	12	f.		"	S
30		Julius	10	m.		"	S
31		Wm.	8	m.		"	S
32		Amelia	5	f.		O.	
33		Matilda	2	f.		"	
34	864/864	ANDERSON, Frank	30	m.	Steamboating 600/	Ger.	
35		Barbary	34	f.	Domestic	"	

1	865/865	PAPE, Fredk.	37	m.	Farmer	200/225 Ger.	
2		Guerdruth	56	f.	Domestic	Hes.	I
3		Amelia	10	f.		O.	S
4		Elisha	8	m.		"	S
5		Clarrie	6	f.		"	
6		Jasper	4	m.		"	
7		Commelia	1	f.		"	
8	866/866	DEARF, Christian	24	m.	Carpenter	"	M
9		Catharine	17	f.	Domestic	/50 "	M
10	867/867	LAPE, Christian	35	m.	Farmer	2000/375 Wit.	
11		Mary	35	f.	Domestic	O.	
12		Thos.	7	m.		"	S
13		Reuben	5	m.		"	
14		David	3	m.		"	
15		Mary	1	f.		"	
16		STARDLEY, Jacob	21	m.	Farm laborer	Wit.	
17	868/868	WARD, Moses	68	m.	Farmer	6000/500 Va.	
18		Mary	63	f.	Domestic	"	
19		Stephen	30	m.	Farmer	O.	
20		Geo. W.	23	m.	Steamboating	"	
21		COLLINGG, Leving	38	f.	Domestic	"	
22		Wm.	13	m.		"	S
23		Mary J.	12	f.		"	S
24		Lucy A.	9	f.		"	S
25	869/869	WARD, Moses	31	m.	Farmer	/150 "	
26		Elisabeth	23	f.	Domestic	"	
27		Roena	3	f.		"	
28		HALEY, Rose	5	f.		"	
29	870/870	GOODHUGH, Neoma	47	f.	Domestic 16,000/800	"	
30		John	17	m.	Farmer	"	S
31		Archabald	16	m.	Farmer	"	S
32	871/871	ROSS, Henry	53	m.	Day laborer	/150 "	I
33		Jane	48	f.	Domestic	"	I
34		Sylvester	29	m.	Boating	"	
35		Margaret	16	f.	Domestic	"	
36		James	15	m.		"	
37		Wm.	9	m.		"	

Page 128   20 July 1860   Sheet 198 verso

1	872/872	WALTON, Jas.	48	m.	Farmer	15,000/1175	Pa.
2		Mariah	37	f.	Domestic		O.
3		Thos.	21	m.	Farmer		"
4		Josephus	20	m.	Farmer		" S
5		Augustus	18	m.	Farmer		" S
6		Nancy	17	f.	Domestic		" S
7		James	15	m.			" S
8		Jeremiah	9	m.			" S
9		John	7	m.			" S
10		Frances	2	f.			"
11	873/873	STEED, Gideon	30	m.	Farmer	/365	"
12		Bethany	30	f.	Domestic		"
13		Charlotta	15	f.			" S
14		Juli anne	13	f.			" S
15		Mary J.	6	f.			"
16		John	5	m.			"
17	874/874	STEED, Geo.	70	m.	Farmer	7500/150	Va.
18		Elisabeth	60	f.	Domestic		O.
19	875/875	YOST, Joel	51	m.	Farmer	7000/1000	"
20		Nancy	43	f.	Domestic		Pa.
21		Anjaline	23	f.	Domestic		O.
22		Manervy	22	f.	Domestic		"
23		Frances A.	15	f.	Domestic		" S
24		Warren	12	m.			" S
25		Geo.	11	m.			" S
26		Nancy E.	10	f.			" S
27		Jas. K.	6	m.			" S
28		WALTON, Nancy	72	f.	Retired		Pa.
29	876/876	JONSON, Hannah	42	f.	Domestic	4000/200	O. I
30		Susianna	30	f.	Domestic		"
31		ATKINSON, Hannah	35	f.	Domestic		"
32	877/877	MALORY, Benjamin	32	m.	Farmer		"
33		Hannah A.	22	f.	Domestic		Va.
34		Wickliff	8	m.			O. S
35		Clarance	4	m.			"
36		John	9/12	m.			"
37	878/878	McINTIRE, David S.	53	m.	Blacksmith	/150	Va.
38		Mary	49	f.	Domestic		O.
39		Catharine	22	f.	Domestic		"

Page 129   20 July 1860   Sheet 199

1	879/879	MALORY, Wm. H.	27	m.	Farmer	9000/3394	O.
2		Amanda J.	22	f.	Domestic		"
3		Orzoro F.	5	f.			"
4		McCOY, Kiziah	55	f.	Domestic		"
5		Mary A.	19	f.	Domestic		" S
6	880/880	ALLEN, Thós.	54	m.	Farmer	/15	Pa.
7		Elizabeth	53	f.	Domestic		Va.

8		ALLEN, Margaret	16	f.	Domestic	O. S
9		Wm.	14	m.		" S
10		Florance	10	f.		" S
11	881/881	CLEMENT, David	23	m.	Shoemaker /50	Va. M
12		Lydia A.	19	f.	Domestic	O. M
13	882/882	BATES, Mary	59	f.	Domestic /100	Eng.
14		Wm.	22	m.	Day laborer	O.
15	883/883	LABARON, Theodore	41	m.	Mast. Engineer 850/200	Pa.
16		Amanda	28	f.	Domestic	"
17		Geo.	18	m.	Apprentice Engineer	" S
18		Theodore	16	m.	Farm laborer	" S
19		Anne	14	f.		" S
20		Mary E.	11	f.		" S
21		Frank	9	m.		" S
22		Mortimer	6	m.		O. S
23		Wm.	4	m.		Va.
24		Marthy	7/12	f.		"
25		McDANIEL, Idea	6	f.		"
26		CLARK, Amos	80	m.	Retired	Conn.
27		Eliza	62	f.	Retired	Pa.
28	884/884	RUTTER, Wm.	39	m.	Farmer 2200/600	O. I
29		Rachel	39	f.	Domestic	Va. I
30		James	19	m.	Farm laborer	O. S
31		Melvin V.	7	m.		"
32	885/885	CASE, Joel	25	m.	Butcher /200	"
33		Elisabeth	24	f.	Domestic	"
34		Eugene	3	m.		"
35		Sarah A.	2/12	f.		"
36	886/886	COLLINS, Jas.	46	m.	Stone mason 1000/200	Scot.
37		Susianna	46	f.	Domestic	"
38		Robert	21	m.	Bricklayer	Pa.
39		Francis	19	m.	Engineer	O.

Page 130	20 July 1860				Sheet 199 verso
1	Jennet	17	f.	Domestic	Pa.
2	Jas.	15	m.	Machinist	" S
3	Clarinda	13	f.		" S
4	Charles	11	m.		Va. S
5	Allen	9	m.		O. S
6	Mary J.	7	f.		" S
7	John K.	5	m.		"
8	Calvin D.	3	m.		"

9	887/887	DOIL, Wm.	50	m.	Blacksmith 3000/300	Ger.
10		Louisa	46	f.	Domestic	"
11		Mini	15	f.	Domestic	O. S
12		Wm.	14	m.		" S
13		Edward	12	m.		" S
14		Elisabeth	8	f.		" S

15		EARLY, Nancy	12	f.			O. S	
16	888/888	UMPHER, Geo.	22	m.	Cabinet-maker	/75	Sax.	
17		Margaret	21	f.	Domestic		"	
18	889/889	MEEK, Jacob	41	m.	Merchant	/1500	Pa.	
19		Anne	40	f.	Domestic		Eng.	
20	890/890	STEENROD, Daniel	58	m.	Farmer	4000/780	Va.	
21		Susianna	54	f.	Domestic		O.	
22		Joseph	34	m.	Farm laborer		"	
23		Nathaniel	22	m.	Teacher		"	
24		Permelia	20	f.	Domestic		"	S
25		Ephraim	8	m.			"	S
26		FALLWELL, Susianna	10	f.			"	S
27		BLAIR, Mary	76	f.	Retired		Md.	
28	891/891	MOZENA, Francis	25	m.	Farmer		O.	
29		Esther	24	f.	Domestic		"	
30		Emma	6	f.			"	
31	892/892	CAIN, Richard M.	31	m.	Farmer	2000/310	"	
32		Mary	31	f.	Domestic		"	
33		Armand	10	f.			"	S
34		Clary	8	f.			"	S
35		Owiner	5	m.			"	S
36		Singleton	4	m.			"	
37		Semantha	1	f.			"	
38		Daniel	69	m.	Retired		Pa.	
39	893/893	COLLENS, Michael	30	m.	Farmer	/300	Ire.	

1		Mary J.	33	f.	Domestic		Ire.	
2		Mary J.	12	f.			Va.	S
3		Margaret A.	10	f.			"	S
4		Eliza	8	f.			"	S
5		Thos.	3	m.			"	
6		Roena	1	f.			"	
7	894/894	LIVELY, James	64	m.	Day laborer	/150	Ire.	
8		Jane	64	f.	Domestic		"	
9	895/895	DAVIS, Lewis	53	m.	Fence builder	/100	N.Y.	
10		Catharine	40	f.	Domestic		Pa.	
11		Mary	19	f.	Domestic		O. S	
12		Joel	18	m.	Farmer		"	
13		Geo.	17	m.	Farmer		"	S
14		Samuel	14	m.			"	S
15		Elisabeth	2	f.			"	
16	896/896	CONLEY, Robert	72	m.	Farm laborer	/250	Pa.	
17		Catharine	62	f.	Domestic		Va.	
18		Amanda	21	f.	Domestic		O.	
19		Margaret	19	f.	Domestic		"	
20		Eliza	16	f.	Domestic		"	S

21		CONLEY, Catharine	13	f.			O. S
22	897/897	DUFF, Anne	51	f.	Domestic	500/100	" I
23		Mary	25	f.	Domestic		" I
24		John	21	m.	Teamster		"
25		Parker	15	m.			"
26		Thos.	14	m.			"
27	898/898	COLVIN, Owen	38	m.	Farm laborer	/50	Ire.
28	899/899	THOMPSON, Jas.	58	m.	Farmer	2500/390	O.
29		Mary A.	57	f.	Domestic		Pa.
30		Stephen	34	m.	Boating		O.
31		Isaac	28	m.	Boating		"
32		Geo. W.	26	m.	Clerk on boat		"
33		Rebecca E.	24	f.	Domestic		"
34		Susianna	19	f.	Domestic		" S
35		Jas.	17	m.	Farmer		"
36		CLARK, Sarah H.	31	f.	Servant		"
37		Earnast	9	m.			"
38		LEES, Marthy	23	f.	Servant		La.

Page 132   21 July 1860   Sheet 200 verso

1	900/900	VARLEY, John	31	m.	Farmer	12,000/7400	Va.
2		Margaret	24	f.	Domestic		Pa.
3		Frank	3	m.			Va.
4		Charles	1	m.			Pa.
5		FINN, Thos.	18	m.	Farm laborer		Ire.
6		BAKER, Emily J.	17	f.	Domestic		Va.
7		BARLEY, Mary J.	34	f.	Domestic		"
8	901/901	STETSON, Jas.	36	m.	Farmer	/380	O.
9		Anne	36	f.	Domestic		"
10		Charles	17	m.	Farm laborer		" S
11		Edward	15	m.	Farm laborer		" S
12		James	13	m.			" S
13		Marshal	11	m.			" S
14		Sarah	8	f.			"
15		Emaline	5	f.			"
16		Martha	1	f.			"
17	902/902	HANNA, James	34	m.	Farmer	/300	Pa.
18		Hariet	35	f.	Domestic		O.
19		Margaret A.	10	f.			" S
20		James	8	m.			" S
21		Nancy C.	6	f.			" S
22		Wm. F.	2	m.			"
23		BROWN, Ephraim	18	m.	Farm laborer		"
24	903/903	MARTIN, Nimrod A.	29	m.	Steamboat Pilot	/200	"
25		Mary A.	27	f.	Domestic		"
26		James	6	m.			"
27	904/904	GILMORE, Martin	45	m.	Farmer	1000/220	"
28		Anne	36	f.	Domestic		"
29		Missouri	18	f.	Domestic		" S
30		Dalice	15	m.			" S

31		GILMORE, Marion	12	m.			O.	S
32		Margaret J.	10	f.			"	S
33		Ezria	4	m.			"	
34	905/905	MARTIN, John	52	m.	Farmer	4000/700	Pa.	
35		Nancy	49	f.	Domestic		O.	
36		Elisabeth	29	f.	Domestic		"	
37		Francis M.	23	m.	Physician		"	
38		Richard	19	m.	Teacher		"	S
39		Charlotta	18	f.	Domestic		"	S

1		Hannah	16	f.			O.	S
2		Matilda	14	f.			"	S
3	906/906	ZINK, Jacob	33	m.	Farmer	1000/300	Sw.	
4		Mary A.	28	f.	Domestic		"	
5		Caroline	12	f.			O.	S
6		Benjamin	11	m.			"	S
7		John	8	m.			"	S
8		Elisabeth	5	f.			"	
9		Wm.	1	m.			"	
10	907/907	LITTLEMAN, Sewell	33	m.	Farmer	800/200	"	
11		Rachel	28	f.	Domestic		"	
12		Geo. B.	3	m.			"	
13		Quilla	1	m.			"	
14	908/908	LITTLETON, Edward	78	m.	Retired	/50	Del.	I
15		Mary	68	f.	Domestic		Conn.	I
16	909/909	CORTSMAN, Fred-						
		erick	40	m.	Farmer	1000/400	Ger.	
17		Barbara	36	f.	Domestic		Pa.	I
18		Mary	14	f.	Domestic		O.	S
19		Ervin	13	m.			"	S
20		Louisa	8	f.			"	S
21		Frederick	4	m.			"	
22		Emily	1	f.			"	
23	910/910	FOLDER, Abraham	50	m.	Farmer	1000/350	Sw.	
24		Barbara	42	f.	Domestic		"	
25		Abraham	13	m.			"	S
26		Martha	10	f.			"	S
27		Eliza	2	f.			O.	
28		Godfrey	1	m.			"	
29	911/911	MILLER, Peter	33	m.	Farmer	300/250	Sw.	
30		Frances	73	f.	Domestic		"	
31		Susianna	24	f.	Domestic		"	
32		Amena	21	f.	Servant		"	
33		Christian	22	m.	Farm laborer		"	
34		Mary	26	f.	Domestic		"	S
35	912/912	CASE, Zadoc	40	m.	Farmer	/600	O.	
36		Hannah	45	f.	Domestic		Va.	

| 37 | | CASE, Malissa | 16 | f. | Domestic | | O. | S |
| 38 | | Hariet | 14 | f. | | | " | S |

1		Emeline	13	f.			O.	S
2		Wm.	8	m.			"	S
3		Robert	6	m.			"	S
4		Joel	4	m.			"	S
5		Zadoc	2	m.			"	
6		Wm.	69	m.	Farmer		Md.	

7	913/913	WESTON, Ephram	39	m.	Baker	300/200	O.	
8		Louisa	37	f.	Domestic		R.I.	
9		Mary	16	f.	Domestic		O.	S
10		Sarah	14	f.			"	S
11		Wm. R.	1	m.			"	
12		JONES, Deborah	64	f.	Domestic		R.I.	

13	914/914	ULLOM, John	65	m.	Farmer	2000/450	Pa.	
14		Susianna	55	f.	Domestic		"	
15		Ismenna	21	f.	Domestic		O.	
16		Elisha	18	m.	Farmer		"	S
17		Peter	16	m.	Farmer		"	S
18		Mathias	11	m.			"	S
19		JACKSON, Emaline	17	f.	Domestic		"	S
20		HARTER, Barbary	84	f.	Retired		Pa.	I

| 21 | 915/915 | GALAGHER, Margaret | 56 | f. | Domestic | /75 | O. | |
| 22 | | Calvin J. | 25 | m. | Farmer | | " | |

23	916/916	SCOTT, Matilda	49	f.	Domestic	/175	"	
24		Wm.	25	m.	Farmer		"	
25		Eliza J.	17	f.	Domestic		"	S
26		Sarah	15	f.	Domestic		"	
27		David	12	m.			"	S
28		Susianna	10	f.			"	
29		Adaline	7	f.			"	

30	917/917	HOWELL, John W.	41	m.	Day laborer		"	I
31		PASCEL, Sarah	54	f.	Domestic		Pa.	I
32		John	25	m.	Farmer		"	
33		Jas.	22	m.	Farmer		"	
34		Jesse B.	19	m.	Farmer		"	

35	918/918	ULLOM, Jacob	29	m.	Farmer	/225	"	
36		Hariet	21	f.	Domestic		"	
37		Mary E.	5	f.			"	S
38		Hariet	4	f.			"	
39		Elbert	1	m.			"	

1	919/919	WARD, Joseph	42	m.	Farmer	/475	O.	
2		Susianna	39	f.	Domestic		"	
3		Seth L.	18	m.	Farm laborer		"	S
4		Mary J.	16	f.	Domestic		"	S

5		WARD, John	14	m.			O. S
6		Andrew	12	m.			" S
7		Elily E.	9	f.			" S
8		Henry	7	m.			"
9		Alexandria	4	m.			"
10		Marthy E.	1	f.			"
11	920/920	DAVIS, Mary	45	f.	Domestic	700/110	" I
12		Emily	15	f.			" S
13		Daniel	13	m.			" S
14		MARTIN, Adaline	18	f.	Domestic		"
15	921/921	BURKHOLDER, John	38	m.	Farmer	1400/300	Sw. I
16		Catharine	38	f.	Domestic		"
17		Elisabeth	14	f.			"
18		Anne	12	f.			O. S
19		Margaret	10	f.			" S
20		Geo.	8	m.			" S
21		Susianna	5	f.			"
22		John P.	3	m.			"
23		Henry	1	m.			"
24		STALL, Jacob	51	m.	Carpenter		Sw.
25	922/922	GOLAWER, Milton	28	m.	Cooper	350/100	O.
26		Sarah J.	22	f.	Domestic		"
27		Nelson	3	m.			"
28		Alphin	1	m.			"
29		Metha	1/12	f.			"
30	923/923	BUCHBLER, Andrew	39	m.	Cheese-maker	/350	Sw.
31		Anne B.	35	f.	Domestic		" I
32		Eliza	11	f.			" S
33		Frederick	10	m.			" S
34		Mary	7	f.			" S
35		Andrew	6	m.			"
36		Rose	4	f.			O.
37		DURIG, Fred	20	m.	Dairyman		Sw.
38	924/924	OBLINGER, Fred-					
		erick	36	m.	Farmer	400/150	"
39		Anne	34	f.	Domestic		"

1		Frederick	14	m.			Sw.
2		Levi	12	m.			" S
3		Godfrey	10	m.			" S
4		Rose	9	f.			" S
5		Jacob	8	m.			O. S
6		Eliza	6	f.			"
7		John	4	m.			"
8		Charles	1	m.			"
9	925/925	LEAP, Henry	36	m.	Farmer	2800/575	Ger.
10		Julia A.	31	f.	Domestic		" I
11		Julia A.	14	f.			O. S
12		Henry	12	m.			" S

13		LEAP, Catharine	10	f.			O.	S
14		Rose A.	7	f.			"	S
15		Godfrey	4	m.			"	
16		Saml.	2	m.			"	
17		Magdeline	1/12	f.			"	
18	926/926	HATHORN, Stephen	38	m.	Farmer	5000/480	Md.	
19		Sarah	37	f.	Domestic		O.	
20		AMBLER, Wm.	64	m.	Farmer	/80	Va.	
21		Nancy	58	f.	Domestic		"	
22		JORDEN, Nancy	16	f.	Domestic		O.	S
23		HEATH, Joshua	15	m.			"	S
24		FOREMAN, Wm.	4	m.			"	
25	927/927	SICKS, David	65	m.	Farmer	4500/450	Pa.	
26		Ruth	55	f.	Domestic		"	
27		Michael	19	m.	Farmer		O.	S
28		Lewis	17	m.	Farmer		"	S
29		Milton	14	m.			"	S
30	928/928	ECKELS, John	44	m.	Farmer	/225	Pa.	I
31		Jane	45	f.	Domestic		Va.	I
32		Armstrong	19	m.	Farmer		Pa.	
33		Wm.	17	m.	Farmer		Va.	
34		John C.	16	m.	Farmer		O.	S
35		Joshua S.	13	m.			"	S
36		David J.	11	m.			"	S
37		Mary J.	9	f.			"	S
38		Kiziah	8	f.			"	S
39		Saml. J.	6	m.			"	S

Page 137   23 July 1860   Sheet 203

1	929/929	COOK, Cephas	40	m.	Farmer	150/	Pa.	
2		Jane	44	f.	Domestic		"	I
3		Nancy	13	f.			O.	S
4		Elisabeth	12	f.			"	S
5		John	10	m.			"	S
6		Saml.	10	m.			"	S
7		Wm.	8	m.			"	S
8		Malissa	5	f.			"	
9		James E.	1	m.			"	
10	930/930	ALLEN, John	24	m.	Farm laborer	/60	Va.	
11		Anne E.	23	f.	Domestic		O.	
12		Jas. R.	5	m.			"	
13		Leondus	1	m.			"	
14	931/931	ROSELL, Jacob	34	m.	Farmer	400/175	"	
15		Arminta	25	f.	Domestic		"	
16		Jas. F.	7	m.			"	S
17		Westley	6	m.			"	
18		Hiley A.	3	f.			"	
19	932/932	FAGINS, Casander	55	m.	Farmer	1000/60	Pa.	I
20		John	22	m.	Day laborer		O.	
21		Hetta	21	f.	Domestic		"	S

22		FAGINS, Martha	16	f.	Domestic		O. S
23		Cassa	14	f.			" S
24	933/933	SYX, Henry	37	m.	Farmer	1600/450	Pa.
25		Clarissa	37	f.	Domestic		O.
26		Sarah E.	14	f.			" 4
27		Wilson	12	m.			"
28		Mary J.	10	f.			"
29		Jas. A.	8	m.			"
30		Ruth M.	6	f.			"
31		Rachel A.	3	f.			"
32		David E.	1	m.			"
33	934/934	AMBLER, John C.	23	m.	Farmer	500/275	"
34		Louisa	31	f.	Domestic		"
35		Stephen K.	5	m.			"
36		Jas. M.	4	m.			"
37		Sarah	1	f.			"
38	935/935	BATES, Richard	52	m.	Farmer	/100	Eng.
39		Martha	50	f.	Domestic		"

Page 138   23 July 1860   Sheet 203 verso

1	936/936	YOHO, John	49	m.	Farmer	5000/525	Va.
2		Sarah	47	f.	Domestic		Pa.
3		John	25	m.	Farmer		O.
4		Jacob	16	m.	Farmer		" S
5		Mary	15	f.	Domestic		" S
6	937/937	LUTHY, Charles	23	m.	Farmer	/100	"
7		Sarah	19	f.	Domestic		"
8		Eliel E.	1	m.			"
9	938/938	SPEAR, Andrew	57	m.	Cooper	800/100	"
10		Susianna	38	f.	Domestic		Pa. I
11		Thos.	12	m.			" S
12		Martha	1/12	f.			O.
13		CORE, Francis	6	f.			" S
14	939/939	WHITE, Ebenezer	43	m.	Farmer	200/550	Va.
15		Elisabeth	43	f.	Domestic		O.
16		Thos. J.	11	m.			" S
17		Virginia E.	9	f.			" S
18		HOWELL, Anne	96	f.	Retired		N.J.
19	940/940	HOWELL, Thos.	41	m.	Farmer	/160	O.
20		Anne E.	9	f.			" S
21	941/941	CRAIG, James	29	m.	Farmer	/150	"
22		Barbary A.	19	f.	Domestic		"
23		Alice	5/12	f.			"
24	942/942	GILMORE, Jas.	72	m.	Farmer	1000/350	Pa.
25		Eleanor	69	f.	Domestic		Va. I
26		Perry	35	m.	Farmer		O.
27	943/943	SPRAIG, William	50	m.	Farmer	/100	"

28		SPRAIG, Mary	46	f.	Domestic		O.	
29		Wm.	22	m.	Day laborer		"	
30		Sarah	20	f.	Domestic		"	
31		John	15	m.			"	S
32		Eliza	13	f.			"	S
33		Jas.	11	m.			"	S
34		Emma	7	f.			"	S
35		Albert	4	m.			"	
36		Amanda	10/12	f.			"	
37	944/944	CAMPBELL, Jas. R.	62	m.	Farmer	800/140	Del.	
38		Margaret	54	f.	Domestic		Va.	
39		Joseph	31	m.	Carpenter		Pa.	

1		Mary	26	f.	Domestic		Pa.	
2		Lidia	24	f.	Servant		"	
3		Elisabeth	21	f.	Servant		O.	
4		James	19	m.	Farmer		"	
5		Jesse W.	17	m.	Farmer		"	S
6		Margaret	10	f.			"	S
7	945/945	WILSON, Westley	57	m.	Farmer	/750	O.	
8		Martha	53	f.	Domestic		Md.	
9		Wm.	22	m.	Day laborer		O.	
10		Henry	20	m.	Day laborer		"	
11		Joseph	18	m.	Day laborer		"	
12		Martha	11	f.			"	S
13		Sarah	9	f.			"	S
14	946/946	ROSELL, Jacob	28	m.	Farmer	800/125	"	
15		Arminta	30	f.	Domestic		"	
16		James	7	m.			"	S
17		Wesley	5	m.			"	
18		Hila A.	3	f.			"	
19	947/947	BOUGHNER, Wm.	35	m.	Farmer	3700/484	"	
20		Rebecca	32	f.	Domestic		"	
21		Mahala	12	f.			"	S
22		Mary M.	10	f.			"	S
23		John M.	8	m.			"	S
24		Manerva O.	7	f.			"	S
25		Elwood	6	m.			"	S
26		Jane	3	f.			"	
27		James	1	m.			"	
28	948/948	WIGGINS, Geo.	52	m.	Day laborer	/50	Va.	I
29		Elila	42	f.	Domestic		O.	I
30		Franklin	19	m.	Boatman		"	
31		Geo.	14	m.			"	S
32		Phebe	9	f.			"	S
33		Jas. M.	6	m.			"	
34	949/949	SYCKS, David	25	m.	Farmer	/100	"	
35		Silome	28	f.	Domestic		"	
36		Mary E.	2	f.			"	

37	950/950	HILL, Jane	41	f.	Domestic	/100	Va.
38		Benjamin	22	m.	Farmer	/700	Pa.
39		Sarah M.	19	f.	Domestic	/250	"

Page 140   23 July 1860   Sheet 204 verso

1	951/951	ADAMS, Jas.	28	m.	Farmer	10,000/1357	Va.
2		Hannah	31	f.	Domestic		Pa.
3		Sarah	7	f.			O. S
4		David N.	6	m.			" S
5		Marshal V.	5	m.			"
6		Ruth A.	4	f.			"
7		Cora J.	3	f.			"
8		James	1/12	m.			"
9	952/952	ADAMS, James Sr.	79	m.	Farm laborer	/150	Ire.
10		Sarah	68	f.	Domestic		"
11		HILL, Jas.	20	m.	Farmer		Pa.
12		Letticia	30	f.			Va.
13	953/953	GRIFFEN, John	40	m.	Farmer	/626	Scot.
14		Nancy	31	f.	Domestic		Va.
15		Isebell	11	f.			O. S
16		Wm.	10	m.			" S
17		James	9	m.			" S
18		John	7	m.			" S
19		Sarah	6	f.			" S
20		Orlena	5	f.			"
21		Mathew	2/12	m.			"
22	954/954	FIEZLY, Abraham	61	m.	Farmer	2400/380	Sw. I
23		Elisabeth	58	f.	Domestic		" I
24		Elisabeth	28	f.	Domestic		"
25		John	21	m.	Farmer		"
26		Frederick	16	m.	Farmer		" S
27	955/955	FIZLEY, Saml.	29	m.	Carpenter	150/	O.
28		Frances	30	f.	Domestic		"
29		Louisa	1	f.			"
30	956/956	BOIR, John	24	m.	Machinest	/50	Ger.
31		Margaret	24	f.	Domestic		"
32	957/057	BERKHOLDER, Jacob	43	m.	Farmer	3000/409	Sw.
33		Mar---	36	f.	Domestic		"
34	958/958	FLOWHOUS, John	29	m.	Farmer	900/175	Ger.
35		Catharine	38	f.	Domestic		"
36		Margaret	11	f.			Va. S
37		Anne	8	f.			" S
38		John	6	m.			O. S
39		Mary	5	f.			" S

Page 141   23 July 1860   Sheet 205

1		Catharine	2	f.		O.
2		Geo.	9/12	m.		"

3	959/959	STEPHENS, Marthy A.	47	f.	Domestic	900/150	Sw.
4		Elisabeth	20	f.	Domestic		O.
5		Peter	16	m.			" S
6		Geo.	15	m.			' S
7		Mary	12	f.			" S
8		Lewis	10	m.			" S
9		Saml.	9	m.			" S
10		Catharine	8	f.			' S
11	960/960	BLITTER, Jacob	39	m.	Farmer	2000/280	Sw.
12		Barbary	41	f.	Domestic		"
13		Jacob	11	m.			O. S
14		Elisabeth	9	f.			" S
15		David	3	m.			"
16		REATS, John	58	m.	Farmer		Sw.
17		Roseanne	49	f.	Domestic		"
18	961/961	SHINHAT, John	53	m.	Farmer	1000/	Ger.
19		Eliza	55	f.	Domestic		"
20		Catharine	16	f.	Domestic		"
21	962/962	RUTTER, Joseph	50	m.	Farmer	900/450	O.
22		Elisabeth	45	f.	Domestic		Pa.
23		Enoch	27	m.	Farmer		O.
24		William	25	m.	Farmer		"
25		David	16	m.	Farmer		" S
26		GRIMES, John	51	m.	Farmer	1000/360	Pa.
27	963/963	SHIMHOUTT, John	25	m.	Farmer	/50	Ger. M
28		Catharine	23	f.	Domestic		" M
29	964/964	FOREST, Hartman	48	m.	Farmer	2300/420	O.
30		Marthy	8	f.			"
31		Henry M.	6	m.			" S
32		Geo.	3	m.			"
33		Reason	3/12	m.			"
34		Joseph	12	m.			" S
35	965/965	MASON, Peter	27	m.	Farmer	/50	Pa.
36		Eleanor	24	f.	Domestic		"
37		Jesse	6	m.			O.
38		Phebe	4	f.			"
39		John	2	m.			"

Page 142   23 July 1860   Sheet 205 verso

1	966/966	BAKER, John	56	m.	Farmer	1200/300	Ger.
2		Barbary	58	f.	Domestic		"
3		Jane	20	f.			O.
4		Frederick	12	m.			" S
5		Matilda H.	9	f.			Mo. S
6		John	26	m.	Farmer		Ger. M
7		Rose A.	23	f.	Domestic		O. M
8	967/967	LAYMAN, John G.	31	m.	Wagon-maker	900/150	Sw.
9		Mary A.	32	f.	Domestic		"
10		Augustus	8	m.			"

11		LAYMAN, Wm.	6	m.			O.
12		Jacob	4	m.			"
13		John	2	m.			"
14		Jesse	10/12	m.			"
15	968/968	LANER, Wm.	51	m.	Farmer	1000/350	Sw.
16		Mary	46	f.	Domestic		"
17		Frederick	20	m.	Farmer		"
18		Christian	18	m.	Farmer		"
19		Mary	16	f.	Domestic		"
20		Elisabeth	9	f.			"
21		Felix	27	m.	Carpenter	/50	O.
22	969/969	LINEBURGER, John	54	m.	Farmer	600/295	Ger.
23		Catharine	48	f.	Domestic		"
24		ROMER, Harman	11	m.			Pa.
25	970/970	CONDON, Denis	25	m.	Shoemaker	/60	Md.
26		Christena F.	19	f.	Domestic		O.
27	971/971	SUPERS, Theadore	62	m.	Miller	4500/350	Ger.
28		Margaret	61	f.	Domestic		"
29		Charles	21	m.	Farmer		"
30	972/972	DAVIS, Joshua	49	m.	Farmer	2000/494	O.
31		Mary	42	f.	Domestic		"
32		Sylbern	19	m.	Farmer		" S
33		Nancy	18	f.	Domestic		"
34		Selkirk	16	m.	Farmer		" S
35	973/973	GRIMES, Wm.	42	m.	Farmer	800/100	Pa.
36	974/974	WIGGINS, Philip	29	m.	Farmer	/250	O.
37		Margaret	18	f.	Domestic		"

1	975/975	ANDERSON, James	60	m.	Farmer	/50	Md.
2		Hannah J.	49	f.	Domestic		"
3		Sarah A.	16	f.	Domestic		O. S
4		Wesley	10	m.			" S
5		Mary	8	f.			" S
6		Joseph	4	m.			"
7	976/967	HALEY, James	62	m.	Farmer	2500/200	Eng.
8		Anjaline	7	f.			O.
9	977/977	BITMER, Jasper	45	m.	Farmer	1000/210	Ger.
10		Catharine	44	f.	Domestic		"
11		John	12	m.			Pa. S
12		Eliza	10	f.			Va. S
13		Wm.	7	m.			" S
14	978/978	HOWELL, Thos. J.	28	m.	Farmer	/250	O.
15		Elinor	31	f.	Domestic		"
16		Mary E.	6	f.			"
17		Rachel	4	f.			

18		HOWELL, Levi	2	m.			O.
19		Nelson	1/12	m.			"
20	979/979	FISTE, Mathew	29	m.	Farmer	400/60	Ger.
21		Catharine	17	f.	Domestic		"
22		John	1/12	m.			O.
23	980/980	FIST, Godily	66	m.	Farmer	1200/250	Ger.
24		Catharine	67	f.	Domestic		"
25	981/981	ROUSENBURGER, God-					
		frey	23	m.	Carpenter	/75	Ger.
26		Christena	28	f.	Domestic		"
27		Andrew	5	m.			Va.
28		Christiana	2	f.			"
29		Catherine	5/12	f.			"
30	982/982	SHAW, Josiah	31	m.	Farmer	/150	"
31		Delila	24	f.	Domestic		"
32		Jas. R.	10	m.			" S
33		Richard	2	m.			"
34		Nancy R.	2/12	f.			"
35	983/983	SHAW, Eseciahire	42	m.	Farmer	/220	Pa.
36		Elisabeth	45	f.	Domestic		"
37		Richard	20	m.	Farmer		O. S
38		Nancy J.	18	f.	Domestic		" S
39		Ruth	14	f.			" S

Page 144   24 July 1860   Sheet 206 verso

1		John	12	m.			O. S
2		Josephus	10	m.			" S
3		Delila	8	f.			" S
4	984/984	SHAW, James	39	m.	Farmer	3000/500	Va.
5		Mary	44	f.	Domestic		O.
6		Jane	15	f.			" S
7		Margaret	13	f.			" S
8		Theadore	9	m.			" S
9		Wm.	7	m.			" S
10		Julia A.	4	f.			"
11		Susianna	1	f.			"
12		HATHWAY, Jeremiah	23	m.	Day laborer	/40	"
13		James	20	m.	Day laborer		Ill. S
14		Robert F.	17	m.	Day laborer		" S
15	985/985	ROOT, Zachariah	77	m.	Retired		Md.
16		Ruth	41	f.	Domestic		Va.
17	986/986	SMITH, Cary M.	48	m.	Farmer	9000/290	O.
18		Margaret	37	f.	Domestic		"
19		Enos	20	m.	Teacher		"
20		Susianna	17	f.	Domestic		" S
21		John	15	m.			" S
22		Jas.	14	m.			" S
23		Isaac	10	m.			" S

24		SMITH, Mary	8	f.			O. S
25		Joseph	6	m.			" S
26		Huldah	4	f.			"
27		Nancy	3/12	f.			"

28	987/987	WIGGENS, Robert	24	m.	Day laborer	/40	"
29		Elisa A.	20	f.	Domestic		"
30		Thos. J.	4	m.			"
31		Eliza J.	1	f.			"

32	988/988	HAYWARD, John	29	m.	Farmer	/225	"
33		Jane	27	f.	Domestic		"
34		Emeline	1	f.			"
35		Earnest	1/12	m.			"

36	989/989	FLOWHOUS, Conrad	52	m.	Farmer	800/250	Ger.
37		Anne	33	f.	Domestic		"
38		John	10	m.			Va.
39		Catharine	8	f.			"

1		Caroline	6	f.			O.
2		Elisabeth	3	f.			"
3		Jacob	7/12	m.			"

4	990/990	HOWELL, Olever	29	m.	Farmer	50/125	"
5		May	25	f.	Domestic		"
6		Hariet	3	f.			"
7		Thos.	1	m.			"

8	991/991	GREENILLE, David	47	m.	Farmer	2500/300	"
9		Mary	37	f.	Domestic		"
10		Sarah A.	12	f.			" S
11		Theadore	10	m.			" S
12		Elisabeth	9	f.			" S
13		Geo.	4	m.			"
14		Catharine	2	f.			"
15		GREENLEY, Sarah	78	f.	Retired		Ire.

16	992/992	HOWELL, Thos.	59	m.	Farmer	400/300	Va.
17		Elisa	48	f.	Domestic		O.
18		Levi	26	m.	Farm laborer		"
19		Huldah	18	f.	Domestic		"
20		Davis	16	m.	Farmer		" S
21		Sydna	14	f.			" S
22		Precilla	11	f.			" S
23		Wm.	9	m.			" S
24		Marshal	7	m.			" S
25		Armanda	5	f.			" S

26	993/993	NOTTS, Lewis L.	63	m.	Farmer	240/300	Pa. I
27		Margaret	64	f.	Domestic		" I
28		Mary	37	f.	Domestic		"
29		Rebecca	33	f.	Domestic		O.
30		Malinda	24	f.	Domestic		"
31		Jas.	37	m.	Farm laborer		Pa.

32	994/994	NOTTS, Geo.	36	m.	Farm laborer	/150	Pa.	I
33		Margaret	37	f.	Domestic		O.	
34		Benjamin	12	m.			"	S
35		Wilson S.	9	m.			"	S
36	995/995	McCURDY, Aaron	43	m.	Farmer	/380	"	
37		Sarah	37	f.	Domestic		"	
38		Rachel	15	f.			"	S
39		John W.	14	m.			"	S

Page 146   24 July 1860   Sheet 207 verso

1		Mary	12	f.			O.	S
2		Martha A.	9	f.			"	S
3		Shanon L.	3	m.			"	
4	996/996	WIGGENS, Philip	55	m.	Farmer	2200/600	Va.	
5		Sarah	56	f.	Domestic		Pa.	
6		Geo.	18	m.	Farmer		"	S
7		David	16	m.	Farmer		"	S
8		HUGHS, Thos.	4	m.			"	
9	997/997	TSCHAPPATT, John	30	m.	Carpenter	/150	"	
10		Margaret	22	f.	Domestic		"	
11		Amanda J.	3	f.			"	
12		Oliver	1	m.			"	
13	998/998	GASTON, Eleanor	52	f.	Domestic	500/100	Eng.	1
14		Levina	18	f.	Domestic		O.	
15		Anne	16	f.	Domestic		"	
16	999/999	FAGINS, Robinson	33	m.	Farmer	/75	"	
17		Eliza J.	32	f.	Domestic		"	
18		Wm.	11	m.			"	S
19		Isibell	9	f.			"	S
20		Martha	7	f.			"	S
21		Saml.	4	m.			"	
22		Sarah	2/12	f.			"	
23	1000/1000	FAGINS, Thos.	35	m.	Day laborer	/100	"	
24		Sarah	33	f.	Domestic		"	
25		Oscar	9	m.			"	S
26		Jane	7	f.			"	S
27		Susianna	4	f.			"	
28		Albert	1	m.			"	
29		McMAHON, Susi-anna	64	f.	Retired		Md.	
30	1001/1001	BESKIRK, Mor-timer	23	m.	Day laborer	/150	O.	
31		Margaret	24	f.	Domestic		"	
32		Amanda J.	1	f.			"	
33	1002/1002	TIE, John	32	m.	Carpenter	650/250	Ger.	
34		Elisabeth	23	f.	Domestic		"	
35		Geo.	4	m.			Va.	
36		Catharine	2	f.			O.	

37	1003/1003	HENTHORN, Jesse	75	m.	Farmer	500/	Va.
38		Hannah	56	f.	Domestic		Pa.
39		Marinda	29	f.	Domestic		O.

Page 147   24 July 1860   Sheet 208

1		Isaac	22	m.	Farmer		O.
2		Nancy	17	f.	Domestic		"
3		Julianne	14	f.			"
4	1004/1004	HENTHORN, Elijah	25	m.	Farmer	/100	"
5		Nancy	24	f.	Domestic		"
6		Eliza J.	3	f.			"
7		Sarah A.	2	f.			"
8		Shannan	1/12	m.			"
9	1005/1005	GATTIN, Lewis	32	m.	Farmer	/100	"
10		Elisabeth	38	f.	Domestic		"
11		Congolton	8	m.			" S
12		Orlando	7	m.			"
13		Jane	5	f.			"
14		Casper	3	m.			"
15		Clarinda	1	f.			"
16	1006/1006	CROUGH, John	36	m.	Farmer	550/150	Ger.
17		Margaret	38	f.	Domestic		"
18		Catharine	9	f.			Va.
19		John	7	m.			"
20		Henry	5	m.			"
21	1007/1007	ARN, Adam	52	m.	Shoemaker		Sw.
22		Elisabeth	40	f.	Domestic		"
23		John	19	m.	Farm laborer		O.
24		Felix	18	m.	Farm laborer		"
25		Marthy	15	f.			" S
26		Rose A.	13	f.			" S
27		Saml.	11	m.			" S
28		Elisabeth	7	f.			" S
29		Mary	5	f.			"
30		Lewis	1	m.			"

(Salem Township Concluded)

(Jas. Okey, Asst. Marshall)

* * *

Jackson Township   P. O. Sardis

Page 148   25 July 1860   Sheet 209

1	1008/1008	DUNN, Joseph	40	m.	Preacher D.	800/275	Pa.
2		Lousinda	40	f.	Domestic		"
3		Israel	17	m.	Farmer		O. S
4		Rachel	13	f.			"
5		Alford	11	m.			" S
6		Saml. S.	8	m.			" S

7		DUNN, Mary	5	f.			O.
8		Marthy	3	f.			"
9	1009/1009	FARMER, Richard	43	m.	Farmer	2500/400	"
10		Marriah	38	f.	Domestic		"
11		Saml.	18	m.	Farmer		"
12		Margaret	14	f.			"
13		Jamima	12	f.			" S
14		Silena E.	10	f.			"
15		Jas.	7	m.			"
16		Napoleon	5	m.			"
17		Stephen	2	m.			"
18		Sophia	1	f.			"
19	1010/1010	TILTON, Sarah	55	f.	Domestic	/75	Md.
20		NORMAN, Richard	30	m.	Farmer	/200	O.
21	1011/1011	M--- Francisco	36	m.	Farmer	4700/700	Md.
22		MOFET, Hannah	32	f.	Domestic		Pa.
23		Saml. B.	10	m.			" S
24		Martha	8	f.			O. S
25		Geo.	5	m.			" S
26		Perry	4	m.			"
27		Margaret	3	f.			"
28		Wm.	1	m.			"
29	1012/1012	ROBINSON, John	49	m.	Farmer	2800/600	Pa.
30		Elisabeth	58	f.	Domestic		Va.
31		Benjamin	19	m.	Farmer		O. S
32		Elisabeth	16	f.	Domestic		" S
33		Melvina	14	f.			" S
34		FOUTY, Thos.	24	m.	Steamboat		Va.
35		Joseph P.	21	m.	Steamboat		O.
36		Lydia	18	f.	Domestic		"
37		HENDERSON, John	15	m.			"
38	1013/1013	ROBINSON, Timo-thy	25	m.	Farmer	/200	Pa.
39		Martha	24	f.	Domestic		"

Page 149   25 July 1860   Sheet 209 verso

1		James	4	m.			O.
2	1014/1014	HOSKINS, Arthur	40	m.	Farmer	/140	"
3		Eliza	39	f.	Domestic		"
4		Prisilla	16	f.	Domestic		" S
5		Sarapta	14	f.			" S
6		Adaline	11	f.			" S
7		Loxley	9	m.			" S
8		Wm.	7	m.			" S
9		Franklin	4	m.			"
10		PEGGS, Preston	28	m.	Farm laborer		"
11	1015/1015	BRAILFORD, Mar-iah	32	f.	Domestic	/40	"
12		Hannah	9	f.			"

13		BRAILFORD, Anja-line	3	f.			O.
14		Drusilla	76	f.	Retired		Pa.
15	1016/1016	JONES, Philip	50	m.	Farmer	/120	Md.
16		Polly B.	39	f.	Domestic		O.
17		Clarissa M.	22	f.	Domestic		"
18		Mary A.	19	f.	Domestic		"
19		Saml.	17	m.	Farmer		"
20		Susianna	15	f.			" S
21		Mahala	13	f.			" S
22		Wm. W.	8	m.			"
23		Silas P.	3	m.			"
24	1017/1017	TILTON, Wm.	72	m.	Farmer	1000/180	Va.
25		Clarissa	64	f.	Domestic		N.Y.
26		BOLDON, Jas.	25	m.	Day laborer		Md.
27	1018/1018	STOUT, Marshal	28	m.	Farmer	/350	Va.
28		Malthena	29	f.			"
29		Henderson	4	m.			"
30		Alsinda	2	f.			"
31		Clarinda	6/12	f.			"
32		NORMAN, Sarah A.	21	f.	Servant		Va.
33	1019/1019	SCOONOVER, Wm.	26	m.	Farmer	/350	O.
34		Christenia	25	f.	Domestic		"
35		Sarah V.	2	f.			"
36	1020/1020	McMAHON, John	72	m.	Physician	1500/800	Va.
37		Elisabeth	69	f.	Domestic		Pa.
38		WATSON, Stephen	44	m.	Farm laborer		O.23
39		KINKADE, Rebecca	15	f.			" S

Page 150   26 July 1860   Sheet 210

1	1021/1021	STEWART, Daniel	50	m.	Farmer	3200/650	Pa.
2		Rachel	37	f.	Domestic		O.
3		Isaac	21	m.	Farmer		"
4		Elisabeth	19	f.	Domestic		"
5		Frances	18	f.	Domestic		"
6		Sarah A.	16	f.	Domestic		"
7		Wm.	12	m.			"
8		John W.	10	m.			"
9		Jas. M.	8	m.			"
10		Joseph F.	4	m.			"
11		Thos. M.	2	m.			"
12		Harvy E.	1	m.			"
13		ACKLEY, Mary	56	f.	Domestic		Pa. I
14	1022/1022	SCHOONOVER, John	49	m.	Farmer	3000/450	"
15		Mary	47	f.	Domestic		" I
16		Jesse	19	m.	Farmer		O. S
17		Nancy	17	f.	Domestic		" S
18		John	14	m.			" S
19		Wesley	7	m.			" S
20		Thos. B.	4	m.			"
21		HENDERSON, Mary	6	f.			" S

22		SCHOONOVER, Danl.	23	m.	Farm laborer	350/150	O.	

23	1023/1023	MARTIN, Theadore	23	m.	Farm laborer	/100	Va.	
24		Elisabeth	21	f.	Domestic		O.	
25		Louisa	1	f.			"	

26	1024/1024	MARTIN, John W.	30	m.	Farmer	500/180	Va.	
27		Eliza J.	29	f.	Domestic		O.	
28		Franklin P.	7	m.			"	S
29		Nancy J.	2	f.			"	

30	1025/1025	GARDER, Josephus	35	m.	Farmer	1500/350	Pa.	
31		Nancy	33	f.	Domestic		O.	
32		Elisabeth	14	f.			"	S
33		Dudily W.	11	m.			"	S
34		Jas. M.	10	m.			"	S
35		Rebecca E.	7	f.			"	S
36		Mary V.	3	f.			"	
37		Ebenezer	1/12	m.			"	

| 38 | 1026/1026 | BITTLE, George | 62 | m. | Farmer | /360 | Pa. | |
| 39 | | Eliza | 48 | f. | Domestic | | Va. | |

Page 151   **26 July 1860**   **Sheet 210 verso**

1		Jane E.	22	f.	Domestic		O.	
2		Wm. D.	20	m.	Boating		"	
3		John H.	18	m.	Farmer		"	
4		ROBERTS, Wm.	72	m.	Farmer		Pa.	

5	1027/1027	HOSKINSON, Arch-						
		ibald	45	m.	Farmer	200/200	O.	
6		Sarah	50	f.	Domestic		"	
7		Oleva	19	f.	Domestic		"	
8		Clarinda	16	f.	Domestic		"	
9		Elisabeth J.	14	f.			"	S
10		Virginia C.	7	f.			"	S
11		Elisabeth E.	4	f.			"	

12	1028/1028	ELSON, Jas.	68	m.	Farmer	700/280	"	I
13		Hariet	58	f.	Domestic		"	I
14		Alexandria	20	m.	Day laborer		"	
15		Henry	17	m.	Day laborer		"	S
16		Jones	14	m.			"	S
17		Fluancy	10	f.			"	S

18	1029/1029	TICE, George	34	m.	Farmer	/370	Dar.	
19		Barbary	35	f.	Domestic		Wit.	
20		Fredrich	8	f.			Pa.	S
21		Mary L.	6	f.			"	S
22		John	5	m.			"	
23		Geo. W.	3	m.			O.	
24		Fredrick W.	1	m.			"	

25	1030/1030	RUSH, Slater B.	38	m.	Farmer	400/50	"	
26		Prudance	36	f.	Domestic		"	
27		John K.	16	m.	Farmer		"	S

28		RUSH, Rachel M.	13	f.			O.	S
29		Caroline	10	f.			"	S
30		Gemima	8	f.			"	S
31		Elisabeth	6	f.			"	S
32		Wm.	2	m.			"	
33		Willas	2	m.			"	
34		Mary B.	1/12	f.			"	
35	1031/1031	BROCK, Geo.	58	m.	Carpenter	700/50	Va.	
36		Elisabeth	48	f.	Domestic		Pa.	
37		Lousinda B.	17	f.	Domestic		O.	
38		Prudance A.	14	f.	Domestic		"	

Page 152   26 July 1860   Sheet 211

1	1032/1932	RUSH, Isaac	44	m.	Farmer	500/	Pa.	
2		Amy	42	f.	Domestic		O.	
3		Isaac O.	20	m.	Farmer		"	
4		Elisabeth	18	f.	Domestic		"	
5		Mary J.	17	f.	Domestic		"	S
6		Delila	14	f.			"	S
7		John C.	11	m.			"	S
8		Geo. G.	9	m.			"	
9		Maywood	8	m.			"	
10		Lorance	5	m.			"	
11		Daniel H.	1	m.			"	
12	1033/1033	BILLARD, Ugene	31	m.	Farmer	600/	Fr.	
13		Susianna	28	f.	Domestic		Ger.	
14		Augustus	7	m.			Sw.	
15		Alcid	4	m.			"	
16		Jas.	1	m.			"	
17	1034/1034	MORE, Elace P.	52	m.	Farmer	3200/600	Pa.	
18		Elisabeth J.	36	f.	Domestic		O.	
19		Malinda J.	11	f.			"	S
20		Ciclia S.	7	f.			"	S
21		Lora	2	f.			"	
22		Anne	68	m.	Domestic		Pa.	
23	1035/1035	CARR, Sanford	39	f.	Farmer	/150	Va.	
24		Susianna	35	f.	Domestic		Sw.	
25		Christopher	16	m.	Farmer		O.	S
26		John	15	m.			"	S
27		Amanda	10	f.			"	S
28		Sanford	8	m.			"	
29		Mary	6	f.			"	
30		Anne	4	f.			"	
31		Martha	1	f.			"	
32	1036/1036	GILMORE, Joseph	66	m.	Farmer	/100	Pa.	
33		Nancy	56	f.	Domestic		"	
34		Wesley	19	m.	Farmer		O.	
35		Otho	17	m.	Farmer		"	
36		Josephus	7	m.			Va.	
37		MARTIN, Jane	5	f.			O.	
38	1037/1037	WILSON, John	30	m.	Boating	/100	"	

39		WILSON, Matilda	28	f.	Domestic		O.	

Page 153   26 July 1860   Sheet 211 verso

1		Mary J.	3	f.			O.	
2		Mahela	1	f.			"	
3	1038/1038	ESTEL, Daniel	36	m.	Farmer	1000/100	Pa.	
4		Eleanor	34	f.	Domestic		Va.	
5		Lousinda	10	f.			O.	S
6		John	8	m.			"	S
7		Margaret	6	f.			"	S
8		Wm.	4	m.			"	
9		Roland	1	m.			"	
10	1039/1039	HUBARD, Jas.	35	m.	Boating	140/50	Va.	
11		Mary	33	f.	Domestic		O.	
12		Mary	14	f.			"	S
13		Sarah	12	f.			"	S
14		Jas. M.	8	m.			"	S
15		Lemina	4	f.			"	
16	1040/1040	BADGER, Chris- topher	30	m.	Farmer	/100	Sw.	
17		Frances	26	f.	Domestic		"	
18		Peter	2	m.			O.	
19		Godfrey	5/12	m.			"	
20	1041/1041	LONGWELL, John	30	m.	Farmer	/100	"	
21		Amanda	28	f.	Domestic		Va.	
22		Absolam	9	m.			O.	
23		John W.	7	m.			"	
24		Adaline	1	f.			"	
25	1042/1042	EARLEY, Benoni	63	m.	Farmer	400/75	Md.	
26		Elisabeth	54	f.	Domestic		Pa.	
27	1043/1043	FAGERT, Francis	41	m.	Farmer	300/65	Als.	
28		Anne	45	f.	Domestic		Sw.	
29		John	16	m.	Farmer		O.	
30		Isaac	14	m.			"	
31		Christopher	10	m.			"	
32		Selona	8	f.			"	
33	1044/1044	WAIT, Oben	31	m.	Farmer		"	
34		Eliza E.	26	f.	Domestic		"	
35	1045/1045	PEGGS, Elias	65	m.	Farmer	/50	Va.	
36		Elisabeth	46	f.	Domestic		N.Y.	
37		RESICKER, Mar- garet	22	f.	Domestic		O.	
38		Christian	20	m.	Day laborer		"	
39		Jacob	18	m.	Day laborer		"	

Page 154   27 July 1860   Sheet 212

1		Wm.	15	m.	Day laborer		O.	S
2		Mary	13	f.			"	S

3	1046/1046	MARTIN, Alex-					
		andria	36	m.	Boating	1000/80	O.
4		Elisabeth	31	f.	Domestic		Va.
5		Mary	2	f.			O.

6	1047/1047	HOSMAN, Benedec	37	m.	Farmer	900/300	Ger.	
7		Elisabeth	32	f.	Domestic		"	I
8		Caroline	3	f.			O.	
9		Elisabeth	1	f.			"	
10		CROPS, Christian	38	m.	Farmer		Ger.	

11	1048/1048	MENDROL, Jacob	59	m.	Farmer	900/175	"
12		Mary	36	f.	Domestic		"
13		John	3	m.			"
14		Alexander	1	m.			O.

15	1049/1049	WALTER, Fred	24	m.	Farmer		Sw.
16		Anne E.	21	f.	Domestic		"
17		Mary L.	9/12	f.			O.

18	1050/1050	WALTERS, Susiana	58	f.	Domestic	4000/700	Sw.
19		Christian	38	m.	Farmer		"
20		John	26	m.	Farmer		"
21		Benjamin	26	m.	Farmer		"
22		Margaret	17	f.	Domestic		"
23		Henry	15	m.			"

24	1051/1051	LEIDFORTH, John	32	m.	Farmer	1400/165	Ger.	
25		Rose A.	34	f.	Domestic		"	I
26		Alexandrine	9	f.			Pa.	
27		Rose A.	6	f.			"	S
28		John	3	m.			"	

29	1052/1052	CASUMAN, John	40	m.	Farmer	/75	Sw.
30		Barbary	39	f.	Domestic		"

31	1053/1053	MERPHY, Jas.	36	m.	Boating	/200	Del.	
32		Rebecca	40	f.	Domestic		Pa.	
33		John	23	m.	Farmer		Del.	
34		Jas. W.	16	m.	Farmer		O.	S
35		Sarah J.	13	f.			"	S
36		Nicholas	10	m.			"	S
37		Ruth A.	8	f.			"	S
38		Mary E.	4	f.			"	
39		Wm. J.	1	m.			"	

Page 155	27 July 1860	Sheet 212 verso

1	1054/1054	CANP, Saml.	29	m.	Farmer	/300	O.
2		Sarah A.	23	f.	Domestic		"
3		Abraham	4	m.			"
4		Mary M.	2	f.			
5		BRAILFORD, Arm-					
		strong	14	m.			"

6	1055/1055	RUTTER, Isaac	26	m.	Farmer	/100	"
7		Lydia	27	f.	Domestic		"

8		RUTTER, Mary E.	6	f.			O.
9		Sarah R.	3	f.			"
10		John M.	1	m.			"
11	1056/1056	FOUTY, John	44	m.	Farmer	2200/750	"
12		Mary J.	28	f.	Domestic		"
13		Thos. W.	10	m.			"
14		Mary E.	8	f.			"
15		Sarah F.	6	f.			Ind.
16		John F.	2	m.			O.
17		Charles W.	1	m.			"
18		Joseph P.	7/12	m.			"
19		MARTIN, Calvin	27	m.	Farm laborer		"
20	1057/1057	SOLEAS, James	34	m.	Farmer	/350	"
21		Sarah J.	22	f.	Domestic		"
22		Wm.	11/12	m.			"
23	1058/1058	SMITTLE, David	22	m.	Boating	/50	"
24		Barbary	19	f.	Domestic		"
25		Henry	2	m.			"
26		Duncon	27	m.	Boating	/50	"
27		Emily	22	f.	Domestic		"
28	1059/1059	MINGLER, John	44	m.	Farmer	/120	Sw.
29		Mary	47	f.	Domestic		"
30		John	21	m.	Boating		"
31		Mary	14	f.			" S
32		Elisabeth B.	13	f.			O. S
33		Godfrey	8	m.			" S
34		Wm.	8	m.			" S
35		Jacob	6	m.			" S
36	1060/1060	DON, Harvy	28	m.	Boating	/50	"
37		Amy	22	f.	Domestic		"
38		Virginia	2	f.			"

Page 156   **27 July 1860**   **Sheet 213**

1	1061/1061	FRAMPTON, David	57	m.	Boating	1400/100	Pa.
2		Amanda	41	f.	Domestic		D.C.
3		Thos. J.	18	m.	Boating		Pa.
4		Jas. L.	16	m.	Farmer		" S
5		Arthur	13	m.			O. S
6		David	11	m.			Pa. S
7		John	9	m.			O. S
8		Wm. H.	6	m.			"
9		Amanda C.	2	f.			"
10		Edward	1/12	m.			"
11	1062/1062	McMAHON, Wm.	47	m.	Farmer	/75	"
12		Mary	46	f.	Domestic		"
13		John G.	23	m.	Sawyer		"
14		Geo. W.	21	m.	Farmer		"
15		Wm. H.	20	m.	Boating		"
16		Mary A.	18	f.	Domestic		" S
17		Alfred D.	16	m.	Farmer		"

18		McMAHON, Susi-					
		anna	14	f.		O.	S
19		Lilly F.	12	f.		"	S
20		Sarah E.	7	f.		"	S
21		Charlotta	6	f.		"	
22		David S.	3	m.		"	
23	1063/1063	SMITTLE, Elisa-					
		beth	46	f.	Domestic	500/180	"	I
24		Ezekiel	19	m.	Farmer		"	
25		Aveline	17	f.	Domestic		"	
26		Gratia	13	f.		"	S
27	1064/1064	FAGGOTT, Wm.	27	m.	Farmer	/360	Va.
28		Catharine	28	f.	Domestic		Ger.
29		Louisa	5	f.		O.
30		Caroline	3	f.		"
31		Mary	4/12	f.		"
32	1065/1065	FAGERT, Michael	49	m.	Carpenter	300/492	Ger.
33		Thecla	46	f.	Domestic		"
34		Geo.	16	m.	Farmer		O.	S
35		Isarel	12	m.		"	S
36		Mary	8	f.		"	S
37		Alfona	3	f.		"
38		SELLERS, Barbary	73	f.	Domestic		Ger.

1	1066/1066	KNIGHT, Susianna	58	f.	Domestic	/125	Va.	I
2		Mary	70	f.	Domestic		"	I
3		HOSKINSON, Nancy	68	f.	Domestic		"	I
4		LEWIS, John	50	m.	Farm laborer		"	I
5	1067/1067	FOUTY, Isaac	26	m.	Boating	/200	"
6		Sarah	23	f.	Domestic		O.
7	1068/1068	WILSON, Wm.	67	m.	Wagon maker	/50	Pa.
8		Wm.	26	m.	Day laborer		"
9		David	21	m.	Day laborer		"
10		Nancy	20	f.	Domestic		O.
11	1069/1069	STEWART, I. D.	46	m.	Quireman	/50	Pa.
12		A. J.	43	m.	Quireman		"
13		ANDERSON, Jas.	28	m.	Blacksmith	/50	Va.
14		NOBLE, Wm.	23	m.	Quireman		Scot.
15		McKENTOSH, Wm.	33	m.	Quireman		"
16		SMITH, Rebecca	40	f.	Domestic		O.
17	1070/1070	RIGHT, Andrew J.	22	m.	Day laborer	/100	Va.
18		Rebecca	21	f.	Domestic		O.
19		John	3/12	m.		"
20	1071/1071	JANA, John M.	44	m.	Merchant	1000/2000	"
21		Silena	24	f.	Domestic		Va.
22		Jacob	19	m.	Boating		O.
23		Anna M.	15	f.		"	S

24		JANA, Jas. A.	4	m.			O.
25		Wm. S.	3	m.			"
26		John F.	10/12	m.			"

27	1072/1072	McFARLON, Joseph	48	m.	Farmer	4000/563	Pa.
28		Gratia	53	f.	Domestic		Mass.
29		KIRKLAND, Wm.	23	m.	Farmer		O.
30		KNIGHT, Elisa-					
		beth	16	f.	Domestic		"

31	1073/1073	MELOTT, John	45	m.	Farmer	/70	"	
32		Mary A.	43	f.	Domestic		Pa.	
33		Alexandria	21	m.	Farmer		O.	
34		Isiah	19	m.	Farmer		"	
35		Augustus	16	m.	Farmer		"	
36		Asberry	14	m.			"	
37		Mary L.	12	f.			"	1
38		John W.	10	m.			"	
39		Susiana	5	f.			"	

Page 158   27 July 1860   Sheet 214

1	1074/1074	BOON, Elam	40	m.	Farmer	600/280	O.	
2		Mary A.	41	f.	Domestic		"	I
3		Sophronia	18	f.	Domestic		"	
4		Nancy	16	f.	Domestic		"	
5		Sarah E.	11	f.			"	S
6		Lemuel	9	m.			"	S
7		Nichlon	6	m.			"	S

8	1075/1075	SHOEMAKER, Jacob	40	m.	Shoemaker	250/150	Ger.	
9		Christena	40	f.	Domestic		"	I
10		Mary	7	f.			O.	
11		Wm.	5	m.			Pa.	
12		GABRIEL, John	50	m.	Carpenter		Ger.	

13	1076/1076	COOPER, Francis					
		L.	27	m.	Farmer	700/180	Pa.
14		Mary	25	f.	Domestic		"
15		Mary J.	5	f.			"
16		John	4	m.			O.
17		Jesse	2	m.			"
18		Sarah	10/12	f.			"
19		Mary	63	f.	Domestic		Pa.

20	1077/1077	FLOWERS, Wm.	77	m.	Farmer	350/100	Eng.
21		Anne	63	f.	Domestic		Pa.
22		Theadore F.	28	m.	Farmer	/100	O.
23		Rachel	24	f.	Domestic		"
24		Wm.	1	m.			"

25	1078/1078	McNEELY, Thos.	36	m.	Farmer	500/100	Pa.
26		Richard	12	m.			O.
27		Anne	10	f.			"
28		Lusinda	6	f.			"
29		Hannah	4	f.			Va.

30	1079/1079	NORMAN, Richard	37	m.	Farmer	/50	"

31		NORMAN, Rebecca	36	f.	Domestic	Md.
32		Jane	16	f.	Domestic	Va. S
33		Rachel	13	f.		O. S
34		Wm.	10	m.		"
35		Susianna	7	f.		"
36		Daniel	6	m.		"
37		Lewis	2	m.		"
38	1080/1080	MAYHUGH, David	35	m.	Farmer 600/260	"
39		Sarah A.	29	f.	Domestic	"

Page 159   28 July 1860   Sheet 214 verso

1		Mary E.	9	f.		O.
2		Margaret	8	f.		"
3		Sarah J.	6	f.		"
4		Amanda	4	f.		"
5		Alexandria	2	m.		"
6		Rebecca	1/12	f.		"
7	1081/1081	ALLEN, Jas.	39	m.	Farmer	"
8		Gemima	25	f.	Domestic	"
9		Jesse	6	m.		" S
10		Saml.	5	m.		"
11		John	3	m.		"
12	1082/1082	BENNET, John	64	m.	Farmer /100	Pa.
13		Rachel	59	f.	Domestic	Md.
14		Elisha	26	m.	Day laborer	O.
15		Amos	24	m.	Day laborer	"
16		Geo. W.	13	m.		" S
17		Jessee	18	m.	Day laborer	" S
18		Simeon	20	m.	Day laborer	"
19	1083/1083	BENNET, Daniel	22	m.	Farmer	" M
20		Gemima	20	f.	Domestic	" M
21		Benjamin	1/12	m.		"
22	1084/1084	BENNET, John	36	m.	Farmer 1200/260	"
23		Lusinda L.	27	f.	Domestic	" I
24		David	6	m.		" S
25		Catharine	4	f.		"
26		Susianna	1/12	f.		"
27	1085/1085	CEHRS, Jacob	32	m.	Farmer 1200/250	Sw.
28		Christina	22	f.	Domestic	O.
29		Fleming	3	m.		"
30		Manerva	1	f.		"
31	1086/1086	CEHRS, Magdelena	68	f.	Domestic /50	Sw.
32		Anne	28	f.	Domestic	"
33		Matilda	7	f.		O.
34		Cornelia	2	f.		"
35	1087/1087	HENTHORN, Eli	51	m.	Farmer /270	"
36		Margaret	47	f.	Domestic 600/	Pa. I
37		Adam	27	m.	Farmer	O.

P. O. Salem   Jackson Township

38		HENTHORN, Eli	19	m.	Farmer		O.	

1		Henry	17	m.	Farmer		O.	
2		Mary F.	15	f.			"	
3		Elisabeth	13	f.			"	
4		Rose A.	10	f.			"	
5		Eliza J.	8	f.			"	
6		Sarah M.	6	f.			"	
7		Peter	3	m.			"	
8	1088/1088	EDDY, Isaac	37	m.	Farmer	800/75	Va.	
9		Easter	42	f.	Domestic		O.	
10		Elisabeth	17	f.	Domestic		"	S
11		Lawrence	16	m.	Farmer		"	S
12		Christiana	14	f.			"	S
13		Francis	12	f.			"	S
14		David	10	m.			"	
15		Isaac C.	7	m.			"	
16		Easter M.	4	f.			"	
17		Peter	2/12	m.			"	
18	1089/1089	REEVES, Elihu	43	m.	Farmer	1500/375	N.J.	
19		Jane	42	f.	Domestic		"	
20		RIGGLES, Adaline	8	f.			Va.	
21		TILFORD, Robt.	13	m.			O.	
22	1090/1090	EDDY, Henry	39	m.	Farmer	1000/200	Va.	
23		Nancy J.	30	f.	Domestic		O.	
24		Susianna	16	f.	Domestic		"	
25		Elisabeth	14	f.			"	
26		Josephus	7	m.			"	
27		Isaac G.	1	m.			"	
28	1091/1091	HENTHORN, John	22	m.	Farmer	/50	"	
29		Lyda A.	22	f.	Domestic		"	
30		Ezra	1	m.			"	
31		Huldah	2/12	f.			"	
32	1092/1092	HENTHORN, Nathan	40	m.	Farmer	/50	"	
33		Hulda	35	f.	Domestic		"	
34		Ruhane	17	f.	Domestic		"	
35		Margaret	13	f.			"	
36		Susiana	10	f.			"	
37		MEADOWS, John C.	15	m.			"	
38		Martin L.	14	m.			"	
39	1093/1093	TRUAX, Geo.	36	m.	Farmer	/200	"	

1		Jane	36	f.	Domestic		O.	
2		Hannah	14	f.			"	
3		Mary	12	f.			"	S
4		Jas.	10	m.			"	S
5		Margaret M.	8	f.			"	S

6		TRUAX, Susiana	5	f.			O.
7		Frances	2	f.			"
8	1094/1094	MYRES, Washing- ton	33	m.	Farmer	1500/250	"
9		Sarah	33	f.	Domestic		"
10		Mary J.	8	f.			" S
11		Geo.	6	m.			" S
12		Jas.	5	m.			" S
13		Wm.	4	m.			"
14		Abraham	1	m.			"
15	1095/1095	HENDERSHOT, Cas- per	32	m.	Day laborer	/250	Ill.
16		Frances	28	f.	Domestic		O.
17		Amos	13	m.			" S
18		Mary	11	f.			" S
19		Julia A.	9	f.			" S
20		Prugance	6	f.			" S
21		Hariet	3	f.			"
22	1096/1096	KENT, Lovetia	56	f.	Domestic	400/200	Pa.
23		Roseberry	19	m.	Farmer		"
24		Benjamin	15	m.	Farmer		"
25		Wm.	3	m.			O.
26	1097/1097	BARKER, Elas	48	m.	Farmer	360/200	Pa.
27		Sarah	43	f.	Domestic		O.
28		Cecelia	18	f.	Teacher		"
29		Emma	17	f.	Teacher		" S
30		Elmira	15	f.			" S
31		Mary	10	f.			" S
32		Martha	10	f.			" S
33		Sarah E.	6	f.			" S
34	1098/1098	BARKER, Jesse	29	m.	Farmer	1000/500	"
35		Mary M.	24	f.	Domestic		Va.
36		Louisa	6	f.			O. S
37		Viola	5	f.			" S
38		Leomi	3	f.			"
39		Susiana	1	f.			"

1		SANFORD, Clark	18	m.	Farm laborer		O.
2	1099/1099	COX, Andrew	27	m.	Farmer	/100	"
3		Lydia A.	27	f.	Domestic		"
4		McNEELY, Eliza	1	f.			"
5	1100/1100	BARKER, Moses	59	m.	Farmer	1500/720	Pa.
6		Sarah	53	f.	Domestic		"
7		Ezra	23	m.	Farmer		"
8		Noah	18	m.	Farmer		O. S
9		Jas.	16	m.	Farmer		" S
10		Geo. W.	14	m.			" S
11		Alvin	13	m.			" S
12		Sarah A.	11	f.			" S

13	1101/1101	STEWART, Peter	45	m.	Farmer	/125	Pa.
14		Martha	44	f.	Domestic	300/	O.
15		Nathan	22	m.	Farm laborer		"
16		John	20	m.	Farm laborer		"
17		Peter	18	m.	Farm laborer		"
18		Eleanor	14	f.			"
19		Elisabeth	12	f.			"
20		Alexandria	11	m.			"
21	1102/1102	BARKER, Elisha	37	m.	Farmer	500/200	Pa.
22		Rachel	36	f.	Domestic		O.
23		Benjamin	6	m.			"
24		John	4	m.			"
25		Sarah	3	f.			"
26		Lydia	3	f.			"
27		Elisha	2	m.			"
28		Delecia	1	f.			"
29	1103/1103	BARKER, Benjamin	27	m.	Farmer	/100	"
30		Mary E.	21	f.	Domestic		"
31		Alvin	6/12	m.			"
32	1104/1104	DENNIS, B. T.	39	m.	Farmer	/160	Va.
33		Lydia	41	f.	Domestic		"
34		Joseph	18	m.	Farmer		O.
35		Lydia A.	12	f.			" S
36		Geo. A.	10	m.			" S
37		FISHER, Wm.	40	m.	Day laborer		" I
38	1105/1105	HENTHORN, Adam	55	m.	Farmer	400/120	Va.
39		Drusilla	28	f.	Domestic		O.

Page 163			30 July 1860			Sheet 216 verso	
1		Jacob	24	m.	Day laborer		O.
2		Adam	20	m.	Day laborer		"
3		Geo.	15	m.			"
4		Martha	12	f.			"
5		Jacob	5	m.			"
6		Sarah	1	f.			"
7	1106/1106	SHOOK, Jas.	47	m.	Farmer	3400/700	Pa.
8		Zilpha	42	f.	Domestic		O.
9		John	24	m.	Boating		"
10		Jacob	22	m.	Farm laborer		"
11		Richard	21	m.	Farm laborer		"
12		Louisa	19	f.	Domestic		"
13		Isaac	15	m.			"
14		Mary E.	13	f.			" S
15		Thos.	11	m.			" S
16		Friend	10	m.			" S
17		Jas.	8	m.			" S
18		Elam	6	m.			" S
19		Benjamin	5	m.			" S
20		Sampson	3/12	m.			"
21	1107/1107	BARKER, John	28	m.	Farmer	/50	"
22		Eleanor	26	f.	Domestic		Pa.

23		BELFORD, John	21	m.	Day laborer		O. I
24		Drusilla	17	f.	Domestic		"
25	1108/1108	HENTHORN, Wm.	30	m.	Farmer	/50	"
26		Catharine	30	f.	Domestic		Pa. I
27		Frances	8	f.			O.
28		Charlotta	3	f.			"
29		Clarissa	8/12	f.			"
30		BELFORD, Darcus	62	f.	Retired		Pa. I
31	1109/1109	HUFMAN, Elinezer	29	m.	Carpenter	/100	O.
32		Dorcas	29	f.	Domestic		"
33		Sylvester	8	m.			"
34		James	6	m.			"
35		Nancy	2	f.			"
36		Daniel	4	m.			"
37	1110/1110	BRAILFORD, Benja-
min	39	m.	Farmer	/150	" I
38		Sarah	41	f.	Domestic		" I
39		Eleanor	19	f.	Domestic		"

1		John	16	m.	Day laborer		O.
2		Nathan	12	m.			"
3		Rebecca	8	f.			"
4		Dorcas	7	f.			"
5		Mary	5	f.			"
6		Wm. H.	4	m.			"
7		Barnabas	18	m.	Farm laborer		"
8	1111/1111	STEWART, Daniel	60	m.	Farmer	/60	Pa. I
9		Maria	39	f.	Domestic		O.
10		Roletta J.	14	f.			"
11	1112/1112	BROWN, Saml. S.	42	m.	Farmer	/100	Pa.
12		Sarah A.	41	f.	Domestic		"
13		Elisabeth	18	f.	Domestic		Va. S
14		Jesse	13	m.			" S
15		Phebe	9	f.			" S
16		John	4	m.			O.
17	1113/1113	BOORAD, Olaver
G.	24	m.	Farmer	/70	Pa.
18		Elisabeth	23	f.	Domestic		"
19		Sattira	1	f.			O.
20		Jas.	2/12	m.			"
21		BROOKS, Jas. A.	20	m.	Farmer		Pa.
22	1114/1114	BAILEY, Benjamin	24	m.	Farmer	/25	O.
23		Mary E.	21	f.	Domestic		Md.
24		Cordelia	1	f.			O.
25		Sarah E.	1/12	f.			"
26	1115/1115	BRIDGMAN, John	62	m.	Farmer	10,000/2520	Vt.
27		Mariah	55	f.	Domestic		Conn.

28		BRIDGMAN, Fran-ces	17	f.	Domestic	O.	S
29		Benjamin	13	m.		"	S
30		Wm.	8	m.		Va.	S
31	1116/1116	SAMOS, Jno.	47	m.	Farmer	/150	O. I
32		Elisabeth	35	f.	Domestic		" I
33		Alexandria	16	m.	Boating		"
34		Delila	13	f.			" S
35		Mary	10	f.			" S
36		Sarah	6	f.			" S
37	1117/1117	DON, Washington	54	m.	Farmer	600/250	N.Y.
38		Vesta	48	f.	Domestic		O.
39		Calvin	21	m.	Boating		"

Page 165   30 July 1860   Sheet 217 verso

1		McKINSY, Mary	24	f.	Domestic	O.	
2		Norcissa	10	f.		"	S
3		Isibell	3	f.		"	
4	1118/1118	CONNER, David	35	m.	Farmer	/100	"
5		Dicia	33	f.	Domestic		"
6		Jane	7	f.			"
7		John	4	m.			"
8		Selane	3	f.			"
9	1119/1119	CALVIN, John	23	m.	Farmer	150/160	" M
10		Eliza J.	21	f.	Domestic		Pa.
11		Jared	4/12	m.			O.
12	1120/1120	CALVIN, Sophia	51	f.	Domestic	150/160	Pa.
13		Raspberry	16	m.	Farmer		O.
14	1121/1121	COOPER, John H.	38	m.	Farmer	800/340	Pa.
15		Mary	42	f.	Domestic		"
16		Saml.	15	m.	Farm laborer		O. S
17		Julia A.	14	f.			" S
18		Caroline	11	f.			" S
19		Mary E.	9	f.			" S
20		Malissy	7	f.			" S
21		John H.	5	m.			" S
22		Eveline	3	f.			"
23	1122/1122	MISHINIC, Jacob	52	m.	Farmer	800/250	Ger.
24		Mary	44	f.	Domestic		"
25		Jacob	20	m.	Farmer		O.
26		Catharine	15	f.			"
27		Caroline	13	f.			"
28		Elisabeth	13	f.			"
29		John	12	m.			"
30		Rebecca	9	f.			"
31		Matilda	9	f.			"
32		Jas.	7	m.			"
33		Louisa	5	f.			"
34		Benjamin	3	m.			"

```
35  1123/1123  ALLEN, Francis    33    m.    Day laborer    /50     Va.
36             Hannah            30    f.    Domestic               O.
37             Winfield           8    m.                           "    S
38             Madison            5    m.                           "
39             Melvina         8/12   f.                            "
```

Page 166   30 July 1860   Sheet 218

```
1   1124/1124  HESS, Wm.         38    m.    Farmer      700/175    O.
2              Mary A.           34    f.    Domestic               Ger.
3              Harmon            10    m.                           Pa.
4              Wm.                8    m.                           "
5              Edward             6    m.                           "
6              John               3    m.                           "

7   1125/1125  BOON, Mahala      47    f.    Domestic      /40      O.
8              Arthur            18    m.    Farm laborer           "
9              Nancy J.           7    f.                           "    S

10  1126/1126  SMITH, Geo.       59    m.    Farmer        /70      Pa.
11             Elisabeth         53    f.    Domestic               "
12             Thos.             31    m.    Boating                "
13             Rachel            22    f.    Domestic               "
14             Elisabeth         19    f.    Domestic               "
15             Matilda           16    f.    Domestic               O.
16             Mahala            12    f.                           "
17             Lemuel            12    m.                           "
18             LINCY, John       13    m.                           "

19  1127/1127  MATHEWS, Isaac    53    m.    Farmer       /100      Pa.
20             Malinda           40    f.    Domestic               O.
21             Jacob             17    m.    Carpenter              "    S
22             Andrew J.         12    m.                           "    S
23             Alexandria         1    m.                           "
24             Lusinda           13    f.                           "    S
25             Marinda           10    f.                           "    S
26             Jonathon           9    m.                           "    S

27  1128/1128  MATHEWS, Elias    42    m.    Farmer       /100      "
28             Sarah A.          38    f.    Domestic               "
29             Andrew            17    m.    Farmer                 "
30             Jacob             15    m.    Farmer                 "
31             Mary E.           13    f.                           "
32             Elias              6    m.                           "
33             Isaac              4    m.                           "
34             David S.           2    m.                           "

35  1129/1129  WILEY, Geo. W.    23    m.    Farmer        /40      "    M
36             Sarah             19    f.    Domestic               "    M
37             Francis M.      1/12   m.                            "

38  1130/1130  WRIGHT, Wm.       34    m.    Farmer     1200/400    Pa.
39             Eleanor           29    f.    Domestic               O.
```

Page 167   30 July 1860   Sheet 218 verso

```
1              Mary              10    f.                           O.
```

2		WRIGHT, John T.	8	m.			O.
3		Elisabeth	5	f.			"
4		SOLES, Manervy	1?	f.			"
5		Isaac	15	m.	Farm laborer		"
5	1131/1131	SOLES, Jared	44	m.	Farm laborer		
						2200/500	Pa.
6		Catharine	38	f.	Domestic		Va.
7		Robert	11	m.			"
8		BURGS, David	18	m.	Farm laborer		O.
9	1132/1132	CINCLAIR, John	34	m.	Farmer	/50	Va.
10		Hester A.	22	f.	Domestic		"
11		Catharine	5	f.			"
12		Wm. F.	3	m.			O.
13		Jaret S.	6/12	m.			"
14		SOLES, Lydia	8	f.			Pa.
15	1133/1133	HISSON, David	55	m.	Farmer	500/170	"
16		Elisabeth	48	f.	Domestic		O.
17		Luthue	30	m.	Boating		"
18		John	17	m.	Farm laborer		"
19		Hannah	15	f.			"
20		David	13	m.			"
21		HISERN, Sarah	9	f.			"
22		David	4	m.			"
23		Henry	28	m.	Farmer		"
24	1134/1134	YOGER, Henry	51	m.	Farmer	1500/450	Ger.
25		Elisabeth	31	f.	Domestic		"
26		Charles	8	m.			O.
27		John	6	m.			"
28		Catharine	3	f.			"
29		Mary	1	f.			"
30		John	83	m.	Retired		Ger.
31	1135/1135	YOGER, John	49	m.	Farmer	1500/550	"
32		Elisabeth	41	f.	Domestic		Pa.
33		Jacob	18	m.	Farmer		"
34		Henry	13	m.			O.
35		David	11	m.			"
36		Conrod	6	m.			"
37		Christian	1	m.			"
38	1136/1136	ESMIRE, Harman	62	m.	Farmer	1000/500	Ger.

1		Elisabeth	61	f.	Domestic		Ger.
2		Henry	26	m.	Farm laborer		"
3		Lewis	19	m.	Farm laborer		Va.
4		Sopha	14	f.			"
5	1137/1137	STALINGS, Jas.	56	m.	Farmer	/75	Md.
6		Marthy	42	f.	Domestic		"
7		Joseph	17	m.	Farmer		"
8		Jas. W.	16	m.	Farmer		"

```
9                STALINGS, Rachel 12   f.                              O.
10                    Isabell       9   f.                              "
11                    Geo.          7   m.                              "
12                    Rebecca       5   f.                              "
13                    Malisy        3   f.                              "

14  1138/1138  FARR, Michael       40   m.   Farmer      /120 Ger.
15                    Elisabeth    30   f.   Domestic           "
16                    Henry         3   m.                      O.
17                    Catharine     1   f.                      "
18                    Margaret    3/12   f.                      "

19  1139/1139  SOLES, Catharine    30   f.   Domestic    /50  Va. I

20  1140/1140  WAGONER, Jacob      62   m.   Farmer      300/160 Ger.
21                    Joanne       55   f.   Domestic            "
22                    Gottlob      15   m.                       "   S
23                    Leeby         9   f.                       "

24  1141/1141  BELEL, Michael      27   m.   Farmer      1000/300 Wit.
25                    Catharine    37   f.   Domestic             "
26                    Catharine    11   f.                     Pa. S
27                    Elisabeth     9   f.                      "  S
28                    Henry         7   m.                      "  S
29                    Wm.           5   m.                      "
30                    John          3   m.                      O.

31  1142/1142  HATHORN, Wm.        35   m.   Farmer      3000/375   "
32                    Mary E.      33   f.   Domestic              "
33                    Ortha L.      4   f.                         "
34            SHOOK, Louisa        19   f.   Domestic              "
35            HANK, Harman         62   m.   Farm laborer   Ger.

36  1143/1143  MACOR, John         51   m.   Farmer      500/320    "
37                    Elisabeth    43   f.   Domestic              "
38                    Catharine    18   f.   Domestic              "
39                    Jacob         9   m.                         O.
```

Page 169   31 July 1860   Sheet 219 verso

```
1            BROWN, Catharine     62   f.   Domestic        Ger.

2   1144/1144  WINTER, John        40   m.   Farmer      600/100    "
3                     Margaret     60   f.   Domestic              "
4                     Mary         11   f.                         "
5                     Gertrude      9   f.                         "
6                     John          7   m.                         "
7                     Henry         5   m.                         "
8                     Catharine     1   f.                         O.

9   1145/1145  EARNES, Fred-
                    erick          45   m.   Shoemaker      Ger.
10                    Mary         34   f.   Domestic            "
11                    Christian     8   m.                     Pa.
12                    Mary          6   f.                      "
13                    Jacob         4   m.                     O.
14                    Louisa        1   f.                      "
```

15	1146/1146	EIKE, Lewis	47	m.	Farmer	600/250	Ger.	
16		Christina	44	f.	Domestic		"	
17		Charles	16	m.	Farm laborer		"	
18		Louisa	14	f.			"	
19		Wm.	6	m.			Pa.	
20		Mary	2	f.			O.	
21	1147/1147	LOHREY, Jacob	46	m.	Farmer	1000/260	Ger.	
22		Getrath	37	f.	Domestic		"	
23		Conrad	19	m.	Farm laborer		"	
24		John	17	m.	Farm laborer		"	
25		Henry	12	m.			O.	
26		Wm.	2	m.			"	
27		GROUSE, John	47	m.	Basket-maker		Ger.	
28	1148/1148	COTHER, Henry	60	m.	Farmer	/200	"	
29		Elisabeth	60	f.	Domestic		"	
30		ROSELY, August	7	m.			O.	
31	1149/1149	SOLES, Stephen	40	m.	Farmer	1000/400	Md.	
32		Catharine	38	f.	Domestic		O.	
33		Isaac	16	m.	Farmer		"	S
34		Jacob	14	m.			"	S
35		Levi	10	m.			"	S
36		Marthy	7	f.			"	S
37		Catharine	5	f.			"	
38		Jas. S.	3	m.			"	
39		Mary A.	1	f.			"	

Page 170   31 July 1860   Sheet 220

1	1150/1150	WEIGL, Lews	55	m.	Farmer	1600/520	Ger.	
2		Anne	48	f.	Domestic		"	
3		Henry	26	m.	Coal-digger		"	
4		Wm.	22	m.	Farm laborer		"	
5		August	20	m.	Farm laborer		"	
6		Anne	18	f.	Domestic		"	
7		John	14	m.			Pa.	S
8		Sarah	11	f.			"	S
9		Mary	10	f.			"	S
10		Jacob	8	m.			O.	S
11		Albert	6	m.			"	S
12		Elisabeth	4	f.				
13	1151/1151	ROSELEIB, Lewis	66	m.	Farmer	400/260	Ger.	I
14		Margaret	40	f.	Domestic		"	I
15		Catharine	17	f.	Domestic		O.	
16		Elisabeth	14	f.			"	
17		Louisa	10	f.			"	S
18		Phebe	8	f.			"	S
19		Christian	6	m.			"	
20		Heneretta	4	f.			"	
21		Sophia	1	f.			"	
22	1152/1152	MOHN, Nicholas	83	m.	Farmer	/50	Ger.	
23	1153/1153	HARTMAN, Andrew	48	m.	Farmer	500/350	"	

24	HARTMAN, Heneretta	46	f.	Domestic	Ger.	
25	Henry	19	m.	Farmer	"	S
26	Doraphy	16	f.	Servant	"	
27	Christian	14	m.		"	S
28	Caroline	11	f.		O.	S
29	John	8	m.		"	S
30	Mary	5	f.		"	
31	Eliza	1	f.		"	

32	1154/1154	HOLZWORTH, Frederick	50	m.	Farmer	1500/400	Ger.
33		Mary	51	f.	Domestic		"
34		Wm.	19	m.	Teacher		Pa.
35		Henry	18	m.	Farm laborer		"
36		Elisabeth	12	f.			O.

37	1155/1155	FROBISH, John	40	m.	Farmer	900/400	Ger. I
38		John	14	m.			O.
39		Elisabeth	12	f.			"

Page 171	31 July 1860	Sheet 220 verso

1	Wm.	10	m.		O.	
2	Sarah	8	f.		"	
3	Jacob	5	m.		"	
4	Philip	3	m.		"	
5	CONER, Barbary	46	f.	Domestic	Ger.	

6	1156/1156	HISON, Elson	29	m.	Farmer	400/275	O.
7		Nancy	31	f.	Domestic		Pa.
8		Jas.	9	m.			O. S
9		David	7	m.			" S
10		Isibell	4	f.			"
11		Eliza J.	1	f.			"
12		COLVIN, Cass B.	21	m.	Farm laborer		"

13	1157/1157	FROBISH, Michael	36	m.	Farm laborer	800/400	Ger.
14		Elisabeth	35	f.	Domestic		"
15		Rose A.	11	f.			O. S
16		James	9	m.			" S
17		Geo.	7	m.			" S
18		Michael	5	m.			" S
19		Frances	4	f.			"
20		Lewis	2	m.			"
21		Charlotta	6/12	f.			"

22	1158/1158	HISSOM, Thomas	32	m.	Farmer	500/200	" I
23		Mary	27	f.	Domestic		Pa.
24		Blenchy	11	f.			O. S
25		Luthur	10	m.			" S
26		Sarah E.	7	f.			" S
26		Jane	3	f.			"

27	1159/1159	CONNER, David	32	m.	Farm laborer	/50	"
28		Dycey	30	f.	Domestic		"

29		CONNER, Nancy	8	f.			O.	
30		John	6	m.			"	
31		Celena	3	f.			"	
32	1160/1160	BIERS, Jacob	30	m.	Farmer	/150	"	I
33		Hariet	27	f.	Domestic		Va.	
34		Isaac M.	4	m.			O.	
35		Nancy	5	f.			"	
36		Wm.	1	m.			"	
37		Susianna	1/12	f.			"	
38	1161/1161	McKNIGHT, Levi	26	m.	Farmer	/150	Va.	
39		Eleanor	24	f.	Domestic		O.	

Page 172   31 July 1860   Sheet 221

1		Mary E.	5	f.			O.	
2		Francis	2	m.			"	
3		Vilinda	2/12	f.			"	
4	1162/1162	SMITH, Job	28	m.	Farmer	/50	Pa.	
5		Sarah J.	21	f.	Domestic		O.	
6	1163/1163	RICHY, Conrod	31	m.	Farmer	500/260	Ger.	
7		Julia	25	f.	Domestic		Pa.	
8		Jacob	19	m.	Boating	400/	Ger.	
9		Jacob	6	m.			O.	
10		John	5	m.			"	
11		Conrod	4	m.			"	
12		Henry	2	m.			"	
13		Harmon	1	m.			"	
14	1164/1164	DARLING, Joseph	50	m.	Farmer	/50	Pa.	I
15		Jane	42	f.	Domestic		Va.	I
16		Prisilla	21	f.	Domestic		"	
17		Elisabeth	19	f.	Domestic		"	
18		Rachel	17	f.	Domestic		"	S
19		Saml.	15	m.			"	S
20		Bates	12	m.			O.	S
21		Adelia	10	f.			"	S
22		Lusinda	8	f.			Va.	S
23		Arminta	5	f.			"	
24		Margaret	1	f.			O.	
25	1165/1165	DUVALL, Zenus	34	m.	Farmer	400/350	"	
26		Rebecca	28	f.	Domestic		"	
27		Arminda	9	f.			"	S
28		Clarinda	6	f.			"	S
29		John	3	m.			"	
30		Wm. A.	8/12	m.			"	
31	1166/1166	COLVIN, Sally	54	f.	Domestic	200/150	Va.	
32		Robert	23	m.	Day laborer		O.	
33		Marshal	15	m.			"	
34		Emily	14	f.			"	
35		Alexandria	12	m.			"	S
36		HISSON, Anne	4	f.			"	
37		COLVIN, Charles	17	m.	Day laborer		"	

38	1167/1167	COLVIN, William	30	m.	Farmer	200/150	O.
39		Constta	30	f.	Domestic		" I

Page 173   31 July 1860   Sheet 221 verso

1		Roba	8	f.			O.
2		Lusinda	5	f.			"
3		Geo.	3	m.			"
4	1168/1168	HISON, Ruth	30	f.	Domestic	200/100	" I
5		Levina	15	f.			" S
6		Susianna	13	f.			" S
7		Alexandria	10	m.			" S
8		Henry	8	m.			" S
9	1169/1169	MARTIN, Gilbert	50	m.	Farmer	400/250	Pa.
10		Susianna	46	f.	Domestic		Va.
11		Mary L.	20	f.	Domestic		O.
12		Maria	16	f.	Domestic		" S
13		Josephene	8	f.			" S
14		Marthy	4	f.			"
15	1170/1170	MILLER, Peter	28	m.	Farmer	300/700	Sw.
16		Elisabeth	22	f.	Domestic		"
17		Carline	4	f.			O.
18		Amelia	1	f.			"
19	1171/1171	BRINFILL, Harison	31	m.	Cooper	150/150	Pa.
20		Magdalena	28	f.	Domestic		O.
21		Matilda	8	f.			" S
22		Wm. H.	3	m.			"
23		Geo. W.	1/12	m.			"
24	1172/1172	CLAY, Benedic	30	m.	Farmer	/50	Ger.
25		Barbary	28	f.	Domestic		"
26		Caroline	1	f.			O.
27	1173/1173	ROLES, John	60	m.	Farmer	300/200	Md.
28		Mariah	60	f.	Domestic		"
29		Elisabeth	31	f.	Domestic		O.
30		Anne	25	f.	Domestic		"
31		Eleanor	20	f.	Domestic		"
32		Jas.	15	m.			" S
33		CAMPBELL, Genney	8	f.			" S
34	1174/1174	ONHOUS, Jacob	30	m.	Farmer	300/	"
35		Rose	30	f.	Domestic		"
36		Jacob	5	m.			" S
37		Wm.	3	m.			"
38		John	1	m.			"
39		MORE, Marthy	8	f.			"

Page 174   31 July 1860   Sheet 222

1	1175/1175	ROLES, Jacob	26	m.	Farmer	/100	O.
2		Eliza	25	f.	Domestic		"

3		ROLES, Adda O.	1	f.			O.
4		Charles	1	m.			"
5	1176/1176	UMENSETTER, John	54	m.	Farmer	/250	Md.
6		Matilda	41	f.	Domestic		Pa.
7		Anjaline	20	f.	Domestic		Va.
8		Mary	18	f.	Domestic		O.
9		Zenda V.	17	f.			" S
10		Gracia	12	f.			" S
11		George	16	m.	Farmer		" S
12		John	10	m.			" S
13		Hannah	7	f.			" S
14		Ebenezer	4	m.			"
15		Sarah	4	f.			"
16		David	6/12	m.			"
17		JESEMIN, Ala-manda	1	m.			"
18	1177/1177	PANE, Stephen W.	24	m.	Farmer	/200	"
19		Elisabeth	22	f.	Domestic		"
20		Mary S.	3	f.			"
21		Wm. B.	1	m.			"
22	1178/1178	PAYERE, Truman	50	m.	Farmer	1000/200	N.Y.
23		Susianna	50	f.	Domestic		Va. I
24		Ruphus	21	m.	Farmer		O.
25		Dickson	19	m.	Farmer		" S
26		SNIDER, Henry	21	m.	Day laborer		"
27	1179/1179	ROLES, Benjamin	24	m.	Farmer	100/50	"
28		Anjalin	20	f.	Domestic		"
29	1180/1180	HASCON, Elson	50	m.	Farmer	/150	" I
30		Charity	53	f.	Domestic		Va. I
31		Monterille	27	m.	Boating		"
32		Clenton	23	m.	Boating		"
33		Theadocia	20	f.	Domestic		"
34		Ezekiel	18	m.	Boating		"
35		Archibald	16	m.	Farmer		O.
36		Vestia	13	f.			"
37		Comantha	11	f.			"
38		Wm. D.	8	m.			"
39	1181/1181	SHOOK, George	31	m.	Farmer	/150	Va.

Page 175   1 August 1860   Sheet 222 verso

Beginning of Cochransville.

1		Belinda	27	f.	Domestic		Va.
2		John	11	m.			" S
3		Rose A.	9	f.			" S
4		Sarah	8	f.			"
5		Elisabeth	7	f.			"
6		Catharine	5	f.			"
7		Ozias	1	m.			"
8	1182/1182	MARTIN, Washing-ton	35	m.	Farmer	/60	O.

9		MARTIN, Susianna	28	f.	Domestic	O.	
10		Sarah M.	10	f.		"	
11		Rebecca A.	8	f.		"	
12		Caroline	6	f.		"	
13		Thos. W.	4	m.		"	
14		David S.	1	m.		"	
15		Sarah	63	f.	Retired	N.Y.	
16	1183/1183	MOSSER, Christian	27	m.	Farmer	/1260 Sw.	I
17		Emily	22	f.	Domestic	O.	I
18		John	4	m.		"	
19		Frederick	2	m.		"	
20		Christian	6/12	m.		"	
21		MOSER, Frederick	23	m.	Farm laborer	Sw.	
22		FELLER, Nicholas	55	m.	Farm laborer	"	
23	1184/1184	ULLOM, Jesse	37	m.	Farm laborer	/100 Pa.	
24		Sarah W.	30	f.	Domestic	"	
25		Jas.	13	m.		"	S
26		Wm.	11	m.		"	S
27		Craven	9	m.		"	S
28		Franklin	7	m.		"	S
29		Ruphus	7	m.		"	S
30		Julian	4	f.		O.	
31		Margaret	2	f.		"	
32	1185/1185	ANDERSON, Ezekiel	35	m.	Farmer	/100 Pa.	I
33		Mary	33	f.	Domestic	"	I
34		Elizabeth	12	f.		"	
35		Wm.	6	m.		"	
36		Matilda	3	f.		"	
37	1186/1186	WHITON, Jas.	70	m.	Farmer	9000/800 Va.	
38		John	40	m.	Farmer	O.	
39		Rachel	38	f.		"	

1		Jane	35	f.	Domestic	O.	
2		COCHRAN, Sarah	33	f.	Domestic	"	
3		Amanda	28	f.	Domestic	"	
4		Isibell	25	f.	Domestic	"	
5		Susianna	21	f.	Domestic	"	
6		WHITON, Ebenezer	34	m.	Farm laborer	"	
7		John	23	m.	Farm laborer	"	
8		Leander	5	m.		"	
9	1187/1187	WITON, Rachel	75	f.	Domestic	9000/800 Pa.	
10		Anne	51	f.	Teacher	O.	
11		Nichlom	35	m.	Steamboat pilot	"	
12		Jermiah	37	m.	Steamboat pilot	"	
13		Rachel	33	f.	Domestic	"	
14		MUSSER, Julia A.	26	f.	Domestic	"	
15		Ruth	24	f.	Domestic	"	
16		PARKER, Wm.	7	m.		"	S

17		WITON, Jas.	43	m.	Pilot		O.	
18		Joseph	30	m.	Farmer		"	
19		Thos.	46	m.	Pilot		"	
20	1188/1188	GARDEN, Charles	27	m.	Farmer	/200	Va.	
21		Manerva	22	f.	Domestic		Ind.	
22		Nellie	3	f.			"	
23		Elisabeth	1	f.			"	
24	1189/1189	GARDEN, Ruth	50	f.	Domestic	20,000/200	Va.	
25		Nicholas	21	m.	Molder		"	
26		James	16	m.	Farmer		"	
27		Henry	25	m.	Farmer		"	
28		Mary	18	f.	Domestic		Ire.	
29		DUNCAN, Mary A.	50	f.	Domestic		Mo.	
30		CLOPLIN, Edward	8	m.			Ind.	
31	1190/1190	RODES, Dickeson	37	m.	Day laborer	/150	O.	
32		Hettereogenia	34	f.	Domestic		"	
33		Cassa	17	f.	Domestic		"	
34		John M.	15	m.			"	
35		Gracia	10	f.			"	
36		Benoni	8	m.			"	
37		Sarah	6	f.			"	
38		Catherine	3	f.			"	
39		Alexandria	6/12	m.			"	

| Page 177 | | | 1 August 1860 | | | | Sheet 223 verso | |

1	1191/1191	LANON, Daniel	32	m.	Tailor	150/80	Va.	
2		Euphama	25	f.	Domestic		"	
3		Sophia A.	11	f.			"	
4		Eliza J.	6	f.			"	
5		Charles N.	2	m.			"	
6	1192/1192	HUBARD, Rosewell	35	m.	Blacksmith	/400	Pa.	
7		Procidence	34	f.	Domestic		O.	
8		Gerome	13	m.			"	S
9		Henry	9	m.			"	S
10		Melvin S.	7	m.			"	S
11		Orbilled	5	m.			"	
12		Charles	3	m.			"	
13		Sarah C.	4/12	f.			"	
14	1193/1193	HUBARD, Ephram	26	m.	Farmer	/200	"	
15		Rachal	19	f.	Domestic		"	
16		Lewis E.	2/12	m.			"	
17	1194/1194	HUBARD, Hariet	56	f.	Domestic	/200	N.Y.	
18		Porter	15	m.			O.	
19		Erastus V.	24	m.	Boating		"	
20	1195/1195	TRIPET, Wm.	59	m.	Farmer	10,000/700	Va.	
21		Elisabeth	54	f.	Domestic		N.J.	
22		Jesse G.	22	m.	Miner		Va.	
23		Mary J.	15	f.			"	
24		Thos. B.	13	m.			"	

25	1196/1196	BOWLES, Jesse	57	m.	Farmer	400/120	Md.
26		Eliza E.	35	f.	Domestic		O.
27		Geo.	19	m.	Farmer		"
28		Jesse	16	m.	Farmer		"
29		Marion	14	m.			"
30		David	11	m.			"
31		Manervy	9	f.			"
32		Wm.	7	m.			"
33		John	4	m.			"
34		Hariet	3	f.			"
35		Mary E.	1	f.			"

36	1197/1197	RUSELL, Charles P.	36	m.	Farmer	4000/1225	Va.
37		Ruth C.	32	f.	Domestic		"

38	1198/1198	DEIST, Rinehart	27	m.	Farmer	400/250	Ger. I
39		Mary	25	f.	Domestic		"

Page 178			1 August 1860			Sheet 224
1		Henry	2/12	m.		O.

2	1199/1199	TUEAL, Daniel	38	m.	Farmer	300/250	"
3		Dianna	28	f.	Domestic		Va.
4		Gratia	11	f.			O. S
5		Consignee	9	m.			" S
6		Virginia	7	f.			" S
7		Cince	5	m.			"
8		Theadora	3	f.			"
9		Staford	1	m.			"

10	1200/1200	TUEL, Daniel	68	m.	Farmer	/100	Va.
11		Mary	68	f.	Domestic		" I
12		BOLEN, Eliza	19	f.	Servant		O.

13	1201/1201	CLUTTER, John	38	m.	Day laborer	/50	"
14		Elisabeth	30	f.	Domestic		"
15		Mary F.	5	f.			"
16		John S.	2	m.			"

17	1202/1202	LISK, John	36	m.	Day laborer	/75	"
18		Sarah	30	f.	Domestic		" I
19		Louisa	7	f.			"
20		Harvy	5	m.			"
21		Arena	3	f.			"
22		Angaline	2/12	f.			"

23	1203/1203	CISSON, L. E.	34	m.	Grocer	800/600	Va.
24		Martha C.	34	f.	Domestic		Pa.
25		Columbia	11	f.			Ill. S
26		Henry H.	7	m.			O. S
27		Margaret	3	f.			Va.
28		Sarah G.	1	f.			O.

29	1204/1204	MARLOW, Isaac	35	m.	Boating	100/175	"
30		Margaret	49	f.	Domestic		"

31		MARLOW, Leonard	22	m.	Boating	O.
32		Mary A.	20	f.	Domestic	"
33		Jas. W.	18	m.	Boating	"
34		John	16	m.	Day laborer	" S
35		David	14	m.		" S
36		Allen	12	m.		" S
37		Hariet J.	5	f.		"
38	1205/1205	CRUMP, John	53	m.	Farmer	6000/500 Va.
39		Ruth	56	f.	Domestic	Pa.

Page 179   1 August 1860   Sheet 224 verso

1		Lewis W.	20	m.	Boating	/150 Va.
2		Jas.	18	m.	Farmer	"
3	1206/1206	CRUMP, David	46	m.	Farmer	/100 O.
4		Eleanor	44	f.	Domestic	"
5		Thos.	16	m.	Day laborer	"
6		Elisabeth	10	f.		"
7		Matilda	7	f.		"
8		Leander	3	m.		"
9	1207/1207	MITCHEL, Thos.	28	m.	Farmer	800/300 "
10		Melvina	24	f.	Domestic	N.Y.
11		Flora	3	f.		O.
12	1208/1208	MITCHEL, John	26	m.	Boating	/100 "
13		Abagal	20	f.	Domestic	Pa.
14	1209/1209	CLINE, Geo. W.	40	m.	Cooper	500/350 O.
15		Mary	45	f.	Domestic	"
16		Charles	19	m.	Merchant	" S
17		Isabelle	15	f.	Servant	" S
18	1210/1210	ARMSTRONG, Robert				
			38	m.	Carpenter	300/300 Pa.
19		Elisabeth	35	f.	Domestic	O.
20		Narcissa	9	f.		"
21	1211/1211	SALISBURG, John	30	m.	Farmer	/350 "
22		Celesta A.	24	f.	Domestic	"
23		Melvina	2	f.		"
24		Francis	6/12	m.		"
25	1212/1212	CRUMP, Wm. H.	24	m.	Merchant	/300 Va.
26		Mary E.	22	f.	Domestic	"
27		J. R.	27	m.	Merchant	/300 "
28	1213/1213	COCHRAN, Geo. W.	27	m.	Farmer	/250 O.
29		Mary	25	f.	Domestic	"
30		Jas. R.	3	m.		"
31		Elisabeth J.	7/12	f.		"
32		BELL, Christena	68	f.	Domestic	Ire.
33		Edward	19	m.	Teacher	/50 O.
34	1214/1214	COCHRAN, Thos.	60	m.	Farmer	9000/750 Va.
35		Mary A.	55	f.	Domestic	"

36		COCHRAN, Mary E.	23	f.	Domestic	O.
37		Melvina	21	f.	Domestic	"
38		Sarah A.	19	f.	Domestic	"
39		Violinda	17	f.	Domestic	"

Page 180   1 August 1860   Sheet 225

| 1 | | Harison | 16 | m. | Farmer | O. |
| 2 | | Friend | 14 | m. | | " |

3	1215/1215	HOTT, Noah	43	m.	Farmer	/200	Va.	I
4		Sarah	42	f.	Domestic		Pa.	I
5		Susianna	19	f.	Domestic		O.	
6		Catharine	17	f.	Domestic		"	
7		Noah P.	15	m.	Farmer		"	
8		John H.	12	m.			"	
9		Sarah E.	9	f.			"	
10		Andrew J.	5	m.			"	
11		James B. F. P.	3	m.			"	

| 12 | 1216/1216 | LITTLE, Saml. | 23 | m. | Farmer | /50 | " |
| 13 | | Lydia | 22 | f. | Domestic | | " |

14	1217/1217	EVONS, Anthony	38	m.	Farmer	/150	"	
15		Deborah	36	f.	Domestic		"	
16		Lusinda	7	f.			"	
17		Anthony	4	m.			"	
18		Francis M.	3	m.			"	
19		Rhoda	1	f.			"	
20		WHITE, Hamilton	12	m.			"	S
21		Jackson	10	m.			"	S
22		John	8	m.			"	

23	1218/1218	BRADFIELD, John	40	m.	Farm laborer	/50	Va.	
24		Gratia	30	f.	Domestic		O.	
25		Elisabeth	14	f.			"	S
26		Charles	13	m.			"	S
27		Joshua	9	m.			Ky.	S
28		John H.	6	m.			"	
29		Arthur	5	m.			"	
30		KID, Elisabeth	75	f.	Domestic		Md.	
31		Eleanor	50	f.	Domestic		Va.	

32	1219/1219	SNIDER, Andrew	42	m.	Farmer	2000/550	Ger.
33		Rebecca	32	f.	Domestic		Va.
34		Margaret	14	f.			"
35		John N.	9	m.			"
36		Josephus	7	m.			"
37		Andrew C.	4	m.			"
38		Eliza	2	f.			"
39		Thomas	2/12	m.			"

Page 181   2 August 1860   Sheet 225 verso

1	1220/1220	BRADFIELD, Joshua					
			30	m.	Farmer	1200/250	O.
2		Caroline	30	f.	Domestic		"
3		Marthy A.	7	f.			"

```
4              BRADFIELD, Mary
               E.              5    f.                              O.
5              Wm.             3    m.                              "
6              Layfayett      2/12  m.                              "

7   1221/1221  KNAPP, Charles A.24   m.   Turner      600/150  Pa.
8              Sarah T.       22   f.   Domestic               O.
9              Ella M.         2   f.                           "
10             Ida M.        3/12  f.                           "

11  1222/1222  KNAPP, Willison 25   m.   Miller      600/150  Pa.
12             Purlina        24   f.   Domestic               O.
13             John W.         4   m.                           "   S
14             Mary M.         2   f.                           "
15             Robert M.     8/12  m.                           "
16             McMULLEN, Pheba
               J.             21   f.   Servant                 "

17  1223/1223  HUBBARD, Begoner 41  m.   Day laborer   /100  Conn.
18             Magdelena      40   f.   Domestic               Va.
19             Sarah E.       13   f.                           O.
20             Frances E.     12   f.                           "
21             Harvy          10   m.                           "
22             Sherman         9   m.                           "
23             Wilsey          7   m.                           "
24             John C.         3   m.                           "

25  1224/1224  JONSON, Enoch   27   m.   Farmer      4500/750  Va.
26             Charlotta      27   f.   Domestic               O.
27             Eva             3   f.                           "
28             Bertha          1   f.                           "
29             Wm.           2/12  m.                           "

30  1225/1225  HUBARD, Thos.   30   m.   Day laborer   /100    "
31             Sitha          25   f.   Domestic               "
32             Harvy C.       10   m.                           "
33             Hariet T.       8   f.                           "
34             Catharine       6   f.                           "
35             Sarah A.        4   f.                           "
36             Mary E.         1   f.                           "

37  1226/1226  WHITNEY, Enoch  22   m.   Farmer       300/100   "
38             Eveline        18   f.                           "
39             John          1/12  m.                           "
```

Page 182   2 August 1860   Sheet 226

```
1   1227/1227  FOLGER, H. L.   31   m.   Farmer      1250/330  Va.
2              Margaret       31   f.   Domestic               "
3              Josephene      13   f.                           O.  S
4              Bushrod F.     10   m.                           "   S
5              Hellen E.       8   f.                           "   S
6              Otho Mc.        5   m.                           "   S
7              Oliver          1   m.                           "

8   1228/1228  McKNIGHT, Char-
               les T.         23   m.   Farmer        /100     "
9              Elisabeth C.   18   f.   Domestic               "
```

```
10          McKNIGHT, Flora
            A.              4/12  f.                                    O.

11 1229/1229 McKNIGHT, Wm.    65   m.     Farmer      1000/200  Va.
12           Margaret         45   f.     Domestic              O.
13           Isaac N.         14   m.                           "     S
14           Clarissa         12   f.                           "     S

15 1230/1230 McKNIGHT, John   35   m.     Farmer      /150      Va.
16           Lucretia         30   f.     Domestic              O.
17           Elisabeth        19   f.                           "
18           Jas. B.           7   m.                           "
19           Theadore          5   m.                           "
20           Semantha          3   f.                           "
21           Mary              1   f.                           "

22 1231/1231 McKNIGHT, Jas. B.28   m.     Farmer      100       Va.
23           Elisabeth        24   f.     Domestic              O.
24           Windfield         4   m.                           "
25           Mary A.           3   f.                           "
26           Viola J.        10/12 f.                           "
27           DYE, Benjamin    42   m.     Day laborer           "

28 1232/1232 SOERGEL, John H. 37   m.     Farmer      600/225   Ger.
29           Julia            30   f.     Domestic              Pa.
30           Mary              8   f.                           "
31           Sarah             4   f.                           O.
32           Wm.               3   m.                           "
33           James             1   m.                           "
34           LUDOLPH, Henry   37   m.     Farmer      400/200   Ger.
35           Catharine        35   f.     Domestic              "
36           John              9   m.                           O.
37           Conrod            7   m.                           "
38           Henry             5   m.                           "
39           Reinhart          3   m.                           "
```

```
1            Caroline          1   f.                           O.

2  1233/1233 McWILLIAM, John  44   m.     Farmer      2500/450  "
3            Marthy           40   f.     Domestic              "
4            Margaret         13   f.                           "     S
5            Hannah           11   f.                           "
6            Josephene E.      9   f.                           "
7            Marthy            7   f.                           "
8            Jas. S.           5   m.                           "
9            John R.           3   m.                           "
10           Mary E.         2/12 f.                            "

11 1234/1234 JUSTICE, George  26   m.     Day laborer  /75      "     I
12           Levitia J.       23   f.     Domestic              "
13           John W.           3   m.                           "
14           Frederick E.      1   m.                           "

15 1235/1235 CALHOON, Saml.   47   m.     Engineer     800/250  Pa.
16           Elisabeth        46   f.     Domestic              O.
```

17		CALHOON, John C.	26	m.	Engineer		O.	
18		Geo. S.	21	m.	Farmer		Pa.	
19		Catharine	18	f.	Domestic		O.	
20		Eliza A.	16	f.	Domestic		"	
21		Alice A.	13	f.			"	
22		Andrew J.	9	m.			"	
23		HUGHS, Mary	6	f.			"	
24		Elisabeth	4	f.			"	
25	1236/1236	CLUTTER, Martin	26	m.	Day laborer	/75	"	
26		Sarah	30	f.	Domestic		Pa.	I
27		Saml.	7	m.			O.	
28		Thos. M.	5	m.			"	
29		Jas. W.	4	m.			"	
30		John L.	1	m.			"	
31		Wm. W.	1/12	m.			"	
32	1237/1237	CLARK, Wm.	53	m.	Farmer	/250	"	
33		Dortha	46	f.	Domestic		Pa.	
34		John	22	m.	Farm laborer		Va.	
35		Jane	20	f.	Domestic		"	
36		Milton	15	m.			"	
37		Sydena	13	f.			"	
38		Jesse	11	m.			"	
39		Benton	7	m.			"	

Page 184   2 August 1860   Sheet 227

1		Marion	6	m.			O.
2		Rachel	2	f.			"
3	1238/1238	BOCHITE, Geo.	53	m.	Farmer	1500/400	Ger.
4		Mary	47	f.	Domestic		"
5		Geo.	23	m.	Boating		O.
6		Bernitt	21	m.	Farm laborer		"
7		John F.	5	m.			"
8	1239/1239	IRVING, Robert	28	m.	Farmer	/50	"
9		Elisabeth	25	f.	Domestic		Pa.
10	1240/1240	RUDOLT, Conrod	60	m.	Farmer	350/150	Ger.
11		Elisabeth	55	f.	Domestic		"
12		Susianna	18	f.	Domestic	300/	Pa.
13	1241/1241	LUNDOLPH, Conrod	65	m.	Farmer	400/250	Ger.
14		Elisabeth	63	f.	Domestic		"
15		Susianne	18	f.	Domestic		Pa.
16	1242/1242	BOWMAN, Fred-					
		erick	38	m.	Farmer	400/200	Ger.
17		Margaret	37	f.	Domestic		"
18		John	2	m.			O.
19		Margaret	1/12	f.			"
20		LUTTER, John	4	m.			"
21		SHIE, Geo.	58	m.	Farmer		Ger.
22	1243/1243	MOOD, Henry	49	m.	Farmer	300/256	Ger.

23		MOOD, Elisabeth	48	f.	Domestic	Ger.
24		Mary	17	f.	Domestic	Pa.
25		Catharine	15	f.		"
26		Margaret	12	f.		"
27		John	7	m.		O.
28	1244/1244	LOHER, Michel	34	m.	Farmer	800/400 Fr.
29		Catharine	39	f.	Domestic	Ger.
30		John	19	m.	Farm laborer	Pa.
31		Frederick	17	m.	Farm laborer	"
32		Rachel	14	f.		"
33		Jacob C.	9	m.		O.
34		Caroline M.	7	f.		"
35		Catharine	4	f.		"
36		Martin G.	1	m.		"
37	1245/1245	WRIGHT, Martin	45	m.	Farmer	300/200 Ger. I
38		Thursa	36	f.	Domestic	" I
39		Barbary	6	f.		Pa.

Page 185			2 August 1860			Sheet 227 verso
1		Frederick	4	m.		O.
2		Joseph	3	m.		"
3		George	8/12	m.		"
4	1246/1246	HANLINE, John	41	m.	Farmer	650/250 Ger.
5		Margaret	32	f.	Domestic	" I
6		John	13	m.		Pa.
7		Sophia	10	f.		"
8		Louisa	7	f.		"
9		Lina	5	f.		"
10		Henry	3	m.		"
11		Geo.	2	m.		"
12		Adam	4/12	m.		"
13	1247/1247	MIRACLE, Jacob	45	m.	Farmer	/100 Ger.
14		Dortha	42	f.	Domestic	"
15		Modice	18	m.		"
16	1248/1248	KREIG, Geo.	29	m.	Farmer	600/200 Ger.
17		Catharine	22	f.	Domestic	"
18		Christiana	6	f.		O.
19		Henry	4	m.		"
20		William	2	m.		"
21		John	5/12	m.		"
22	1249/1249	BYER, Conrod	50	m.	Farmer	400/200 Ger.
23		Elisabeth	54	f.	Domestic	"
24		Elisabeth	17	f.	Domestic	O.
25		Daniel	14	m.		"
26	1250/1250	CLUTTER, John T.	68	m.	Farmer	400/50 Pa.
27		Catharine	62	f.	Domestic	Del.
28		Jas. W.	19	m.	Farmer	O.
29		Jas. J.	8	m.		" S
30	1251/1251	JUSTICE, Geo. W.	30	m.	Farmer	/50 "

P. O. Cochransville   Jackson Township

31		JUSTICE, Lavitia	27	f.	Domestic	O.
32		John W.	3	m.		"
33		Frederick A.	1	m.		"
34	1252/1252	SCARBROUGH, Wm.	35	m.	Farmer	800/160 Md.
35		Elsey	24	f.	Domestic	O.
36		STEWARD, Ezekiel	16	m.	Farm laborer	"

(Jackson Township Concluded)

(Jas. Okey, Ass't. Marshal)

* * *

P. O. Calais   Seneca Township

__Page 1__   4 June 1860   Sheet 229

1	1/1	STEPHEN, Elijah	32	m.	Farmer	3100/465	O.
2		Sarah A.	26	f.	Domestic		Pa.
3		John W.	8	m.			O. S
4		James R.	6	m.			" S
5		Mary L.	4	f.			" S
6		Joseph M.	2	m.			"
7		Lucy J.	2/12	f.			"
8		WILLIS, Mary E.	16	f.	Domestic		"
9		CLEVELAND, Frank-					
		lin	19	m.	Farm laborer		"
10	2/2	BRIDGEMAN, William	26	m.	Farmer	/150	Va. I
11		Mary	21	f.			O.
12		Rachel L.	10/12	f.			"
13		James	20	m.	Farm laborer		Va.
14		HEARL, Nancy	60	f.	Domestic		"
15	3/3	EDGAR, John	29	m.	Farmer	/100	Pa.
16		Ann	27	f.	Domestic		O.
17		George	6	m.			" S
18		William T.	4	m.			"
19		Elisabeth	3	f.			"
20		Ruth	71	f.	Domestic		Pa. I
21	4/4	JOHNSON, John	44	m.	Farmer	/40	"
22		Mariah	34	f.	Domestic		"
23		Appollo	16	m.	Farm laborer		O.
24		Nancy	13	f.			"
25		David	11	m.			"
26		Levi	9	m.			"
27		Emma	7	f.			"
28		John H.	2	m.			"
29	5/5	GALLAGHER, Nancy	45	f.	Farmer	1200/100	Ire.
30		Lydia A.	20	f.	Domestic		O.
31		Mary E.	18	f.	Domestic		" S
32		Rosanna	16	f.	Domestic		" S
33		Sarah J.	13	f.			" S
34		John	9	m.			" S

35		GALLAGHER, Annie	6	f.			O.
36		Edmund	5	m.			"
37	6/6	DAILY, Vincent	25	m.	Farmer	/150	" I
38		Mariah	26	f.	Domestic		"
39		John M.	1	m.			"
40		BALT, Bazel	30	m.	Laborer		Va.

Page 2		4 June 1860				Sheet 229 verso	
1	7/7	DAILY, James	58	m.	Farmer	2500/412	O.
2		Rachel	49	f.	Domestic		" I
3		Peter	23	m.	Farm laborer		"
4		Elisabeth	20	f.	Domestic		"
5		Robert	18	m.	Farm laborer		"
6		John	15	m.			" S
7		Margaret	14	f.			" S
8		Rachel	11	f.			" S
9		JONES, Hannah	11	f.			" S
10		MAHOLLAND, Rachel	30	f.	Domestic		"
11	8/8	RAILING, John	28	m.	Farmer	/100	" I
12		Jane	21	f.	Domestic		" I
13		Eliza A.	5	f.			"
14		Solomon	3	m.			"
15		Rosanna	1	f.			"
16	9/9	CARPENTER, Jacob	45	m.	Farmer	1000/300	"
17		Rebecca	44	f.	Domestic		" I
18		Mary	20	f.	Domestic		" I
19		Francina	16	f.			" S
20		James	14	m.			" S
21		Lavina	13	f.			" S
22		Elisabeth	11	f.			" S
23		Lydia	9	f.			"
24		Anise	7	f.			"
25		Jacob	5	m.			"
26		Nancy J.	3	f.			"
27		GILMORE, Sarah	9	f.			" S
28		Josiah	1	m.			"
29	10/10	CARPENTER, John Sr.	76	m.	Farmer	4800/82	Va.
30		Rosanna	66	f.	Domestic		Pa.
31		Mary	16	f.	Domestic		O. S
32	--/11	CARPENTER, John Jr.	30	m.	Farm laborer	/100	" I
33		Nancy	27	f.	Domestic		" I
34		Jacob	6	m.			"
35		John	2	m.			"
36		Mary J.	2	f.			"
37	11/12	CARPENTER, Giles-					
		pie	28	m.	Farm laborer	/150	" I
38		Savilla	27	f.	Domestic		" I
39		Mary	8	f.			"

Page 3   4 June 1860   Sheet 230

```
1              CARPENTER, Robert    6   m.                              O.
2                Margaret E.        4   f.                              "
3                Vincent            2   m.                              "
4                Daniel             1   m.                              "

5   12/13      CARPENTER, James    38   m.   Farmer        /100         "   I
6                Ann               38   f.   Domestic                   "   I
7                Samuel            15   m.   Farm laborer               "   S
8                David            12   m.                              "   S
9                Jesse             11   m.                              "   S
10               Savilla            9   f.                              "
11               John               6   m.                              "
12               Julitta            4   f.                              "
13               Eliza E.           1   f.                              "
14  GILLMORE, John                 16   m.   Farm laborer               "   S
15               Mary J.           14   f.                              "   S

16  13/14      CARPENTER, David
               Sr.                69   m.   Farmer      2900/100   Va. I
17               Mary Sr.          65   f.   Domestic                   "   I
18               Mary Jr.          20   f.   Domestic                   O.
19               George             1   m.                              "

20  14/15      CARPENTER, Robert   23   m.   Farm laborer   /110        "
21               Mariah            19   f.   Domestic                   "   I

22  15/16      CARPENTER, David
               Jr.                33   m.   Farmer        /115         "
23               Sarah             29   f.   Domestic                   "
24               Andrew             6   m.                              "
25               Emiline            4   f.                              "

26  16/17      MORRIS, Elijah      31   m.   Farmer        /500    Pa.
27               Barbary           23   f.   Domestic               O. I
28               Hannah             3   f.                              "
29               Henry              1   m.                              "
30  BOROUGH, Tabitha                9   f.                              "
31  BENNETT, Richard               22   m.   Farm laborer               "   I

32  17/18      BOTKIN, Robert      26   m.   Farm laborer   /240        "
33               Mary              22   f.   Domestic                   "
34               Wm. M.             1   m.                              "

35  18/19      POWELL, Burr        48   m.   Farmer      2000/600   Va.
36               Susanna           38   f.   Domestic                   "
37               Daniel            20   m.   Miller                 O.
38               William           19   m.   Farm laborer               "
39               Nancy             17   f.   Domestic                   "
40  HANEY, Mary                    20   f.   Domestic               Md.
```

Page 4   4 June 1860   Sheet 230 verso

```
1   18/19      POWELL, Eliza       15   f.   Domestic               O.  S
2                Mary              14   f.                              "   S
3                Manley            12   m.                              "   S
4                James              9   m.                              "
```

5		POWELL, Catharine	8	f.		O. S
6		Ruth	6	f.		" S
7		George	3	m.		"
8		John F.	1	m.		"
9		BOTKIN, Jehue	23	m.	Farm laborer	"
10	19/20	DAWSON, John	43	m.	Master Mason /75	Va.
11		Elisabeth	46	f.	Domestic	"
12		Amanda	20	f.	Domestic	" I
13		James	19	m.	Mason	" S
14		Martha E.	18	f.	Domestic	" S
15		John D.	17	m.	Farm laborer	"
16		POWELL, Tabitha	67	f.	Domestic	"
17		RHINEHART, James N.	2	m.		O.
18		POWELL, Jackson	24	m.	Master Carpenter	Va.
19	20/21	NEWLON, Wilson	48	m.	Farmer	Pa.
20		Hannah	50	f.	Domestic	"
21		Mary P.	23	f.	Domestic	"
22		Isabella	19	f.	Domestic	Va.
23		William H.	18	m.	Farm laborer /225	" S
24		Joseph W.	16	m.	Farm laborer	" S
25		George W.	14	m.		O. S
26		Benjamin F.	10	m.		" S
27	21/22	McCOLLEY, Craten	27	m.	Blacksmith /150	"
28		Lrenzo	20	f.	Domestic	"
29		Hannah M.	2	f.		"
30		not named	1/12	m.		"
31	22/23	MERCER, James T.	30	m.	Farmer /750	Va.
32		Sarah	22	f.	Domestic	O.
33		Latona M.	2	f.		"
34		Myra V.	7/12	f.		"
35	23/24	STEPHENS, Washing-				
		ton	40	m.	Farm laborer	"
36		Margaret	35	f.	Domestic	"
37		John	14	m.		" S
38		Andrew	5	m.		" S
39	24/25	STEPHENS, Edward	23	m.	Farm laborer	"
40		Jane	1	f.		"

1		Sarah	25	f.	Domestic	O.
2		Mariah	9	f.		" S
3	25/26	VERNON, Jacob	53	m.	Farmer 42,900/7350	Pa.
4		Catharine	55	f.	Domestic	"
5		John	23	m.	Farm laborer	"
6		Catharine	18	f.	Domestic	O. S
7		Carrolton	14	m.		" S
8		Sarah	87	f.	Nothing	Pa.
9		OKEY, William	16	m.	Farm laborer	O. S
10	26/27	JONES, John M.	38	m.	Millwright /300	"

11		JONES, Sarah A.	38	f.	Domestic	O.	
12		Mary L.	11	f.		"	S
13		Albert M.	8	m.		"	S
14		Charles W.	5	m.		"	S
15	27/28	ADAMS, William	40	m.	Master Carpenter		
					400/200	Pa.	
16		Cynthia	40	f.	Domestic	"	
17		Rachel	14	f.		O.	S
18		Elisabeth	12	f.		"	S
19		Mary	10	f.		"	S
20		Catharine	6	f.		"	S
21		Agnes A.	4	f.		"	
22		Nancy E.	10/12	f.		"	
23		Andrew	19	m.	Carpenter	Pa.	
24		CLARK, Calvin	2	m.		O.	
25	28/29	CARPENTER, George	43	m.	Nothing /50	"	
26		Jane	36	f.	Domestic	"	
27		John	17	m.	Farm laborer	"	
28		Joseph	15	m.	Farm laborer	"	S
29		George W.	11	m.		"	S
30		HENNING, John	3	m.		"	
31	29/30	CARPENTER, Joseph	34	m.	Farmer /200	"	I
32		Barbary	29	f.	Domestic	"	I
33		Wesley	13	m.		"	S
34		Enoch	11	m.		"	S
35		Arrilla	8	f.		"	S
36		William	3	m.		"	
37		Elijah	2/12	m.		"	
38		GILLMORE, Ann	18	f.	Domestic	"	
39	30/31	ELLSWORTH, Lawren					
		F.	37	m.	Farmer 4000/665	"	
40		Mary	30	f.	Domestic	Pa.	

1		Celestia J.	13	f.		O.	S
2		Sarah V.	12	f.		"	S
3		Carline	9	f.		"	S
4		James W.	7	m.		"	S
5		Sevellin H.	5	m.		"	
6		not named	3	f.		"	
7		Leroy W.	4/12	m.		"	
8		RAILING, Henry	55	m.	Farm laborer	Pa.	
9		CARRICK, Benjamin	18	m.	Farm laborer	O.	S
10	31/32	RAILING, Solomon	23	m.	Farm laborer /150	"	M
11		Mary J.	19	f.	Domestic	"	M
12		James	9	m.		"	S
13	32/33	CURRY, Merh	51	m.	Farmer /450	"	
14		Mary	54	f.	Domestic	Md.	
15		James W.	25	m.	Farm laborer	O.	
16		George E.	23	m.	Farm laborer	"	

```
17              CURRY, Nancy E.    20   f.   Domestic              O.
18              Jacob L.           18   m.   Farm laborer          "
19              Susanna            16   f.   Domestic              "

20  33/34  REED, William          39   m.   Farmer        /100    "
21              Sarah A.           32   f.   Domestic              Va.
22              Mary A.            11   f.                         O.   S
23              Henrietta           9   f.                         "   S
24              Elizabeth J.        6   f.                         "   S
25              John P.             4   m.                         "
26              Emily               2   f.                         "
27              William C.       8/12   m.                         "

28  34/35  JONES, James E.        29   m.   Farmer     400/200    "
29              Mary E.            26   f.   Domestic              "
30              Mary A.             5   f.                         "
31              William P.          3   m.                         "
32              Mariah           9/12   f.                         "
33              Sarah            9/12   f.                         "

34  35/36  PORTER, Alexander      39   m.   Farmer     800/70     Pa.
35              Sarah A.           27   f.   Domestic              O.
36              William            20   m.   Farm laborer          "

37  36/37  JOHNSON, William
                C.                 39   m.   Blacksmith  400/100   Pa.
38              Jane               47   f.   Domestic              Va.
39              John               14   m.                         O.   S
40              Mary J.            13   f.                         "    S
```

Page 7   5 June 1860   Sheet 232

```
1               James R.           10   m.                         O.   S
2               William G.          8   m.                         "    S

3   37/38  PORTER, James R.       28   m.   Farmer    1000/200    "    I
4               Hannah             77   f.   Domestic              Pa.
5               HAGUE, Pierson N.  12   m.                         O.   S

6   38/39  RUCKER, Allen          45   m.   Farmer    3425/500    Va.
7               Lucretia           44   f.   Domestic              Me.  I
8               Jason              22   m.   Farm laborer  /150    O.
9               Mary J.            17   f.   Domestic              "
10              Nancy A.           13   f.                         "    S
11              Pascal             11   m.                         "    S
12              Emily E.            8   f.                         "    S
13              Jesse M.            3   m.                         "    S

14  39/40  RUCKER, Vincent        24   m.   Farmer        /250    "
15              Lydia              27   f.   Domestic              "
16              Rebecca L.          4   f.                         "
17              Genevia             2   f.                         "
18              THOMAS, Rebecca    68   f.   Domestic              Pa.
19              Edward             25   m.   Farm laborer          O.

20  40/41  SLACK, James           56   m.   Farmer        /150    Va.
21              Martha             30   f.   Domestic              Md.
```

22		SLACK, John W.	16	m.	Farm laborer	O.	S
23		James T.	14	m.		"	S
24		Thomas B.	12	m.		"	S
25		Rachel J.	7	f.		"	S
26		Leander R.	2	m.		"	
27	41/42	STEPHEN, Andrew J.	27	m.	Farmer	/200	"
28		Margaret E.	20	f.	Domestic		"
29		William H.	5/12	m.			"
30	42/43	STEPHEN, John	54	m.	Farmer	9000/1500	"
31		Jane	52	f.	Domestic	Pa.	
32		Louisa J.	22	f.	Domestic	O.	
33		Lucinda	18	f.	Domestic	"	S
34		John R.	13	m.		"	S
35		Sarah E.	11	f.		"	S
36		STERKEY, Orlando	20	m.	Farm laborer	"	S
37	43/44	CARPENTER, Aaron	43	m.	Farmer	3000/600	"
38		Jane	43	f.	Domestic	Del.	
39		Robert	19	m.	Farm laborer	O.	S
40		Mariah	17	f.	Domestic	"	S

Page 8			5 June 1860			Sheet 232 verso	
1		Aaron	15	m.		O.	S
2		William	14	m.		"	S
3		Reason	11	m.		"	S
4		Moses	10	m.		"	S
5		Rachel	6	f.		"	
6		Benjamin F.	4	m.		"	
7		Daniel	1	m.		"	
8	44/45	CARRICK, George	24	m.	Farm laborer	/50	"
9		Eliza J.	1	f.			"
10	45/46	JOHNSON, Samuel	44	m.	Farmer	3000/400	"
11		Margaret	41	f.	Domestic	Pa.	
12		James T.	16	m.	Farm laborer	O.	S
13		Mary J.	14	f.		"	S
14		John	12	m.		"	S
15		Lydia	11	f.		"	S
16		Menander	8	m.		"	S
17		Joseph	5	m.		"	
18		Francis	2	m.		"	
19		Esbon	4/12	m.		"	
20	46/47	WINDHAM, George	69	m.	Farmer	/100	Md.
21		Elisabeth	64	f.	Domestic	Pa.	
22		William	24	m.	Farm laborer	/100	O.
23		Aquilla	17	m.	Farm laborer		"
24		RITZ, Elisabeth	84	f.	Nothing	Pa.	
25		BAILEY, Sarah	14	f.		O.	
26		RUCKER, Catharine	6	f.		"	
27		Joseph	3	m.		"	
28	47/48	WINDHAM, Joseph R.	27	m.	Farmer	/200	"	M
29		Rebecca	19	f.	Domestic		"	M

30	48/49	HAGUE, Benjamin	36	m.	Farmer	2500/790	O.	
31		Ruth	31	f.	Domestic		"	
32		Mary D.	11	f.			"	S
33		Samuel M.	6	m.			"	S
34	49/50	BUNTING, Thomas A.	66	m.	Master Mason	/50	Pa.	
35		Catharine	56	f.	Domestic		"	
36	50/51	MILLER, Adam	32	m.	Farmer	/150	O.	
37		Eliza E.	22	f.	Domestic		"	
38		Mariah J.	5	f.			"	
39		Sarah C.	3	f.			"	
40		Josiah	11/12	m.			"	

Page 9   5 June 1860   Sheet 233

1	51/52	PRYER, George	33	m.	Farmer	600/300	O.	
2		Nancy	20	f.	Domestic		"	
3		Eber H.	1	m.			"	
4		Eliza J.	6/12	f.			"	
5	52/53	PRYER, James	61	m.	Farmer	/100	Pa.	I
6		Sarah	60	f.	Domestic		Va.	
7		Sarah	18	f.	Domestic		O.	
8		James W.	16	m.	Farm laborer		"	S
9	53/54	PRYER, Nathan	26	m.	Farmer	1000/350	"	
10		Susanna	24	f.	Domestic		"	
11	54/55	PRYER, John	28	m.	Farmer	1600/550	"	
12		Francina	26	f.	Domestic		"	
13		James V.	6	m.			"	S
14		Jefferson E.	4	m.			"	
15		Asberry T.	3	m.			"	
16	55/56	PRYER, Joshua	35	m.	Farmer	1600/600	"	
17		Sarah E.	29	f.	Domestic		"	
18		James J.	10	m.			"	S
19		Mary A.	8	f.			"	S
20		Sarah J.	7	f.			"	S
21		David H.	6	m.			"	S
22		George F.	5	m.			"	S
23		Francis M.	3	m.			"	
24		Levi	9/12	m.			"	
25	56/57	BARLOW, Zachariah	47	m.	Farmer	/250	"	
26		Mary	42	f.	Domestic		"	
27		Elisabeth	21	f.	Domestic		"	
28		William	20	m.	Apprentice Carpenter		"	
29		Jefferson	18	m.	Farm laborer		"	
30		Margaret A.	15	f.	Domestic		"	S
31		Phebe	14	f.			"	S
32		Levi W.	12	m.			"	S
33		Martha J.	10	f.			"	S
34		Charles B.	8	m.			"	S
35		Mariah F.	6	f.			"	S
36		Mary C.	4	f.			"	
37		Sarah J.	2	f.			"	

```
38  57/58  WINDHAM, George Jr.38  m.   Farmer        /350    O.
39           Sarah             40  f.   Domestic               "
40           Elisabeth         17  f.                          "      4
```

Page 10   6 June 1860   Sheet 233 verso

```
1            Jesse             14  m.                          O. S
2            Lucinda            8  f.                          "  S
3            George             5  m.                          "
4            Joseph             3  m.                          "
5            RUCKER, Emily     11  f.                          "  S

6   58/59  DANFORD, William    45  m.   Farmer     8500/1840   "
7            Phebe             42  f.   Domestic               "
8            Joseph N.         23  m.   Laborer                "
9            Stephen           22  m.   Farmer                 "
10           Nancy J.          18  f.   Domestic               "  S
11           John M.           16  m.   Farm laborer           "  S
12           Mary              14  f.                          "  S
13           William M.        12  m.                          "  S
14           Margaret E.       10  f.                          "  S
15           Cloe T.            8  f.                          "  S
16           Samuel C.          7  m.                          "  S
17           James H.           3  m.                          "
18           Charles M.         1  m.                          "

19  59/--  UNOCCUPIED

20  60/60  REED, James R.      37  m.   Farmer     1600/450   O.
21           Ann M.            42  f.   Domestic              Md.
22           Edward            17  m.   Farm laborer          O. S
23           James             15  m.   Farm laborer           "  S
24           Sarah A.          13  f.                          "  S
25           John B.           12  m.                          "  S
26           Rachel             9  f.                          "  S
27           Leah               7  f.                          "
28           George H.          5  m.                          "
29           Charles W.         2  m.                          "

30  61/61  DAILY, James A.     36  m.   Farmer     2900/375    "
31           Nancy             36  f.   Domestic               "
32           John              11  m.                          "  S
33           Margaret J.        5  f.                          "
34           William            1  m.                          "
35           RUCKER, Pascal    78  m.   Farm laborer  /300   Va.

36  62/62  RUCKER, Sarah       46  f.   Farmer      780/350   Me. I
37           Martin            19  m.   Farm laborer          O. S
38           Elisabeth         17  f.   Domestic               "
39           William           15  m.   Farm laborer           "
40           Jane              13  f.                          "  S
```

Page 11   6 June 1860   Sheet 234

```
1            Martin A.         10  m.                          O. S

2   63/63  RUCKER, Joseph      28  m.   Farmer     2560/400    "
3            Mary A.           23  f.   Domestic               "
```

4		RUCKER, Henry M.	4	m.			O.	
5		Sarah A.	2	f.			"	
6		William G.	9/12	m.			"	
7		WILSON, Mary A.	10	f.			"	S
8	64/64	ALLEN, Jacob	26	m.	Farmer	700/400	"	
9		Eunice	24	f.	Domestic		"	
10		Calita	6	m.			"	
11		Eliza	1	f.			"	
12	65/65	PORTER, William	67	m.	Farmer	480/150	Md.	
13		Harriet	54	f.	Domestic		Del.	
14	66/66	SHEMAN, John	37	m.	Farmer	600/250	Bav.	
15		Upolona	21	f.	Domestic		"	
16		John	7	m.			"	
17		Frank	33	m.	Farm laborer		"	
18	67/67	KENT, John	43	m.	Farmer	4500/2000	O.	
19		Elisabeth	47	f.	Domestic		"	
20		William	18	m.	Farm laborer		"	S
21		Sarah A.	15	f.	Domestic		"	S
22		Danford	10	m.			"	S
23	68/68	FOWLER, Hilary	43	m.	Farmer	2000/300	Md.	
24		Rebecca	34	f.	Domestic		"	
25		William H.	14	m.			O.	S
26		John H.	12	m.			"	S
27		Mary J.	10	f.			"	S
28		Robert F.	7	m.			"	S
29		Andrew M.	5	m.			"	S
30	69/69	MECHEM, Jesse E.	47	m.	Farmer	7710/1347	"	
31		Margaret	48	f.	Domestic		Va.	
32		Carlo C.	20	m.	Student of science		O.	S
33		James	19	m.	Farm laborer		"	S
34		Homer	13	m.			"	S
35		Adaline	5	f.			"	
36		RUCKER, John	33	m.	Farm laborer		"	
37		KELLEY, Delille	22	f.	Domestic		"	
38	70/70	RUCKER, Samuel	23	m.	Farmer	800/280	"	
39		Mary	27	f.	Domestic		■	
40		Charles	2	m.			"	

Page 12			6 June 1860			Sheet 234 verso		
1		PORTER, Mary E.	8	f.			O.	
2	71/71	RUCKER, Lucy	55	m.	Farmer	/500	Me.	
3		Larkin	16	m.	Farm laborer		O.	
4		Warren	19	m.	Farm laborer		"	
5		BLAKE, Mary J.	17	f.	Domestic		"	
6	72/72	RUCKER, Sanford	22	m.	Farm laborer	800/200	"	
7		Ruth P.	19	f.	Domestic		"	
8		William W.	4/12	m.			"	

9	73/73	MASSIE, Josiah	45	m.	Farmer	4000/600	O.	
10		Mary	48	f.	Domestic		"	
11		Hariet	16	f.	Domestic		"	S
12		Sarah	11	f.			"	
13		Levina C.	9	f.			"	
14		Martha	5	f.			"	
15		Monty J.	3	f.			"	
16	74/74	SCOTT, John W.	30	m.	Farmer		"	
17		Ruth	23	f.	Domestic		"	I
18		Isaac P.	7	m.			"	S
19		Elisabeth	6	f.			"	
20		Matthew A.	3	m.			"	
21		William T.	2	m.			"	
22	75/75	MASSIE, Azariah	30	m.	Farmer	1500/100	"	
23		Elisabeth	29	f.	Domestic		"	
24		Alexander	8	m.			"	S
25		Isaac F.	5	m.			"	
26		Charles M.	1/12	m.			"	
27		Mary	76	f.	Domestic		"	
28		KELLY, Lucinda	15	f.	Domestic		"	
29	76/76	ALLEN, John	75	m.	Farmer	600/300	Md.	I
30		Mary	63	f.	Domestic		Va.	
31		William	23	m.	Clerk		O.	
32		Amanda	15	f.	Domestic		"	S
33	77/77	RUCKER, Lewis	32	m.	Farmer	1400/300	"	
34		Margaret	29	f.	Domestic		"	I
35		Thomas F.	10	m.			"	S
36		Lucy C.	7	f.			"	S
37		John L.	5	m.			"	S
38		Nancy E.	2	f.			"	
39	78/78	HANSON, Elijah	44	m.	Farmer	900/300	"	
40		Ellen	39	f.	Domestic		Md.	

1		William	19	m.	Farm laborer		O.	
2		John	17	m.	Farm laborer		"	S
3		Noah	15	m.	Farm laborer		"	S
4		Henry	12	m.			"	S
5		Mary J.	10	f.			"	S
6		Charles	6	m.			"	S
7		James	3	m.			"	
8	79/79	ROBINSON, Thomas	48	m.	Farmer	1100/300	Pa.	
9		Emily A.	41	f.	Domestic		O.	
10		James W.	21	m.	Student		"	S
11		John O.	19	m.	Farm laborer		"	S
12		Nathaniel	15	m.	Farm laborer		"	S
13		Rachel J.	7	f.			"	S
14	80/80	HUNT, John	33	m.	Farmer	1100/200	"	
15		Sarah	25	f.	Domestic		"	

16		HUNT, Thomas F.	6	m.			O. S
17		Mary J.	3	f.			"
18		James H.	2/12	m.			"
19	81/81	HUNT, Thomas	38	m.	Farmer	800/150	Md.
20		Elisabeth	36	f.	Domestic		O.
21		Mary A.	17	f.	Domestic		"
22		Jane	15	f.	Domestic		" S
23		James	13	m.			" S
24		Isabella	11	f.			" S
25		John	9	m.			" S
26		George	7	m.			" S
27	82/82	KENELLER, William	33	m.	Farmer	1400/300	"
28		Eliza	17	f.	Domestic		"
29		James	11	m.			" S
30	83/83	KENELLER, Margaret	38	f.	Farmer	1200/200	"
31		Margaret Jr.	6	f.			" S
32		John	8	m.			" S
33		CASEY, Samuel	22	m.	Farm laborer		"
34	84/84	ROBINS, Leah	45	m.	Farmer	/300	Va.
35		Daniel	25	m.	Farm laborer		O.
36		Alexander	17	m.	Farm laborer		" S
37		James	15	m.	Farm laborer		" S
38		Catharine	13	f.			" S
39		Montgomery	10	m.			" S
40		John	10	m.			" S

Page 14			7 June 1860				Sheet 235 verso
1		Oliver	4	m.			O.
2		Lihue	21	m.	Farmer		" 6
3	85/85	YINTZ, John	64	m.	Farmer	600/300	Bav.
4		Christena	45	f.	Domestic		"
5		Mary	13	f.			" S
6		John	5	m.			O.
7	86/86	YINTZ, Joseph	36	m.	Farmer	4700/550	Bav.
8		Mary A.	34	f.	Domestic		"
9		Elisabeth	16	f.	Domestic		O.
10		Barbary	14	f.			"
11		George	12	m.			" S
12		Apolona	11	f.			" S
13		Mary A.	9	f.			" S
14		Margaret	6	f.			" S
15		Hannah	6	f.			"
16		Clara	3	f.			"
17		Phermina	1	f.			"
18	87/87	MILIGAN, Hugh	36	m.	Farmer	/100	"
19		Sarah	32	f.	Domestic		Pa.
20		Isabella	18	f.	Domestic		O.
21		John	16	m.	Farm laborer		" S
22		James A.	14	m.			" S

23		MILIGAN, Elisabeth	10	f.			O.	S
24		Robert S.	6	m.			"	
25		William	2	m.			"	

26	88/88	DOTSON, George	22	m.	Farmer	1250/350	"	
27		Martha	22	f.	Domestic		Md.	
28		George S.	4	m.			O.	

| 29 | 89/89 | DOTSON, William | 27 | m. | Farmer | 600/400 | Md. | |
| 30 | | Rebecca | 60 | f. | Domestic | | " | |

31	90/90	MILLIGAN, Alex.	37	m.	Farmer	700/100	Va.	
32		Hester	33	f.	Domestic		O.	
33		John W.	7	m.			"	S
34		George W.	7/12	m.			"	

35		MILLIGAN, James	31	m.	Farmer	700/350	"	
36		Isabella	74	f.	Domestic		Ire.	
37		James Jr.	14	m.			"	S

38	92/92	DAY, Thomas	59	m.	Farmer	1200/500	Md.	
39		Sarah A.	58	f.	Domestic		"	
40		Sarah E.	30	f.	Domestic		"	

1		ADY, Joseph	19	m.	Farm laborer		O.	
2		CURREN, Ruth J.	6	f.			"	S
3		CRANDLE, Sarah E.	18	f.			"	

4	93/93	WILLIAMS, Joseph B.	34	m.	Physician	700/400	"	
5		Mary	32	f.	Domestic		"	
6		Reed	10	m.			"	S
7		Joseph B.	7	m.			"	S
8		Josephine	4	f.			"	
9		John H.	2	m.			"	
10		William T.	22	m.	Farm laborer		"	

11	94/94	LEWELLEN, Jonathon	34	m.	Farmer	3000/750	"	
12		Sinah	35	f.	Domestic		"	
13		Emily	13	f.			"	S
14		Elisabeth	12	f.			"	S
15		Mary	9	f.			"	S
16		Amanda	8	f.			"	S
17		Robert	6	m.			"	S
18		Joseph	4	m.			"	
19		Sarah A.	2	f.			"	
20		Sinah E.	7/12	f.			"	

21	95/95	CARPENTER, Joseph	33	m.	Farmer	1000/600	"	
22		Matilda A.	27	f.	Domestic		"	
23		Sarah A.	2	f.			"	
24		Ellen	6/12	f.			"	
25		JOHNSON, William	18	m.	Farm laborer	/80	"	S

| 26 | 96/96 | HOGUE, Isaac | 22 | m. | Farm | /500 | O. | |
| 27 | | Susan | 21 | f. | Domestic | | " | |

28		HOGUE, Mary J.	1	f.			O.	
29	97/97	REED, John B.	41	m.	Farmer	2600/575	"	
30		Catharine	32	f.	Domestic		Pa.	
31		Shannon	7	m.			O.	
32		Mary	6	f.			"	
33		Edward	4	m.			"	
34		Clarrissa	2	f.			"	
35	98/98	CUNNINGHAM, William	45	m.	Farm laborer		"	
36		ALLEN, Jane	45	f.	Domestic		"	
37		Anthoney	15	m.	Farm laborer		"	S
38		Eleanor	13	f.			"	S
39	99/99	BRISTOR, John	26	m.	Farmer	/300	"	M
40		Catharine	18	f.	Domestic		"	M

Page 16   7 June 1860   Sheet 236 verso

1	100/100	ALLEN, Ambrose	22	m.	Farmer	/200	O.	
2		Mary	18	f.	Domestic		"	
3		William W.	6/12	m.			"	
4	101/101	HUNT, Henry	26	m.	Farmer	/150	"	
5		Sarah	22	f.	Domestic		"	
6		Mary A.	2	f.			"	
7	102/102	HUNT, William Sr.	60	m.	Farmer	2050/150	Md.	
8		Ann	61	f.	Domestic		"	I
9		James	20	m.	Farm laborer		O.	
10	103/103	HUNT, William Jr.	29	m.	Farmer	/200	"	
11		Nancy	28	f.	Domestic		"	
12		Charles	5	m.			"	S
13		George	3	m.			"	
14		WHITTAM, Mariah	52	f.	Domestic		"	
15	104/104	BIRKHART, Andrew	27	m.	Farmer	/50	Bav.	
16		Hannah	23	f.	Domestic		"	
17		John	3	m.			O.	
18		Peter	1	m.			"	
19		Mary	2/12	f.			"	
20	105/105	KNEHM, Peter	54	m.	Farmer	1400/600	Fr.	
21		Catharine	52	f.	Domestic		"	
22		John	22	m.	Farm laborer		"	M
23		Nicholas	20	m.	Farm laborer		"	
24		Nick	16	m.	Farm laborer		"	
25		Elias	15	m.	Farm laborer		"	
26		Simon	13	m.			O.	S
27		Joseph	11	m.			"	S
28		BAKER, Mariah	76	f.	Domestic		Fr.	
29		KNEHM, Ann	18	f.	Domestic		"	M
30	106/106	BAKER, Dominah	46	m.	Farmer	1500/500	Bav.	
31		Mary	51	f.	Domestic		"	
32		John	21	m.	Farm laborer		O.	

33		BAKER, Elisabeth	19	f.	Domestic		O.	
34		Caroline	17	f.	Domestic		"	
35		William	15	m.	Farm laborer		"	
36		Mary	11	f.			"	
37		Ann	8	f.			"	
38	107/107	BIDENHAYH, Casper	39	m.	Farmer	1400/350	Kni-hessen	
39		Terrissa	35	f.	Domestic		"	
40		Mary A.	12	f.			Pa.	

Page 17   8 June 1860   Sheet 237

1		John	11	m.			Pa.	S
2		Henry	8	m.			O.	S
3		Francis	6	m.			"	S
4		Michael	4	m.			"	
5		Charles	3	m.			"	
6		Joseph	1	m.			"	
7	108/108	DEMENT, Josiah	27	m.	Farmer	/450	"	
8		Mary	27	f.	Domestic		"	I
9		Elisabeth	6	f.			"	S
10		Sarah	2	f.			"	
11		PORTER, Nancy	19	f.	Domestic		"	
12		Mary E.	4/12	f.			"	
13	109/109	DEMENT, William	26	m.	Farmer	/165	"	
14		Hariet	23	f.	Domestic		"	
15		Eleanor	4	f.			"	
16		Ann M.	9/12	f.				
17	110/110	MERKLE, John	40	m.	Farmer	2000/400	Pa.	
18		Sarah A.	36	f.	Domestic		Va.	I
19		Robert	17	m.	Farm laborer		O.	
20		Emily	15	f.	Domestic		"	S
21		Corline	13	f.			"	S
22		Eli	12	m.			"	S
23		Elisabeth	9	f.			"	S
24		Henry	7	m.			"	S
25		Susanna	5	f.			"	
26		Lydia A.	2	f.			"	
27		Barbary E.	1	f.			"	
28		John W.	4	m.				
29	111/111	FOLGER, Izrael	26	m.	Farmer	/300	"	
30		Mariah	26	f.	Domestic		"	
31		Campsadell	5	f.			"	
32		Calista	3	f.			"	
33		Rufus	2	m.			"	
34		Marion	6/12	m.				
35		Susanna	60	f.	Domestic		Va.	
36	112/112	ULRICH, Valentine	39	m.	Farmer	1100/300	Bav.	
37		Mariah	14	f.			"	S
38		Catharine	12	f.			"	S
39		Peter	10	m.			"	S

40 113/--- UNOCCUPIED

Page 18		8 June 1860			Sheet 237 verso

1	114/113 BLOCK, George	23	m.	Farmer	/250 Bav. M
2	Catharine	24	f.	Domestic	O. M
3	WYSENT, Philamin	5	f.		" S
4	115/114 LUTZ, Joseph	23	m.	Carpenter	/150 Bav.
5	Mary A.	21	f.	Domestic	"
6	116/116 EVERLY, George	36	m.	Farmer	1200/350 Wir.
7	Caroline	21	f.	Domestic	"
8	Jacob	7	m.		O. S
9	Elisabeth	4	f.		"
10	Mary	2	f.		"
11	117/116 WYSENT, Jacob	39	m.	Farmer	4000/500 "
12	Catharine	45	f.	Domestic	Fr.
13	Barbary	18	f.	Domestic	O.
14	Jacob	15	m.	Farm laborer	" S
15	Francis	14	m.		": S
16	Catharine	12	f.		" S
17	Valentine	11	f.		" S
18	Joseph	8	m.		" S
19	John	7	m.		" S
20	Peter	4	m.		"
21	Adam	2	m.		"
22	Simon	1	m.		"
23	118/117 BIRKHART, David	28	m.	Farmer	1500/ Ger.
24	Catharine	22	f.	Domestic	" I
25	John	2	m.		O.
26	Mary	8/12	f.		"
27	119/118 BIRKHART, John G.	34	m.	Farmer	Ger.
28	Lena	27	f.	Domestic	"
29	Mary	6	f.		O.
30	John	4	m.		"
31	Theobold	2	m.		"
32	Catharine	1	f.		"
33	120/119 PRYOR, Christian	21	m.	Farmer	/125 "
34	Elisabeth	22	f.	Domestic	"
35	Arminta A.	1	f.		"
36	121/120 BREDEN, Daniel	45	m.	Farmer	600/275 Md.
37	Nancy	51	f.	Domestic	"
38	James	22	m.	Laborer	O.
39	William	20	m.	Laborer	"
40	Jane	18	f.	Domestic	"

Page 19		8 June 1860			Sheet 238

1	Mary	16	f.	Domestic	O. S
2	Susanna	12	f.		" S
3	Richard	7	m.		" S

		Name	Age	Sex	Occupation	Value	Birthplace		
4		DOTSON, Rebecca	24	f.	Domestic		Md.		
5	122/121	HERLAN, Jacob	54	m.	Farmer	1200/300	Bad.		
6		Jane	41	f.	Domestic		Pa.		
7		Peter	22	m.	Farm laborer		O.		
8		Mariah	20	f.	Domestic		"		
9		Jacob	15	m.	Farm laborer		"	S	
10		Louisa	12	f.			"	S	
11		John	11	m.			"	S	
12		Sarah A.	8	f.			"	S	
13		Lucy	2	f.			"		
14	123/122	BUNTING, William	41	m.	Farmer	/150	"		
15		Clarissa	34	f.	Domestic		"		
16		Elisabeth	13	f.			"	S	
17		Josiah	7	m.			"	S	
18		Washington	4	m.			"		
19		William	3	m.			"		
20		Sarah C.	1	f.					
21	124/123	KISER, Henry	40	m.	Farmer	2000/500	Ham.		
22		Eve	71	f.	Domestic		"		
23		Margaret	33	f.	Domestic		"		
24		Elisabeth	18	f.	Domestic		"		
25		TUY, Caroline	17	f.	Domestic				
26		KISER, Jacob	12	m.			O.	S	
27		Frank	10	m.			"	S	
28		Adam	9	m.			"		
29		Francis	7	m.			"		
30		Eve	5	f.			"		
31		John	2	m.			"		
32	125/124	ALLEN, Joel	54	m.	Farmer	1200/400	Pa.		
33		Martha	51	f.	Domestic		Va.		
34		Joel	15	m.	Farm laborer		O.	S	
35		William W.	12	m.			"	S	
36		Elisabeth A.	10	m.			"	S	
37		Julian	8	f.			"	S	
38	126/125	RIGHERT, Joseph	34	m.	Farmer	600/150	Bav.		
39		Mary	30	f.	Domestic		"		
40		STEINOLA, Rachel	16	f.	Domestic				

Page 20   8 June 1860   Sheet 238 verso

		Name	Age	Sex	Occupation	Value	Birthplace		
1	127/126	FOLGER, Robert	41	m.	Farmer	/175	Va.	I	
2		Nancy	40	f.	Domestic		"	I	
3		James H.	18	m.	Farm laborer		"	S	
4		Mary E.	15	f.	Domestic		"	S	
5		Isaac J.	14	m.			"	S	
6		John W.	12	m.			"	S	
7		Susan J.	10	f.			"	S	
8		Amanda	8	f.			"	S	
9		Robert	6	m.			"		
10		George W.	4	m.			"		
11		Webster	7/12	m.			O.		
12	128/127	DANFORD, Benjamin	40	m.	Farmer	10,120/1810	"		

13		DANFORD, Ann	33	f.	Domestic		Pa.	
14		Jesse M.	12	m.			O.	S
15		Rebecca J.	10	f.			"	S
16		Robert V.	9	m.			"	S
17		Mary A.	5	f.			"	
18		Lucretia F.	3	f.			"	
19		Samuel W.	1	m.			"	
20		Nancy E.	7	f.			"	
21	129/128	DEMENT, Vincent	59	m.	Farmer	3300/400	Va.	
22		Elisabeth	53	f.	Domestic		O.	I
23		Silas	17	m.	Farm laborer		"	S
24		SNYDER, Amelia	17	f.	Domestic		"	
25	130/129	POLLSGRAF, Michael	50	m.	Farmer	2400/700	Bav.	
26		Elisabeth	50	f.	Domestic		"	
27		Lina	20	f.	Domestic		O.	
28		Rachel	19	f.	Domestic		"	
29		Mary	17	f.	Domestic		"	
30		Barbara	15	f.	Domestic		"	
31		Lewis	13	m.			"	
32		Eve	11	f.			"	S
33		Louisa	10	f.			"	S
34		Christina	9	f.			"	S
35		George	3	m.			"	
36		KINLEHEREN, Christopher	31	m.	Farm laborer		Ger.	
37	131/130	BIRKHART, Philip	50	m.	Farmer	2500/650	Bav.	
38		Modalana	46	f.	Domestic		"	
39		Wendele	16	m.	Farm laborer		"	
40		George M.	15	f.?	Domestic ?		"	

1		Modolena	13	f.			Bav.	
2		Elisabeth	11	f.			"	
3		John	7	m.			O.	
4		Frederick	5	m.			"	
5	132/131	BRISTOR, James	22	m.	Farmer	/300	"	
6		Hannah M.	21	f.	Domestic		Va.	
7		William M.	3	m.			O.	
8		Sarah J.	2	f.			"	
9	133/132	SOVILLE, Hannah	59	f.	Domestic	300/50	Pa.	
10		Thomas	20	m.	Laborer		O.	
11		Adam	24	m.	Farmer			
12	134/133	BAKER, Joseph	57	m.	Farmer	/200	"	I
13		Elisabeth	46	f.	Domestic		"	
14		Margaret	12	f.			"	S
15		Martin	10	m.			"	S
16		Nelson	8	m.			"	S
17		Mary A.	2	f.			"	
18	135/134	BAKER, John	56	m.	Farmer	4000/450	"	

19		BAKER, Elisabeth	52	f.	Domestic	O. I
20		Sarah	33	f.	Domestic	" I
21		James	30	m.	Farm laborer	" I
22		Elijah	26	m.	Farm laborer /150	"
23		Andrew	23	m.	Farm laborer	" I
24		Lucinda	21	f.	Domestic	" I
25		John F.	15	m.	Farm laborer	"
26		Eliza E.	12	f.		"
27		Francis M.	1	m.		"
28	136/137	COULTERS, Robert	37	m.	Farmer 1200/300	"
29		Thamer	35	f.	Domestic	"
30		George W.	12	m.		" S
31		Caroline	10	f.		" S
32		Hannah E.	8	f.		" S
33		Amelia J.	5	f.		" S
34		Mary A.	2	f.		"
35	137/136	FOLGER, Philip	38	m.	Farmer 600/450	Va.
36		Mary	36	f.	Domestic	O.
37		James	16	m.	Farm laborer	S
38		Elisabeth	13	f.		S
39		Eli	7	m.		S
40		Ann M.	4	f.		

1	138/137	HANNAHS, Barbara	34	f.	Domestic /50	Ger.
2		Mary E.	4	f.		O.
3	139/138	EDGAR, Moses	22	m.	Farmer /40	" M
4		Catharine	21	f.	Domestic	" M
5	140/139	PORTER, Joseph	40	m.	Laborer	Del.
6		Catharine	18	f.	Domestic	O.
7		Rachel	16	f.	Domestic	"
8		Hariet	14	f.		"
9		William	12	m.		"
10		Mary	8	f.		"
11		Sarah	6	f.		"
12	141/140	CARPENTER, Samuel B.	39	m.	Farmer 1000/250	"
13		Mary	36	f.	Domestic	" I
14		Elijah	17	m.	Farm laborer	" S
15		Sarah	14	f.		" S
16		Henry D.	12	m.		" S
17		Andrew	6	m.		" S
18		Robert	4	m.		"
19		Samuel	1	m.		"
20	142/141	CARPENTER, David of Jr.	40	m.	Farmer /75	"
21		Catharine	27	f.	Domestic	"
22		Mary E.	10	f.		" S
23		George W.	7	m.		" S
24		Rachel	5	f.		"

25		CARPENTER, Josiah	1/12	m.				O.	
26	143/142	CARPENTER, Reason	40	m.	Farmer	1000/250	"	
27		Rachel	34	f.	Domestic		"	I
28		Mary	16	f.	Domestic		"	
29		Jane	14	f.			"	S
30		Robert	13	m.			"	S
31		William	11	m.			"	S
32		Margaret	8	f.			"	S
33		Drusilla	6	f.			"	
34		Sarah E.	4	f.			"	
35		Nancy	1	f.			"	
36	144/143	CARPENTER, John D.	42	m.	Farmer	1000/170	"	I
37		Louisa	36	f.	Domestic		"	I
38		George	17	m.	Farm laborer		"	S
39		Nancy	15	f.	Domestic		"	S
40		Vincent	13	m.			"	S

Page 23		9 June 1860		Sheet 240

1		Elias	11	m.				O.	
2		Mary E.	9	f.				"	
3		Eliza A.	7	f.				"	
4		Asberry	4	m.				"	
5	145/144	CARPENTER, Vincent	46	m.	Farmer	8000/700		"	
6		Eleanor	32	f.	Domestic			"	
7		Randolph	21	m.	Farm laborer	/100		"	S
8		John	20	m.	Farm laborer			"	S
9		Elijah	18	m.	Farm laborer			"	S
10		Abel	12	m.				"	S
11		Joseph	8	m.				"	S
12		SNYDER, Caroline	18	f.	Domestic			"	
13	146/145	WINDHAM, John	44	m.	Farmer	/150		"	
14		Rebecca	36	f.	Domestic			"	I
15		Thomas	22	m.	Farm laborer			"	
16		Catharine	13	f.				"	S
17		Emily	11	f.				"	S
18		Louisa	9	f.				"	S
19		George	7	m.				"	
20		Sarah E.	4	f.				"	
21		Lucinda	2	f.				"	
22		John	10/12	m.				"	
23	147/146	MERKLE, Jacob	63	m.	Farmer	2500/450		Pa.	
24		Christena	62	f.	Domestic			"	
25		Jacob	23	m.	Farm laborer			"	
26		Christopher	20	m.	Farm laborer			"	
27		Nancy	18	f.	Domestic			"	
28		CRAFFORD, Eliza	13	f.				"	S
29	148/147	STACKHOUSE, William	49	m.	Farmer	/300		"	I
30		Mary A.	45	f.	Domestic			Va.	I
31		Rebecca	22	f.	Domestic			O.	

32		STACKHOUSE, Mary A.	16	f.	Domestic		O. S
33		William	13	m.			" S
34		John F.	6	m.			" S
35	149/148	WISE, Robert	38	m.	Farmer	/150	"
36		Eleanor	30	f.	Domestic		" I
37		William	8	m.			" S
38		Lucinda	12	f.			" S
39		Eliza A.	5	f.			"
40		Asberry	2	m.			"

Page 24   11 June 1860   Sheet 240 verso

1		Mary J.	4/12	f.			O.
2	150/149	SEARS, John Sr.	62	m.	Farmer	2500/400	Md. I
3		John, Jr.	21	m.	Farm laborer		O.
4		BUMELER, William E.	27	m.	Farm laborer		Md.
5		Rebecca	25	f.	Domestic		O.
6		Mary E.	3	f.			"
7		Sarah E.	1	f.			"
8		SEARS, Francis	19	f.	Domestic		
9	151/150	BETTS, Joseph	45	m.	Farmer	1600/500	" I
10		Jane	39	f.	Domestic		" I
11		James	21	m.	Farm laborer		"
12		Margaret	18	f.	Domestic		" S
13		Martha J.	16	f.	Domestic		" S
14		Elisabeth	7	f.			" S
15		John	5	m.			"
16		George	3	m.			"
17		Amanda	4/12	f.			
18	152/151	HANNAHS, James	38	m.	Farmer	2400/800	"
19		Ann	38	f.	Domestic		Ger.
20		Mariah J.	18	f.	Domestic		O.
21		John T.	16	m.	Farm laborer		" S
22		Philip W.	14	m.			" S
23		Barbary E.	12	f.			" S
24		Eli M.	10	m.			" S
25		Adam J.	8	m.			" S
26		Mary A.	6	f.			"
27		Margaret A.	3	f.			"
28		Sarah A.	8/12	f.			
29	153/152	GAMLS, John	40	m.	Farmer	2300/600	Fr.
30		Catharine	40	f.	Domestic		"
31		Angeline	6	f.			O. S
32		Terrissa	4	f.			"
33		Mary P.	2	f.			
34	154/153	CLEGG, Richard	51	m.	Farmer	2400/400	Pa.
35		William	26	m.	Farm laborer		O. I
36		Thomas	17	m.	Farm laborer		" S
37		Sarah E.	11	f.			" S
38		Rachel	19	f.	Domestic		"

39	155/154	CLEGG, Samuel	28	m.	Farmer	/50	O.	
40		Lydia	26	f.	Domestic		"	I

Page 25   11 June 1860   Sheet 241

1		Mary	4	f.			O.	
2		John R.	5	m.			"	
3		Jacob	1	m.			"	
4	156/155	RIBBLE, Frederick	55	m.	Farmer	1200/400	Bav.	
5		Eve	42	f.	Domestic		"	
6		Jacob	17	m.	Farm laborer		O.	
7		Louisa	15	f.	Domestic		"	
8		Charles	14	m.			"	S
9		Daniel	10	m.			"	S
10	157/156	McLING, Philip	57	m.	Farmer	1800/400	Bav.	
11		Elisabeth	62	f.	Domestic		"	
12		NOTTS, Lewis	28	m.	Farm laborer	/400	"	
13		Christene	17	f.	Domestic		"	
14		Philip	1	m.			O.	
15	158/157	CHRISTMAN, Philip	33	m.	Farmer	1500/425	Bav.	
16		Rosanne	25	f.	Domestic		"	
17		Christene	6	f.			O.	
18		Philip	4	m.			"	
19		Lana	2	f.			"	
20		Eve	3/12	f.			"	
21	159/158	CHRISTMAN, Jacob	62	m.	Farmer	2600/450	Bav.	
22		Eve	58	f.	Domestic		"	
23		Jacob	23	m.	Farm laborer		"	
24		Catherine	19	f.	Domestic		"	
25		John	16	m.	Farm laborer		"	
26		Barbary	12	f.			"	
27	160/159	CHRISTMAN, Lewis	64	m.	Farmer	800/200	"	
28		Godfrey	27	m.	Farmer	450/250	"	
29		Christina	59	f.	Domestic		"	
30		Catharine	22	f.	Domestic		"	
31		Jacob	4	m.			O.	
32		Christena	3	f.			"	
33		Henry	3/12	m.			"	
34	161/160	REED, Robert	45	m.	Farmer	1000/300	"	
35		Mariah	34	f.	Domestic		"	
36		Royal O.	20	m.	Farm laborer		"	
37		Orison	19	m.	Farm laborer	/75	"	
38		Horace	17	m.	Farm laborer		"	
39		Francis M.	16	f.	Domestic		"	
40		Prudence	14	f.			"	S

Page 26   11 June 1860   Sheet 241 verso

1		Linna C.	12	f.			O.	S
2		Lucius	9	m.			"	S
3		Andrew	7	m.			"	S

4		REED, William	2	m.		O.
5		Lydia A.	5/12	f.		"
6	162/161	STEPHENS, Elisa-beth	21	f.	Domestic	" I
7		BAKER, Andrew	5	m.		"
8		MORRIS, Robert	1	m.		"
9	163/162	HAYS, George H.	38	m.	Farmer	/400 Md.
10		Elisabeth	32	f.	Domestic	O.
11		James	6	m.		" S
12		Margaret J.	5	f.		" S
13		Charles	3	m.		"
14	164/165	HICKMAN, John	31	m.	Farmer	/250 "
15		Hester	26	f.	Domestic	" I
16		Edward	7	m.		"
17		William	5	m.		"
18		Sarah E.	3	f.		"
19		James	1	m.		
20	165/164	WELLS, James	42	m.	Farmer	3000/750 Pa.
21		Julitta	39	f.	Domestic	O.
22		William S.	19	m.	Farm laborer	"
23		Eliza	16	f.	Domestic	" S
24		John	14	m.		" S
25		Nancy	12	f.		" S
26		Julitta J.	10	f.		" S
27		Elisabeth	8	f.		" S
28		James	6	m.		" S
29		Bird	4	f.		"
30		Elijah	1	m.		"
31	166/165	SCOFIELD, John S.	34	m.	Farmer	400/275 Va.
32		Jane	36	f.	Domestic	O.
33		MORRIS, Mary E.	14	f.		" S
34		SCOFIELD, John	8	m.		" S
35		Barbara E.	5	m.		" S
36		Robert W.	3	m.		"
37	167/166	SMELLWOOD, William T.	40	m.	Farmer	600/300 Md.
38		Mary A.	28	f.	Domestic	Can.
39		TRUAX, Mary A.	5	f.		O. S
40		WAITS, Thomas	17	m.	Laborer	"

Page 27   11 June 1860   Sheet 242

1	168/167	ATKINSON, Mitchele T.	55	m.	Farmer	7000/650 O.
2		Nancy	50	f.	Domestic	"
3		Margaret A.	18	f.	Domestic	" S
4		Lydia L.	14	f.		" S
5		Isaac B.	16	m.	Laborer	" S
6		Phebe L.	12	f.		" S
7		Lucius W.	9	m.		" S
8		Homer F.	7	m.		" S
9		Milton M.	4	m.		"

10	169/168	BAKER, Andrew	36	m.	Farmer	2000/300	O.	I
11		Nancy	33	f.	Domestic		"	I
12		Lydia	21	f.	Domestic		"	I
13		Matilda	19	f.	Domestic		"	S
14		Elijah	17	m.	Farm laborer		"	S
15		Mary	15	f.	Domestic		"	S
16		Jacob	13	m.			"	S
17		Sarah	11	f.			"	S
18		John	7	m.			"	
19		Henry	6	m.			"	
20		Andrew	4	m.			"	
21		John Mc.	2	m.			"	
22		Andrew	2/12	m.			"	
23		Julitta	2/12	f.			"	
24	170/169	MERCER, George	25	m.	Farm laborer	/100	"	
25		Nancy J.	4	f.			"	
26		Emiline	2	f.			"	
27	171/170	BAKER, Jacob Jr.	42	m.	Farmer	1000/500	"	I
28		Jane	43	f.	Domestic		"	I
29		Jacob Sr.	86	m.	Nothing	4000/50	"	I
30		Mary A.	17	f.	Domestic		"	
31		RUCKER, Josiah	28	m.	Farm laborer		"	
32		BAKER, William	14	m.			"	S
33		Samuel	12	m.			"	S
34		Lydia	9	f.			"	S
35		Margaret	7	f.			"	
36		Jacob	4	m.			"	
37		Mariah	2	f.			"	
38		REYNOLDS, Lydia	17	f.	Domestic		"	
39	172/171	JOHNSON, Daniel	30	m.	Farm laborer	/80	"	I
40		Mary	30	f.	Domestic		"	I

Page 28   12 June 1860   Sheet 242 verso

1		Peter	12	m.			O.	S
2		Sarah J.	11	f.			"	
3		Ezekiel	9	m.			"	S
4		Nancy	6	f.			"	S
5		Hester A.	4	f.			"	
6		Olla	3	f.			"	
7		Margaret	4/12	f.			"	
8	173/172	ECKELS, Daniel	37	m.	Farm laborer	/75	"	
9		Elisabeth	35	f.	Domestic		Pa.	
10		Lafayette	14	m.			O.	S
11		James T.	12	m.			"	S
12		Mary C.	10	f.			"	S
13		John	8	m.			"	
14		Philip	6	m.			"	
15		George	3	m.			"	
16		Alexander	9/12	m.			"	
17	174/173	STEPHENS, Julian	64	m.	Farmer	5500/400	Va.	
18		Alexander A.	38	m.	Farmer	4000/450	O.	

19		STEPHENS, Levina	38	f.	Domestic		O.	
20		Solomon	8	m.			"	S
21		WISE, Enoch	26	m.	Farm laborer		"	I

22	175/174	KNOPP, Daniel	35	m.	Farmer	800/300	Bav.	
23		Lena	28	f.	Domestic		"	
24		Jacob	6	m.			"	
25		Lena	5	f.			O.	
26		Catharine	3	f.			"	
27		Daniel	6/12	m.			"	

28	176/175	STEPHENS, Appollo	25	m.	Farmer	4800/900	"	
29		Mary	22	f.	Domestic		"	
30		Jacob	5	m.			"	
31		Sarah C.	3	f.			"	
32		Nancy	1	f.			"	

33	177/176	WEST, William	33	m.	Farmer	/100	"	
34		Sophia	35	f.	Domestic		"	I
35		Jacob	14	m.			"	S
36		Margaret J.	12	f.			"	S
37		Mary A.	10	f.			"	S
38		Morris	6	m.			"	
39		Wilson	4	m.			"	
40		Rachel	9/12	f.			"	

Page 29   12 June 1860   Sheet 243

1	178/177	RICH, Daniel	27	m.	Farmer	1700/850	Pa.	
2		Lana	20	f.	Domestic		O.	
3		Leonidas	10/12	m.			"	
4		BOYD, Sarah	50	f.	Domestic		Pa.	I

5	179/178	COEN, James	39	m.	Farmer	700/200	"	
6		Sarah A.	35	f.	Domestic		O.	
7		Henry	14	m.			"	S
8		Thomas J.	11	m.			"	S
9		Elisabeth	7	f.			"	
10		Margaret	5	f.			"	
11		James	3	m.			"	
12		Nancy J.	1	f.			"	

13	180/179	HICKMAN, Daniel	60	m.	Farmer	/200	Pa.	
14		Martha A.	57	f.	Domestic	"		I
15		James	17	m.	Farm laborer	"		S

16	181/180	HOWILER, Benjamin	22	m.	Farmer	/400	O.	
17		Nancy	18	f.	Domestic		"	
18		Nancy J.	9/12	f.				

19	182/181	MORGAN, George W.	30	m.	Farmer	/200	"	I
20		Mary	22	f.	Domestic		"	
21		Eli	3	m.			"	
22		Catherine	1	f.			"	

| 23 | 183/182 | WELLS, William | 63 | m. | Farmer | 5400/1200 | Pa. | I |
| 24 | | Nancy | 61 | f. | Domestic | | " | I |

25		WELLS, Appollo	23	m.	Farm laborer		O.	
26		STREET, Mary A.	20	f.	Domestic		"	
27	184/183	CARPENTER, David	51	m.	Farmer	/100	"	I
28		Delille	48	f.	Domestic		"	I
29		Hannah	16	f.	Domestic	•	"	
30		Zephaniah	14	m.			"	
31		Mary	11	f.			"	S
32		Abel	3	m.			"	
33		Viletta	8/12	f.			"	
34		Samuel	22	m.	Farm laborer		"	
35		Rebecca	20	f.			"	
36	185/184	CARPENTER, Richard	30	m.	Farm laborer	/100	"	
37		Ann	26	f.	Domestic		"	
38		Demerris	8	m.			"	
39		Arius	6	m.			"	
40		Ariam	4	f.			"	

Page 30   12 June 1860   Sheet 243 verso

1		Mary F.	2	f.			O.	
2		Philip	9/12	m.			"	
3	186/185	STEPHENS, Modalina	81	f.	Domestic	800/	Md.	
4	187/186	HOWILER, Joseph	28	m.	Farmer	3500/800	Bav.	
5		Lana	28	f.	Domestic		O.	
6		Benjamine	7	m.			"	S
7		Mary L.	5	f.			"	S
8		FLOYD, Meris T.	20	m.	Farm laborer		"	
9	188/187	NORRIS, Thomas B.	65	m.	Farmer	1200/400	D.C.	
10		Jane	54	f.	Domestic		Pa.	I
11		Catharine	36	f.	Domestic		O.	
12		Elisabeth	14	f.			"	S
13	189/188	MORRIS, George	28	m.	Farmer		"	
14		Catharine	24	f.	Domestic		"	
15		James M.	5	m.			"	
16		Nancy J.	4	f.			"	
17		Mary A.	1	f.			"	
18		Isaac	8	m.			"	S
19	190/189	CRAFFORD, John	26	m.	Farmer	/150	O.	I
20		Nancy	26	f.	Domestic		"	I
21		Ariam	8	f.			"	S
22		William S.	7	m.			"	S
23		James	3	m.			"	
24		Greenbury	1	m.			"	
25	191/190	MILLER, John	43	m.	Farmer	/250	"	I
26		Sarah	43	f.	Domestic		"	I
27		Sarah	19	f.	Domestic		"	
28		Mary	19	f.	Domestic		"	
29		Rebecca	16	m.			"	S
30		Francis	14	m.			"	S

31		MILLER, Julitta	5	f.			O.
32		Charity	3	f.			"
33		Eliza	7/12	f.			"
34	192/191	MILLER, Peter	38	m.	Farmer	/40	Pa. I
35		Rhoda	27	f.	Domestic		O. I
36		Mary E.	9	f.			" S
37		Catharine	7	f.			" S
38		Nancy J.	5	f.			"
39		John	3	m.			"
40		STEPHEN, John	18	m.	Farm laborer		"

1	193/192	STEPHEN, Alexander					
		D.	36	m.	Farmer	5400/900	O.
2		Mary	36	f.	Domestic		"
3		Samuel	16	m.	Farm laborer		" S
4		CARPENTER, Samuel					
		H.	12	m.			" S
5		STEPHEN, James	6	m.			" S
6		Julitta	1	f.			"
7	194/193	RICHARDSON, John	41	m.	Farmer	/50	" I
8		Eleanor	36	f.	Domestic		" I
9		Samuel	15	m.	Farm laborer		" S
10		Jemima	13	f.			" S
11		Henry	11	m.			" S
12		Mary A.	9	f.			" S
13		Rachel	8	f.			"
14		Elisabeth	8	f.			"
15		John	6	m.			"
16		Gilespie	2	m.			"
17	195/194	STEPHEN, Andrew	32	m.	Farmer	1600/300	"
18		Sarah	33	f.	Domestic		"
19		Nancy	12	f.			" S
20		Julitta	11	f.			" S
21		Margaret	9	f.			" S
22		Elijah	4	m.			"
23		Eliza	10/12	f.			"
24	196/195	STEPHEN, Jacob	22	m.	Farm laborer	/50	"
25		Margaret	26	f.	Domestic		"
26	197/196	WARNER, James	21	m.	Farmer	/250	Pa.
27		Mary	24	f.	Domestic		O.
28		Joanna	1	f.			"
29		Letitia	2/12	f.			"
30		CARPENTER, John B.	23	m.	Farmer	/200	"
31	198/197	THETCHER, Daniel	34	m.	Farmer	500/150	Pa.
32		Mary	25	f.	Domestic		O. I
33		Samuel	11	m.			" S
34		Nancy	7	f.			"
35		Margaret	5	f.			"
36		Mary	3	f.			"
37		William T.	2	m.			

38	199/198	CARPENTER, Joseph	55	m.	Farmer	/80	O.	
39		Martha	50	f.	Domestic		Pa.	I
40		SUMMERS, Annie	30	f.	Domestic		O.	I

Page 32   12 June 1860   Sheet 244 verso

1		CARPENTER, Nancy	10	f.			O.	S
2		Silas	9	m.			"	S
3		Hannah E.	5	f.			"	
4		SUMMERS, Elisha	4	m.			"	
5		Rhuhama	1	f.			"	

6	200/199	STEPHENS, Valentine						
		S.	35	m.	Farmer	1300/1030	"	
7		Barbary	37	f.	Domestic		"	
8		Sylvester	14	m.			"	S
9		Mary E.	11	f.			"	S
10		John	8	m.			"	S
11		Julian	2	f.			"	
12		not named	4/12	f.			"	

13	201/200	BOWERSOCK, John S.	32	m.	Farmer	/50	"	
14		Eliza J.	29	f.	Domestic		"	I
15		Mary R.	10	f.			"	S
16		Sarah C.	6	f.			"	
17		Eliza F.	3	f.			"	
18		Cyntha J.	1	f.			"	

19	202/201	SNYDER, John	83	m.	Farmer	/150	Va.	
20		Rachel	50	f.	Domestic		Pa.	I
21		John	25	m.	Farm laborer		O.	
22		George	23	m.	Farm laborer		"	
23		Margaret	21	f.	Domestic		"	
24		Rachel	13	f.			"	S
25		Francis	15	m.	Farm laborer		"	S

| 26 | 203/202 | BIRKHART, John | 34 | m. | Farmer | 1200/ | Bav. | |
| 27 | | Mary | 37 | f. | Domestic | | " | |

| 28 | 204/203 | SHUMAN, Henry | 40 | m. | Laborer | | Pa. | |

Begining of Calais.

29	205/204	GREENELTCH, Louisa						
		E.	40	f.	Domestic	100/50	O.	
30		Sarah E.	17	f.	Domestic		"	
31		John	12	m.			"	S
32		Hulda	6	f.			"	S
33		Francis	3	m.			"	

34	206/205	GREEN, James	55	m.	Farmer		N.J.	
35		Lucy	45	f.	Domestic		Pa.	
36		RHINEHART, Sarah	56	f.			"	23
37		GREEN, Lucy	22	f.	Domestic		"	
38		James M.	20	m.	Farm laborer	/200	O.	
39		John S.	18	m.	Farm laborer		"	S
40		Joseph	14	m.			"	S

Page 33				13 June 1860			Sheet 245	
1		GREEN, Rhinehart	10	m.			O.	S
2		Eliza A.	6	f.			"	S
3		Charles F.	2	m.			"	
4	207/206	McJILTON, John	46	m.	Physician	/150	D.C.	
5		Mary	39	f.	Domestic		O.	
6		Hariet	18	f.	Domestic		"	S
7		Thomas	12	m.			"	S
8		Catharine	10	f.			"	S
9		John	8	m.			"	S
10		Loretta	6	f.			"	S
11		Frederick	4	m.			Ill.	
12		Mary A.	1	f.			O.	
13	208/207	SHACKLEE, George					"	
		W.	38	m.	Lawyer	400/600	"	
14		Rachel	26	f.	Domestic		"	I
15		George	4	m.			"	S
16		Warren E.	3	m.			"	S
17		Martha A.	1	f.			"	
18		ECKELS, Martha	28	f.	Domestic		"	I
19	209/208	McBRIDE, Abram	28	m.	Laborer	/175	"	
20		Eunice	27	f.	Domestic		"	
21		Scelia	4	f.			"	
22		Everet	2	m.			"	
23		Mary L.	3/12	f.			"	
24	210/209	HARDESTY, James L.	46	m.	Tobacco Packer	/50	Md.	
25		Rebecca	46	f.	Domestic		"	
26		Alexander	14	m.			O.	S
27		Sarah A.	7	f.			"	S
28		Charles	6	m.			"	S
29		David	3	m.			"	
30		Mary	1	f.			"	
31	211/210	McKEE, James H.	25	m.	Wheelwright	/150	Va.	
32		Eliza	22	f.	Milliner		Eng.	
33	---/211	OUTLAND, Joseph	32	m.	Wheelwright	240/200	O.	
34		Phebe D.	32	f.	Domestic		"	
35		Lydia	9	f.			"	S
36		Thomas O.	6	m.			"	S
37		Florence	4	f.			"	S
38		Caroline	2	f.			"	
39	212/212	RICHARDSON, Joseph						
		W.	22	m.	Teacher	/175	Pa.	
40		Calista	18	f.	Domestic		O.	

Page 34			13 June 1860			Sheet 245 verso	
1		Forest C.	2	m.			O.
2		James W.	5/12	m.			"

3	213/213	KELLEY, Sebastian					
		C.	25	m.	Laborer	/150	O.
4		Sarah E.	20	f.	Domestic		"
5		Mary J.	2	f.			"
6		Margaret L.	9/12	f.			"
7	214/214	STOCKDALE, Ruth	30	f.	Domestic	400/100	"
8		Miriam	9	f.			" S
9		Sarah E.	7	f.			" S
10	215/215	TUTTLES, Levi	34	m.	Cabinet-maker		
						500/1000	Pa.
11		Sarah E.	29	f.	Domestic		Md.
12		John W.	19	m.			O. S
13		William	9	m.			" S
14		Mary	4	f.			" S
15		Charles R.	6/12	m.			"
16		Nancy	15	f.	Domestic		" S
17		John	25	m.	Cabinet-maker	/150	Pa.
18		SEARS, David T.	31	m.	Master Carpenter		
						/200	Md.
19	216/216	RUTTER, William	37	m.	Farmer	200/200	Pa.
20		Harriet	41	f.	Domestic		Eng.
21		William	7	m.			O. S
22		George	5	m.			" S
23	217/217	LANEY, William D.	45	m.	Merchant	100/500	"
24		Lydia A.	26	f.	Domestic		Pa.
25		Esbon F.	10	m.			O. S
26		Catharine	6	f.			"
27		not named	2/12	m.			"
28		same	2/12	m.			"
29	218/218	DEMENT, Elisabeth	31	f.	Domestic	300/200	Md.
30		Josephine	15	f.	Domestic		O.
31		Louisa E.	13	f.			" S
32		Jenny L.	11	f.			" S
33		John	6	m.			"
34		Mary	3	f.			"
35		William	11/12	m.			"
36	219/219	GOODHART, John H.	40	m.	Farmer-Blacksmith		
						4000/500	Va.
37		Naomi	32	f.	Domestic		O.
38		Mary E.	10	f.			" S
39		George W.	8	m.			" S
40		Daniel	5	m.			" S

Page 35   13 June 1860   Sheet 246

1		BIROUGH, Jane	43	f.	Domestic		Pa.
2	220/220	STOCKDALE, Thomas	71	m.	Laborer	/50	Md. I
3		Lydia	71	f.	Domestic		"
4	221/221	SHAKLEE, Solomon	37	m.	Blacksmith	/200	O.
5		Jane	29	f.	Domestic		" I

6		SHAKLEE, Amanda	11	f.			O.	S
7		Charles	9	m.			"	S
8		Sarah J.	6	f.			"	S
9		Lorenzo F.	4	m.			"	
10		Franklin	11/12	m.			"	
11		HENNING, William	30	m.	Lawyer	400/100	Pa.	

12	222/222	DAVIDSON, William	23	m.	Shoemaker	/100	O.
13		Martha	20	f.	Domestic		"

14	223/223	OGLEBEY, Joseph H.	21	m.	Merchant	/6000	"
15		Sarah	62	f.	Domestic	1500/150	Pa.

16	224/224	WEHR, Joseph	33	m.	Farmer	3000/1000	O.
17		Nancy	31	f.	Domestic		"
18		Louisa J.	6	f.			"
19		Henrietta	3	f.			"
20		Richard O.	8/12	m.			"
21		MILLER, Joseph	29	m.	Tobacco packer		"

22	225/225	BALL, Farlon	44	m.	Farmer	450/350	Va.
23		Eleanor	45	f.	Domestic		O.
24		Sarah A.	21	f.	Domestic		"
25		William	19	m.	Blacksmith		"
26		Eliza E.	17	f.	Domestic		"
27		Farlon A.	15	m.			"	S
28		George	13	m.			"	S
29		Emma	10	f.			"	S
30		Embrozena	9	f.			"	S

31	226/226	CLEVELAND, Thaddeus S.	41	m.	Farmer-Merchant 1600/500		Me.
32		Mary	48	f.	Domestic		O.
33		Sarah E.	17	f.	Domestic		"	S
34		Hannah J.	15	f.	Domestic		"	S
35		Wellington N.	12	m.			"	S
36		Henry	6	m.			"	S
37		Margaret	52	f.	Domestic	100/	"

38	227/227	GAMLS, Nicholas	25	m.	Tanner	400/600	Mos.
39		Mary	21	f.	Domestic		O.
40		Elisabeth	7/12	f.			"

Page 36	13 June 1860	Sheet 246 verso

1	228/228	GAMLS, John	23	m.	Saddler	800/150	Mos.
2		Charlotte	27	f.	Domestic		O.
3		Barbary E.	1	f.			"
4		YOCKEY, Samuel	16	m.	Apprentice Saddler		"
5		Philip	25	m.	Shoemaker		"

6	229/229	SPRIGGS, John P.	27	m.	Lawyer-Teacher 480/350		"
7		Lucinda	30	f.	Domestic		"
8		Rosalia	1	f.			"
9		RUCKER, Lucy E.	9	f.			"	S

(Seneca Township Concluded)

(J. P. Spriggs, Ass't Marshall).

* * *

Franklin Township   P. O. Summerfield

13   14 June 1860

14	230/230	REED, Edward	73	m.	Farmer	16,500/3080	Pa.
15		Mary	65	f.	Domestic		"
16		Martha	22	f.	Domestic		O.
17		OKEY, Emanuel	24	m.	Farm laborer		"
18		MELOT, Madisson	10	m.			" S

19	231/231	REED, George	39	m.	Farmer	"
20		Rebecca	24	f.	Domestic	Pa.
21		John	1	m.		O.
22		Jane	2/12	f.		"
23		CHAMBERS, Eliza	14	f.		" S

24	232/232	MERCER, Joshua	33	m.	Farmer /100	"
25		Eliza A.	26	f.	Domestic	"
26		Susan B.	7	f.		"
27		Samuel	4	m.		"
28		John	2	m.		"
29		CASEY, Elisabeth	13	f.		" S

30	233/233	FORSHEY, John	24	m.	Farmer	"
31		Catharine	22	f.	Domestic	"

32	234/234	YUNG, James	51	m.	Farmer /140	Pa.
33		Hester	55	f.	Domestic	Va.
34		Margaret	24	f.	Domestic	O.
35		Mary W.	21	f.	Domestic	"
36		CASEY, Shaderick	22	m.	Farm laborer	"

37	235/235	CASEY, William	54	m.	Farmer 2100/600	Pa.
38		Nancy	55	f.	Domestic	" I
39		Mary	16	f.	Domestic	O. S
40		YUNG, Margaret	27	f.	Domestic	"

Page 37   14 June 1860   Sheet 247

1	236/236	WARFIELD, William	48	m.	Farmer /300	Md.
2		Mary J.	38	f.	Domestic	"
3		John	12	m.		" S
4		Elisabeth	3	f.		O.
5		not named	4/12	m.		"

6	237/237	AUG, John S.	31	m.	Farmer 2000/250	"
7		Elisabeth	31	f.	Domestic	"
8		William A.	7	m.		" S
9		Robert W.	4	m.		"
10		Aaron W.	2	m.		"
11		STIGLER, Nathan	17	m.	Farm laborer	"

```
12 238/238 McPHERSON, John W. 27  m.   Farmer        /300    O.
13            Malissa           27  f.   Domestic              "
14            Mary E.            4   f.                         "
15            Sarah E.          1   f.                         "

16 239/239 McPHERSON, L. F.   60  m.   Farmer        /2000   Va.
17            Mariah            54  f.   Domestic              O.
18            Mariah E.         33  f.   Domestic              "
19            Joseph W.         7   m.                         "     S

20 240/240 TAYLOR, Silas      35  m.   Farmer        /200     "
21            Elisabeth A.      33  f.   Domestic              "
22            Martha J.         14  f.                         "     S
23            Samuel W.         12  m.                         "     S
24            John W.           8   m.                         "     S
25            Leah E.           6   f.                         "
26            Joseph W.         4   m.                         "
27            Fletcher M.       1   m.                         "

28 241/241 GIBSON, Samuel     23  m.   Farmer        1200/275  "
29            Wilamina          21  f.   Domestic              "
30            Rebecca J.        1   f.                         "
31            William           26  m.   Farmer        1200/300  "
32            KAIN, Alvira J.   12  f.                         "     S

33 242/242 DOTSON, John       35  m.   Farmer        2000/450  Md.
34            Margaret          30  f.   Domestic              O.
35            William           10  m.                         "     S
36            James M.          6   m.                         "     S
37            Rebecca           8   f.                         "     S
38            Martha            4   f.                         "

39 243/243 SCOTT, Henry       26  m.   Farmer        /250     "     M
40            Ruth A.           24  f.   Domestic              "     M
```

Page 38   14 June 1860   Sheet 247 verso

```
1  244/244 HANES, Hiram H.    29  m.   Master Carpenter
                                                     500/200   O.
2            Ann E.            23  f.   Domestic              "
3            Elisabeth A.      3   f.                         "
4            KAIN, Joanna      9   f.                         "     S

5  245/245 GIBSON, Richard    43  m.   Farmer        5600/855  Md.
6            Wilamina          37  f.   Domestic              "
7            John              16  m.   Farm laborer          O.  S
8            Samuel            13  m.                         "   S
9            William           11  m.                         "   S
10           Martha A.         4   f.                         "
11           FORSHEY, Lucinda  19  f.   Domestic              "

12 246/246 SMITH, John        65  m.   Horse keeper  /300     Pa.
13           Sarah             61  f.   Domestic              O.
14           Mary              11  f.                         "   S
15           Margaret          3   f.                         "

16 247/247 DEVOE, Joseph      58  m.   Farmer        3000/760  Md.
17           Elisabeth C.      54  f.   Domestic              "
```

18		DEVOE, Thomas	18	m.	Farm laborer	O.	S
19		Alfred R.	16	m.	Farm laborer	"	S
20		Martha J.	14	f.		"	S
21		Terrisa A.	12	f.		"	S
22		Joseph O.	10	m.		"	S
23		BOEN, Christina A.	18	f.	Domestic	"	
24	248/248	DILLON, Hugh	47	m.	Farmer	Pa.	I
25		Catharine	51	f.	Domestic	"	I
26		Elwood	24	m.	Farm laborer	O.	
27		Samuel	21	m.	Farm laborer	"	
28		Jacob	19	m.	Farm laborer	"	
29		Henry	17	m.	Farm laborer	"	
30		Jane	14	f.		"	
31		Hugh	12	m.		"	
32		Margaret	9	f.		"	
33		Catharine	6	f.		"	
34		Benjamin	4	m.		"	
35	349/349	BROWN, Matthew	43	m.	Farmer 5000/800	"	
36		Hannah	41	f.	Domestic	"	
37		Stephen	20	m.	Farm laborer	"	S
38		Catharine	16	f.	Domestic	"	
39		Asa	12	m.		"	
40		Nancy	9	f.		"	

Page 39   15 June 1860   Sheet 248

1		Mary A.	5	f.		O.	
2		Hariet	1	f.		"	
3		John W.	21	m.	Farm laborer	"	
4	250/250	LIGHT, Jacob	56	m.	Farm laborer	"	I
5		Rachel	32	f.	Domestic	Va.	I
6		Matthias	21	m.	Farm laborer	O.	
7		James.	19	m.	Farm laborer	"	
8		Mary A.	14	f.		"	
9		Thomas	5	m.		"	
10		Robert	1	m.		"	
11	251/251	DRAPER, William	49	m.	Farmer 2920/600	Pa.	
12		Margaret	35	f.	Domestic	"	
13		Joseph	23	m.	Farm laborer	Va.	
14		Eve	21	f.	Domestic	O.	
15		Adam	18	m.	Farm laborer	"	S
16		Charles R.	6	m.		"	S
17		Ludwell	2	m.		"	
18		ANTLE, Mary A.	54	f.	Domestic	"	
19	252/252	PICKENS, Alexander	49	m.	Farmer 1600/500	"	
20		Catharine	49	f.	Domestic	"	
21		OGLE, Susan	12	f.		"	
22	253/253	HARDESTY, Fleming	27	m.	Farmer	"	
23		Elisabeth	29	f.	Domestic	"	I
24		Charles E.	6	m.		"	S
25		Albert M.	4	m.		"	
26		Ann M.	1	f.		"	

27	254/254	PORTER, Ezekiel	45	m.	Farmer	2500/450	Va.	
28		William	31	f.	Domestic		Md.	
29		Nancy	18	f.	Domestic		O.	
30		Samuel	16	m.	Farm laborer		"	S
31		William	14	m.			"	S
32		John	12	m.			"	S
33		Thomas	8	m.			"	S
34		Charles	2	m.			"	
35		Sarah A.	5	f.			"	
36		James F.	1/12	m.			"	
37		BERNES, Nathan	31	m.	Farm laborer		"	I
38	255/255	WEENER, Thomas	42	m.	Farmer	1100/	Bav.	
39		Eve	42	f.	Domestic		"	
40		Mary	13	f.			"	

Page 40   15 June 1860   Sheet 248 verso

1		Louisa	10	f.			Pa.	
2		Caroline	5	f.			0.23	
3	256/256	STOFFLE, James	24	m.	Farmer	1500/450	Bav.	
4		Mary	29	f.	Domestic		"	I
5		John	7	m.			Pa.	S
6		Mary	5	f.			"	S
7		William	2	m.			O.	
8		Stephen	10/12	m.			"	
9		PAMALI, Philip	23	m.	Farm laborer		Bav.	
10	257/257	YUNG, William	46	m.	Farmer	/400	Va.	
11		Margaret	45	f.	Domestic		Pa.	
12		George	22	m.	Student		"	S
13		Minerva	19	f.	Teacher		Va.	
14		Rebecca	15	f.	Domestic		O.	
15		Mary	14	f.			"	S
16		Joseph	12	m.			"	S
17		Martha	10	f.			"	S
18		Abigail	8	f.			"	S
19		Lina	5	f.			"	S
20		not named	3/12	f.			"	
21	258/258	LEISURE, Isaac	28	m.	Farmer	/300	Va.	
22		Elisabeth	32	f.	Domestic		Pa.	I
23		John	11	m.			O.	3
24		Mary E.	9	f.			"	S
25		Isaac	7	m.			"	S
26		Harvy	2	m.			"	
27		Izrael	4	m.			"	
28	259/259	PENNINGTON, Otho	23	m.	Farmer	/100	"	I
29		Sarah	22	f.	Domestic		"	I
30		Jesse M.	2	m.			"	
31		James W.	1	m.			"	
32	260/260	WISE, Jacob	34	m.	Farmer	1600/300	"	
33		Mary	31	f.	Domestic		"	I
34		Sarina J.	12	f.			"	S

35		WISE, Martha A.	10	f.			0. S
36		John W.	7	m.			"
37		James E.	5	m.			"
38		Mary E.	3	f.			"
39	261/261	DEARTH, Hiram	33	m.	Farmer	1200/300	" I
40		Hester J.	26	f.	Domestic		"

Page 41   15 June 1860   Sheet 249

1		William A.	7	m.			0. S
2		James M.	5	m.			" S
3		Ephraim A.	10/12	m.			"
4	261/261	WISE, James	25	m.	Farmer	/100	"
5		Mary C.	21	f.	Domestic		"
6		John W.	3	m.			"
7	262/262	WISE, William	32	m.	Farmer	1200/325	"
8		Margaret	18	f.	Domestic		"
9	263/263	DENNIS, William	33	m.	Farmer	1200/525	"
10		Hariet	27	f.	Domestic		Pa.
11		Mary A.	7	f.	Domestic		0. S
12		Martha L.	5	f.			" S
13		Patience S.	2	f.			"
14		KAIN, John	11	m.			" S
15	264/264	SWAIN, William G.	47	m.	Farmer	800/400	Md. I
16		Mary A.	42	f.	Domestic		Pa.
17		Matilda	18	f.	Domestic		0.
18		Hariet	15	f.	Domestic		" S
19		James C.	13	m.			" S
20		Martha	10	f.			" S
21		Mary A.	9	f.			" S
22		Nancy J.	7	f.			" S
23		Mahala	5	f.			"
24		Mariah C.	1	f.			"
25	265/265	DUM, Arthur	58	m.	Farmer	2600/600	Md.
26		Salina	56	f.	Domestic		Pa.
27		Jeremiah	26	m.	Farm laborer		0.
28		Elias	26	m.	Farm laborer		"
29		Martha J.	18	f.	Domestic		"
30		Arthur	14	m.			" S
31		William E.	12	m.			" S
32	266/266	AUG, Yung	39	m.	Farmer	5000/450	"
33		Mary E.	33	f.	Domestic		"
34		Washington	7	m.			"
35		John	5	m.			"
36		Eliza	3	f.			"
37		NOVILLE, Richard	12	m.			" S
38	267/267	CRANDLE, Thomas B.	54	m.	Farmer	/400	Md.
39		Elisabeth	44	f.	Domestic		" I
40		Mary	21	f.	Domestic		"

Page 42   15 June 1860   Sheet 249 verso

1		CRANDLE, Richard	19	m.	Farm laborer		Md.	
2		Sarah	18	f.	Domestic		"	
3		Alice	16	f.	Domestic		"	S
4		Catharine	13	f.			"	S
5		Mariah J.	11	f.			O.	S
6		George	8	m.			"	S
7		Thomas W.	5	m.			"	S
8		John	2	m.			"	
9	268/268	COURTNEY, Joseph	46	m.	Farmer	/150	Va.	
10		Mary	43	f.	Domestic		"	I
11		Luiter	18	m.	Farm laborer		"	S
12		Robert	16	m.	Farm laborer		"	S
13		Joseph	14	m.			"	S
14		Catharine	13	f.			"	S
15		James B.	7	m.			O.	
16		Charles C.	4	m.			"	
17	269/269	CRANDLE, James	23	m.	Farmer	/250	Md.	
18		Eliza J.	20	f.	Domestic		O.	
19		MERSH, Catharine	8	f.			"	S
20	270/270	SWAIN, Thomas E.	25	m.	Farmer	/200	"	
21		Lydia A.	26	f.	Domestic		"	I
22		John W.	4	m.			"	
23		Melvina	2	f.			"	
24	271/271	SMITH, Joseph	55	m.	Farmer	1300/380	Va.	I
25		Mary A.	45	f.	Domestic		"	
26		Nancy J.	16	f.	Domestic		O.	
27		Wilson	14	m.			"	S
28		Lydia	13	f.			"	S
29	272/272	SOUTHERS, William	33	m.	Farmer	/400	"	
30		Mary E.	24	f.	Domestic		"	I
31		Albert	11/12 m.				"	
32	273/273	BERNETT, Benjamin	31	m.	Farmer	800/	"	
33		Margaret	25	f.	Domestic		"	
34		John A.	7	m.			"	S
35		Amelia	5	f.			"	S
36		George W.	3	m.			"	
37		Mary J.	8/12 f.				"	
38	274/274	McGILL, Robert	65	m.	Weaver	150/150	Ire.	
39		Barbary	57	f.	Domestic		Pa.	I
40		TUTTLE, Annie	60	f.	Domestic		Md.	I

Page 43   16 June 1860   Sheet 250

1	275/275	MERSH, Charles H.	57	m.	Farmer	1200/250	Md.	
2		Eliza J.	27	f.	Domestic		O.	
3		Charles J.	3	m.			"	
4		Amelia E.	1	f.			"	
5	276/276	CURTIS, Amos	31	m.	Farmer	500/200	"	I

6		CURTIS, Elisabeth	28	f.	Domestic	O.	I
7		Alvira	9	f.		"	S
8		Mary A.	8	f.		"	S
9		Sarah A.	6	f.		"	S
10		Nancy E.	4	f.		"	
11		James R.	3	m.		"	
12		Joseph L.	8/12	m.		"	
13	277/277	SWAIN, James	60	m.	Farm laborer	/100	Md.
14		Eleanor	48	f.	Domestic		"
15		Thomas	7	m.			O.
16	278/278	ADIS, John	27	m.	Farm laborer	/100	Md. I
17		Martha	23	f.	Domestic		O. I
18		Elisabeth	3	f.			"
19		Jane	1	f.			"
20	279/279	PEPPER, Minor	69	m.	Farmer	1100/330	Del.
21		Elisabeth	64	f.	Domestic		"
22		Andrew	26	m.	Farm laborer		Va.
23		Alfred	19	m.	Farm laborer		O.
24		Mary	21	f.	Domestic		"
25	280/280	DULY, Nathaniel	44	m.	Farmer	2200/500	Md. I
26		Mary	32	f.	Domestic		O. I
27		Sarah A.	17	f.	Domestic		" S
28		Lydia M.	15	f.			"
29		William H.	15	m.	Farm laborer		" S
30		Marion	6	m.			"
31		Stephen	3	m.			"
32	281/281	MURRY, Isaac	51	m.	Farmer	5500/1500	Md.
33		Elisabeth	51	f.	Domestic		O.
34		Elisabeth	24	f.	Domestic		"
35		Mary A.	23	f.	Domestic		"
36		George	22	m.	Farm laborer		"
37		Darcus	19	f.	Domestic		" S
38		Marion	18	m.	Farm laborer		"
39		Eliza J.	10	f.			" S
40		Cyntha E.	8	f.			" S

Page 44   15 June 1860   Sheet 250 verso

1	282/282	FORSHEY, Abram	68	m.	Farmer	1500/50	Va.
2		Sarah	64	f.	Domestic		"
3		Thomas	26	m.	Farm laborer	/200	O.
4		Rachel	28	f.	Domestic		"
5		Sarah F.	7	f.			" S
6		Absalom	5	m.			" S
7		Mary A.	3	f.			"
8		James A.	1	m.			"
9	283/283	FORSHEY, Eljah	33	m.	Farm laborer	/150	" I
10		Hetta	34	f.	Domestic		" I
11		Sarah J.	13	f.			" S
12		Cain	11	m.			" S
13		David	9	m.			" S

14		FORSHEY, Jacob	6	m.			O.	S
15		Mary M.	4	f.			"	
16		Naomi M.	2	f.			"	
17		Jasper	1	m.			"	
18	284/284	SMITH, John B.	30	m.	Music Teacher	/30	"	
19		Margaret	30	f.	Domestic		"	I
20		Mariah J.	9	f.			"	S
21		Hariet J.	8	f.			"	S
22		John L.	5	m.			"	
23		Abram V.	8/12	m.			"	
24	285/285	LEISURE, William	31	m.	Farmer	/100	Va.	I
25		Nancy	33	f.	Domestic		"	I
26		Levi	10	m.			"	
27		Melissa	9	f.			"	
28		William	7	m.			"	
29		John	4	m.			"	
30		Eliza A.	2	f.			"	
31		Rachel J.	4/12	f.			"	
32	286/286	LEISURE, John	59	m.	Farmer	600/175	Va.	I
33		Nancy	58	f.	Domestic		"	I
34		John	19	m.	Farm laborer		O.	
35	287/287	PEPPER, Hanson	26	m.	Farmer	/400	"	M
36		Naomi	18	f.	Domestic		"	M
37		Albert W.	2	m.			"	
38	288/288	FORSHEY, David	44	m.	Farmer	1250/300	"	
39		Thomas	21	m.	Farm laborer		"	
40		Mary J.	18	f.	Domestic		"	

Page 45   16 June 1860   Sheet 251

1		Emiline	15	f.	Domestic		O.	
2		John	14	m.			"	S
3		Susan	12	f.			"	S
4		Eliza	10	f.			"	S
5		Mariah	8	f.			"	S
6		William	6	m.			"	S
7		Hariet	1	f.			"	
8	289/289	LISTER, James	42	m.	Farmer	1250/250	N.Y.	I
9		Mary	39	f.	Domestic		O.	I
10		Hester	17	f.	Domestic		"	S
11		Thomas	15	m.	Farm laborer		"	S
12		Matilda	13	f.			"	
13		James	12	m.			"	
14		Samuel	10	m.			"	
15		Matthew	6	m.			"	
16		William M.	1	m.			"	
17	290/290	FORSHEY, Nathaniel	24	m.	Farmer	400/150	"	
18		Mary E.	23	f.	Domestic		Pa.	
19		Isadora	1	f.			O.	
20		Mary J.	12	f.			"	S

```
21 291/291 FORSHEY, Solomon   70  m.   Farmer        1500/250  Pa.
22         Sarah              25  f.   Domestic                O.
23         Stephen D.         2/12 m.                          "

24 292/292 FORSHEY, Elias     23  m.   Farm laborer  /75       "    I
25         Mary J.            20  f.   Domestic                "

26 293/293 KING, John         37  m.   Farmer        1000/200  "
27         Martha M.          36  f.   Domestic                "    I
28         Samuel             17  m.   Farm laborer            "    S
29         Amos               16  m.   Farm laborer            "    S
30         Elisabeth          14  f.                           "    S
31         Mary E.            12  f.                           "    S
32         Matthew            10  m.                           "    S
33         Thomas              6  m.                           "    S
34         Hannah              5  f.                           "
35         Hariet              3  f.                           "
36         Andrew              2  m.                           "
37         John               4/12 m.                          "
38         Elizabeth          78  f.   Domestic                Md.

39 294/294 WATSON, James L.   39  m.   Shoemaker     /500      Va.
40         Elisabeth          38  f.   Domestic                "
```

Page 46   16 June 1860   Sheet 251

```
1          Elias              14  m.                           O.  S
2          Samuel             11  m.                           "   S
3          William             9  m.                           "   S
4          Jane                7  f.                           "
5          James               5  m.                           "
6          Mary                3  f.                           "
7          Leonidas           8/12 m.                          "

8  295/295 MORRIS, Levi       35  m.   Farmer        /300      "
9          Rachel A.          27  f.   Domestic                "
10         Eliza A.            9  f.                           "   S
11         Melissa             8  f.                           "
12         Nancy               5  f.                           "
13         John W.            11/12 m.                         "
14         Ann                72  f.   Domestic                Md.

15 296/296 ANTLE, Thomas      62  m.   Farmer        1500/400  Pa.  I
16         Mary               60  f.   Domestic                "
17         Samuel             18  m.   Farm laborer            "
18         Thomas             12  m.                           "

19 297/297 MORRIS, James      46  m.   Farmer        /300      O.
20         Elisabeth          19  f.   Domestic                "
21         Rachel J.           1  f.                           "
22         William            17  m.   Farm laborer            "   S
23         John               17  m.   Farm laborer            "   S
24         Nelson             15  m.   Farm laborer            "   S

25 298/298 DRAPER, Isaac      29  m.   Farmer        1200/300  Va.
26         Nancy              36  f.   Domestic                Pa.
27         HAGERMAN, Peter    19  m.   Farm laborer            O.
28         FRAZIER, Sarah J.  14  f.                           "
```

29	299/299	ROBINS, Stephen	28	m.	Farmer	600/250	O.
30		Eleanor	23	f.	Domestic		"
31		William	4	m.			"
32		Wilber	1	m.			"
33		FLORE, Mary J.	10	f.			" S
34	300/300	ROBBINS, Levi	50	m.	Farmer	1800/400	"
35		Sarah	28	f.	Domestic		"
36		Swasey	21	m.	Farm laborer		"
37		Levi	19	m.	Farm laborer		" S
38		Wesley	10	m.			" S
39		Danford	2	m.			"
40		SMITH, James	11	m.			" S

Page 47   16 June 1860   Sheet 252

1	301/301	MERICAL, William	35	m.	Farmer	/200	O.
2		Elisabeth	24	f.	Domestic		" I
3		John	11	m.			" S
4		William	8	m.			"
5		Rachel A.	4/12	f.			"
6	302/302	BIRKHART, Joseph	28	m.	Farmer	800/200	Bav.
7		Barbary	32	f.	Domestic		"
8		Margaret	7	m.			O.
9		John	5	m.			"
10		Barbary	3	f.			"
11		Mary	2	f.			"
12		Catharine	1	f.			"
13		Joseph	3/12	m.			"
14	303/303	SWICK, Michael	58	m.	Farmer	2800/800	Bav.
15		Catharine	45	f.	Domestic		"
16		Barbary	15	f.	Domestic		"
17		Mary	10	f.			"
18		Catharine	6	f.			O.
19		Martin	22	m.	Farm laborer		Bav.
20		Orris	19	m.	Carpenter		"
21		George	17	m.	Farm laborer		"
22		Joseph	15	m.	Farm laborer		" S
23		John	12	m.			"
24		Peter	2	m.			O.
25	304/304	SHAHEN, Leander	20	m.	Farmer	/100	"
26		Elisabeth E.	19	f.	Domestic		"
27	305/305	SHAHEN, Mary	41	f.	Domestic		"
28		Abner	19	m.	Farm laborer		"
29		Thomas	17	m.	Farm laborer		"
30		Randolph	14	m.			" S
31		Mary J.	12	f.			" S
32		Albert	6	m.			"
33		Louisa A.	4	f.			"
34	306/306	FORSHEY, Hamilton	42	m.	Farmer	/100	"
35		Martha	39	f.	Domestic		" I
36		Elijah	17	m.	Farm laborer		"
37		Eliza	15	f.	Domestic		"

38		FORSHEY, Emily	13	f.		O.	S
39		Charlotte	11	f.		"	S
40		Nancy	9	f.		"	S

Page 48			18 June 1860			Sheet 252 verso

1		Malinda	7	f.		O.
2		Narcussus	5	f.		"
3		Bathia	3	f.		"
4		Andrew H.	2/12	m.		"

5	307/307	FORSHEY, George	29	m.	Farmer	/150	"
6		Catharine	27	f.	Domestic		"
7		Cadelia	6	f.			"
8		Jane M.	4	f.			"
9		Hariet L.	1	f.			"
10		Benjamin	1/12	m.			"

11	308/308	FORSHEY, Richard	45	m.	Farmer	300/175	"	
12		Bathia	43	f.	Domestic		"	
13		Asa	17	m.	Farm laborer		"	
14		Eliza J.	13	f.			"	S
15		Sebastien	11	m.			"	S
16		Rachel	8	f.			"	
17		Mary A.	5	f.			"	

18	309/309	MALET, Miles	38	m.	Farmer	4400/750	"	
19		Margaret	29	f.	Domestic		"	
20		Clarissa	12	f.			"	S
21		Mary	7	f.			"	S
22		Joseph	5	m.			"	S
23		George	1	m.			"	
24		FORSHEY, Elisha	24	m.	Farm laborer		"	

25	310/310	KING, Thomas	40	m.	Farmer	500/275	"	
26		Mary	36	f.	Domestic		"	I
27		Mariah	17	f.	Domestic		"	
28		Nancy	15	f.	Domestic		"	
29		Mary	13	f.			"	
30		Shaderick	9	m.			"	
31		Robert	5	m.			"	
32		Ann	3	f.			"	
33		Elisabeth	3	f.			"	

34	311/311	GIRE, Harmon	30	m.	Farmer	1100/200	Old.
35		Modelana	25	f.	Domestic		
36		Chritena	6	f.			O.
37		John	4	m.			"
38		Henry	2	m.			"

39	312/312	HUGHES, David	23	m.	Farmer	/375	"
40		Mary	23	f.	Domestic		"

Page 49			18 June 1860			Sheet 253

1		Alvira	2	f.	O.
2		Ballet	6/12	f.	"

3	313/313	HUGHES, Benjamin	50	m.	Farmer	8600/1600	Pa.
4		Elisabeth	40	f.	Domestic		"
5		Thomas	19	m.	Farm laborer		O. S
6		Uriah	17	m.	Farm laborer		" S
7		Allen	15	m.	Farm laborer		" S
8		Theodore	13	m.			" S
9		Winfield	12	m.			" S
10		Elisabeth	8	f.			"
11		DUNLAP, Jane	20	f.	Domestic		La.
12		CURTIS, Bennet	15	m.	Farm laborer		O. S
13		Albert	11	m.			" S
14		Mary	9	f.			" S
15		Church	6	f.			" S
16	314/314	STARKEY, Henry	37	m.	Farmer	/300	"
17		Mary	34	f.	Domestic		"
18		Minor	15	m.	Farm laborer		" S
19		Malinda	10	f.			" S
20		Margaret	7	f.			" S
21		Mary A.	5	f.			"
22		George	3	m.			"
23	315/315	BARLOW, George	43	m.	Farmer	1200/500	"
24		Mary A.	40	f.	Domestic		" I
25		Zachariah	19	m.	Farm laborer		" S
26		Benjamin	17	m.	Farm laborer		" S
27		John W.	14	m.			" S
28		Margaret E.	9	f.			" S
29		Mary C.	5	f.			"
30	316/316	CLAY, John	55	m.	Farmer	600/175	Pa. I
31		Province	45	f.	Domestic		O. I
32		Zachariah	25	m.	Farm laborer	/75	"
33		Elisabeth	23	f.	Domestic		"
34		Margaret	19	f.	Domestic		"
35		Sarah	14	f.			"
36		Martha	1	f.			"
37	317/317	LEMASTER, Septamus	35	m.	Farmer	500/150	Va.
38		Mary	31	f.	Domestic		O.
39		Emmer	11	m.			" S
40		Maranda	13	f.			" S

Page 50　　　　　　19 June 1860　　　　　Sheet 253 verso

1		Jasper	10	m.			O. S
2		Richard	6	m.			"
3		Isaac	2	m.			"
4		Elisabeth J.	10/12	f.			"
5	318/318	WELLS, William	31	m.	Farmer	/200	"
6		Permina	26	f.	Domestic		Pa. I
7		James	1	m.			O.
8	319/319	PICHET, Joseph	47	m.	Farm laborer		"
9		Mary E.	44	f.	Domestic		"
10		William	16	m.			"
11		Theodore	14	m.			"

12		PICKET, Amelia	12	f.		O.
13		Catharine J.	8	f.		"
14	320/320	CAVANAGH, Malchi	41	m.	Farmer /300	Pa.
15		Annie	44	f.	Domestic	Md. I
16		George A.	22	m.	Farm laborer	O.
17		Albert A.	19	m.	Farm laborer	"
18		Louisa J.	15	f.	Domestic	" S
19		Mariah	13	f.		" S
20		John R.	11	m.		" S
21		William T.	8	m.		" S
22		Sarah E.	3	f.		"
23	321/321	CAVANAGH, Timothy	69	m.	Farmer 1200/200	Pa.
24		Mariah	66	f.	Domestic	"
25		FRYMAN, Mary	93	f.	Domestic	"
26		CURREN, Hannah	9	f.		O.
27	322/322	ROBINS, William	25	m.	Farmer /200	"
28		Elisabeth	22	f.	Domestic	" I
29		Onna C.	6	f.		"
30	323/323	SMITH, Josiah	30	m.	Farmer 500/200	" I
31		Caroline	28	f.	Domestic	" I
32		William B.	8	m.		" S
33		James	6	m.		" S
34		John H.	1	m.		"
35	324/324	BERNETT, John	50	m.	Farmer 1200/200	Md.
36		Nancy	49	f.	Domestic	Va. I
37		William	20	m.	Farm laborer	O. I
38		Jacob	17	m.	Farm laborer	"
39		Catharine	14	m.		" S
40	325/325	THOMPSON, Albert P.	32	m.	Farmer /250	Pa.

1		Rachel M.	29	f.	Domestic	Pa.
2		Thomas L.	9	m.		O. S
3		Albert F.	7	m.		" S
4		Amanda E.	3	f.		"
5		Mary A.	1	f.		"
6		not named	1/12	m.		"
7		Ann	62	f.	Domestic 3100/250	Pa.
8	326/326	HEARTLY, John S.	25	m.	Farmer /300	O.
9		Ellen	23	f.	Domestic	Pa.
10		William R.	3	m.		O.
11		Allen C.	2	m.		"
12		Sarah M.	8/12	f.		"
13	327/327	CLEGG, Thomas	31	m.	Farmer 600/200	"
14		Elisabeth	27	f.	Domestic	" I
15		Harmina	11	f.		" S
16		John	9	m.		" S

17		CLEGG, Lucinda	7	f.			O.	S
18		Richard	5	m.			"	
19		Samuel R.	1	m.			"	
20	328/328	THOMPSON, Joseph	53	m.	Farmer	1600/225	Pa.	
21		Anne S.	47	f.	Domestic		"	
22		Margaret A.	17	f.	Domestic		"	S
23		Fremen C.	15	m.	Farm laborer		"	S
24		Hirem N.	12	m.			"	S
25		Clara J.	10	f.			"	S
26		Albert S.	6	m.			"	S
27		Emily R.	4	f.			"	
28	329/329	THOMPSON, William	29	m.	Farmer	/300	"	
29		Mary E.	24	f.	Domestic		O.	
30		Ida A.	3	f.			"	
31		Hortense	2	f.			"	
32		Emeretta	1/12	f.			"	
33	330/330	STEED, Jonas A.	22	m.	Farm laborer	/125	"	
34		Sarah E.	25	f.	Domestic		Pa.	
35	331/331	BARLOW, George	84	m.	Farmer	1500/200	Md.	I
36		Margaret	65	f.	Domestic		"	
37	332/332	STARKEY, Benjamin	60	m.	Farmer	2600/500	Pa.	M
38		Melissa	43	f.	Domestic		Va.	M
39		WIRE, Verl J.	18	f.	Domestic		O.	
40		Wm.	16	m.			"	

Page 52   19 June 1860   Sheet 254 verso

1		Dow	7	m.			O.	S
2	332/332	STALLINGS, Knnilus	33	m.	Farmer	/50	Md.	I
3		Martha A.	24	f.	Domestic		O.	
4		Margaret E.	6	f.			"	
5	333/333	MERICAL, Isaac	35	m.	Farmer		"	
6		Patience	27	f.	Domestic		"	
7		Hannah J.	9	f.			"	
8		Margaret	7	f.			"	
9		Martha	5	f.			"	
10		Meranda	1	f.			"	
11		John	74	m.	Farmer	1200/150	"	
12	334/334	KING, Elijah	45	m.	Farmer	/200	"	
13		Mary	42	f.	Domestic		"	I
14		Adaline	16	f.	Domestic		"	
15		John	11	m.			"	
16		Jehu	8	m.			"	
17		Amanda E.	6	f.			"	
18		Melissa	3	f.			"	
19		Albert	1	m.			"	
20		William	24	m.	Farm laborer		"	I
21		Ann	23	f.	Domestic		"	
22		Rachel J.	3	f.			"	
23		Thomas S.	2	m.			"	

24	335/335	McELFRESH, Cornelius A.	25	m.	Farmer	/100	O. I
25		Catharine	22	f.	Domestic		" I
26		Welcome L.	3	f.			"
27		Martha	7/12	f.			"
28	336/336	STARKEY, Edward	31	m.	Farmer	600/300	"
29		Catharine	26	f.	Domestic		"
30		John	9	m.			" S
31		Willis	2	m.			"
32		George	16	m.	Farm laborer		"
33	337/337	LONG, Simeon	33	m.	Farmer	600/300	Eng.
34		Hannah	40	f.	Domestic		Va. I
35		Joseph	15	m.	Farm laborer		O.
36	338/338	THORNTON, Elijah	45	m.	Farmer	1600/750	Va. I
37		Mary J.	34	f.	Domestic		O.
38		Reuben	17	m.	Farm laborer		" S
39		John	13	m.			" S
40		Elisabeth	11	f.			" S

Page 53   19 June 1860   Sheet 255

1		Lucetta	8	f.			O. S
2		Richerd	6	m.			" S
3		Amanda	4	f.			"
4		Malchi	2	m.			"
5		Albert	2/12	m.			"
6	339/339	MORRIS, Robert	33	m.	Farmer	1200/300	" I
7		Rebecca	30	f.	Domestic		" I
8		William	14	m.			" S
9		Mary J.	11	f.			" S
10		Levi T.	9	m.			" S
11		Charlotte	3	m.			"
12	340/340	McKEE, James	20	m.	Farm laborer		N.Y. M
13		Theressa	22	f.	Domestic		Eng. M
14	341/341	RAY, George	30	m.	Farmer	600/150	Pa. I
15		Mary E.	25	f.	Domestic		N.Y.
16		William A.	8	m.			O. S
17		George	7	m.			" S
18		Jasper	5	m.			" S
19		Lilian	3	f.			"
20	342/342	STALLINGS, David	46	m.	Farmer	1600/500	Md.
21		Ann	40	f.	Domestic		" I
22		William	21	m.	Farm laborer		O.
23		Mary J.	17	f.	Domestic		"
24		John	15	m.	Farm laborer		" S
25		David	14	m.			" S
26		Susan	11	f.			" S
27		TURNER, Melissa J.	1	f.			"
28	343/343	COULTER, David	44	m.	Farmer		" I
29		Eliza	40	f.	Domestic		Va. I

30		COULTER, Lydia	7	f.			Va.	S
31		Mariah M.	5	f.			"	S
32		Cordelia	6	f.			"	
33		Hugh	3	m.			"	
34	344/344	ROBINSON, Hugh	40	m.	Farmer	4500/1000	Ire.	
35		Elisabeth	34	f.	Domestic		O.	
36		George	8	m.			"	S
37		Francis M.	5	m.			"	S
38		Mary J.	12	f.			"	S
39	345/345	McVEY, Thomas	25	m.	Farmer	/100	"	M
40		Margaret	20	f.	Domestic		"	M

Page 54   20 June 1860   Sheet 255 verso

1	346/346	McVEY, Elias	23	m.	Farmer	/150	O.	M
2		Sarah J.	18	f.	Domestic		"	M
3	347/347	MERICAL, Thomas	44	m.	Farmer	/75	"	
4		Charlotte	40	f.	Domestic		"	
5		John	21	m.	Farm laborer		"	S
6		Margaret	19	f.	Domestic		"	S
7	348/348	MERICAL, Jesse	47	m.	Farmer	2300/750	"	
8		Meranda	32	f.	Domestic		"	I
9		Adam S.	19	m.	Farm laborer		"	S
10		William J.	15	m.	Farm laborer		"	S
11		John I.	12	m.			"	S
12		Caroline	16	f.	Domestic		"	
13		McVEY, Emily	12	f.			"	S
14		Mary	10	f.			"	S
15		Ann	8	f.			"	
16		Hariet J.	7	f.			"	
17		Sarah A.	5	f.			"	
18		Ellen S.	1	f.			"	
19	349/349	McVEY, Benjamin	49	m.	Farmer	2850/750	"	
20		Nancy A.	52	f.	Domestic		"	
21		Ann	18	f.	Domestic		"	S
22		George	15	m.	Farm laborer		"	S
23		Benjamin	13	m.			"	S
24	350/350	HOGUE, Stephen	38	m.	Farmer	2100/450	Va.	
25		Elisabeth	37	f.	Domestic		O.	
26		Joseph	15	m.	Farm laborer		"	S
27		Moses	13	m.			"	S
28		Lucinda	11	f.			"	S
29		Nelson	9	m.			"	S
30		Ann	7	f.			"	S
31		Miller	3	m.			"	
32		Jane	1	f.			"	
33	351/351	MERICAL, Samuel	39	m.	Farmer	600/150	"	
34		Nancy	37	f.	Domestic		Ire.	
35		Elisabeth A.	16	f.	Domestic		O.	S
36		John A.	10	m.			"	S

37		MERICAL, Ellen V.	7	f.			O.	S
38		Jesse F. S.	3	m.			"	
39	352/352	McELFRESH, Adam	21	m.	Farmer	/200	"	M
40		Sarah	19	f.	Domestic		"	M

Page 55   20 June 1860   Sheet 256

1	353/353	McELFRESH, Joshua	46	m.	Farmer	2250/800	Md.	I
2		Mary A.	47	f.	Domestic		"	
3		William	18	m.	Farm laborer		O.	S
4		Mary J.	14	f.			"	S
5		Irvin	11	m.			"	S
6		Henry	9	m.			"	S
7	354/354	HANSON, Nancy	39	f.	Farmer	2300/500	"	I
8		Sarah	22	f.	Domestic		"	
9		Isaac	16	m.	Farm laborer		"	S
10		Deborah	13	f.			"	S
11		William	10	m.			"	S
12		Mary E.	7	f.			"	S
13		Henry	5	m.			"	"
14		Edward	1	m.			"	
15		MILLIGAN, Edward	22	m.	Farm laborer		"	
16	355/355	ST. JHON, Michael	51	m.	Farmer	1250/300	Fr.	
17		Sarah	57	f.	Domestic		"	
18		Catharine	21	f.	Domestic		O.	
19		Christien	19	m.	Farm laborer		"	S
20		Lewis	17	m.	Farm laborer		"	S
21	356/356	McELFRESH, Henry	40	m.	Farmer	1500/1150	Md.	
22		Mary	36	f.	Domestic		O.	
23		Hariet	17	f.	Domestic		"	
24		Hannah	15	f.	Domestic		"	
25		James W.	13	m.			"	S
26		Mariah	13	f.			"	S
27		Rachel	9	f.			"	S
28	357/357	McELFRESH, William	35	m.	Farm laborer		"	S
29		Elisabeth	24	f.	Domestic		"	I
30		Nathaniel	13	m.			"	
31		Cornelius	9	m.			"	
32		Henry	7	m.			"	
33		John W.	4	m.			"	
34		Samuel W.	3	m.			"	
35		Hannah E.	1	f.			"	
36	358/358	BORTON, Aaron	32	m.	Farmer	1600/450	"	
37		Ellen	33	f.	Domestic		"	
38		Lucinda	9	f.			"	S
39		Mary E.	6	f.			"	S
40		William	3	m.			"	

Page 56   20 June 1860   Sheet 256

1		Mary	1	f.			O.
2		BERNES, William	81	m.	Farm laborer		Md.

3		WILSON, Asa	13	m.			O.	S
4	359/359	MILLIGAN, William	50	m.	Farmer	1200/575	"	
5		Ann	44	f.	Domestic		Pa.	
6		Calvary	19	m.	Farm laborer		O.	S
7		Mary	15	f.	Domestic		"	S
8		Caroline	13	f.			"	S
9		Cowden	10	m.			"	S
10		Sarah	9	f.			"	S
11		Rebecca	6	f.			"	S
12		John F.	2	m.			"	
13	360/360	NEIHART, Lewis	28	m.	Farmer	/750	Bav.	
14		Mariah	26	f.	Domestic		Pa.	
15		Catharine	2	f.			O.	
16		Elisabeth	1	f.			"	
17	361/361	NEIHART, Valentine	56	m.	Farmer	1500/350	Bav.	
18		Catharine	54	f.	Domestic		"	
19	362/362	NEIHART, Frederick	26	m.	Master Carpenter	/200	"	
20		Barbary	21	f.	Domestic		Md.	
21		Frederick	6	m.			O.	
22		Henry	1	m.			"	
23	363/363	COHERT, Jacob	31	m.	Farmer	575/250	Bav.	
24		Elisabeth	28	f.	Domestic		"	
25		HOOFMAN, Margaret	50	f.	Domestic		"	
26		David	10	m.			"	
27	364/364	WILHELM, David	38	m.	Farmer	1500/400	"	
28		Mary	36	f.	Domestic		"	I
29		Elisabeth	12	f.			O.	S
30		Mary	10	f.			"	S
31		Margaret	8	f.			"	
32		Daniel	6	m.			"	
33		Henrietta	3	f.			"	
34		not named	1/12	m.			"	
35	365/365	McGOVENS, William	24	m.	Farmer		"	
36		Martha	20	f.	Domestic		"	
37	366/366	TURNER, Richard	39	m.	Farmer	1500/	Md.	I
38		Elisabeth	40	f.	Domestic		"	I
39		John R.	14	m.			"	S
40		Samuel	12	m.			O.	S

Page 57		20 June 1860				Sheet 257
1		Sarah B.	10	f.		O.
2		Margaret A.	8	f.		"
3		Joseph	6	m.		"
4		Susan E.	4	f.		"
5		Melissa	1	f.		"
6	367/367	WILSON, William	25	m.	Farmer /200	"
7		Hariet	21	f.	Domestic	"
8		Sarah E.	3	f.		"

9		WILSON, Mary E.	2	f.			O.
10		Thomas W.	7/12	m.			"
11	368/368	WILSON, John	26	m.	Farmer	/205	"
12		Mary E.	21	f.	Domestic		"
13		Sarah M.	3	f.			"
14		Martha A.	1	f.			"
15		CHAMBERS, Susan J.	17	f.			" S
16	369/369	DECEMBER, Peter	44	m.	Farmer	650/200	Bav.
17		Mary	12	f.			"
18	370/370	MOORE, Josiah	52	m.	Farmer	1000/500	Pa.
19		Nancy	52	f.	Domestic		" I
20		Thomas	18	m.	Farm laborer		O.
21		Robert	13	m.			"
22	371/371	TURNER, Randolph	30	m.	Farmer	500/200	Pa.
23		Elisabeth	23	f.	Domestic		O.
24		Hiram	1	m.			"
25	372/372	BARLOW, Joshua	29	m.	Master Carpenter 25/100		"
26		Lucinda	27	f.	Domestic		"
27		Coleman	6	m.			" S
28		Mary J.	1	f.			"
29	373/373	HOGUE, William	26	m.	Farmer	600/200	"
30		Elisabeth	31	f.	Domestic		" I
31	374/374	SLOAN, John	55	m.	Farmer	6000/900	Pa.
32		Susan	52	f.	Domestic		" I
33		John Jr.	23	m.	Farm laborer		O.
34		Peter	21	m.	Farm laborer		" I
35		William	19	m.	Farm laborer		" S
36		Elisabeth	17	f.	Domestic		" S
37		Jane	13	f.			" S
38		Campsadell	9	f.			" S
39		SCOTT, Thomas	19	m.	Farm laborer		"
40	375/375	SLOAN, Oliver	29	m.	Farmer	1200/250	"

Page 58   20 June 1860   Sheet 257 verso

1		Mary J.	28	f.	Domestic		O.
2		Emiline	8	f.			" S
3		William H.	6	m.			"
4		James	1	m.			"
5	376/376	MALSTON, Andrew	44	m.	Farmer	/50	Pa.
6		Sarah	35	f.	Domestic		O. I
7		Melinda	13	f.			"
8		Robert	8	m.			"
9		Lorenzo	6	m.			"
10		Andrew	4	m.			"
11		Sarah	2	f.			
12	377/377	HOLDEN, John	39	m.	Farmer	1400/300	"

13		HOLDEN, Mahala	36	f.	Domestic		O.	
14		Mary A.	15	f.	Domestic		"	S
15		Martha J.	13	f.			"	S
16		James M.	11	m.			"	S
17		Sarah E.	8	f.			"	S
18		John W.	6	m.			"	S
19		Jacob A.	4	m.			"	
20		McKEE, Mary	68	f.	Domestic		Pa.	
21	378/378	WHEELER, John W.	50	m.	Farmer	4000/1100	"	
22		Rachel	52	f.	Domestic		Va.	
23		Elijah	25	m.	Farm laborer		O.	
24		James	21	m.	Farm laborer		"	S
25		Allen	19	m.	Farm laborer		"	S
26		Edward	17	m.	Farm laborer		"	S
27		Eliza A.	15	f.	Domestic		"	S
28		Robert	12	m.			"	S
29		Mariah	10	f.			"	S
30	379/379	WHEELER, William	85	m.	Nothing		Pa.	I
31		Mary	85	f.	Nothing		"	I
32		Sarah	16	f.	Domestic		O.	S
33	380/380	FAREN, Irvin	40	m.	Carpenter	/25	"	
34		Christena	41	f.	Domestic		"	I
35		Edward	19	m.	Farm laborer		"	
36		Aaron	17	m.	Farm laborer		"	
37		Francis	15	m.	Farm laborer		"	S
38		Alfred	11	m.			"	S
39		Henrietta	8	f.			"	
40		Melissa	5	f.			"	

Page 59			20 June 1860				Sheet 258	
1		Charles	2	m.			O.	
2	381/381	MOORE, John	33	m.	Farmer	/15	Pa.	
3		Elisabeth	27	f.	Domestic		O.	
4		Melissa	5	f.			"	
5		David T.	3	m.			"	
6		Elial	1	m.			"	
7		Thomas	18	m.	Farm laborer		"	
8	382/382	CROE, Peter	41	m.	Farmer	1000/450	"	
9		Hulda	45	f.	Domestic		"	I
10		William	18	m.	Farm laborer		"	
11		Louisa	14	f.			"	
12		Nancy	6	f.			"	
13		Elisabeth	4	f.			"	
14	383/383	EARLY, Alexander	61	m.	Farmer	/15	Pa.	
15		Almyra	38	f.	Domestic		O.	I
16		William	8	m.			"	
17		Wesley	4	m.			"	
18		Ruth A.	1	f.			"	
19	384/384	GIVINS, David	42	m.	Farmer	1500/500	Pa.	
20		Charity	43	f.	Domestic		"	I

21		GIVINS, Thomas	19	m.	Farm laborer		O.	
22		Sarah	18	f.	Domestic		"	
23		John	14	m.			"	S
24		Ellen	13	f.			"	
25		Tacy	11	f.			"	
26		Sesen	10	f.			"	S

27	385/385	JOHNSON, John	73	m.	Farmer	1600/300	Ire.	
28		Margaret	30	f.	Domestic		"	
29		Flora T.	3	f.			O.	

30	386/386	DAILY, Vincent	45	m.	Farmer	/300	"	
31		Margaret	43	f.	Domestic		"	
32		James	18	m.	Farm laborer		"	23
33		Thomas	13	m.			"	23
34		Peter	11	m.	Farm laborer		"	
35		Oliver	11	m.			"	
36		McKEE, Thomas	88	m.			"	1

37	387/387	WHEETIN, Mary	40	f.	Farmer	/100	Pa.	I
38		Phebe	18	f.	Domestic		O.	
39		Minerva	15	f.	Domestic		"	S
40		Theodore	13	m.			♥	S

| Page 60 | | | 21 June 1860 | | | | Sheet 258 verso | |

| 1 | | William | 10 | m. | | | O. | S |
| 2 | | Mary A. | 8 | f. | | | " | S |

3	388/388	McVEY, Joseph	32	m.	Farmer	1200/400	"	
4		Isabelle	26	f.	Domestic		"	I
5		William	11	m.			"	S
6		Jacob	9	m.			"	S
7		Elisabeth	7	f.			"	S
8		John	5	m.			"	
9		Freemen	3	m.			"	
10		Mary W.	2	f.			"	

11	389/389	CECIL, Hazel	51	m.	Farmer	2500/600	"	I
12		Sarah	52	f.	Domestic		"	I
13		Rhoda	19	f.	Domestic		"	S
14		Sarah A.	17	f.	Domestic		"	S
15		Phena	14	f.			"	S

16	390/390	DARNEL, Andrew	25	m.	Farm laborer		"	I
17		Catharine	24	f.	Domestic		"	
18		Mariah	4	f.			"	
19		Julian	2	f.			"	
20		Mary	1/12	f.			"	

21	391/391	MOBLEY, Amos	26	m.	Farmer	/150	"	
22		Margaret	21	f.	Domestic		"	
23		Sarah J.	2	f.			"	

24	392/392	CRAIG, Sarah	40	f.	Domestic	1450/300	Pa.	
25		David	14	m.			O.	S
26		Roseberry	12	f.			"	S
27		James T.	10	m.			"	S

28		CRAIG, Deborah	8	f.			"	O. S
29	393/393	MALSTON, Sarah	35	m.	Domestic		"	I
30		Cornelius	15	m.	Laborer		"	S
31		Hannah	8	f.			"	
32		James M.	5	m.			"	
33		Eliza M.	2	f.			"	
34	394/394	WINLAND, Alexander	38	m.	Farmer	1200/275	"	I
35		Hannah J.	35	f.	Domestic		"	
36		John L.	5	m.			"	
37		Mary	3	f.			"	
38		Margaret J.	8/12	f.			"	
39		AMOS, Malen	22	m.	Farm laborer		"	

40 395/--- UNOCCUPIED

Page 61   21 June 1860   Sheet 259

1	396/395	WINLAND, John	27	m.	Farmer	/600	O.	
2		Mariah	27	f.	Domestic		"	I
3		James	4	m.			"	
4		Mary E.	2	f.			"	
5	397/396	WISE, Amos	22	m.	Farm laborer		"	
6		Mary	21	f.	Domestic		"	I
7		Anne E.	3	f.			"	
8		George W.	6/12	m.			"	
9	398/397	TURNER, James F.	30	m.	Farmer	/500	"	
10		Jane	25	f.	Domestic		"	I
11		Henry	5	m.			"	S
12		James W.	3	m.			"	
13		John D.	2	m.			"	
14		Elbrige	7/12	m.			"	
15	399/398	TURNER, Elbridge	58	m.	Farm laborer		Md.	I
16		Elisabeth	68	f.	Domestic		Pa.	I
17	400/399	WINLAND, Jacob	34	m.	Farmer	2000/250	O.	
18		Mariah	31	f.	Domestic		"	
19		William	14	m.			"	S
20		John H.	11	m.			"	S
21		Sindarilla	9	f.			"	S
22		Hannah	5	f.			"	
23		Winfield S.	3	m.			"	
24		Isadora	10/12	f.			"	
25	401/400	GIVENS, Daniel	47	m.	Farmer	1900/300	Pa.	
26		Jemima A.	47	f.	Domestic		"	
27		George W.	20	m.	Farm laborer		O.	
28		Susan	17	f.	Domestic		"	S
29		Sarah	15	f.	Domestic		"	S
30		Lydia	12	f.			"	S
31		Hannah	8	f.			"	
32		Daniel S.	22	m.	Farm laborer		"	
33	402/401	McCONNELL, John	35	m.	Farm laborer	200/400	"	

34	McCONNELL, Sarah	33	f.	Domestic		O.	
35	Levi	13	m.			"	S
36	Henry	11	m.			"	S
37	Isabella	7	f.			"	S
38	Sarah A.	3	f.			"	

39	403/402	DENNIS, Joseph	35	m.	Farmer	500/225	Va.	I
40		Hester	28	f.	Domestic		N.Y.	I

Page 62   21 June 1860   Sheet 259 verso

1	Fred W.	11	m.			O.	S
2	Moses W.	9	m.			"	S
3	Mary E.	6	f.			"	S
4	Sarah C.	3	f.			"	
5	Abram	1	m.			"	

6	404/403	MAHONA, John	34	m.	Farmer	500/200	"	I
7		Louisa	25	f.	Domestic		"	I
8		William T.	13	m.			"	S
9		Elisabeth	11	f.			"	S
10		Sarah A.	6	f.			"	S
11		Hannah	4	f.			"	
12		John A.	2	m.			"	
13		Alexander	1	m.			"	

14	405/404	CALVERT, Jacob J.	66	m.	Farmer	1700/600	Pa.	
15		Mary	63	f.	Domestic		Va.	
16		Margaret E.	27	f.	Teacher		O.	S
17		James W.	25	m.	Farm laborer		"	
18		John D.	21	m.	Farm laborer		"	
19		Elce T.	19	f.	Domestic		"	S

20	406/405	GARDNER, Joseph	31	m.	Farmer	500/200	"	
21		Isabella	33	f.	Domestic		"	I
22		William J.	12	m.			"	S
23		Mary L.	9	f.			"	S
24		Wesley K.	7	m.			"	S
25		Andrew	5	m.			"	S
26		Melissa	3	f.			"	
27		not named	4/12	m.			"	
28		BOLTON, Jane	47	f.	Domestic		Pa.	I

29	407/406	McCONNELL, Wesley	23	m.	Teacher		"	
30		CAREY, Robert	40	m.	Farmer	/100	Del.	
31		Mary	43	f.	Domestic		"	
32		Martha M.	15	f.			O.	S
33		Samuel	13	m.			"	S
34		John T.	11	m.			"	S
35		George R.	9	m.			"	S
36		Robert S.	7	m.			"	S

37	408/407	LUBURG, John	46	m.	Farmer	1500/440	Md.	
38		Susan	41	f.	Domestic		Pa.	
39		Rachel A.	13	f.			O.	S
40		Wesley	12	m.			"	S

Page 63				21 June 1860			Sheet 260	
1	409/408	WELLS, David	31	m.	Farmer	/200	O.	I
2		Rebecca A.	39	f.	Domestic		Md.	I
3		Ala J.	6	f.			O.	S
4		Amos A.	3	m.			"	
5		not named	1	f.			"	
6	410/409	WELLS, Elisabeth	56	f.	Farmer	1600/275	O.	I
7		Ann	22	f.	Domestic		"	
8		Samuel	21	m.	Farm laborer		"	
9		Thomas M.	17	m.	Farm laborer		"	
10		Liza A.	17	f.	Domestic		"	
11		David D.	15	m.	Farm laborer		"	
12	411/410	HINES, Thomas	43	m.	Farmer	2000/525	"	
13		Elisabeth	35	f.	Domestic		"	
14		Joseph	20	m.	Farm laborer		"	S
15		Susan	18	f.	Domestic		"	S
16		Daniel	16	m.	Farm laborer		"	S
17		William	13	m.			"	S
18		Edward	11	m.			"	S
19		Theodore	9	m.			"	S
20		Elisabeth	7	f.			"	S
21		Margaret	5	f.			"	S
22		George	3	m.			"	
23		Atty	2/12	m.			"	
24	412/411	HINES, Joseph	47	m.	Farmer	9040/1000	Va.	
25		Hester	41	f.	Domestic		O.	
26		Woodman	19	m.	Farm laborer		"	S
27		George	17	m.	Student		"	S
28		Hiram	15	m.	Farm laborer		"	S
29		Thomas	13	m.			"	S
30		Elisabeth	11	f.			"	S
31		Nahem	8	m.			"	S
32		BEMES, Bazel	34	m.	Farm laborer		"	
33	413/412	ANTLE, John H.	24	m.	Farmer		"	M
34		Susannah E.	21	f.	Domestic		"	M
35	414/413	WILSON, Samuel J.	35	m.	Farmer	1250/320	O.	
36		Catharine	27	f.	Domestic		"	
37		Mary J.	9	f.			"	S
38		Martha E.	7	f.			"	S
39		William C.	3	m.			"	
40		Elisabeth M.	1	f.			"	

Page 64				22 June 1860			Sheet 260 verso	
1	415/414	COX, Joseph	31	m.	Farmer	1250/300	Md.	
2		Margaret	23	f.	Domestic		O.	I
3		James W.	9	m.			"	S
4		Mary E.	4	f.			"	
5		John J.	1	m.			"	
6		Jeremiah	20	m.	Farm laborer		"	
7	416/415	COX, James	61	m.	Farmer	1400/1200	Md.	

8		COX, Matilda	54	f.	Domestic	Md. I
9		Franklin	23	m.	Farm laborer	O.
10		Rebecca A.	18	f.	Domestic	"
11		Marinda	9	f.		" S
12	417/416	COX, Wesley	27	m.	Farm laborer /275	"
13		Lucinda	19	f.	Domestic	"
14	418/417	WILSON, William	48	m.	Farmer 2800/600	Va.
15		Mary	46	f.	Domestic	"
16		William	16	m.	Farm laborer	O. S
17		Henry	14	m.		" S
18		James	11	m.		" S
19		Winfield	9	m.		" S
20		Martha	8	f.		" S
21		Theodore	4	m.		"
22	419/418	WILSON, Thomas	25	m.	Student	"
23		Rachel	24	f.	Domestic	"
24		Oscar F.	1	m.		"
25	420/419	WILSON, Thomas Sr.	50	m.	Farmer 4000/700	Va.
26		Sarah	48	f.	Domestic	"
27		Nancy	21	f.	Domestic	O.
28		George	19	m.	Farm laborer	" S
29		Susan	16	f.	Domestic	" S
30		Martha	7	f.		" S
31		Henry	15	m.	Farm laborer	" S
32	421/420	STALLINGS, James				
		Jr.	33	m.	Farmer 3000/600	Md.
33		Mariah	32	f.	Domestic	O.
34		Edward	11	m.		" S
35		Joseph	9	m.		" S
36		Margaret B.	3	f.		"
37		STEWART, Thomas	17	m.	Farm laborer	"
38	422/421	LINGO, Henry H.	37	m.	Miller 1500/300	"
39		Sarah	35	f.	Domestic	"
40		Jane E.	10	f.		" S

Page 65   22 June 1860   Sheet 261

1		Edward T.	6	m.		O. S
2		William H.	5	m.		" S
3		Benjamin A.	1	m.		"
4	423/422	OSHAL, James	60	m.	Farmer 4000/200	Pa.
5		Sarah	56	f.	Domestic	Va. I
6		John	21	m.	Farm laborer	O.
7		Thomas W.	20	m.	Farm laborer	"
8		Mary E.	17	f.	Domestic	"
9	424/423	OSHAL, William W.	33	m.	Farmer 1000/200	"
10		Elisabeth	30	f.	Domestic	"
11		Rhoda	7	f.		"
12		Sarah A.	5	f.		" S
13		William	1	m.		"

14		OSHAL, Peter M.	31	m.		Farmer	800/200	O.	
15		Harriet	27	f.		Domestic		"	
16		Uphona	2	f.				"	
17		James	1	m.				"	
18	425/424	OSHAL, James F.	28	m.		Farmer	/225	"	
19		Margaret	26	f.		Domestic		"	
20		Joseph	4	m.				"	
21		James	2	m.				"	
22		William	6/12	m.				"	
23		COURCY, Joshua	26	m.	M.	Farm laborer			
24	426/425	HAWKINS, Elisabeth	36	f.		Farmer		"	
25		Mary	15	f.		Domestic		"	S
26		John	13	m.				"	S
27		Jane	10	f.				"	S
28		Benjamin	8	m.				"	S
29		Oswell	6	m.				"	S
30		Ann M.	4	f.				"	
31		Mary	80	f.		Domestic		Pa.	I
32	427/426	CURTIS, Benjamin	104	m.	B.	Nothing		Va.	I
33	428/427	CURTIS, Harrisson	54	m.	M.	Farmer	1000/300	"	
34		Cloe	51	f.	M.	Domestic		"	I
35		Francis	21	f.	M.	Domestic		"	I
36		Eliza J.	16	f.	M.	Domestic		"	
37		John	23	m.	M.	Farm laborer		"	I
38		Mary J.	23	f.	M.	Domestic		"	I
39		Ross	4	m.	M.			O.	
40		Mariah	6	f.	M.			"	

Page 66   22 June 1860   Sheet 261 verso

1		David A.	1	m.				O.	
2	429/428	CURTIS, Jacob	35	m.	B.	Farmer	600/200	Va.	I
3		Mary J.	31	f.	M.	Domestic		"	I
4		Rebecca	2	f.	M.			O.	
5		Melvina	8/12	f.	M.			"	
6		BIRK, John	10	m.	M.			Va.	
7	430/429	ARMSTRONG, Joseph	40	m.	M.	Farm laborer		"	
8		Mary	40	f.	M.	Domestic		"	
9		Martha	14	f.	M.			"	S
10		Elisabeth	12	f.	M.			"	S
11		Ann	12	f.	M.			"	
12		William	10	m.	M.			"	
13		Jacob R.	6	m.	M.			"	
14		Elias	4	m.	M.			"	
15		Mary A.	2	f.	M.			"	
16	431/430	CARMICHAEL, Joshua	27	m.		Farmer	/100	"	
17		Nancy	25	f.		Domestic		"	
18		Thompson	3	m.				"	
19		Woodman	1	m.				"	
20	432/431	CARMICHAEL, William	33	m.		Farmer	2500/1000	"	

21		CARMICHAEL, Mary					
		A.	32	f.	Domestic	O.	
22		Alexander	13	m.		"	S
23		Gardner	11	m.		"	S
24		Monroe	9	m.		"	S
25		Caroline	6	f.		"	S
26	433/432	OKEY, Gardner	32	m.	Farmer	1000/475	"
27		Melissa	26	f.	Domestic		"
28		Alcena	7	f.		"	S
29		Carolina	4	f.		"	
30		George	1	m.		"	
31		Charles	13	m.		"	S
32		HUNT, Bun	25	m.	Farm laborer	"	I
33	434/433	ANTLE, Isaac	50	m.	Farm laborer	/150	"	I
34		Nancy	50	f.	Domestic		"	I
35		Ellen	24	f.	Domestic		"	I
36		William	19	m.	Farm laborer		"	I
37		Rebecca	17	f.	Domestic		"
38		Isaac	15	m.	Farm laborer		"
39		Thomas	11	m.		"	S
40		Edward	9	m.		"	S

1		Joseph	7	m.		"	S
2		Jasper	7	m.		"	
3		Cis	4	f.		"	
4	435/434	WELLS, William	30	m.	Farmer	300/150	"
5		Margaret	26	f.	Domestic		"	I
6		Atkinson	7	m.		"	S
7		Mary A.	5	f.		"	S
8		John	3	m.		"
9		Jesse W.	6/12	m.		"
10	436/435	LOGAN, Joseph	28	m.	Farmer	300/200	Pa.
11		Elisabeth	21	f.	Domestic		"
12		John C.	1	m.		O.
13	437/436	MERKEE, Joseph H.	50	m.	Farmer	7000/350	"
14		Mary	49	f.	Domestic		Pa.
15		William H.	27	m.	Farm laborer	/1000	O.
16		Joseph	20	m.	Farm laborer		"
17		Mary A.	18	f.	Domestic		"	S
18		Fletcher	16	m.	Farm laborer		"	S
19		Orange S.	13	m.		"	S
20		George T.	4	m.		"
21		BOLTON, Irvin	20	m.	Farm laborer		"
22	438/437	ROBINS, Isaac	54	m.	Farmer	1800/350	N.C.	I
23		Sarah	60	f.	Domestic		N.J.	I
24		PARSONS, Hariet E.	16	f.	Domestic		O.
25		ROBBINS, John W.	7	m.		"	S
26		HUNT, William	23	m.	Farm laborer		"	I
27		John A.	3	m.		"

```
28 439/438 LOGAN, Abia       65  m.   Laborer        /75    Pa.
29          Mary             57  f.   Domestic              O. I
30          Peter            24  m.   Laborer               "  I
31          John             19  m.   Laborer               "
32          Sarah A.         15  f.   Domestic              "

33 440/439 GARDNER, Samuel   57  m.   Farmer      600/250 Unkn.I
34          McFADDEN, Mary   27  f.   Domestic              "  I
35          Enos             28  m.   Farm laborer          "
36          Mariah J.         4  f.                         O.
37          William           3  m.                         "
38          Alonzo            2  m.                         "
39          Andrew           23  m.   Farm laborer          "

40 441/--- UNOCCUPIED
```

Page 68　　　　　　　　　22 June 1860　　　　　　Sheet 262 verso

```
 1 442/440 BAINUM, Levi      38  m.   Farmer      3000/700  O.
 2          Mary             41  f.   Domestic              "
 3          Nancy            15  f.   Domestic              "  S
 4          Sarah E.         13  f.                         "  S
 5          Rachel            8  f.                         "  S
 6          Fanny             6  f.                         "  S
 7          Levi              4  m.                         "
 8          Mary J.           2  f.                         "
 9          LOGAN, David     21  m.   Farm laborer          "

10 443/441 KELLEY, Peter     68  m.   Laborer             Pa.
11          Sarah            59  f.   Domestic              "  I
12          Martha           17  f.   Domestic              "
13          William          14  m.                         "
14          Rachel           13  f.                         "
15          John             10  m.                         "  S
16          James            10  m.                         "  S

17 444/442 WYMEN, William    30  m.   Laborer             O.
18          Mary J.          22  f.   Domestic              "
19          John W.           3  m.                         "
20          James             1  m.                         "

21 445/443 KNOPP, William    40  m.   Farmer      1800/600 Va. I
22          Mary             42  f.   Domestic            Md.
23          Jane             18  f.   Domestic              "
24          Sarah            16  f.   Domestic              "
25          William           6  m.                         "
26          David             2  m.                         "

27 446/444 SILLS, Mary       77  f.   Domestic        /200 Pa.
28          Matilda          27  f.   Domestic            O.
29          Emily            24  f.   Domestic              "

30 447/445 HICKS, Thompson   23  m.   Farm laborer          "  I
31          Hester A.        19  f.   Domestic              "  I
32          William           1  m.                         "

33 448/446 CURTIS, Elisabeth 44  f. M. Domestic           Va. I
34          Margaret         22  f. M. Domestic             "
```

35		CURTIS, George W.	21	m. M.	Laborer		Va.
36		William	18	m. M.	Laborer		"
37		John	16	m. M.	Laborer		"
38		Mary	15	f. M.	Domestic		"
39		Benjamin	11	m. M.			"
40		Smith	7	m. M.			"

Page 69   22 June 1860   Sheet 263

1		Elisabeth	4	f. M.			Va.
2	449/447	CURTIS, Harvy	30	m. M.	Farmer	800/400	"
3		Edmona	25	f. M.			"
4		Hamilton	3	m. M.			O.
5		Rosetta	4/12	f. M.			"
6		John W.	10	m. M.			"
7		James W.	11	m. M.			"
8	450/448	LAYENT, George	37	m.	Farmer	800/1200	Pa.
9		Mahala	31	f.	Domestic		O.
10		Catharine	11	f.			" S
11		Mary	9	f.			" S
12		Ann E.	7	f.			" S
13		John W.	4	m.			"
14		Mahala L.	3	f.			"
15		George	4/12	m.			"
16	451/449	CURTIS, Benjamin	40	m. M.	Laborer	/100	Va. I
17		Julia	33	f. M.	Domestic		" I
18		Mary E.	16	f. M.	Domestic		" S
19		Noah	14	m. M.			" S
20		Sarah F.	10	f. M.			" S
21		Ester C.	8	f. M.			O.
22		Reuben	5	m. M.			"
23		Hannah J.	3	f. M.			"
24		Cornelius	9/12	m. M.			"
25	452/450	HAGERMAN, Peter	46	m.	Farmer	2000/500	Va.
26		Lavina	42	f.	Domestic		" I
27		James	16	m.	Farm laborer		O.
28		Susanna	14	f.			"
29		Isaac	12	m.			"
30		Martha A.	9	f.			"
31		John	7	m.			"
32		William	5	m.			"
33		Sarah	2	f.			"
34	453/451	FLEMING, John	57	m.	Farmer	1800/300	Pa.
35		Margaret	53	f.	Domestic		"
36		Moses	23	m.	Farm laborer		"
37		Margaret J.	19	f.	Domestic		" S
38		John W.	17	m.	Farm laborer		O. S
39	454/452	KING, Isaac	40	m.	Farmer	2000/1380	Pa.
40		Ruth	60	f.	Domestic		"

Page 70   23 June 1860   Sheet 263 verso

1		William	35	m.	Farm laborer	Va.

2	455/453	ARMSTRONG, Peter	23	m.	M.	Farmer	400/200	Va.
3		Hannah	60	f.	M.			"	I
4		Amanda	21	f.	M.			"
5		Clarissa	18	f.	M.			"	S
6		Josephine	14	f.	M.			"

7	456/454	STALLINGS, James Sr.	61	m.	Farmer	3000/650	Md.	I
8		Margaret	61	f.	Domestic		"	I
9		Richard	20	m.	Farm laborer		O.
10		Almae	6	f.			"	S

11	457/455	FLANDERS, Nehemiah	25	m.	Farmer	800/300	"
12		Jane M.	21	f.	Domestic		"
13		John W.	9/12	m.			"

14	458/456	OKEY, Edward	35	m.	Farmer	/400	"
15		Catharine	27	f.	Domestic		"
16		James	4	m.			"
17		John	2	m.			"
18		Margaret	3/12	f.			"
19		Woodman	14	m.			"	S

20 459/--- UNOCCUPIED

Beginning of Stafford.

21	460/457	TOSSEL, John E.	34	m.	Shoemaker	250/200	Ger.
22		Mary E.	37	f.	Domestic		"
23		Oscar	10	m.			"	S
24		Hulda	17	f.	Domestic		"	S
25		Henry	9	m.			"	S
26		Terrissa	8	f.			"	S
27		Elisabeth	3	f.			O.
28		Lewis	1	m.			"

29	461/458	CATLETT, John	23	m.	Blacksmith	/150	"
30		Sarah	25	f.	Domestic		"
31		MARTIN, Mary	8	f.			"	S
32		Myre	7	m.			"	S
33		Jehu	5	m.			"
34		William	3	m.			"
35		CATLETT, John T.	2/12	m.			"

36	462/459	GIBENS, Birden	38	m.	Wagoner	250/250	"	I
37		Mary	42	f.	Domestic		"	I
38		Martha	16	f.	Domestic		"	S
39		Homer W.	14	m.			"	S
40		Sarah	10	f.			"	S

1		Ann M.	9	f.			O.
2		William	6	m.			"
3		Alexander	3	m.			"

4	463/460	BARNETT, Andrew	64	m.	Farmer	2000/100	Md.
5		Amelia	66	f.	Domestic		"

```
6          BARNETT, Jacob L.  35   m.     Tobacco Packer
                                                      1250/125   O.

7  464/461 EATON, John W.       25   m.     Tobacco Packer /250    "
8          Emily                22   f.     Domestic               '
9          William E.            2   m.                            "

10 465/462 CAIN, John B.        69   m.     Cabinet-maker
                                                      4400/200  S.C.
11         Patience             67   f.     Domestic            Pa.
12         Joseph W.             5   m.                          O.  S
13         John N.              36   m.     Laborer      /175     "

14 466/463 ULLMAN, Peter        33   m.     Blacksmith  800/150 Ger.
15         Margaret             24   f.     Domestic            O.
16         John F.               7   m.                          "     S
17         William H.            4   m.                          "     S
18         SLACK, George        16   m.     Student              "     S

19 ---/464 BROOKS, John         23   m.     Blacksmith  200/175  O.  M
20         Nancy                16   f.     Domestic             "   M

21 467/465 WELLS, Charles       68   m.     Grocer      4300/500 Va.
22         Rachel               66   f.     Domestic             "
23         RORMERS, Martha M.   20   f.     Domestic             O.

24 468/466 BARNETT, Rebecca     36   f.     Domestic             "
25         John                 37   m.     Farmer      6500/6000 "
26         Mariah C.            11   f.                          "     S
27         Amelia J.             9   f.                          "
28         William H.            7   m.                          "     S
29         John W.               6   m.                          "     S
30         James R.              4   m.                          "
31         Charles H.            2   m.                          "

32 469/467 HAWKINS, Reuben      49   m.     Merchant    5000/400 Pa.
33         Jane                 45   f.     Domestic             "
34         Louisa J.            18   f.     Domestic             "    2
35         William              17   m.     Tobacco Packer       O.  S
36         Jacob S.             14   m.                          "   S
37         Reuben L.            11   m.                          "   S
38         Albert                8   m.                          "   S

39 470/468 BROCK, John W.       38   m.     Cabinet-maker
                                                      400/300    "
40         Mariah               36   f.     Domestic            Pa.
```

```
1          Nathaniel            15   m.     Student              O.  S
2          John W.              11   m.                          "   S

3  471/469 WOODMAS, Hugh        55   m.     Tanner       /250   Scot.
4          Jane                 48   f.     Domestic            Eng.
5          Jane E.              22   f.     Domestic             O.
6          Henrietta            20   f.     Teacher              "
7          Leonard              16   m.     Laborer              "   S
8          Emily                14   f.                          "   S
```

9		WOODMAS, Herbert	9	m.		O. S
10		Grace	5	f.		" S
11	472/470	HILL, Hannah	48	f.	Domestic 100/100	Del.
12		Ananias	20	m.	Tobacco Packer	O.
13		Hannah J.	17	f.	Domestic	"
14		Mary M.	15	f.	Domestic	" S
15		Martha E.	13	f.		" S
16	473/471	STEEL, William	49	m.	Miller 15,300/4500	Scot.
17		Elisabeth	45	f.	Domestic	Va.
18		John	20	m.	Student	O. S
19		David	17	m.	Laborer	" S
20		George	14	m.		" S
21		W. Glaston	5	m.		" S
22		SIMPSON, Mary	14	f.		" S
23	474/472	JONES, James	55	m.	Mechanic /150	N.J.
24		Hester A.	34	f.	Domestic	Pa.
25		Joseph	22	m.	Teacher	O. S
26		William H.	14	m.		" S
27		Ann R.	12	f.		" S
28		Albert F.	3	m.		"
29		Edwin S.	11/12	m.		"
30	475/473	THOMPSON, Irvin	26	m.	Minister, W. M.	
31		Eliza	22	f.	Domestic	
32		George	6	m.		O. S
33		Greenville	4	m.		"
34		Charles	2	m.		"
35	476/474	STEEL, Stephen	36	m.	Master Carpenter /100	"
36		Elisabeth	28	f.	Domestic	"
37		Mary	6	f.		"
38		James E.	4	m.		"
39		Lydia E.	2	f.		"
40		John	1/12	m.		"

1	477/475	HATFIELD, Thomas C.	33	m.	Minister, M.E. /250	Pa. M
2		Martha	29	f.	Domestic	" M
3		Martha E.	11	f.		Va. S
4		William	7	m.		" S
5		Thomas J.	5	m.		"
6	478/476	STEWART, William	57	m.	Tobacco Packer 150/300	Pa.
7		Sarah	47	f.	Domestic	"
8		Mary C.	22	f.	Domestic	O. I
9		Lavina J.	16	f.	Domestic	" S
10	479/477	BOTTOMFIELD, Shad- erich	26	m.	Shoemaker 125/100	"
11		Sarah	20	f.	Domestic	"
12	480/478	YOCKEY, Charles	33	m.	Cabinet-maker 1250/100	Ger.

13		YOCKEY, Melinda	25	f.	Domestic		O.	
14		Charles W.	7	m.			"	S
15		Charlotte	5	f.			"	S
16		Mary E.	4	f.			"	
17		Martha M.	6/12	f.			"	
18	481/479	SMITH, Alexander	42	m.	Tobacco Packer	150/150	Va.	
19		Sarah	38	f.	Domestic		"	
20		Louisa A.	21	f.	Domestic		"	
21		James W.	14	m.			"	S
22	482/480	MASON, George	33	m.	Physician	1000/3500	"	
23		Jennet	26	f.	Domestic		"	
24		James L.	5	m.			"	S
25		William P.	2	m.			"	
26	483/481	CARMICHAEL, David	38	m.	Farmer	800/	Va.	
27		Nancy	30	f.	Domestic		"	I
28		Edward	13	m.			O.	S
29		James	11	m.			"	S
30		Hariet	9	f.			"	S
31		William	7	m.			"	S
32		Mary J.	4	f.			"	
33		Sarah E.	1	f.			"	
34	484/482	KELLEY, George	42	m.	Laborer		Va.	I
35		Milla	35	f.	Domestic		"	I
36		Elisabeth	16	f.	Domestic		"	
37		William	13	m.			"	S
38		Lucy	11	f.			"	
39		George	6	m.			"	
40		Hulda	1	f.			"	

| Page 74 | | | 25 June 1860 | | | Sheet 265 verso | |

1	485/483	TETERS, Tap	41	m. M.	Blacksmith	/150	Va.	I
2		Mary J.	41	f.	Domestic		"	
3		Elisabeth	17	f. M.	Domestic		"	
4		Clem	14	m. M.			"	
5		Jesse A.	11	m. M.			"	
6		Evaline	9	f. M.			"	
7		Ann E.	7	f. M.			"	
8		WALTER, John	39	m.	Crippled		"	I
9	486/484	FREMEN, Turner	44	m. M.	Cooper	100/50	"	I
10		Polly	60	f. M.	Domestic		"	I
11		Sarah	48	f. M.	Domestic		"	I
12		Jane	20	f. M.	Domestic		"	
13		Albert	19	m. M.	Laborer		"	S
14		Mary	16	f. M.	Domestic		"	S
15		Jacob	11	m. M.			"	S
16		George	9	m. M.			"	
17		Minor	6	m. M.			"	
18		Tea	3	m. M.			O.	
19	487/485	SMITH, Isaac	41	m.	Merchant	4000/1500	"	

20		SMITH, Mary E.	27	f.	Domestic		O.	
21		Mary K.	12	f.			"	S
22		Virginia	2	f.			"	
23		WERY, William S.	22	m.	Merchant	1000/1000	"	
24	488/486	KIGER Jacob	48	m.	Shoemaker	250/150	Pa.	I
25		Anny	49	f.	Domestic		Va.	
26		John A.	3	m.			O.	
27	489/487	BROWN, Hugh	41	m.	Saddler	600/100	Ire.	
28		Mary A.	37	f.	Domestic		O.	
29		Elisabeth	18	f.	Domestic		"	S
30		James	16	m.	Student		"	S
31	490/488	BOTTOMFIELD, Hiram	53	m.	Shoemaker	300/400	"	
32		Jane G.	27	f.	Domestic		"	
33		William S.	7	m.			"	S
34		James S.	3	m.			"	
35		Osawatamie	6/12	m.			"	
36		SWARTWOOD, Thomas	22	m.	Shoemaker		"	
37		BALL, Joseph	27	m.	Saddler	300/300	"	
38	491/489	OKEY, Woodman	68	m.	Justice of Peace		Md.	
39		Sarah	45	f.	Domestic		O.	
40		HANES, Theodocia	12	f.			"	S

1		Amanda J.	8	f.			O.	S
2	492/490	BUCKINGHAM, James	38	m.	Farmer	/75	Md.	
3		Patience	15	f.	Domestic		O.	S
4		Charles	14	m.			"	S
5		Mary J.	12	f.			"	S
6		John T.	10	m.			"	S
7		SINGER, George	23	m.	Saddler		"	
8	493/491	EATON, Shepherd	49	m.	Inn-keeper	700/250	O.	
9		Sarah A.	45	f.	Domestic		Va.	
10		Sarah E.	23	f.	Domestic		O.	
11		Martha E.	22	f.	Domestic		"	S
12		Hannah J.	15	f.	Domestic		"	S
13		Mariam	8	f.			"	S
15	494/492	MORTON, William L.	37	m.	Mechanic	/150	"	
16		Hester A.	32	f.	Domestic		"	
17		George H.	3	m.			"	

18   (Franklin Township Concluded)

                              (J. P. Spriggs, Ass't. Marshall)

* * *

21	495/493	JOHNSON, Nancy	44	f.	Farmer	500/235	Pa.	I
22		CAREY, Sarah	60	f.	Domestic		Del.	
23	496/494	CARMICHAEL, James	71	m.	Farmer	700/100	Pa.	
24		Mary A.	33	f.	Domestic		"	I
25		Levi	1	m.			O.	
26	497/495	JOHNSON, James	35	m.	Farmer	/250	N.Y.	I
27		Mary C.	25	f.	Domestic		Del.	I
28		Sarah E.	8	f.			O.	
29		George W.	6	m.			"	
30		Eli	2	m.			"	
31		Wesley	6/12	m.			"	
32	498/496	ADAMS, John	45	m.	Farmer	1200/350	Md.	
33		Elisabeth	38	f.	Domestic		O.	
34		James W.	18	m.	Farm laborer		"	S
35		John W.	16	m.	Farm laborer		"	S
36		Stephen C.	12	m.			"	S
37		William	10	m.			"	S
38		Rebecca	2	f.			"	
39	499/497	CREYTON, John W.	79	m.	Farmer	500/150	Ire.	
40		Delilla	64	f.	Domestic		Va.	I

End of Stafford.

Page 76   26 June 1860   Sheet 266 verso

1	500/498	GALLAGHER, Abner	23	m.	Farm laborer	/50	O.	I
2		Michel	21	f.	Domestic		"	I
3		John A.	1	m.			"	
4	501/499	AMOS, Daniel	76	m.	Farmer		Md.	I
5		Rebecca	60	f.	Domestic		"	
6	502/500	AMOS, Joshua	36	m.	Farmer	1000/425	"	
7		Rachel	35	f.	Domestic		O.	I
8		John	18	m.	Farm laborer		"	
9		Mary J.	15	f.	Domestic		"	S
10		Henry R.	13	m.			"	S
11		Eliza J.	12	f.			"	S
12		Hannah	8	f.			"	S
13		Elisabeth E.	6	f.			"	S
14		William	3	m.			"	
15		Celia	1	f.			"	
16	503/501	WHITTAM, Benjamin	64	m.	Farmer	600/125	Va.	
17		Josias	23	m.	Farm laborer		O.	
18		Perry	21	m.	Farm laborer		"	
19		Mariah	18	f.	Domestic		"	
20		PRICE, Edward	15	m.	Farm laborer		"	S
21		Ruth	6	f.			"	
22	504/502	JONES, William	28	m.	Farmer	800/300	O.	
23		Martha	18	f.	Domestic		"	
24		Rebecca A.	3	f.			"	

| 25 | | JONES, John W. | 1 | m. | | O. |
| 26 | | Rebecca | 60 | f. | Domestic | Md. I |

| 27 | 505/503 | CARROLL, Ruth | 58 | f. | Domestic | Pa. |
| 28 | | Susan | 51 | f. | Domestic | " |

29	506/504	DENNIS, Absalom	36	m.	Farmer	800/225	Md. I
30		Anne	33	f.	Domestic	O. I
31		Rebecca	9	f.		" S
32		Morgan	8	m.		" S
33		William	6	m.		" S
34		Ruth A.	4	f.		"
35		Margaret E.	1	f.		"

36	507/505	JOHNSON, Peter	59	m.	Farmer	N.Y.
37		Hester	55	f.	Domestic	" I
38		Peter	22	m.	Farmer	600/150	O. M
39		Amy	19	f.	Domestic	" M

| 40 | 508/506 | METCALF, Jacob | 39 | m. | Farmer | 1200/285 | " |

| Page 77 | | | 26 June 1860 | | | Sheet 267 |

1		Mary	33	f.	Domestic	O.
2		Sarah E.	14	f.		" S
3		Reuben	13	m.		" S
4		Susanna	11	f.		" S
5		Lydia C.	5	f.		" S
6		Enoch	2	m.		"
7		Jacob	2/12	m.		"
8		Nelson	16	m.	Farm laborer	" S

9	509/507	UNGER, August	30	m.	Farmer	500/300	Sax.
10		Caroline	27	f.	Domestic	"
11		Emiline	5	f.		O.
12		Charles	3	m.		"
13		Lewis	6/12	m.		"

14	510/508	SWARTZ, Henry	32	m.	Farmer	675/100	"
15		Frederick	30	f.	Domestic	"
16		Edward	4	m.		"
17		Terrissa	2	f.		"
18		Henry	8/12	m.		"

| 19 | 511/509 | SWARTZ, John | 61 | m. | Farmer | 400/ | Ger. |
| 20 | | Caroline | 60 | f. | Domestic | " |

21	512/510	METZ, Cono	35	m.	Farmer	400/150	"
22		Christena	34	f.	Domestic	"
23		Elisabeth	4	f.		O.
24		Caroline	2	f.		"
25		Christena	6/12	f.		"

26	513/511	SNOWBERRY, Peter	34	m.	Farmer	400/	Ger.
27		Catharine	36	f.	Domestic	"
28		Jacob	8	m.		O.
29		Cate	5	f.		"
30		Lana	4	f.		"

31		SNOWBERRY, Peter	1	m.			O.
32	514/512	SCHRADER, Jacob	36	m.	Farmer	400/	Ger.
33		Catharine	30	f.	Domestic		"
34		Margaret	6	f.			O.
35		Phebe	4	f.			"
36		John	2	m.			"
37		Jacob	1	m.			"
38	515/513	DENNIS, Absalom	69	m.	Farmer	/75	Va.
39		Jane	44	f.	Domestic		Md. I
40		David	24	m.	Laborer		O. I

Page 78   26 June 1860   Sheet 267 verso

1		George	22	m.	Farm laborer	/110	O. I
2		MARTIN, William	15	m.	Farm laborer		" S
3		DENNIS, Lemuel	11	m.			" S
4		Albert	6	m.			" S
5	516/514	BATREM, Michael	57	m.	Farmer	2500/600	Bav.
6		Elisabeth	54	f.	Domestic		"
7		Henry	30	m.	Farm laborer		"
8		Caroline	8	f.			O.
9		Catharine	7	f.			"
10		Frederick	5	m.			"
11		Elisabeth	4	f.			"
12		Emily	1	f.			"
13	517/515	MARTIN, Henry	25	m.	Farmer	1200/350	"
14		Lydia	24	f.	Domestic		" I
15		Margaret E.	1	f.			"
16		Eleanor	60	f.	Farmer	/250	" I
17		Margaret	32	f.	Domestic		" I
18		John	16	m.	Farm laborer		"
19	518/516	JOHNSON, John	75	m.	Nothing		N.J.
20		Rachel	70	f.	Domestic		" I
21		John, Jr.	30	m.	Farmer	800/	O.
22		Eliza	29	f.	Domestic		"
23		Mary E.	1	f.			"
24	519/517	BODY, Henry	25	m.	Farmer	1800/500	Br.
25		Phebe	25	f.	Domestic		Ham.
26		Elisabeth	5	f.			O.
27		Henry	4	m.			"
28		William	1	m.			"
29		KIMINACH, Phebe	58	f.	Domestic		Ham.
30	520/518	KELLY, Thomas	27	m.	Farm laborer	/50	Pa. I
31		Elisabeth	25	f.	Domestic		O.
32		Alexander	4	m.			"
33		George W.	3	m.			"
34		Sarah M.	8/12	f.			"
35	521/519	SEBAAH, Michael	60	m.	Farmer	700/250	Bav.
36		Catharine	60	f.	Domestic		"
37		Lewis	59	m.	Farm laborer		"

38		SEBAAH, Elisabeth	56	f.	Domestic	Bav.
39		Jacob	24	m.	Farm laborer	"

40	522/520	KIMINACH, Michael	55	m.	Farmer	800/355 Bav.

Page 79   26 June 1860   Sheet 268

1		Margaret	50	f.	Domestic	Ham.
2		Philip	16	m.	Farm laborer	"

3	523/521	MERSHALL, Chris-				
		tian	28	m.	Farmer	2200/300 Sax.
4		Cadeline	25	f.	Domestic	O.
5		Henry	8	m.		"
6		Cadaline	5	f.		"
7		Christian	3	m.		"
8		Charles	1	m.		"
9		MILLINGHOUSER,				
		Mary	16	f.	Laborer	"

10	524/522	SHOUP, Lawrence	51	m.	Farmer	/200 Bav.
11		Catharine	47	f.	Domestic	"
12		FELNER, John	16	m.	Farm laborer	O.

13	525/523	DAY, Thomas B.	30	m.	Farmer	2000/1350 "
14		Mary E.	25	f.	Domestic	"

15	---/524	STEWART, W. T. M.	31	m.	Farmer	2000/800 "	
16		Sarah A.	34	f.	Domestic	"	
17		John T.	13	m.		"	S
18		George	6	m.		"	S

19	526/525	HANDSHUMAKER, Chris-					
		tian	56	m.	Farmer	3000/450 Bav.	
20		Dartha	56	f.	Domestic	"	
21		Jacob	18	m.	Farm laborer	O.	
22		Philip	23	m.	Farm laborer	"	
23		Adam	15	m.	Farm laborer	"	S

24	527/526	HANDSHUMAKER, Val-				
		entine	27	m.	Farmer	/150 Bav.
25		Elisabeth	19	f.	Domestic	O.

Beginning of Lebanon.

26	528/527	KIRKPATRICK, John	58	m.	Farmer	3000/600 "
27		Mary	58	f.	Domestic	Pa.
28		Henry C.	18	m.	Farm laborer	O.
29		DAVIDSON, Thomas E.	1	m.		"
30		MONEHAN, Mary A.	18	f.	Domestic	"

31	529/528	LINGBACH, Henry	20	m.	Master Blacksmith		
						200/100 Ger.	M
32		Catharine	21	f.	Domestic	"	M
33		Catharine	1/12	f.		"	

34	530/529	RIDGWAY, John M.	33	m.	Tobacco Packer	
						1000/150 O.

35		RIDGWAY, Elisa-beth	32	f.	Domestic		O.	
36		William	10	m.			"	S
37		Samuel M.	8	m.			"	S
38		Charles	6	m.			"	S
39		Cornelia J.	3	f.			"	
40		Mariam	9/12	f.			"	

Page 60   26 June 1860   Sheet 268 verso

1	531/530	BROWN, Perry	39	m.	Tobacco Packer	250/150	O.	
2		Elisabeth	44	f.	Domestic		Va.	I
3		Alice	16	f.	Domestic		O.	
4		Ann	9	f.			"	S
5	---/531	BROWN, Silas	19	m.	Tobacco Packer		"	
6		Nancy J.	18	f.	Domestic		"	
7	532/532	CRAFFORD, Alexander	28	m.	Cabinet-maker	1000/300	O.	
8		Jane	31	f.	Domestic		"	
9		Sarah A.	6	f.			"	S
10		Margaret	1	f.			"	
11		BIDENHARN, Otto	23	m.	Merchant	500/8000	Han.	
12		MASTERS, T. M.	22	m.	Clerk	1000/	O.	
13	533/533	CRAFFORD, James	54	m.	Cabinet-maker	350/150	Md.	
14		Sarah	48	f.	Domestic		O.	I
15		Mary A.	18	f.	Domestic		"	
16		Phebe	16	f.	Domestic		"	S
17		Angeline	13	f.			"	S
18		James	7	m.			"	S
19		Lecellen	4	f.			"	
20	534/534	WOODARD, James H.	25	m.	Tobacco Packer	30/100	Md.	
21		Margaret	23	f.	Domestic		O.	
22		James	3	m.			"	
23		Drusilla	1	f.			"	
24	535/535	RICHARDSON, Samuel	31	m.	Physician	50/200	Pa.	
25		Rebecca	29	f.	Domestic		Va.	
26		Alonzo	9	m.			O.	S
27		Ellen	6	f.			"	S
28		Otto	9/12	m.			"	
29	536/536	KIRKPATRICK, James	31	m.	Miller	1000/200	"	
30		Amanda	28	f.	Domestic		"	
31		Martha	1	f.			"	
32		CAMEL, William	64	m.	Nothing		Va.	
33	537/537	MASTERS, William J.	25	m.	Cooper	250/100	O.	
34		Mary M.	30	f.	Domestic		Ger.	

```
35          MASTERS, M. Levina   3    f.                                    O.
36               George O.       1/12 m.                                    "

37 538/538 McPEEK, Alexander    23    m.    Tobacco Packer /75              "
38               Rachel          21    f.    Domestic                        "
39               Lincven         3/12 m.                                    "

40 539/--- UNOCCUPIED
```

Page 81   27 June 1860   Sheet 269

```
1  540/539 MERIDETH, Rollin     29    m.    Master Carpenter
                                                    600/150  Va.
2                Jane C.         24    f.    Domestic             O.  I
3                Martha          5     f.                         "   S
4                Charles W.      4     m.                         "

5  541/540 NOSTELLER, Nancy
                J.               33    f.    Domestic        /75  O.  I
6                Mary A.         9     f.                         "   S
7                Eliza J.        7     f.                         "   S

8  542/541 HIZZY, Alexander     45    m.    Carpenter   250/125  Md.
9                Elisabeth       51    f.    Domestic             Va. I
10               Mariah          18    f.    Domestic             O.
11               James M.        13    m.                         "   S

12 543/542 BELL, Jesse          43    m.    Tobacco Packer /100  "
13               Drusilla        29    f.    Domestic             "   I
14               Mary L.         7     f.                         "   S
15               Sarah J.        5     f.                         "   S
16               Henry           2     m.                         "
17               Amina A.        3/12  f.                         "

18 544/543 KIRKPATRICK, Wm. L.  29    m.    Laborer     240/200  "
19               Sabina          28    f.    Domestic             "
20               Jonathan        4     m.                         "
21               Mary E.         3     f.                         "
22               Bustamenta      1     m.                         "

23 545/544 RIDGEWAY, Charles
                W.               31    m.    Merchant  2350/5000  "
24               Caroline M.     28    f.    Domestic             Va.
25               Amelia          7     f.                         O.  S
26               Permelia        4     f.                         "   S
27               Emilazetta      4     f.                         "
28               Rusell          4/12  m.                         "
29          RAKE, Eliza J.       20    f.    Domestic             "
30               John            23    m.    Tobacco Packer       "

31 546/545 MORGAN, George       60    m.    Shoemaker   300/100  Md. I
32               Margaret        56    f.    Domestic             "   I

33 547/546 MASTERS, William     55    m.    Tanner      500/300  O.
34               Charlotte       50    f.    Domestic             Pa.
35               Nancy           16    f.    Domestic             O.  S
36               John W.         13    m.                         "   S
```

37		MASTERS, Richard	9	m.			O. S
38	548/547	DAY, Thomas L.	30	m.	Miller	1100/175	"
39		Elisabeth	20	f.	Domestic		"
40		Magga P.	1	f.			"

Page 82   27 June 1860   Sheet 269 verso

1		John	1/12	m.			O.
2	549/548	ASHBAUGH, Frederick	61	m.	Physician	450/200	Pa.
3		Phebe	58	f.	Domestic		"
4	560/559	SEBACH, John	28	m.	Farm laborer	/150	Bav.
5		Catharine	25	f.	Domestic		"
6		Eve	5	f.			O.
7		Christena	3	f.			"
8		Adam	2	m.			"
9	561/560	SHANKLIN, Isaac	34	m.	Tobacco Packer	/150	"
10		Catharine	30	f.	Domestic		Ger.
11		Edward S.	12	m.			O. S
12		Newton	10	m.			" S
13		Vachel	8	m.			" S
14		Charlotte	7	f.			" S
15		James	4	m.			"
16		Isaac	3	m.			"
17	362/361	SIDLER, Charles	30	m.	Master Shoemaker	800/300	Br.
18		Lina	22	f.	Domestic		O.
19		Catherine	3	f.			"
20		Mary A.	1	f.			"
21	563/562	HANNAH, John	50	m.	Farmer	4000/1600	Pa.
22		Elisabeth	56	f.	Domestic		Md. I
23		Paron	21	m.	Farm laborer		O.
24		Hannah	14	f.			"
25	---/563	WILSON, Rachel	24	f.	Domestic		"
26		Oscar P.	1	m.			"
27		LENGE, Carey L.	2	m.			"
28	564/564	DAY, Francis	35	m.	Merchant	500/150	Md.
29		Eliza	22	f.	Domestic		Va. I
30		John W.	6	m.			O. S
31		Sarah T.	5	f.			" S
32		James E.	3	m.			"
33		GALLAGHER, William	21	m.	Shoemaker		"
34	565/565	CURRENS, Thomas W.	34	m.	Farmer	/275	"
35		Mary A.	29	f.	Domestic		Md.
36		Sarah A.	8	f.			O. S
37		Ruth	6	f.			" S
38		Thomas H.	5	m.			" S
39		STRAKER, Samuel	27	m.	Farm laborer		Md.

End of Lebanon.

40 566/566 RAKE, Abrem   43 m.   Farmer   1200/300 O. I

1		Mary A.	30	f.	Domestic		O.	
2		Sarah E.	15	f.	Domestic		"	S
3		Matilda	11	f.			"	S
4		Amanda	4	f.			"	
5		Minerva	2	f.			"	
6		Elisabeth	22	f.	Domestic		"	

7	567/567	DAY, Lewis	64	m.	Farmer	800/300	Va.	
8		Elisabeth	62	f.	Domestic		N.J.	I
9		Martha M.	6	f.			O.	S

10	568/568	DAY, Milton	23	m.	Farm laborer	/100	"	
11		Matilda	23	f.	Farm laborer		"	
12		Alexander A.	1	m.			"	

13	569/569	OLIVER, James	36	m.	Farmer	300/175	Del.	
14		Mercy	39	f.	Domestic		Va.	I
15		Phebe	10	f.			O.	
16		Levi	9	m.			"	
17		Lyman	9	m.			"	
18		Sarah E.	4	f.			"	

19	570/570	MASTERS, Thomas	31	m.	Farmer	/150	"	
20		Mary J.	31	f.	Domestic		"	
21		Charles C.	4	m.			"	
22		Hariet A.	2	f.			"	

23	571/571	MASTERS, Andrew	25	m.	Farm laborer	/125	"	
24		Filina	22	f.	Domestic		"	
25		Samuel A.	9/12	m.			"	

26	572/572	BEARDMORE, Thomas	30	m.	Farmer	1500/350	Eng.	
27		FROGGART, Ann	48	f.	Domestic		"	
28		Mary	19	f.	Domestic		"	
29		William	9	m.			"	S
30		BEARDMORE, Samuel	74	m.			"	

31	573/573	STEWART, William	60	m.	Farmer	800/300	Pa.	
32		Martha	53	f.	Domestic		"	
33		William H.	20	m.	Farm laborer		O.	S
34		James	16	m.	Farm laborer		"	S
35		David	15	m.	Farm laborer		"	S
36		Martha E.	6	f.			"	S

37	574/574	McCOLLEY, John	54	m.	Farmer	600/300	Ire.	
38		Nancy	45	f.	Domestic		O.	
39		Mary E.	17	f.	Domestic		"	S
40		Margaret	15	f.	Domestic		"	S

| 1 | John F. | 13 | m. | | O. | S |
| 2 | Isabella | 12 | f. | | " | S |

3		McCOLLEY, Christi-ana	8	f.			O. S
4		James J.	3	m.			"
5	575/575	WORKMAN, Abrem	38	m.	Farmer	1500/350	"
6		Elisabeth	38	f.	Domestic		"
7		Elisabeth	14	f.			"
8		Jacob	12	m.			"
9		Mary R.	7	f.			"
10		Wesley	5	m.			"
11		Jane	2	f.			
12	576/576	STEWART, Charles	27	m.	Farmer	/50	"
13		Darcus A.	23	f.	Domestic		"
14	577/577	CURRENS, Stephen	30	m.	Farmer	/100	"
15		Jane	26	f.	Domestic		"
16	578/578	EWING, Absalom	43	m.	Farmer	1000/325	"
17		Comfort	46	f.	Domestic		Va.
18		Sarah E.	17	f.	Domestic		O.
19		Nancy R.	16	f.	Domestic		"
20		James B.	14	m.			" S
21		Mary M.	6	f.			"
22	579/579	HIST, John	48	m.	Farmer	/400	Pa.
23		Ann	43	f.	Domestic		"
24		William H.	17	m.	Farm laborer		O. S
25		John M.	14	m.			" S
26		Clark J.	11	m.			" S
27		Sarah I.	9	f.			"
28		Nancy F.	6	f.			"
29		Hariet M.	3	f.			"
30	580/580	FLANIGAN, William	32	m.	Farmer	/100	"
31		Mary M.	30	f.	Domestic		" I
32		Michael	8	m.			"
33		Thomas W.	6	m.			"
34		Matthew S.	4	m.			"
35		Francis M.	1	m.			"
36	581/581	CARROLTON, Benja-min	34	m.	Farmer	1000/350	"
37		Rachel	27	f.	Domestic		"
38		Joseph J.	7	m.			" S
39		Mary E.	4	f.			"
40		George L.	2	m.			

Page 85	28 June 1860	Sheet 271

1	582/582	FLANIGAN, John	59	m.	Farmer	550/100	Pa.
2		Sarah J.	24	f.	Domestic		O. I
3		Mary	20	f.	Domestic		" I
4		Lucinda	17	f.	Domestic		"
5		Calvin M.	29	m.	Farm laborer	/100	"
6	583/583	DICKENS, Samuel	44	m.	Farmer	1200/400	Va.

7		DICKENS, Delille	44	f.	Domestic		O.	
8		William	17	m.	Farm laborer		"	S
9		Adam	14	m.			"	S
10		John	12	m.			"	
11		Samuel	10	m.			"	
12		Thomas	8	m.			"	
13		Robert	4	m.			"	
14		Albert	4/12	m.			"	
15		Elisabeth	16	f.	Domestic		"	
16		Joseph	19	m.	Farm laborer		"	
17	584/584	ADAMS, Seth	36	m.	Farmer	3500/1400	"	I
18		Mary	36	f.	Domestic		"	I
19		Harvey H.	15	m.	Farm laborer		"	S
20		Louisa E.	14	f.			"	S
21		Lucinda J.	12	f.			"	S
22		John C.	10	m.			"	S
23		Seth	8	m.			"	S
24		James M.	6	m.			"	
25		Sarah E.	4	f.			"	
26		Charles W.	1	m.			"	
27		WARD, Seth	16	m.	Farm laborer		"	S
28		HALL, John	20	m.	Farm laborer		"	
29	585/585	ADAMS, James M.	21	m.	Farmer	/150	"	I
30		Martha S.	19	f.	Domestic		"	
31		Abbey	2	f.			"	
32		Louisa J.	6/12	f.			"	
33		McMILLEN, Martha	19	f.	Domestic		"	
34	586/586	WITDEMS, George	27	m.	Farmer	/250	"	
35		Elisabeth	26	f.	Domestic		"	I
36		Samuel A.	7	m.			"	
37		George W.	3	m.			"	
38		Alice H.	3/12	f.			"	
39	587/587	SCOTT, Abijah	33	m.	Farmer	/100	"	
40		Mary	23	f.	Domestic		"	

Page 86   28 June 1860   Sheet 271 verso

1		Catherine	8	f.			O.	S
2		Henry	5	m.			"	
3		Albert	1	m.			"	
4	588/588	KENEY, John	33	m.	Farmer	1000/200	"	
5		Susan	39	f.	Domestic		"	I
6		William D.	10	m.			"	S
7		James H.	8	m.			"	S
8		Lorenzo E.	7	m.			"	S
9		Catherine R.	5	m.			"	
10		Nathan W.	3	m.			"	
11	589/589	HALL, Henry	55	m.	Farmer	1000/300	"	
12		Mary	57	f.	Domestic		"	I
13		Nancy	27	f.	Domestic		"	
14		Menassa	20	m.	Farm laborer		"	

15		WORTHINGTON, Wm.	7	m.			O.
16		Armintha	5	f.			"
17		Ira W.	1	m.			"
18		HALL, Sarah	57	f.	Domestic		"
19		Henry	24	m.	Harness maker		"
20	590/590	HALL, Thomas	48	m.	Farmer	900/250	Md.
21		Mary	46	f.	Domestic		O.
22		James	18	m.	Farm laborer		" S
23		Rebecca	11	f.			" S
24		Martha	6	f.			"
25		Thomas	3	m.			"
26	591/591	SCOTT, Benjamin	36	m.	Farmer	/125	"
27		Elisabeth	26	f.	Domestic		" I
28		John	14	m.			" S
29		Hannibal	10	m.			" S
30		Harvey	9	m.			" S
31		Caroline	5	f.			"
32		Richard	1/12	m.			"
33	592/592	HUCHESSON, Eben-					
		ezer	47	m.	Farmer	3500/1000	Pa.
34		Rhoda	41	f.	Domestic		O.
35		John J.	21	m.	Farm laborer		" S
36		Samuel T.	19	m.	Farm laborer		" S
37		Isaac F.	17	m.	Farm laborer		" S
38		Sarah E.	15	f.	Domestic		" S
39		Salathiel	13	m.			" S
40		Jane	5	f.			"

Page 87   28 June 1860   Sheet 272

1		Enzy	3	f.			O.
2	593/593	CATLETT, William	24	m.	Farmer	/175	"
3		Hannah	21	f.	Domestic		"
4		John H.	2	m.			"
5		Henry	8/12	m.			"
6	594/594	McCOLLEY, Thomas	50	m.	Farmer	400/100	Ire. I
7		Charlotte	45	f.	Domestic		"
8		John	20	m.	Farm laborer		"
9		Arch	18	m.	Farm laborer		"
10		Mary J.	16	f.	Domestic		"
11		William	14	m.			" S
12		Alexander	12	m.			" S
13		Robert	8	m.			" S
14	595/595	LAW, Matthew	39	m.	Farmer	1800/500	O.
15		Elisabeth	36	f.	Domestic		"
16		Samantha	15	f.	Domestic		" S
17		John W.	13	m.			" S
18		Samuel N.	13	m.			" S
19		Fletcher M.	7	m.			" S
20	596/596	SHOAF, Daniel	42	m.	Farmer	250/150	D.G.
21		Philippi	32	f.	Domestic		"

22	597/597	MORRILL, Archbold	35	m.	Farmer	1200/400	O.	
23		Sarah J.	31	f.	Domestic		"	
24		Hannah J.	1	f.			"	
25		Mary	18	f.	Domestic		"	
26	598/598	MERIDETH, Thomas	53	m.	Farmer	2900/650	Va.	
27		Milla	48	f.	Domestic		"	
28		Davis	20	m.	Farm laborer		O.	
29		James B.	16	m.	Farm laborer		"	S
30		Alvira	14	f.			"	S
31		George	12	m.			"	S
32		William E.	11	m.			"	S
33	599/599	RIDGWAY, Elza	56	m.	Farmer	1800/400	"	
34		Jane	50	f.	Domestic		"	
35		Percilla	25	f.	Domestic		"	
36		William	18	m.	Farm laborer		"	
37		James	16	m.	Farm laborer		"	
38		Elza	14	m.			"	S
39	600/600	WEST, Eber	58	m.	Farmer	500/400	Va.	
40		Lydia	58	f.	Domestic		Pa.	

Page 88   28 June 1860   Sheet 272 verso

1		John	25	m.	Farm laborer		O.	
2		James	23	m.	Farm laborer		"	
3		Melissa	21	f.	Domestic		"	
4		Sarah	19	f.	Domestic		"	
5		Simon	16	m.	Farm laborer		"	S
6		Jacob	14	m.			"	S
7		Wallas	12	m.			"	S
8		Martha	10	f.			"	S
9		Ezra	8	m.			"	S
10	601/601	WEST, William Sr.	55	m.	Farmer	1000/200	Va.	
11		DELONG, Thomas	19	m.	Farm laborer		O.	S
12		James	13	m.			"	S
13	602/602	WEST, William Jr.	30	m.	Farmer	550/200	"	
14		Hannah	27	f.	Domestic		"	
15		William A.	7	m.			"	
16		Hannah M.	5	f.			"	
17		Ann M.	3	f.			"	
18		Thomas O.	10/12	m.			"	
19	603/603	TIPPANS, Elijah	46	m.	Farmer	1000/350	"	
20		Charlotte	41	f.	Domestic		"	I
21		William	21	m.	Farm laborer		"	S
22		Rachel A.	19	f.	Domestic		"	S
23		Elisabeth	17	f.	Domestic		"	S
24		Napoleon	16	m.	Farm laborer		"	S
25		Susan	14	f.			"	S
26		Merrilla	12	f.			"	S
27		John	10	m.			"	S
28		Caroline	7	f.			"	S
29		Thomas	3	m.			"	

30	604/604	CONER, Jonathon	42	m.	Farmer	1000/250	O.
31		Mary J.	37	f.	Domestic		" I
32		Adam	17	m.	Farm laborer		". S
33		John W.	16	m.	Farm laborer		" S
34		Richard	9	m.			" S
35		Joseph E.	7	m.			" S
36		Thomas C.	5	m.			"
37		Sarah P.	2	f.			"
38	605/605	CASEY, Samuel J.	52	m.	Farmer	1300/450	"
39		Barbary	40	f.	Domestic		"
40		John T.	19	m.	Farm laborer		"

Page 89   28 June 1860   Sheet 273

1		Margaret	15	f.	Domestic		O.
2		Angeline	11	f.			" S
3		Susanna	9	f.			" S
4		William	7	m.			" S
5		Marion	5	m.			" S
6		Robert	3	m.			"
7		Adaline	22	f.	Domestic		"
8	606/606	DAVIS, John	60	m.	Farmer	900/225	O.
9		Elisabeth	55	f.	Domestic		"
10		Bradford	15	m.			" S
11	607/607	MILLS, Isaah	39	m.	Farmer	1000/400	" I
12		Nancy	39	f.	Domestic		"
13		Louisa	17	f.	Domestic		" S
14		Caroline	13	f.			" S
15		Sarah	8	f.			" S
16		Mary E.	4	f.			"
17		ALLEN, Matilda	21	f.			" I
18	608/608	GROVES, George	47	m.	Farmer	600/200	"
19		Catharine	44	f.	Domestic		Md.
20		James	18	m.	Farm laborer		O. S
21		Sarah	16	f.	Domestic		" S
22		William	14	m.			" S
23		Caroline	11	f.			" S
24		Sarah E.	7	f.			" S
25	609/609	SIMONS, Solomon	46	m.	Farmer	3000/550	"
26		Melinda	43	f.	Domestic		" I
27		Morris	23	m.	Farm laborer		"
28		Brice	20	m.	Farm laborer		"
29		Angeline	18	f.	Domestic		" S
30		Margaret	15	f.	Domestic		" S
31		John B.	13	m.			" S
32		Samuel	8	m.			" S
33		Solomon	5	m.			"
34	610/610	SIMONS, Warton	26	m.	Farmer	/150	"
35		Barbary	21	f.	Domestic		"
36		Madisson	3	m.			"
37		Amanda	1	f.			"

38	611/611	EATON, Samuel	40	m.	Farmer	1500/350	Pa.
39		Mary A.	33	f.	Domestic		" I
40		Margaret J.	14	f.			O. S

Page 90   28 June 1860   Sheet 273 verso

1		William	12	m.			O. S
2		Elisabeth A.	9	f.			" S
3		John	5	m.			"
4		George	3	m.			"
5		Peter	6/12	m.			"
6	612/612	CLINE, Levi	67	m.	Farmer	500/225	"
7		Sarah	63	f.	Domestic		Va. I
8		Roseberry	22	m.	Farm laborer		O.
9	613/613	CLINE, Milton	27	m.	Farm laborer	/50	" I
10		Lydia C.	28	f.	Domestic		" I
11		Eliza J.	6	f.			"
12		William	3	m.			"
13		Angeline	2	f.			"
14		Sarah	1	f.			"
15		Mary E.	2/12	f.			"
16	614/614	FLEMING, Jacob	40	m.	Farmer	1700/450	"
17		Charlotte	41	f.	Domestic		"
18		Elisabeth A.	17	f.	Domestic		" S
19		Narcis	16	f.	Domestic		" S
20		Thomas	14	m.			" S
21		Enoch	12	m.			" S
22		Isaac	5	m.			"
23		Lucretia	3	f.			"
24		Mary F.	1	f.			"
25	615/615	CLINE, William	54	m.	Farmer	1600/400	"
26		Rachel	54	f.	Domestic		" I
27		Enoch	30	m.	Farm laborer		"
28		Hariet	25	f.	Domestic		"
29		Orpha	21	f.	Domestic		"
30		Rhama	45	f.	Domestic		" I
31	616/616	CLINE, Ira	26	m.	Farm laborer	/125	"
32		Melinda	25	f.	Domestic		"
33		Sarah E.	3	f.			"
34		Mary L.	8/12	f.			"
35	617/617	BENNET, Elisabeth	50	f.	Farmer	1000/125	" I
36		Nathan	22	f.	Farm laborer		" I
37	618/618	RICE, Henderson	41	m.	Farmer	1000/300	Va.
38		Elisabeth	41	f.	Domestic		Md. I
39		Edmond M.	12	m.			O. S
40		Alice C.	9	f.			" S

Page 91   29 June 1860   Sheet 274

1		William N.	8	m.			O. S
2		Oscar M.	5	m.			" S

3	619/619	WILLIAMS, Simon	39	m.	Farmer	400/275	O.
4		Rhine	23	f.	Domestic		" I
5		Matthias	15	f.	Domestic		" S
6		Daniel	13	m.			" S
7		Hannah	13	f.			" S
8		William	6	m.			" S
9		Susanna	8/12	f.			"
10		Barbary	16	f.	Domestic		" MS
11	620/620	JACKMAN, Samuel	38	m.	Farmer	1000/225	"
12		Margaret	33	f.	Domestic		"
13		Nancy J.	6	f.			" S
14		Mary C.	6/12	f.			"
15		GEORGE, James A.	20	m.	Farm laborer		"
16	621/621	KEENE, John	38	m.	Farmer	/110	"
17		Jane	30	f.	Domestic		"
18		Richard	12	m.			" S
19		Sarah J.	8	f.			" S
20		Margaret E.	5	f.			"
21		Melissa A.	1	f.			"
22	622/622	JOY, George	25	m.	Farm laborer	/25	"
23		Elisabeth	21	f.	Domestic		" I
24		Nancy	3	f.			"
25		John W.	1	m.			"
26	623/623	ADAMS, John	47	m.	Farmer	1600/175	" I
27		Matilda	44	f.	Domestic		"
28		John	14	m.			"
29		William	12	m.			"
30		Modalene	5	f.			"
31		FLANIGAN, Emanuel	22	m.	Farm laborer		"
32	624/624	ADAMS, Isaac	35	m.	Farmer	300/75	" I
33		Lucretia	32	f.	Domestic		" I
34		Isaah	11	m.			" S
35		Frederick	9	m.			" S
36		Mary J.	7	f.			" S
37		Ira	5	m.			"
38		Rachel	1	f.			♥
39	625/625	ADAMS, George	67	m.	Farmer	600/250	" I
40		Abba	53	f.	Domestic		" I

1		Rhoda	20	f.	Domestic		" I
2		Jane	15	f.	Domestic		"
3	626/626	McDOEL, Madisson	23	m.	Farm laborer	/50	" M
4		Mary E.	18	f.	Domestic		" M
5	627/627	ENGLISH, William	34	m.	Farmer	500/250	"
6		Jane	32	f.	Domestic		"
7		John C.	11	m.			" S
8		George W.	9	m.			" S

9		ENGLISH, James F.	7	m.			O.
10		Marion S.	4	m.			"
11		Wilson S.	2	m.			"
12		Milton C.	1/12	m.			"
13		McDOEL, Catharine	24	f.	Domestic		"
14	628/628	MORGAN, Henry	57	m.	Farmer	400/200	Pa. I
15		Margaret	55	f.	Domestic		Va. I
16		Jane	30	f.	Domestic		O. I
17		Julian	8	f.			"
18		William	6	m.			"
19		Margaret	4	f.			"
20		Mariah	1	f.			"
21	629/629	McPEEK, Jesse	36	m.	Farmer	800/450	"
22		Rachel	40	f.	Domestic		" I
23		HOUSE, James	77	m.	Nothing		Pa.
24		ARMSTRONG, Bayard	9	m.			O. S
25	630/630	MUSSNER, Adam	45	m.	Farmer	2000/500	Fr.
26		Elisabeth	42	f.	Domestic		"
27		Philip	18	m.	Farm laborer		Pa.
28		Sarah C.	17	f.	Domestic		"
29		Abagail	15	f.	Domestic		"
30		Henry L.	11	m.			O. S
31		Sophia M.	4	f.			"
32	631/631	WEBER, Valentine	47	m.	Farmer	2500/580	Bav.
33		Catharine	50	f.	Domestic		"
34		Jacob	20	m.	Farm laborer		O.
35		William	19	m.	Farm laborer		" MS
36		Catherine A.	3	f.			"
37		Francis J.	15	f.	Domestic		" MS
38	632/632	SMITH, Philip	87	m.	Farmer	300/100	Fr.
39		Elisabeth	74	f.	Domestic		"

40 633/--- UNOCCUPIED

Page 93			29 June 1860				Sheet 275
1	634/634	WALTERS, Joseph	50	m.	Farmer	200/150	Dar.
2		Catharine	37	f.	Domestic		Fr.
3		Catharine	15	f.	Domestic		Pa. S
4		Mary A.	14	f.			" S
5		Joseph	12	m.			" S
6		Caroline	8	f.			O. S
7		Henry	6	m.			" S
8		John W.	3	m.			"
9	635/635	MASTERS, John	28	m.	Farmer		"
10		Martha	24	f.	Domestic		"
11		Ross W.	4	m.			"
12		John W.	2	m.			"
13	636/636	KEEN, Richard	35	m.	Farmer	1600/450	"
14		Ann	27	f.	Domestic		"

15		KEEN, Simon P.	26	f.	Farm laborer		O.	
16	637/636	BENNET, John	52	m.	Farmer		Pa.	I
17		Sally	51	f.	Domestic		Va.	I
18		Susan	24	f.	Domestic		O.	I
19		Richard	21	m.	Farm laborer		"	I
20		Sarah J.	20	f.	Domestic		"	I
21		Hannah P.	14	f.			"	
22		John W.	12	m.			"	
23		James F.	9	m.			"	
24	638/637	MILLER, John	40	m.	Farmer	1500/450	"	
25		Elisabeth	50	f.	Domestic		"	I
26		Benjamin	17	m.	Farm laborer		"	S
27		Mary A.	16	f.	Domestic		"	S
28		Amanda	14	f.			"	S
29		Margaret	12	f.			"	S
30		J. Madisson	7	m.			"	S
31		Marion	6/12	m.			"	
32	639/638	MASTERS, Thomas	66	m.	Farmer	2000/400	N.J.	
33		Mary	47	f.	Domestic		O.	I
34		Thomas C.	11	m.			"	S
35		Henry C.	9	m.			"	S
36		George W.	7	m.			"	S
37		William H.	4	m.			"	
38		SHEMKS, Eliza J.	21	f.	Domestic		"	
39	640/639	CLAREY, Samuel	34	m.	Farmer	250/100	"	
40		Ann	35	f.	Domestic		"	

Page 94			29 June 1860			Sheet 275 verso		
1		Martin V.	12	m.			O.	S
2		Cordelia A.	8	f.			"	S
3		Daniel J.	6	m.			"	S
4		Sarah D.	4	f.			"	S
5	641/640	HOLIDA, Peter	59	m.	Farmer		Bav.	
6		Francis	25	m.	Farmer	300/90	"	
7		Susan	47	f.	Domestic		O.	I
8		Amy	8	f.			"	S
9		BIRKHAMER, William	19	m.	Farm laborer		"	
10		Philip	10	m.			"	S
11		Barbary	14	f.			"	S
12	642/641	POWELL, Andrew	30	m.	Farmer	/50	"	
13		Margaret	32	f.	Domestic		"	I
14	643/642	BRIGHT, Carlisle	46	m.	Farmer	/125	Pa.	I
15		Rachel	57	f.	Domestic		O.	I
16		Jacob	23	m.	Farm laborer		"	I
17		Frances	16	f.	Domestic		"	
18		Joseph	19	m.	Farm laborer		"	
19		Deborah	15	f.	Domestic		"	
20	644/643	McKNIGHT, Francis	50	m.	Farmer	400/100	"	
21		Rebecca	44	f.	Domestic		"	

22		McKNIGHT, Mary J.	16	f.	Domestic		O.
23		John	10	m.			"
24		Louisa	8	f.			"
25		Nathan	4	m.			"
26	645/644	PARKS, John	23	m.	Farmer	400/100	"
27		Ruth	18	f.	Domestic		"
28		Mary E.	2	f.			"
29	646/645	DALRIMPLE, Jesse	26	m.	Laborer		" I
30		Ruth A.	21	f.	Domestic		"
31		Rachel A.	5	f.			"
32		John W.	3	m.			"
33		George M.	1	m.			"
34	647/646	HUGHES, Benjamin	21	m.	Farmer	/75	" M
35		Sarepta	20	f.	Domestic		" M
36		LUCKEY, William	25	m.	Farm laborer		"
37	648/647	LUCKEY, Jesse	49	m.	Farmer	3500/600	"
38		Mary	36	f.	Domestic		Va. I
39		Richard	21	m.	Farm laborer		O.
40		Lucinda	17	f.	Domestic		"

Page 95		29 June 1860				Sheet 276	
1		Joseph	15	m.	Farm laborer		O.
2		Cornelius	13	m.			"
3		George	11	m.			"
4		Mary	8	f.			"
5		John C.	3	m.			"
6		Albert W.	3/12	m.			"
7	649/648	KEEN, John	33	m.	Farmer	/125	"
8		Jane	29	f.	Domestic		"
9		Richard	12	m.			" S
10		Sarah J.	7	f.			" S
11		Margaret E.	5	f.			" S
12		Melissa A.	1	f.			
13	650/649	DALRIMPLE, John D.	23	m.	Farm laborer		" I
14		Martha A.	21	f.	Domestic		" I
15		James M.	7/12	m.			
16	651/650	VANNOY, Burris	56	m.	Farmer	/195	"
17		Jane	50	f.	Domestic		" I
18		Edmund	19	m.	Farm laborer		"
19		David	16	m.	Farm laborer		
20	652/651	MILLER, Thomas	41	m.	Farmer	3000/650	"
21		Sarah A.	19	f.	Domestic		"
22		Sarah A.	20	f.	Domestic		" I
23		Martin	15	m.	Farm laborer		" S
24		Rebecca J.	14	f.			" S
25		Nancy	11	f.			" S
26		Rachel	6	f.			"
27		George W.	6/12	m.			

28		MILLER, Jacob	75	m.	Laborer	/800	Pa. I
29		James	17	m.	Farm laborer		O.
30	653/652	MILLER, Abrem	38	m.	Farmer	500/200	" I
31		Eliza	34	f.	Domestic		"
32		Crafford J.	9	m.			" S
33		Phebe J.	7	f.			" S
34		Margaret G.	5	f.			"
35		Hannah E.	2	f.			"
36	654/653	WARNICK, Matthew	27	m.	Blacksmith	/300	"
37		Margaret	31	f.	Domestic		"
38		Mary C.	3	f.			"
39		John T.	2	m.			"
40	655/654	DYER, John	26	m.	Blacksmith	/50	"

Page 96   29 June 1860   Sheet 276 verso

1		Sarah E.	20	f.	Domestic		O.
2		Thomas	8/12	m.			"
3		EARLY, Elisabeth	24	f.	Domestic		"
4		MILLER, John	19	m.	Farm laborer		"
5	656/655	BROWN, John	27	m.	Farmer	400/150	"
6		Mary	26	f.	Domestic		" I
7		Barbary E.	3	f.			"
8		Jacob	1	m.			"
9	657/656	FLEMING, Philip	40	m.	Farmer	1500/300	Bav.
10		Catharine	35	f.	Domestic		"
11		Philip	11	m.			O.
12		Elisabeth	9	f.			"
13		John	5	m.			"
14		Caroline	3	f.			"
15	658/657	McKNIGHT, William	26	m.	Farmer	/125	" I
16		Susanna	23	f.	Domestic		" I
17		Sarah J.	4	f.			"
18		BRIGHT, Francis	17	f.	Domestic		"
19	659/658	PARKS, James	35	m.	Farmer	400/150	"
20		Nancy	32	f.	Domestic		"
21		Serena J.	9	f.			"
22		David	7	m.			"
23		Lewis	5	m.			"
24		Mary E.	3	f.			"
25	660/659	MARTIN, William	31	m.	Farmer	1800/250	"
26		Sarah	31	f.	Domestic		" I
27		Western T.	6	m.			"
28		Mary E.	4	f.			"
29		Jennet	3/12	f.			"
30	661/660	PARK, Walter	60	m.	Farmer	1200/500	Scot.
31		Eliza	54	f.	Domestic		"
32		James	21	m.	Farm laborer		O.

33		PARK, John	18	m.	Farm laborer		O. S
34		Eliza J.	17	f.	Domestic		" S
35		William	15	m.	Farm laborer		" S
36		Mary A.	11	f.			" S
37	662/661	BLOIR, Morgan	40	m.	Farmer	/50	"
38		Mary	38	f.	Domestic		"
39		David	4	m.			"
40		Mary J.	2	f.			"

Page 97   30 June 1860   Sheet 277

1		BLOIR, Morgan Sr.	78	m.	Laborer		O.	
2		Mary	70	f.			"	
3	663/662	BAPST, August	35	m.	Farmer	300/	Bav.	
4	664/663	NICHOLSON, John	25	m.	Farmer	/125	O.	
5		Sarah	20	f.	Domestic		"	
6		Charles C.	2	m.			"	
7		Thadus B.	6/12	m.			"	
8	665/664	ORANGE, Calvin J.	35	m.	Laborer		Pa.	
9		Isabella	26	f.	Domestic		"	
10		Nancy J.	8	f.			"	
11		Mary E.	6	f.				
12		Thomas S.	5	m.			O.	
13		John W.	3	m.			"	
14	666/665	JOHNSON, William	60	m.	Farmer	800/300	"	
15		Nancy	60	f.	Domestic		"	
16		Samuel	14	m.			"	
17	667/666	JOHNSON, Abrem	25	m.	Farmer	500/200	"	
18		Nancy	21	f.	Domestic		"	I
19		William	4	m.			"	
20		Caroline	2	f.			"	
21	668/667	NUNN, Hannah	40	f.	Domestic		"	
22		Henry	18	m.	Laborer		"	
23		Winfield	4	m.			"	
24	669/668	DENNIS, Moses	40	m.	Farmer	/150	"	
25		Mary	36	f.	Domestic		"	
26		Sarah J.	17	f.	Domestic		"	S
27		John	16	m.	Farm laborer		"	S
28		Absalom	15	m.	Farm laborer		"	S
29		Flora	8	f.			"	S
30		Alexander	2	m.			"	
31		Benjamin F.	4/12	m.			"	
32	670/669	HICKS, Jacob	45	m.	Farmer	1000/400	Va.	I
33		Hariet	44	f.	Domestic		"	
34		Samuel	18	m.	Farm laborer		O.	S
35		Margaret	14	f.			"	S
36		Robert L.	10	m.			"	S
37		Smith	8	m.			"	S

```
38            HICKS, Jacob I.      3   m.                          O.
39            RUCKER, Ara         38   f.   Domestic               "
40            Elisabeth A.       7/12  f.                          "
```

Page 98   2 July 1860   Sheet 277 verso

```
 1  671/670  CRAIG, James H.     39   m.   Farmer      500/350   O.
 2            Elisabeth          37   f.   Domestic              Eng.  I
 3            John T.            13   m.                         O.    S
 4            James H.           11   m.                         "     S
 5            David O.            9   m.                         "     S
 6            Charles L.          5   m.                         "
 7            William H.          3   m.                         "
 8            Barbara J.          1   f.                         "
 9            Sylvester M.       16   m.   Farm laborer          "

10  672/671  WISE, Elisabeth     66   f.   Domestic             Pa.   I
11            Agnes A.           21   f.   Domestic             O.    I
12            Joseph             24   m.                        "     4
13            Louisa             15   f.   Domestic             "

14  673/672  McPEEK, Joseph      24   m.   Farmer      550/350  "
15            Jane               24   f.   Domestic             "
16            Lydia L.           12   f.                        "

17  674/673  McCONNELL, Charles  30   m.   Farmer     1000/350  "
18            Isabella           30   f.   Domestic             "
19            Mary J.            10   f.                        "     S
20            William             7   m.                        "     S
21            George              1   m.                        "

22  675/674  ROBINS, John        47   m.   Farmer     1000/275  "     I
23            Catharine          51   f.   Domestic             Pa.   I
24            NUNN, Jane         15   f.   Domestic             O.
25            FISHER, Elisabeth   8   f.                        "     S

26  676/675  FISHER, Isaac       33   m.   Farmer      /100     "
27            Elisabeth          33   f.   Domestic             "
28            Catharine          10   f.                        "     S
29            Hester A.           6   f.                        "
30            Thomas H.           4   m.                        "
31            Martha M.           2   f.                        "

32  677/676  IRVIN, James        45   m.   Farmer      /275     Pa.   I
33            Mahala             32   f.   Domestic             Va.   I
34            George W.          14   m.                        O.    S
35            Catharine A.        9   f.                        "     S

36  678/677  PARSONS, William    29   m.   Farmer      /175     "     I
37            Catharine M.       20   f.   Domestic             "

38  679/678  PARSONS, Smith      23   m.   Farmer      /65      "     I
39            Eliza A.           25   f.   Domestic             "     I
40            George            7/12  m.                        "
```

Page 99   2 July 1860   Sheet 278

```
 1  680/679  PARSONS, George     55   m.   Farmer      500/200  Va.   I
```

```
2              PARSONS, Catharine  54   f.   Domestic                  Del. I
3              HASHMAN, John       23   m.   Farm laborer               O. I
4                 Mary J.          21   f.   Domestic                   "
5                 Catharine         1   f.                              "

6   681/680    HUPP, Hiram         50   m.   Farmer        400/175    Va. I
7                 Ruth             45   f.   Domestic                   O.
8                 William          15   m.   Farm laborer               "
9                 Francis          14   m.                              "
10                Ruth              9   f.                              "
11                Hiram             8   m.                              "
12                Hannah            6   f.                              "
13                Deborah E.        4   f.                              "
14                Delille           2   f.                              "

15  682/681    CROOK, John         23   m.   Farm laborer    /50        "
16                Mary             19   f.   Domestic                   "
17                Ruth A.        10/12  f.                              "

18  683/682    LINDEMOOD, Neri     38   m.   Farmer         /1120     Va.
19                Mary             36   f.   Domestic                  Pa. I
20                John W.          15   m.   Farm laborer               O. S
21                Christiana       13   f.                              "  S
22                James M.         11   m.                              "  S
23                Louisa            9   f.                              "  S
24                Charles           7   m.                              "
25                Mary A.           5   f.                              "
26                Adrian            3   m.                              "
27                Irvin B.          1   m.                              "

28  684/683    LINDEMOOD, Jacob    71   m.   Gunsmith 10,000/2285     Va.
29                Christena        63   f.   Domestic                   "

30  685/684    LINDEMOOD, Menassa  40   m.   Farmer         /600        "
31                Fanny            31   f.   Domestic                   O.
32                John             17   m.   Farm laborer               "  S
33                Jonathon         10   m.                              "  S
34                Diana             7   f.                              "  S
35                Margaret          6   f.                              "
36                James             4   m.                              "
37                George H.         3   m.                              "
38                Neri C.           1   m.                              "
39            McFADDEN, James      22   m.   Farm laborer              Md.

40  686/685    LINDEMOOD, Ryan     33   m.   Farmer         /1260     Va.
```

```
1                 Mary J.          23   f.   Domestic                   O.
2                 John H.           9   m.                              "
3                 Jacob             7   m.                              "
4                 Jemima A.         1   f.                              "
5             GIVENS, Daniel M.    22   m.   Farm laborer               "
6             FOX, Martha          18   f.   Domestic                   "

7   687/686    TAYLOR, Alfred      34   m.   Farmer        500/250      "
8                 Ruth             28   f.   Domestic                   "  I
9                 William N.        2   m.
```

```
10          TAYLOR, Richard    14    m.                              O.
11              Rhoda          12    f.                              "    S
12              Julian          9    f.                              "    S
13              Eliza M.      1/12   f.                              "

14 688/687  ROBINSON, James    29    m.    Farmer        /200        "    I
15              Eliza          27    f.    Domestic                  "    I
16              Asa             9    m.                              "
17              William         7    m.                              "
18              John            3    m.                              "

19 689/688  CARTER, Jeremiah
                P.             45    m.    Farmer     1000/200  N.J.
20              Rachel         40    f.    Domestic                  O.   I
21              David M.       17    m.    Farm laborer              "    S
22              William        11    m.                              "    S
23              Benjamin        3    m.                              "
24              Joseph        4/12   m.                              "
25              Sarah          14    f.                              "
26              Mary A.         2    f.                              "

27 690/689  MILLER, George W.  46    m.    Farmer     3500/700  Pa.
28              Sarah          41    f.    Domestic                  O.   I
29              Rachel         20    f.    Domestic                  "    S
30              Sarah          18    f.    Domestic                  "    S
31              Mary           17    f.    Domestic                  "    S
32              David          15    m.    Farm laborer              "    S
33              Deborah A.     13    f.                              "    S
34              Elisabeth      10    f.                              "    S
35              Susanna         8    f.                              "    S
36          ADAMS, James       19    m.    Farm laborer              "    S

37 691/690  GROP, Dennis       32    m.    Farmer        /100  Va.
38              Amelia         32    f.    Domestic                  O.

39 692/691  CONNER, David      28    m.    Farmer     1200/300       "    I
40              Rebecca        48    f.    Domestic                  "    I
```

Page 101   4 July 1860   Sheet 279

```
1  693/692  CONER, Joseph      32    m.    Farmer     1000/400  O.
2               Leah C.        30    f.    Domestic                  "
3               Minerva A.     11    f.                              "
4               Adaline         3    f.                              "
5               Richard A.      1    m.                              "

6  694/693  CONER, Stephen     38    m.    Farmer     1500/425       "
7               Elisabeth      33    f.    Domestic                  "
8               Eliza J.       14    f.                              "    S
9               Nancy E.       11    f.                              "    S
10              Hannah A.      10    f.                              "    S
11              Robert          8    m.                              "    S
12              William D.      5    m.                              "
13              John            1    m.                              "

14 695/694  JACKSON, William   25    m.    Farm laborer   /200       "
15              Margaret       23    f.                              "
```

16		JACKSON, Edward	5	m.			O.	
17		Henry	2	m.			"	
18	696/695	SALSBERRY, John J.	42	m.	Farmer	/250	"	I
19		Elisabeth	52	f.	Domestic		"	I
20		James	20	m.	Farm laborer		"	
21		Ellen	17	f.	Domestic		"	S
22		Daniel	15	m.	Farm laborer		"	S
23		Susanna	12	f.			"	S
24		MILLER, Daniel	9	m.			"	
25		HILL, Phebe	63	f.	Domestic		Pa.	I
26	697/696	MILLER, Frederick	51	m.	Farmer	1560/600	O.	I
27		Nancy	40	f.	Domestic		"	I
28		Hester	25	f.	Domestic		"	I
29		Abram	24	m.	Laborer		"	
30		Rebecca	22	f.	Domestic		"	I
31		Frederick	19	m.	Farm laborer		"	
32		Jacob	17	m.	Farm laborer		"	
33		Moses	15	m.	Farm laborer		"	
34		Harvey	13	m.			"	
35		Daniel	10	m.			"	
36		Nancy J.	8	f.			"	
37		Elisabeth	6	f.			"	
38		Ann	20	f.	Domestic			
39	698/697	MARTIN, Thomas	37	m.	Farmer	2000/600	"	
40		Abagail	39	f.	Domestic		"	I

Page 102   4 July 1860   Sheet 279 verso

1		Sarah G.	10	f.			O.	S
2		Robert J.	5	m.			"	S
3		Mary E.	2	f.			"	
4		George W.	3/12	m.			"	
5	699/698	THOMPSON, James	41	m.	Farmer	/120	"	
6		Catharine	37	f.	Domestic		"	
7		Rachel	14	f.			"	S
8		Liza A.	9	f.			"	S
9		Sarah J.	7	f.			"	S
10		Martha	4	f.			"	
11		Tabitha E.	1	f.			"	
12	700/699	KINKADE, Andrew	58	m.	Farmer	800/200	Pa.	I
13		Rachel	20	f.	Domestic		O.	I
14		Deborah	16	f.	Domestic		"	
15		SULIVEN, John	16	m.	Farm laborer		"	
16		KINKADE, Edward	3	m.			"	
17	700/700	KINKADE, Benjamin	29	m.	Farm laborer	/75	"	I
18		Melinda	24	f.	Domestic		"	I
19		Elisabeth	7	f.			"	
20		Rachel A.	5	f.			"	
21		Mary E.	3	f.			"	
22	701/701	CRONIN, Andrew	36	m.	Farm laborer	/125	"	
23		Rebecca	36	f.	Domestic		"	I

24		CRONIN, Michael	12	m.			O.	S
25		John	10	m.			"	S
26		Ann	8	f.			"	
27		Daniel	6	m.			"	
28		Hulda	3	f.			"	
29		Mathias	8/12	m.			"	
30	703/702	MARTIN, Robert	64	m.	Farmer	3600/500	Pa.	
31		Elisabeth	66	f.	Domestic		Va.	I
32		Henry	16	m.	Farm laborer		O.	S
33		James	13	m.			"	S
34		Elisabeth	11	f.			"	S
35		Melinda	7	f.			"	
36		KINKADE, Daniel	20	m.	Farm laborer		"	I
37		MILLER, Lucy A.	14	f.			"	S
38	704/703	DAVIS, Drusilla	63	f.	Farmer	1500/350	Md.	I
39		John	40	m.	Nothing		O.	I4
40		Kinsey	36	m.	Farm laborer		"	

Page 103   4 July 1860   Sheet 280

1	705/704	McVEY, Samuel	42	m.	Farmer	3000/800	Pa.	
2		Elisabeth	41	f.	Domestic		O.	I
3		Jacob	15	m.	Farm laborer		"	S
4		Mary A.	14	f.			"	S
5		Rachel J.	12	f.			"	S
6		Nancy E.	10	f.			"	S
7		Elisabeth	8	f.			"	S
8		Cynthia A.	4	f.			"	
9	706/705	PARKS, David	30	m.	Farmer	350/125	"	
10		Elisabeth	21	f.	Domestic		"	
11		Sarah E.	4	f.			"	
12		George L.	2	m.			"	
13		Francis	1	m.				
14	707/706	McFADDEN, William	24	m.	Farmer	/300	Md.	
15		Louisa	23	f.	Domestic		O.	
16		Mary E.	3	f.			"	
17		Nancy	1	f.				
18	708/707	McFADDEN, George	48	m.	Farmer	1500/500	Md.	
19		Emily	33	f.	Domestic		Pa.	
20		Mary	13	f.			O.	S
21		Hamilton	11	m.			"	S
22		Margaret	9	f.			"	S
23		Washington	7	m.			"	S
24		Louisa	5	f.			"	S
25		Elisabeth	3	f.			"	
26		George	1	m.			"	
27	709/708	WEST, William	77	m.	Farmer	800/275	Md.	
28		Jane	30	f.	Domestic		Pa.	
29		Mary A.	28	f.	Domestic		"	
30		Chalmer	2	m.			O.	
31	710/709	McFADDEN, John	20	m.	Farmer	/150	"	

32		McFADDEN, Sarah A.	19	f.	Domestic		O.
33		Lewis A.	6/12	m.			"
34	711/710	McFADDEN, William	24	m.	Farmer	/150	"
35		Deborah	23	f.	Domestic		" I
36		John P.	3	m.			"
37		Samuel R.	1	m.			"
38	712/711	PARKS, James	49	m.	Farmer	700/200	"
39		Elisabeth	33	f.	Domestic		" I
40		Margaret	19	f.	Domestic		"

Page 104   4 July 1860   Sheet 280 verso

1		Wesley	16	m.	Farm laborer		O.
2		John	6	m.			"
3	713/712	PARKS, David Sr.	57	m.	Farmer	375/205	Pa.
4		Sarah	62	f.	Domestic		Va. I
5		Thomas	22	m.	Farm laborer		O.
6		PARMER, Hannah	46	f.	Domestic		Va. I
7		Martha J.	12	f.			O. S
8	714/713	LINDAMOOD, Wesley	33	m.	Farmer	/650	Va.
9		Nancy	31	f.	Domestic		O.
10		Christina	13	f.			" S
11		Elisabeth	12	f.			" S
12		Martin	10	m.			" S
13		Mary M.	8	f.			" S
14		Isabella	4	f.			"
15		Walter	2	m.			"
16	715/714	GARDNER, George	32	m.	Farmer	/75	" I
17		Sarah A.	31	f.	Domestic		" I
18		John W.	5	m.			"
19		Mary L.	3	f.			"
20		William T.	1	m.			"
21	716/715	DEARTH, James	62	m.	Farmer	500/220	" I
22		Sarah	58	f.	Domestic		" I
23		Hester	22	f.	Domestic		"
24		William	17	m.			"
25	717/716	DEARTH, Randolph	35	m.	Farmer	400/200	" I
26		Tabitha	32	f.	Domestic		"
27		Sarah	12	f.			"
28		Ruth	11	f.			"
29		Owen	4	m.			"
30	718/717	DEARTH, Samuel	31	m.	Farmer	400/200	"
31		Susan J.	26	f.	Domestic		"
32		Smith	4	m.			"
33		Randolph	1	m.			"
34	719/718	DEARTH, Owen	27	m.	Farmer	400/100	"
35		Sarah E.	18	f.	Domestic		"
36		Hester A.	3	f.			"
37		Hariet E.	6/12	f.			"

38	720/719	KINSEY, Benjamin	39	m.	Farmer	2000/350	O.	
39		Mary A.	32	f.	Domestic		"	
40		Francis A.	11	m.			"	S

Page 105   5 July 1860   Sheet 281

1		William	8	m.			O.	S
2		John W.	6	m.			"	S
3		Mahala	3	f.			"	
4		Margaret	16	f.	Domestic		"	
5	721/720	ROBINSON, Asa W.	50	m.	Laborer	/25	Va.	
6		Jane	55	f.	Domestic		N.J.	I
7	722/721	CARPENTER, Lewis	32	m.	Farmer	/50	O.	
8		Phebe	32	f.	Domestic		"	I
9		Sylvester	4	m.			"	
10		Sidney E.	2	f.			"	
11	7?3/722	DYE, Irvin	25	m.	Farmer	500/150	"	
12		Nancy	24	f.	Domestic		"	
13		Mary A.	6	f.			"	
14		Joseph	4	m.			"	
15		Nancy J.	2	f.			"	
16	724/723	MACKEY, Matthew	28	m.	Farmer	500/250	"	
17		Melissa	24	f.	Domestic		"	I
18		Henry	13	m.			"	S
19		Abrem	10	m.			"	S
20		Ruth E.	8	f.			"	S
21		Eliza J.	4	f.			"	
22		Hannah M.	3	f.			"	
23		Margaret I.	1/12	f.			"	
24	725/724	WINLAND, Hannah	60	f.	Farmer	2000/500	Pa.	
25		William	22	m.	Farm laborer		O.	
26		James	18	m.	Farm laborer		"	
27		John H.	11	m.			"	S
28		Rhoda E.	13	f.			"	S
29	726/725	DAVIS, John	36	m.	Farmer	400/200	"	I
30		Emiline	46	f.	Domestic		Va.	I
31		MOORE, Benjamin	22	m.	Farm laborer		O.	
32		DAVIS, Henry	16	m.	Farm laborer		"	S
33		Russell	12	m.			"	S
34		John A.	11	m.			"	S
35		Elisabeth	9	f.			"	S
36		Margaret A.	6	f.			"	S
37	727/726	LINDEMOOD, Abram	57	m.	Farmer	1000/600	Va.	
38		Frances	45	f.	Domestic		"	
39		William	25	f.	Domestic		"	
40		Mary A.	20	f.	Domestic		O.	

Page 106   5 July 1860   Sheet 281 verso

1		Milo	17	m.	Farm laborer		O.	S

2		LINDEMOOD, Sarah E.	15	f.	Domestic		O.	S
3		John	12	m.			"	S
4		Diana	10	f.			"	S
5		Amanda J.	4	f.			"	
6		Mary F.	2	f.			"	
7		Abrem	5/12	m.			"	
8		George W.	5/12	m.			"	
9	728/727	LINDEMOOD, Edmund	26	m.	Farmer	/100	Va.	
10	729/728	KIRKBRIDE, William	51	m.	Farmer	1500/300	O.	
11		Joanna	36	f.	Domestic		"	
12		Dudly	21	m.	Farm laborer		"	
13		Mary	12	f.			"	S
14		Dennis G.	10	m.			"	S
15		Lucetta	8	f.			"	S
16		May	5	f.			"	S
17		Emma	1	f.			"	
18	730/729	BOMAN, Henry	41	m.	Farmer	/125	"	
19		Ann	42	f.	Domestic		"	
20		Mary A.	13	f.			"	S
21		John	11	m.			"	S
22		Joshua	9	m.			"	S
23		Percilla J.	7	f.			"	S
24		Sarah E.	3	f.			"	
25	731/730	McVEY, Thomas	24	m.	Farmer	/135	"	
26		Lucinda	18	f.	Domestic		"	
27		Harlet	1	f.			"	
28	732/731	McVEY, Margaret	57	f.	Domestic	1000/50	"	I
29		Mary A.	14	f.			"	S
30		Elisabeth	75	f.	Domestic		Pa.	
31	733/732	McVEY, John	33	m.	Farmer	/150	O.	
32		Nancy J.	22	f.	Domestic		"	I
33		Jesse	3	m.			"	
34	734/733	BURTON, Lorenzo	31	m.	Farmer	400/125	"	
35		Ann E.	29	f.	Domestic		"	
36		Camsadel	1	f.			"	
37		NEEDS, Mary	13	f.			"	S
38	735/734	SUTTON, Henry	30	m.	Farmer	/150	"	
39		Mary A.	25	f.	Domestic		"	I
40		Willis M.	5	m.			"	

1		WHITTEM, Hannah J.	19	f.	Domestic		O.	
2	736/735	WEST, Samuel	30	m.	Farmer	400/175	"	
3		Rebecca	25	f.			"	
4		Sarah E.	9	f.			"	S
5		Mary J.	7	f.			"	S
6		John A.	5	m.			"	S

7		WEST, Martha E.	4	f.			O.
8		Catharine V.	1	f.			"
9	737/736	HILL, Daniel	45	m.	Farmer	600/200	"
10		Eliza	42	f.	Domestic		"
11		Joseph	23	m.	Farm laborer		"
12		Mary	21	f.	Domestic		" I
13		Reason	19	m.	Teacher		"
14		Margaret	17	f.	Domestic		"
15		Elza	15	m.	Farm laborer		" S
16		James	13	m.			" S
17		Daniel	11	m.			" S
18		Henry	10	m.			" S
19		Nancy A.	6	f.			" S
20		John A.	4	m.			"
21	738/737	KIRKBRIDE, Ranson	35	m.	Farmer	800/350	" I
22		Sarah	28	f.	Domestic		"
23		Henry	18	m.	Farm laborer		" S
24		Dycen	10	m.			" S
25		Mary E.	9	f.			" S
26		Alfred	8	m.			" S
27		Margaret	7	f.			"
28		Rhoda	8/12	f.			"
29	739/738	WILLISSON, Amos	58	m.	Farmer	700/350	"
30		Elisabeth	54	f.	Domestic		" I
31		Emiline	11	f.			" S
32		Nancy E.	9	f.			" S
33	740/739	WILLISSON, Jere	28	m.	Farmer	/100	"
34		Mary	26	f.	Domestic		" I
35		John A.	7	m.			" S
36		Madisson	5	m.			" S
37		Simon P.	4	m.			"
38		Milton	6/12	m.			"
39	741/740	SCOTT, Hugh	27	m.	Farmer	/75	"
40		Hester	24	f.	Domestic		" I

1		Elisabeth M.	5	f.			O.
2		James H.	2	m.			"
3		Sarah C.	1	f.			"
4	742/741	SCOTT, Matthew	63	m.	Farmer	2000/450	Pa.
5		Elisabeth	53	f.	Domestic		Va. I
6		Nathaniel	23	m.	Teacher		O.
7		Matthew	25	m.	Farm laborer		"
8		James	21	m.	Farm laborer		"
9		Thomas	11	m.			" S
10		Sarah	18	f.	Domestic		" S
11		Harriet	16	f.	Domestic		" S
12	743/742	HODGE, William	84	m.	Nothing	/75	Pa.
13		Samuel	38	m.	Farmer	2000/450	"

14		HODGE, Catharine	30	f.	Domestic		O.	
15		John W.	8/12	m.			"	
16	744/743	HODGE, Martha	40	f.	Domestic		"	
17		Mary A.	45	f.	Domestic		"	
18		TIPPANS, Luther	12	m.			"	S
19	745/744	MERTIN, John	23	m.	Farmer	/50	"	
20		Sarah	19	f.	Domestic		"	
21		Mary E.	2	f.			"	
22		Ephraim J.	5/12	m.			"	
23	746/745	MERTIN, Urias	21	m.	Farmer	/300	"	
24		Mary B.	17	f.	Domestic		"	
25		George W.	5/12	m.			"	
26		POOL, Thomas	12	m.			"	
27	747/746	NEWELL, James	43	m.	Farmer	/100	Pa.	I
28		Sarah	43	f.	Domestic		O.	I
29		Benoni	18	m.	Farm laborer		"	S
30		Isaac	16	m.	Farm laborer		"	S
31		John	13	m.			"	S
32		Thomas J.	11	m.			"	S
33		Sarah M.	9	f.			"	S
34		William J.	7	m.			"	
35		Benett W.	2	m.			"	
36	748/747	McFADDEN, John Sr.	60	m.	Farmer		"	
37		Mary A.	55	f.	Domestic		"	

(Bethel Township Concluded)

(J. P. Spriggs, Ass't. Marshall)

* * *

P. O. Graysville   Washington Township

Page 109   5 July 1860   Sheet 283

1	749/748	MERTIN, Ephraim	51	m.	Farmer	2300/500	O.	
2		Susana	42	f.	Domestic		"	I
3		Margaret	18	f.	Domestic		"	
4		William	13	m.			"	S
5		James P.	12	m.			"	S
6		Sarah A.	9	f.			"	S
7		Liza A.	7	f.			"	S
8		Martha J.	5	f.			"	S
9		Elizabeth	4	f.			"	
10		Mahala	2	f.			"	
11	750/749	PARIS, Peter	80	m.	Nothing			
12		James	27	m.				5
13	751/750	WILLISSON, James	32	m.	Farmer	/250	O.	I
14		Alinda	28	f.	Domestic		"	
15		Eli	6	m.			"	

16		WILLISSON, Eliza- beth	4	f.			O.
17		Mary A.	2	f.			"
18	752/751	ENLOW, James	53	m.	Farmer	1950/400	Pa.
19		Margaret	54	f.	Domestic		O.
20		HENTHORN, Rachel	36	f.	Domestic		" I
21		James M.	18	m.	Farm laborer		"
22	753/752	HENTHORN, Stephen	48	m.	Farmer	4000/1200	"
23		Sarah	49	f.	Domestic		Pa.
24		William	22	m.	Farm laborer		O.
25		Alexander	20	m.	Farm laborer		"
26		George	11	m.			" S
27		Margaret	16	f.	Domestic		" S
28		Isabella	15	f.	Domestic		" S
29		POOL, William	17	m.	Farm laborer		" S
30	754/753	HENTHORN, Adam	21	m.	Farm laborer	/75	" M
31		Sarah A.	20	f.	Domestic		" M
32	755/754	DALRIMPLE, William	33	m.	Farm laborer		Md.
33		Elisabeth	24	f.	Domestic		Pa.
34		Rebecca J.	6	f.			O.
35		Elisabeth	4	f.			"
36		Sarah P.	2	f.			"
37	756/755	FERRELL, James P.	41	m.	Farmer	2500/415	"
38		Elisabeth	32	f.	Domestic		Va.
39		Richard B.	7	m.			O. S
40		William J.	3/12	m.			"

Page 110   6 July 1860   Sheet 283 verso

1	757/756	SCOTT, William	31	m.	Farmer	/200	O.
2		Jane	27	f.	Domestic		"
3		Mary F.	5	f.			"
4		Richard O.	2	m.			"
5		Effa	8/12	f.			"
6		Robert B.	8/12	m.			"
7		PARMER, Martha	41	f.	Domestic		" I
8	758/757	GROVE, David	48	m.	Farmer	/300	"
9		Sarah	40	f.	Domestic		"
10		Elisabeth	18	f.	Domestic		" S
11		Agnes A.	14	f.			" S
12		John H.	11	m.			" S
13		Parker W.	9	m.			" S
14		Isaac F.	7	m.			" S
15		Mary L.	2	f.			"
16		William C.	9/12	m.			"
17	759/758	HANEY, Evan	51	m.	Farmer	3000/675	Md.
18		Nancy	40	f.	Domestic		O.
19		Chesman	19	m.	Farm laborer		" S
20		Elisabeth A.	16	f.	Domestic		" S
21		Nancy	15	f.	Domestic		" S

22		HANEY, Lydia	10	f.			O.	S
23		Rachel	6	f.			"	S
24		Casander	1	f.			"	
25		POOL, John	19	m.	Farm laborer		"	

26	760/759	DERBAN, Henry	31	m.	Farmer	1500/400	Md.	
27		Sarah	20	f.	Domestic		O.	I
28		Zephalinda	2	f.			"	
29		James D.	7/12	m.			"	
30		SMITH, Elisabeth	9	f.			"	

31	761/760	CLINGMAN, Samuel	36	m.	Farmer	1500/250	Pa.	
32		Terrissa	34	f.	Domestic		O.	
33		Sarah A.	7	f.			"	
34		Samuel D.	4	m.				
35		William	1	m.			Va.	

36	762/761	CLINE, Isaac	49	m.	Farmer	600/250	O.	
37		Mary	48	f.	Domestic		"	
38		Rhna (?)	23	f.	Domestic		"	

39	---/762	CLINE, Jonathon	21	m.	Farm laborer		"	
40		Barbary	18	f.	Domestic		"	

Page 111   6 July 1860   Sheet 284

1		George	18	m.	Farm laborer		O.	S
2		Rachel	16	f.	Domestic		"	S
3		Daniel	14	m.			"	S
4		Benjamin F.	12	m.			"	S
5		Albert M.	9	m.			"	S

6	763/763	SMITH, Elijah	36	m.	Tobacco Packer		"	
7		Rachel	60	f.	Domestic		Pa.	I
8		Frederick	6	m.			O.	

9	764/764	THOMAS, Isaac	50	m.	Farmer	1600/500	"	
10		Louisa	42	f.	Domestic		"	
11		Mariah	20	f.	Domestic		"	
12		David	10	m.			"	S

13	765/765	THOMAS, William	19	m.	Farmer	/50	"	M
14		Charlotte	17	f.	Domestic		"	M

15	766/766	PROVINCE, Jesse S.	31	m.	Farmer	800/300	Pa.	
16		Mahala	24	f.	Domestic		O.	
17		James N.	5	m.			"	S
18		Sarah E.	3	f.			"	
19		Thomas	1	m.			"	

20	767/767	GREY, William	35	m.	Farmer	800/325	"	
21		Catharine	25	f.	Domestic		"	
22		Sarah J.	5	f.			"	
23		George	3	m.			"	
24		Martha	9/12	f.				

25	767/767	JOHNSON, James	46	m.	Farmer	/75	"	I

26		JOHNSON, Matilda	50	f.	Domestic	O. I
27		Mary J.	17	f.	Domestic	"
28		David	9	m.		"
29		Sarah F.	3	f.		"
30	768/768	DUNDASS, John	45	m.	Farmer	1000/300 Ire.
31		Fathy	38	f.		" 5
32		William	16	m.	Farm laborer	O.
33		Jane	13	f.		"
34		Sarah	12	f.		"
35		Robert	10	m.		"
36		John	5	m.		"
37		Atha	7	m.		"
38		James	2	m.		"
39	769/769	FLOWERS, David	52	m.	Farmer	1500/400 Pa.
40		Mary A.	46	f.	Domestic	"

Page 112			6 July 1860			Sheet 284 verso
1		Mary M.	20	f.	Domestic	O. S
2		David M.	18	m.	Farm laborer	" S
3		John M.	16	m.	Farm laborer	" S
4		Aquilla J.	14	m.		" S
5		Susanna C.	12	f.		" S
6		Hannah H.	8	f.		" S
7		Archbold F.	6	m.		"
8	770/770	HOOD, John	21	m.	Farmer	/75 " MI
9		Mariah	22	f.	Domestic	" MI
10		David W.	1/12	m.		"
11		McBETH, Sarah J.	14	f.		"
12	771/771	HOOD, Benjamin	69	m.	Farmer	/100 Md. I
13		Nancy	53	f.	Domestic	O. I
14		David	21	m.	Farm laborer	"
15		Sarah	18	f.	Domestic	"
16		Jane	15	f.	Domestic	"
17		Thomas	19	m.	Farm laborer	"
18		Eliza	10	f.		"
19	772/772	HOOD, Hezekiah	24	m.	Farmer	/50 " I
20		Margaret E.	24	f.	Domestic	" I
21		Rebecca A.	3	f.		"
22		Mary J.	2	f.		"
23	773/773	FOX, Thomas	40	m.	Farmer	/125 "
24		Mary	38	f.	Domestic	"
25		Finley	13	m.		"
26		William	11	m.		"
27		Mary	9	f.		"
28		George	6	m.		"
29	774/774	MEED, Walter C.	55	m.	Farmer	/150 Md.
30		Mary H.	42	f.	Domestic	Pa. I
31		Benjamin	22	m.	Tobacco Packer	O.
32		Thomas	21	m.	Tobacco Packer	"

33		MEED, Theodore	18	m.	Tobacco Packer		O.	
34		Mary	16	f.	Domestic		"	
35		Sarah A.	14	f.			"	
36		George	12	m.			"	S
37		Lucetta	8	f.			"	S
38		Jane R.	5	f.			"	
39	775/775	HALL, Rhna (?)	48	m.	Farmer	500/150	"	
40		Rachel	30	f.	Domestic		"	I

Page 113   6 July 1860   Sheet 285

1		Benj. F.	11	m.			O.	S
2		Sarah J.	9	f.			"	
3		John T.	6	m.			"	
4		Rachel A.	3	f.			"	
5		William H.	1	m.			"	
6		Sarah	50	f.	Domestic		"	
7	776/776	EDWARDS, Benj.	35	m.	Farmer	1200/300	"	
8		Ethalinda	34	f.	Domestic		"	
9		Alvira	11	f.			"	
10		Mary	9	f.			"	
11		Pressha J.	7	f.			"	
12		John	5	m.			"	
13		Minerva	1	f.			"	
14	777/777	BODKIN, Richard	53	m.	Farmer	600/150	Pa.	
15		Rachel	43	f.	Domestic		O.	
16		Amanda	16	f.	Domestic		"	S
17		Elma A.	14	f.			"	S
18		Hariet A.	11	f.			"	S
19		John	4	m.			"	
20		James	2	m.			"	
21	778/778	PROVINCE, Jesse	57	m.	Farmer	500/225	Pa.	I
22		Cecela	54	f.	Domestic		"	I
23		Uriah	23	m.	Farm laborer		"	
24		Nathan	20	m.	Farm laborer		"	S
25		Amanda	17	f.	Domestic		"	S
26		Susanna	15	f.	Domestic		"	S
27		Rebecca	13	f.			"	S
28		Mary M.	11	f.			O.	S
29	779/779	CURRY, John	34	m.	Farmer	1800/500	Ire.	
30		Margaret	27	f.	Domestic		"	
31		Elisabeth	2	f.			O.	
32		Susanna	1	f.			"	
33		Elisabeth	74	f.	Domestic		Ire.	
34		PARKER, James	18	m.	Farm laborer		O.	S
35		CURRY, Christena	15	f.	Domestic		"	S
36	780/780	TAYLOR, William	21	m.	Farmer	/75	Ire.	
37		Susana	20	f.	Domestic		"	
38	781/781	DENBO, Thomas	35	m.	Farmer	/50	O.	
39		Ann	30	f.	Domestic		"	

40   DENBO, Mary   4   f.   O.

Page 114   7 July 1860   Sheet 285 verso

1   Sarah   2   f.   O.

2 782/782 GARDNER, Chris-
            tian   40   m.   Farmer   800/300 Ger.
3   Rachel   42   f.   Domestic   Md. I
4   John   19   m.   Cripple   Va.
5   Elisabeth   14   f.   O. S
6   James   9   m.   "   S
7   Hariet   8   f.   "   S
8   Sarah J.   6   f.   "   S
9   Ann M.   4   m.   "   S
10   Rachel   2   f.   "
11   JONES, Gesper   18   m.   Farm laborer /40   "

12 783/783 THOMAS, Abrem   45   m.   Farmer   1500/300 Pa.
13   Phebe   40   f.   Domestic   O.
14   Joseph   21   m.   Farm laborer   "
15   James   17   m.   Farm laborer   " S
16   Lorenzo   14   m.   " S
17   Mervin   11   m.   " S
18   Samuel M.   6   m.   "
19   John   6/12   m.   "

20 784/784 PROVINCE, Joseph   40   m.   Farmer   400/100 O.
21   Miller   30   f.   Domestic   "
22   John   8   m.   " S
23   Mary J.   6   f.   " S
24   Milla   4   f.   "

25 785/785 HANEY, Nicholas   26   m.   Farmer   /150   " M
26   Hannah   16   f.   Domestic   " M

27 786/786 MORELL, Thomas   27   m.   Farmer   800/350 "
28   Evaline   23   f.   Domestic   "
29   CALHOON, John W.   12   m.   "

30 787/787 PROVINCE, Benjamin 26   m.   Farmer   /225   " I
31   Eunice   21   f.   Domestic   "
32   Franklin P.   3   m.   "
33   Mary J.   1   f.   "

34 788/788 MORELL, George   40   m.   Farmer   2000/645 O.
35   Catharine   37   f.   Domestic   "
36   John W.   12   m.   " S
37   George T.   10   m.   " S
38   Mary J.   8   f.   " S
39   James L.   1   m.   "
40   CRANSON, Nancy   57   f.   Domestic   Ire. I

Page 115   7 July 1860   Sheet 286

1 789/789 FURGESSON, James   44   m.   Farmer   /200 Ire.
2   Mary   42   f.   Domestic   " I

```
3              FURGESSON, Joseph   18   m.    Farm laborer          O.  S
4              William            17   m.    Farm laborer          "   S
5              Elisabeth          16   f.    Domestic              "   S
6              Martha             14   f.                          "   S
7              Robert             12   m.                          "   S
8              Mary A.            10   f.                          "   S
9              Nathaniel           8   m.                          "   S
10             Margaret            7   f.                          "   S
11             Marion              1   m.                          "
```

```
12  790/790   KENEY, Milton      38   m.    Farmer       1600/300  "
13             Leah               37   f.    Domestic              "   I
14             Roswell            15   m.    Farm laborer          "   S
15             Sarah J.           14   m.                          "   S
16             Mary C.            12   f.                          "   S
17             Abel H.             8   m.                          "
18             Mariah L.           5   f.                          "
19             John W.             3   m.                          "
```

```
20  791/791   EARLY, Jonathon    62   m.    Farmer        300/150  Pa.
21             Matilda            52   f.    Domestic              "   I
22             William B.         27   m.    Farm laborer          O.
23             Edward             22   m.    Farm laborer          "   I
24             Sarah              19   f.    Domestic              "
25             Izrael             17   m.    Farm laborer          "   S
26             Matilda            14   f.                          "   S
27             Isaac B.            7   m.                          "   S
```

```
28  792/792   RHINARD, Henry     21   m.    Farmer        300/75   O.
29             Emily              21   f.    Domestic              "
30             Lydia               2   f.                          "
```

```
31  793/793   BATRON, Jesse      56   m.    Farmer         /100    "
32             Mary               51   f.    Domestic              Va. I
33             Jacob B.           21   m.    Farm laborer          O.
34             William            18   m.    Farm laborer          "
35             Ruth A.            16   f.    Domestic              "
36             Robert              8   m.                          "
```

```
37  794/794   MORRELL, William   28   m.    Farmer       1000/500  "
38             Eliza              20   f.    Domestic              "
39             Agnes               4   f.                          "
40             Amanda              1   f.                          "
```

Page 116   7 July 1860   **Sheet** 286 verso

```
1   795/795   MORRELL, Margaret  55   f.    Domestic     1000/100  Md.
```

```
2   796/796   SCOTT, James       55   m.    Farmer       2000/675  Va.
3             Mary               53   f.    Domestic              Pa. I
4             Thomas             21   m.    Farm laborer          O.  S
5             James B.           18   m.    Farm laborer          "   S
6             Alexander          17   m.    Farm laborer          "   S
7             HILL, Precias       5   f.                          "
8             SCOTT, Frances     44   f.    Domestic              "   4
```

```
9   797/797   SCOTT, Richard     30   m.    Nothing       400/100  "
10             Rachel             25   f.    Domestic              "
```

11		SCOTT, William	4	m.		O.
12		James T.	1	m.		"
13	798/798	SMITH, Jesse	63	m.	Farmer	/75	Pa. I
14		Sarah	51	f.	Domestic		Va. I
15		Melinda	26	f.	Domestic		" I
16		Zachariah	24	m.	Farm laborer		" I
17		Catharine	20	f.	Domestic		" I
18		Lorenzo	11	m.			"
19		James	8	m.			"
20		Melissa	4	f.			"
21		Jackson	4	m.			"
22	799/799	SMITH, Elisha	36	m.	Farmer	2800/230	"
23		Eunice	31	f.	Domestic		" I
24		Louisa	13	f.			"
25		Harvy	10	m.			"
26		Elisabeth	8	f.			"
27		Nathaniel	6	m.			"
28		Daniel	4	m.			"
29		Amanda	2	f.			"
30		Luzetta	9/12	f.			"
31	800/800	CATLETT, Alex.	29	m.	Farmer	/50	Va. I
32		Emily	28	f.	Domestic		N.Y. I
33		Jane	9	f.			O.
34		Samuel	8	m.			" S
35		Mariah	3	f.			"
36		John	1	m.			"
37	801/801	ROSE, Frederick	44	m.	Farmer	1500/300	H.K.
38		Rebecca	39	f.	Domestic		O.
39		Ruth A.	19	f.	Domestic		" S
40		Frederick R.	17	m.	Farm laborer		" S

Page 117   7 July 1860   Sheet 287

1		Simon	16	m.	Farm laborer		O. S
2		Sarah A.	13	f.			" S
3		Amelia L.	11	f.			" S
4		Franklin	6	m.			" S
5	802/802	BLAIR, David	33	m.	Farmer	/275	"
6		Isabella	26	f.	Domestic		"
7		Lana	8	f.			"
8		Ezekiel	6	m.			"
9		Joshua W.	2	m.			"
10	803/803	BLAIR, Ezekiel	68	m.	Farmer	1000/240	Md.
11		Sarah	69	f.	Domestic		N.J. I
12		Lucinda	25	f.	Domestic		O.
13		Henry	13	m.			"
14		Archela	23	f.	Domestic		"
15		James W.	3/12	m.			"
16	804/804	BLAIR, Philip	45	m.	Farmer	1500/300	O.
17		Susanna	46	f.	Domestic		" I

18		BLAIR, Silas	16	m.	Farm laborer		O.	S
19		Hamilton	14	m.			"	S
20		Nancy	10	f.			"	S
21		Eli	9	m.			"	
22		Sylvester	7	m.			"	
23		Sarah J.	4	f.			"	
24		POWELL, Diana	25	f.	Domestic		"	

25	805/805	POWELL, Hiram	22	m.	Farmer	/100	"	
26		Mary A.	19	f.	Domestic		"	
27		William D.	3/12	m.			"	

28	806/806	BATTIN, Samuel	22	m.	Farmer	/100	"	
29		Angeline	20	f.	Domestic		"	
30		Percilla	2	f.			"	
31		William P.	1/12	m.			"	

32	807/807	CLINE, Jonathon	22	m.	Farmer	400/225	"	
33		Matilda	22	f.	Domestic		Pa.	I
34		Matthias	2	m.			O.	
35		Rachel	1/12	f.			"	
36		PROVINCE, John	16	m.	Farm laborer		"	S

| 37 | 808/808 | TAYLOR, Greenberry | 30 | m. | Miller | /100 | Va.| M |
| 38 | | Malinda J. | 20 | f. | Domestic | | " | M |

| 39 | 809/809 | LAMPING, Frederick A. | 43 | m. | Merchant | 30,000/30,000 | Old. | |
| 40 | | Casander | 43 | f. | Domestic | | O. | |

Page 118   9 July 1860   Sheet 287 verso

1		Josaphine	18	f.	Domestic	O.	S
2		William	16	m.	Clerk	"	S
3		George	14	m.		"	S
4		Otha	12	m.		"	S
5		Arasmus	9	m.		"	S
6		Clemens A.	2	m.		"	
7		Frederick A.	1	m.		"	
8		BREIDENSTEIN, Emily	19	f.	Domestic	H.K.	
9		FRENCH, Elisabeth	77	f.	Nothing	Md.	
10		RHIENES, Gerhart	28	m.	Clerk	Old.	
11		KISTER, Andrew	22	m.	Farm laborer	H.K.	
12		SMITH, Samuel	34	m.	Tobacco Packer	O.	

| 13 | 810/810 | WAY, Thomas A. | 54 | m. | Farmer | 12,035/5000 | Md. | |
| 14 | | Lydia J. | 10 | f. | | | O. | |

15	---/811	CAMEL, Levi	60	m.	Farm laborer		Del.	I
16		Ann	60	f.	Domestic		O.	
17		Levi	20	m.	Farm laborer		"	
18		Martha J.	22	f.	Domestic		"	
19		Lydia A.	17	f.	Domestic		"	

| 20 | 811/812 | EATON, David of J. | 35 | m. | Farmer | /325 | " | |

21		EATON, Deborah A.	33	f.	Domestic		O.	
22		Amanda J.	5	f.			"	
23		Mary	3	f.			"	
24		Nathan	1	m.			"	

25	812/813	FLINT, David D.	20	m.	Farmer	/50	"	
26		Mary A.	29	f.	Domestic		"	
27		Charlotte	10/12	f.			"	

28	813/814	LATHAM, Louisa	41	f.	Farmer	1500/	"	I
29		Mary	18	f.	Domestic		"	
30		James	20	m.	Farm laborer		"	S
31		Anfield	16	m.	Farm laborer		"	
32		John	14	m.			"	S
33		Joseph	12	m.			"	S
34		Malen	10	m.			"	S
35		Sabina	3	f.			"	

36	814/815	SPIKER, David	40	m.	Wagon-maker	/125	"	
37		Catharine	36	f.	Domestic		"	
38		Adalantic	11	m.			"	
39		Margaret	8	f.			"	
40		Martha	5	f.			"	

Page 119   9 July 1860   Sheet 288

1		Sophronius	3	m.			O.	
2		Monroe	1	m.			"	

3	815/816	WHITE, Rachel	57	f.	Domestic	600/675	Pa.	

4	816/817	WHITE, William	27	m.	Farmer	1400/225	O.	
5		Marinda	21	f.	Domestic		"	I
6		Arsula	3	f.			"	
7		Louisa B.	1	f.			"	
8		PUGH, Hannah	40	f.	Domestic		"	

9	817/818	MARSHALL, Lavina	45	f.	Farmer	/150	Va.	
10		Orval	20	m.	Farmer		O.	
11		MORGAN, Hannah	28	f.	Domestic		"	I
12		Peter	1	m.			"	

13	818/819	EATON, David of A.	37	m.	Farmer	700/1300	Md.	
14		Hannah	35	f.	Domestic		"	
15		Deborah	11	f.			O.	S
16		Lorenzo D.	8	m.			"	S
17		Angeline	3	f.			"	

18	819/---	UNOCCUPIED

19	820/820	FORACRE, James	44	m.	Farmer	800/375	Pa.	
20		Hannah	39	f.	Domestic		"	
21		Sarah	18	f.	Domestic		O.	S
22		Albert	16	m.	Farm laborer		"	S
23		William	12	m.			"	S
24		Joshua	7	m.			"	S

25	821/821	BROWN, Moses	38	m.	Farmer	700/250	"	

26		BROWN, Lydia	38	f.	Domestic		O.	I
27		William	12	m.		"	S
28		Mary	10	f.		"	S
29		Josephine	2	f.		"	
30		WILLIAMSON, Hannah	98	f.	Domestic	Md.	I
31		BROWN, Rebecca	35	f.	Domestic	O.	I
32		Lavina	8	f.		"	
33	822/822	WILLIAMSON, George	24	m.	Farmer	/50	"	M
34		Perlina	32	f.	Domestic		"	M
35		DENBO, Jane	10	f.		"	
36		George	3	m.		"	
37	823/823	WHITE, Thomas	24	m.	Farmer	1200/300	"
38		Elisabeth	25	f.	Domestic		"
39		Melissa	5	f.		"	
40		Anne A.	4	f.		"	

Page 120   9 July 1860   Sheet 288 verso

1		HENTHORN, Samuel	18	m.	Farm laborer		O.	
2	824/824	HARMON, John	31	m.	Farmer	1400/500	"
3		Matilda	29	f.	Domestic		"
4		Catharine	9	f.		"	S
5		Mary E.	6	f.		"	S
6		James R.	4	m.		"	
7		Isaac	2	m.		"	
8		Peter	6/12	m.		"	
9	825/825	BROWN, Andrew	31	m.	Farmer	/75	"
10		Catharine	16	f.	Domestic		"
11		Margaret J.	9/12	f.		"	
12		CLINE, Diana	25	f.	Domestic		"	I
13		Andrew C.	5	m.		"	
14	826/826	WILLIAMSON, Isaac	30	m.	Farmer	6500/800	"
15		Abagail	24	f.	Domestic		"
16		Madisson	12	m.		"	S
17		Samuel R.	7	m.		"	S
18		Lorenzo D.	2	m.		"	
19		REECE, James	19	m.	Farm laborer		"	S
20	827/827	CLINE, David	49	m.	Farmer	2000/450	"
21		Jane	45	f.	Domestic		"	I
22		Samuel	19	m.	Farm laborer		"	S
23		Cornelius	17	m.	Farm laborer		"	S
24		Matilda	15	f.	Domestic		"	S
25		Ruth	13	f.		"	S
26		Mary	11	f.		"	
27		Jane	4	f.		"	
28		Sarah E.	3	f.		"	
29	828/828	CLINE, Noah	25	m.	Farmer	/150	"
30		Clia A.	24	f.	Domestic		"
31		Caroline	3	f.		"	
32		Charlotte	2	f.		"	

33		CLINE, Eli	1/12	m.			O.
34	829/829	CLINE, Eli	33	m.	Farmer	2000/550	"
35		Milla	28	f.	Domestic		" I
36		Jane	6	f.			"
37		Franklin	4	m.			"
38		Andrew	2	m.			"
39	830/830	CLINE, Nathaniel	30	m.	Farmer	1600/400	"
40		Ellen	24	f.	Domestic		"

Page 121   9 July 1860   Sheet 289

1		Ross	5	m.			O.
2		Eunice	4	f.			"
3		William H.	3	m.			"
4		John M.	1	m.			"
5	831/831	CLINE, Joseph M.	34	m.	Farmer	3000/650	"
6		Sarah J.	28	f.	Domestic		"
7		Johnson	6	m.			"
8		Emily J.	4	f.			"
9		Alonzo	2	m.			"
10	832/832	CLINE, Henry	27	m.	Farmer	/200	" I
11	833/833	CLINE, George	58	m.	Farmer	6500/750	"
12		Elisabeth	20	f.	Domestic		"
13		Lavina	18	f.	Domestic		" S
14		Henry	15	m.	Farm laborer		" S
15		Sarah J.	13	f.			" S
16		William H.	11	m.			" S
17		John W.	7	m.			" S
18	834/834	ALLEN, David	40	m.	Farmer	/250	"
19		Ann E.	30	f.	Domestic		"
20		Andrew	8	m.			" S
21		Isaah	6	m.			"
22		Jemima	1	f.			"
23		CHERDEN, William	13	m.			" S
24		GRIFFEN, Alvira	16	f.	Domestic		" S
25		ALLEN, Joseph	60	m.			" 5
26		GRIFFEN, Thomas W.	61	m.	Painter		Md.
27	835/835	ALLEN, Simon	24	m.	Farmer	/100	O. M
28		Elisabeth	20	f.	Domestic		" M
29	836/836	WILLIAMSON, Lei-sure	37	m.	Farmer	2000/600	" I
30		Jemima	29	f.	Domestic		" I
31		Harvy	12	m.			" S
32		William	9	m.			" S
33		Nancy	8	f.			" S
34		Joseph E.	5	m.			"
35		Mary	3	f.			"
36		Isaah	1	m.			"
37		DENBO, Nancy	14	f.			"

38	837/837	NOLTON, John	35	m.	Farmer	2000/600	O.
39		Mary	28	f.	Domestic		" I
40		Sarah E.	1	f.			"

Page 122   9 July 1860   Sheet 289 verso

1		William P.	1/12	m.			O.
2		Cornelius	14	m.			" S
3		David	12	m.			" S
4		Nancy J.	9	f.			" S
5		Andrew C.	5	m.			" S
6	838/838	CLINE, Thomas	47	m.	Farmer	4500/580	"
7		Sarah	48	f.	Domestic		"
8		Isaac	20	m.	Farm laborer		"
9		Isaah	18	m.	Farm laborer		" S
10		Martin	16	m.	Farm laborer		" S
11		Martha	14	f.			" S
12		David	12	m.			" S
13		William T.	10	m.			" S
14	839/839	NOLTON, Andrew	29	m.	Farmer	/125	"
15		Willian	22	f.	Domestic		" I
16		Esau	4	m.			"
17		Stacy H.	3	m.			"
18		Lemuel	1/12	m.			"
19	840/840	JONES, Enos	50	m.	Farmer	200/125	"
20		Emily F.	50	f.	Domestic		"
21		Gasaway	20	m.	Farm laborer		"
22		Nancy	18	f.	Domestic		"
23		Susan	14	f.			"
24		Henry F.	12	m.			"
25		Archeleus	7	m.			"
26		Enos	5	m.			"
27		Rachel	3	f.			"
28		Phebe E.	1	f.			"
29		Alva	22	m.	Farm laborer		"
30	841/841	RHINARD, Isaac	88	m.	Nothing	2500/200	Pa.
31		Hester	73	f.	Domestic		Ire.
32		Effa	18	f.	Domestic		O. S
33		John	14	m.			" S
34	842/842	FLINT, Jacob	55	m.	Farmer	4000/850	Vt.
35		Eliza	54	f.	Domestic		Va.
36		Oliver	20	m.	Farm laborer		O. S
37		Loretta	18	f.	Domestic		"
38		Joseph P.	14	m.			"
39		APPLEN, Rebecca	58	f.	Domestic		N.H.
40	843/843	SNODGRASS, Francis	36	m.	Mechanic	/100	Pa.

Page 123   9 July 1860   Sheet 290

1		Lucinda	26	f.	Domestic		O.
2		Marion	6/12	m.			"

3		SNODGRASS, James	6	m.			O.	
4	844/844	RHINARD, James	48	m.	Farmer	6000/1000	Pa.	
5		Rachel	44	f.	Domestic		"	I
6		Esther	23	f.	Domestic		O.	
7		John M.	21	m.	Farm laborer		"	S
8		Hamilton	17	m.	Farm laborer		"	S
9		Jane	15	f.	Domestic		"	S
10		James K.	14	m.			"	S
11		Rebecca	11	f.			"	S
12		George W.	9	m.			"	S
13		Margaret	4	f.			"	
14		Victoria	2	f.			"	

15	845/845	STILL, James L.	25	m.	Farm laborer		"	
16		Nancy	25	f.	Domestic		"	
17		James W.	1	m.			"	

18	846/846	SMITH, Samuel	42	m.	Farmer	/400	Pa.	
19		Adaline	38	f.	Domestic		Va.	
20		James W.	16	m.	Farm laborer		O.	S
21		John B.	14	m.			"	S
22		Alonzo M.	12	m.			"	S
23		Thomas J.	10	m.			"	S
24		Francis M.	6	m.			"	
25		Samuel A.	4	m.			"	
26		Mary C.	1	f.			"	
27		Alice A.	20	f.	Domestic		"	

28	847/847	BELL, Alexander	48	m.	Minister, M. E. 4500/800		Ire.	
29		Christiana	46	f.	Domestic		Pa.	
30		Catharine	18	f.	Domestic		O.	S
31		John D.	16	m.	Farm laborer		"	S
32		Margaret E.	14	f.			"	S
33		Christiana	9	f.			"	S
34		James A.	7	m.			"	S

35	848/848	HAMLIN, Richard	72	m.	Farmer	2200/450	Pa.	
36		Margaret	50	f.	Domestic		O.	I
37		Henry	22	m.	Farm laborer		"	I
38		Sarah	24	f.	Domestic		"	I
39		Richard	20	m.	Farm laborer		"	
40		Philip	13	m.			"	

Page 124   10 July 1860   Sheet 290 verso

1		HEREN, Nancy J.	13	f.			O.	S
2		HAMLIN, Nancy J.	11	f.			"	S
3		Rosanna	9	f.			"	S
4		Leonard	4	m.			"	

5	849/849	HAMLIN, Rufus	31	m.	Farmer	/75	"	I
6		Mary A.	29	f.	Domestic		"	
7		Nancy	8	f.			"	
8		Elisabeth	7	f.			"	
9		Sarah	5	f.			"	

10		HAMLIN, Charlotte	4	f.			O.	
11		James W.	3	m.			"	
12		Mary E.	1	f.			"	
13	850/850	HAMLIN, Eli	28	m.	Farmer	1100/100	"	I
14		Hariet	17	f.	Domestic		"	
15		Hannibal	17	m.	Farm laborer		"	
16	851/851	BOHLEN, Samuel	46	m.	Farmer	125/50	Sw.	
17		Mary A.	29	f.	Domestic		O.	
18		Henry	6	m.			"	
19		Samuel	1	m.			"	
20	852/852	CLINE, John	44	m.	Farmer	/125	"	
21		Mary	42	f.	Domestic		"	I
22		Charlotte	19	f.	Domestic		"	
23		Amanda	18	f.	Domestic		"	
24		Nancy	17	f.	Domestic		"	
25		Jane	14	f.			"	
26		Sarah	10	f.			"	
27		William	5	m.			"	
28		Eunice	4	f.			"	
29		John T.	1	m.			"	
30	853/853	MORELAND, Elias	57	m.	Farmer	1600/250	Va.	
31		Elisabeth	53	f.	Domestic		O.	I
32		Darcus	18	f.	Domestic		"	
33		Elias N. J.	16	m.	Farm laborer		"	S
34		William C.	10	m.			"	S
35	854/854	HILL, Luther	26	m.	Farmer	700/200	O.	
36		Amanda	26	f.	Domestic		"	
37		Mary	5	f.			"	
38		James	3	m.			"	
39		Lavina	2	f.			"	
40		Lazetta	6/12	f.			"	

Page 125　　　　　　　　10 July 1860　　　　　　　　Sheet 291

1		Jennetta	6/12	f.			O.	
2	855/855	HILL, John	67	m.	Farmer	800/350	N.Y.	
3		Margaret	61	f.	Domestic		Pa.	
4		Charles	35	m.	Farm laborer	1000/	O.	
5		Ezra	29	m.	Farm laborer		"	
6		Porter	27	m.	Farm laborer		"	I
7		Phebe	26	f.	Domestic		"	
8		Susan	24	f.	Domestic		"	
9		Margaret	22	f.	Domestic		"	
10		Weltha	19	f.	Domestic		"	
11		John	16	m.	Farm laborer		"	
12	856/856	CLINE, Samuel N.	33	m.	Farmer	2000/400	"	
13		Sarah A.	27	f.	Domestic		"	I
14		Madisson	9	m.			"	S
15		Isaac P.	7	m.			"	S

16		CLINE, Hiram	5	m.			O. S
17		Mary J.	3	f.			"
18		Luther	1	m.			"
19		Eunice	1/12	f.			"
20	857/857	PIATT, Jacob	40	m.	Farmer	150/150	"
21		Ellen	40	f.	Domestic		" I
22		John	18	m.	Farm laborer		"
23		Nancy	16	f.	Domestic		" S
24		David	14	m.			" S
25		Robert	12	m.			" S
26		Jacob	8	m.			" S
27		Nathaniel	6	m.			" S
28		Simon	4	m.			"
29		Sarah A.	2	f.			"
30	858/858	HARMON, Andrew	56	m.	Farmer	4000/400	Pa. I
31		Jane	54	f.	Domestic		" I
32		GRIFFEN, Thomas	14	m.			O.
33	859/859	HARMON, John	25	m.	Farmer	/100	"
34		Cynthia	23	f.	Domestic		"
35		Maxell	4	m.			"
36		Russell	1	m.			"
37	860/860	CLINE, Martin V.	20	m.	Farm laborer		"
38		Frances	18	f.	Domestic		"
39		Rosanna	5	f.			"
40	861/861	HARMON, Henry	23	m.	Farmer	/150	" M

Page 126   10 July 1860   Sheet 291 verso

1		Nancy	20	f.	Domestic		O. M
2	862/862	COSS, George	48	m.	Farmer	5000/550	Va. I
3		Sarah	40	f.	Domestic		Md. I
4		Margaret	22	f.	Domestic		O.
5		Elisabeth	20	f.	Domestic		" S
6		Mahala	18	f.	Domestic		" S
7		John	16	m.	Farm laborer		" S
8		Sarah M.	14	f.			" S
9		George W.	12	m.			" S
10		Mary J.	10	f.			" S
11		Solomon	8	m.			" S
12		Jacob	6	m.			"
13		Lovina	4	f.			"
14		David	10/12	m.			"
15		WILLIAMS, Margaret	80	f.	Domestic		Md.
16	863/863	SMITH, Robert	34	m.	Farmer	150/75	O.
17		Melinda	33	f.	Domestic		" I
18		William	9	m.			" S
19		John M.	2	m.			"
20		Jasper N.	3/12	m.			"
21	864/864	BROWN, Abel	56	m.	Farmer	300/200	"

22		BROWN, Abagail	50	f.	Domestic		O.	
23		Wesley	24	m.	Farm laborer		"	
24		Rachel	10	f.			"	

25	865/865	BAKER, John	54	m.	Farmer	/50	"	
26		Susan	55	f.	Domestic		Pa. I	
27		James	20	m.	Farm laborer		O.	
28		William	18	m.	Farm laborer		"	
29		Theodore	14	m.			"	

30	866/866	BAKER, Andrew	24	m.	Farm laborer		"	
31		Margaret	20	f.	Domestic		"	
32		Sarah E.	2	f.			"	
33		Susan A.	8/12	f.			"	

34	867/867	BAKER, David	29	m.	Farmer	400/200	"	
35		Sarah	24	f.	Domestic		"	
36		Joseph W.	4	m.			"	
37		John A.	1	m.			"	

38	868/868	POWELL, Mary	48	f.	Farmer	600/275	Pa. I	
39		Atty	20	m.	Farm laborer	200/100	O.	
40		Dartha L.	18	f.	Domestic		"	

Page 127   10 July 1860   Sheet 292

1		Thomas	16	m.	Farm laborer		O.	S
2		Mary J.	14	f.			"	S
3		William R.	11	m.			"	S

4	869/869	POWELL, Chris- topher	29	m.	Farmer	200/200	"	
5		Hester A.	21	f.	Domestic		"	
6		Caleb	3	m.			"	
7		Andrew	8/12	m.			"	

8	870/870	BROWN, Lewis	36	m.	Farm laborer		"	I
9		Ruth A.	35	f.	Domestic		"	I
10		Nancy J.	9	f.			"	S
11		Beni	7	m.			"	S
12		John	5	f.			"	
13		Uriah	3	m.			"	
14		Frederick J.	8/12	m.			"	

15	871/871	SNYDER, John	37	m.	Farmer	350/200	"	I
16		Lucinda	35	f.	Domestic		"	I
17		Hesekiah	13	m.			"	S
18		Eliza	12	f.			"	S
19		Mary E.	8	f.			"	S
20		Armintha A.	3	f.			"	
21		George	6/12	m.			"	

22	872/872	WAY, Joshua	51	m.	Farmer	2500/950	Md.	
23		Lucinda	45	f.	Domestic		O.	
24		George	20	m.	Farm laborer		"	S
25		William	17	m.	Farm laborer		"	S
26		Thomas	11	m.			"	S

```
27          WAY, James          9   m.                              O.  S
28          Clara               4   f.                              "

29  873/873 LUCKEY, Joseph      80  m.   Farmer      1000/300  Pa.   I
30          Tabitha             75  f.   Domestic              Va.   I
31          Catharine           40  f.   Domestic              "
32          Joseph              18  m.   Farm laborer          "
33          WILLIAMS, James      5  m.                          "

34  874/874 DRAKE, Thomas       48  m.   Farmer       500/500  "    I
35          Hannah              46  f.   Domestic              "
36          William             22  m.   Farm laborer          "    I
37          Benjamin            21  m.   Farm laborer          "    I
38          John                19  m.   Farm laborer          "
39          Thomas              17  m.   Farm laborer          "
40          George W.           14  m.                          "
```

```
1           Mary E.             12  f.                              O.
2           Wesley              10  m.                              "
3           Frederick            8  m.                              "
4           Casnder              6  f.                              "
5           Esther A.            2  f.                              "
6           Sarah A.            23  f.   Domestic                   "    I

7   875/875 FINEY, Elijah M.    30  m.   Farmer       800/200  "
8           Adaline             26  f.   Domestic              "    I
9           Francis M.           6  m.                          "
10          Peter W.             4  m.                          "
11          Nancy J.             2  f.                          "
12          WORLEY, Mary J.     19  f.   Domestic              "
13          HALL, William       12  m.                          "

14  876/876 COOPER, John        27  m.   Farmer        /400  N.Y.
15          Catharine           22  f.   Domestic              O.
16          Mary S.              4  f.                          "
17          Irvin B.             1  m.                          "
18          BROWN, James        14  m.                          "    S
19          COOPER, Anthony     75  m.   Farmer      1800/     Pa.   I

20  877/877 POWELL, Abner       90  m.   Nothing       /100  Va.
21          Catharine           50  f.   Domestic              Pa.   I
22          Joseph              15  m.   Farm laborer          O.
23          George W.           12  m.                          "
24          John D.             10  m.                          "
25          Josiah C.            7  m.                          "
26          Anthony              3  m.                          "

27  879/879 PIATT, Thomas       47  m.   Farmer      4000/1200 O.
28          Emily               45  f.   Domestic              "    I
29          Nancy               23  f.   Domestic              "
30          William             19  m.   Farm laborer          "    S
31          Mary A.             17  f.   Domestic              "
32          John M.             14  m.                          "    S
33          Thomas              10  m.                          "    S
34          Emily                7  f.                          "
```

35	880/880	GATTIN, Dennis	25	m.	Farmer	/300	O.	
36		Elisabeth	21	f.	Domestic		"	
37		William H.	1	m.			"	
38	881/881	BENNETT, Elijah	32	m.	Laborer		"	
39		Sarah	25	f.	Domestic		"	
40		Nancy	6	f.			"	

Page 129   11 July 1860   Sheet 293

1		Levi	1	m.			O.	
2	882/882	FISHER, Samuel S.	31	m.	Farmer	3000/700	"	M
3		Margaret J.	27	f.	Domestic		"	M
4		ROSE, Rhinehart	17	m.	Farm laborer		"	
5	883/883	PARIS, John	48	m.	Farmer	2000/600	Va.	
6		Phebe	49	f.	Domestic		O.	I
7		McGowen	25	m.	Farm laborer		"	
8		Joseph	23	m.	Carpenter		"	
9		Tabitha	21	f.	Domestic		"	I
10		Mary A.	18	f.	Domestic		"	
11		Lewis	12	m.			"	S
12		Eliza	6	f.			"	
13	884/884	GREEN, Isaac T.	29	m.	Farmer	/200	"	
14		Elisabeth	25	f.	Domestic		"	
15		Sarah C.	6	f.			"	
16		Thomas F.	4	m.			"	
17	885/885	WARWICK, Thomas	63	m.	Master Mason	400/100	Pa.	
18		Rachel	66	f.	Domestic		Va.	
19		Rachel	19	f.	Domestic		O.	
20	886/886	FISHER, Samuel	31	m.	Farmer	800/200	"	
21		Mary	28	f.	Domestic		"	
22		Eunice	6	f.			"	
23		Thomas W.	4	m.			"	
24		HALL, George	27	m.	Farm laborer	600/	"	
25	887/887	McNEACE, James	50	m.	Farmer	5000/800	Ire.	
26		Matilda	50	f.	Domestic		"	
27		Alexander	19	m.	Farm laborer		"	
28		William	17	m.	Farm laborer		"	
29		Eliza	16	f.	Domestic		"	
30		James	15	m.			"	
31		Matilda	12	f.			O.	
32	888/888	DYE, Joseph	48	m.	Farmer & Cabinet-maker	1500/350	"	
33		Mary	48	f.	Domestic		Pa.	I
34		Elisabeth A.	19	f.	Domestic		O.	
35		Joseph M.	18	m.	Farm laborer		"	
36		Susanna	14	f.			"	
37		Mary P.	9	f.			"	
38	889/889	DYE, George	23	m.	Farm laborer		"	M

39		DYE, Margaret	20	f.	Domestic		O. M
40	890/890	DYE, John	24	m.	Farmer		"

1		Mary	29	f.	Domestic		O.	
2		Ann E.	5	f.			"	
3	891/891	DYE, Isaac	28	m.	Farmer	400/200	"	
4		Eleanor	25	f.	Domestic		"	I
5		Hulda J.	5	f.			"	
6		Franklin	3	m.			"	
7		Ara R.	1	f.			"	
8	892/892	PHILIPS, Alfred	31	m.	Farmer	600/325	"	
9		Lucinda	30	f.	Domestic		"	
10		Nancy J.	6	f.			"	
11		Sarah N.	3	f.			"	
12		William A.	1	m.			"	
13	893/893	HUPP, John	21	m.	Farmer		"	
14		Mary	21	f.	Domestic		"	I
15		Jackson	1	m.			"	
16	894/894	POLTIN, Joshua	28	m.	Farmer	/100	"	I
17		Eliza	23	f.	Domestic		"	
18		William W.	7	m.			"	
19		John C.	5	m.			"	
20		George T.	1	m.			"	
21	895/895	ALLEN, David	50	m.	Farmer	4000/740	Pa.	
22		Sarah	48	f.	Domestic		O.	I
23		Philip	19	m.	Farm laborer		"	
24		Ezekiel	17	m.	Farm laborer		"	S
25		Sarah	15	f.	Domestic		"	S
26		Perlina	13	f.			"	S
27		David	12	m.			"	S
28		Henry	7	m.			"	
29		Louisa	4	f.			"	
30		Elijah	2	m.			"	
31	896/896	ALLEN, Lewis	22	m.	Farmer	/175	"	
32		Ellen	20	f.	Domestic		"	
33	897/897	FISHER, Thomas S.	35	m.	Farmer	1200/410	"	
34		Mary T.	37	f.	Domestic		"	
35		Simon	14	m.			"	S
36		Ruth A.	12	f.			"	S
37		Rebecca J.	9	f.			"	S
38		Samuel S.	7	m.			"	S
39		Mary M.	4	f.			"	
40		JOHNSON, Chrian	74	f.	Domestic		Pa.	

1	898/989	DEVON, John W.	22	m.	Farmer	/300	O.

2		DEVON, Mary J.	21	f.	Domestic		O.
3		James H.	2	m.			"
4		Daniel B.	2/12	m.			"
5	899/899	PIATT, Benjamin	31	m.	Farmer	1000/350	"
6		Phebe	27	f.	Domestic		"
7		Benjamin	7	m.			"
8		Robert	3	m.			"
9		Anne E.	6/12	f.			"
10		WATSON, Benjamin	82	m.	Nothing		Pa. I
11	900/900	DEARTH, George	24	m.	Farm laborer	/50	O. IM
12		Mary J.	17	f.	Domestic		" M
13		Eliza J.	49	f.	Domestic		"
14		Elisabeth	11	f.			"
15	901/901	ALLEN, Avery	25	m.	Farm laborer	/75	"
16		Nancy	24	f.	Domestic		"
17		Sarah A.	6	f.			"
18		Perlina	1	f.			"
19	902/902	GALLAUGHER, Henry	40	m.	Laborer		"
20		Levice	38	f.	Domestic		"
21		Sarah I.	9	f.			"
22		John	6	m.			"
23		Mary E.	1	f.			"
24	903/903	MERKLE, David	25	m.	Farmer		"
25		Hannah	23	f.	Domestic		" I
26		Moses	2	m.			"
27		Martha	6/12	f.			"
28	904/904	MERKLE, Moses	65	m.	Farmer	2000/150	Md.
29		Sarah	60	f.	Domestic		" I
30		Aaron	20	m.	Farm laborer		O.
31		Matthias	14	m.			"
32	905/905	MERKLE, Jacob	23	m.	Farmer		"
33		Mahala	22	f.	Domestic		"
34		William H.	4	m.			"
35		Matthias	3	m.			"
36		Sarah J.	2	f.			"
37		Lucinda	1	f.			"
38	906/906	MERKLE, John	28	m.	Farmer	/250	"
39		Hannah	24	f.	Domestic		"
40		Philip	4	m.			"

1		William	2	m.			O.
2		Cornelius	1/12	m.			"
3	907/907	CHRISTY, Thomas	26	m.	Farmer	/400	"
4		Darcus	22	f.	Domestic		"
5		Cornelius	8/12	m.			"

6	908/908	DEVORE, Daniel	50	m.	Farmer	3000/500	Pa.	
7		Elisabeth A.	33	f.	Domestic		O.	
8		Luther R.	12	m.			"	S
9		Margaret J.	11	f.			"	S
10		Isaac W.	9	m.			"	S
11		Alexander	6	m.			"	S
12		Samuel H.	3	m.			"	
13		David H.	6/12	m.			"	
14	909/909	NOLTIN, Cornelius	26	m.	Farmer	/1050	"	
15		Nancy	29	f.	Domestic		"	
16		WINLAND, Margaret	13	f.			"	S
17		Urana	8	f.			"	S
18		James	5	m.			"	
19		NOLTIN, Elisabeth	3	f.			"	
20		DRUM, Eliza	24	f.	Domestic		"	
21		Mary E.	2	f.			"	
22	910/910	NOLTIN, John	56	m.	Farmer	6000/2500	"	
23		Elisabeth	54	f.	Domestic		Va.	I
24		Mariah	20	f.	Domestic		"	
25		Elisabeth	14	f.			"	S
26		WEAVER, Henry	9	m.			"	S
27	911/911	EATON, Abijah	58	m.	Farmer	1500/800	Pa.	
28		Angeline	47	f.	Domestic		O.	
29		Lana	12	f.			"	S
30		Lydia E.	10	f.			"	S
31	912/912	BIGLEY, James	28	m.	Farmer	/200	"	
32		Elisabeth	27	f.	Domestic		"	
33		Nancy A.	6	f.			"	
34		Emma J.	4	f.			"	
35		Samuel H.	6/12	m.			"	
36	913/913	CHRISTY, Jane	40	f.	Domestic		"	
37		Mary M.	18	f.	Domestic		"	
38	914/914	CHRISTY, Finley	24	m.	Farmer	1000/250	"	
39		Mary A.	20	f.	Domestic		"	
40		James A.	1/12	m.			"	

1	915/915	BEARDMORE, Isaac	40	m.	Farmer	1600/300	Eng.	
2		Ann	41	f.	Domestic		"	I
3		Elisabeth	17	f.	Domestic		"	
4		Thomas	15	m.	Farm laborer		"	S
5		John W.	10	m.			"	S
6		Sarah A.	6	f.			O.	
7		Isaac	4	m.			"	
8		Clara F.	1	f.			"	
9	916/916	CECIL, Joshua	29	m.	Minister, U.B.	/400	"	
10		Rebecca E.	29	f.	Domestic		"	
11		Levi T.	9	m.			"	S
12		Mary E.	7	f.			"	S

13		CECIL, Rebecca J.	5	f.			O.	S
14		Canarissa	3	f.			"	
15		Ann M.	1	f.			"	
16	917/917	CECIL, Amon	25	m.	Farmer	/300	"	
17		Elisabeth	24	f.	Domestic		"	
18		John N.	6	m.			"	S
19		Sophia J.	3	f.			"	
20	918/918	FARA, George	24	m.	Farmer	/225	"	I
21		Hariet	24	f.	Domestic		"	I
22		Nancy E.	4	f.			"	
23		Margaret A.	3	f.			"	
24		ANDERSON, Robert	20	m.	Farm laborer		"	I
25		DENIMS, Stephen	22	m.	Farm laborer		"	I
26	919/919	FARRA, Isaac	55	m.	Farmer	1600/250	Pa.	
27		Ann	54	f.	Domestic		"	I
28		Helen	20	f.	Domestic		O.	I
29		Thamer	19	f.	Domestic		"	
30		John	16	m.	Farm laborer		"	
31		Asberry	4	m.			"	
32	920/920	McJILTON, Camel	35	m.	Farmer	/150	"	
33		Nancy	27	f.	Domestic		"	
34		Hariet C.	10	f.			"	
35		Thomas	9	m.			"	
36		George	7	m.			"	
37		Camel	5	m.			"	
38		Eli	2	m.			"	
39		Miles	2/12	m.			"	
40	921/921	BURTIN, John	59	m.	Farmer	1500/150	Pa.	

Page 134   12 July 1860   Sheet 295 verso

1		BURTON, Eleanor	47	f.	Domestic		Va.	
2		Elisabeth	15	f.	Domestic		"	
3		Angeline	13	f.			O.	
4	922/922	MORTIMORE, John	30	m.	Farm laborer	/50	"	I
5		Rebecca E.	28	f.	Domestic		"	I
6		Sarah C.	7	f.			"	
7		William	6	m.			"	
8		Susanna	2	f.			"	
9		Hariet E.	1	f.			"	
10	923/923	COLLINS, Sarah	59	f.	Domestic	1200/200	Pa.	
11	924/924	NICHOLSON, William	53	m.	Farmer	500/300	"	
12		Nancy	55	f.	Domestic		Va.	I
13		Lavina	17	f.	Domestic		O.	
14	925/925	CLENDENING, James	32	m.	Farm laborer		"	
15		Amanda	27	f.	Domestic		"	
16		Reason	7	m.			"	
17		John W.	4	m.			"	

18		CLENDENING, James F.	2	m.			O.	

19	926/926	VESS, J. W.	40	m.	Farmer	/350	Va.	
20		Sarah J.	39	f.	Domestic		O.	
21		Albert	15	m.	Farm laborer		"	S
22		Alfred	13	m.			"	S
23		Thomas	11	m.			"	S
24		William	9	m.			"	S
25		John	7	m.			"	S
26		Hiram	5	m.			"	
27		Mary E.	1	f.			"	

28	927/927	DRAKE, Nathan	25	m.	Farmer	/200	"	I
29		Sarah A.	22	f.	Domestic		"	I
30		George W.	4	m.			"	
31		Sarah E.	2	f.			"	

32	928/928	SHEPHERD, William	40	m.	Farmer	600/280	"	
33		Mary	35	f.	Domestic		"	
34		BATTIN, John	10	m.			"	S
35		PCLTON, Mary	6	f.			"	

36	929/929	HUBBERT, Thomas	42	m.	Farmer	2000/675	Va.	
37		Lydia A.	40	f.	Domestic		"	
38		James O.	19	m.	Farm laborer		O.	S
39		George	18	m.	Farm laborer		"	S
40		Daniel H.	17	m.	Farm laborer		"	S

Page 135   12 July 1860   Sheet 296

1		Elisabeth	15	f.	Domestic		O.	S
2		Levina	14	f.			"	S
3		Thomas	12	m.			"	S
4		Alexander	10	m.			"	S
5		William W.	7	m.			"	S
6		Lydia L.	3	f.			"	
7		Joseph	2	m.			"	

8	930/930	MAPLE, John N.	40	m.	Farmer	1400/350	"	
9		Catharine	35	f.	Domestic		"	
10		Alexander	15	m.	Farm laborer		!	S
11		Edwin R.	13	m.			"	S
12		Samantha A.	10	f.			"	S
13		George P.	8	m.			"	S
14		John N.	5	m.			"	
15		Charles C.	10/12	m.			"	

16	931/931	DRAKE, John	34	m.	Farmer	1500/400	"	I
17		Margaret	26	f.	Domestic		"	I
18		Mariah J.	12	f.			"	S
19		William	10	m.			"	S
20		Mary C.	7	f.			"	
21		George	5	m.			"	
22		Randolph	3	m.			"	
23		Nancy	1	f.			"	

24	932/932	HALL, Isaac	30	m.	Farmer	500/400	"	

```
25              HALL, Elisabeth J.  23    f.    Domestic                      O.
26                 Orpha             2    f.                                  "
27                 Hernanda        6/12   m.                                  "
28                 Calvin           17    m.    Farm laborer                  "

29  933/933  SHAFER, Joseph C.      29    m.    Farmer            /265        "
30                 Eliza J.         25    f.    Domestic                      "    I
31                 Elisabeth J.      7    f.                                  "
32                 James W.          1    m.                                  "

33  934/934  UNDERWOOD, John        28    m.    Farmer            /100   Ind.  I
34                 Margaret E.      20    f.    Domestic                 O.   I
35                 Simon R.          2    m.                             "

36  935/935  SHAFER, John           62    m.    Farm laborer      /100   Md.
37                 Hannah           57    f.    Domestic                 Pa.  I
38                 Daniel W.        16    m.    Farm laborer            O.

39  936/936  SHAFER, John V.        34    m.    Farmer          550/250   "
40                 Mary A.          33    f.    Domestic                 "    .
```

```
1                  Josiah            9    m.                             O.  S
2                  Rachel A.         6    f.                             "
3                  Hannah M.         4    f.                             "
4                  Eliza J.          2    f.                             "
5                  Isaac W.         21    m.    Farm laborer            "
6                  Phebe A.         13    f.                             "

7   937/937  WOODFORD, Mary         43    f.    Domestic        1400/200  Md.  I
8                  Lucinda          17    f.    Domestic                 O.
9                  Louisa           15    f.    Domestic                 "
10                 Mariah C.        12    f.                             "    S
11                 Frances J.        3    f.                             "
12                 John             56    m.    Farmer          1400/400  "

13  938/938  McCONNELL, John        29    m.    Farmer            /200    "
14                 Sarah A.         26    f.    Domestic                 "
15                 Josiah B.         6    m.                             "    S
16                 James W.          4    m.                             "
17                 Willis H.         2    m.                             "
18                 Winfield P.    2/12   m.                             "

19  939/939  GATCHEL, Nathan        43    m.    Farmer         2500/420   Pa.
20                 Elisabeth        46    f.    Domestic                 "
21                 John D.          18    m.    Farm laborer            O.  S
22                 Jeremiah W.      16    m.    Farm laborer            "   S

23  940/940  BEEVER, Peter          53    m.    Farmer         4200/750   Va.
24                 Elisabeth        54    f.    Domestic                 O.  I
25                 James            20    m.    Farm laborer            "   S
26                 Emily            15    f.    Domestic                 "
27                 Thomas W.        11    m.                             "   S
28              HALL, Enoch         20    m.    Farm laborer            "
29                 Elias            21    m.    Farm laborer            "

30  941/941  HICKINBOTTOM,
                   John             44    m.    Farmer         1000/250   Eng.
```

31		HICKINBOTTOM,						
		Elisabeth	51	f.	Domestic		Eng.	
32		William	19	m.	Farm laborer		"	
33	942/942	HANA, John	47	m.	Farmer	600/150	"	
34		Hannah	50	f.	Domestic		"	
35	943/943	BEARDMORE, John	38	m.	Farmer	2800/600	"	
36		Nancy	36	f.	Domestic		O.	
37		Thomas	16	m.	Farm laborer		"	S
38		John W.	14	m.			"	S
39		Elisabeth	12	f.			"	S
40		Sarah	9	f.			"	S

Page 137			12 July 1860				Sheet 297	
1		Nancy	7	f.			O.	S
2		Mary E.	5	f.			"	
3		Julian	2	f.			"	
4	944/944	McNIGHT, Benia	59	m.	Farmer	1500/275	Va.	I
5		Jane	53	f.	Domestic		Md.	I
6		Uriah	22	m.	Farm laborer		O.	
7		LITTLE, Sarah	15	f.	Domestic		"	S
8		TIPPANS, Clarkson	7	m.			"	
9	945/945	DRUMOND, Jesse	25	m.	Shoemaker		"	
10		Mary A.	20	f.	Domestic		"	
11	946/946	COX, William	23	m.	Farm laborer		"	M
12		Semantha	18	f.	Domestic		"	M
13	947/947	SMITH, Archibald	40	m.	Farmer	600/250	Ire.	
14		Mary	36	f.	Domestic		"	
15		REECE, Margaret	20	f.	Domestic		O.	
16	948/948	SMITH, Samuel	36	m.	Farmer	2000/500	"	
17		Nancy J.	24	f.	Domestic		"	
18		Olive A.	5	f.			"	
19		Dent C.	3	m.			"	
20		Porter S.	2	m.			"	
21		Mary E.	10/12	f.			"	
22	949/949	JOY, Benjamin	57	m.	Farmer	1500/400	Md.	I
23		Susan	49	f.	Domestic		Va.	I
24		Isaac	17	m.	Farm laborer		O.	S
25		Hannah	14	f.			"	S
26		Samuel	12	m.			"	S
27	950/950	EATON, John	30	m.	Blacksmith	/200	"	
28		Delille	23	f.	Domestic		"	
29		Mary A.	3	f.			"	
30		Martha J.	1	f.			"	
31	951/951	EATON, William	30	m.	Blacksmith	600/200	"	
32		Rebecca	23	f.	Domestic		"	
33		James	3	m.			"	

34		EATON, Samuel	1	m.			O.
35	952/952	COSS, Benjamin	46	m.	Farmer	2000/350	"
36		Elisabeth	56	f.	Domestic		Va. I
37		William	17	m.	Farm laborer		Md.
38		John	15	m.	Farm laborer		O.
39		Henry	9	m.			"
40		Mary M.	7	f.			"

Page 138   13 July 1860   Sheet 297 verso

1	953/953	WATSON, John	69	m.	Farmer	600/400	Scot.	
2		Margaret	73	f.	Domestic		"	
3		James	37	m.	Farmer	2100/3000	"	
4		John A.	12	m.			O.	S
5		Smith H.	10	m.			"	S
6		James A.	8	m.			"	S
7		Mary	6	f.			"	S
8		Archibald J.	4	m.			"	
9		CAREMEN, Mary	18	f.	Domestic		Bav.	
10	954/954	McCUE, George	31	m.	Farmer	2000/800	O.	
11		Sarah J.	27	f.	Domestic		"	
12		Cyrus	7	m.			"	S
13		Lewis C.	5	m.			"	S
14		John W.	4	m.			"	
15		William	90	m.	Nothing		Ire.	
16		WILLIAMSON, Jane	18	f.	Domestic		O.	
17	955/---	UNOCCUPIED						
18	956/955	WINTERS, Henry	33	m.	Farmer	1700/600	"	
19		Sarah R.	28	f.	Domestic		"	
20		John	9	m.			"	S
21		Margaret	7	f.			"	S
22		Catharine	5	f.			"	S
23		Elisabeth	3	f.			"	
24		Jane	1	f.			"	
25		SCOTT, Matthew	22	m.	Farm laborer		"	
26	957/956	HARMON, Elisabeth	56	f.	Farmer	3000/750	Pa. I	
27		Daniel	21	m.	Farm laborer		O.	
28		Alexander	16	m.	Farm laborer		"	S
29		Peter	12	m.			"	S
30		Elisabeth	13	f.			"	S
31		RICHARDS, Mary	10	f.			"	S
32	958/957	KIMBALL, Joseph	26	m.	Farmer		"	
33		Catharine A.	24	f.	Domestic		"	
34		Hannah J.	2	f.			"	
35	959/958	HARMON, James	27	m.	Farmer	/200	"	
36		Elisabeth A.	34	f.	Domestic		"	
37		Mary L.	2	f.			"	
38		PIATT, Mary E.	4	f.			"	
39	960/959	SWANEY, Hugh	65	m.	Farmer	300/50	Ire.	

40   SWANEY, Bridget   55 f.   Domestic   Ire.

1   CLARK, Samuel   23 m.   Farm laborer   O.

2 961/960 STATES, Daniel D. 33 m.   Farmer   1000/400 Pa.
3   Sarah   31 f.   Domestic   "
4   George W.   8 m.   O.
5   James B.   4 m.   "
6   Henry   3/12 m.   "

7 962/961 FRANCIS, John   52 m.   Farmer   1000/300   "
8   Amelia   48 f.   Domestic   "
9   MOTT, Mary J.   7 f.   "

10 963/962 MAN, Abrem   42 m.   Farmer   5400/1300 "
11   Julian   36 f.   Domestic   Md. I
12   Clarkson   15 m.   Farm laborer   "   S
13   Clarissa J.   12 f.   "   S
14   Thomas F.   10 m.   "   S
15   Vachel H.   1 m.   "
16   PIATT, Lavina   18 f.   Domestic   "

17 964/963 SMITH, Isaac   26 m.   Farm laborer   /200 "
18   Sarah A.   24 f.   Domestic   "
19   James H.   1 m.   "
20   TRUAX, Ann V.   18 f.   Domestic   "

21 965/964 WHITE, John   40 m.   Farm laborer   /300 "   M
22   Elisabeth   25 f.   Domestic   "   M
23   Malinda J.   15 f.   Domestic   "
24   Julian   12 f.   "
25   George   8 m.   "

26 966/965 ACKLEY, Wilson   18 m.   Farm laborer   "
27   UNDERWOOD, Mordica 58 m.   Miller   /20 Pa.
28   Deborah   52 f.   Domestic   N.J. I
29   Martha   12 f.   O.

30 967/966 HALL, George   42 m.   Farmer   3500/600   "
31   Margaret   38 f.   Domestic   "   I
32   Henderson   19 m.   Farm laborer   "
33   Sarah   17 f.   Domestic   "
34   Mary   16 f.   Domestic   "
35   Philip   14 m.   "
36   Rachel   12 f.   "
37   Samantha   7 f.   "
38   Saverta   3 f.   "

39 968/967 DILLON, Henry   35 m.   Farmer   1500/400   "
40   Cyntha   34 f.   Domestic   "   I

1   David   11 m.   O. S
2   John   10 m.   " S

3		DILLON, Mary J.	7	f.			O.	S
4		Lucy A.	5	f.			"	
5		Nancy	4	f.			"	
6		Henry	2	m.			"	
7	969/968	BEAVER, John	28	m.	Farmer	3500/1200	"	
8		Elisabeth	25	f.	Domestic		"	
9		Mary E.	4	f.			"	
10		Armintha J.	2	f.			"	
11		RIDGEWAY, Ara	20	f.	Domestic		"	
12		HALL, William	20	m.	Farm laborer		"	
13	970/969	DAUGHERTY, David	30	m.	Farmer	1600/330	"	
14		Margaret	27	f.	Domestic		"	I
15		Mary J.	6	f.			"	
16		Jacob	4	m.			"	
17		Nancy C.	2	f.			"	
18		Cyntha	4/12	f.			"	
19		SHAFER, Philip	11	m.			"	S
20	971/970	COX, John	34	m.	Farmer	1200/500	"	
21		Mary	27	f.	Domestic		"	
22		Minerva J.	8	f.			"	S
23		Clarinda	6	f.			"	
24		Mary E.	3	f.			"	
25		Sarah M.	10/12	f.			"	
26		Rebecca	37	f.	Domestic			
27		John	16	m.	Farm laborer			
						1000/	"	S
28		Josephas	6	m.			"	
29	972/971	DAUGHERTY, Daniel	33	m.	Farmer	850/300	"	
30		Barbary	27	f.	Domestic		"	
31		David	4	m.			"	
32		Sarah	3	f.			"	
33		Armstrong	2/12	m.			"	
34	973/972	DAUGHERTY, William	50	m.	Farmer	/275	Ire.	
35		Nancy	57	f.	Domestic		O.	I
36		Thomas	19	m.	Farm laborer		"	S
37		John	17	m.	Farm laborer		"	S
38		Michael	14	m.			"	S
39		Hugh	13	m.			"	S
40		Nancy J.	10	f.			"	

1		Cornelius	7	m.			O.
2	974/973	DAUGHERTY, Jacob	32	m.	Farmer	1200/300	"
3		Frances	22	f.	Domestic		"
4		John W.	3	m.			"
5		Sarah E.	1	f.			"
6	975/974	DAUGHERTY, Edward	50	m.	Farmer	1600/400	Ire.
7		Sarah	47	f.	Domestic		O.
8		John	22	m.	Farm laborer		"

9		DAUGHERT.Y, Margaret	18	f.	Domestic		O. S
10		Mary	16	f.	Domestic		" S
11		Sarah	14	f.			" S
12		Martha	12	f.			" S
13		Cornelius	10	m.			"
14		Catharine	8	f.			"
15		Emily E.	3	f.			"
16	976/975	DAUGHERTY, Simon	26	m.	Farmer	1200/300	"
17		Mary	23	f.	Domestic		"
18		Edward	8	m.			"
19		Margaret	6	f.			"
20		Sarah	2	f.			"
21	977/976	DAUGHERT.Y, Samuel	27	m.	Farmer	/350	"
22		Rache] A.	25	f.	Domestic		"
23		Lewis S.	2	m.			"
24	978/977	HICKEMBOTTON, Thomas	40	m.	Farmer	1200/300	Eng.
25		Elisabeth	32	f.	Domestic		"
26		John	10	m.			O. S
27		Ellen A.	8	f.			" S
28		Isaac B.	7	m.			" S
29		William	4	m.			"
30		James H.	2	m.			"
31		Abner	3/12	m.			"
32	979/978	LACHFORD, Jonathon	34	m.	Farmer	/50	Eng.
33		Hester	22	f.	Domestic		"
34	980/979	DUCHER, James	30	m.	Farmer	/200	O.
35		Mary	30	f.	Domestic		"
36	981/980	BIRES, Abner	36	m.	Farmer	1600/650	"
37		Mary A.	32	f.	Domestic		"
38		Sarah M.	13	f.			" S
39		Jarret	11	m.			" S
40		Catharine	6	f.			" S

Page 142		13 July 1860				Sheet 299 verso	
1		Rebecca J.	2	f.			O.
2		Elias J.	2/12	m.			"
3		BENNETT, Elijah	20	m.	Farm laborer		" I
4	982/981	WEAVER, George	25	m.	Farmer	/150	Pa.
5		Phebe	29	f.	Domestic		" I
6		Axie	3	f.			O.
7		Lemuel	2	m.			"
8		Margaret	6/12	f.			
9	983/982	CLINE, Isaac	54	m.	Farmer	1500/550	"
10		Elisabeth	51	f.	Domestic		" I
11		Andrew	28	m.	Farm laborer		"
12		Charlotte	15	f.			" S

13		CLINE, Nancy C.	13	f.			O.	S
14		Sarah A.	10	f.			"	S

15	984/983	BIRES, Amos	25	m.	Farm laborer	/100	"	
16		Lucy	22	f.	Domestic		"	
17		Orion L.	1	m.			"	

18	985/984	SLACK, William	23	m.	Farmer	/200	"	
19		Lucinda	25	f.	Domestic		"	
20		Alba V.	4	m.			"	
21		George R.	3	m.			"	
22		William H.	1	m.			"	

23	986/985	BATTIN, Aaron	50	m.	Farmer	/200	"	
24		Charity	44	f.	Domestic	2000/	"	
25		SLACK, John	29	m.	Farm laborer		"	
26		Adanah V.	12	m.			"	
27		Sedwick	16	m.	Farm laborer		"	

Beginning of Graysville.

28	987/986	HAMILTON, Thomas	41	m.	Blacksmith	/400	Va.	
29		Mary A.	40	f.	Domestic		Pa.	
30		Mary M.	16	f.	Domestic		O.	S
31		Nancy D.	14	f.			"	S
32		Thomas M.	12	m.			Pa.	S
33		Samuel	9	m.			O.	S
34		John W.	7	m.			"	S
35		Rachel R.	2	f.			"	

36	988/987	BERICKMAN, Pearson						
		A.	38	m.	Blacksmith	/200	Pa.	
37		Dellille	32	f.	Domestic		O.	I
38		Randolph	10	m.			"	S
39		Elisabeth R.	8	f.			"	S
40		John K.	6	m.			"	S

Page 143   14 July 1860   Sheet 300

1	989/988	HALL, Isaac	52	m.	Farmer	1500/600	Va.	I
2		Eunice	22	f.	Domestic		O.	
3		Jesse	20	m.	Farm laborer		"	
4		Joanna	16	f.	Domestic		"	
5		Simon	14	m.			"	S
6		Jere	11	m.			"	S

7	990/989	WESTBROOK, Wm. A.	44	m.	Farmer	1200/320	"	
8		Mariah	45	f.	Domestic		"	
9		Martha M.	18	f.	Domestic		"	
10		Hariet A.	17	f.	Domestic		"	
11		Darcus J.	15	f.	Domestic		"	
12		Mariah W.	13	f.			"	S
13		Armintha	10	f.			"	S
14		John W.	8	m.			"	S
15		Amanda	6	f.			"	
16		Sarah B.	4	f.			"	

| 17 | 991/990 | FOGLE, George | 36 | m. | Physician | 600/300 | Va. | |

18		FOGLE, Celina	30	f.	Domestic		Va.	
19		Ann A.	13	f.			"	S
20		Armintha J.	10	f.			O.	S
21		Mary E.	7	f.			"	S
22		Alice V.	5	f.			"	S
23		Margaret L.	3	f.			"	
24		Martha C.	1	f.			"	
25	992/991	HALL, Enoch	40	m.	Tobacco Packer			
						400/100	"	I
26		Elisabeth J.	35	f.	Domestic		"	I
27		William A.	13	m.			"	S
28		Nancy A.	10	f.			"	S
29		Mary A.	10	f.			"	S
30		Amanda J.	8	f.			"	
31		Julian	6	f.			"	
32		James	2	m.			"	
33	993/992	KINKADE, James	32	m.	Teacher	/100	"	
34		Amanda	28	f.	Domestic		"	
35		Levi L.	2	m.			"	
36		Louise	1/12	f.			"	
37		Hannah V.	14	f.			"	S
38		Joseph V.	11	m.			"	S
39	994/993	ROSE, Thomas	38	m.	Physician	/300	Va.	
40		Nancy	36	f.	Domestic		O.	

1		John W.	16	m.	Clerk		O.	
2		George W.	9	m.			"	S
3		Thomas J.	7	m.			"	S
4		Albert M.	3	m.			"	
5		Lucinda	1	f.			"	
6		GROVE, Elisabeth	18	f.	Domestic		"	S
7	995/994	ROBINSON, Wm. T.	40	m.	Merchant			
						60,000/2,000	Va.	
8		Verta B.	27	f.	Domestic		"	
9		Ann A.	13	f.			"	S
10		William A.	6	m.			"	S
11		Frederick	2	m.			"	
12		CRONY, Elisabeth	18	f.	Domestic		"	
13	996/995	JOY, Mark	26	m.	Tobacco Packer 30/50		"	
14		Mary	27	f.	Domestic		"	
15		Elisabeth J.	5	f.			"	S
16		George L.	3	m.			"	
17		Mary M.	1	f.			"	
18		HALL, John	42	m.	Laborer		"	
19	997/996	MILLER, Jacob	28	m.	Grocer 1400/800		"	
20		Rebecca	22	f.	Domestic		"	I
21		Elisabeth A.	7	f.			"	
22		Mary E.	5	f.			"	
23		Irvin H.	1/12	m.			"	

24	998/997	DILLON, William	70	m.	Nothing	/150	Va.	I
25		Sarah	37	f.	Domestic		"	
26		Elam	30	m.	Teacher	270/200	O.	
27		Nancy	22	f.	Domestic		"	
28		Elva	20	f.	Domestic		"	
29		WILCOX, Isaac	12	m.			"	S

30	999/998	DILLON, William	33	m.	Physician	250/500	Va.	
31		Rachel A.	30	f.	Domestic		O.	I
32		Elam	10	m.			"	S
33		Abner	8	m.			"	S
34		Jonathon	6	m.			"	S
35		William G.	4	m.			"	

36	1000/999	WARNICA, Fred-erick	29	m.	Cabinet-maker	/150	Br.	
37		Catherine	27	f.	Domestic		Sw.	
38		Lilly	5	f.			O.	

| 39 | 1001/1000 | GEPHART, George | 41 | m. | Blacksmith | /700 | Md. | |
| 40 | | Mary A. | 43 | f. | Domestic | | Eng. | I |

Page 145   14 July 1860   Sheet 301

1		Thomas R.	16	m.	Tobacco Packer		O.	S
2		Mary L.	14	f.			"	S
3		Eliza J.	11	f.			"	S
4		Mariah L.	9	f.			"	S
5		Samuel P.	7	m.			"	S
6		Rebecca A.	5	f.			"	
7		Amelia L.	2	f.			"	
8		SMITH, Samuel	30	m.	Tobacco Packer		"	
9		HUGHES, Joseph	18	m.	Tobacco Packer		"	

10	1002/1001	JOY, Eli	29	m.	Blacksmith	/125	"	
11		Sarah A.	19	f.	Domestic		"	
12		Mary L.	1	f.			"	

13	1003/1002	TRAVERSE, John	30	m.	Shoemaker	/100	"	
14		Mary A.	20	f.	Domestic		"	
15		Josiah	1	m.			"	
16		Mariah T.	4/12	f.			"	
17		BARNHART, Mary J.	10	f.			"	

18	1004/1003	GATCHEL, John	29	m.	Merchant	1000/500	"	
19		Rachel	25	f.	Domestic		N.Y.	
20		Deborah	73	f.	Domestic		Md.	

| 21 | 1005/1004 | DYE, John L. | 36 | m. | Wagon-maker | /300 | O. | |
| 22 | | Sarah | 78 | f. | Domestic | 650/ | Md. | I |

23	----/1005	LUCAS, Abagail	38	f.	Domestic		O.	
24		DYE, Elza	25	m.	Laborer		"	
25		Lucy A.	6	f.			"	
26		LUCAS, William	2/12	m.			"	
27		John	27	m.	Teacher			

28	1006/1006	STECKHOUSE,						
		Jacob	35	m.	Shoemaker	750/200	O.	
29		Louisa	30	f.	Domestic		"	I
30		Mary L.	15	f.	Domestic		"	S
31		Rebecca A.	11	f.			"	S
32		Elisabeth A.	6	f.			"	
33		SLACK, Zedder	18	m.	Apprentice	Shoemaker	"	
34	1007/1007	POWELL, Isaac	40	m.	Merchant	1000/500	"	
35		Jane	35	f.	Domestic		"	
36	1008/1008	BARBER, Arte	20	m.	Clerk		Pa.	
37		KETTERER, George	22	m.	Clerk		O.	
38	1009/1009	EDDINGTON, Jona-						
		thon	28	m.	Blacksmith	/100	Va.	
39		Phebe	25	f.	Domestic		O.	
40		John W.	7	m.			"	S

Page 146			14 July 1860				Sheet 301 verso	
1		BUTTIN, William	20	m.	Blacksmith		O.	
2	1010/1010	JOY, Jesse	31	m.	Shoemaker	/100	"	
3		Susanna	28	f.	Domestic		"	I
4		Mary A.	8	f.			"	S
5		Thomas W.	7	m.			"	S
6		Margaret J.	5	f.			"	S
7		Benjamin F.	3	m.			"	
8		James W.	1/12	m.			"	
9	1011/1011	KELLER, George	43	m.	Wagoner	1000/300	"	
10		Mary A.	38	f.	Domestic		Ire.	
11		Frances J.	16	f.	Domestic		O.	
12		Hirem	14	m.			"	S
13		Sarah D.	12	f.			"	S
14		Charles H.	8	m.			"	S
15		John W.	6	m.			"	S
16		Margaret L.	4	m.			"	
17		George	1	m.			"	
18		CRAWFORD, John	28	m.	Saddler	100/	Ire.	
19		WILLIS, James	22	m.	Grocer	/200	O.	
20	1012/1012	BROWN, Edward A.	35	m.	Shoemaker	800/100	"	
21		Sarah A.	26	f.	Domestic		"	
22		Hopewell	15	m.	Nothing		"	S
23	1013/1013	GRIM, John	72	m.	Farmer	250/200	Md.	
24		Margaret	69	f.	Domestic		"	I
25		William	29	m.	Farm laborer		"	
26	1014/1014	POLIN, George	44	m.	Grocer	2000/100	O.	
27		Margaret	40	f.	Domestic		"	I
28		John	18	m.	Clerk		"	
29		Hery J.	15	m.			"	S
30		Margaret E.	9	f.			"	S
31		Vincent	5	m.			"	

32		POLIN, George W.	2	m.			O.	
33	1015/1015	POLIN, James	21	m.	Carpenter	/100	"	
34		Elisabeth	20	f.	Domestic		"	
35	1016/1016	HAL , Jesse	44	m.	Farmer	1000/220	Va.	I
36		Eliza	44	f.	Domestic		Pa.	
37		Mershall	17	m.	Farm laborer		O.	
38		Ellis	16	m.	Farm laborer		"	S
39		Catharine	14	f.			"	S
40		Sarah	7	f.			"	S

Page 147   14 July 1860   Sheet 302

1		Evaline	4	f.			C.	
2		Amos	2	m.			"	
3	1017/1017	WIPLEBY, Joseph	36	m.	Farmer	1500/450	"	
4		Lucinda	32	f.	Domestic		Pa.	
5		William J.	12	m.			O.	S
6		George S.	10	m.			"	S
7		John H.	7	m.			"	S
8		Frances L.	5	f.			"	S
9		Sarah E.	1	f.			"	
10	1018/1018	OKEY, James	54	m.	Farmer	2700/500	"	
11		Catharine	51	f.	Domestic		"	
12		Elisabeth	21	f.	Domestic		"	
13		Lewis O.	16	m.	Farm laborer		"	S
14		David	14	m.			"	S
15		James W.	11	m.			"	S
16	1019/1019	OKEY, Cornelius	23	m.	Farmer	/200	"	
17		Sarah	21	f.	Domestic		"	
18		Sylvester	2	m.			"	
19		William A.	1	m.			"	
20	1020/1020	DEVORE, James	30	m.	Farmer	1500/400	"	I
21		Mary A.	21	f.	Domestic		"	I
22		William H.	3	m.			"	
23		Sarah E.	2	f.			"	
24		Calvin	6/12	m.			"	
25	1021/1021	NOLTIN, William	24	m.	Farm laborer	/150	"	M
26		Melissa	16	f.	Domestic		"	M
27	1022/1022	SHUTZ, William	49	m.	Farmer	3500/850	Pa.	
28		Catharine	37	f.	Domestic		"	I
29		Peter	19	m.	Farm laborer		O.	S
30		George	17	m.	Farm laborer		"	S
31		James	15	m.	Farm laborer		"	S
32		Elisabeth	14	f.			"	S
33		Mary A.	8	f.			"	S
34		Rachel	4	f.			"	
35		Hester	1	f.			"	
36		John	23	m.	Farm laborer			

(Washington Township Concluded)

(J. P. Spriggs, Ass't. Marshall)

* * *

Wayne Township   P. O. Woodsfield

Page 148	17 July 1860			Sheet 302 verso	

1	1023/1023 BERICKMAN, Sam-					
	uel	42	m.	Farmer	/150	Pa.
2	Mary	34	f.	Domestic		O.
3	Isaac	15	m.	Farm laborer		"
4	Sarah J.	13	f.			" S
5	Martin A.	10	m.			" S
6	John W.	8	m.			" S
7	Margaret H.	4	f.			"
8	Mary L.	2	f.			"
9	1024/1024 BAKER, David	25	m.	Farmer	2200/300	"
10	Mary J.	19	f.	Domestic		"
11	Sarah J.	2	f.			"
12	Jacob N.	1	m.			"
13	Sarah	68	f.			Pa.
14	1025/1025 POLIN, George	29	m.	Farmer	300/100	O. I
15	Sarah	24	f.	Domestic		" I
16	John M.	5	m.			"
17	James H.	3	m.			"
18	Henry J.	1/12	m.			"
19	1026/1026 BAKER, Jackson	30	m.	Farmer	1100/275	"
20	Eve A.	29	f.	Domestic		"
21	Catharine	11	f.			"
22	Margaret J.	10	f.			"
23	Sarah	8	f.			"
24	Martin	6	m.			"
25	John	5	m.			"
26	Mary E.	3	f.			"
27	George	1	m.			"
28	1027/1027 BAKER, Isaac	46	m.	Farmer	1000/210	"
29	Sarah	44	f.	Domestic		Pa.
30	Margaret J.	18	f.	Domestic		O.
31	Isaac J.	5	m.			"
32	1028/1028 BAKER, Daniel	25	m.	Farm laborer		
					400/200	"
33	Mary J.	22	f.	Domestic		" I
34	Clarinda E.	3	f.			"
35	Margaret	1	f.			"
36	CRONE, Joseph	17	m.	Farm laborer		"
37	1029/1029 WINLAND, James	57	m.	Farmer	5500/600	"
38	Margaret	50	f.	Domestic		" I
39	Louisa E.	13	f.			" S
40	1030/1030 WINLAND, Henry	22	m.	Farm laborer		"

Page 149   17 July 1860   Sheet 303

1		WINLAND, Mary E.	19	f.	Domestic		O.
2		Henry M.	6/12	m.			"
3		Margaret J.	13	f.			" S
4		Worna	9	f.			" S
5		James	6	m.			" S
6		LUTHER, Elias	17	m.	Farm laborer		" S
7	1031/1031	WHITTICKER, Sit-ner	24	m.	Farmer	/250	"
8		Julian	19	f.	Domestic		"
9		James	4	m.			"
10		George	1	m.			"
11	1032/1032	STEED, James	38	m.	Farmer	1000/425	"
12		Mary	34	f.	Domestic		"
13		Margaret	16	f.	Domestic		"
14		Elisabeth A.	14	f.			"
15		John M.	12	m.			"
16		Henry W.	9	m.			"
17		Hannah M.	7	f.			"
18		George A.	5	m.			"
19		Mary L.	2	f.			"
20		James M.	6/12	m.			
21	1033/1033	FISHER, Joshua	44	m.	Farmer	700/200	" I
22		Sarah	42	f.	Domestic		"
23		Mary A.	21	f.	Domestic		"
24		Sarah J.	19	f.	Domestic		"
25		Margaret E.	17	f.	Domestic		"
26		Elisabeth	13	f.			"
27		Melissa	10	f.			"
28		William	8	m.			"
29		Matilda	5	f.			"
30		Louisa	4	f.			"
31		Hannah S.	1	f.			
32		LOWE, Mary	60	f.	Domestic		Pa.
33	1034/1034	DAUGHERTY, Ste-phen	28	m.	Farmer	/200	O.
34		Ann	26	f.	Domestic		"
35		Sarah	10	f.			" S
36		Thomas	8	m.			" S
37		Clarissa J.	6	f.			"
38		Stephen	5	m.			"
39		Jasper	4	m.			"
40		Margaret A.	2	f.			"

Page 150   17 July 1860   Sheet 303 verso

1		Mary E.	3/12	f.			O.
2	1035/1035	DAUGHERTY, Jere-miah	26	m.	Farm laborer	/100	"
3		Sarah	24	f.	Domestic		"
4		James M.	6	m.			

```
5           DAUGHERTY,
            George         4    m.                              O.
6           Peter          3    m.                              "
7           Matthew        2    m.                              "
8           Barbary E.     2/12 f.                              "

9   1036/1036 DAUGHERTY, Mat-
            thew           47   m.   Farmer      2000/450 Ire.
10          Mary           36   f.   Domestic             O.
11          Margaret       10   f.                        "
12          Thomas         3    m.                        "

13  1037/1037 DAUGHERTY,
            Stephen Sr.    34   m.   Farmer      2000/500 Ire.
14          Mary A.        28   f.   Domestic             Va.
15          Margaret       9    f.                        O.  S
16          Hannah         7    f.                        "   S
17          Mary C.        6    f.                        "   S
18          Rebecca A.     5    f.                        "
19          Barnard        3    m.                        "
20          Stephen O.     1    m.                        "
21          Margaret       44   f.   Domestic             Ire.
22          Catherine      42   f.   Domestic             "
23          McENESPIE, Re-
            becca          20   f.   Domestic             Va.
24          MILLER, James  20   m.   Farm laborer         "

25  1038/1038 STRICKLAND, Jor-
            dan            23   m.   Farmer               O.
26          Mary           23   f.   Domestic             "
27          Matilda J.     8/12 f.                        "

28  1039/1039 EARLY, William 49  m.   Farmer      /50    "
29          Sarah          42   f.   Domestic             "   I
30          Sarah E.       10   f.                        "   S

31  1040/1040 EARLY, John J. 21  m.   Farmer      800/125 "   M
32          Catharine      19   f.   Domestic             "   M

33  1041/1041 WILLISSON, Jere-
            miah           73   m.   Farmer      500/300 Pa. I
34          Hannah         75   f.   Domestic             Va. I
35          William        20   m.   Farm laborer         O.
36          Sarah A.       17   f.   Domestic             "

37  1042/1042 NALLEY, Marion 28  m.   Farm laborer         "
38          Sarah J.       19   f.   Domestic             "
39          Levi J.        4    m.                        "
40          George W.      2    m.                        "
```

```
1   1043/1043 NALLEY, Levi   72  m.   Farmer      3500/650 O. I
2           Rebecca        60   f.   Domestic             "
3           Jemima         28   f.   Domestic             "
4           Levi J.        14   m.                        "
5           MERTIN, John W. 12  m.                        "
```

6	1044/1044	NALLEY, Levi Jr.	40	m.	Farmer	/100	O.
7		Louisa	38	f.	Domestic		"
8		Mary E.	4	f.			"
9		Sylvester	2	m.			"
10		Virginia	4/12	f.			"
11	1045/1045	MARTIN, John	45	m.	Farmer	/100	"
12		Elisabeth	35	f.	Domestic		"
13		Rachel A.	16	f.	Domestic		" S
14		Milton J.	10	m.			" S
15		Mary C.	8	f.			"
16		Thomas	4	m.			"
17		Isaac	2	m.			"
18		Louisa M.	2/12	f.			
19	1046/1046	BAKER, John	46	m.	Farmer	1200/500	"
20		Elisabeth	39	f.	Domestic		"
21		Milton D.	21	m.	Farm laborer		"
22		Ellen J.	13	f.			" S
23		ADAMS, George W.	14	m.			Va. S
24	1047/1047	NALLEY, John	45	m.	Farmer	/75	O. I
25		Sarah	39	f.	Domestic		" I
26		William	5	m.			"
27		George	3	m.			"
28		Margaret	2	f.			"
29		HINES, Maxell	13	m.			" S
30		Sarah	9	f.			"
31		David	15	m.	Farm laborer		"
32	1048/1048	MOSSE, George	56	m.	Farmer	/100	"
33		Martha	53	f.	Domestic		" I
34		John	18	m.	Farm laborer		" S
35		George R.	16	m.	Farm laborer		" S
36	1049/1049	BAKER, Isaac T.	30	m.	Farm laborer	/50	"
37		Arsula	25	f.	Domestic		"
38		George	4	m.			"
39		Martha I.	7	f.			" S
40		John	3	m.			"

Page 152   17 July 1860   Sheet 304 verso

1		Lucinda J.	2	f.			O.
2	1050/1050	NALLEY, Zach-					
		ariah	43	m.	Farm laborer		" I
3		Elisabeth	32	f.	Domestic		"
4		Melinda	16	f.	Domestic		"
5		John M.	12	m.			"
6		Obadiah	10	m.			"
7		Rebecca	8	f.			"
8		Margaret	2	f.			"
9		Alfred	5	m.			
10	1051/1051	CECIL, Stephen	35	m.	Farmer	/50	"
11		Elisabeth	28	f.	Domestic		"

```
12                CECIL, Jacob D.    1   m.                            O.
13                Melissa A.         4   f.                            "

14  1052/1052 BAKER, Henry          30   m.    Farmer         /200     "
15                Elisabeth         26   f.    Domestic                "
16                Sarah E.           5   f.                            "
17                Leander C.         3   m.                            "
18                George F.          1   m.                            "

19  1053/1053 EARLY, Alfred        31   m.    Farm laborer   /25      "
20                Hester           24   f.    Domestic                "
21                Mary L.            6   f.                            "
22                Sarah E.           3   f.                            "
23                Robert C.          1   m.                            "

24  1054/1054 MOSSE, John          54   m.    Farmer  20,300/3800  Pa.
25                Emily            50   f.    Domestic                O.
26                Albert B.        17   m.    Farm laborer            "    S
27                William S.       15   m.    Farm laborer            "    S
28                Louisa C.        12   f.                            "    S
29                Henry H.          5   m.                            "    S
30                NALLEY, Joseph   18   m.    Farm laborer            "    S
31                ADAMS, Virginia  12   f.                            "    S
32                FARNSWORTH,
                  Louisa           18   f.    Domestic                "    S
33                LATTY, John E.    3   m.                            "

34  1055/1055 BAKER, Isaac         34   m.    Carpenter      /75      "
35                Arsula           27   f.    Domestic                "    I
36                Martha E.         8   f.                            "    S
37                George W.         5   m.                            "    S
38                John W.           4   m.                            "
39                Mary J.           1   f.                            "

40  1056/1056 WOODRING, James      20   m.    Farm laborer   /30      "    M
```

```
1                 Jane             18   f.    Domestic                O. M

2   1057/1057 LATTY, Samuel        26   m.    Farmer       500/600   Pa.
3             HALL, Peter          14   m.                           O.

4   1058/1058 LATTY, John          76   m.    Farmer       500/300   Pa.
5                Ann               67   f.    Domestic                "    I
6                John              22   m.    Farm laborer           Va.
7             HALL, Margaret       24   f.    Domestic                O.  I

8   1059/1059 KINKADE, Rhona       24   m.    Farmer       400/225    "
9                Elisabeth         25   f.    Domestic                "
10               James M.           3   m.                            "
11               David W.           2   m.                            "
12               Elisabeth A.    1/12  f.                            "

13  1060/1060 ROUSE, George        25   m.    Farmer        /50       "
14               Rachel A.         20   f.    Domestic                "
15               James M.           1   m.                            "
```

16	1061/1061	MORRIS, Wilson	32	m.	Farmer	1500/350	O.
17		Hannah J.	19	f.	Domestic		"
18		Virginia E.	10/12	f.			"
19	1062/1062	KENEY, George	24	m.	Farm laborer		" M
20		Nancy	25	f.	Domestic		" M
21		Jane	18	f.	Domestic		"
22	1063/1063	MORRIS, David	37	m.	Farmer	1500/350	"
23		Margaret A.	36	f.	Domestic		Pa.
24		Joseph H.	16	m.	Farm laborer		O. S
25		Thomas W.	12	m.			" S
26		George S.	10	m.			" S
27		William F.	8	m.			" S
28		Rachel J.	6	f.			" S
29		Mary H.	4	f.			"
30		David L.	1	m.			"
31	1064/1064	MORRIS, William	28	m.	Farmer	/200	"
32		Susanna	25	f.	Domestic		"
33		Mary L.	8	f.			" S
34		Daniel H.	6	m.			" S
35		David A.	4	m.			"
36		Robert W.	2	m.			"
37		Jacob W.	6/12	m.			"
38	1065/1065	DEARTH, James	26	m.	Farmer	400/100	"
39		Mary	24	f.	Domestic		"
40		William	9	m.			" S

Page 154		18 July 1860				Sheet 305 verso	
1		John	7	m.			O. S
2		Barbary	4	f.			"
3	1066/1066	SHUMAN, Jacob	55	m.	Farmer	1000/350	"
4		Mary	18	f.	Domestic		"
5		Jesse	32	m.	Farm laborer		"
6	1067/1067	STRICKLAND,					
		Robert	37	m.	Farmer	1000/350	Va.
7		Louisa	35	f.	Domestic		O.
8		John	14	m.			"
9		Jacob	12	m.			"
10		Lucy	6	f.			"
11	1068/1068	DEARTH, William	55	m.	Farmer	1500/700	Pa. I
12		Mary A.	52	f.	Domestic		O. I
13		Mary C.	20	f.	Domestic		"
14		Susan	13	f.			" S
15		COON, Jane E.	8	f.			"
16	1069/1069	JOHNSON, Benja-					
		min	33	m.	Farmer	400/150	"
17		Elisabeth	23	f.	Domestic		"
18		Joseph	4	m.			"
19		Mary A.	1	f.			

Wayne Township		P. O. Woodsfield					515

```
20 1070/1070 KISER, James      38  m.   Farm laborer  /175   O. I
21          Emily J.          32  f.   Domestic            "
22          Susan             11  f.                       "
23          Mary E.            9  f.                       "
24          William C.         6  m.                       "
25          Louisa J.          3  f.                       "

26 1071/1071 STRICKLAND,
            Joshua            41  m.   Farmer      1500/400 Va.
27          Margaret A.       33  f.   Domestic            O.
28          Benjamin F.       14  m.                       "  S
29          Jacob M.           6  m.                       "  S
30          Nancy J.          12  f.                       "  S
31          Mary M.            1  f.                       "

32 1072/1072 MILBERN, Sarah    46  f.   Domestic            Va.
33          Diana             17  f.   Domestic            "
34          Rhoda E.          14  f.                       "  S
35          Samuel W.         11  m.                       "  S

36 1073/1073 STRICKLAND,
            Joseph            69  m.   Farm laborer        "
37          Nancy             65  f.   Domestic            "

38 1074/1074 HINES, Kinsey D. 21  m.   Farm laborer  /25   "  M
39          Samantha          16  f.   Domestic            O. M

40 1075/1075 STRICKLAND,
            Jordan            23  m.   Farmer        /50   Va.
```

Page 155		18 July 1860				Sheet 306

```
1           Mary              24  f.   Domestic            O.
2           Matilda          8/12 f.                       "

3 1076/1076 SPARKS, Joseph    45  m.   Laborer             Pa. I
4           Percilla          40  f.   Domestic            "  I
5           John              15  m.   Laborer             O.
6           James             10  m.                       "
7           Sarah              7  f.                       "
8           Joseph             3  m.                       "

9 1077/1077 FULKERSON,
            Tobias S.         38  m.   Farmer      1200/300 Pa.
10          Mary A.           33  f.   Domestic            O.
11          Margaret E.       11  f.                       "  S
12          William A.         9  m.                       "  S
13          Jacob T.           6  m.                       "  S
14          James H.           4  m.                       "
15          George W.          2  m.                       "

16 1078/1078 PIFER, Adam       24  m.   Farm laborer        Ger. M
17          Hannah J.         20  f.   Domestic            O. M
18          Joseph W.        2/12 m.                       "

19 1079/1079 BISHOP, Wesley    48  m.   Farmer      1000/500 Va. I
20          Amanda            48  f.   Domestic            "  I
```

21		BISHOP, William					
		J.	22	m.	Farm laborer	O.	
22		Martha J.	21	f.	Domestic	"	
23		Thomas W.	20	m.	Farm laborer	"	I
24		John I.	18	m.	Farm laborer	"	
25		Amanda	17	f.	Domestic	"	
26		Reuben	14	m.		"	S
27		Charles M.	12	m.		"	S
28		Benjamin F.	10	m.		"	S
29		Emily E.	3	f.		"	
30	1080/1080	HUCHESSON, John	50	m.		/50	Unk. 5
31		Elisabeth	60	f.	Domestic	O.	
32		Matilda	19	f.	Domestic	"	
33		William A.	15	m.	Farm laborer	"	
34	1081/1081	SNIDER, Andrew	56	m.	Farmer	500/225	Va.
35		Elisabeth	56	f.	Domestic	O.	I
36		William	20	m.	Farm laborer	"	
37		James	19	m.	Farm laborer	"	
38	1082/1082	BONAN, Samuel	40	m.	Farm laborer	/50	"	I
39		Sarah J.	36	f.	Domestic	"	
40		Melissa	12	f.		"	

1		Ann E.	2	f.		O.	
2		Nancy C.	1	f.		"	
3	1083/1083	CONER, Catharine	41	f.	Farmer	600/300	"
4		Sylvanus	20	m.	Farm laborer	"	I
5		John W.	19	m.	Farm laborer	"	
6		Sarah E.	15	f.	Domestic	"	
7		Charlotte M.	13	f.		"	
8		Henry M.	4	m.		"	
9		Mary E.	2	f.			
10	1084/1084	WILLISSON, John	44	m.	Farmer	1500/475	"
11		Margaret	39	f.	Domestic	"	
12		Jacob	18	m.	Farm laborer	"	S
13		Hannah E.	16	f.	Domestic	"	S
14		David K.	14	m.		"	S
15		John M.	12	m.		"	S
16		William H.	6	m.		"	S
17	1085/1085	WILLISSON, Lewis	22	m.	Farmer	/100	"
18		Louisa	19	f.	Domestic	"	
19		Sylvester B.	2/12	m.		"	
20	1086/1086	MOSSE, Joseph	60	m.	Farmer	1200/300	Md.
21		Sarah	59	f.	Domestic	Pa.	
22		Elisabeth	29	f.	Domestic	O.	
23		Amon	25	m.	Farm laborer	"	
24		Rebecca	23	f.	Domestic	"	
25		Pernina	20	f.	Domestic	"	
26		Sabina	18	f.	Domestic	"	

27		MOSSE, Martha	16	f.			0.23	
28	1087/1087	MARTIN, Stephen	30	m.	Farm laborer	/50	"	
29		Mahala	29	f.	Domestic		"	I
30		Sarah C.	18	f.	Domestic		"	
31		John	14	m.			"	
32		Stephen A.	9	m.			"	
33		Martha A.	7	f.			"	
34		Isaac	5	m.			"	
35		Margaret E.	2	f.			"	
36	1088/1088	NOSSINGER, Edward	34	m.	Farmer	/400	"	
37		Nancy	38	f.	Domestic		"	
38		Simon	6	m.			"	
39		John L.	4	m.			"	
40		Mary J.	2	f.			"	

Page 157   18 July 1860   Sheet 307

1		DRUM, Amanda J.	16	f.			0.	
2	1089/1089	DAUGHERTY, Mary	49	f.	Domestic	4000/1000	"	
3		James	27	m.	Farm laborer		"	
4		Isaac	21	m.	Farm laborer		"	
5		Edward	19	m.	Farm laborer		"	S
6		Hester	18	f.	Domestic		"	S
7		David	16	m.	Farm laborer		"	S
8		Daniel W.	9	m.			"	S
9	1090/1090	LOWE, James	32	m.	Farmer	/250	"	
10		Nancy	28	f.	Domestic		"	
11		Nancy J.	2	f.			"	
12		DAUGHERTY, Margaret	14	f.			"	S
13		Mary A.	12	f.			"	S
14	1091/1091	BEAVER, John	75	m.	Farmer	3000/400	Va.	
15		Nancy	70	f.	Domestic		"	
16		CLINE, Sarah	20	f.	Domestic		O.	
17		HALL, Amanda	8	f.			"	S
18	1092/1092	GREY, John	76	m.	Farmer	7000/1100	Ky.	
19		Sarah	60	f.	Domestic		Va.	
20		BALEY, Rebecca	17	f.	Domestic		O.	
21	1093/1093	GREGORY, John	25	m.	Farmer	/100	"	
22		Arminda	26	f.	Domestic		"	I
23		Milton	6	m.			"	
24		Sarah	4	f.			"	
25		Nancy J.	3	f.			"	
26		Joel	2/12	m.			¥	
27		SOUTH, Thomas	14	m.				
28	1094/1094	GREY, Rachel	51	f.	Farmer	1500/400	N.Y.	
29		Marinden	20	m.	Farm laborer		O.	
30		Alfred	18	m.	Farm laborer		"	

31		GREY, Jane	16	f.	Domestic		O.	
32		James T.	13	m.			"	
33	1095/1095	UPHOLE, James	25	m.	Farmer	400/	"	M
34		Catharine	22	f.	Domestic		"	M
35	1096/1096	JOHN, Armstrong	42	m.	Farmer	750/200	Pa.	
36		Mary	34	f.	Domestic		"	
37		Armstrong W.	16	m.	Farm laborer		O.	S
38		John A.	13	m.			"	S
39		Hannah J.	15	f.	Domestic		"	S
40		Samuel J.	11	m.			"	S

Page 158   19 July 1860   Sheet 307 verso

1		Sarah E.	9	f.			O.	S
2		William J.	8	m.			"	S
3		Isaac N.	3	m.			"	
4		George W.	5/12	m.			"	
5	1097/1097	JOHN, Barbary	78	f.	Domestic		Pa.	
6		Hannah	55	f.	Domestic		"	
7	1098/1098	OSBERN, James T.	24	m.	Farmer	300/120	O.	
8		Charlotte M.	24	f.	Domestic		"	
9		Sarah E.	5	f.			"	
10		Mary E.	1	f.			"	
11	1099/1099	RUCKER, John	24	m.	Farmer	600/125	"	
12		Arminda E.	22	f.	Domestic		"	
13		Caroline	2	f.			"	
14		Sarah E.	1/12	f.			"	
15	1100/1100	UPHOLE, John	54	m.	Farmer	600/325	Md.	I
16		Ann	40	f.	Domestic		O.	
17		Henry	22	m.	Farm laborer		"	I
18		George W.	20	m.			"	
19		Mary	18	f.	Domestic		"	
20		LANDES, Sarah	7	f.			"	
21	1101/1101	YOHO, Daniel	54	m.	Farmer	700/200	Va.	
22		Elisabeth	42	f.	Domestic		O.	
23		Clarissa	13	f.			"	
24		Clarinda	11	f.			"	
25		Matilda	7	f.			"	
26		Daniel D.	3/12	m.			"	
27	1102/1102	HENDRICKS, Henry B.	35	m.	Farmer	/200	Pa.	
28		Catharine	36	f.	Domestic		Va.	I
29		John T.	8	m.			"	
30		William G.	6	m.			"	
31		Jane	4	f.			"	
32		Hariet H.	3	f.			"	
33		Jared	1	m.			"	
34		Daniel	70	m.	Nothing		Pa.	

35	1103/1103	DUCHER, Dillus	64	m.	Farmer	/300	N.Y.
36		Hannah	50	f.	Domestic		"
37		Eunice L.	20	f.	Domestic		"
38		Mary D.	10	f.			" S

39	1104/1104	DAUGHERTY, James	53	m.	Farmer	1200/500	Ire.
40		Hester	52	f.	Domestic		O.

Page 159   19 July 1860   Sheet 308

1		Arthur	26	m.	Farm laborer	800/	O.
2		Hannah	23	f.	Domestic		"
3		Nancy J.	20	f.	Domestic		" S
4		Catharine	17	f.	Domestic		" S
5		James T.	3	m.			"
6		Garrisson O.	6	m.			" S

7	1105/1105	McDANIEL, Joseph	55	m.	Farmer	/100	Pa. I
8		Charlotte	46	f.	Domestic		" I
9		Sarah J.	17	f.	Domestic		" S
10		Mary E.	16	f.	Domestic		" S
11		Susan	12	f.			" S
12		Amanda	10	f.			" S
13		Nancy	9	f.			" S
14		Rhuhend	7	f.			"
15		Eliza A.	4	f.			"
16		Margaret	1	f.			"

17	1106/1106	GREY, Samuel	47	m.	Farmer	3000/800	"
18		Mary	32	f.	Domestic		Md.
19		John	23	m.	Farm laborer		O.
20		Sarepta	16	f.	Domestic		"
21		Bradford	13	m.			"
22		EDDINGTON, Smith	34	m.	Farm laborer	/40	Va. I

23	1107/1107	DRUM, Simon	62	m.	Farmer	9000/1350	Pa.
24		Ludia	63	f.	Domestic		"
25		Sarah	30	f.	Domestic		O.
26		James	25	m.	Farm laborer	/90	"
27		STARKEY, Martha	10	f.			" S

28	1108/1108	STACKHOUSE, Ja- cob	35	m.	Chair-maker		"
29		Lucy	36	f.	Domestic		"
30		Elisabeth	10	f.			"
31		Harmon	8	m.			"
32		William H.	6	m.			"
33		James J.	4	m.			"
34		Nancy M.	2	f.			"
35		Mary J.	12	f.			"

36	1109/1109	CONER, Thomas	33	m.	Farmer	600/200	" I
37		Rachel	20	f.	Domestic		"
38		John	24	m.	Farm laborer		"

39	1110/1110	NALLEY, Mary	39	f.	Domestic		" I
40		Sarah A.	16	f.	Domestic		" S

Page 160   19 July 1860   <u>Sheet 308 verso</u>

#	Household	Name	Age	Sex	Occupation	Value		
1		NALLEY, John W.	14	m.			O.	S
2	1111/1111	DAUGHERTY, John	48	m.	Farmer	1200/225	"	
3		Julian	43	f.	Domestic		"	I
4		Sarah	19	f.	Domestic		"	
5		Eleanor	18	f.	Domestic		"	
6		Nancy	16	f.	Domestic		"	S
7		John	14	m.			"	S
8		Daniel	12	m.			"	S
9		Jane	9	f.			"	S
10		Elisabeth	6	f.			"	S
11		Joshua	4	m.			"	
12		Martha	2	f.			"	
13	1112/1112	CLINE, Nelson	29	m.	Farmer	/75	"	
14		Margaret	26	f.	Domestic		"	
15		Mary J.	2	f.			"	
16		Nancy	6/12	f.			"	
17	1113/1113	CONGER, Mary	57	f.	Domestic	2500/325	"	I
18		Stephen	27	m.	Farmer		"	I
19		John	24	m.	Farm laborer		"	
20		David	19	m.	Farm laborer		"	
21		Pluma	14	f.			"	
22		Juliet	14	f.			"	
23	1114/1114	-----, Mary	24	f.	Domestic		"	I
24		Hulda	7	f.			"	
25		Nazel	5	m.			"	
26		Zachariah	3	m.			"	
27		Enos	1	m.			"	
28	1115/1115	BROWN, John	23	m.	Farm laborer		"	I
29		Mary C.	15	f.	Domestic		"	
30	1116/1116	LONG, Michael	42	m.	Farmer	800/200	"	
31		Charlotte	37	f.	Domestic		"	I
32		Jefferson	18	m.	Farm laborer		"	
33		Hannah	13	f.			"	
34		Stacy J.	11	f.			"	
35		Matilda	8	f.			"	
36		George W.	5	m.			"	
37		Martha A.	2	f.			"	
38	1117/1117	LONG, Margaret A.	22	f.	Domestic		"	M
39	1118/1118	LOWE, John	22	m.	Teacher	/200	"	
40		Mary E.	17	f.	Domestic		Va.	

Page 161   19 July 1860   <u>Sheet 309</u>

#	Household	Name	Age	Sex	Occupation	Value		
1		Mary E.	6/12	f.			O.	
2	1119/1119	LONG, Jacob	46	m.	Farmer	800/200	"	
3		Hannah	47	f.	Domestic		Pa.	

4		LONG, Lucinda	22	f.	Domestic	O. M
5		Margaret	21	f.	Domestic	"
6		William	17	m.	Farm laborer	"
7		Mary C.	15	f.	Domestic	"
8		Bradford	13	m.		" S
9		Theodore	11	m.		" S
10		Charlotte	9	f.		" S
11	1120/1120	CRAWFORD, George	22	m.	Farm laborer	"
12		Montervail	2	m.		"
13		Jacob R.	1/12	m.		"
14		MOOSE, Joseph	22	m.	Farm laborer	" M
15	1121/1121	CRONIN, Aaron	44	m.	Farmer 1200/400	" I
16		Eliza	40	f.	Domestic	" I
17		Isaac	20	m.	Farm laborer	"
18		Mary	19	f.	Domestic	"
19		Percilla	17	f.	Domestic	"
20		Rebecca	14	f.		"
21		William	12	m.		"
22		Sarah J.	10	f.		"
23		Howard	8	m.		"
24		Rachel	6	f.		"
25		Sylvester	4	m.		"
26		Andrew	2	m.		"
27	1122/1122	CRONIN, Samuel	38	m.	Chair-maker /75	"
28		Julian	13	f.		" S
29		Melissa	11	f.		" S
30		Patrick	9	m.		" S
31		Leonard	7	m.		" S
32		Lucy	4	f.		" S
33	1123/1123	FARNSWORTH,				
		Howard	39	m.	Farmer	"
34		Nancy	24	f.	Domestic	"
35		Sylvester	6	m.		"
36		Malength	4	m.		"
37		Elisabeth E.	2	f.		"
38		Asberry	1/12	m.		"
39	1124/1124	GREE, Nancy	43	f.	Domestic 2500/500	"
40		John	21	m.	Farmer	"

Page 162   20 July 1860   Sheet 309 verso

1		Levosure	19	m.	Farmer	O.
2		Penelope	17	f.	Domestic	"
3		Elisabeth	15	f.	Domestic	"
4		Jane	12	f.		"
5		George	10	m.		"
6		Mary A.	7	f.		"
7	1125/1125	HOWELL, Aaron	66	m.	Farmer 2000/350	" I
8		Elisabeth	65	f.	Domestic	Md. I
9		Hamilton	20	m.	Farm laborer	O.
10	1126/1126	HOWELL, Aaron Jr.	26	m.	Farm laborer	"

11		HOWELL, Jane	25	f.	Domestic	O.	
12		William C.	3	m.		"	
13		Lena L.	1	f.		"	
14	1127/1127	KEYSER, Simon	36	m.	Farmer	1000/350	"
15		Mary A.	36	f.	Domestic	"	I
16		Mary M.	14	f.		"	
17		William	11	m.		"	
18		Benjamin	9	m.		"	
19		Susanna	6	f.		"	
20		Sylvester	10/12	m.		"	
21		JOHNSON, Susan	67	f.	Domestic	"	
22	1128/1128	CRONIN, James	47	m.	Farmer	4400/1350 Pa.	
23		Naomi	42	f.	Domestic	Va.	I
24		Alexander	22	m.	Farm laborer	O.	
25		Crawford	19	m.	Farm laborer	"	S
26		Harriet	15	f.	Domestic	"	S
27		Albert	11	m.		"	S
28		Caroline	9	f.		"	S
29		Amos	6	m.		"	S
30		Martha A.	3	f.		"	
31		James M.	1	m.		"	
32		Margaret	44	f.	Domestic	"	
33		GREGORY, Jackson	3	m.		"	
34	1129/1129	CRONIN, George	22	m.	Farm laborer	"	
35		Ann E.	22	f.	Domestic	"	
36	1130/1130	COHERN, William	55	m.	Farmer	800/150 Ire.	
37		Catharine A.	41	f.	Domestic	Md.	
38		James	20	m.	Farm laborer	Pa.	
39		Sarah	22	f.	Domestic	"	
40		John	12	m.		O.	S

Page 163   20 July 1860   Sheet 310

1		Mary J.	10	f.		O.	S
2		Levi	8	m.		"	S
3		Susan	3	f.		"	
4		Mahala	6/12	f.		"	
5	1131/1131	COHERN, William	30	m.	Farm laborer	Pa.	
6		Sarah	30	f.	Domestic	O.	
7		James	6	m.		"	S
8		Martha A.	3	f.		"	
9		William T.	1	m.		"	
10	1132/1132	MORRIS, Thomas	67	m.	Farmer	2000/300 Pa.	
11		Phebe	43	f.	Domestic	"	
12		CLARK, James W.	19	m.	Farm laborer	"	
13		HOWARD, Mariah	14	f.		"	S
14		MATLOCK, Lewis	26	m.	Farm laborer	O.	
15	1133/1133	SMITH, Bazel	26	m.	Farmer	/175	"
16		Elisa J.	24	f.	Domestic	"	
17		Mary	3	f.		"	
18		Matilda	2	f.		"	

19	1134/1134	MORRIS, James H.	38	m.	Farmer	1200/200	Pa.	
20		Lydia G.	39	f.	Domestic		"	
21		William A.	14	m.			Va.	S
22		Francis M.	12	m.			"	S
23		Martha A.	10	f.			"	S
24		Sarah E.	7	f.			O.	S
25		Joseph E.	5	m.			"	S
26		Sylvester P.	4	m.			"	
27		Ida M.	2/12	f.			"	
28	1135/1135	PIFER, George	25	m.	Farmer	/150	Ger.	
29		Mary	21	f.	Domestic		"	
30	1136/1136	BAKER, Sinclair	60	m.	Farmer	600/475	Va.	
31		Margaret	60	f.	Domestic		"	I
32		Thomas J.	27	m.	Farm laborer		O.	I
33		Susan E.	33	f.	Domestic		"	I
34		Margaret J.	12	f.			"	
35		William	24	m.	Farm laborer		"	I
36	1137/1137	FRANK, Oscar	33	m.	Farmer	1200/450	Sax.	
37		Caroline	30	f.	Domestic		Bav.	
38		Henry	8	m.			O.	
39		August	6	m.			"	
40		Charles	4	m.			"	

Page 164   20 July 1860   Sheet 310 verso

| 1 | | Flora | 3 | f. | | | O. | |

Beginning of Lewisville.

2	1138/1138	PFIFER, Henery	60	m.	Farmer	600/150	Bav.	
3		Elisabeth	50	f.	Domestic		"	
4		Henry	18	m.	Farm laborer		O.	
5	1139/1139	DEIL, Henry	60	m.	Farmer	3000/675	Dar.	
6		Elisabeth	60	f.	Domestic		"	5
7		John W.	28	m.	Farmer		"	
8		Catharine	23	f.	Domestic		O.	
9		Henry C.	4	m.			"	
10		John W.	2	m.			"	
11		Canrad	24	m.	Farm laborer		Dar.	
12	1140/1140	BUTT, Mark	65	m.	Farmer	500/300	"	
13		Catharine	66	f.	Domestic		"	
14		Michael	25	m.	Farm laborer		"	
15		Barbary	22	f.	Domestic		"	
16		Mary	19	f.	Domestic		"	
17	1141/1141	CASTNER, Kaneth	62	m.	Farmer	800/150	Bav.	
18		Catharine	62	f.	Domestic		"	I
19		Jacob	38	m.	Farmer		"	
20		George	19	m.	Farm laborer		"	
21	1142/1142	ROSE, Simon	30	m.	Farmer	1200/400	H.K.	
22		Sarah A.	29	f.	Domestic		O.	

23		ROSE, Samuel	10	m.			O.		
24		Mary	8	f.			"		
25		Frederick	6	m.			"		
26		Elisabeth	4	f.			"		
27		George	8/12	m.			"		
28		SMITH, Robert	23	m.	Farmer		"		
29		DEIL, Casper	1	m.			"		
30	1143/1143	McVEY, Samuel	37	m.	Farmer	/400	"		
31		Margaret	30	f.	Domestic		Md.	I	
32		Thomas	18	m.	Farm laborer		O.	S	
33		Rachel	16	f.	Domestic		"	S	
34		Jacob	14	m.			"	S	
35		David	12	m.			"	S	
36		Benjamin	10	m.			"	S	
37		Miles	8	m.			"	S	
38		Mary	6	f.			"	S	
39		Mariah	10/12	f.			"		
40	1144/1144	VIVER, Fred	36	m.	Farmer	400/450	Ger.		

Page 165   20 July 1860   Sheet 311

1		Elisabeth	27	f.	Domestic		Ger.		
2		Jacob	10	m.			O.		
3		Lena	8	f.			"		
4		Margaret	6	f.			"		
5		Elisabeth	4	f.			"		
6		George	3	m.			"		
7		Henry	1	m.			"		
8	1145/1145	LAFFAREE, Isa-bella	54	f.	Domestic	800/300	Pa.		
9	1146/1146	LAFFAREE, Sam-uel	25	m.	Farmer		O.		
10		Phebe	22	f.	Domestic		"		
11		James M.	2	m.			"		
12		Mary A.	5/12	f.					
13		MERSHALL, Elisa-beth	82	f.	Domestic		Pa.		
14	1147/1147	LAFFAREE, Costen	27	m.	Farmer		O.		
15		Elisabeth	28	f.	Domestic		"		
16		Smittson	4	m.			"		
17		Thomas	3	m.			"		
18		Mary E.	1	f.					
19	1148/1148	DYRE, William	24	m.	Farmer	200/100	"	M	
20		Rebecca	17	f.	Domestic		"	M	
21	1149/1149	POLIN, Nathaniel	58	m.	Farmer	600/500	Va.		
22		Mariam	36	f.	Domestic		O.	I	
23		Margaret A.	12	f.			"	S	
24		Jane	7	f.			"		
25		David	5	m.			"		
26		William	4	m.			"		
27		John	1	m.			"		

28	1150/1150	STACKNER, Lewis	42	m.	Farmer	1200/300	Bav.	
29		Barbary	33	f.	Domestic		"	
30		Caroline	11	f.			O.	S
31		Elisabeth	10	f.			"	S
32		Frederick	8	m.			"	S
33		Lana	6	f.			"	
34		Lewis	4	m.			"	
35		John	2	m.			"	
36	1151/1151	ORN, John	55	m.	Farmer	1200/400	Bav.	
37		Elisabeth	65	f.	Domestic		"	
38		RISE, George	25	m.	Farmer		"	
39		Catharine	22	f.	Domestic		"	
40		Henry	2/12	m.			O.	

Page 166			20 July 1860				Sheet 311 verso	
1	1152/1152	BOWMAN, Jacob	25	m.	Farmer		Pa.	
2		Louisa	23	f.	Domestic		Bav.	
3	1153/1153	SMITH, Sarah	32	f.	Domestic	400/150	O.	I
4		Mary	13	f.			"	S
5		Elisabeth	11	f.			"	S
6		Juliet	9	f.			"	S
7		Pluma	6	f.			"	S
8	1154/1154	SMITH, Aaron	30	m.	Farmer	/200	"	
9		Rachel	25	f.	Domestic		"	I
10		Eliza	7	f.			"	
11		Julia	6	f.			"	
12		Samuel	5	m.			"	
13		Howard	3	m.			"	
14		Sarah	1	f.			"	
15		Mary	61	f.	Domestic	1200/200	Va.	I
16		David	14	m.			O.	S
17		CONGER, Jackson	5	m.			"	
18	1155/1155	KEOHLER, Peter	46	m.	Farmer	800/150	Ger.	
19		Elisabeth	32	f.	Domestic		"	
20		Peter	14	m.			"	S
21		Charles	12	m.			"	S
22		Caroline	10	f.			"	S
23		Frederick	5	m.			"	
24		Sally A.	3	f.			"	
25		Mary	2/12	f.			O.	
26	1156/1156	SMITH, Anson	34	m.	Farmer	200/150	"	
27		Pernina	35	f.	Domestic		"	
28		Mary A.	16	f.	Domestic		"	S
29		Catharine A.	14	f.			"	S
30		Anson	1	m.			"	
31		Jeremiah	11	m.			"	S
32		Roseberry	9	m.			"	S
33		Sarah A.	8	f.			"	S
34		Clara	6	f.			"	S
35		Aaron	3	m.			"	
36	1157/1157	KNIGHT, Valen-tine	43	m.	Farmer	800/200	"	

37		KNIGHT, Rachel	35	f.	Domestic		O.	I
38		Josiah	16	m.	Farm laborer		"	S
39		Mary	13	f.			"	S
40		Charles	11	m.			"	S

Page 167   21 July 1860   Sheet 312

1		Elisabeth	8	f.			O.	S
2		John W.	2	m.			"	
3		Frances	77	f.	Domestic		Va.	
4	1158/1158	TURNER, John	33	m.	Farmer	/150	O.	I
5		Elisabeth	32	f.	Domestic		"	
6		Levi	13	m.			"	S
7		William	11	m.			"	S
8	1159/1159	KNIGHT, Lemuel	49	m.	Farmer	800/75	Va.	
9		Thamer	30	f.	Domestic		O.	I
10		Similaa	13	f.			"	S
11		Mary J.	10	f.			"	S
12		Benjamin	8	m.			"	S
13		James W.	7	m.			"	S
14		Sarah E.	4	f.			"	
15		John W.	1	m.			"	
16	1160/1160	EDWARDS, Mahlon	38	m.	Farmer	1500/900	Va.	
17		Rachel	32	f.	Domestic		O.	
18		Maranda J.	6	f.			"	
19		Mortimor	4	m.			"	
20		William H.	3	m.			"	
21	1161/1161	ROUSE, Thomas	47	m.	Farmer	2000/600	O.	I
22		Elisabeth	36	f.	Domestic		Va.	
23		Denton	22	m.	Farm laborer		O.	
24		Edward	19	m.	Farm laborer		"	S
25		Matilda	17	f.	Domestic		"	S
26		Nancy	15	f.	Domestic		"	S
27		Margaret	13	f.			"	S
28		Mahala	8	f.			"	S
29		Mary	6	f.			"	
30		Rachel	2	f.			"	
31	1162/1162	McVEY, Samuel	72	m.	Farmer	2500/450	Pa.	I
32		Jane	73	f.	Domestic		"	I
33		FORSHEY, Nancy	21	f.	Domestic		"	
34		GREY, Anice	15	f.	Domestic		"	
35		George	2/12	m.			"	
36	1163/1163	McVEY, Jehue	25	m.	Farmer	/150	"	
37		Margaret	21	f.	Domestic		"	
38		Amy	3	f.			"	
39		Armintha	1	f.			"	
40	1164/1164	HUFFMAN, Michael	40	m.	Farmer	1500/400	Bav.	

Page 168   21 July 1860   Sheet 312 verso

1		Mary	32	f.	Domestic		Bav.

2		HUFFMAN, Lewis	11	m.		O.
3		Frederick	16	m.	Farm laborer	"
4		Caroline	3	f.		"
5		Elisabeth	1	f.		"
6	1165/1165	GIVENS, Joseph	42	m.	Farmer	1200/425	" I
7		Lucinda	38	f.	Domestic	"
8		Melissa	19	f.	Domestic	" S
9		John	18	m.	Farm laborer	" S
10		Daniel	15	m.	Farm laborer	" S
11		Hannah	13	f.		" S
12		Susan	11	f.		" S
13		Lydia	10	f.		" S
14		Jacob	6	m.		" S
15		Milla	5	f.		"
16		Joseph H.	2	m.		"
17	1166/1166	BUTT, Lewis	53	m.	Farmer	2000/480	Bav.
18		Catharine	53	f.	Domestic	"
19		Eve	8	f.		O.
20		Jacob	6	m.		"
21		Lewis	4	m.		"
22		John	1	m.		"
23		Frederick	5/12	m.		"
24		Adam	83	m.		Bav.
25	1165/1165	KNUPP, Adam	65	m.	Farmer	4000/400	"
26		Caroline C.	55	f.	Domestic	"
27		Frederick	20	m.	Farm laborer	"
28		Phebe	14	f.		"
29	1166/1166	DEARTH, Mordica	44	m.	Farmer	800/475	O. I
30		Susanna	46	f.	Domestic	Va.
31		Isaac	24	m.	Farmer	O. M
32		Jacob	22	m.	Farm laborer	"
33		Permelia J.	20	f.	Domestic	"
34		Nancy	18	f.	Domestic	"
35		Lucinda	16	f.	Domestic	"
36		Theodore B.	14	m.		"
37	1167/1167	STOFFLE, Michael	54	m.	Farmer	800/450	Bav.
38		Margaret	48	f.	Domestic	"
39		Michael	24	m.	Farm laborer	"
40		Caroline	20	f.	Domestic	"

1		Philip	15	m.	Farm laborer		O.
2		Margaret	11	f.		"
3		STENBAUGH, Mar-				
		garet	68	f.	Domestic	Bav.
4	1168/1168	SHAFFER, Charles	35	m.	Farmer	1500/450	"
5		Mary	24	f.	Domestic	"
6		John	3	m.		O.
7		George	1	m.		"
8		John	87	m.	Nothing	Bav.
9		Mary	65	f.	Domestic	"

10	1169/1169	STOFFLE, John	51	m.	Farmer	2000/330	Bav.
11		Mariah	45	f.	Domestic		Fr.
12		Margaret	13	f.			Pa. S
13		John	11	m.			O. S
14		Frederick	8	m.			"
15		Henry	6	m.			"
16		Jacob	4	m.			"
17		George	2	m.			"
18		Mariah	1/12	f.			"
19	1170/1170	BUTT, Jacob	50	m.	Farmer	1200/300	Bav.
20		Sophia	30	f.	Domestic		
21		Catharine	19	f.	Domestic		O.
22		Elisabeth	15	f.	Domestic		"
23		Sophia	10	f.			
24		RAPP, Catharine	40	f.	Domestic		Bav.
25	1171/1171	GIVENS, Daniel	76	m.	Farmer	1200/100	Md.
26		Mary	23	f.	Domestic		O. I
27		Sarah M.	5	f.			"
28		David	2	m.			"
29		Amanda J.	7	f.			
30	1172/1172	GIVENS, Joseph	23	m.	Farm laborer	/75	"
31		Lucinda	18	f.	Domestic		"
32		Mary E.	1	f.			"
33	1173/1173	GIVENS, Andrew	38	m.	Farmer	1500/375	"
34		Ann	32	f.	Domestic		"
35		Oliver	13	m.			"
36		Louisa	15	f.	Domestic		"
37		James	11	m.			"
38		Henry	8	m.			"
39		Rachel	6	f.			"
40		John	1	m.			"

Page 170   24 July 1860   Sheet 313 verso

1	1174/1174	SPENTZ, James	27	m.	Farmer	/150	O.
2		Elisabeth	19	f.	Domestic		"
3		George	4	m.			"
4		Arthur	1	m.			"
5	1175/1175	WATKINS, Denton	64	m.	Farmer	600/250	Md.
6		Mahala	54	f.	Domestic		"
7		Irvin	20	m.	Farm laborer		O. S
8		Taylor	18	m.	Farm laborer		" S
9		Milton	15	m.	Farm laborer		" S
10		Hamberlind	13	m.			" S
11		ROUSE, Matilda	18	f.	Domestic		" S
12	1176/1176	CASH, Reason	55	m.	Farmer	3000/450	"
13		Susanna	50	f.	Domestic		Md. I
14		Hannah	20	f.	Domestic		O. S
15		Isaah	17	m.	Farm laborer		" S
16		Darcus	15	f.	Domestic		" S
17		Jonathon	12	m.			" S

18	1177/1177 CASH, David	28	m.	Farmer	/200	O.		
19	Martha A.	25	f.	Domestic		"		
20	Elisabeth	5	f.			"		
21	Reason	3	m.			"		
22	Solomon	1	m.			"		
23	1178/1178 McMULLEN, Asa	43	m.	Farmer	1500/400	Va.	I	
24	Mary	40	f.	Domestic		O.		
25	Nancy J.	17	f.	Domestic		"		
26	Rachel	15	f.	Domestic		"	S	
27	William	13	m.			"	S	
28	Spencer S.	9	m.			"	S	
29	John	6	m.			"	S	
30	Mordica H.	5	m.			"		
31	Thomas C.	3	m.			"		
32	Malan	3	m.			"		
33	TIMMONS, Susan	51	m.	Domestic		Pa.		
34	Sarah	12	f.			O.	S	
35	Elisabeth A.	5	f.			Ind.		
36	1179/1179 WINLAND, Hugh	20	m.	Farmer	500/100	O.		
37	Elisabeth	28	f.	Domestic		"	I	
38	Henry	2	m.			"		
39	Percilla	1	f.			"		
40	Elisha	1/12	m.			"		

Page 171   24 July 1860   Sheet 314

1	FORSHEY, Benja-min	8	m.			O.		
2	1180/1180 WINLAND, William	37	m.	Farmer	/100	"		
3	Susan	28	f.	Domestic		"		
4	Charles	12	m.			"	S	
5	Elisabeth	11	f.			"	S	
6	Henry	9	m.			"	S	
7	William L.	6	m.			"	S	
8	Mary E.	4	f.			"		
9	Matilda	3	f.			"		
10	Elias	1	m.			"		
11	1181/1181 COULTAS, Richard	36	m.	Farmer	500/150	"		
12	Percilla	28	f.	Domestic		"		
13	William	7	m.			"	S	
14	Joshua	6	m.			"		
15	Nancy	2	f.			"		
16	Oliver	1	m.			"		
17	1182/1182 WINLAND, James	22	m.	Farmer	/75	"	I	
18	Jane	21	f.	Domestic		"	I	
19	Sylvestor	2	m.			"		
20	Miles J.	1	m.			"		
21	1183/1183 JENNINGS, Elias	40	m.	Laborer		"		
22	Elisabeth	40	f.	Domestic		"		
23	Sarah	17	f.	Domestic		"		
24	1184/1184 BARBER, James	30	m.	Farmer		"		

25		BARBER, Eliza	30	f.	Domestic		O.
26		Margaret J.	12	f.			"
27		Mary A.	10	f.			"
28		George	8	m.			"
29		Elisabeth	6	f.			"
30		Susan	4	f.			"
31		Charlotte	2	f.			"
32		POLIN, Howard	14	m.			"
33	1185/1185	SMITH, Andrew	42	m.	Farmer	/400	"
34		Julian	40	f.	Domestic		"
35		Mary J.	16	f.	Domestic		" S
36		Martha A.	14	f.			" S
37		Charlotte	12	f.			" S
38		Elisabeth	10	f.			" S
39		Harvy J.	8	m.			"
40		Sarah	6	f.			"

Page 172   24 July 1860   Sheet 314 verso

1		Juliana	5	f.			O.
2		Amanda	2	f.			"
3		WILBER, Edward	14	m.			"
4	1186/1186	SMITH, John	37	m.	Farmer	1800/500	" I
5		Mary	32	f.	Domestic		"
6		Louisa	13	f.			" S
7		Riley	12	m.			" S
8		George W.	10	m.			" S
9		Melissa	8	f.			" S
10		James M.	6	m.			" S
11		Sarah	4	f.			"
12		John	1	m.			"
13	1187/1187	BLITZ, Henry	27	m.	Farmer	/100	H.D.
14		Mary	22	f.	Domestic		Bav. I
15		Phebe	5	f.			Pa.
16		Elisabeth	3	f.			O.
17		Catharine	1	f.			"
18	1188/1188	FABER, Henry	62	m.	Farmer	500/200	Bav.
19		Elisabeth	58	f.	Domestic		"
20	1189/1189	FABER, Jacob	29	m.	Farmer	300/175	Bav.
21		Elisabeth	22	f.	Domestic		"
22		Elisabeth	3	f.			O.
23		Mary	1	f.			"
24	1190/1190	BRUBAUGH, Henry	38	m.	Farmer	/50	Bav.
25		Catharine	36	f.	Domestic		"
26		Caroline	8	f.			"
27		Frederick	6	m.			"
28		Philip	4	m.			"
29		Mary	2	f.			O.
30		Jacob	2/12	m.			"
31	1191/1191	BIRKHART, Peter	25	m.	Farmer	700/150	Bav.

32		BIRKHART, Catharine	21	f.	Domestic		Bav.
33		Frederick	2	m.			O.
34	1192/1192	GROSS, Adam	30	m.	Farmer	900/200	Bav.
35		Elisabeth	27	f.	Domestic		"
36		Mary	2	f.			O.
37	1193/1193	BAUGH, John	40	m.	Farmer	1400/400	Bav.
38		Christena	40	f.	Domestic		"
39		John	15	m.	Farm laborer		"
40		Henry	13	m.			"

Page 173   24 July 1860   Sheet 315

1		Catharine	10	f.			Bav.	
2		Adam	4	m.			"	
3	1195/1195	BLAZER, Benjamin	34	m.	Farmer	500/325	O.	
4		Sarah	31	f.	Domestic		"	I
5		Eliza	12	f.			"	S
6		David	10	m.			"	S
7		Howard	8	m.			"	S
8		Elias	6	m.			"	S
9		Hulda	4	f.			"	
10		Sylvester	1	m.			"	
11	1196/1196	BUTT, Baltzer	29	m.	Farmer	500/100	Bav.	
12		Catharine	28	f.	Domestic		"	
13		Charles	6	m.			O.	
14		Baltzer	4	m.			"	
15		Louisa	2	f.			"	
16	1197/1197	GETNER, Artem	44	m.	Farmer	1000/250	Bav.	
17		Margaret	40	f.	Domestic		"	
18		Adam	17	m.	Farm laborer		"	
19		Louisa	14	f.			"	
20		Catharine	11	f.			"	S
21	1198/1198	McVEY, Isaac	45	m.	Farmer	400/100	Bav.	
22		Ann	48	f.	Domestic		Va.	
23		Lemuel	30	m.	Shoemaker		O.	
24		Mary A.	7	f.			"	
25		Martha M.	6	f.			"	
26		Elisabeth	2	f.			"	
27	1199/1199	McVEY, George W.	27	m.	Farm laborer	/200	"	
28		Mahala A.	26	f.	Domestic		"	
29		Isaac	8	m.			"	
30		William	6	m.			"	
31		Elisabeth J.	4	f.			"	
32		Samuel J.	2	m.			"	
33	1200/1200	MOORE, Jonathan	30	m.	Farmer	/125	Pa.	
34		Elisabeth	23	f.	Domestic		O.	
35		Lazetta	5	f.			"	
36		Hariet	4	f.			"	

37		MOORE, John W.	8	m.			O.	S
38	1201/1201	MATLOCK, Lucre-tia	47	f.	Domestic	600/100	"	
39		Andre	20	m.	Farm laborer		"	
40		Thomas	13	m.			"	S

1		Mary A.	12	f.			O.	S
2		David	10	m.			"	S
3		John	6	m.			"	
4	1202/1202	FARNSWORTH, Robert	38	m.	Farmer	400/150	"	
5		Percilla	32	f.	Domestic		"	
6		William	14	m.			"	S
7		John	12	m.			"	S
8		Mahala	10	f.			"	S
9		Samuel	7	m.			"	
10		Jacob	3	m.			"	
11		INMAN, Stephen	50	m.	Chair-maker			
12	1203/1203	JOHNSON, Patrick	30	m.	Farmer	/100	Ire.	
13		Susan	29	f.	Domestic		O.	
14		John	8	m.			"	
15		William	5	m.			"	
16		Francis	2	m.			"	
17	1204/1204	PRYOR, Euphron-ius	37	m.	Farmer	4000/800	"	
18		Susanna	37	f.	Domestic		"	
19		William H.	16	m.	Farm laborer		"	S
20		Elisabeth	14	f.			"	S
21		Hannah	12	f.			"	S
22		Isaac	10	m.			"	S
23		Lydia A.	8	f.			"	S
24		John	6	m.			"	S
25		Samuel	3	m.			"	
26	1205/1205	HICKS, Jeremiah	37	m.	Farm laborer	/50	"	I
27		Rachel	35	f.	Domestic		"	
28		Amanda M.	15	f.	Domestic		"	
29		Sarah J.	10	f.			"	
30		James E.	5	m.			"	
31		Woodman T.	1/12	m.			"	
32	1206/1206	WORLEY, James	45	m.	Farmer	1800/500	"	
33		Deborah	39	f.	Domestic		Md.	I
34		Sarah A.	16	f.	Domestic		O.	S
35		Jacob A.	12	m.			"	S
36		Catharine	10	f.			"	S
37		Juliana	8	f.			"	S
38		John H.	5	m.			"	S
39		Susan A.	1	f.			"	
40	1207/1207	MARSH, James	33	m.	Blacksmith	/40	Va.	

1		MARSH, Elisabeth	33	f.	Domestic	O.	
2		Abram	3	m.		"	
3		John W.	1	m.		"	
4	1208/1208	PRYOR, Smiley	52	m.	Farmer	2800/600	" I
5		Mary	47	f.	Domestic		" I
6		Adaline	22	f.	Domestic		"
7		Clia	20	f.	Domestic		"
8		Joseph	18	m.	Farm laborer		" S
9		Sarah	16	f.	Domestic		" S
10		William A.	12	m.			" S
11		Smiley	8	m.			" S
12		Hartless	6	m.			"
13		PHILIPS, Thomas					
		T.	3	m.			"
14	1209/1209	PRYOR, John	24	m.	Farm laborer	/350	"
15		Hariet	22	f.	Domestic		"
16		Mary E.	1	f.			"
17	1210/1210	McFREDERICK,					
		Andrew	42	m.	Farmer	2500/420	Pa.
18		Angeline	35	f.	Domestic		O.
19		Mary J.	15	f.	Domestic		" S
20		Irvin	13	m.			" S
21		Ruth	11	f.			" S
22		John	9	m.			" S
23		Rachel A.	8	f.			" S
24		James	6	m.			" S
25		William	5	m.			"
26		Elisabeth	3	f.			"
27		Joseph A.	1	m.			"
28	1211/1211	HARRIS, John W.	57	m.	Teacher		D.C.
29		Cloe E.	37	f.	Teacher		N.Y.
30		THOMAS, Sarah A.	57	f.	Domestic		N.J.
31		JOHNSON, Margaret					
		E.	13	f.			O. S
32	1212/1212	POWELL, John	59	m.	Farmer	3000/550	Md.
33		Catharine	50	f.	Domestic		O. I
34		Jacob	19	m.	Farm laborer		"
35		Susan	18	f.	Domestic		" S
36		Julian	24	f.	Domestic		"
37		Hannah	16	f.	Domestic		"
38		Margaret	14	f.			" S
39		Joseph	10	m.			"
40	1213/1213	POWELL, Andrew	30	m.	Farmer	/400	"

1		Alvira	26	f.	Domestic	O. I	
2		Mary A.	10	f.		" S	
3		David	8	m.		" S	

4		POWELL, Catharine	5	f.			O.
5		Elisabeth	3	f.			"
6		John	10/12	m.			"
7	1214/1214	McCONNELL, John	73	m.	Farmer	600/300	Ire.
8		Jane	66	f.	Domestic		Pa.
9	1215/1215	JACKMAN, Susan	32	f.	Domestic	600/	O.
10		Theodore	10	m.			" S
11		Edward	8	m.			" S
12		PORTER, James	26	m.	Farm laborer	/100	"
13	1216/1216	McCONNELL, Alex	38	m.	Farmer	/200	"
14		Mary	31	f.	Domestic		"
15		Ellen J.	10	f.			" S
16		Cordelia A.	8	f.			" S
17		Mary C.	6	f.			" S
18		John A.	5	m.			"
19		Susan E.	4	f.			"
20		Francis A.	1	m.			"
21	1217/1217	JACKMAN, Nancy	60	f.	Domestic	1200/325	Pa. I
22		Margaret	33	f.	Domestic		O.
23		Susan	26	f.	Domestic		"
24		Alexander	30	m.	Farmer		"
25		Catharine	24	f.	Domestic		"
26		Elisabeth	22	f.	Domestic		"
27		Adam	21	m.	Farm laborer		"
28	1218/1218	MAXWELL, William	32	m.	Farmer	/125	Pa.
29		Luticia	32	f.	Domestic		O.
30		Catharine C.	10	f.			" S
31		Joseph A.	9	m.			" S
32		Nancy A.	6	f.			" S
33		Clara J.	1	f.			"
34	1219/1219	BIGLEY, Joseph	59	m.	Farmer	2000/315	"
35		Elisabeth	59	f.	Domestic		Pa.
36	1220/1220	HARTSHORN, Sam-					
		uel	48	m.	Farmer	3000/700	O.
37		Susana	48	f.	Domestic		Pa. I
38		James	21	m.	Farm laborer		O.
39		Nancy J.	16	f.	Domestic		"
40		Martha A.	14	f.			"

1		Cephas D.	12	m.			O. S
2		Samuel H.	6	m.			" S
3	1221/1221	HARTSHORN, George	24	m.	Farmer	/250	"
4		Ann M.	23	f.	Domestic		"
5		Johnathon	1	m.			"
6	1222/1222	HARTSHORN, Wil-					
		liam	22	m.	Farmer	/50	"
7		Sarah	21	f.	Domestic		" I

8		HARTSHORN, Lu-ticia A.	1	f.			O.	
9	1223/1223	JONES, Christian	33	m.	Farmer	1200/375	"	
10		Mary A.	30	f.	Domestic		"	
11		David	6	m.			"	
12		John W.	4	m.			"	
13		Rachel J.	2	f.			"	
14	1224/1224	HENDERSHOT, George W.	37	m.	Farmer	1200/350	"	
15		Belinda	32	f.	Domestic		"	
16		Elias	12	m.			"	S
17		David	11	m.			"	S
18		Rebecca J.	6	f.			"	S
19		George L.	3	m.			"	
20		Jonathon	6/12	m.			"	
21		George	72	m.	Nothing		Pa.	
22		Elisabeth	69	f.	Domestic		"	I
23	1225/1225	SLOAN, George W.	34	m.	Farmer	2000/550	O.	I
24		Hannah	34	f.	Domestic		"	I
25		Mary A.	12	f.			"	S
26		Amos	10	m.			"	S
27		Elisabeth	8	f.			"	S
28		Martha	6	f.			"	S
29		Lucinda	6/12	f.			"	
30		Elias	72	m.	Nothing		Pa.	
31	1226/1226	EDDINGTON, Charles	26	m.	Farmer	/125	Va.	
32		Martha	23	f.	Domestic		O.	I
33		John W.	6	m.			"	
34	1227/1227	NOLTON, Calvin P.	47	m.	Farmer	1600/1000	"	
35		Sarah	44	f.	Domestic		"	I
36		Martha A.	20	f.	Domestic		"	I
37		Joseph	17	m.	Farm laborer		"	S
38		James	16	m.	Farm laborer		"	S
39		Thomas	14	m.			"	S
40		George	12	m.			"	S

1		Eunice	10	f.			O.	S
2		Frederick	8	m.			"	S
3		John W.	2	m.			"	
4	1228/1228	KELLEY, Edward	56	m.	Farmer	1500/300	Md.	
5		Fanny	82	f.	Domestic		"	
6		Margaret	70	f.	Domestic		"	
7	1229/1229	WILLIAMS, Levi	49	m.	Farmer	2000/400	Pa.	
8		Lucinda	34	f.	Domestic		"	
9		Charlotte	17	f.	Domestic		Va.	S
10		Melissa	16	f.	Domestic		O.	S
11		Jacob	12	m.			"	S

12		WILLIAMS, Sarena	8	f.			O. S
13		Martin L.	5	m.			"
14		Mary E.	3	f.			"
15		Sarepta	1	f.			"
16	1230/1230	HAYS, Isaac	22	m.	Farm laborer	/50	O. I
17		Elisabeth A.	21	f.	Domestic		Va. I
18		Mary M.	1/12	f.			O.
19	1231/1231	SCARBROUGH, John	40	m.	Farmer	600/300	Md. I
20		Elisabeth	40	f.	Domestic		Pa.
21		Sarena	12	f.			O. S
22		Annie	10	f.			" S
23		William T.	7	m.			" S
24		Joseph	6	m.			"
25		Abba	2	f.			"
26	1232/1232	ELLIS, Joseph	76	m.	Farmer	1200/400	Del.
27		Elisabeth	76	f.	Domestic		Md. I
28		MOORE, Thomas	12	m.			O.
29	1233/1233	WATSON, Robert	20	m.	Farmer	/50	" M
30		Mahala	19	f.	Domestic		" M
31	1234/1234	SCARBROUGH, Ste-phen	25	m.	Farmer		O.
32		Eliza	20	f.	Domestic		Eng.
33		Emmer	3	f.			O.
34		Levi	1	m.			"
35	1235/1235	BOOTH, John H.	56	m.	Farmer	1800/650	Eng.
36		Mary A.	53	f.	Domestic		"
37		Isaac	33	m.	Farmer		"
38	1236/1236	-----, Thomas	29	m.	Farmer		"
39		Elmyra	28	f.	Domestic		O.
40		Nancy J.	5	f.			"

1		Johile	3	m.			O.
2		Mary A.	1	f.			"
3	1237/1237	WEAVER, Samuel	22	m.	Farmer	/50	"
4		Hannah	17	f.	Domestic		"
5		Mary E.	8/12	f.			"
6	1238/1238	SCARBROUGH, Jo-seph	67	m.	Farmer	500/100	Md.
7	1239/1239	EDDINGTON, John	38	m.	Farmer	600/225	"
8		Lydia	38	f.	Domestic		Pa. I
9		Mary	15	f.	Domestic		O. S
10		Nancy J.	10	f.			" S
11		Peter	8	m.			" S
12		Loretta	1	m.			"
13	1240/1240	KENEY, Ann	50	f.	Domestic	600/200	O.

14		KENEY, Richard	22	m.	Farmer		O.
15		Deborah	20	f.	Domestic		"
16		Jane	17	f.	Domestic		"
17		Alfred	15	m.	Farm laborer		"
18		Edward	11	m.			"
19		MILLER, John	5	m.			"
20	1241/1241	EDDINGTON, Peter	32	m.	Farmer	400/100	Va.
21		Sarah	29	f.	Domestic		O.
22		Ann	4	f.			"
23		Mary L.	3	f.			"
24		Thornton	10/12	m.			"
25	1242/1242	KINEY, Frederick	30	m.	Farm laborer		O.
26		Nancy	28	f.	Domestic		"
27	1243/1243	CHAPMAN, Alfred	40	m.	Farm laborer		Pa.
28		Elisabeth	32	f.	Domestic		O. I
29		James W.	7	m.			"
30		Thomas	6	m.			"
31		George W.	4	m.			"
32		Henry H.	3	m.			"
33		Mary A.	3/12	f.			"
34	1244/1244	ALLEN, Levi	43	m.	Farmer	1600/600	Md.
35		Sarah	40	f.	Domestic		O. I
36		Reuben	24	m.	Farm laborer		"
37		Harriet	19	f.	Domestic		"
38		Sarah C.	10	f.			"
39		George W.	6	m.			"
40	1245/1245	ODEN, William	60	m.	Farmer	1400/400	Md.

Page 180   25 July 1860   Sheet 318 verso

1		Cate A.	43	f.	Domestic		Md.
2		William A.	18	m.	Farm laborer		O. S
3		Rachel A.	15	f.	Domestic		"
4		Elisabeth J.	12	f.			" S
5		Margaret	10	f.			" S
6		Nathan	7	m.			" S
7		Frances J.	3	f.			"
8		Mary M.	1	f.			"
9	1246/1246	EDDINGTON, William C.	76	m.	Farmer	1500/350	Va.
10		Mary	65	f.	Domestic		" I
11		WAGGLE, William	15	m.	Farm laborer		O.
12	1247/1247	EDDINGTON, Benj.	30	m.	Farmer		"
13		Matilda	28	f.	Domestic		"
14		Mary M.	1	f.			"
15	1248/1248	HIGHMAN, David	60	m.	Farmer	1200/500	Pa.
16		Jane	56	f.	Domestic		" I
17		Duncan	23	m.	Farm laborer		O.
18		David	18	m.	Farm laborer		" S
19		Hannah	15	f.	Domestic		" S

20		HIGHMAN, Sarah T.	10	f.			O. S
21	1249/1249	HIGHMAN, Marquis	28	m.	Farmer	400/200	"
22		Mary	26	f.	Domestic		"
23		Melissa	4	f.			"
24		Jane	2	f.			"
25		David	1	m.			"
26	1250/1250	JONES, Jeremiah	49	m.	Farmer	1000/250	Pa.
27		Margaret	47	f.	Domestic		" I
28		Henry	19	m.	Farm laborer		"
29		Nancy C.	17	f.	Domestic		"
30		John N.	15	m.	Farm laborer		" S
31		Barbary E.	13	f.			"
32		Andrew J.	8	m.			" S
33	1251/1251	SMITH, George	49	m.	Farmer	3000/450	Pa.
34		Lucinda	45	f.	Domestic		" I
35		Madisson	18	m.	Farm laborer		O. S
36		Martha	13	f.			" S
37		Mary	8	f.			" S
38	1252/1252	SMITH, David	22	m.	Farm laborer		"
39		Margaret	19	f.	Domestic		"
40		Milton	1/12	m.			"

Page 181   25 July 1860   Sheet 319

1	1253/1253	SHAKLEE, Timothy	60	m.	Farmer		O.
2		Jane	55	f.	Domestic		"
3		Lorenzo	19	m.	Farm laborer		"
4		EDDALEON, Clar-					
		issa	9	f.			"

(Wayne Township Concluded)

I do hereby certify that there is (181) one hundred
and Eighty-one Pages of free inhabitants in my district
and I do further certify that the Enumeration was made
according to my oath and instructions to the best of my
knowledge and belief.

Calais, Monroe County, Ohio, August   1860.

J. P. Spriggs, Asst. Marshall

Sworn to and Subscribed before me this 17th day of
August, A. D. 1860,

William Henning

Mayor of the Town of Calais.

Number of inhabitants in	Seneca Township	1406
	Franklin Township	1560
	Bethel	1340
	Washington	1554
	Wayne	1324
	Total	7184

```
Number of Farms              Seneca        175
                             Franklin      177
                             Bethel        177
                             Washington    185
                             Wayne         165

                             Total         879

Number of Deaths             Seneca         14
                             Franklin       18
                             Bethel         13
                             Washington     20
                             Wayne          13

                             Total          78

Number of Pages              Schedule No. 1  181
                                      No. 3   03
                                      No. 4   46
                                      No. 5    1
                                      No. 6    1

                                             232
```

Number of Manufacturing Establishments, Seneca Tn. 54

* * *

Switzerland Township   P. O. Cameron

Page 1			11 July 1860				Sheet 321
1	1/1	TSHAPPAT, Jacob	55	m.	Farmer	3000/700	Sw.
2		Susanna	50	f.	Wife		"
3		William	27	m.	Farm laborer		O.
4		Cessilla	23	f.	Domestic (Scarlet Fev.)		
5		Luisa	20	f.	Domestic		O.
6		Samuel	16	m.	Farm laborer		" S
7		David	14	m.			" S
8		Albert	12	m.			" S
9		Mary	9	f.			" S
10	2/2	TSHAPPAT, Phillip	24	m.	Farmer	/200	" M
11		Catharine	20	f.	Wife		Sw. M
12	3/3	SCHARMAN, Christian	71	m.	Farmer	500/100	H.D.
13		Julia	60	f.	Wife		"
14	4/4	SCHARMAN, Adam	37	m.	Farmer	500/200	"
15		Elisabeth	36	f.	Wife		"
16		Elisabeth	6	f.			O.
17	5/5	WORKMAN, Stephen	38	m.	Farmer	500/150	"
18		Sarah	36	f.	Wife		"
19		Andrew	14	m.			" S
20		Sarah E.	14	f.			" S

21		WORKMAN, John R.	10	m.		O.	S
22		Samuel S.	9	m.		"	S
23	6/6	BEAM, Adam	60	m.	Farmer	1500/300 Pa.	
24		Mary	50	f.	Wife	"	
25		John	23	m.	Farm laborer	O.	S
26		Mary J.	21	f.	Domestic	"	S
27		Jacob	15	m.		"	S
28		Martha	13	f.		"	S
29		Hannah	11	f.		"	S
30		Arminda	9	f.		"	S
31		Susanna	5	f.		"	S
32		Fellena	4	f.		"	
33	7/7	LETZSEH, August	48	m.	Farmer	1500/300 Sax.	
34		Amalia	37	f.	Wife	"	
35		Emely	20	f.	Domestic	"	S
36		Charles	16	m.		O.	S
37		Wilhelmina	14	f.		"	S
38		August	11	m.		"	S
39		Mary	7	f.		"	S

Page 2   11 & 12 July 1860   Sheet 321 verso

1		William	6	m.		O.	S
2		Elisabeth	5	f.		"	
3		John	3	m.		"	
4		Harvey	2	m.		"	
5	8/8	NEIPERT, Godfried	69	m.	Farmer	/400 Sax.	
6	9/9	VANEST, David	72	m.	Farmer	500/200 N.J.	
7		Sally	66	f.	Wife	"	
8		John	27	m.	Farm laborer	O.	I
9	9/9	WHEELER, Benjamin	38	m.	Farmer	1000/150 Md.	
10		Sarah E.	25	f.	Wife	O.	
11		George W.	19	m.	Farm laborer	"	S
12		Elsy	16	f.	Domestic	"	S
13		SHIN, Ruth	14	f.		"	S
14		Emely J.	13	f.		"	S
15		William	9	m.		"	S
16		Jacob A.	2	m.		"	
17		Albert	3/12	m.		"	
18	10/10	GARLOCH, Andrew	33	m.	Farmer	/50	"
19		Nancy	38	f.	Wife	Va.	
20		Sarah Ann	10	f.		O.	S
21		Rachel	9	f.		"	S
22		Mary J.	7	f.		"	S
23		Melinda	5	f.		"	S
24		William Dandny	3	m.		"	
25		Adanora	1	f.		"	
26	11/11	PRIOR, David	42	m.	Farmer	700/100 O.	
27		Harriet	36	f.	Wife	"	
28		Mary E.	16	f.	Domestic	"	S

29		PRIOR, Rebecca	15	f.			0.	S
30		Madison	12	m.			"	S
31		Arthur	10	m.			"	S
32		Harvey	7	m.			"	S
33		Clarissa	5	f.			"	S
34		William	1	m.			"	
35	12/12	LOY, George	49	m.	Farmer	/50	"	
36		Nancy	45	f.	Wife		"	
37		Elisabeth	22	f.	Domestic		"	
38		Mary	20	f.	child		"	S
39		William	18	m.	child		"	S

Page 3   12 July 1860   Sheet 322

1		Jacob	14	m.			0.	S
2		David	12	m.			"	S
3		Andrew	11	m.			"	S
4		Catharine	9	f.			"	S
5		Mary	6	f.			"	S
6		Phebe	4	f.			"	
7	13/13	MEEKER, David	33	m.	Farmer	1800/200	0.	
8		Margaret	33	f.	Wife		"	
9		Peter	8	m.			"	S
10		Samuel	6	m.			"	S
11		Mandy J.	1	f.			"	
12		George W.	3/12	m.			"	
13	14/14	WORKMAN, William	38	m.	Farmer	1600/400	"	
14		Agnes	35	f.	Wife		"	
15		Amos	16	m.	child		"	S
16		Sarah E.	12	f.			"	S
17		Albert	8	m.			"	S
18	15/15	SPRAGUE, Robert A.	38	m.	Cooper	300/150	"	
19		Mary	35	f.	Wife		"	
20		William	15	m.			"	S
21		Rachel	9	f.			"	S
22		Terxahan	6	f.			"	S
23		John	2	m.			"	
24	16/16	HUBACHER, Benedict	54	m.	Farmer	600/150	Sw.	
25		Sarah	47	f.	Wife		0.	
26		Henry	17	m.	Domestic		"	S
27		Mary	12	f.			"	S
28		Charlotte	12	f.			"	S
29		John	10	m.			"	S
30		Luisa	8	f.			"	S
31		William	4	m.			"	
32	17/17	BROCK, William H.	50	m.	Farmer	2500/425	"	
33		Mary	45	f.	Wife		"	
34		Elisabeth	24	f.	Domestic		"	
35		Oddy	18	m.	child		"	S
36		Abel	15	m.			"	S
37		Daniel	12	m.			"	S

38		BROCK, Millissa	5	f.			O.	
39		Philimon	1	m.			"	

Page 4   13 July 1860   Sheet 322 **verso**

1	18/18	WHEELER, Samuel	30	m.	Farmer	/60	O.	
2		Jane	22	f.	Wife		"	
3		James M.	3	m.			"	
4		William	1	m.			"	
5	19/19	SHUTTS, George	33	m.	Farmer	1500/325	Va.	
6		Margaret	30	f.	Wife		O.	
7		Robert H.	7	m.			"	S
8		Sarah J.	4	f.			"	
9		John M.	2	m.			"	
10	20/20	SHUTTS, James	29	m.	Farmer	/150	"	
11		Mary	23	f.	Wife		"	
12		William	6	m.			"	S
13		Clary	1	f.			"	
14	21/21	BROCK, John	54	m.	Farmer	1800/400	Va.	
15		Rachel	31	f.	Wife		"	
16		Joseph	23	m.	child		O.	
17		William	20	m.	child		"	
18		Levi	15	m.			"	S
19		Mary E.	12	f.			"	S
20		John	6	m.			"	S
21		Daniel	3	m.			"	
22		Mary E.	2	f.			"	
23	22/22	MAHLON, Thomas	26	m.	Farmer	/235	"	
24		Barbary	19	f.	Wife		"	
25		Johnson	3/12	m.			"	
26	23/23	STARKEY, Mary	27	f.	Farmer	/50	"	
27		Adaline	8	f.			"	S
28		Clara	4	f.			"	S
29		William B.	2	m.			"	
30	24/24	POWELL, Adonijah	56	m.	Farmer	1400/40	"	
31		Harriet	48	f.	Wife		"	
32		David	14	m.			"	S
33		MEEKER, Thomas	19	m.	Farm laborer		"	S
34		THOMAS, Margaret	13	f.	Domestic		"	S
35		POWELL, Barnebas	26	m.	Teacher	/300	"	
36	25/25	GARLOCH, Jacob	30	m.	Farmer	800/100	"	
37		Messi Jane	29	f.	Wife		"	
38		David	7	m.			"	S
39		Joseph	4	m.			"	

Page 5   13 July 1860   Sheet 323

1	26/26	BUCK, Martain	44	m.	Farmer	/130	Wir.	
2		Christina	49	f.	Wife		"	
3		George	16	m.	child		"	S

4		BUCK, Mathias	15	m.			Wir.	S
5		Gottlieb	8	m.			"	S
6	27/27	BLUE, John	75	m.	Farmer	800/60	Va.	
7		Eliza	57	f.	Wife		Md.	
8	28/28	DAVIS, Samuel	25	m.	Farm laborer	/40	Pa.	
9		Margaret A.	24	f.	Wife		O.	
10		William	4	m.			"	
11		Nancy	4	f.			"	
12		Mary E.	1	f.			"	
13	29/29	MOGLICH, Phillip	50	m.	Farmer	1000/170	Pr.	
14		Mary	45	f.	Wife		"	
15		Elisabeth	16	f.	child		"	S
16		Jacob	12	m.			"	S
17		William	2	m.			O.	
18	30/30	BLUE, Abraham	40	m.	Farmer	/250	"	
19		Mary Ann	33	f.	Wife		"	
20		Cardilla	14	f.			"	S
21		John	11	m.			"	S
22		Silas	9	m.			"	S
23		Aron	7	m.			"	S
24		Abraham	5	m.			"	S
25		Mary E.	2	f.			"	
26	31/31	HEADLEY, Aron	26	m.	Farmer	500/200	"	
27		Lavina	23	f.	Wife		"	
28		Barbara	4	f.			"	
29		James	2	m.			"	
30	32/32	WEIL, Jacob	37	m.	Farmer	700/300	Als.	
31		Mary J.	30	f.	Wife		O.	
32		Mary Ann	12	f.			"	S
33		Albert G.	11	m.			"	S
34		Alexander	3	m.			"	S
35		Mandy Jane	2	f.			"	
36	33/33	McVEIGH, Napoleon	32	m.	Farmer	/100	"	
37		Jemima	28	f.	Wife		"	
38		Narcissa	3	f.			"	
39		Clerissa	1	f.			"	

Page 6   14 July 1860   Sheet 323 verso

1	--/34	McVEIGH, Jarome	22	m.	Farmer	/435	O.	
2		Dartha M.	29	f.	Domestic		"	
3	34/35	RUBLE, David	57	m.	Farmer	5000/500	"	
4		Nancy	55	f.	Wife		Pa.	
5		Susann	30	f.	Teacher	/100	O.	
6		Mary	18	f.	child		"	S
7		Katherine	16	f.	child		"	S
8		READER, Martin	19	m.	Farm laborer		"	S
9	35/36	RUBLE, John	30	m.	Farmer	/285	"	

10		RUBLE, Nancy J.	22	f.	Wife		O.		
11		Milton	4	m.			"		
12		Ochron	8/12	m.			"		
13		Harriet	8/12	f.			"		
14	36/37	SMITH, Elisabeth	69	f.	Farmer	500/340	Va.		
15		Mann	29	m.	Farm laborer		O.		
16		Johannah	36	f.	Domestic		"		
17		Seletheal	40	m.	child		"	6	
18		Seevers	22	m.	child		"	46	
19		Elisabeth	20	f.	child		"		
20	37/38	SCHRAGER, James	32	m.	Farmer	500/100	Pa.		
21		Sarah	35	f.	Wife		O.		
22		Sarah	8	f.			"	S	
23		Mary	7	f.			"	S	
24		James	5	m.			"	S	
25		Susanna	4	f.			"		
26		Madison	2	m.			"		
27		John M.	10/12	m.			"		
28	--/39	SCHRAGER, Jacob	69	m.	Farm laborer	/25	Pa.		
29	38-40	GAITZ, John	23	m.	Apprentice tanner	/240	O.		
30		Rachel	29	f.	Wife		"		
31	39/41	SANDROG, Catharine	58	f.	Farmer	600/50	H.D.		
32		Nikolas	19	m.	Farm laborer		"		
33	40/42	BROWNIGER, Abel	33	m.	Farmer	/320	O.		
34		Harriet	27	f.	Wife		"		
35		Joseph K.	7	m.			"	S	
36		Andrew J.	3/12	m.			"		
37		MOSSE, Arrina	22	f.	Domestic		"		
38	41/43	BROWN, William	29	m.	Farmer	/575	"		
39		Sarah	25	f.	Wife		"		

Page 7			14 July 1860				Sheet 324	
1		Mathias	5	m.			O.	
2		Menerva	3	f.			"	
3	42/44	BROWN, Abel	42	m.	Farmer	/600	"	
4		Maria	31	f.	Wife		"	
5		Mary L.	9	f.			"	S
6		Susanna	8	f.			"	S
7		Arlof	4	m.			"	
8		Clark	4/12	m.			"	
9	43/45	EARLEY, Samuel	41	m.	Farmer	400/150	Md.	
10		Sarah	30	f.	Wife		O.	
11		Permely	9	f.			"	S
12		Madison	6	m.			"	
13	44/46	BROWN, Jacob	69	m.	Farmer	2000/600	Va.	
14		Nancy	67	f.	Wife		"	

15	45/47	BOLES, John	45	m.	Farmer	300/270	O.	
16		Susanna	50	f.	Wife		Sw.	
17		Eunis	17	f.	child		O.	
18		Mary M.	15	f.			"	S
19		Emeline	12	f.			"	S
20		Sarah	80	f.	Domestic		Pa.	

21	46/48	BRILL, John	29	m.	Master Blacksmith			
						300/500	H.K.	
22		Mary	28	f.	Wife		Sw.	
23		William	4	m.			O.	
24		George	2	m.			"	
25		Metilda	4/12	f.			"	

26	47/49	KOERNER, Agustus	42	m.	Farmer	1400/420	Han.	
27		Millasina	42	f.	Wife		"	
28		Christian	19	m.	child		O.	S
29		August	15	m.			"	S
30		Emmely	13	f.			"	S
31		Charles E.	11	m.			"	S
32		John	9	m.			"	S
33		Johanna	7	f.			"	S
34		Adolph	5	m.			"	S
35		George	3	m.			"	
36		Doris	6/12	f.			"	

37	48/50	WATSON, Jacob	32	m.	Farmer	/25	"	
38		Mary J.	29	f.	Wife		"	
39		Rosina	7	f.			"	

Page 8			16 July 1860			Sheet 324 verso		
1		Hester Ann	5	f.			O.	
2		Leander	3	m.			"	
3		Amanda	1	f.			"	

4	49/51	WATSON, Hester	53	f.		/30	Md.	
5		Harvy	8	m.			O.	S

6	50/52	SCHAFFER, Jacob	54	m.	Farmer	2000/525	Wir.	
7		Katharina	53	f.	Wife		"	
8		Adam	25	m.	child		"	
9		George	21	m.	child		O.	
10		Gottlieb	16	m.	child		"	S
11		Mary	19	f.	child		"	S
12		Katharine	14	f.			"	S
13		Elisabeth	10	f.			"	S

14	51/53	SCHAFER, Godfried	28	m.	Farmer	/50	Wir.	
15		Elisabeth	20	f.	Wife		"	

16	52/54	STEINER, Charlotta	45	f.	Farmer	1800/650	Als.	
17		John	20	m.	Farm laborer		O.	
18		Caroline	10	f.			"	S

19	53/55	KIMPBAL, Frieder-			Steamboatman			
		ick	36	m.		1100/3000	H.D.	

20		KIMPBAL, Mary	31	f.	Wife		Pa.
21		Louis	14	m.			O. S
22		George	13	m.			" S
23		Eliza	9	f.			" S
24		Frederick	6	m.			" S
25		Katharine	4	f.			" S
26		Mary	2	f.			"
27		MILLER, H. C.	26	m.	Steamboatman	/150	H.K.
28		Katharine	21	f.	Wife		"
29		Sarah J.	1	f.			Pa.
30	54/56	BAUMBERGER, John	58	m.	Farmer	1400/500	Sw.
31		Elisabeth	33	f.	Wife		"
32		John	24	m.	Master Blacksmith /150		"
33		Louis	20	m.			"
34		July	8	f.			O. S
35		Caroline	6	f.			"
36		Jacob	3	m.			"
37		Albert	1	m.			"
38	55/57	OTHO, George	46	m.	Farmer	/150	Han.
39		Mary S.	44	f.	Wife		"

Page 9   17 July 1860   Sheet 325

1		Mary B.	20	f.	child		Han.
2		Barbara	19	f.	child		"
3		Jacob	17	m.	child		" S
4		Christina	10	f.			" S
5		Charley	6	m.			O. S
6	56/58	ZLEINDEN, Ulrich	62	m.	Farmer	1000/305	Sw.
7		Elisabeth	39	f.	Wife		"
8		Charlotta	18	f.	child		O. S
9		John	16	m.	child		" S
10		Katharine	11	f.			" S
11		Luisa	6	f.			" S
12	57/59	FANKHOUSER, Dan-iel	47	m.	Farmer	1500/700	Sw.
13		Magdelena	43	f.	Wife		"
14		Magdelena Jr.	22	f.	child		O.
15		John	18	m.	child		" S
16		Samuel	17	m.	child		" S
17		Mary	15	f.			" S
18		Charlotta	14	f.			" S
19		Caroline	12	f.			" S
20		Jacob	6	m.			" S
21	58/60	FROELICH, Jacob	68	m.	Farmer	3000/420	Als.
22		Elisabeth	68	f.	Wife		"
23		Christian	31	m.	Farm laborer	/300	Pa.
24		Jacob	28	m.	Wagon-maker	/100	O.
25	59/61	FROLICH, William	40	m.	Farmer	/300	Pa.
26		Rebecca	34	f.	Wife		O.

27		FROLICH, Elisabeth	6	f.			O.
28	60/62	BURRY, David	60	m.	Farmer	900/310	Sw.
29		Anna	63	f.	Wife		"
30		John	25	m.	Farm laborer		"
31		Rosina	21	f.	Domestic		"
32		Jacob	6	m.			O.
33		Elisabeth	4	f.			"
34		DIRRIG, Rosina	66	f.	Domestic	1400/220	Sw.
35	61/63	DIRRIG, Christian	67	m.	Farmer		"
36		Elisabeth	60	f.	Wife		"
37		Caroline	20	f.	Domestic		"
38		Peter	18	m.	Domestic		"
39		Mary	8/12	f.			O.

Page 10   17 July 1860   Sheet 325 verso

1		John	33	m.	Farmer		Sw.	
2	62/64	HENNY, Daniel	29	m.	Farmer	300/200	"	
3	63/65	SCHNEGG, Christian	69	m.	Farmer	2500/685	"	
4		Christian, Jr.	34	m.	Master Carpenter	/200	"	
5		Mary	33	f.	Wife		"	
6		Jacob	11	m.			O.	S
7		Samuel	10	m.			"	S
8		Luisa	9	f.			"	
9		William	7	m.			"	S
10		Elisabeth	6	f.			"	
11		Charlotta	5	f.			"	
12		Christian	3	m.			"	
13		John	1	m.			"	
14	64/66	FOX, Jacob	58	m.	Farmer	1500/1100	Wir.	
15		Jacob Jr.	25	m.	Farmer	/100	"	
16		Gottlieb	24	m.	Farm laborer		"	
17		Christoph	18	m.	child		"	
18		Johanna	32	f.	Domestic		"	
19	65/67	KUNZIG, Urs	67	m.	Farmer	3500/1000	Sw.	
20		Ann	58	f.	Wife		"	
21		Christian	35	m.	Domestic		"	
22		John	25	m.	Domestic		O.	
23	66/68	HARMANN, John	53	m.	Master Tailor	500/100	Bav.	
24		Johanna	44	f.	Wife		Sax.	
25		Johanna	16	f.	child		O.	
26		Mary	12	f.			"	S
27		Henry	5	m.			"	S
28	67/69	BIRKEY, John	34	m.	Farmer	500/300	Sw.	
29		Sachria	33	f.	Wife		O.	
30		Sarah M.	9	f.			"	S
31		John	6	m.			"	S

32		BIRKEY, Emely	2	f.		O.	
33	68/70	FISHER, Conrad	42	m.		200/300 H.D.	
34		Katharine	40	f.		"	
35		Caroline	15	f.		O.	
36		Katharine	11	f.		"	S
37		John	9	m.		"	S
38		Conrad	7	m.		"	S
39		Mary	4	f.		"	

<u>Page 11</u>   18 July 1860   <u>Sheet 326</u>

1		George	1	m.		O.	
2	69/71	ZANGGER, John	36	m.	Farmer	3000/1185	"
3		Presilla	27	f.	Wife		"
4		Luisa	7	f.			" S
5		Samuel	5	m.			" S
6		Harriet	4	f.			"
7		Anna	9/12	f.			"
8		Barbara	59	f.	Domestic		Sw.
9	70/72	KIMPBLE, John	44	m.	Steamboatman		
						1800/425	H.D.
10		Sophia	44	f.	Wife		"
11		John	15	m.			O. S
12		Henry	13	m.			Pa. S
13		Samuel	6	m.			O. S
14		Emeline	2	f.			"
15		Katarine	74	f.	Domestic		H.D.
16		HABERMEHL, Fried-					
		rick	27	m.	Artist	/200	"
17	71/73	WORKMAN, Amos	30	m.	Farmer	/450	O.
18		Caroline	27	f.	Wife		"
19		Alonzo	6	m.			"
20		William Jr.	28	m.	Farm laborer		"
21	72/74	TIDD, William	57	m.	Farmer	800/225	N.J.
22		Sarah	48	f.	Wife		"
23		Albert	23	m.	Farm laborer		O.
24		Alexander	19	m.	Farm laborer		"
25		Melissa	16	f.	child		" S
26		Henry	14	m.			" S
27		Richard	12	m.			" S
28		Isaac	9	m.			" S
29	73/75	WORKMAN, David	46	m.	Farmer	1500/850	"
30		Mary	49	f.	Wife		"
31		Elisabeth	20	f.	child		" S
32		Mary Ann	17	f.	child		" S
33		Lusinda	15	f.	child		" S
34		Margaret	12	f.			" S
35	74/76	KANZIG, Christian	32	m.	Day laborer		Sw.
36		Charlotta	28	f.	Wife		Pa.
37		John	6	m.			"
38		David	4	m.			O.

39		KANZIG, Emeline	2	f.			O.

1	75/77	DAVIS, Jacob	50	m.	Teacher	1500/490	O.	
2		Mary	45	f.	Wife		"	
3		Mary J.	20	f.	child		"	
4		Thomas	18	m.	child		"	S
5		Jane	16	f.	child		"	
6		Jacob	14	m.			"	S
7		Eliza	9	f.			"	S
8		John	6	m.			"	
9		William	4	m.			"	
10		CROSIER, Margaret	69	f.	Domestic		"	
11	76/78	MEEKER, Andrew	28	m.	Farmer	600/150	"	
12		Jane	65	f.	Domestic		Md.	
13		Sally	17	f.	Domestic		O.	
14		THOMAS, Nancy	7	f.	Domestic		"	
15	77/79	TRACY, Elisha	57	m.	Farmer	800/185	Pa.	
16		Mary	53	f.	Wife		Md.	
17		Samuel	25	m.	Farm laborer		O.	
18		Daniel	20	m.	child		"	
19		SNIDER, Mary E.	5	f.	Domestic		"	
20		James D.	3	m.	Domestic		"	
21	78/80	FOX, Nickolas	52	m.	Farmer	300/150	Bav.	
22		Elisabeth	51	f.	Wife		"	
23		Margaret	23	f.	child		"	
24		Jacob	14	m.			"	S
25		LINCH, Janey	10	f.	Domestic		Pa.	S
26	79/81	REIGSEGGER, Peter	50	m.	Farmer	2000/600	Sw.	
27		Lohuhemnrey	46	f.	Wife		O.	
28		Henry	20	m.	Teacher		"	
29		Levi	17	m.	Teacher		"	S
30		William	14	m.			"	S
31		John	12	m.			"	S
32		Luisa	10	f.			"	S
33		Rachel	8	f.			"	S
34		Emma	1	f.			"	
35	80/82	RUFF, Michael	59	m.	Farmer	600/225	Als.	
36		Margret	52	f.	Wife		"	
37		John	21	m.	child		O.	
38		George	15	m.	child		"	S
39		Jacob	10	m.			"	S

1		Emely	9	f.			O.	S
2	81/83	HIRTH, Phillip	37	m.	Farmer	800/125	Bav.	
3		Ann Barbera	34	f.	Wife		Sw.	
4		Luisa	9	f.			O.	S
5		Alexander	6	m.			"	S
6		Mary Ann	4	f.			"	S

7		HIRTH, Margeret	2	f.			O.	
8		Theodore	3/12	m.			"	
9	82/84	LAPP, George	45	m.	Farmer	2500/2485	Als.	
10		Elisabeth	38	f.	Wife		"	
11		Elisabeth Jr.	7	f.			O.	S
12		Mary	5	f.			"	
13		Samuel	3	m.			"	
14		Carolina	1	f.			"	
15		ELIGER, Edward	13	m.	Farm laborer		"	S
16	83/85	RUPP, Jacob	31	m.	Physician	/470	Sw.	
17		Elisabeth	26	f.	Wife		"	
18		Jas. Emil	2	m.			O.	
19	84/86	EYER, Louis	76	m.	Farmer	400/110	Als.	
20		Louis Jr.	40	m.	Farm laborer		"	
21		Elisabeth	33	f.	Wife		O.	
22		Martha Allen	4	f.			"	
23		Elisabeth	2	f.			"	
24		William H.	2/12	m.			"	
25	85/87	KREBS, Elisabeth	46	f.	Farmer	400/120	Sw.	
26		John	21	m.	Farm laborer		"	
27		Rosina	16	f.	child		O.	S
28		Mary Ann	11	f.			"	S
29		Carolina	8	f.			"	S
30		HARTMAN, John	4	m.			"	
31		LONG, John W.	2	m.			"	
32		Rosina	6/12	f.			"	
33	86/88	ROTH, John	36	m.	Farmer	1500/290	Sw.	
34		Mary	35	f.	Wife		"	
35		Mary J.	14	f.			O.	S
36		Rosina	12	f.			"	S
37		Friedrich	10	m.			"	S
38		Luisa	8	f.			"	S
39		John	7	m.			"	S

Page 14   21 July 1860   Sheet 327 verso

1		Henry	4	m.			O.	
2		Adolph	1	m.			"	
3	87/89	ROTH, Jacob	28	m.	Farmer	2000/465	Sw.	
4		Mary	22	f.	Wife		O.	
5		Ellen	1	f.			"	
6		A. Mary	42	f.	Domestic		"	
7		MULLET, Mary	13	f.	Domestic		"	S
8	88/90	ISALY, Christian	54	m.	Farmer	1800/500	Sw.	
9		Verena	50	f.	Wife		"	
10		Mary E.	32	f.	child		"	
11		John	30	m.	child		O.	
12		Salome	16	f.	child		"	S
13		Jacob	14	m.			"	S
14		Mary	12	f.			"	S
15		Josephine	10	f.			"	S

16		ISALY, Caroline	5	f.			O. S
17	89/91	SCHAFFER, George	55	m.	Farmer	2000/400	Wir.
18		Mary	47	f.	Wife		"
19		Barbary	19	f.	child		O.
20		Luisa	9	f.			" S
21		Ellen	3	f.			"
22		DETRICH, Friedrich	14	m.	Farm laborer	/50	Wir. S
23	90/92	AFFOLTER, Jacob	61	m.	Farmer	1500/100	Sw.
24		GROPP, Friederich					
		Mark	39	m.	Domestic		Han.
25		Charlotta	41	f.	domestic		"
26		KESERMAN, Jacob	40	m.	domestic		Sw.
27	91/93	YOST, William	57	m.	Farmer	2000/680	"
28		Mary	38	f.	Wife		"
29		John	16	m.	child		O. S
30		William	11	m.			" S
31		Caroline	6	f.			" S
32		Samuel	4	m.			"
33		Mary Ann	3/12	f.			"
34	92/94	BREITIGAM, Marger-et	67	m.	Farmer	800/70	Sax.
35		Henry	35	m.	Farm laborer		"
36		Christian H.	26	m.	Farm laborer		"
37	93/95	KELLER, Barbara	49	f.	Farmer	800/150	Sw.
38		Jacob	12	m.			O.
39	94/96	HEIGER, John W.	40	m.	Farmer	1800/422	Sw.

Page 15			21 July 1860				Sheet 328
1		Elisabeth	38	f.	Wife		Sw.
2		Elisabeth Jr.	15	f.			O. S
3		Samuel	10	m.			" S
4		Jacob	9	m.			" S
5		Adaline	7	f.			" S
6		Luisa	5	f.			" S
7		Edward	4	m.			"
8		Daniel	2	m.			"
9		Theophil	5/12	m.			"
10		William	5/12	m.			"
11	95/97	KAMPFER, Fried-erich	29	m.	Farmer	2500/380	"
12		Mary	28	f.	Wife		"
13		John W.	6	m.			" S
14		Mary L.	4	f.			"
15		Friederich	2	m.			"
16		Robert E.	1	m.			"
17		FRANZ, Gottlieb	16	m.	Farm laborer		"
18	96/98	ISALI, Eugen	24	m.	Farmer	800/135	"
19		Rosina	23	f.			"
20		Charles	1	m.			"

21	97/99	YENNI, John	60	m.	Teacher	1600/1000 Sw.	
22		Elisabeth	53	f.	Wife	"	
23		John	25	m.	child	O.	
24		Samuel	18	m.	child	"	S
25		Rosina	14	f.		"	
26		Julius	10	m.		"	S

27	98/100	REISER, John W.	50	m.	Master Cabinet-maker /200 Sw.	
28		Mary	52	f.	Wife	"
29		John	23	m.	Cabinet-maker	"
30		Samuel	14	m.		"	S
31		Charles	8	m.		"	S

32	99/101	TREIBER, Michael	51	m.	Master Shoemaker 700/230 Als.	
33		Katharine	46	f.	Wife	"
34		Jacob	20	m.	child	O.
35		Friederich	19	m.	child	"
36		Katharine	17	f.	child	"
37		Michael	16	m.	child	"	S
38		Henry	10	m.		"	S
39		John	9	m.		"	S

1		Luisa	8	f.		O.
2		Mary	4	f.		"

3	100/102	KIEFER, Henry	56	m.	Farmer	1800/325 Als.	
4		Mary	34	f.	Wife	Wir.	
5		Henry	17	m.	child	O.	S
6		Sophia	15	f.		"	
7		Friedericka	13	f.		"	
8		Friederich	12	m.		"	S
9		Rosina	10	f.		"	S
10		Christina	8	f.		"	S
11		Jacob	7	m.		"	S
12		Elisabeth	5	f.		"	
13		John	4	m.		"	
14		Samuel	2	m.		"	

15	101/103	LAPP, Michael	46	m.	Farmer	3000/1095 Als.	
16		Elisabeth	44	f.	Wife	Sw.	
17		John	20	m.	child	O.	
18		Mary	18	f.	child	"	
19		Michael	16	m.	child	"	S
20		Henry	13	m.		"	S
21		Elisabeth	9	f.		"	S
22		George	7	m.		"	S
23		Luisa	4	f.		"	

24	102/104	FANKHOUSER, Nicko-las	58	m.	Farmer	1700/385 Sw.	
25		Anna	47	f.	Wife	"	
26		Daniel	22	m.	child	O.	
27		John W.	21	m.	child	"	

28		FANKHOUSER, Sam-					
		uel A.	19	m.	child		O.
29		Joseph A.	17	m.	child		" S
30		Friederich F.	16	m.	child		" S
31		Christian T.	14	m.			" S
32		Charles L.	12	m.			" S
33		Jacob Aug.	10	m.			" S
34		Elisabeth R.	5	f.			"
35		Anna	43	f.	Domestic		Sw.
36	103/105	MEHL, George	56	m.	Farmer	2000/700	Als.
37		Elisabeth	48	f.	Wife		"
38		George	25	m.	child		"
39		Katharine	23	f.	child		"

Page 17   24 July 1860   Sheet 329

1		Mary	16	f.			O.
2		Caroline	14	f.			" S
3		Charles	12	m.			" S
4		Friederich	10	m.			" S
5	104/106	HUGI, Jacob	41	m.	Farmer	1600/350	Sw.
6		Rachel	41	f.	Wife		Ind.
7		Mary	6	f.			O. S
8		John	5	m.			" S
9		Louis	3	m.			"
10		Caroline	1	f.			"
11	105/107	MILLER, Jacob Jr.	29	m.	Farmer	900/180	Bav.
12		Sophia	30	f.	Wife		Als.
13		John J.	4	m.			O.
14		Elisabeth	2	f.			"
15	106/108	BECK, Mary	67	f.	Farmer	1200/320	Sw.
16		Charles	23	m.	Steamboatman		"
17		Theophil	18	m.	Farm laborer		"
18		Rudolf	16	m.	Farm laborer		"
19		STILLA, Mary	14	f.	Domestic		"
20	107/109	LAMNERZOLL, John	33	m.	Farmer	1800/230	Sax.
21		Margeret	28	f.	Wife		H.D.
22	108/110	STRAUCH, John	44	m.	Farmer	1800/375	"
23		Mary	40	f.	Wife		"
24		Katharine	16	f.	child		O.
25		John	14	m.			" S
26		Henry	11	m.			" S
27	109/111	GRAPLY, Andrew	24	m.	Minister, Meth. P.	/110	Bad.
28		Mary A..	24	f.	Wife		O.
29		Susanna C.	1	f.			"
30	110/112	BLETTLER, Jacob	62	m.	Farmer	1200/320	Sw.
31		Christian	19	m.	child		O.
32		Elisabeth	18	f.	child		"
33		Luisa	16	f.	child		" S

34		BLETTLER, Frieder-					
		ich	13	m.		O.	S
35		Mary A.	5	f.		"	S
36	111/113	KINDELBERGER, Fried-					
		erich	57	m.	Farmer	1600/1430 Bav.	
37		Margeretta	56	f.	Wife	"	
38	112/114	HUBACHER, Nickolas	37	m.	Farmer	Sw.	
39		Anne Mary	38	f.	Wife	Als.	

Page 18   24 July 1860   Sheet 329 verso

1		Elisabeth	16	f.	child	O.	
2		Mary	15	f.		"	S
3		Luisa	13	f.		"	S
4		Lina	11	f.		"	S
5		Samuel	10	m.		"	S
6		John	8	m.		"	
7		Charles	6	m.		"	
8		Caroline	3	f.		"	
9		George W.	10/12	m.		"	
10		Nickolas Sr.	73	m.	Domestic	Sw.	
11		Elisabeth	73	f.	Domestic	"	
12	113/115	SCHLAPBACH, Peter	51	m.	Master Weaver		
					200/30	"	
13		Elisabeth	46	f.	Wife	"	
14		Wilhelmina	21	f.	child	O.	
15		David	17	m.	child	"	S
16		John	13	m.		"	S
17		Amalia	9	f.		"	
18		Jacob	4	m.		"	
19		David	2	m.		"	
20	114/116	DANKWERTH, Charles	48	m.	Farmer	3500/595 Han.	
21		Christina	50	f.	Wife		
22		Emelia	19	f.	child	Va.	M
23		FORNEY, John	25	m.	Farm laborer	O.	M
24		DANKWERTH, Charles	14	m.		Va.	S
25		Christina	12	f.		"	S
26		Henry	10	m.		"	S
27		HANKEY, William	15	m.	Farm laborer	"	S
28	115/117	YENNI, Friederich	32	m.	Farmer	1500/270 Sw.	
29		Rosina	33	f.	Wife	O.	
30		Daniel	9	m.		"	S
31		Mary E.	6	f.		"	S
32		Luisa	4	f.		"	
33		Caroline	3	f.		"	
34		Rosina	1	f.		"	
35	116/118	MILLER, Jacob Sr.	63	m.	Farmer	1200/260 Bav.	
36		Rosina	65	f.	Wife	"	
37		Philip	26	m.	Farm laborer	"	
38		Eliza	22	f.	Farm laborer	H.K.	
39		Christina	36	f.	Domestic	Bav.	

Page 19					25 July 1860			Sheet 330

1	117/119	BAY, Bernhard	64	m.	Farmer	1500/205	Als.	
2		Magdelena	62	f.	Wife		"	
3		Phillip	19	m.	child		"	
4		Luisa	27	f.	Domestic		"	
5		BAUER, Elisabeth	4	f.			O.	
6	118/120	SCHAFER, Frieder-						
		ich	23	m.	Farmer	1700/215	Wir.	
7		Elisabeth	25	f.	Wife		O.	
8		Theodore	6	m.			"	S
9		Edward	3	m.			"	
10		AFFOLTER, Mary	66	f.	Domestic		Sw.	
11	119/121	LEIFER, Philip	43	m.	Farmer	1500/500	Als.	
12		Salome	40	f.	Wife		"	
13		Phillip	19	m.	child		O.	S
14		Henry	17	m.	child		"	S
15		E. William	15	m.			"	S
16		Elisabeth	7	f.			"	
17		Caroline	4	f.			"	
18		Mary	2	f.			"	
19	120/122	BERGER, John	64	m.	Farmer	600/175	Sw.	
20		Katharine	59	f.	Wife		"	
21		BUHLMAN, Mary	4	f.			"	
22	121/123	BORN, Mary	69	f.		/1000	Sw.	
23		KESERMAN, Mary	68	f.		/1000	"	
24	122/124	RIST, George	36	m.	Master Carpenter/50		Bad.	
25		Ann Mary	37	f.	Wife		"	
26		George	12	m.			"	
27		Elisabeth	8	f.			"	S
28		Caroline	1	f.			O.	
29		Christina	15	f.			Bad.	
30	123/125	LOEB, Christian	66	m.	Farmer	1500/570	Wir.	
31		Darothea	65	f.	Wife		O.	
32		Adam	21	m.	Farm laborer		"	
33	124/126	LOEB, John	30	m.	Cabinet-maker	/1300	Wir.	
34		Rosina	21	f.	Wife		O.	
35		William	1	m.			"	
36	125/127	BOLTZ, Christian	55	m.	Farmer	3500/685	Pr.	
37		Christina	47	f.	Wife		"	
38		William	22	m.	child		Pa.	
39		Louis	21	m.	child		"	

Page 20					25 July 1860			Sheet 330 verso

1		Katharine	17	f.	child		O.	
2		Caroline	4	f.			"	
3	126/128	WALTER, Friederich	47	m.	Farmer	1800/650	Als.	
4		Margeret	43	f.	Wife		Pr.	

5		WALTER, Friederich	16	m.	child		O.	S
6		Luisa	14	f.			"	S
7		Jacob	12	m.			"	S
8		Michael	3	m.			"	
9	127/129	KOCHER, Jacob	30	m.	Farmer	/75	Sw.	
10		Mary J.	29	f.	Wife		O.	
11		William	14	m.			"	S
12		David	12	m.			"	S
13		Philip	10	m.			"	
14		Elisabeth	7	f.			"	
15		Robert L.	5	m.			"	
16		John W.	4	m.			"	
17	128/130	DAVIS, Michel	57	m.	Farmer	5000/500	Va.	
18		Clarinda	52	f.	Wife		"	
19		James	28	m.	Boatman	/300	O.	
20		William	26	m.	Boatman		"	
21		Emely J.	23	f.	child		"	S
22		Louisiana	19	f.	child		"	S
23		Leonore	14	f.			"	S
24		Michal	11	m.			"	S
25	129/131	BARBERET, Ignaz	47	m.	Farmer	5000/500	Bav.	
26		Katharina	39	f.	Wife		"	
27		John	33	m.	child		Va.	
28		Michel	20	m.	child		"	
29		Johanna	17	f.	child		"	
30		Nickolas	14	m.			"	S
31		Eunis	11	f.			"	S
32		Mary	8	f.			"	S
33		Eliza	6	f.			"	
34		George	4	m.			"	
35		Emma	2	f.			"	
36	130/132	WYKERT, H. J.	45	m.	Farmer	600/250	Va.	
37		July	43	f.	Wife		"	
38		Elisabeth J.	17	f.	child		"	
39		Nancy Ann	16	f.	child		"	

1		Thomas B.	14	m.			O.	S
2		Francis E.	12	m.			"	S
3		Rachel	9	f.			"	S
4		Clerinda	1	f.			"	
5	131/133	BOSTON, W. L.	30	m.	Teacher	/200	O.	
6		Sarah	30	f.	Wife		"	
7		Lucinda	8	f.			"	S
8		Charlotta	4	f.			"	
9		William	2	m.			"	
10	132/135	KIRKBRIDE, Mar-						
		garet	45	f.	Farmer	1200/170	Ire.	
11		Cornelius	27	m.	child		O.	
12		Katharina	25	f.	child		"	
13		Clerinda	23	f.	child		"	

14		KIRKBRIDE, Mathias	21	m.	child	O.	
15		Rosa	18	f.	child	"	
16		Thomas	12	m.		"	S
17		Mary	10	f.		"	S
18		George W.	7	m.		"	
19		McTAGE, Stephen	89	m.	Domestic	Ire.	
20	133/135	KREBS, Anna	65	f.	Farmer	2500/450	Sw.
21		Christian	40	m.	Farm laborer		"
22		Samuel	23	m.	Farm laborer	O.	
23		Charlotta	21	f.	child	"	
24		Mary	18	f.	child	"	
25		DAVIS, Lee	8	m.		"	S
26		BLARE, George	22	m.	Steamboatman	"	
27		Margaret O.	5/12	f.		"	
28	134/136	LORENZ, Michael	50	m.	Farmer	2500/650	Als.
29		Magdelena	45	f.	Wife		"
30		Michael	22	m.	child	O.	
31		Friederich	21	m.	child	"	S
32		Magdelena Jr.	19	f.	child	"	S
33		Henry	18	m.	child	"	S
34		Elisabeth	14	f.		"	S
35		John	3	m.		"	
36	135/137	STEPHEN, Frieder-ich	65	m.	Farmer	1500/225	Als.
37		Elisabeth	67	f.	Wife		"
38		Henry	34	m.	child	/200	"
39		John	33	m.	child	O.	

Page 22			26 July 1860			Sheet 331 verso	
1		Friederich	23	m.	Farm laborer	O.	
2		Sarah	21	f.	child	"	
3		RUBI, Mary	22	f.	Domestic	"	
4		Mary A.	10/12	f.		"	
5		John F.	10/12	m.		"	
6	136/138	LOEB, Mathias	44	m.	Farmer	1500/500	Wir.
7		Dorothea	37	f.	Wife		"
8		Fridericka	16	f.	child	O.	S
9		Mary	13	f.		"	S
10		Katharine	9	f.		"	S
11		Margareta	9	f.		"	S
12		Charles	5	m.		"	
13		Luisa	3	f.		"	
14	137/139	BEISER, Adam	40	m.	Farmer	1000/655	Wir.
15		Barbara	41	f.	Wife		"
16	138/140	BEISER, Godfried	68	m.	Vine Gardener	/400	"
17		Sophia	69	f.	Vine Gardener		"
18	139/141	LEIFER, Magdelena	68	f.	Farmer	800/300	Als.
19	140/142	HOFFMAN, Henry	58	m.	Farmer	1200/320	Bay.
20		Elisabeth	46	f.	Wife		"

21		HOFFMAN, Elisabeth				
		Jr.	20	f.	child	Bav.
22		Friederich	11	m.		O. S
23		Louis	9	m.		" S
24		Mary K.	7	f.		" S
25		FRIEDERICH, Magde-				
		lena	2	f.		Va.
26		RAUCH, Jacob	80	m.	Domestic	Bav.
27	141/143	WINGERTER, Jacob	46	m.	Farmer	1600/400 Bav.
28		Katharine	41	f.	Wife	Wir.
29		Luisa	11	f.		Va. S
30		Gustavus	9	m.		" S
31		Hermann	6	m.		" S
32		Eliza	4	f.		O.
33		Melinda	3/12	f.		"
34.		Jerome	11	m.	Farm laborer	Va. S
35	142/144	KELLER, Jacob	40	m.	Farmer	/200 Sw.
36		Katharine	40	f.	Wife	Wir.
37		Katharine Jr.	4	f.		O.
38		John Jas.	2	m.		"
39	143/145	KOCHER, Alexander	31	m.	Farmer	/295 "

Page 23			27 July 1860			Sheet 332
1		Huldah	29	f.	Wife	O.
2		Mary Ann	9	f.		" S
3		Luisa	7	f.		" S
4		Sally	6	f.		" S
5		Caroline	4	f.		"
6		Elisabeth	1	f.		"
7	144/146	BLARE, Huldah	54	f.	Farming	1000/30 "
8		James	32	m.	child	"
9		SMITH, Thomas	33	m.	Day laborer	"
10		BLARE, Oliver	21	m.	Steamboatman	"
11	145/147	BLETTLER, Emanuel	25	m.	Farmer	2000/260 "
12		Mary	21	f.	Wife	"
13		Delary J.	1	f.		"
14		John W.	10	m.		" S
15		Sary	4	f.		"
16	146/148	SMITH, Thomas	53	m.	Farmer	1500/230 "
17		Experience	47	f.	Wife	"
18		Huldah	14	f.		" S
19		Jefferson	10	m.		"
20		George	4	m.		"
21	147/149	STILLA, William	62	m.	Farmer	1600/250 Pr.
22		Elisabeth	44	f.	Wife	Sw.
23		John	19	m.	child	O. S
24		Mary	17	f.	child	"
25		Julius	14	m.		" S
26		Theodore	10	m.		" S

27	148/150	ROTH, John W. Jr.	35	m.	Farmer	1600/360	Sw.
28		Rosina	33	f.	Wife		Wir.
29		Mary	11	f.			O.
30		Rosina	9	f.			"
31		Elisabeth	6	f.			"
32		Caroline	4	f.			"

33	149/151	BAUER, Joseph	33	m.	Farmer	1500/245	Bad.	
34		Theresia	34	f.	Wife		"	
35		Joseph	10	m.			O.	S
36		Elisabeth	7	f.			"	S
37		William	5	m.			"	
38		Carolina	3	f.			"	
39		Theresia	6/12	f.			"	

Page 24   **27 July 1860**   **Sheet 332 verso**

1		Elisabeth	70	f.	Domestic		Bad.
2		Leonhard	60	m.	Farm laborer		"

3	150/152	STEILE, Casper	39	m.	Farmer	600/180	Wir.	
4		Magdelena	38	f.	Wife		"	
5		Lorenz	9	m.			O.	S
6		Christian	8	m.			"	S
7		Katharine	5	f.			"	S
8		Paulina	4	f.			"	
9		Ameline	3/12	f.			"	

10	151/153	ROTH, John	30	m.	Farmer	3000/325	Sw.
11		Friedericka	24	f.	Wife		Wir.
12		Christian	1	m.			O.
13		William	10/12	m.			"

14	152/154	ROTH, John W. Sr.	70	m.	Farmer	/400	Sw.
15		Katharine	65	f.	Wife		"
16		FOX, Barbara	11	f.	Domestic		Wir.
17		BECKER, Theophil	21	m.	Domestic		Bad.

18	153/155	SOLLAND, John	45	m.	Farmer	50/25	Sw.

19	154/156	WOLF, Rudolf	39	m.	Farmer	250/105	"
20		Anna B.	52	f.	Wife		"
21		Magdelena	3	f.			O.

22	155/157	BEIELER, John	49	m.	Farmer	300/300	Sw.

23	156/158	LEHMAN, Anna	55	f.	Farming	400/200	"
24		John	24	m.	Farm laborer		O.
25		Jacob	17	m.	Farm laborer		"
26		Mary	83	f.	Domestic		Sw.

27	157/159	STALETER, Peter	66	m.	Farmer	200/65	"
28		Katharina	65	f.	Wife		"

29	158/160	RABEL, Friedericka	55	f.	Farming	1500/250	Wir.
30		Luisa	23	f.	child		"
31		Adam	20	m.	child		O.

32		RABEL, Fredericka	15	f.		O. S
33		William	10	m.		" S
34		Caroline	6	f.		" S
35	159/161	BORRER, Katharina	63	f.	Farming 1200/200	Sw.
36		RABEL, Christian	32	m.	Farm laborer	Wir.
37		Carolina	28	f.	Wife	Sw.
38		Emmanuel	5	m.		O.
39		John	2	m.		"

Page 25   28 July 1860   Sheet 333

1		Katharine	3/12	f.		O.
2	160/162	GEER, Jonathon	48	m.	Farmer /40	Va.
3		Rebecca	48	f.	Wife	"
4		Charles	24	m.	child	"
5		Elisabeth	23	f.	child	"
6		Alexander	17	m.	child	"
7		James	13	m.		"
8		William	21	m.	Day laborer	"
9		Richard	19	m.	Day laborer	"
10		Martin	16	m.	Day laborer	"
11		Thomas	14	m.		"
12		STEWARD, Clerissa	15	f.	Domestic	"
13		Rebecca	16	f.	Domestic	"
14	161/163	MORELAND, Clarkston	47	m.	Master Carpenter /50	N.Y. M
15		Ann	41	f.	Wife	Eng. M
16		KINNY, Elisabeth J.	21	f.	child	Pa.
17		E. Isreal	19	m.	child	"
18		Mary K.	17	m.	child	Va.
19		Prissilla	9	f.		O.
20		Margaret A.	4	f.		"
21	162/164	HARRIS, John	67	m.	Farmer 4000/365	Va.
22		Drewsilla	60	f.	Wife	O.
23		Thomas	27	m.	Teacher	Va. S
24		Leonavis	20	f.	child	" S
25		Franklin	17	m.	child	" S
26		Millisa	13	f.		" S
27		Octaviana	10	f.		"
28	163/165	NEIHARD, Jacob	67	m.	Farm laborer /50	Bav.
29		Margaret	40	f.	Wife	O.
30		John	18	f.	child	"
31		Luisa	12	f.		" S
32		Jacob	10	m.		" S
33		Mary Ann	9	f.		" S
34		Henry	8	m.		" S
35		Caroline	6	f.		"
36		Margaret Ann	4	f.		"
37	164/166	BROWN, Isaac	57	m.	Farmer /120	"

38		BROWN, Abel	27	m.	child	O.
39		William	23	m.	child	"

1		Robert	21	m.		O.	
2		Lidy Ann	15	f.		"	
3		Barbary J.	15	f.		"	
4	165/167	BROWN, George	33	m.	Farmer	1050/285	"
5		Mary	31	f.	Wife	Va.	
6		Orleth	12	m.		O.	S
7		Leander	10	m.		"	S
8		Robert G.	8	m.		"	S
9		Barbary L.	7	f.		"	S
10		Nancy J.	5	f.		Ind.	
11		Adaline	4	f.		O.	
12		Rachel T.	3	f.		"	
13		Albert G.	1	m.		"	
14	166/168	FANKHOUSER, Jacob	27	m.	Farmer	/60	"
15		Mary	23	f.	Wife		"
16		William	5	m.			"
17		Mary B.	2	f.			"
18	167/169	ZINGG, Felix	30	m.	Farmer	1400/1300	Sw.
19		Elisabeth	31	f.	Wife		"
20		John A.	5	m.			O.
21		Mary L.	2	f.			"
22		Caroline	6/12	f.			"
23		Mary	72	f.	Domestic	/1000	Sw.
24	168/170	ZINGG, John W.	41	m.	Farmer	3500/500	"
25		Magdalena	34	f.	Wife		Fr.
26		Edward	13	m.			O. S
27		William	9	m.			" S
28		Charles	5	m.			"
29		Rosa	4	f.			"
30		Henry	5/12	m.			"
31	169/171	WHITE, William	25	m.	Farmer	1800/345	"
32		Nickolas	35	m.	Farm laborer	/100	Sw.
33		Jacob	28	m.	Farm laborer	/100	"
34		Rosina	32	f.	Domestic		"
35		Daniel	6	m.			O.
36		Oddy	5	m.			"
37		Barbara	65	f.	Domestic		Sw.
38	170/172	STEPHENS, Solome	61	f.		/2000	Als.
39	171/173	FANKHOUSER, John	33	m.	Farmer	600/355	O.

1		Elisabeth	28	f.	Wife	O.
2		Caroline	6	f.		"
3		William	3	m.		"

4		FANKHOUSER, Charles 1		m.			O.	

5	172/174	LEHMAN, John	53	m.	Farmer	300/230	Sw.	
6		Elisabeth	52	f.	Wife		"	
7		Charles	25	m.	child		"	
8		Friederich	21	m.	child		O.	
9		Gottlieb	20	m.	child		"	
10		Luisa	16	f.	child		"	S

11	173/175	FANKHOUSER, Mary	65	f.	Farming	1000/130	Sw.	
12		Arnold	24	m.	child		O.	
13		Friederich	34	m.	Farm laborer	/400	"	
14		WHITE, Mary L.	13	f.	Domestic		"	

15	174/176	FANKHOUSER, Samuel	38	m.	Farmer	1600/315	"	
16		Mary	32	f.	Wife		Sw.	
17		Caroline	8	f.			O.	S
18		Mary	6	f.			"	S
19		Samuel	4	m.			"	
20		Luisa	3	f.			"	
21		Paulina	2	f.			"	
22		Elisabeth	4/12	f.			"	

23	175/177	NIPPERT, Eva	72	m.	Farming	1800/650	Als.	
24		Friederich	30	m.	Farm laborer		"	
25		Elisabeth	27	f.	Wife		Bav.	
26		Jacob A.	6	m.			O.	S
27		Elisabeth	5	f.			"	S
28		Mary	4	f.			"	
29		Charles	2	m.			"	
30		George	6/12	m.			"	

31	176/178	WALTER, Nickolas	52	m.	Farmer	1800/2400	Sw.	
32		Mary	39	f.	Wife		"	
33		Elisabeth	15	f.			O.	S
34		Mary Ann	13	f.			"	S
35		Christian	12	m.			"	S
36		Nickolas	8	m.			"	S
37		Mary	8	f.			"	S
38		John	8	m.			"	S
39		Caroline	6	f.				

Page 28   30 July 1860   Sheet 334 verso

1		Samuel	3	m.			O.	
2		William	1	m.			"	
3		FLURY, Joseph	60	m.	Domestic	/300	Sw.	
4		BANDI, Nickolas	45	m.	Master Mason	/100	"	

5	177/179	HESSIG, Jacob	57	m.	Farmer	1000/75	"	
6		Elisabeth	46	f.	Wife		Als.	
7		Caroline	7	f.			O.	S
8		Magdelena	5	f.			"	
9		Luisa	2	f.			"	
10		Margaret	3/12	f.			"	

11	178/180	SCHROTER, Fried-erich	38	m.	Farmer	1600/185	Pr.	

			Name	Age	Sex		Value	
12			SCHROTER, Katharine	37	f.	Wife		Sw.
13			John	17	m.	child		O.
14			Elisabeth	15	f.			" S
15			Luisa	13	f.			" S
16			Rosina	10	f.			" S
17			Charles	4	m.			"
18			Paulina	2	f.			"
19			Katharine	5/12	f.			"
20	179/181	BIGLER, John		27	m.	Farmer	1000/280	"
21			Ann Eliza	24	f.	Wife		Sw.
22			Alexander	11	m.			O. S
23			Paulina	9	f.			" S
24			John	7	m.			" S
25			Charles	5	m.			"
26			Charlotta	2	f.			"
27			Magdelena	37	f.	Domestic		Sw.
28	180/182	BIGLER, Christian Jr.	36	m.	Farmer	600/205	"
29			Elisabeth	27	f.	Wife		"
30			Friederich	10	m.			O. S
31			Caroline	9	f.			" S
32			Mary Ann	8	f.			" S
33			Rosina	6	f.			" S
34			Jacob	5	m.			"
35			William	3	m.			"
36			Daniel	1	m.			"
37	181/183	FANKHOUSER, Sophia	62	f.	Farming	1500/345	Sw.
38			Luisa	31	f.	Domestic	/100	O.
39			Friederich	21	m.	Domestic		"

Page 29		31 July 1860					Sheet 335
1		Charlotta	20	f.			O.
2		Magdelena	17	f.			"
3		Phillip	14	m.			" S
4	182/184	BIGLER, Christian	64	m.	Farmer	2000/345	Sw.
5		Mary Ann	52	f.	Wife		"
6		Luisa	23	f.	Domestic		O.
7		Godfried	21	m.	child		"
8		Elisabeth	19	f.	child		"
9		Caroline	16	f.	child		" S
10		Samuel	15	m.			" S
11	183/185	SCHMALZ, Friederich	45	m.	Farmer	450/200	Sw.
12		Mary Ann	40	f.	Wife		"
13		Rosina	17	f.	child		O. S
14		Mary	14	f.			" S
15		Friederich	11	m.			" S
16		Margaret	4	f.			"
17		John	4/12	m.			"
18	184/186	WALTER, Henry	41	m.	Farmer	1700/485	Als.

19		WALTER, Mary C.	40	f.	Wife		Als.	
20		Mary	9	f.			O.	S
21		Luisa	6	f.			"	S
22		Friederich	4	m.			"	
23		Henry	2	m.			"	
24		Darotha	73	f.	Domestic	/50	Als.	
25	185/187	ANSHUTZ, Peter	61	m.	Farmer	1500/305	"	
26		Magdelena	54	f.	Wife		Sw.	
27		Luisa	21	f.	child		Va.	
28		Phillip	18	m.	child		O.	
29		Rebecca	16	f.	child		"	
30		Jacob	13	m.			"	S
31	186/188	BLARE, James	55	m.	Farmer	1000/140	Va.	
32		Experiance	22	f.	child		O.	
33		Wilson	19	m.	child		"	
34		James	17	m.	child		"	
35		FANKHOUSER, Margaret	18	f.	Domestic		"	
36	187/189	BANDI, Nickolas	45	m.	Farmer	700/400	Sw.	
37		Barbara	38	f.	Wife		Bav.	
38		Luisa	7	f.			O.	S
39		Friederich	5	m.			"	S

Page 30   1 August 1860   Sheet 335 verso

1		Emely	2	f.			O.	
2		Carolina	6/12	f.			"	
3		DESQUE, Friederich	78	m.	Domestic		Bav.	
4	188/190	WEISGERBER, Ferdinand	42	m.	Minister, Ger. Evang. /50		Sax.	
5		Carolina	26	f.	Wife		Han.	
6		Henry	6	m.			Ind.	S
7		August	4	m.			"	
8		Luisa	1	f.			O.	
9	189/191	RUCHTZ, Samuel	51	m.	Master Tailor 150/200		Sw.	
10		Mary	56	f.	Wife		"	
11		Elisabeth	21	f.	Domestic		Pa.	
12		Sarah	20	f.	Domestic		"	
13		Mary	9	f.			O.	S
14		Mary Magdelin	3	f.			"	
15	190/192	WINZENRIED, Samuel	40	m.	Farmer	1600/800	Sw.	
16		Ann Barbara	39	f.	Wife		"	
17		Luisa	8	f.			O.	S
18		Carolina	7	f.			"	S'
19		Mary Ann	6	f.			"	S
20		Charles	4	m.			"	
21		Friederich	2	m.			"	
22		Samuel	8/12	m.			"	

23		WINZENRIED, John	50	m.	Domestic	/200	Sw.	
24		Anna	49	f.	Domestic		"	
25	191/193	URBAN, Jacob	43	m.	Farmer	800/125	Als.	
26		Anna	39	f.	Wife		Sw.	
27		Jacob	19	m.	child		O.	
28		Margaret	17	f.	child		"	
29		John	16	m.	child		"	S
30		Samuel	15	m.			"	S
31		Lina	13	f.			"	S
32		Mary	11	f.			"	S
33		Elisabeth	8	f.			"	S
34		Sophia	6	f.			"	S
35		Silma	2	f.			"	
36		August	1	m.			"	
37	192/194	LAGINBUHL, John	62	m.	Farmer	300/200	Sw.	
38		Mary Ann	59	f.	Wife		"	
39	193/195	GRALL, Henry	41	m.	Farmer	1800/215	Als.	

Page 31   2 August 1860   Sheet 336

1		Eva	42	f.	Wife	Als.	
2		Elisabeth	19	f.	child	O.	
3		Magdelane	18	f.	child	"	
4		Luisa	16	f.	child	"	
5		Caroline	15	f.		"	S
6		Salome	13	f.		"	S
7		Charlotta	11	f.		"	S
8		Eva	9	f.		"	S
9		Henry	7	m.		"	S
10		August	4	m.		"	S
11		Charles	2	m.		"	
12		Henry Friederich	1	m.		"	
13		George	5	m.		"	
14	194/196	NICKLAUS, Friederich	46	m.	Farmer	1500/150	Bav.	
15		Rachel	43	f.	Wife		"	
16		Friederich	17	m.	child		N.Y.	S
17		Henry	15	m.			"	S
18		Louis	14	m.			"	S
19		Valentine	12	m.			O.	S
20		John	9	m.			"	S
21		Luisa	8	f.			"	S
22		Katharine	5	f.			"	
23		George	3	m.			"	
24		PFEFFER, Friederich	77	m.	Domestic	/50	Bav.	
25	195/197	ZIMMERLY, Jacob	55	m.	Farmer	1000/200	Sw.	
26		Elisabeth	50	f.	Wife		Bav.	
27		Julianna	20	f.	child		O.	
28		Jacob	18	m.	child		"	
29		Phillip	16	m.	child		"	S
30		Elisabeth	14	f.			"	S

31		ZIMMERLY, Carolina	12	f.			O.	S
32		Luisa	10	f.			"	S
33	196/198	KOCHER, Rudolf	33	m.	Farmer	800/215	"	
34		Huldah	31	f.	Wife		"	
35		John	15	m.			"	S
36		Alexander	12	m.			"	S
37		Christian	9	m.			"	S
38		Mary	7	f.			"	S
39		Isaac	6	m.			"	

Page 32   3 August 1860   **Sheet 336 verso**

1		Andy	4	m.			O.	
2		Samuel	2	m.			"	
3	197/199	WOLF, Henry	64	m.	Farmer	/86	H.D.	
4		Mary	64	f.	Wife		"	
5		KANZIG, Mary	6	f.	Domestic		O.	
6	198/200	KUNZIG, Urs Jr.	41	m.	Farmer	/220	Sw.	
7		Elisabeth	42	f.	Wife		"	
8		Jacob	8	m.			O.	S
9		Caroline	6	f.			"	
10		Charles	4	m.			"	
11		Elisabeth	2	f.			"	
12	199/201	BAUER, Adam	45	m.	Farmer	500/156	H.D.	
13		Sarah	40	f.	Wife		Sw.	
14		Barbara	12	f.			O.	S
15		Daniel	10	m.			"	S
16	200/202	STAUFER, David	47	m.	Farmer	550/180	Sw.	
17		Anna	33	f.	Wife		"	
18		Samuel	7	m.				
19		Carolina	3	f.			O.	
20		Godfried	6/12	m.			"	
21	201/203	ZESSIGER, John	37	m.	Farmer	1800/385	Sw.	
22		Elisabeth	36	f.	Wife		"	
23		Friederich	14	m.			O.	S
24		Charles	13	m.			"	S
25		Caroline	12	f.			"	S
26		Elisabeth	10	f.			"	S
27		Luisa	9	f.			"	S
28		John	7	m.			"	S
29		Rudolf	6	m.			"	S
30		Jacob	4	m.			"	
31		William	2	m.			"	
32		Charlotta	5/12	f.			"	
33	202/204	KELLER, Christian	80	m.	Farmer	200/100	Sw.	
34		Katharine	71	f.	Wife		"	
35		John	14	m.			O.	
36	203/205	KELLER, Margaret	61	f.	Farmer	300/200	Sw.	
37		Edward	9	m.			O.	

```
38 204/206 HARDY, Rudolf        70  m.    Farmer      300/300  Sw.
39         Mary                 65  f.                          "
```

```
1  205/207 LEMLY, George        36  m.    Farmer      1500/400 O.
2          Rebecca              25  f.    Wife                  "
3          John R.               2  m.                          "

4  206/208 LEMLY, Robert        65  m.    Farmer      3000/650 Pa.
5          Jane                 56  f.    Wife                 Va.
6          Barbara              21  f.    child                O.
7          Lusinda              18  f.    child                 "
8          Jane                 16  f.    child                 "    S
9          Sarah                14  f.    child                 "    S
10         Peter Sr.            50  m.    Domestic       /600   "
11         Peter Jr.            25  m.    Farm laborer          "

12 207/209 FREIDIGER, John      52  m.    Farmer       200/1395 Sw.
13         Elisabeth            55  f.    Wife                  "
14         Jacob                25  m.    Farm laborer         O.
15         Mary Ann             21  f.    child                 "
16         Luisa                21  f.    child                 "
17         Ferena               18  f.    child                 "
18         Julyan               16  f.    child                 "    S
19         Samuel               14  m.                          "    S
20         Diana                10  f.                          "    S
21         LEIBUNDGUT, Ulrich   80  m.    Domestic       /50   Sw.

22 208/210 FARNEY, Macaabi      60  m.    Farmer      1600/470  "
23         Margeretta           45  f.    Wife                 Bav.
24         John                 25  m.    Farm laborer         O.
25         Mary                 20  f.    child                 "
26         Catharine            18  f.    child                 "
27         Luisa                16  f.    child                 "
28         Charles              14  m.                          "    S
29         Rosa                 12  f.                          "    S
30         Caroline             10  f.                          "    S
31         Eliza                 7  f.                          "    S
32         Jacob                 3  m.                          "
33         Charlotta             2  f.                          "

34 209/211 DOTAN, Charles       60  m.    Farmer      1600/520 Sw.
35         Mary                 51  f.    Wife                Wir.
36         Charles Jacob        23  m.    Farm laborer         O.
37         John                 21  m.    Farm laborer          "
38         Mary                 17  f.    child                 "
39         William              12  m.                          "    S
```

```
1          Caroline             10  f.                         O.

2  210/212 DOTAN, Charles Jr.   25  m.                          "
3          Johanna              20  f.                          "
4          George W.             1  m.                          "

5  211/213 LUTHY, Christian     55  m.    Farmer      1500/600 Sw.
```

6		LUTHY, Rosina	50	f.	Wife		Sw.
7		Luisa	20	f.	child		O.
8		Rosa	18	f.	child		"
9		Elisabeth	16	f.	child		" S
10		Caroline	14	f.			" S
11		Mary	12	f.			" S
12		Samuel	8	m.			" S
13		Emily	5	f.			" S
14		William	3	m.			"

15	212/214	SHINDLER, Chris-tian	41	m.	Farmer	1800/260	Sw.
16		Elisabeth	46	f.	Wife		"
17		Elisabeth Jr.	24	f.	child		O.
18		Mary Ann	22	f.	child		"
19		Luisa	21	f.	child		"
20		John	17	m.	child		"
21		Rosina	16	f.	child		"
22		Samuel	15	m.			" S
23		Charlotta	14	f.			" S
24		Christian	11	m.			" S
25		Katharine	9	f.			" S
26		Jacob	7	m.			" S
27		Paulina	4	f.			"

28	213/215	MEYER, Jacob	69	m.	Farmer	3000/325	Als.
29		Anna	58	f.	Wife		"
30		George	30	m.	Master Carpenter	/50	O.
31		John	18	m.	child		O.
32		LENTZ, Charles	6	m.			" S

33	214/216	FANKHOUSER, Christ.	32	m.	Farmer	2000/370	"
34		Rosina	32	f.	Wife		"
35		Charles	7	m.			" S
36		Mary	5	f.			" S
37		Charlotta	3	f.			"
38		Emma	6/12	f.			"

Page 35   **6 August** 1860   Sheet 338

1		IMHOFF, Mary	68	f.	Domestic	/300	Sw.
2		Christian	24	m.	Farm laborer	/100	O.
3		John	25	m.	Farm laborer	/100	"

4	215/217	EIGGISBERGER, Jacob	35	m.	Master Blacksmith 550/250		Bav.
5		Mary Ann	32	f.	Wife		O.
6		William	6	m.			" S
7		Charles	4	m.			"
8		Jacob	3	m.			"
9		Rosa	1	f.			
10		LUDY, John	19	m.	Apprentice Blacksmith		Sw.

11	216/218	STAGNER, Godfried	35	m.	Farmer	1500/500	Als.
12		Rosina	34	f.	Wife		"
13		Rosina Jr.	12	f.			O. S

14	STAGNER, Leonore	9	f.		O.	S
15	July	7	f.		"	S
16	Luisa	5	f.		"	
17	Wilhelmina	1	f.		"	
18	HARMAN, Phillip	13	m.		"	
19 217/219	LEHMAN, Nickolas	46	m.	Farm laborer 100/200 Sw.		

(Switzerland Township Concluded)

(Jacob Tschappat, Asst. Marshall)

* * *

* * *